THE
GI's
WAR

Other Books by the Author:

KAMIKAZES

GUADALCANAL

THE MILITARISTS

JAPAN'S WAR

U-BOATS: A PICTORIAL HISTORY

AMERICA'S WARS and MILITARY EXCURSIONS

HITLER'S WAR

THE GI's WAR

THE STORY OF AMERICAN SOLDIERS IN EUROPE IN WORLD WAR II

Edwin P. Hoyt

McGRAW-HILL BOOK COMPANY
New York   St. Louis   San Francisco
Hamburg   Mexico   Toronto

All maps courtesy United States Army.

1 2 3 4 5 6 7 8 9 DOC DOC 8 9 2 1 0 9 8

ISBN 0-07-030627-3

LIBRARY OF CONGRESS CATALOGING-IN-PUBLICATION DATA

Hoyt, Edwin Palmer.
  The GI's war.

  1. World War, 1939–1945—Campaigns—Europe.
2. World War, 1939–1945–Campaigns—Africa, North.
3. Soldiers—United States—History—20th century.
I. Title.
D756.3.H68   1988   940.54'12'73   87–29868
ISBN 0–07–030627–3

Book design by Eve Kirch

This book is dedicated to all the dogfaces who fought in World War II, especially those who fought in the North African and European theaters of operation, and most especially to the thousands of men and women who helped me write this book.

CONTENTS

Contents

ACKNOWLEDGMENTS

Hundreds of people, in America and abroad, contributed to the preparation of this book. I have told parts of the war stories of many of them, but there are just as many stories that I was unable to use. I am grateful to all who replied to my letters and took time away from their busy lives to participate in this book.

Following is a list of people and organizations that were particularly helpful:

Norman Robert Adolph, Robert Alexander, John A. Aller, Ned J. Allred, Eugene Amburgey, Leon N. Armer, Harry A. Bailey, Ray Baranouskas, William S. Beasley, F. Julian Becton, Robert O. Beer, William T. Belvin, Arthur W. Berg, George E. Berry, Jr., E. B. Billingsley, Sidney Bingham, Jr., Sumpter Blackmon, William S. Boice, John Boisky, Chester H. Bope, Charles Bortzfield, T. A. Bradley, Sr., Chuck Brehm, Gerald H. Briggs, Sr., Floyd E. Brooks, Joseph Kirkland Brown, Carleton F. Bryant, John M. Buckingham, William R. Buster, J. T. Butler, James P. Calk, Arthur E. Campbell, Daniel S. Campbell, Arthur L. Carter, Arthur L. Chaitt, Charles Chattaway, Gerard E. Chretien, R. W. Christie, John Chrzan, Theodore V. Ciampi, A. W. Clark, Dayton Clark, Ralph Clausen, Shelton R. Clemmer, Tom Clevenger, Lydon B. Cole, Walter Condon, Beatrice Contrella, John Purley Cooper, Jr., Kenneth Cord, Ernst Corrado, Mrs. J. J. P. Corrigan, Albert N. Crawford, Roy E. Creek, David J. Dallessandro, Herman Dammer,

Richard Dantini, Joseph Davey, Irwin J. Degnan, Edward James Dehné,
Richard A. Dickson, J. C. Doherty, George W. Dohmann, Mrs. John P.
Downing, Charles H. Doyle, Leo A. Duffy, Sr., Howard H. Dukes, John D.
Dulkeleu, William Darien Duncan, R. P. Eaton, Charles Edman, Jr., A. C.
Bill Edson, Harold Eisen, Edward R. Elburn, Edward Ellsberg, Robert J.
Emert, Otto Euteneur, Julian Johnson Euell, Elsie Fagerland, Dan Farket,
Samuel Ferguson, Mrs. Henry C. Flory, William H. Francis, Harvey R.
Fraser, Mrs. Ralph Freeman, Wes Frels, P. S. Gage, Jr., F. M. Garner,
Max Gartenberg, James M. Gavin, Hobart R. Gay, James K. Gaynor, Joseph
S. Gemski, Frank M. Gervasi, Frank J. Givens, Frank Globuschutz, Howard
C. Goodson, Samuel McC. Goodwin, Louis M. Gosorn, John L. Gray, Verdie
M. Guest, Jr., Vincent Haba, Bill Haemmel, Phil Haig, Ira Hall, Jr., Perry
T. Hall, Tom P. Hall, John E. Hammond, James W. Hardin, Paul D.
Harkins, Thomas L. Harris, Chester Harvey, George W. Hassell, Karl E.
Henion, Richard W. Herklotz, Richard L. Higgins, Charles Hlavaty, George
D. Hoffman, Barnett Hoffner, Henry Holt, Jr., Ellis H. Hopfenberg, A.
Horneman, Gerald Houseman, Robert Houson, Donald E. Houston, Mary
E. Houston, Priscilla D. Hoye, Earl Hurt, Stanley Hutek, Thomas F. Inglis,
Carl A. Johnson, Charles H. Johnson, Al Jordan, Frank V. Kalich, E. L.
Kaufmann, Frank Kerch, Jr., Harry W. O. Kinnard, Royal Kleinhardt, John
J. Klinovsky, George Kobe, Amil Kohutek, Henry Kraft, Walter E. Kraft,
Eddie Krause, Denny Kurir, Thomas F. Lancer, Allen Langdon, Eugene L.
Lash, Harold M. Lawrence, Laurence J. Legere, A. H. Lindblad, Lorton S.
Livingston, Frank M. London, Kenneth P. Lord, Dave Lusk, Edward S.
Luther, Donald E. MacDonald, James F. McDonnell, Andrew McFadzean,
Robert E. McFee, Harold R. McGuire, A. MacIvor, A. F. S. MacKenzie, T.
G. McMahon, William G. Malone, M. D. Matthews, Burdette E. Maust, Carl
O. Meier, Gino J. Merli, Karl A. Michel, Curtis W. Miller, Joseph W. Miller,
Arden V. Mischke, John J. Moglia, Robert C. Murphy, Edward B. Nagel,
T. H. Nixon, F. Novak, Ross Novelli, Carlos C. Ogden, William R. Ogden,
Leif Oistad, Morris Olson, Carl F. Oran, Walter Outerson, G. R. Parker,
Bud Pierson, Edwin P. Pierson, Paul W. Pifer, Harry Plisevich, R. L. Poland,
John Popp, Lorne D. Porter, Kenneth Powell, Frank G. Prassel, Robert H.
Pratt, John Prewit, Robert J. Rader, Harold C. Radford, George F. Rankin,
Mike Ranney, Teresa E. Rash, Glenn E. Rathbun, J. B. Ratner, Robert J.
Rausch, Paul A. Reed, Russell P. Reeder, Jr., Frank Riccio, Mary Rizzotto,
J. Milnor Roberts, Mr. and Mrs. Walter B. Roberts, Tony Roman, John Rose,
George Rosie, Harry Rybiski, Edward J. Salkoski, Alan J. Saly, Richard
W. Sargent, Ralph Savarese, Jack A. Scales, A. L. Scarborough, Sr., Leo

H. Scheer, D. Zane Schlemmer, Roland L. Schoepf, William M. Schrader, J. L. Semmes, Harold A. Shebeck, Thomas L. Sherburne, Jr., Philip Sherman, Peter Shian, Edward L. Shields, Floyd S. Simmons, Albert W. Smith, Robert G. Smith, Kay Snetzer (widow of Robert E. Snetzer), Andrew Sotak, Henry G. Spencer, Alfred Stanford, Archie W. Stewart, Jr., Harry P. Storke, Francis H. Strickler, Reuben H. Stussel, Norman R. Stultz, Emil P. Sulkosky, W. A. Sullivan, Travis L. Surratt, Edwin V. Sutherland, Raymond Tarabusi, Lewis C. Taunton, Manuel James Tavis, Wilfred M. Thornton, Dick Thrift, Robert D. Trathen, Alfred L. Turner, Guy C. Turner, Gilbert Unger, James Aleard Van Fleet, William Van Houten, Robert G. Von Staden, R. Clint Wakefield, W. J. Waldmann, Lucian L. Walkup, Glen Warkentien, John L. Warliels, Ralph Watson, Carl F. Weast, Malcolm G. Wentworth, Charles T. Wesner, Richard S. Whitcomb, Thomas G. Wickham, John G. Williams, Marion F. Williams, Robert Hays Williams, S. Lane Wilson, W. F. Winton, Jr., Edward Wayne Wood, Rex Wriggle, Norman R. Zehr, and Elwood J. Zeitz.

Department of the Army, Chief of Military History and Center of Military History, Washington, D.C. (Robert N. Waggoner); Department of the Army Community Relations Division, Office of the Secretary of the Army, Washington, D.C. (Mae E. Pomeroy); Eighty-second Airborne Division Association, Inc., Bloomington, Indiana; Eighty-second Airborne Division Association, Philadelphia Chapter; Kentucky Historical Society, Frankfort, Kentucky; Modern Military Field Branch, Military Archives Division, National Archives (Richard L. Boylan); Ninetieth Division Association, Raytown, Missouri (C. D. Steel); N.W. All Airborne Association; 101st Airborne Division Association, Kalamazoo, Michigan; Reserve Officers Association of the United States, Washington, D.C. (J. Milnor Roberts); Second Armored Division Association; 741st Tank Battalion, Pittsburg, Kansas; Texas Thirty-sixth Division Association; Twentieth Engineer Combat A Association of World War II (George Rankin); U.S. Army Military History Institute, Department of the Army, Carlisle Barracks, Pennsylvania (Richard J. Sommers); United States Military Academy, West Point (Egon A. Weiss, librarian); Veterans of Foreign Wars of the United States; and many many more associations contacted through the soldiers who participated in this book.

And ever grateful thanks to Dr. Dean Allard, Head of the Operational Archives Branch, Naval Historical Center, Department of the Navy, Washington, D.C.

AUTHOR'S NOTE

In the normal sense of the word, this book is not a "war history." As my editor pointed out, there are many misspelled words in this book, especially place names, because the dogfaces—my heroes—were not familiar with the geography of the strange places in which they were fighting, and they most often heard the place names rather than read them. But that's how it was for the GIs, their war was not a nice neat package of maps and geographical descriptions, but a dirty business in which they often did not get their socks off for weeks at a time.

Names, places, numbers, and even the stories of various military actions are recounted here as they were perceived by the dogfaces, mostly enlisted men and junior officers.

The editor suggested that I really ought to clean up the quotations from the dogfaces, turning the grammar and syntax into the sort one reads in the erudite histories of the war. But I preferred to leave the dogface language just as it was in their diaries, letters, and conversations and on the tapes they made for me. Also, as the editor pointed out, sometimes the GIs' account of a battle did not square with the official history or with any other account. This is true, but it is also what this book is all about. This is the story of the dogface war as the dogfaces fought it, told from their point of view, with all their perceptions, misconceptions, and errors. It is not the same war you read about in General Eisenhower's memoirs, although it is

more like the one described in General Bradley's book *Soldier*. There was no
space to accommodate the official accounts for comparison.

Many times the details recalled by my heroes do not conform to the official "facts." For example, at the Falaise pocket Colonel Campbell, the provost marshal of the Fifth Corps, recalled the task he faced in handling 20,000
POWs in a matter of hours. It was pointed out to me that historians said
100,000 German prisoners were taken at the Falaise gap. Perhaps, but not
by Colonel Campbell's Fifth Corps. There were other American units and
Canadians present at that time and place.

No, this book is not a history in the ordinary sense of the word. It is a
book about the sights and sounds and feel of battle, the dreadful boredom of
some aspects of combat, the constant danger and the discomfort.

There are atrocities in this book, atrocities committed by both sides. Some,
especially the Germans, say the American generals encouraged atrocities
with their advice to the soldiers invading Normandy that prisoners of war
were not wanted during the first thirty-six hours. During the trial of the
German officers responsible for the Malmédy massacre of Christmas 1944
the Germans pleaded that they were simply following the same policy that
the Americans invoked on D day. You, the reader, will have to make up
your own mind about that.

Other harsh and sometimes vicious actions are described in this book
too, descriptions that you will not find in other books. I have included them
because I promised to do so and feel that they are a part of the fabric of the
war. Atrocities are not unique to the enemy side.

When I began collecting material for this book in 1980, I was told by
some GIs, mostly enlisted men, that they would participate only if I was
willing to "tell it like it was" and not like it has been told in the various war
histories. On the other side, a number of high-ranking officers, usually staff
officers, refused to participate because I asked questions indicating disagreement and disapproval concerning some of the actions of the brass hats, usually disapproval voiced by enlisted men. Such matters as the disastrous
Rapido River crossing in Italy are cases in point. I made a pledge to the
enlisted men that I would tell the story of their war as it was, as they saw
and lived through it, and as far as I know I have kept that pledge. This book
is the story of the dogface war in all its gory glory.

E. P. H.

PREFACE

This book is about soldiers in World War II. It is not primarily a book about generals or other high-ranking officers, nor is it a book about military strategy and tactics. Rarely did the common soldiers know anything about the military strategy they were deploying, and very seldom anything about tactics, except in their immediate vicinity. Soldiers have been called pawns on the chessboard of war, and that is a very accurate description of the employment of the soldier.

When I say "soldier," I am talking about the field soldier: the GI; the "dogface"; the slogging, leather-booted, tin-hatted, dirty-shirted soldier of the line. Kilroy and his friends. But this description refers to company and field grade officers, too—including a few colonels—officers like Red Reeder, who led his men into battle with such vigor that he lost a leg almost at the beginning of the Normandy campaign, and even Brig. Gen. Theodore Roosevelt, Jr., the happy warrior who died of a heart attack in Normandy. But mostly this is the tale of the adventures of Privates Ogden, Haemmel, Adolph, Miller, Thornton, and Moglia, Corporal Chattaway and Sergeant Elburn, Lieutenant Downing and Captain Shebeck, and hundreds of others whose stories, or parts of them, appear in this book. When the generals and the colonels come in, it is either to use their activities to follow the course of the war or to explain elements of military practice. The stories that follow have almost all been told before, either by the men themselves or by their

chosen biographers. So, too, have the "big" stories of the war in Europe
been told by competent historians, both American and British. Those stories, by and large, are beyond the purview of this book. In other words, this
is not the story of the U.S. Army in World War II but the story of the Army
of the United States in that war. The officers and men of the U.S. Army—
the regulars—were the nucleus of the army of the United States.

The regular officers were dedicated career men, many of whom had spent
more than twenty years in the wilderness of a civilian economy in which
Congress looked with deep suspicion on military expenditures of any sort.
By and large they were good men: the stern and taciturn George Marshall;
the genial and accommodating Dwight Eisenhower; the fatherly, shrewd Omar
Bradley; the dashing, wild George Patton; and a hundred other general officers and a thousand colonels. There were, of course, some bad apples, and
the dogfaces were the first to spot them. There were also some unlucky generals, some of them taking the rap for defeats and errors for which the real
responsibility lay much further up the line. For the most part, the fates of
these professionals are matters of concern within the professional military
establishment. Any criticism of senior officers in this book is a direct reflection of what the GIs thought at the time. Sometimes the GI assessment
was wrong. In many cases what seemed to be the personal idiosyncrasies of
a senior officer turned out to be his method of leading troops. Thus, General
Patton's irritating and sometimes impossible uniform regulations (How can a
mechanic work on the underside of a tank with his tin hat on?) were his
means of jerking the members of the Second Corps in Africa back to attention and of creating a sense of pride among them after a series of defeats had
left them virtually in a state of shock. Patton's slapping of the soldiers in
Sicily was another indication of such gestures—one that cost him dearly—
when the American public rose up in anger at his "brutality" and he was
removed from command.

The public was joined by the dogfaces. One of the soldiers Patton slapped
was an infantryman from the Sixteenth Infantry, which had served the general very well in both north Africa and Sicily. In the words of one of the GIs,
"After that there were 50,000 GIs on Sicily who would like nothing better
than to have a shot at General Patton."

The incident was a very good reminder to the members of the military
that no matter what, they served the people of the United States and not vice
versa.

*

There are other tales in this book that seem to reflect badly on the regular army, particularly the army of prewar days—such as the story of Private Ogden at Fort Monroe and the company commander and sergeant who chose to impose their peculiar discipline on him. As many others have stated, that sort of thing was not uncommon in the peacetime army, whose enlisted men were not notably of the gentler order of Americans. Discipline was strict because it had to be to maintain order. The problems appeared when the old order came up against a new situation in which millions of young Americans joined the armed forces intending only to defeat the enemy and then get back to their civilian pursuits. There was some friction; there had to be. But it is a compliment to the officers of the regular army that there was so little friction, and that General Marshall and his subordinates managed to make soldiers out of raw civilians between 1941 and the landing of the invasion forces in north Africa in November 1942.

Those American soldiers of north Africa were still pretty green. But as Sergeant Ogden said later, twenty-four hours in combat makes a soldier. And that is what happened. The First Armored Division took a terrible shellacking in its initial encounters with the enemy, partly because of the inferiority of the American Sherman tank to the German Tiger and because of the absence of an adequate U.S. antitank gun. However, the American defeat at Kasserine Pass occurred partly because the American officers in charge were inexperienced, and the Germans simply outmaneuvered them. The British felt quite strongly about American inexperience. But that deficiency did not last long, and ultimately the Americans responded brilliantly by improvising; nobody had ever heard of using 105-millimeter howitzers as antitank weapons until the second battle of Kasserine Pass.

The American infantry had plenty to learn, too. But the Americans did learn—all of them—with great speed, and by the time of the Normandy invasion the gloomy prediction of Lord Ismay in the summer of 1941 that the Americans would never be able to stand up to the Germans proved to be, as Winston Churchill said it would be, an inaccurate assessment. The creation and the employment of this enormous American military machine was the great accomplishment of the officers and noncoms of the U.S. Army. And for that Americans should be forever grateful to the professionals who kept the military fires burning between 1919 and 1941 and who then put together the machinery in such a short time.

One other point: throughout the war in Europe there was more than a little friction between the Allies, and that between the British and Americans was most noticeable. Again, it is not the purpose of this book to dwell on the differences, except as they affected the GIs. Many, but not all, of the British who had been in the war for three years at the time of the North African invasion were noticeably contemptuous of their inexperienced American allies. But they made the mistake of underestimating the American capacity to learn. Particularly in the matter of logistics, the British system was far inferior to the American, and was so proved. The British, still suffering from the loss of almost an entire generation of young men in the war of 1914–1918, were extremely cautious in their management of battles; the Americans were much more daring and not very complimentary about the British method. Another element, not usually mentioned in the matter of intra-Allied antagonisms, is the cousinly relationship of British and Americans—a sense of mutual irritation that goes back to the war of the Revolution, and is liable to break out at any time. The epitome of all this was Gen. George S. Patton, Jr., who detested the British, denigrated them at every opportunity, and really believed the war could have been fought much better without them. That was, of course, an extreme notion, but such extremity was a part of General Patton, and was part of what made him America's most dashing field commander.

In spite of the irritations; the international, interservice, and intraservice rivalries; and the errors, incompetence, and arrogance in some places, together the Allies did a magnificent job in winning the European war against a determined and skillful enemy. There is plenty of credit to go around. This book is an attempt to give some of that credit to the GIs who slogged through the mud, whose biographers were Ernie Pyle, Bill Mauldin, and the writers for *Stars and Stripes* and *Yank* magazine. The archetype of these dogfaces is too often pictured as that cartoon character "The Sad Sack." There were sad sacks in the army of the United States, plenty of them, but there were also men of incredible bravery. And in between there were millions of officers and men who went into the service because they felt an obligation or were drafted to fight for their country and who, when the chips were down, performed in a manner that surprised them as much as anyone. So above all, here's to the dogface, the American GI, the citizen soldier of the United States. May he forever appear in the future as he has in the past, in time of need.

Edwin P. Hoyt
Corporal, Army of the United States (1941–1943)
19109959
Betterton, Maryland, 1988

1

THE

SUMMER

OF 1940

**75% OF BEF REPORTED SAFELY OUT OF FLANDERS;
ALLIES ATTACK ON SOMME, WIN ABBEVILLE AREA.
ROOSEVELT WARNS WAR IMPERILS WHOLE WORLD.**

PLEA TO CONGRESS

PRESIDENT ASKS POWER TO CALL OUT NATIONAL GUARD IF NEEDED

BILLION MORE FUNDS

ALL CONTINENTS MAY BE INVOLVED, SAYS NEW DEFENSE MESSAGE

By Felix Belair, Jr.
Special to the New York Times

WASHINGTON, May 31—Warning that "all continents may become involved in a world-wide war" President Roosevelt in a special message today asked Congress for "over $1,000,000,000" in supplemental appropriations for preparedness and for specific authority to call the National Guard and Army Reserves to active duty if needed to safeguard neutrality and for the national defense.

1

> Further enlargement of the defense forces, for which out-
> lays of more than $3,300,000,000 are pending in Congress,
> were necessary, the President said, in view of the success of
> blitzkrieg tactics on the Flanders Front.

Hitler was moving fast. The slow, almost torpid warfare of the winter of
1940 had ended and the "phony war" had proved to be a German deception.
When the panzer divisions swept through Belgium around the end of the
Maginot line, the British had just managed to save three-quarters of their
Flanders army through the almost miraculous Dunkerque evacuation. British
and French communiqués spoke of "success" against Nazi positions along
the Somme, but from America it was much easier to see that the reality lay
in the German High Command's laconic assessment that the Flanders and
Artois campaigns were virtually ended. Three French armies had been destroyed or captured and most of the British force was out of action.

One June day Pvt. William Richard Ogden, 6999701, was pulling kitchen
police at Fort Monroe, Virginia—permanent KP. He had been serving for
six months without a day off. Private Ogden was a soldier of the U.S. Army,
the old army. He had enlisted in 1939 at the age of 16, with stars in his
eyes. The stars were soon gone.

"The problem was that a soldier was considered to be an amoeba—the
lowest form of life on this earth—and perhaps in a way it was true. Most of
us in those days were either bums, ex-convicts, or men who chose to go into
the army instead of going to jail. So the military in those days were really
considered to be nothing but savages. GI meant government issue—a GI
can, which is a garbage can. We were called dogfaces, because of JoJo the
dogface boy. We wore tags, dog tags. So from then on we were dogfaces.
The term GI, meaning soldier, didn't come into being until after the draft."

In the old army an enlisted man had no privileges. He actually gave up
his citizenship rights when he enlisted, Private Ogden had discovered. Even
if he had been 21, he still could not have voted. He could not say anything
negative about an officer, a mayor, a senator, any of those—it theoretically
might mean a general court-martial, a dishonorable discharge, and six months
in the guardhouse.

Private Ogden got paid $21 a month. After money out for necessities
such as haircuts, shaving cream, and the like, he had about $12 a month.
This lasted a week, and the rest of the month he was dead broke. He used

to go scouting around the camp to see how to pick up some money. Monroe is a very old fort, built before the Civil War, and it is laced with old tunnels. One day Ogden came upon a steel door covered over with concrete, and he broke through it. Inside he found a cavern the size of a Quonset hut, filled with long cases. Each case contained brand new .50-caliber rifles, with triangular bayonets, all packed in Cosmoline. The weapons were new—in 1865—bought but never issued during the Civil War.

"Like a fool, I reported this to my commanding officer. A few days later these extremely valuable antique rifles were put up for sale *to officers*." Ogden went to his commanding officer and asked if he could buy one since he had discovered them. He was turned down flat. Who did he think he was? He was only an enlisted man.

A few more incidents of this sort, and Ogden had gained a reputation as a troublemaker. That's how he got put on permanent KP, by orders of the first sergeant, with the approval of the captain.

Not long afterward, Private Ogden appealed to the mess sergeant for some time off, and the mess sergeant agreed. Ogden took off, but he made the mistake of staying in the barracks. That very morning he was found by the first sergeant, who personally escorted him back to the mess hall and told the mess sergeant that Private Ogden was permanent KP, *permanent*.

A little later that day, Private Ogden erupted. He went straight to the first sergeant's office. He did not knock. He did not speak. He picked up the large wooden nameplate the first sergeant kept proudly on his desk, and beat the sergeant over the head with it. Then he walked into the captain's office, grabbed his commanding officer by the necktie, pulled him across the desk, emptied a bottle of ink onto his head, and then struck the captain on the head with the bottle. He threw the captain back into his chair and walked out.

He was arrested and put up for general court-martial under Section 8 of the U.S. Army Articles of Discipline, the paragraph that said "unadjustable to military service."

An officer from nearby Fort Story was assigned to conduct Private Ogden's defense. When this officer learned what had happened and of the cruel and unusual punishment visited on Private Ogden, he made sure the facts were made known to the office of the inspector general of the army. Suddenly all charges were withdrawn. Even the old U.S. Army could not stomach that sort of discipline once the facts were officially established. The alternative to dropping the charges would have to have been a court-martial of the first sergeant and the captain as well as of the private.

Private Ogden was transferred across Hampton Roads to Fort Story, to the organization of the officer who had defended him. In four months he rose from buck private to sergeant. Times had changed, even though the United States was just beginning to pull up its military socks. Sergeant Ogden was a professional soldier, but the army in which he was now serving was no longer ruled by caste, and the enlisted men were no longer as reviled as they had been. A private could be the kid brother of the captain just as easily as not. The army was now the army of the United States; the vast majority of people who were coming into it had absolutely no interest in soldiering as a profession. There was a national defense problem. That was what it was all about.

Not all the West Point officers of the U.S. Army were like Private Ogden's superiors at Fort Monroe. Many were like Capt. Russell Potter Reeder, son of a professional soldier and graduate of the U.S. Military Academy in the class of 1926. Captain Reeder was a company officer serving in the Panama Canal Zone in 1940 and a friend to his men. He had to deal with a post quartermaster who loaded the company messes down with canned artichokes ("damned pinecones") and a commanding general who took an inordinate interest in the condition of the brass doorknobs in the barracks. But Captain Reeder coped—as he did the time on maneuvers when the supply officer of the "attacking force" discovered that he had miscalculated and that the men would have nothing to eat but tuna fish, coffee, and bread for 8.2 meals on the last three days of the maneuvers. Captain Reeder gave his best sergeant some money and five men and sent them out to forage for food. They brought back chickens, sweet potatoes, papayas, mangoes, bananas, pineapples, limes, and sugar. Company L of the Third Infantry never performed better than in those maneuvers.

Life for Captain Reeder was not easy. When he had graduated from the academy and become a second lieutenant, his pay was so low ($143 a month) that the West Point authorities lectured graduating seniors against getting married. There were "perks": the commissary and the post exchange where soldiers could buy food at low prices and liquor and cigarettes without taxes. The officers had golf courses to play on, and a certain amount of leisure. But the life of a professional army officer between the wars was certainly no bed of roses. The changes of 1940 were going to make a big difference.

*

Barnett Hoffner was also a professional soldier, but in a different way. In 1936, in the middle of the Great Depression, Hoffner had enrolled at Long Island University, but he soon decided that college was a dead end. He had always been interested in the military. His family had a military tradition; several members had served in the Austrian army.

At about this time, two of his brother's friends who were in the Marine Corps had come to the house, and he was impressed. So in March 1936 Barnett Hoffner enlisted in the marines for four years. He enjoyed it immensely. It was tough training, the sort that stuck with a man: in 1988 Hoffner could still remember the number of his Marine Corps 1903 Springfield rifle— 868449.

Hoffner was married in 1940. He would have been willing to sign over with the marines, but his wife was adamant against the idea. Discharged, Hoffner went to work for the Veterans Administration in Washington. So while some men were coming in, Barney Hoffner was going out.

*   *   *

On June 1, 1940, in King's Town, on the Eastern Shore of Maryland, a 22-year-old farm boy named Edward Elburn was hoeing vegetables at the Bramble farm where he had been working for three months. Ed Elburn had grown up in King's Town, as had his father and grandfather before him. Elburn was a name well known on the shore, along with Usilton, Anthony, Turner, and Cooper. This branch of the Elburn tribe ran a greenhouse and did a little dry-land farming, as did so many of the Eastern Shore families. Corn was the cash crop, corn that was planted in the early spring and grew in the summer heat until it was picked dry in September and October. Corn and the fruits of the Chesapeake Bay kept the Eastern Shore going. Some of the farmers were also watermen, but not so many in the 1930s. Many of them supplemented their cash crops with venison and wild goose in the fall, for this section of the Eastern Shore was a major flyway for the Canada geese that arrived by the hundreds in September and remained amid the corn stubble until April.

Ed Elburn knew nothing of President Roosevelt's plea to Congress for a more powerful American defense force. The Baltimore papers came over to the shore by ferry, but they did not always arrive on schedule. The Delaware papers came in but were mostly useful for their ads, since Kent and Queen Anne's counties were oriented to shopping in Dover. So Ed Elburn, at 22, didn't spend a lot of time reading the newspapers other than the weekly *Kent*

County News, which had the distinction of starting out as *The Chestertown Spy*, a colonial newspaper. What most of the people of the shore lacked in worldly goods they made up for with a powerful tradition of independence and pride in the history of the shore.

The first settlement in Maryland had been made in Queen Anne's County, on Kent Island. Over in Kent County, Chestertown's "Tea Party" was not so well known as Boston's, but it was almost an exact replica. In the days before the Revolution the Chester River, which separated Chestertown and King's Town, had created a port city to rival Baltimore. The shore in those days had been the natural highway from the southern colonies to Philadelphia and New York. George Washington had ridden north this way more than once, and men from the shore had fought in all their country's wars, from the Revolution on. But in other times, the people of the shore minded their own business and blessed the fact that their Delaware, Maryland, Virginia (Delmarva) peninsula was cut off from the hectic world of business and industry by the Chesapeake Bay. The bay was their livelihood, their recreation, and their protection from the hurly-burly world. One reached the Eastern Shore by driving down the Jersey coast or by crossing the bay on a ferry. There was no other access except by air. A few Baltimoreans maintained big houses on the shore, and more came on the ferry to Betterton, to stay in the resort hotels or the cottages there and dip their feet into the bay at Betterton beach. But by and large the Eastern Shore was as it always had been, an entity unto itself, and that was just how shore folk liked it.

In 1935, after Ed Elburn had graduated from Church Hill High School, he joined the National Guard. His unit was the medical detachment of the 115th Regiment of the Twenty-ninth Division. The regiment was very old; it could trace its history back to the frontier militia formed in Maryland before the Revolution. Two companies had marched from Frederick to Boston in August 1775. During the Civil War, Marylanders and Virginians had fought on both sides. After the war the Twenty-ninth was reactivated with a yin-yang shoulder patch of blue and gray, symbolizing the reunification of north and south.

The Chestertown contingent, a part of the medical detachment, was very small, as befitted a little town on the Eastern Shore. It consisted of twenty-eight men, under the command of Dr. Frank Hines of Chestertown, who had the rank of major when he thought to claim it. Joining the guard was as much a social activity as anything else. At the meetings in the Chestertown armory the boys learned first aid from Doc Hines, and practiced on each other. For two weeks each summer they went to camp. Since the Twenty-ninth Division was a combination of Maryland and Virginia National Guard units, in Elburn's first year the boys went to Union Gap, Virginia, the next year to Camp Ritchie, over in the mountains of the western shore, a real beauty spot later to be glorified as the presidential summer palace at Camp David. The next summer they went to Manassas. They were outfitted in World War I uniforms: blue-denim fatigue jackets and trousers, and mustard-colored wool khakis with 3-foot-long wraparound leggings and tight-fitting blouses. At camp they learned close order drill, how to march with the infantry. Ed Elburn qualified with the 1903 Springfield rifle and had a big bruise on his right cheek to help him remember what the sergeant said about keeping that rifle butt up against his shoulder the next time. As a medic, Private Elburn would not carry a gun, but in battle, as the sergeant said, he might want to defend himself in case of need.

Ed Elburn liked the guard. He liked the camaraderie and the amusements when the members got together for a picnic or a bull roast. He liked going to camp. There was only one thing he did not like:

"Maryland's western mountains are full of rattlesnakes. I carried a medical packet with a little iodine, a pair of scissors, some tape, and ammonia inhalers. Most of my first aid consisted of patching up blisters on the guys during the marches. I also had a snake bite kit, a little scalpel, and a piece of rubber tubing. What worried me was thinking about using that kit. The doc said all I had to do was cut the wound, and then suck the venom and spit it out. I wondered if I would really have the guts to do it."

Since his outfit never ran into any rattlesnakes on march, Medic Elburn did not have to answer the question. He was a company aid man without a lot to do. At the meeting in the Chestertown armory Doc Hines mentioned the news, but there really wasn't a lot to say about it.

As far as Ed Elburn was concerned the events in Washington, just 85 miles away, could have been occurring on the moon.

He was completely unaware of the enormous struggle over the President's twin calls for mobilization of the National Guard and the Army Reserve, and enactment of a national selective service law to provide for a new, citizen army. He knew nothing of the state of training of even his own regiment and division, and certainly nothing of the jeering of the Axis powers at the presidential call for a strong defense.

"The United States can never successfully intervene in the European war," wrote Luigi Barzini, one of Benito Mussolini's pet journalists in Il Duce's newspaper *Il Popolo D'Italia*. He continued:

The United States Regular Army consists of 200,000 mercenaries, with a complement of playboy National Guards who specialize in picnics.... American in-
tervention is a race between a tortoise and an automobile.... There is not a
single man in the United States today who would fight for the Poles, the Belgians,
the Norwegians and the Dutch, and die on the battlefield with the sweet names
of Reynaud and Churchill on his lips. Americans are prepared to do everything
to help the Allies without going to war. Even if the United States openly inter-
venes, it cannot increase its present mediocre exportation.

As the weeks rolled along, France fell to the Germans and Britain prepared
to fight off a German amphibious invasion. In August came the air Battle of
Britain, which eliminated the danger of invasion. Ed Elburn, Pfc. Elburn of
the Maryland National Guard, knew very little about all that; he became
aware of the war in a different way. News of the sinking of American ships
had also come that summer, and with it word of changes in the American
military establishment. He paid more attention to the debate in Washington,
for the calling up of the National Guard, if it happened, was going to concern Ed Elburn and his friends.

In August the National Guard bill was passed and signed by President
Roosevelt. The mobilization began in twenty-six states. In October the 115th
Regiment was called back for another week of duty at Camp Ritchie, a week
that Pfc. Elburn remembered very well:

"It was cold. I mean cold. We had a little stove in the barracks that
looked like an overturned ice cream cone, sitting in a box of sand. We kept
it going all night long to try to keep warm, and the stove set fire to the floor
underneath the sand. The fire brigade had to come with their CO_2 equipment, and it made a terrible mess."

During that week Pfc. Elburn learned that he could get out of the National
Guard, if he wished to quit. But there was a kicker. On September 16 the national selective service bill had been signed into law by President Roosevelt. As
the guard officers informed the men, if they got out they would then be subject
to the draft law that called on all men from 21 to 35 to register. They might not
be called in the raffle immediately, but... So Pfc. Elburn elected to stay in,
knowing that early in 1941 the 115th was going into active service.

Other units were already seriously engaged in the deadly business of preparing for war. Early in August Lt. Gen. Hugh A. Drum, commander of the

U.S. First Army, assembled his forces at Ogdensburg, New York, for mobilization maneuvers. Hanson W. Baldwin of the *New York Times* went upstate to observe the enormous clusters of pyramidal tents that flowed across the fields like anthills. Lest there be some mistake, General Drum addressed the troops. "We must drop the doctrine of defensive war," he warned. "To know that, all you have to do is see what happened to France." America had to mobilize, train its manpower to fight, and organize its industry for war. There could be no defensive war. The United States must build for offense.

General Drum and the commanders of the three other American armies all mobilized their forces at field centers that first week of August for war maneuvers. They were beginning a job that at times seemed impossible, training civilians to become soldiers in just a few months. Sixty percent of those assembled at Ogdensburg were the rawest of the raw.

And who was to train these military tyros?

One of the instructors was Cpl. Charles Chattaway, assistant squad leader, First Rifle Platoon, Company A, 110th Infantry Regiment, of the Twenty-eighth Division. The regiment was a National Guard unit from Monongahela, Pennsylvania, but all that was forgotten in the summer of 1940. Charles Chattaway took off his dairy store clerk's apron and put on his uniform. Off to Ogdensburg he went *on his first summer encampment*.

"...pyramidal tents with latrines at the end of each company street... GI cans on the company street during the hours of darkness, to avoid trips to the latrine... often the targets of raiding parties from adjacent companies... shooting craps, which proved an expensive pastime for this neophyte.

"After two weeks of squad, platoon, and company exercises, we returned home to our armory. We resumed weekly drills of two hours each, for which we received one day's army pay, payable quarterly—a dollar a day—most welcome in these post-Depression days. Our company commander, a prominent local citizen, made a practice of advancing loans to individuals, to be paid when the quarterly checks were received. Our first sergeant, manager of a local clothing store, arranged for credit on the same basis."

General Drum's references that summer to "offensive war" did not sit well with many Americans, particularly those of the "America First" persuasion. At Ann Arbor, Michigan, students of the University of Michigan were circulating petitions against compulsory military training, calling it "a major step toward preparation for an involvement in war." Former President Herbert Hoover agreed: "I have not thought it necessary," he said of the draft. Ohio's

Senator Robert Taft and all America's Charles A. Lindbergh agreed with
him. The nation was still badly split on the need for preparations, but the
Roosevelt administration was forging ahead. The War Department had already undertaken the total reorganization of American forces on the basis of
lessons learned by observation in Europe. One of the first steps had been
the creation of an armored corps of two divisions, which would have 18,000
men and 1400 tanks, to develop "great striking power" at speeds of 50 miles
per hour. It was a concept openly aping the German panzer organization.
The First Armored Division began organizing at Fort Knox, the Second Armored Division at Fort Benning. But so undeveloped were America's sinews
of war that when the Second Armored Division held its first review that fall
there were not enough vehicles to mount the men, so they paraded on foot.
The only really effective unit was Col. George S. Patton, Jr.'s Sixty-eighth
Armored Regiment, which had a full complement of tanks. In fact, Colonel
Patton was just about the only senior officer in the division who knew anything at all about tanks, and his were light tanks, which the Germans would
have found almost laughable.

During that August of 1940 the U.S. Second Army was holding its maneuvers at Camp McCoy, Wisconsin. For three weeks some 60,000 troops of
regular army, National Guard, and reserve units from seven midwestern states
maneuvered through a large area of west central Wisconsin. One young officer involved in this activity was Lt. Harold A. Shebeck, a 1937 graduate of
Ripon College, who was by profession a high school social science teacher
and athletic coach in South Dakota. But for three years Lieutenant Shebeck
had been far more conscious of the dangers of war than most Americans. In
1938 he had gone to Camp McCoy, then a tent camp with no permanent
facilities, training in the Corps Area Service Command. The command had
to decide what facilities would be needed to build a camp of 30,000 men,
just in case the unthinkable should happen and America should have to arm
itself. All sorts of problems had to be solved, for example:

Given the size of a GI loaf of bread and the capacity of a GI oven and the
amount of bread allotted to each man per day, how many ovens, bakeries,
bakers, pots, pans, spoons, and so forth, would be needed to produce the
daily bread requirements for 30,000 troops?

Lieutenant Shebeck persisted in wading through such problems, and by
August 1940 he was attached to a machine gun company of the Wisconsin
National Guard as the guardsmen conducted their maneuvers with the Second Army. There was a certain carnival atmosphere to it all: every night the
men in the camps adjourned to one of the temporary beer stands that were

set up in the area, and a couple of thousand men surged around each 12-foot-square beer stand, each soldier trying to get a glass of beer.

Lieutenant Shebeck, being of an inquiring turn of mind, had some disquieting thoughts about the future. He saw that a quarter of the men had no weapons. Saplings were cut from small trees to improvise. His machine gun company had only half its machine guns. The company was supposed to have 37-millimeter antitank guns, but it had none. Instead, small forked trees were cut, and a small log was put across the crotch to make a "gun."

"Here we were one year after World War II had started and there was this noticeable lack of equipment in our armed forces. It made me wonder if our leaders were aware of what was happening in Europe."

They—at least President Franklin Roosevelt and his advisers—were very much aware of what was happening in Europe, and of what was likely to happen to the United States if Hitler was allowed to overrun the continent of Europe, destroying the fighting capacity of Great Britain, the last obstacle to German control of western Europe. But that knowledge was only slowly working itself into the consciousness of the American people. Sergeant Ogden was a professional. The army, war or peace, was his life. Pfc. Elburn and Corporal Chattaway were in the guard more or less as a lark, and for the extra money they earned by attending training sessions at the armory and at camp in the summer. Lieutenant Shebeck, older and better educated, was more thoughtful and concerned. And then there was another type—the kid just out of high school, looking for kicks.

John J. Moglia was a Long Island boy, who grew up in Hempstead, about 25 miles from New York City. Life "on the island" in those days was not the life of the modern commuter. The Long Island kids called New Yorkers "city slickers," and the city kids called the Long Islanders "hicks from Hicksville" and "clam diggers."

In the summer of 1940 the war excitement reached into Hempstead. Moglia and his friends began talking about going into the service. They argued about the best service. Moglia liked the U.S. Army Air Corps.

"We talked a lot, but when it came to take the plunge we could never get together to make the move. There was always some excuse: 'My girlfriend doesn't want me to,' 'My folks are against it,' 'I don't think I should leave my job.'

"I did manage to get one of my friends in a weak moment to visit the Coast Guard recruiting office. I was accepted but my friend was 1 pound underweight and was turned down. The recruiting officer suggested that he eat a few bananas and come back. He didn't like bananas so he declined and suggested that we try the navy. He was accepted there, but I was not because my teeth were not even.

"Next we went to the marines. I was accepted but when I found that the initial hitch was four years I thought that was too long. My friend agreed. So my friend and I went home to think it over. Just about then, it was September, came the draft registration for everybody over 21. After that I was the only one of the group that was still interested in giving up civilian life before I had to. So I struck off on my own and one day in November I headed for the Army Air Corps recruiting station in Jamaica, Long Island. It so happened that the Air Corps recruiter was out to lunch, but next door a crafty army sergeant had already eaten and decided to use me as dessert. The old sarge was a shrewdy. Told me he'd just finished a big steak and a cold beer; yes, army life was great. Oh, yes, the army had airplanes. Sure, I could later get to fly one. Maybe I'd rather become a mechanic.

"He gave me a short written test, and told me how smart I was. He gave me a brief physical; that is, he ascertained that I could see, I could hear, and he saw that I was breathing. He said there was no question about my being able to eat army food with my uneven teeth. I was going to get along in the army just fine.

"'Would you like to go to the Philippines?' he asked.

"'No. I have an uncle there. I want to make it on my own.'

"'How about Hawaii?'

"'Same problem.'

"He then mentioned Panama, which sounded fine. I knew I was going to end up in some exotic place.

"'Hm.' He thought awhile. 'How about Fort Jay?'

"He was really interested in where I ought to go. I had never heard of Fort Jay but since it was probably in Panama, I agreed. He told me the army would call me when they needed me and not to worry. I was all set. It would be a few weeks. He sent me home.

"At Christmastime the army decided they needed me. On January 2, 1941, then, I had the word and I said farewell to friends and family and headed for the main army recruiting station on Whitehall Street in New York City. I arrived there bright and early with 55 cents in my pocket and great expectations in my heart.

"While waiting for the physical and written tests I had to use the men's room and headed there. A very officious corporal told me to go back to my seat. I told him I would, right after I went to the men's room. He grabbed me and called me an unpleasant name and so I grabbed him and invited him to step outside. A medical officer intervened and suggested that I go to the rest room and then return to my seat. This was just what I had been saying. Later I discovered that the recruiters were paid a bounty for each new recruit and that is why the corporal acted as he did. I was money in the bank. He didn't want to take a chance of losing me.

"During the physical examination all recruits were stark naked and as each doctor examined a part of us he put a mark there with something like lipstick. Before we were finished we were tattooed from head to foot. A doctor told me to bend over and spread my cheeks. I discovered I had two sets of cheeks. I was blindfolded and spun around, made to jump off a chair, and was turned upside down. What a strange exam!

"After two hours of this someone discovered I had been given the wrong examination. I had indicated that I was going to become a flier, so the doctors assumed I was applying for the Air Corps and gave me the exam for flying cadets. After they learned their mistake, the rest went fast.

"'You're going to Fort Jay. Here's your ticket.'

"They also gave me a slip that told me how to get to the docks.

"'Be there at two o'clock.'

"I picked up my bag and left. At last I was on my way to adventure. I was no longer a civilian. I had 55 cents in my pocket and I was ready for the ocean voyage.

"When I reached the dock, there was no ship in sight.

"I panicked. My first day in the service, and already I was AWOL.

"I saw an MP. I apologized to him for missing my ship.

"'What should I do?'

"'Wait for the next one. It'll be along in thirty minutes.'

"Ocean liners sailing on thirty-minute schedules? Suddenly something seemed strange. I dared ask the MP: 'Where the heck is Fort Jay?'

"He pointed. Out there in the harbor was a little island. Governor's Island, he said. Fort Jay. It was the base of the Sixteenth Infantry Regiment. 'Subway soldiers,' he called them.

"The ferry came and I took it and finally got to where I was going. I didn't sleep that night. It was cold and wet and distinctly not Panama. I was homesick, and the foghorns and buoy bells kept me awake. The next day I had another 'ocean voyage' across the harbor to Fort Wadsworth, Staten Island. There I was issued uniforms and gear, and became a member of Company E of the Sixteenth Infantry. I was also told by a sergeant that the only thing I was going to fly was a 1903 Springfield rifle and a bayonet."

*

In every state, America was mobilizing. Everywhere progress was being made. By December the Second Armored Division managed a divisional march from Fort Benning to Panama City, Florida, 600 miles, the longest march ever made anywhere by an American armored division. Back at Fort Benning, as America's leading tank tactician, Colonel Patton got two quick promotions, up to major general and command of the Second.

For Corporal Chattaway and his buddies of the 110th Infantry, training in the Monongahela armory in that fall of 1940 consisted of close order drill, small-bore rifle shooting, and classes on military subjects. One of the company officers took them out to his farm where he had established a .30-caliber-rifle range.

By the fall of 1940 Chattaway and his friends began to anticipate induction into the federal service for a twelve-month period because of the war in Europe. Most of them welcomed the opportunity of serving for a year, provided their jobs would be secure: "It seemed an extension of the good times at the summer encampments."

In January 1941 the company began a recruiting drive, and one result was Corporal Chattaway's promotion to squad leader, with the three inverted V stripes of a buck sergeant. Then came February 3. That day every man of the company received this message:

Company Order No. 2

1. Pursuant to Executive Order No. 8633, of January 14, 1941, and in compliance with General Order No. 3, The Adjutant General's Office, of January 27, 1941, you are ordered to report to the State Armory at 8:00 a.m. Monday, February 17, 1941, for the purpose of induction into the Federal Service.

By Order of
Captain, 110th Infantry (Rifle)
Commanding

"We reported to the armory on February 17, each man drew his equipment.... [We each had] a physical examination and we began training. We were billeted in the drill hall on cots and took our meals in local restaurants, as our cooks had departed with the advance detail to attend Cook's and Baker's School.

"On the evening of February 27 we took leave of our families, sweethearts and friends, entraining for Indiantown Gap Military Reservation, arriving the next morning at a bleak, cold, and snow-covered Lickdale, Pennsylvania, within hiking distance of our new home. Most arrived with mixed emotions, neither depressed nor elated, but apprehensive."

They were right to be apprehensive; they were taking the first step to war.

2

AMATEUR
SOLDIERS

February 13, 1941: Maj. Gen. Milton A. Reckord, commander of the Twenty-ninth Division, called it "the day the 'era of the armory' ended." It was the day he signed the order that transformed Pfc. Ed Elburn and 6926 other enlisted men of the division from weekend warriors to dogfaces.

It happened in the general's office at Fort George G. Meade, a brand-new installation just going up about halfway between Baltimore and Washington, D.C. Pfc. Elburn and the others of his detachment were assembled at the Chestertown armory on the Eastern Shore. They put on their OD (olive drab) wool uniforms with the black neckties and garrison caps with the eagle on them, and they were told that they would report for duty at Fort Meade, along with the others of their regiment, as well as the men of the 175th Regiment. This was the Fifty-eighth Infantry Brigade, the Maryland infantry. The Virginians of the 116th Regiment and the 176th Regiment made up the Eighty-eighth Infantry Brigade. The infantry was supported by the Fifty-fourth Artillery Brigade (three regiments), as well as medical, quartermaster, combat engineer, signal, military police, and other units including the 104th Observation Squadron (Air), which consisted of a handful of overage biplanes. All this was the division. The organization would change substantially, but this had been the National Guard way for years. It was going to take some toughening and some learning to make real soldiers out of these weekend warriors, and no one knew it better than the U.S. High Command. But one had to start somewhere, and for the Twenty-ninth Division it was Fort Meade.

The new dogfaces were hustled into brand-new unpainted barracks, through the mud that surrounded virtually every building in the camp, and there they were told to make themselves at home in their new home. It was a little rugged in some of those barracks, the ones where the doors hadn't yet been hung, or the windows either. The barracks' stoves had been installed as hastily as the barracks themselves had been built, but while the buildings smelled at first of green lumber, that smell was soon overpowered by the musty odor of smoke from the leaky barracks' stoves.

Those stoves had many uses. One day at one of the New Jersey installations, a very tough officer of the day got word that a pair of cooks who had just made corporal had acquired two bottles of whiskey and had it in the barracks, prepared to celebrate. He came stomping in with a sergeant and they searched. But they found nothing. Just as they were walking toward the end of the barracks and the door to the outside, an enormous explosion shook the stove and smoke and ashes came pouring out. That, the two ex-corporals soon learned, was the effect of a hot stove on two bottles of whiskey.

The training began. Training for what? Officers like Gen. George C. Marshall and Gen. Omar Bradley knew it would be training for war, and so did General Reckord and some of the others. But to many, even those who were doing the training, the war was still far from the American shore. In Washington the politicians were debating every issue that involved U.S. relations with Britain, Germany, and the other powers. The America First Committee's leading spokesman, hero Charles A. Lindbergh, was telling the American public that there was no reason for the United States to become involved in the war of Europeans. In Washington Senator Burton K. Wheeler of Montana and some of the other leftovers from the old isolationist days of the 1920s were expressing their agreement.

President Roosevelt, who knew the temper of the country was not yet ready to accept full-scale involvement, had gone on record at the end of 1940 with a promise that American troops would be sent abroad only in case of attack on America itself.

So these young men were training for the defense of the United States. Training with what?

To begin with, they had the old-fashioned soup-plate helmets of World War I. They wore woolen undershirts and long drawers, and either the OD uniform or the blue fatigues and canvas leggings over their high-top laced brown workshoes. Some had really old uniforms, with knee breeches instead of long trousers. In the cold they wore the long OD overcoats; the officers had the choice of short coats, which were much easier to move around in, but there was nothing like that for the enlisted men.

The infantry weapon was the Springfield 1903 .30-caliber rifle. This fire-power was augmented by the .30-caliber water-cooled machine gun and the newer .50-caliber machine gun. The 37-millimeter antitank gun was guar-anteed to be a "tank killer."

The trouble was that there weren't enough weapons to go around, espe-cially when the new draftees began to arrive. At Fort Meade they waited for 10,000 draftees that March. That was a larger force of men than the Twenty-ninth Division had been able to muster.

At Indiantown Gap Military Reservation, Corporal Chattaway's 110th Infan-try settled in quickly. In a few days pass privileges were given, and soon some of the boys were going home the 200 miles every weekend. It got bet-ter: they were allowed to keep personal cars on the post, and with a little luck they could arrange their duty so that they could drive home and back on Wednesdays, as well as weekends.

The 110th was training with the old Springfield rifles. They had wooden machine guns and wooden tubes for mortars. Corporal Chattaway was made "mortar section sergeant." His job was to train three squads of his company in the use of the 60-millimeter mortar. Simple? It might have been if they had had any mortars, but they did not. On the firing range they used an old 3-inch Stokes mortar, firing 81-millimeter ammunition—until a shell exploded in the tube, wounding several members of the squad and leaving the old mortar tube shattered.

Those 10,000 young men who had no military experience at all began com-ing into Fort Meade in March. They came off the farm, out of the factory, out of the ranks of traveling salesmen; soon they would be joined by young men just out of school. They were the rawest of recruits for the military, now to undergo the thirteen-week basic training program that would "make them into soldiers."

Off they went, the new recruits, segregated from the "old soldiers" of the guard units, off to the woods along the Pennsylvania Railroad tracks, off to the sandy loblolly pine forest along Jessup Road.

*

It was the same everywhere. When Pvt. John Moglia arrived at Fort Wadsworth with E Company of the Sixteenth Infantry Regiment, he and the other $21-a-month heroes slept on canvas cots in the halls of the buildings. Although he had enlisted, and was not a draftee, it made no difference.

"We were not allowed to mingle with the regulars; we ate separately as well. My uniform was of World War I vintage, wrap leggings and all. Say, did they itch!

"I used to get up half an hour before reveille in order to get dressed properly. We weren't allowed off post for a month either. I don't blame them. You should have seen this sorry looking bunch of rookies.

"For a treat they issued us the new semiautomatic M-1 Garand rifle. We didn't get to fire them until several months later at the marine camp at Wakefield, Massachusetts, however. We fired .22-caliber rifles in the basement of our quarters for qualification in arms.

"For evening entertainment we were paired off and allowed to knock each others' heads off in the boxing ring. All arguments were settled this way, too. A friend of mine, Bob Natarus, had some Golden Gloves experience, but didn't tell anyone. We had several bull sergeants who liked to get a recruit in the ring and hammer on him. In those days anyone with stripes on his sleeve was a god.

"Bob kept ridiculing this one bully sergeant. I suggested that he keep quiet or else he would have his head dislodged. He told me he would welcome the opportunity and finally he had his reward: the bully ordered him into the ring.

"I was Bob's second.

"'When do you want me to knock him out, John?' he asked me. 'Or perhaps I should just play with him a bit first?'

"Well, to the surprise of all, Bob gave our sergeant friend a real going over and knocked him out in the third round. Guess who was then on KP, latrine duty, coal duty, and so forth, for the next month?"

John's pal Bob was also a pool shark, another fact he concealed from his rube friends of the training unit. Playing the bumpkin at the table in the dayroom, he let everybody beat him, and lost some money. Then suddenly he seemed to learn—real fast—and cleaned house.

They trained. Oh, how they trained!

They were brought up from 3-mile hikes to 10-mile hikes and then to 25-mile hikes with light pack and 35-mile hikes with heavy pack.

"During the last few miles sometimes my butt was dragging," said Private Moglia. "The powers that were had an excellent idea, however. About a mile or so from camp we were met by a drum and bugle corps who 'played us home.' It's amazing how all that fatigue and soreness disappeared when those drums and bugles began to play their magic. We were no longer tired nor had we any pain. Suddenly we were, without command, marching in step and at attention.

"The song says I could have danced all night. Well, I could have marched all day."

And the drum and bugle corps had another bit of magic: on payday. On this special day the men did not have to fall out for reveille; they just got into Class A uniform to report for pay. Twenty-one dollars a month. How sweet that music was:

> Pay day, pay day,
> What will you do with a drunken soldier?
> Pay day, pay day,
> Put him in the guard house til he's sober.
> Pay day, pay day ...

The pay table was the collection point for charitable donations: 10 cents for the Old Soldiers' Home, something for the Red Cross. Canteen and movie tickets were sold there, too, by the book. If you bought a book at the pay table, you got extra tickets. You could spend the chits for beer, cigarettes, candy, shaving cream, and so forth.

On payday the post became a magnet for taxi drivers, girls, and anybody else looking to make a fast buck. Moglia's buddy Bob was alert in the dayroom. Here and there a crap game sprang up, also poker games. If you had any canteen tickets left near the end of the month, they were a big item.

This was still the old army. Moglia's company ate family style in the mess hall; each table had a noncommissioned officer in charge, at the head of the table. All plates were turned down, and all cups were upside down. The soldiers came into the mess hall, sat at their tables, and waited until the mess sergeant gave the command to turn plates. Then they turned the plates over, and the NCO at the table supervised the passing of food dishes. If you wanted sugar, salt, and the like, you asked that it be passed. You did not intercept the food as it came along—shortstopping was strictly forbidden, and for doing it you could get extra duty or something dumped on your head.

Private Moglia's training instructors worried about their boys—but not a lot. One of the recruits (he claimed to have been a hunting guide in upstate New York) got lost while walking his guard post around the coast artillery pieces on the shore, and walked off a dock into 20 feet of water. After the

splash, the officer of the day appeared in a hurry. He was really concerned—
for the M-1 rifle. The rifles were in such short supply that every one in the
army counted. A possible flap was avoided when both man and piece were
recovered and dried off.

Discipline was tough, and strange. Recruits were not permitted to talk to
officers in public. One day, in front of company headquarters, Lt. Albert
Smith saw that sad sack Private Moglia in his World War I leggings and all,
and asked him if he had been measured yet for a new uniform. Moglia replied. Five minutes later he was standing in front of the first sergeant's desk
getting a gigging, and facing hours of extra duty. The lieutenant came in and
got him out of the jam. Fortunately, said the private later, that officer survived the war to become *Colonel* Smith.

Thus were heroes made at Fort Wadsworth.

Ultimately the thirteen-week transformation period ended, and Private
Moglia became Pfc. Moglia, earning $36 a month. The regiment moved up
to Fort Devens, Massachusetts, and there the First Infantry Division ("Big
Red One") was put together for the first time since it had been disbanded
after World War I.

Finally the infantrymen of the Sixteenth Infantry got to fire their new
M-1 rifles on the firing range at Camp Wakefield. It was not easy. Pfc. Moglia
never did master that weapon as fired from the offhand (standing) position.
Nor did many of his comrades. It was a matter of considerable importance in
the camp, because unit competition was fierce, but finally when the statis-
tics were in, all units found difficulties. Only one man of the regiment managed to make a perfect score at all distances with the M-1 in offhand position.

As at Fort Meade, and all across the country, the training intensified. It
had to. These "soldiers" were all still rookies. It had been twenty-three years
since Americans had heard any shots fired in anger, and only a handful of
top sergeants and senior officers knew what war was all about.

So there were marches. And marches. And more marches. At Fort Meade
the cold weather of the winter of 1941 was a blessing in disguise: it meant
that Pfc. Elburn and his buddies didn't have to push the old two-wheel-drive
trucks out of the mud that piled up along the roads in the wet weather. Up
north at Fort Devens, it meant marches through the frozen New Hampshire
countryside. One night on a march toward Nashua, Pfc. Moglia got his first
glimpse of the Northern Lights. That was one wonder. Another was awak-
ening the next morning with the feeling that it had been raining during the
night. He and two others had been sleeping in an isolated area, to get away
from the mob, and that had been the place chosen by their buddies for re-

lief. There was something about bivouacking on the bare ground that created a lot of bladder activity. So three recruits learned something, the army
way, the hard way.

It was cold, cold, cold on that march, and when they got back to Fort
Devens, they were immediately issued tropical uniforms, pith helmets, short
pants, long socks—the works. Two weeks later they were issued skis, ski
pants, ski boots, parkas, heavy mittens, and face masks. Since no orders
were given about disposition of the equipment, a number of the brave youths
decided they would learn to ski unassisted. For the next twenty-four hours
the medics did a lively business in sprains, twists, turns, and breaks. The
next day all winter gear was abruptly recalled.

But the reason for the recall had nothing to do with the sprains and breaks.
The men of the Sixteenth Infantry were now to be trained in assault landings
from seagoing vessels. The first step: the outline of landing craft was drawn
on the ground at Fort Devens using white marking tape around a boat-shaped
area the size of an infantry squad.

"We would crouch in our 'assault boats' and upon command would rush
forward 'over the bow' and charge the enemy. Later we went to Buzzard's
Bay and boarded a former army transport that had previously been sunk. We
were going to do some real landings in Higgins boats, we were told. Those
were the plywood landing craft developed in the early 1940s."

The proceedings were disturbed by a strike of the civilian crew of the old
army transport, who did not care for army ways (no smoking on deck). That
settled, the landings could proceed, and did. The brave soldiers of the Sixteenth Infantry landed on the shores at Buzzard's Bay one gloomy morning to
be greeted by a horde of newsreel and still cameramen.

A few days later, Pfc. Moglia saw a newspaper photograph of himself
and his platoon "storming the beach," but the photo was part of an adver-
tisement. "U.S. Marines Drink Borden's Milk" was the caption.

While the First Infantry Division was learning to storm beaches near Cape
Cod, the same sort of activity was taking place virtually nationwide.

In April the army was still getting lots of volunteers. Thomas G. Wickham of
Muskegon, Michigan, was 19 years old. He had spent one year in college
and he was feeling restless. Perhaps, he thought, he would try a year in the
army—anyone under 21 could volunteer for one year's duty with automatic
release then—and then go back to college.

Wickham's father, a disabled World War I veteran, was very much opposed to the idea, but he finally signed the papers and took his son down to the train. It was off to Kalamazoo then for recruit Wickham, and after passing the test there, he went on to Fort Custer, near Battle Creek. There he got his uniform: another pair of those World War I–issue trousers, tight in the legs, to be worn with leggings, and an overcoat and blouse two sizes too small.

On Easter Sunday, all buttoned up in Class A uniform, the recruits marched out for Sunday sunrise services. They stood at attention for an hour, and Wickham thought he was going to faint because his overcoat and blouse were so tight. One soldier did pass out. He was left to lie there until the service ended.

From the processing center at Fort Custer, where during the second week he got a new uniform that fit, Private Wickham went to Fort Monmouth, New Jersey, and found that he had been arbitrarily assigned to the Signal Corps. At first he felt cheated. Then he shook off the self-pity and decided to learn Morse code and be a radio operator. After all, it was only for a year.

But first there was basic training.

Morning: Calisthenics, then school. The army basic manual, general orders, first aid, gas drill, Morse code, flag and radio operations.

Lunch.

Afternoon: Close order drill. Then field signal exercises. Also weapons practice. In those days soldiers in the Signal Corps carried .45-caliber revolvers—not semiautomatic Colt pistols. The men had to learn proficiency. They also stood guard duty, KP, latrine duty, garbage detail, and area police details. It wasn't the infantry, which Wickham had wanted, but he adjusted.

April 7, 1941: Arthur Campbell, a lawyer from Seattle, was called to active duty with the army. Captain Campbell had been in World War I in France, but now he was Lieutenant Colonel Campbell, assigned to the headquarters of the Washington-Alaska Military District in Seattle.

In May 1941 those infantrymen Private Wickham so admired were moving back and forth on heavy training schedules. The men of the 110th at Indiantown Gap had spent a good deal of time during the winter months sodding and seeding the training grounds. That spring the reason became evident: Indiantown Gap was to be a major training installation. Artillery units from the Twenty-ninth Division came up that May, and Corporal Chattaway and his Twenty-eighth Division friends went south to Camp A. P. Hill near Fredericksburg for regimental exercises. So did the regiments of the Twenty-ninth.

That summer of 1941 seemed hotter than usual to the soldiers marching, marching everywhere. In July Private Wickham was graduated from radio school and sent to Selfridge Field, Michigan, to join the Thirty-eighth Signal Platoon. Almost immediately the unit was ordered to move out to Louisiana for maneuvers. Private Wickham managed one twenty-four-hour pass, hitchhiked back to Muskegon, and—almost immediately it seemed—turned around and hitchhiked back to Selfridge Field.

The platoon packed up and headed south, through southern Michigan, Indiana, Kentucky, and Tennessee. The men crossed the Mississippi at Memphis, and then went down into Arkansas and onto Esler Field, near Camp Beauregard, Louisiana.

They pitched pyramidal tents and put up two shacks: one was the mess hall and the other was the latrine and showers.

"God it was *hot!* Rain clouds would form every day. After a short deluge that turned the clay soil to gumbo, the sun came out and baked the ground hard again."

There was little for a radioman to do, so Private Wickham became a telephone lineman. After "burning a few poles" (sliding down by accident), he got the hang of climbing. Then it was out to the field in pup tents, stringing line for the maneuvers. The GIs called the Louisiana maneuvers "the wooden gun war," because all their machine guns and mortars for protecting the airfield were yellow wooden stakes with the stenciled designations ".30-caliber machine gun" and "60-mm mortar." The planes that came in to attack the airfield dropped sacks of flour. If they hit the runway, the airfield was deemed "out of commission."

After the Louisiana maneuvers, the platoon was sent up to Spartanburg, South Carolina, for war games. It was the same set of maneuvers over again. One night the "enemy" bombed the airfield, and an attack by paratroops was announced. Wickham and his friends spent the night in a slit trench, watching their commanding officer running about giving orders as if something was really going to happen. That was the purpose of those war games, to pretend that something might happen so that the High Command would have some indication of the state of readiness of this new American army that had begun to burgeon just a year earlier.

*

September 17, 1941: Lieutenant Colonel Campbell was ordered to Fort Benning to take the battalion commander and staff officer's course at the Infantry School. Mrs. Campbell came along and found a place to live nearby.

On October 5, 1941, the first American airborne unit was brought into being, the 504th Parachute Battalion, at Fort Benning. The commanding officer was Maj. Richard Chase. One of his staff officers was Capt. Reuben H. Tucker. Capt. Doyle Yardley was commander of Company C. Soon Capt. Edson D. Raff joined up.

Most of the men knew nothing about parachutes. Now they were to learn. They learned how to pack parachutes, and how to jump. And they learned the parachutists' prayer: *God bless the silkworm.*

Soon the men were qualified jumpers, Class 9, Fort Benning Jump School.

For the holidays the battalion put on the biggest spread many of the men had ever seen: oyster cocktail, olives, mixed pickles, cream of celery soup, celery hearts, roast turkey with oyster dressing, cranberry sauce, giblet gravy with rice, apple and date salad, asparagus tips, candied sweet potatoes, mince pie, creamed cauliflower, creamed peas, ambrosia, pound cake, hot rolls, grapes, ice cream, crackers, tangerines, oranges, apples, bananas, and coffee or lemonade. It was the greatest meal the men of the battalion would ever have in all their years of service.

Captain Reeder was promoted to major. He was graduated from the Fort Benning Battalion Command School in November 1941, and was assigned to Fort Ord, California. He had leave before reporting to the Thirty-second Infantry; he spent it finding a house for his family at Carmel and playing golf at Pebble Beach. It sounded like a cushy assignment, joining the Thirty-second Infantry in this pleasant climate. But Reeder and his brother, a navy flier, had talked over the world situation and both were sure that war for the United States was just around the corner.

3

CAROLINA
MOON

The army was changing fast in that summer and fall of 1941. Brig. Gen. Omar Bradley, commander of the Infantry School at Fort Benning, was running ninety-day wonders through the courses, to make combat officers of them. Officers who had previously tried to map out their careers in a sensible fashion suddenly found themselves cast in entirely new roles: Capt. Maxwell D. Taylor, a student of the Japanese language in Tokyo in 1939, spent the spring and early summer of 1941 on a special mission in Latin America, trying to figure out the hemispheric defenses that would be needed against the German threat. That mission was led by Lt. Col. Matthew B. Ridgway. Taylor was chosen because he also had a thorough knowledge of Spanish. Thus was sacrificed this officer's knowledge and understanding of the Japanese people and their language and customs. By late summer 1941 Taylor was a major, working at the seat of army power, the office of Chief of Staff George C. Marshall in Washington, a place where young officers who performed well got noticed by people who counted. It was a whole new army: no longer was a man commissioned, hopeful of ascending the ladder in five-year leaps, second lieutenant to first lieutenant, then to captain, to major, and the all-important jump to lieutenant colonel which brought gold braid to the full-dress uniform cap. The dangers and pitfalls along the road were many: physical disability pushed a man onto the retirement list immediately; the competition within the service was fierce, for every spring a whole new class of West Point cadets were graduated and they became second lieutenants pushing up from below; and very occasionally some deserving noncom was reborn into the ranks of "officers and gentlemen."

If an officer survived in this peacetime army, he might retire as a colonel, if he was lucky. Beyond that, only the miraculously fortunate could rise to the rank of brigadier general or even higher. Why, it seemed just months earlier that Gen. George C. Marshall had been commandant of the army barracks at Fort Vancouver, Washington, where his greatest responsibility had been supervision of the Pacific war games.

All this was changing, and fast. The new young officers had to be brought along, because men such as General Reckord of the Twenty-ninth Division were overage in grade and unfit, for the most part, for combat command. General Reckord, after all, had been a regimental commander in World War I (115th Infantry) and had served now for many years in the National Guard. Even now, General Bradley was looking around for some younger man to take his job as commander at Fort Benning, because Marshall wanted Bradley to organize a fighting division that could be taken overseas. So promotions and changes were coming very fast for the regular army officers, who had been waiting patiently throughout their careers. The problem was and would be to make sure that the men who got the important leadership posts were round pegs in round holes. There would be a great deal of sorting out over the next few months.

On the eastern seaboard, as noted, the first major show was the Carolina maneuvers, held in and around Fort Bragg, North Carolina.

Whatever training the men had undergone before was simple compared to what they now faced. Pfc. Elburn and the others of the Twenty-ninth Division were camped first near the artillery range of Fort Bragg, in the dust of the scrub oak forest that was so sandy the tent pegs would not always hold. The companies posted guards to slow traffic on the roads and keep the sand down so that the food in the mess tents would be edible. The area was full of sand, fleas, mosquitoes, and snakes.

Each division was pitted against another for the exercises. The purpose was to knock out the enemy by "killing" or capturing its men. The Twenty-ninth Division, for example, was to fight the Twenty-eighth Division.

Corporal Chattaway's 110th Infantry went into camp in winterized pyramidal tents between Wadesboro and Lilesville. They were lucky.

The Sixteenth Infantry arrived for the maneuvers minus most of its heavy weapons. Pfc. Moglia was assigned as a BAR (Browning automatic rifle) man and scout during the First Division's war game. His company immediately became lost, logistically speaking, and was cut off from the battalion by the enemy. It was a truly desperate situation, because the men had no emergency rations, and they got very hungry that night. Next morning, telling the men that under no condition could they leave their positions, their lieutenant went to a nearby farmhouse, where he was welcomed royally by the farm family and fed an old-fashioned North Carolina farm breakfast of bacon, eggs, coffee, cake, and grits. Scout Moglia, determined to do his job and follow his leader, found his own farmhouse, and ate eggs, sausages, coffee, and grits, served to him by the farmer's daughter.

Refreshed, the lieutenant then led his company forth from entrapment, and Scout Moglia sniffed out the terrain ahead.

They were soon surprised by an "enemy" tank. The tank pulled up in front of Moglia's platoon position, and a helmeted figure stood up in the turret and announced that Moglia and his buddies were now prisoners of war.

What to do?

The infantrymen were armed with grenades—Bull Durham roll-your-own cigarette tobacco bags filled with sand. Moglia stood up and pitched a "grenade" at the tank, hitting the figure who was standing in the turret—all the better to command his captives—smack in the kisser.

"Dead men can't take prisoners," Pfc. Moglia shouted.

Whereupon, out of the forest came the umpires, to adjudge the case. The "dead" tank commander turned out to be a colonel, and seeing this, Pfc. Moglia melted off into the scrub oak, yielding the case to whomever wanted to argue.

Soon a New England horse cavalry unit moved into action on the side of Moglia's force. The horsemen surrounded the whole platoon of tanks and went riding around, like Indians surrounding a wagon train, firing their .45-caliber pistols and shouting, "Surrender! You're surrounded!"

It was a great show from early October until December. The warriors fought all week, and then took the weekends off. Passes let the soldiers descend on Charlotte, Wadesboro, and other towns to whoop it up on Saturday night. There was more fighting in these towns on weekends than in the field all week, Maj. Gen. Lloyd Fredendall, observing the carnage here and there, announced to his staff. By Monday the battlers were almost too tired to resume the war.

"The troops were divided into two armies, the blues (us) and the reds (enemy). At first, in early October, everyone wanted to be assigned to the red army, because those troops wore cool blue-denim fatigue uniforms in the fighting, while the blue army was outfitted in OD wool."

But as October became November and the Carolina air cooled down, the blues were glad to have the wool, particularly since one of the rules of this combat was that no campfires were permitted. But the GI could find a way: the "battle" raged around the farms of the area, and most of the farmers were most sympathetic to the young men, such very young men. They would come out, with their wives and daughters and sons, bearing pies and cakes and other goodies, and would sympathize with the citizen soldiers sitting around their chilly bivouacs.

"Why don't you build a fire?"

"Can't. Against orders."

"Dang the orders. This is my farm. I'm feeling a mite chilly."

And so, in a jiffy, a nice warm campfire was blazing, and everyone huddled around with their hands out—until an angry officer would show up and move the outfit away from the farm. But the next evening it would be the same somewhere else along the battle perimeter, as the officers fought "the enemy" and the soldiers fought the cold. The observers complained that "the goddamn countryside looked like an amusement park." If this were a real war, they said, all the enemy had to do was zero the artillery in and half the red army would be dead already.

While the guardsmen and reservists were fighting the battle of the blues and reds in North Carolina, the war machine was gearing up from Maine to California. Joseph W. Miller, a Kansas City boy, was living the happy life of a bachelor after his university graduation in 1936. He had found a job with one of the expanding New Deal agencies of the federal government and had plenty of money to spend. Then came the Selective Service Act, and since he was a very young bachelor with no ties, Joe Miller was regarded as extremely eligible for the draft. He was 1-A and high on the list.

When the draft board began sniffing at his heels, Joe Miller tried to enlist in the navy. But when he put on glasses to read the eye chart, a bored petty officer turned him down. So the government took its course, and on November 4, 1941, Joe Miller received a message from Washington that began: "Greetings..."

Joe was drafted and became Pvt. Joseph Miller. His first destination was the reception center at Fort Leavenworth. From there he was cut out of the herd with a group of others and sent to the Engineering Basic Training School at Fort Leonard Wood, Missouri. Private Miller was learning close order drill and the nomenclature of weapons and how to make a bed army style, while Pfc. Elburn and Pfc. Moglia and Corporal Chattaway fought the battle of North Carolina.

There was no such thing as a C ration or a K ration in Carolina that fall of 1941. In the morning when the soldiers set out for the day's war, each man was given three sandwiches—one bologna, one cheese, and one jelly—and a piece of fruit. The canny GI's approach was to get close to a farmhouse and a handout to augment this ration. As far as Pfc. Moglia could tell, the farmers' wives seemed to spend most of their time cooking, because his unit was forever being offered pies and cakes and hot homemade food.

Pfc. Moglia remembered Thanksgiving Day as the best time of all during the maneuvers. The platoon had taken position very near a farmhouse. Moglia was sitting on a rock near the house eating Donkey Dick—bologna—for his lunch and thinking about Long Island and happy holidays of the past. A woman came out of the house, looked at his bologna sandwich, and asked if that was his Thanksgiving dinner.

"Yes," said Pfc. Moglia, with all the wistfulness he could muster.

In a few moments he found himself sitting on the enclosed porch of the farmhouse, at a porch table, eating a real Thanksgiving dinner.

Up came his platoon leader.

"What in the hell are you doing?"

"Eating," said Pfc. Moglia, taking another bite.

"I'm going to put you on report, *Private* Moglia. Get your ass off that porch, and keep your eyes peeled.... The enemy..."

Fortunately, just then a large unit of the red army did appear, firing weapons and making plenty of noise, and in the confusion Pfc. Moglia got off the hook and retained his stripe.

It got colder, but the maneuvers continued. One day Moglia and his buddy, Al Klimek, challenged each other to take a bath. The process involved cutting a hole through the top of a frozen pond near their camp. They did, and survived. The platoon sergeant asked caustically why the two of them were wearing purple underwear, but they survived.

As the "war" drew to a close, the Sixteenth Infantry's base camp moved down near the town of Star, North Carolina. When the weekend came, the older warriors headed for town and some excitement. Pfc. Moglia and Pfc. Jim Pizzi went the other way, hunting a good dinner, on the basis of Moglia's

Thanksgiving experience. The plan was to go up to a nice-looking house and ask to "buy" some coffee and maybe a piece of cake.

It was a grand ploy. They knocked at a door and it opened. There stood a very pretty young woman.

"Ma," she said, "the U.S. Army has come to call."

So her ma came to the door and so did her pa. They were Mr. and Mrs. Albert Davis, and they had nine children, from 1 to 16 years old. "The army" had already met the 16-year-old and they now met the others. The Davises invited the soldiers to stay for dinner. Since that was their purpose, they did.

It was a long table, with a lazy susan and a lot of dishes on it, and they all helped themselves. The house had no electricity or central heating. The water supply system consisted of a kitchen pump, and Mrs. Davis was real proud of that—it was right there inside the house.

"After supper was over we sat by the fireplace for a chat, and Ma Davis reached up by the fireplace for a twist of chewing tobacco. She offered us a chew. We declined, but sat there, watching her, a nursing mother, nursing her baby and chawing. Occasionally she sprayed the fireplace logs with tobacco juice."

The soldiers went away that evening, but the next weekend Mr. Davis came to camp to invite Moglia to spend the weekend with his family.

"Impossible," said the platoon leader. "Pfc. Moglia is engaged in a military exercise."

"Who's in charge here?" asked Mr. Davis. "A colonel?"

"Yes."

"I want to see him."

So Mr. Davis was taken to see the colonel. He explained that his wife had cooked a special dinner for Pfc. Moglia and his daughter had baked a cake. He also explained that he was a taxpayer and he paid the colonel's salary.

"Furthermore," he said, "I want John to go rabbit hunting with me."

So, to the surprise of all the platoon, Pfc. Moglia took off that weekend and went rabbit hunting with Mr. Davis and feasting with the whole tribe. What a weekend! What a war!

The war training of this new army of the United States went on everywhere. Late in September Lieutenant Shebeck had been sent down to General Bradley's command at Fort Benning as a student in the rifle and heavy weap-

ons course. He and some 200 other company grade officers, including a pair
of marines, had come from National Guard and reserve units all over the
country. It was a matter of teaching the teachers; these men were to take
their information and teach their own units when they got back. They had
twelve weeks to learn expertise in the M-1 rifle, the .45-caliber pistol, light
and heavy machine guns, 60- and 81-millimeter mortars, and the 37-milli-
meter antitank gun. They also were to learn map reading, scouting, and patrolling—and how to teach all these skills to men down to the squad level.
All in twelve weeks.

By the end of the first week in December Shebeck was pooped. Most of
the students had taken off that weekend for big parties in Atlanta or Columbus, but he and half a dozen others had elected to sleep away the time instead.

                    *   *   *

So had some of the GI and gob clients of the Iwilei district whorehouses of
Honolulu, who were snoring away vigorously at the sides of their diminutive
companions when the Japanese bombs started falling. Warren Adachi, who
lived near Pearl Harbor, got some friends together and took his truck down
to the base to try to help. He was turned away by the MPs.

Herbert Yamamura was ironing clothes in the family laundry in Kona
when the radio announcer screamed that Pearl Harbor had been attacked.

Makoto Sakamoto was working on a new building for the navy near Ford
Island when the bombs fell. He dived for cover.

Fumio Kido heard the explosions at Hickam Field and saw the Japanese
insignia on the planes. He was disgusted: "Oh, them dumb buggahs. Now
they get it."

There were time differences: three hours to the Pacific coast.

In Seattle, Henry Gosho, the son of a local druggist, was on his way to
choir practice when he heard the radio announce the Japanese attack.

Six hours to the east coast.

Lieutenant Shebeck was sacked out at about one o'clock in the afternoon, when one of his classmates came running into the BOQ, shouting.
This particular officer did things like that. As everybody in the class knew,
he could be up to anything, anything at all.

"The Japanese have just attacked Pearl Harbor!"

"Sure," said Lieutenant Shebeck. "Where's Pearl Harbor?"

"Hey you guys, no kidding. The Japs have attacked Pearl Harbor."

"Listen," said one of the other officers, "you can get yourself in big trouble if you run around spreading rumors like that. Buzz off."

So the messenger, deflated, went off to more salubrious climes to deliver his message, and the young officers in the BOQ resumed their relaxing afternoon. But then someone turned on the radio, and a Columbus station broke into a program of dance music with an emergency announcement:

"The Japanese have just bombed the U.S. Pacific Fleet base at Pearl Harbor. The extent of the damage is not yet known."

So there it was. Pearl Harbor. The U.S. Pacific Fleet.

The afternoon wore away. A very subdued group of young infantry officers hung around the BOQ, not saying very much, twisting the radio dial to get what little information was being released about the disaster to the fleet. As the others came trouping back from Atlanta and Columbus, they were told. Most of them already had the word, for it had spread very quickly through America that day.

Major Reeder left his wife and children sleeping in their Carmel house that Sunday morning and drove along the Seventeen Mile Drive to the Pebble Beach golf course. He played eighteen holes with the assistant pro and won $5. Then he bought a new wedge and practiced recovering from a sand trap for half an hour. He walked into the clubhouse to hear the radio blaring the news of the Japanese attack on Pearl Harbor. He hurried home. Although he had fourteen more days of leave coming, he got his gear together and reported in at Fort Ord that day.

The fort was in a flap. The commanding officer of the Thirty-second Infantry, Colonel Culin, told him the regiment was to evacuate the fort that day. They marched at 6:30 that evening, for they had been told to expect a Japanese invasion of California. Major Reeder took over the Second Battalion. He and his 900 men were responsible for the protection of the 150 miles of coastline from Point Lobos to Pismo Beach, including San Simeon, the ranch castle of William Randolph Hearst. The battalion's command post was at Camp San Luis Obispo.

He had three huge portable guns, French *Grande Puissance Filloux*, which fired 95-pound projectiles for 10 miles. He had twenty-four jeeps. The job was patently impossible. Fortunately the Japanese did not arrive, although nearly every hour brought a new rumor that they were coming.

The battalion's one encounter with the enemy was secondhand. A Japanese submarine had sunk an American freighter off the California coast; when the lifeboats reached shore, the men of the Thirty-second Infantry gave them a hand. That was all.

When the North Carolina maneuvers ended, the Thirty-eighth Signal Platoon loaded up its communications gear and started back for Selfridge Field. Up through Tennessee the soldiers went, and on December 7 they traveled all day without a stop in any town. In the evening, as their convoy rolled into Marion, Indiana, where they were to put up for the night at the local armory, they heard people on the sidewalks shouting something about the bombing of Pearl Harbor. That didn't mean very much to anybody. When the trucks were parked and the bedrolls pulled out, the men went inside the armory and there got the full story of what had happened in Hawaii that morning. The medical officer had a portable radio, and most of the men clustered around it long into the night to hear the news reports.

"This was war!"

In the morning they moved nonstop to Selfridge Field, and there they learned what war meant. All furloughs were canceled. That was what it meant—just then—to Private Wickham and his friends.

Early in December, with the blue army having defeated the red army and all the action ended, Pfc. Moglia's Sixteenth Infantry also started back up north to its base. The men traveled through Pennsylvania, and whenever they stopped to camp, the country people rallied around with cider, milk, salami, bread, fruitcake, beer, and cookies. En route they were told that they might have leave if they were not too far from home, because they would not have to be back to duty for two weeks. Some of the men took advantage of the offer and left the convoy. Pfc. Moglia was in no hurry. He decided to wait until they arrived back at Fort Devens. Then he would clean up his uniforms and go on leave with a light heart.

Alas, he arrived back at camp on the day Pearl Harbor was attacked, and instead of going on leave, he went on guard duty around the officers' quarters. That was what the war meant just then to Pfc. Moglia.

When the Japanese struck, Pvt. Joseph Miller was not halfway through his basic training course. But the coming of war speeded up everything. What was needed—and fast—were men who could manage to sort out personnel. Someone noticed that Private Miller was a college graduate with work experience in personnel. He was pulled into the classification section of the G-1 office, to help process the thousands of recruits who were pouring into the camp, thousands who would be coming ever faster as the pace stepped up.

Pvt. Joe Miller was delighted. It seemed that he had found a "home" in the army for the duration, and a cushy job, not too far from his real home.

"No hero, I, this work suited me to a T."

That was what war meant then to Private Miller.

William G. Haemmel was a high school senior. He lived with his widowed mother in a four-room apartment in the South Bronx section of New York City. All day long on December 7 he had been studying for midterm examinations. Late in the afternoon he turned on the radio and heard a news broadcaster describing an angry, milling crowd in front of the Japanese Embassy in Washington.

What was this all about? Had the Japanese really been using poison gas in China? That had been the rumor for the past few days. He listened. It was only at the end of the newscast, when the announcer summed up, that Bill Haemmel learned of the Japanese attack on Pearl Harbor.

War came to Corporal Chattaway's company when the soldiers were tented down on a snow-covered hillside at Camp A. P. Hill in Virginia. They were on their way back up to Indiantown Gap Military Reservation. It was almost Christmas. Then they had January to get through, and then came February, which would mean the end of their twelve-month tour of duty. They had been expecting to go home then and resume their lives. But now?

In a matter of hours, they knew. Their tour of duty was extended "for the duration." Duration of what?

John P. Downing was in his last year at the University of Michigan. He held a commission as a first lieutenant in the Army Reserve, which he had acquired through years in the National Guard. He was old for college (29); that was because he was a Depression child and had been forced to stop school from time to time and earn the money needed to go back to school. The day after Pearl Harbor he was ordered to take a physical exam at Fort Wayne and report for active duty. He managed to get deferred until the end of the semester, but that would be the end of it. There was no question of finishing up the college year. Uncle Sam needed Lieutenant Downing, and needed him in a hurry.

Lieutenant Colonel Campbell's course at the Infantry School was shortened, and the class was graduated on December 8. He had expected two weeks of leave. It was canceled and he was told to report immediately back to his post in Seattle. Campbell drove 3560 miles in six days to get there.

To the new civilian soldiers in the service there was nothing personal about the war at the outset, but the newspapers and other news media began bringing the war home to America with details about Pearl Harbor, about the fighting on Wake Island, the loss of Guam, and the war in the Philippines.

From the moment that President Roosevelt went before Congress to denounce the Japanese attack, the pressure began to build.

The GIs learned what "duration" meant.

Duration meant the duration of the war that the Japanese had begun and the Germans and the Italians would soon join, a war that would not end until Hitler and Mussolini had been defeated and the Japanese had been properly punished for their infamous attack on the people of the United States. That was what the war meant to everybody.

4

THE WAY
OVERSEAS

It was evening in England on December 7, 1941, when Prime Minister Winston Churchill learned that the Japanese had attacked Pearl Harbor. It was a measure of his growing dependence on the United States that the prime minister was dining that evening at his country house, Chequers, with U.S. Ambassador John G. Winant and U.S. Special Ambassador W. Averell Harriman. The prime minister did not try to conceal his pleasure at the thought that Britain would now have the complete cooperation of the United States in the war:

> No American will think it wrong of me if I proclaim that to have the United States at our side was to me the greatest joy. I could not foretell the course of events. I do not pretend to have measured accurately the martial might of Japan, but now at this very moment I knew the United States was in the war, up to the neck and in to the death. So we had won after all!

Or had they? After the initial euphoria it became evident that most Americans were far more concerned with the war against Japan than the struggle in Europe. No matter that Hitler and Mussolini were hurrying to declare war on the United States; it was the Japanese who had attacked the United States, not the Germans, not the Italians.

Despite all the dangers of a trans-Atlantic voyage, despite the hiatus in leadership of the British war effort that his absence would necessarily create, despite the new crisis created by the sinking of the *Repulse* and the *Prince of Wales* and the attack toward Singapore by the Japanese, Churchill decided that he must go to America to persuade President Roosevelt to devote the major American war effort to the struggle in Europe, not in Asia. Britain's lifeline was the endless convoy, bringing supplies from the New World. Admiral Dönitz's submarine menace was growing stronger every week. The lifeline must not be cut; the Americans must realize the dangers and fight the war in Europe first.

That was the purpose of Churchill's mission to America—first persuading the Americans and then planning how they could help to carry the war against Hitler.

Prime Minister Churchill had to go before the House of Commons on December 10 with the bad news of the *Repulse* and the *Prince of Wales* sinking—two real shockers to the British nation, which had long held the battleship and the battle cruiser to be the most powerful vessels on the seas. Sunk by aircraft! What a shock indeed.

He also had to prepare the government for this new change in the war.

While he was doing so, on December 11, Lieutenant Shebeck at Fort Benning was out on a field problem in the Harmony Church area of the reservation. Suddenly a jeep came roaring up in a cloud of dust and stopped near the little knot of men. Out jumped a lieutenant colonel.

"Germany and Italy have just declared war on the United States," he said. And like the White Rabbit, without further ado, he jumped back into the jeep and sped off, to find another group of men and deliver the breathless message.

Well, so what? After December 7 it didn't take a genius to figure out what was going to happen. Lieutenant Shebeck and his comrades were distinctly underwhelmed. They went back to their field problem.

What the message did mean in practical terms was a new spurt in the training program. Lieutenant Shebeck and his friends were graduated from their course ten days later. General Bradley, who had not yet managed to find someone to succeed him so that he could take a combat command, handed out the diplomas. Immediately after came their marching orders: Lieutenant Shebeck was assigned to the Infantry Training Center at Camp Wolters, Texas.

Lieutenant Shebeck had planned to get married after graduation to a young lady who was teaching school in North Dakota. He had been expecting to take a little leave before taking his post. His fiancée had come from North Dakota to Fort Benning, and they expected to enjoy a brief honeymoon. That had certainly seemed a reasonable enough idea to an army that early in December was giving two weeks' leave to the survivors of the North Carolina massacres. But December 7 changed everything. Leave? Let not Lieutenant Shebeck be ridiculous. Didn't he know there was a war on? It was December 21, and he was to report for duty at Camp Wolters on December 24. So without a wedding ring (it had not arrived in time), without the bride's trousseau (it had gotten mixed up in the luggage aboard some train), and while a taxi waited to take them to the railroad station to catch the train, the couple were married. They caught the train and spent their wedding night in a day coach between Columbus, Georgia, and New Orleans. On December 24, while Prime Minister Churchill met with Secretary of State Cordell Hull in Washington to discuss the fall of Wake Island and other disasters in the Pacific, Lieutenant Shebeck reported for duty at Camp Wolters and was immediately assigned as commander of Company B, 164th Infantry Training Battalion. This was how the brass was going to put together an army in a hurry. Shebeck and two other officers had 254 men who were taking thirteen weeks of basic infantry training; these would help man the new divisions that had to be created.

As Lieutenant Shebeck began snapping his unit into line, Prime Minister Churchill continued his American mission. Churchill presented three position papers on the war. He persuaded President Roosevelt that America should combine with Britain in 1942 to attack in north Africa. He secured the formation of a Combined Chiefs of Staff Committee (headquartered in Washington) to control the strategic decisions of the global war effort against the Rome-Berlin-Tokyo Axis. He secured the promise of quick dispatch of bomber and fighter squadrons of the U.S. Army Air Corps to England.

Churchill had come to America hoping that perhaps four divisions of American troops could be dispatched swiftly to Northern Ireland and more U.S. troops to Iceland. But he had come without real knowledge of the state of American defenses in December 1941.

Churchill described what he found:

Owing to the shipping stringency this will not be possible on any very large scale during 1942. Meanwhile the United States Army is being raised from a strength of a little over thirty divisions and five armoured divisions to a

total strength of about sixty divisions and ten armoured divisions. About
3,750,000 men are at present held or about to be called up for the Army
and Air Force (over a million). Reserves of man-power are practically unlimited, but it would be a misdirection of war effort to call larger numbers
to the armed forces in the present phase.

It does not seem likely that more than between a quarter and a third of the
above American forces can be transported to actual fighting fronts during the
year 1942. In 1943 however the great increases in shipping tonnage resulting
from former and recent shipping programmes should enable much larger bodies
to be moved across the oceans, and the summer of 1943 may be marked by
large offensive operations, which should be carefully studied meanwhile.

There was, as Churchill learned but did not dwell upon, another reason
for his difficulty in securing troops: the American forces simply did not have
40,000 available troops who were well enough trained to be dispatched to
Northern Ireland. President Roosevelt felt that he might have to send 50,000
men to the Pacific in the near future, just to hold the lines. The American
war effort was gearing up, but it was going to take some time for Lieutenant
Shebeck and those other graduates of Fort Benning to train the recruits so
that they would have a chance to survive in battle.

During the Washington meetings General Marshall called on the prime minister and asked him some tough questions. He had agreed that in the next
few months he would send 30,000 American soldiers to Northern Ireland.
How was he going to get them there? The prime minister offered him the two
great British liners, *Queen Mary* and *Queen Elizabeth*, the only 80,000-ton
passenger ships in the world, for this purpose. But even these two great vessels could carry only about 8000 troops each on a voyage if there was to be
sufficient flotation gear to save all the troops in case of disaster. Because of
the urgent situation, Churchill suggested, in effect, that they say to hell with
disaster, and load the ships to the brim. Marshall went away with his face
set in a mold that indicated he was not very pleased with the answer.

While these momentous decisions were in the making in the seats of power,
the men who would be carried in those vessels were being hurried along in
their training.

Corporal Chattaway's 110th Infantry was ordered to move from Indiantown
Gap to Camp Livingston, Louisiana, and on January 9 the long motor trek

south began. Movement also occurred in another way as the army expanded: Corporal Chattaway was jumped two grades to become a staff sergeant, the rank designated by the table of organization as a weapons platoon sergeant of Company A.

The declaration of war by the Germans and their dispatch of a half-dozen submarines to strike at shipping off the American coast created an enormous surge of activity. The fact was that the Army Air Forces and the navy had only a handful of planes and virtually no small vessels capable of combating the submarine threat. And as far as the army was concerned, its principal new job was to protect everything from invasion. To the Twenty-ninth Division this meant a new responsibility: defense of the Atlantic coast from Cape Hatteras to New Jersey. The 116th's 75-millimeter guns were taken to the shore around Hatteras and pointed out to sea. Motorized patrols covered all the beaches. In the sands where even jeeps dare not go, sentries walked 6-mile posts through sunshine, wind, and storm. At Fort Meade one of the four division regiments was kept on twenty-four-hour alert. It was a sign of the progress of the army that the alert division could be completely motorized to react to invasion. New lessons had to be learned: blackouts for air defense, dispersion of motor pools. In January Pfc. Elburn's 115th Infantry was scattered over Pennsylvania and Virginia guarding factories, railroad bridges, docks, and warehouses. Elburn's Second Battalion was on guard duty at Norfolk, ready for the Nazi shock troops—or as ready as they could be, with just about a year of training. The shortage of weapons was still so severe that the 175th Regiment, in training at Fort Meade, had to give up its machine guns to meet the needs of the 115th, on guard duty.

In January 1942 Pfc. Elburn and Pfc. Moglia might have met, had things turned out a bit differently. A military maneuver was planned in Washington to prove and improve American shore defenses. The First Division, in training in Massachusetts, was to "invade" the Virginia coast while the Twenty-ninth Division was to defend it and push the invaders back into the cold January Atlantic.

Considering the state of training of the army troops and the condition of the Atlantic in January, the navy thought the army was nuts. The Wehrmacht certainly was not about to launch an invasion across thousands of miles off rigid sea. But Washington decreed that the mock invasion was to be held, so Pfc. Moglia and his buddies of the Sixteenth Infantry were loaded aboard the transport USS *Wakefield* and moved out down the coast. The GIs were told they were going to Puerto Rico, which was all right with them, a winter vacation paid for by Uncle Sam.

But off the Virginia coast at Cape Henry, the vacation-bound GIs were treated to a rude surprise. On January 12 they were ordered out in full kit to prepare for an amphibious invasion of the beach. Pfc. Moglia had a lot of experience in rushing off the "bow" of that tape-made "landing craft" and assaulting the enemy, but this would be a little different. The men would go over the side of the *Wakefield*, down the landing nets into Higgins boats, and then would be decanted ashore by the navy, to attack the Twenty-ninth Division and conquer.

The morning of January 12 dawned foul and gray. A force 5 wind was blowing, and the whitecaps were up. Squalls slapped across the decks of the *Wakefield*, stinging the faces of anyone unlucky enough to be up there.

It was, announced the navy, too rough to make any amphibious landings.

"Nonsense," said the army, "the show must go on."

The matter was appealed to a higher authority, who ruled for the army, and so the first Higgins boat was put over the side and the assigned load of GIs scrambled down in the cold, over those slippery nets, into the boat.

Then...Crunch, crash, smash, gurgle, gurgle, gurgle. Down went the wreckage of the Higgins boat along the side, and the navy came to rescue the floundering soldiers.

"See," said the navy, "it's too damned rough to launch landing craft."

"The hell you say," said Pfc. Moglia's battalion commander. "My men are tough. Put another boat over the side."

And so Pfc. Moglia and the rest of his squad clambered over the rail and down the slippery nets, half falling into the bouncing Higgins boat. The navy coxswain lost no time in moving fast toward the shore, the boat bouncing and smashing in the heavy sea. They made it into shallow water; then a huge wave poured in across the stern of the slowing Higgins boat, pooping them, as the navy men say. The Higgins boat capsized under all that weight, throwing most of the men into the water. Fortunately they were close enough to the beach to scramble ashore, except for Pfc. Moglia and the coxswain, who were trapped in the wrecked Higgins boat, the anchor having shifted in the wreck and the line holding them both down. Luckily, the coxswain was a real seaman and did not go on duty without his work knife. He got it loose and slashed the anchor line. Then the sailor and soldier struggled ashore, coughing and spitting up seawater.

There were no casualties, but Pfc. Moglia's boatload was also the lone invasion force on the beach. Having seen what had happened to two of the Higgins boats, the navy had objected again and this time had triumphed. The "invasion" was called off.

Whatever had happened to the Twenty-ninth Division the men of the First

Division did not know, but the doughty defenders were nowhere to be seen in the miserable weather. Obviously somebody with intelligence had decided it was too foul for war games.

The stranded invasion force wandered around; and by lunchtime the troops were growing hungry because, as usual, they did not have any emergency rations with them. Pfc. Moglia, as scout, wandered into a watermelon field and considered the theft of a melon. His honesty was saved when a farmer showed up. Moglia asked if he could buy a melon.

"Sure."

"How much?"

"A quarter."

Pfc. Moglia reached into the wet trousers of his OD uniform. No cash. All he had was 15 cents in soggy postage stamps. The farmer took it, and Moglia and his friends ate the watermelon.

Eventually they were found by the "defenders," and when the weather settled down a little they were dispatched by small boat back to the *Wakefield*. That trip wasn't smooth either. It was nearly dusk. It had been a long and hungry day, and they were just about in time for chow. The boat came up on the leeward side of the ship, out of the wind, and the soldier passengers prepared to climb up the landing nets, which were still hanging there. Just then, the galley crew decided it was time to dump the garbage, and the ascending warriors were plastered with potato peelings, leftover gravy, and all the other delicacies of the garbage can. The men came over the side sputtering and dripping garbage. The officer of the deck took one look and called the army liaison officer. This crew was filthy. No, they could not go into the messdeck. Let them go below and get a shower and a change of clothing, and then...

So Pfc. Moglia's squad did not arrive home precisely in glory. But after a hot shower and a change, what a tale they had to tell the others. The only thing that spoiled their mood was the *Wakefield*'s turning around and heading north, away from the direction of Puerto Rico and back to the cold climes of Massachusetts.

Early in 1942 the military leaders in Washington decided that Japanese invasion of the California coast was not imminent, and the Thirty-second Infantry was sent into the desert to learn desert warfare. Major Reeder was promoted to lieutenant colonel and made executive officer of the regiment. Then, without notice, he was transferred to General Marshall's staff in Washington.

*

After the bombing of Pearl Harbor the military authorities did not know what to do with the large Japanese and Japanese-American population of Hawaii. On the mainland the people of Japanese origin were thrown into concentration camps. But such people amounted to more than a third of the population of Hawaii, and in a sense the islands *were* an ideal concentration camp. The Japanese certainly weren't going anywhere. The invocation of martial law seemed enough.

One of the early acts of the military was to discharge all the Japanese-American members of the Hawaii Territorial Guard. The two National Guard regiments were also to be discharged. "Not trustworthy" was the reason. But then fair-minded civilians in Hawaii went to bat for the Japanese-Americans, and the army reversed itself. Wheels in Washington began to turn to make soldiers out of nisei.

The men of the Sixteenth Infantry did not know it, but while they had been "invading" the Virginia coast, great decisions were being made in Washington and London which would control their lives from that point on. Churchill's Washington visit had settled matters: a tendency in some quarters in Washington to turn attention toward Asia was reversed, and it was agreed that Hitler and Mussolini must be knocked out first, while the war in the Pacific would be maintained as virtually no more than a holding action.

Planning for action in Europe was speeded up. Lieutenant Colonel Campbell was recalled from Seattle and took the Union Pacific streamliner bound for Camp Beauregard, Louisiana. He was to join the headquarters of the Fifth Corps. When he arrived, he was told that the Fifth Corps was about to go overseas and he had better get his shots: typhoid, typhus, and yellow fever. Where were they going? No one would say. When? No one would say.

So in the winter of 1942, as the U-boats played havoc with Allied shipping off the coast of the United States, the frantic pace of training grew even faster. Men who had no battle experience, commanded by officers who had no battle experience, had to be made ready to fight under generals whose battle experience was either nil or very limited. And they had about six months to learn how to survive.

5

TO VERDANT
SHORES

In February 1942 the war began to come home to people along the Eastern Shore of the United States in a very personal manner. It was one thing to read in the newspapers about the bombing in China, the collapse of British forces in Malaya, the capture of Hong Kong, the fighting in the Philippines, and, of course, the bombing of London and the titanic struggle in north Africa, where General Rommel seemed to be defeating the British. Even further afield was the war that raged on the Russian front. What was at hand was the German U-boat campaign in American waters, a campaign that soon had the beaches from Cape Hatteras south running black with oil from sunken tankers. General Drum declared a state of emergency along the east coast; cities began to blackout (turn off the lights). The question of censorship was quickly raised, but a compromise was reached with the media, which by and large worked very well. The newspapers and radio stations stopped delivering weather reports, lest they aid the enemy, and they withheld information about ship sailings and troop movements. There were some slips, but not too many. Few Americans yet had any personal sense of loss, but to millions of Americans—despite the self-censorship of much of the news—the attacks began to bring home a growing understanding that this war was real.

Despite President Roosevelt's offhand assurances that American troops should be able to get overseas to help the British in short order, the movement could not be made that fast. By February Churchill and Roosevelt were in agreement that Operation Gymnast (the British-American invasion of French north Africa) would have to be delayed for several months. So must Operation Magnet (the movement of American troops to Northern Ireland). The British reason was shipping; the American reason was state of training. Behind both was the disastrous speed with which the Japanese were moving in the Pacific; this strained the resources of both allies. President Roosevelt had to abandon any immediate consideration of moving American troops to Iceland to free the British.

At the end of the first week of February 1942, officer candidate Joseph Miller was just about finished with his studies and training to become a second lieutenant in the Army of the United States. His eagerness for this prospect was anything but boundless:

"I still can't work up much enthusiasm for the idea of being a second looey, but I suppose I've got to try to make it now. If I thought I could get back my job as an interviewer, I'd do my damnedest to flunk out. But if I did flunk they'd probably ship me right out to Singapore or somewhere."

He was about to be graduated and sent to Fort Belvoir, Virginia, to perfect his engineering skills. The only welcome part as far as he was concerned was that he would soon be only thirty-three minutes from Washington, and would be able to do some tourist rubbernecking.

More classes of officers destined for infantry service were assigned to Gen. Omar Bradley's care at Fort Benning. He still had not managed to arrange affairs at this vital training center so that he could get away. As ordered, on February 12, 1942, Lt. John P. Downing arrived to take the weapons refresher course. While Downing was struggling with the field problems, General Bradley finally broke loose and, in March, moved down to Camp Claiborne, Louisiana, to organize the Eighty-second Division.

The Fifth Corps was going overseas, but Lieutenant Colonel Campbell was not to go immediately. He moved up to Fort Dix, New Jersey, and between conferences on matters such as operations and supply, the colonel had time for some sightseeing of his own. Mrs. Campbell came back east to celebrate her birthday with her husband. They went to Philadelphia and saw the Liberty Bell, and Colonel Campbell bought some uniforms. They went on to New York and stayed at the Hotel New Yorker. They saw Eddie Cantor in the musical *Banjo Eyes*, and then went to the Hawaiian Room of the Lexington Hotel (very popular with westerners). On Easter Sunday they went to St. Thomas's Church on Fifth Avenue for the services; afterward they watched the Easter parade. They rode a double-decker bus up to 185th Street and Riverside Drive and then they returned and had lunch at Rockefeller Center, where they watched the ice skating on the rink. They went to Atlantic City and then came back to New York, staying at the Commodore Hotel this time. They had dinner at Jensen's Hofbrau and ended up the night at Jack White's 18 Club.

This last entertainment was a farewell celebration, for the colonel was about to go overseas at last. On May 10 Mrs. Campbell started home to Seattle, and the next day Colonel Campbell sailed for the British Isles on the *Queen Mary* with other officers of the Fifth Corps. The British were getting troops for Northern Ireland at last. U.S. Fifth Corps headquarters was set up in Belfast.

From this point on, it would be meetings and planning, preparing for the arrival of hundreds of thousands of American GIs into Britain.

*   *   *

At the end of May 1942 the army organized the Hawaiian Provisional Battalion, an all-nisei unit. The men were to be sent to the mainland for training because if there was a Japanese invasion of Hawaii, which still seemed very possible, their presence in the islands could be more than a little confusing.

In June they went to Camp McCoy, Wisconsin, for infantry training.

In the spring of 1942 the 503d Parachute Infantry Regiment was activated and sent to Fort Bragg, North Carolina. An airborne command was also established.

Maj. Edson Raff became executive officer of the 503d; Captain Tucker left the 504th. And in June 1942 the Second Battalion of the 503d Parachute Infantry (which would become the 509th in one of those confusing army changes of designation) was sent to England to train with the British airborne forces.

That spring the war was going badly for England in the African campaign. The Germans were making a major assault on Malta, which meant the British had to expend enormous effort at sea and in the air in the Mediterranean

theater. The Americans sent the carrier *Wasp* to help out, but that was not
the sort of help the British needed. As the Russians kept saying, what was
needed were more fronts against the Germans. What England needed from
America, in addition to the supply line, were troops to come into the field.
General Marshall went to England to discuss the problems. He was in Britain
as General Bradley began to put together the Eighty-second Division down
in Louisiana. Marshall had to tell Churchill that it would be September before he could find even two and a half divisions to put into action. The political leaders were talking about bringing thirty American divisions over to
Europe. But the military men had to have time—and more time.

General Bradley was still in the throes of organizing the Eighty-second
Division in May, when Lieutenant Downing graduated from school and was
assigned to the First Division at Camp Blanding, Florida. It was an indication of the hurry-hurry-hurry philosophy that had overtaken the new army
that Downing and his fellow officers were given only one day as travel time
from Fort Benning to Camp Blanding. He was assigned to Company F of the
Eighteenth Infantry Regiment, introduced to Colonel Sherburne, the CO, and
shown his quarters. The company orderly pointed out the equipment that
had been drawn for the lieutenant: footlocker, gas mask, washbasin, helmet,
1903 Springfield, cartridge belt, suspenders, compass, shelter halves, poles,
pins, ropes and a bedding roll for making up a pup-tent bed, blankets, sheets,
field glasses, musette bag, canteen, cup, mess gear, and first aid packet.
The orderly held out a memorandum receipt, and the lieutenant signed it.
The orderly told him about the laundry rules and messing, and then he left.
From that point on, Lieutenant Downing was on his own. There were no dog
robbers (personal servants for officers) in the new army.

Lieutenant Downing learned something else that day about this new army:
the importance of rank. Three of his class from Fort Benning had come to
the Eighteenth. He outranked one of the officers, but the other outranked
him. Such matters would come to be very important. Later, a regimental
roster was put together, showing the history of each officer by rank and date
of rank. Among the lieutenants there was fierce competition because so many
of them were of such recent vintage. "Rank among lieutenants is like chas-
tity among whores" was the old army saying. But the lieutenants would have
to learn who preceded whom on the roster, and salute accordingly. That little bit of "chicken shit," however, was yet to come. On that first day Lieutenant Downing "bumped" the experienced leader of the Company F weapons
platoon and became the new leader. As it happened, no one cared a great
deal just then, because opportunity was everywhere for the experienced. The

man he bumped was on his way to Army Air Corps flight training. Later that same day Downing went to a parade to see off a cadre selected from the First Division to activate the new Seventy-ninth Division. So many changes were made in the Eighteenth Infantry that in two weeks Downing found himself installed as company executive officer.

He still had plenty to learn, but the army was accommodating in hurrying the procedure. Within a few weeks the Eighteenth was ordered to Fort Benning for maneuvers. At Benning the soldiers were assigned a new area in the wilds of the reservation near Cusseta. And there they set up camp.

Meanwhile, affairs were going very well for the Eighty-second Division, but not for the Twenty-eighth Division on the other side of the Red River. Sergeant Chattaway's 110th Infantry was a part of this division. The Twenty-eighth was having more than its share of problems. One problem was the cannibalization of the division to create new units. Many of the noncoms had been sent to Officer Candidate School; the same had happened to many National Guard divisions. For these noncoms had some experience, and experienced leadership was the major need of the day.

The Twenty-eighth Division had another problem in common with National Guard divisions: cliquism. The guard units were made up of men from the same towns and cities; many of these troops either were related, had gone to school together, or had business associations back home. For example, here is a list of the original hometown headquarters of the constituent units of the 110th Regiment, of the Pennsylvania National Guard, now federalized:

Regimental headquarters	Washington
Headquarters company	Altoona
Medical detachment	Connellsville
Headquarters, First Battalion	Washington
Company A	Monongahela
Company B	New Brighton
Company C	Somerset
Company D	Monessen
Headquarters, Second Battalion	Altoona
Company E	Mt. Pleasant
Company F	Indiana
Company G	Altoona

Company H	Washington
Headquarters, Third Battalion	Greensburg
Company I	Greensburg
Company K	Waynesburg
Company L	Blairsville
Company M	Latrobe
Band	Altoona
Antitank company	Connellsville
Service company	Scottdale

So favoritism was a real problem. When a noncom moved out to OCS or into a cadre to form a new regiment, the officers chose "one of the boys" to fill his spot. The officers often addressed one another, and sometimes enlisted men too, by their first names; it was hard for Cousin Bill to call Cousin Charlie "Sir."

In addition to the problems caused by Washington's insatiable demand for "cadres," morale began to decline as draftees came into this and other regiments and found themselves facing a tight little club in which they were denied membership. This was a problem throughout the war; where tough commanders solved it, as in the case of General Bradley's Twenty-eighth Division, the division performed admirably. Where the tough command was lacking and the "old boyism" was allowed to persist, as with the Twenty-seventh Division (New York National Guard), which went to the Pacific, the results were disastrous. Maj. Gen. Ralph Smith, commander of the Twenty-seventh, was criticized for the conduct of the division at the Gilbert Islands and later at the Marshalls and finally was removed from command at the height of the battle for Saipan. Sensing the impending disaster of cronyism (as few leaders did), General Bradley took the tough step of breaking up those old hometown cliques, transferring officers and noncoms around the division to get them away from their friends.

General Bradley's wholesale transfers caused a lot of grousing at the time, but the result within three months was a hardening of discipline and a toughening of the division.

No such problem existed with the Eighteenth Infantry, which was already supplying cadres for new units and taking in new officers like Lieutenant Downing.

At Fort Benning's bivouac area Lieutenant Downing spent his first night on the ground. He had three blankets in his bedroll. When he put it down, he saw that the officer across from him had an air mattress. How soft! he thought. That was hardly soldiering. But as the night wore on and the ground got harder, how *soft*, he thought—and the next day, commandeering the company jeep, he went to town and bought an air mattress. Within a week he also had a kapok sleeping bag. He was learning the difference between the GI way and the right way.

At Benning that summer Lieutenant Downing's Second Battalion was not directly involved in the maneuvers, so they trained: close order drill, foxhole digging, foxhole filling, road marches, gun drill, and the local obstacle course, which consisted largely of a mudhole too broad to leap across. The object, said a fellow officer of waggish ways, was to make everybody so angry they wanted to get into combat to escape training.

They also had lectures: Articles of War lectures, military courtesy lectures, and sex lectures.

The chaplain told you not to do it.

The surgeon told you what to do after you had done it, and showed that great historic film, the *V.D. Special*.

The battalion commander told you what the army would do to you if you didn't follow the advice of the chaplain and did it and then didn't follow the advice of the surgeon and got it.

One Saturday night Lieutenant Downing drew special military police duty in the city of Columbus. The city had a big police force. Fort Benning had its own MPs. The division had its own MP company. But this was the Saturday night after payday, and not all of the above sufficed. So on Saturday nights this force was augmented from the infantry regiments by groups of officers and men who were to arrest other men, as Lieutenant Downing put it "for doing the things they themselves would probably be doing if they hadn't been detailed to the police job."

Lieutenant Downing took his special MPs to the Columbus city jail and reported to the assistant provost marshal who had set up shop there. Downing's task was to supervise the search of all the men brought in, remove their valuables and money, and safeguard these until the drunks sobered up.

Business at the jail began to boom at about 8 p.m., when the first drunk showed up. Soon they were reeling in before their captors in sixes and sevens. They were brought into the receiving room, frisked by an MP, who handed the valuables to Downing, who put them into an envelope, sealed it, and wrote the owner's name and amount of money on the outside. The man was then led to the drunk tank, a large, dim room with a concrete floor and a steel barred cage inside for the aggressive. The steel door of the drunk tank clanged shut, and the miscreant was safe. He could lie down anywhere on the floor. If he got obstreperous, he was pushed into the barred cage in the middle, to fight with other obstreperous drunks.

As the hours passed, the drunks piled up, noisy drunks, snoring drunks, sick drunks, belligerent drunks. All in a mass. The room smelled of vomit and whiskey, sweat and urine.

At midnight, when curfew came to Columbus, the number of arrivals slowed down. Finally, at around 3 a.m. it was time to go home. All the unit officers and special MPs were assembled and the provost marshal called out:

"All men from the Sixteenth Infantry. . . . "

"All men from the Twenty-sixth Infantry. . . . "

"All men from the First Engineers. . . . "

"All men from the Eighteenth Infantry. . . . "

As the units were called out, the sobering drunks began to get up and weave toward the door. As the men of the Eighteenth came along, Lieutenant Downing asked each man his name and company and handed him his envelope. Outside, the special MPs loaded the Eighteenth's drunk contingent into trucks and carted them back to camp. They were sorted out by unit and delivered to their camp areas, and Downing and his MPs went "home" to sack out. Nobody got shafted except the drunk-tank gladiators. They went on report to the regimental commander; all the rest went back to work to learn their jobs.

In mid-June Prime Minister Churchill came to the United States once again. The failure of the planners to come up with a program of attack that could utilize some American forces right away made him fearful that the United States was going to turn its power back toward the Pacific.

There certainly was reason for that British concern. The Japanese had moved like lightning across southern Asia, virtually to the shores of Australia. Their threat there had been stopped by Admiral King's insistence on the invasion of Guadalcanal Island, over the objections of General MacArthur and many others of the army. King had used navy troops—U.S. Marines— but there were not enough marines to go around. Army troops and Army Air Corps units were also needed to stem the tide of the Japanese in the South Pacific, and Admiral Nimitz of the navy's Pacific Fleet and General MacArthur of the army's Southwest Pacific Command were crying for help.

One of the things that had to be done in a hurry was to build air bases, land installations, and sea bases in the Pacific. In the prewar past all such work had been contracted out to civilians, but it was not reasonable to depend on civilians in a war zone. Problems of danger, labor, and management were too great. So military units had to be organized in a hurry to enlist and draft specialists who could run bulldozers and other heavy equipment and who could plan and build bases under the most unfavorable conditions.

Thus, on May 10, 1942, a young mechanic from Muskogee, Oklahoma, enlisted in the Naval Reserve as a chief machinist's mate in the new Naval Construction Service. He did not go to duty immediately. One of the first enlistees, he had to wait for the navy to get going. He waited for assignment. The navy, heretofore telling Nimitz and MacArthur that they would have to get along with what they had in hand, realized that no matter what President Roosevelt had promised about priorities, there were certain needs.

Churchill, so preoccupied with so many enormous problems, sensed this change and feared that matters would get out of hand. Although Britain's situation was more perilous than it had been at Christmas, with the U-boats wreaking havoc along the American coast, Churchill insisted on coming to America. So great was the menace of the U-boats that spring, and so great was Churchill's need for haste, that he flew the Atlantic, a most dangerous procedure for a political leader, given the state of the art of flying at that time. But given the need to reinforce President Roosevelt's intention to first concentrate efforts against Germany, Churchill had to talk faster than the Japanese were acting. There had been talk about an Operation Roundup, which was to be a cross-Channel attack, but it could not be launched, obviously, for at least a year. Given that problem, the Americans had to be drawn physically into the European battle before then, if their interest in the European war was to be sustained.

On June 20, while Churchill was in Washington, he received the dreadful word that Tobruk had fallen to Rommel's forces, with 33,000 British and Australian soldiers taken prisoner. Most dreadful: as at Singapore, the British force surrendered to an enemy of about half its strength. This, of course, was a problem of leadership, and was recognized as such in Washington.

What could the Americans do? Even if they wanted to throw the First Division and perhaps the Twenty-ninth into Africa, the operation would require planning and transportation. That would take at least three or four months given the state of shipping and the paucity of military hardware, for the United States had only begun six months before to address these problems in terms of practical need.

Churchill asked immediately for Sherman tanks. General Marshall said that the first Shermans were just coming off the production lines. They were being put into the hands of the underarmed American armored divisions. But if the British needed tanks, they would be taken away from the GIs. And they were. Three hundred seventy Sherman tanks and a hundred self-propelled 105-millimeter guns were taken from the U.S. Army, put onto ships, and sent immediately to the Suez Canal.

· That need, emphasized by the Tobruk surrender, turned out to be Churchill's best card in this new adventure in Washington. He did not have to argue about what must happen and when. The Germans must be stopped in Africa. What could the Americans do to help stop them?

Not much, said General Lord Ismay gloomily. He was British chief of staff and had accompanied Churchill on this trip to America, and down to the Carolinas to watch the Forty-seventh Infantry and other units in maneuvers. The awkward Americans—some units still without their mortars; the Second Armored Division without its new tanks; the American paratroops just being organized into two divisions (they saw 1000 men drop, and that represented the best America could put up)—did not make much of a show for the combat-hardened British.

"What do you think of it?" Churchill asked Ismay when the show was over.

"To put these troops against continental troops would be murder," said Ismay.

Fortunately for the Allied war effort, Churchill did not communicate Ismay's gloom to Roosevelt or General Marshall. Otherwise, those parachute troops, infantry, and armored divisions might have gone the other way, to the Pacific. As it was, Roosevelt and Marshall promised to get Americans overseas to England as quickly as possible.

At the end of June the Eighteenth Infantry was told to get ready to move to Indiantown Gap Military Reservation. How times had changed. For Indiantown Gap was now the staging area for troops bound overseas. That's not what the men were told, however. They were told nothing at all. The company wag had his way: the troops were so sick of the mudhole they were in that they were ready to go to Pennsylvania.

They went in army fashion: hurry up and wait. Washington had ordered their movement most expeditiously. Army had ordered their movement by the end of the month. Corps had ordered their arrival at Indiantown Gap on June 30. Division had ordered the troop movement for 8 a.m. Regiment said

7:00. Battalion said 6:00. The company commander had them rousted out into the rain at 5:00 to a quick breakfast. Lieutenant Downing, as executive officer of the company, did not have any troops to roust out, so he assembled all his personal gear and went to the spot where the orderly tent had stood until an hour earlier. There was First Sergeant Merrill, lying on his blown-up air mattress, underneath his overcoat, smoking a cigarette. They waited in companionable silence, in the rain, until they heard the whine of the 2½-ton trucks coming up the road, double-clutching. The men had assembled where they were told to go, and they stood around sheeplike in little knots, half asleep in the growing dawn. They had to be herded into the deuce-and-a-half. Merrill was up, bawling out orders and numbers and moving around calling off names.

Then, out of the confusion, order: all were loaded. A handful of men in a half-track were left to police the area, and the column moved off toward the railroad yards. They were on their way. A day on the train, and then Indiantown Gap. What luxury! They were back in barracks, two-story wooden temporary barracks, built for Corporal Chattaway's outfit; the green grass around them was sowed by Corporal Chattaway and friends. The enlisted men slept in black iron cots in long rows. The sergeants were two and three to a room at each end of the barracks. Lieutenant Downing had the great luxury of a room to himself in the BOQ, a cubicle on the second floor of his barracks, with a window. He fell into bed that first night and slept hard, to be awakened the next morning by an enormous racket outside his window. It took him a moment to realize where he was and what the noise was. It was the blaring of the regimental band, playing "Happie Heinie," the regimental anthem, a piece of music created by a World War I bandmaster from two old German marches. Lucky fellow, Downing, to have a room just above the parade ground.

Training, training, and more training—the old army way. The company officers were all assigned to special weapons training—after hours. Downing was just fresh out of weapons school at Fort Benning; that made no difference, said the company commander. He took the training.

More changes. A new regimental commander, Lieutenant Colonel Greer. A meeting, to introduce all the new regimental officers, shavetails fresh out of OCS. One of them was a real rarity: Lieutenant Hobratschk. He had been a sergeant stationed on Oahu Island on Pearl Harbor day. He was the only officer in the regiment who had heard a shot fired in anger.

More surprises. A new commander came to F Company—Captain Williams, who had been an aide to Maj. Gen. Terry Allen, commander of the

First Division! So it was musical chairs again, and Lieutenant Downing reverted to his old weapons platoon job.

The pace quickened. They got ID cards and dog tags. They shipped all their belongings home (one footlocker was to be shipped overseas for an officer and one barracks bag for a dogface). They got shots. They got rid of the regimental shields on their caps. They changed to wool uniforms. They got the new bucket helmets. Officers and sergeants were issued the new carbines.

Throughout the division, men who had leave coming got it for the most part. In the Sixteenth Infantry Pfc. Moglia went home to Long Island.

One night he dreamed that he was on a ship; as they approached the land, he saw the greenest fields he had ever seen. And when they landed he heard the people speaking the same language he spoke, but they drove on the left side of the road. Funny! And the people were very friendly. "How ridiculous!" he said when he woke up, because the scut through the regiment was that they were headed for the Pacific war. The Japanese drove on the left, and their land was green, but he had no intention of landing there just then; besides, he knew they would not be very friendly. It was all ridiculous.

"Where are you going now, John?" asked his Uncle Pete.

"Oh, on secret maneuvers, they say," lied Pfc. Moglia, knowing he was going to the Pacific. "We'll be back in a couple of months."

"I'll bet you're going to England," said Uncle Pete, who seemed to have been something of an armchair strategist. "I suppose you'll be marrying one of those English girls? Pick out a nice one."

"Hell, no! Too many pretty American girls. The English are stuffed shirts. No sense of humor. Besides, we aren't going to England anyhow."

So Pfc. Moglia went back to Indiantown Gap. He had been selected for Officer Candidate School, but when the call came he was on leave, so it all had to be started over again.

He was detached from Company E of the Sixteenth Infantry and told that new orders were being written to send him to OCS. No, he didn't have to move out of the barracks for a few days. But then, one morning at three o'clock, Pfc. Moglia was awakened rudely by the platoon sergeant of his old platoon and told to get up. They were moving out.

"Go away," said Pfc. Moglia. "I'm no longer assigned to the Sixteenth."

"The hell you aren't," said the sergeant, pulling him out of bed.

The bad news was confirmed by the first sergeant, so Pfc. Moglia packed up his A bag and his B bag, tossing out half his gear, and waited. He went outside. All the phone booths were nailed shut. He looked outside the regimental area. A double line of guards ringed the perimeter.

It was the same at the Eighteenth Infantry barracks. Big Red One—the U.S. Army First Infantry Division—was getting ready to move out. It was July 31. Before daylight came, the troops were in train cars, on their way to Brooklyn, each soldier carrying his A bag, full field equipment, helmet, gas mask, webbed belt, ammunition pouches, two water canteens, and weapons.

The next morning they hit the docks. They saw the French liner *Normandie* tied up. All around them stevedores were yelling and cranes were moving huge boxes into openings in the side of an enormous ship. It got hot that August morning, and in his place in line Lieutenant Downing began to sweat.

Someone came along dispensing white paper bags. Lunches. He took one.

Soon Lieutenant Downing was sweating so much that the chest of his field jacket was stained. His head ached from the weight of the new helmet and liner. The line moved. He was called to a table, near a gangplank, where a white-haired second lieutenant with a chest covered with ancient ribbons checked his name off on a register and a GI gave him two cards, one a cabin assignment, one a mess card. He staggered up the gangplank, and was met at the top by a blue-uniformed steward.

"Are you an officer?" the steward inquired in an unbelieving, very British voice.

"Yes," said Lieutenant Downing. He understood the distrust: no British officer would be loaded down like a camel.

But the steward looked at his cards, shrugged at the incomprehensible ways of the Yanks, and showed the lieutenant to a passageway. Downing went down to the cabin. It was one which in peacetime would have been assigned for two people. Now there were five double-deck bunks in the cabin. He threw his gear onto an upper bunk. He smelled bananas. He remembered lunch and took from the pocket of his field jacket the white paper sack. It was redolent of smashed banana and looked greasy. He went to the porthole, saw that it was on the seaward side, and dropped the bag overboard.

He arranged his gear and then went below to find the men of his company. They were down, down, down, in a large room dominated by 3-foot-high tables. Underneath the tables were mattresses, above were slung hammocks. Up and down, all around, struggled the men, trying to find a place to dump their belongings and bunk. Next to the entrance to the huge room, First Sergeant Merrill had set up his command post and was dispensing orders: KP, abandon ship, messing, fire regulations, air raid drill, when to go on deck, when not to go on deck, weapons inspections, sentry duty, a training program, and latrine duty. While Lieutenant Downing was in attendance, new orders began to arrive, countermanding some of the orders on Sergeant Merrill's table. He began to curse, picked up his overseas cap, slammed it onto his head, and then began sorting out men to do this and that. Lieutenant Downing picked up his duty orders and escaped gratefully to try to find his way back up to his quarters.

As was to be expected, given the fact that Pfc. Moglia's position was not entirely clear, he had a much harder time of it. His unit came up to the docks where two big ships were berthed. The soldiers marched onto the quay and waited. As names were called, they picked up their barracks bags and moved to one ship or the other. Finally all were aboard, except one Pfc. John Moglia.

There was no question about what had happened. The platoon sergeant, the first sergeant, even the captain might have been certain that Pfc. Moglia was going along with Company E, but the company clerk had not gotten the word, so Moglia was not on the company roster. He went up to an MP guarding the right ship. The MP looked at his clipboard.

"You're not on the manifest. Try the other one."

He went to an MP guarding the left ship.

"You're not on the manifest."

"What do I do now?" Moglia asked the MP.

"Go back to your unit."

"What unit? Everybody's on these ships."

"Sorry, buddy, go on back to the Gap."

"How do I get back there?"

"That's your problem. We're getting ready to sail."

Suddenly, on the deck of the ship on the right, Moglia noticed a familiar face. It was the battalion personnel sergeant. After much yelling and sergeantly maneuvering, Pfc. Moglia was taken aboard the ship. He learned that he had boarded the *Duchess of Bedford*. The ship on the left was the *Malaga*. He did not know where he was going or when he would get there.

*

Neither, at the moment, did Lieutenant Downing in his far more lordly quarters aboard his ship. It did not take him long to learn that he was aboard the *Queen Mary*. Winston Churchill had kept his promise to General Marshall. Britain's great liners were now in the service of the Allies, transporting American troops to England for the great battles to come.

6

OVER THERE...

July 1942: Aboard the *Queen Mary,* on the morning after boarding, Lieutenant Downing looked out the porthole and discovered that they were still at the dock. After breakfast he was summoned to the lounge for a meeting of officers. Major General Allen was there, and so was the ship captain. The general noted the obvious, that they were on their way overseas, and then introduced the captain. The captain gave a little lecture on abandoning ship. There were not enough lifeboats, he said casually, for the men, but the life rafts would work—as long as the men just clung to the sides and no one got aboard the rafts.

After this inspiring lecture, a British general made an almost incomprehensible speech about how tough the Germans were. Then General Allen said a few words about how he believed in the division, and that was the end of it.

"It wasn't a morale builder," said Lieutenant Downing.

But something else that happened that day was.

Lieutenant Downing had some really good news for Company F, Eighteenth Infantry: the Second Battalion was to furnish all the extra kitchen help needed on the ship to accommodate the 16,000 troops going across. Virtually every man was detailed to some kitchen job. So all across the Atlantic F Company would eat first class.

When the men were not doing that, they were practicing "abandon ship" and learning about the British. Lieutenant Downing instructed his men in the British marks of rank, and they yawned. He instructed them in the values of British pounds, shillings, and pence, and the crapshooters all hung on his every word.

The *Queen Mary*, at 35 knots, quickly outdistanced her overage American destroyer escort and was at sea, alone, for the crossing. The troops saw nothing (but heard daily scuttlebutt reports of U-boat packs searching for them) until the fifth day, when planes flew overhead. They had their air escort into the Western Approaches, the most dangerous of all British waters because of the submarines. And then the green-brown land came into view, the green-brown hills of Scotland, and a small town of brick and stone buildings on the shore. They had arrived at Gourock, Scotland. A handful of limp barrage balloons hung above the harbor. A handful of freighters sat, lazily pulling at their anchors. A handful of small boats charged about the harbor, dropping off civilians and blue-uniformed British naval officers, or drab-dressed army officers.

And that day Company F of the Eighteenth Infantry went ashore. The men were hustled through the dock area with the others of the regiment. They stopped to fill their canteen cups with big drinks of tea ladled out by smiling British women wearing thick coats and scarves over their heads against the damp. A Highland officer in kilt, knee socks, and low shoes walked up to the battalion commander, saluted smartly, and introduced himself. The soldiers were led to rail coaches, and one officer was designated mess officer. He produced something new: K rations. Lieutenant Downing got a dinner ration, soybean meal crackers, a stick of gum, three Chelsea cigarettes, a package of synthetic lemon powder, paper-wrapped lumps of sugar advertising Joe's Steak House, a few pieces of candy, and finally a can of cheese laced with bits of bacon. He thought it was great!

It was afternoon when they started out across Scotland. A British officer came through the railcar, stopping at each compartment, to show the Americans how to put down the blinds.

"Blackout, you know. The Jerries sometimes come over to strafe."

The train moved. The night wore on, and the junior officer poker game did too. The night won, and the poker game subsided; the junior officers slouched in their seats, squirming as they tried to sleep. They pulled down windows and looked out into the night. They came to stations, but all the signs had been removed to confuse any German paratroopers. Even when they would ask a Briton on the platform the name of the place, the answer didn't mean anything to them.

Around dawn they began breaking out the K rations again. This time Lieutenant Downing did not think so much of his.

At about 7 a.m. the train stopped at Tidworth station. The Americans got their equipment and went outside. They had arrived. It was misty and damp. The officers found their platoons and got the men lined up, sleepy and yawning, and marched them off the platform in columns of twos. The men were led through a village, and then along a tree-lined road. They passed a single British sentry in battle dress who was guarding a gate. After passing through the gate, they marched along a road lined with brick buildings. They had arrived: their new home was the old British cavalry barracks of Tidworth on the Salisbury Plain.

Lieutenant Downing and Sergeant Merrill found the barracks for the company and saw the men inside. Then Downing went off to the BOQ, called Candahar Barracks "after some obscure Indian frontier battle." Inside he found that the advance detail had failed, and no quarters had been assigned. An officers' roster with date of rank had to be found so that rooms could be given out in order of precedence. No one had such a list. Nothing could be done. Downing found a side room with an unoccupied table, lay down, and went to sleep. He woke up at lunchtime, but there was no lunch. Another foul-up. It was the next day before the administrative mess was all sorted out and a meal was served: boiled mutton, boiled cabbage, boiled potato, boiled brussel sprouts, bread, and tea.

They were in England, no doubt about it!

At the end of the first week the division's equipment still had not arrived; there were no weapons, so no weapons drills could be staged. Thus the officers and men were given permission to go to London. All 15,000 men of the division had the same idea at the same time. The army and the British laid on buses and trains, but the confusion was enormous. Nobody, you see, was used to dealing with 15,000 Yanks all in a bunch. But they made it, somehow, into London.

All these Americans, the first the British had seen in bulk, were real oddities, and everyone wanted to help. The British railmen learned to say "round trip," meaning "return trip." The Americans had plenty to learn, too. About queuing for tickets and for taxis. By raising their ranks a few notches (the British were not yet acquainted with American rank badges) Downing and his friends got rooms at the Piccadilly Hotel; then they went pub crawling. They looked for girls, didn't find any, and got back to the hotel late and a little drunk. On Sunday it was back to Tidworth. The equipment began to arrive. And then the training began.

*

Lieutenant Colonel Campbell was rushing about, worrying about the training of the Fifth Corps, of which Lieutenant Downing was going to be a small part. The colonel went to tank exhibitions and examined beaches, all in behalf of the corps. He met General Mark Clark and other increasingly important American officers. He also met Al Jolson, Merle Oberon, Frank McHugh, and Allen Jennings, American film stars who came to entertain the troops. RHIP. He was a real utility infielder. They made him acting G-3 and he met Amon Carter, publisher of the Fort Worth *Star Telegram*, who was on a junket to England. Busy, busy, busy.

Aboard the *Duchess of Bedford* the men of the Sixteenth Infantry rolled about like peas in pods in the confines of their bunk rooms, marching dutifully—if a little wobbly—to latrines, to mess, up on deck for a breath of air, and back down to the sweaty smell of the bunk room.

After the ship had been at sea for several days, the men were called on deck to hear a message from Brig. Gen. Theodore Roosevelt, Jr., assistant division commander of the First Infantry Division, who was bringing this second contingent of the division along. Now, for the first time, they learned where they were going. They were on their way to England.

That was the bombshell. The rest of the message was devoted to promoting Anglo-American unity. The British, said General Roosevelt, were kind and friendly people, but the GIs had to be on their good behavior as ambassadors of goodwill.

British? "Yuck!" was the consensus of Company E. Why in hell were they going to Britain? The Limeys were stuffed shirts, and they couldn't fight. They ran away at Dunkerque, didn't they?

(Fortunately for Allied amity the men of Company E did not know about Singapore and Tobruk.)

The Sixteenth Infantry landed at Liverpool. Yes, thought Pfc. Moglia, the grass was the greenest green he ever saw; yes, the people spoke his language. Yes, they drove on the left. His dream had come true.

As the men were boarding the railway cars, there suddenly arose a loud commotion on the platform. A mongrel dog, a good part of him bulldog, was running up and down the platform. "Whitey," the G Company mascot, had suddenly escaped! He had been smuggled on board the *Duchess of Bedford* by someone in the company (a court-martial offense, but wasn't everything?).

The men of Company G were whistling and shouting, trying to get Whitey aboard the train. Whitey was running up and down the platform, tongue out, licking new friends and looking for old ones.

General Roosevelt looked on and grinned.

"Hey, get that dog out of sight. Here's the general," somebody shouted.

"Look at that English dog," Roosevelt said, pointing. "He seems to like us."

"Hey, that's Whitey. He's not English."

"Nonsense, soldier," said General Roosevelt, looking sharply at the offending young man who had said those unwise words. "He has to be an English dog. He barks like an English dog. Somebody pick him up. We'll take him with us."

What the general didn't say was that on several occasions in Carolina, Virginia, and Georgia he had been on road marches with G Company, and Whitey had been trotting along at the general's side all the time. What the dogfaces did not yet know, the general knew: how to keep people off report.

Pfc. Moglia and his company were loaded onto trains, and they, too, headed for the Salisbury Plain. But they came in daylight, through the most populous part of the country, and as their trains chugged along, people waved and grinned and shouted from houses and fields along the track.

"Hello, Yanks."

"Bless you, Yanks."

So everything the young Americans had been snarling about the Limeys suddenly stopped coming out. But it was still a queer place, this England. As the train approached Tidworth station, they saw women driving lorries and trains. Strange. As they arrived, so did a reception committee and a British brass band to play them into the compound. The drummer was wearing a huge tiger skin.

General Roosevelt picked Pfc. Moglia and his buddy Pfc. George Racol to be his personal honor guard. In full field kit they led the parade to Tidworth Barracks, stepping out smartly. The tune was the "Colonel Bogie March." The men of the Sixteenth Infantry felt 10 feet tall. The crowds cheered:

"Welcome Yanks."

"Thank God you're here."

"We love you, Yanks."

From then on, every time Pfc. Moglia heard that particular march, he got goose bumps. It was a long, long time before the movie *The Bridge on the River Kwai*.

*

The plans for this American arrival in England had been months in the making. Just after the Churchill visit to Washington in 1941, the Eighth Corps headquarters at Jacksonville, Florida, had orders from Washington to send Gen. Roscoe Woodruff, the commander of the corps, and his intelligence officer, Col. Thomas L. Sherburne, to England for briefing on the coming large-scale movement of American troops to Britain. Sherburne was to stay on and work with the British to plan all the details. The American party was greeted royally in London, put up at Claridge's (Claridge's and the Savoy were the top hotels), and briefed about all the British plans for the future. The British intelligence officers opened the box: they told the Americans of deception plans to persuade the Germans that the Pas de Calais would be the target of the Allied cross-Channel attack; they told them how all German intelligence agents had been captured and dealt with or turned to become Allied agents. They unveiled the methods they used to bug neutral embassies, many of which, sadly, were not as neutral as they ought to have been. But the British used that too—they played on the neutrals and got their pro-German reactions through them.

The general went home to America. Colonel Sherburne stayed on in London, moved out of Claridge's to Grosvenor House (only third-level accommodations), and set to work. Later, he returned to Washington to keep the commanders of the Fifth Corps and the Eighth Corps informed of the military planning in London, for from the beginning these two corps had been designated by the Americans as the units that would lead the fighting in Europe.

The war, then, was going on simultaneously on two levels: the practical, active war, which in the summer of 1942 the British were fighting in Africa, and the war of the future, the planning war, for operations months in the offing or operations that might be canceled at any moment.

For a long time—by the American standards of 1942, six months was a very long time—the planning war had been in progress. As noted, the Fifth Corps was assembled at Camp Beauregard at Alexandria, Louisiana, early in 1942, before it moved on to Fort Dix. In May 1942, even before the First Division was sent to England, Fifth Corps headquarters moved to Lurgan, Northern Ireland. The Americans might not be able to send the British those divisions they wanted in the north, but they sent them a corps command—as a down payment on the promise.

Sergeant Ogden was in England! Six months after Pearl Harbor he had come over with an advance medical unit. Then he was sent to SHAEF (Supreme

Headquarters Allied Expeditionary Force) headquarters, the pre-Eisenhower headquarters. He became a courier of secret documents from Gen. Frederick Morgan's office to the coding and decoding room, located across London in a huge underground bunker. It was all very spooky.

Then he went to the replacement depot and was sent to Tidworth Barracks.

Back in April, Adm. "Dicky" Mountbatten, who was in charge of special operations (meaning ways of making the enemy's life miserable, or dingbat propositions, depending on how one looked at it), had put forth a plan for a nuisance raid on Dieppe. One of the purposes of the raid would be to provide a test of the German shore defenses. Operation Rutter, as it was called, was approved in May by the British chiefs of staff and set up for July. Then it was delayed, and then it was delayed again. But when it became apparent that no real operation against the Germans on the French coast could be mounted in 1942, the Dieppe raid again went onto the calendar.

While all this was going on, Sergeant Ogden and nine other volunteer Americans who could handle .50-caliber machine guns were detailed, very secretly, to work with the British. They were assigned to five British E-boats specially mounted with twin .50-caliber guns. The only reason Americans were involved was that the British did not make the .50-caliber guns, and they were not familiar with them; they needed men who knew how to use them.

Every night for two months before the Dieppe raid, those boats were out, racing up and down the French coast, strafing the shores, and getting the Germans used to their presence. They came in as close as 100 yards.

Then came August, and the Dieppe raid, where troops of the Canadian Second Division went in, 5000 strong, and struck disaster. The Germans were supposed to have only some communications troops at Dieppe, and the raid was supposed to be a "piece of cake," but in the preceding weeks the Germans had moved a first-class regiment to the area. Among the Canadians 18 percent of the 5000 men lost their lives and about 2000 were taken prisoner. The fiasco was covered by those E-boats, with their American gunners, who stood offshore during the whole operation—landing and withdrawal. Only one boat was lost.

When the boats arrived back in England, the American gunners were warned that they were never to mention the Dieppe Raid, on pain of court-martial. And they never did. Sergeant Ogden swore that not even his battalion commander was ever told what had really happened. The fact is that Sergeant Ogden and his fellow gunners may have been the first American ground troops in American uniform to fight against the Germans during World War II!

Now that the dam had broken, thousands of Americans began coming into England. The Army Air Corps became the U.S. Army Air Forces, and the Eighth Air Force was designated to work out of Britain. In preparation for the move across the Channel—now scheduled for 1943—units such as the 816th Aviation Engineers Battalion came in August. Those engineers would build airstrips and other installations on the other side of the Channel, after D day.

Little by little, then, the Americans were beginning to take their place in the land war against the Germans. Others were getting ready.

In the 110th Infantry, just before the mass transfers in the Twenty-eighth Division ordered by General Bradley, Sergeant Chattaway was promoted to first sergeant of A Company. Then he was switched in the same job to K Company.

Lt. Joseph Miller got his commission just before June 1942. The authorities at Fort Belvoir courteously asked all the new graduates to apply for the sort of engineering assignment they wanted. Lieutenant Miller picked topographic engineers—he was a photography nut. Sure, said the personnel officers, and they assigned him with all the other new lieutenant Millers and a whole segment of "M's" to a new black service regiment being formed at Camp Gordon, Georgia. This was a remnant of the old army, the segregated black units, not trusted for combat but used for labor, commanded by white officers.

Lieutenant Miller got on fine with his troops, but he hated Georgia. Still, he was just getting acclimated to the life—officers' mess, post officers' club, and not much to do—when suddenly he was jerked out of somnolence and assigned to the Twentieth Combat Engineer Regiment, training at Camp Blanding, Florida, for very quick shipment overseas. The Twentieth had been having its troubles. It had been activated by a bunch of "good ol' boys" from the south, but then personnel assigned just about an equal number of Yankees from New York, New Jersey, and Pennsylvania (including a large sprinkling of Polish- and Italian-Americans). The mixture was like a Molotov cocktail just ready for a match, and one wild night, just before Lieutenant Miller arrived, a line was drawn down a company street and the War Between the States was fought all over again. Thus there were some transfers out, and some transfers in: e.g., Lieutenant Miller.

The commanding officer of the Twentieth Engineers was Col. Eugene Caffey, a career soldier who had spent the peacetime years in the adjutant general's department, a fact that someone in officer personnel decided would make him the ideal commander of engineer troops: he didn't know "doodely squat" about what engineers were supposed to do in combat, his subordinates learned very quickly. But what the colonel did not know about his job, he made up for with fiery enthusiasm for combat and military discipline. When Lieutenant Miller and the other draft of new officers arrived at Camp Blanding, they were greeted by the colonel, who informed them in the most vivid language that they had joined a "fighting outfit" and he was going to make sure that they had a chance to find a glorious death "fighting these people."

Any lack of confidence this pep talk might have left unfilled was remedied by the colonel's attitude toward military discipline:

Sparked by what he did know from the adjutant general's office, the colonel loved courts-martial. Every time a GI came back late on pass or got drunk and was put on report, the colonel convened a court-martial. So many men were convicted of offenses that the regiment had to build its own stockade. There the men worked at hard labor, and *worked* out their sentences.

Those who were not in the stockade spent the days loading up the Twentieth's vehicles and equipment on railcars, for they were destined soon to go overseas. The first stop would be Camp Kilmer, New Jersey, and then the port of embarkation. At Camp Kilmer the Twentieth Engineers seemed to spend most of their time in "shit storms" engineered by their colonel. The saving grace, for the officers—not the enlisted men—was the nearness to New York City. The company officers could get loose most weekends to go to New York and blow off the steam the colonel had built up in them all week long. The bright lights of Manhattan undoubtedly lighted up many darkened souls and the soothing potions of the bars put out many fires.

Lieutenant Miller and the others of the Twentieth were all psyched up to go overseas. On Saturday, September 19, Lieutenant Miller went off to New York for the weekend to stay at the Hotel New Yorker and do what soldiers did on leave. He returned to camp, thoroughly dragged out, on Sunday night. There he learned that all the regiment's trucks and equipment had been commandeered and given to another outfit (a company officer would never learn which one, but it was the Twenty-ninth Division's engineers) who were sailing just then for England.

The Twenty-ninth Division had been modernized (turned from a four-regiment division into a three-regiment division) and moved up and down the east coast throughout the summer of 1942. General Reckord had been retired and succeeded by Maj. Gen. Leonard T. Gerow. Pfc. Elburn had made sergeant, still a medic, still with the 115th.

All spring the soldiers' training had largely been in jungle warfare, which convinced just about everyone the division was destined for the Pacific, particularly after the fall of Corregidor to the Japanese was announced in May. But they had then participated in the Sixth Corps maneuvers in the Carolinas. They did not know—no one outside Washington and London knew—that the fall of Tobruk had put a real supercharger on Washington's movement to get American troops overseas to Europe. On September 6, without warning, Washington informed General Gerow that he was to be ready "immediately" to move his division.

Men were on leave. Men were off at training schools. Men were in the process of being reassigned to OCS and other units. Everyone was called back. All the division yin-yang blue-and-gray identification marks were erased from everything. The Twenty-ninth Division was rushed up to Camp Kilmer, to supersede the Twentieth Engineers and other outfits waiting there, scheduled for shipment overseas. The Twenty-ninth was going to England in a hurry. The men loaded aboard the *Queen Mary* and the *Queen Elizabeth* and sailed.

No one knew exactly when the Twenty-ninth was going to be needed, or where. What they did know in Washington was that Operation Torch—the American invasion of French north Africa—was on. That had finally been settled early in August, and Gen. Dwight D. Eisenhower was appointed Allied commander in chief in Africa. The Americans would have it no other way, particularly after the debacles at Dunkerque and Tobruk. For what was true in London—a basic distrust of the fighting qualities of the American allies—was equally true in Washington—a distrust of the fighting abilities of the British. Many Americans, from Pfc. Moglia to Maj. Gen. George S. Patton, Jr., held the British in very low regard. Politically speaking, Prime Minister Churchill (perhaps because of his American mother) sensed the dangers and accommodated himself to them admirably. The Americans would be in charge; to lead the campaign they had chosen their most genial and adaptable general. But the British would have plenty of safeguards to be sure the war did not get off the track.

*   *   *

In England that summer of 1942 the Allies were planning the details of the invasion of north Africa. Maj. William Yarborough arrived to become Gen. Mark Clark's staff man for airborne operations. The paratroop battalion had already arrived and was quartered on an estate near Hungerford, Berkshire. Lieutenant Colonel Raff was keeping his men in shape.

The training of the American paratroopers included the use of new British radar devices, Rebecca and Eureka, which were supposed to guide a plane to any point. But—someone had to place Eureka on the spot first.

This job was to be done in north Africa by Lieutenant Hapgood of the U.S. Army Signal Corps. He had come to England to learn from the English. That fall he was sent back to America, with his two suitcases (Eureka and Rebecca), ostensibly to be discharged from the army. This was to confuse enemy agents. His next destination was to be north Africa.

The parachute troops were to fly from England to north Africa, where they would drop to capture two aerodromes, called A and B on the contour maps kept under guard in the command post.

The men were toughened by long road marches with full pack and were taken on flights to 10,000 feet, without oxygen, to accustom them to the hardship of the long air trip to Africa. On September 26 the troops were air-dropped in Northern Ireland, for practice. That was the last drop before combat.

But the problem apparent all that autumn was that the troop carrier planes were not ready, and their crews were not sufficiently trained in celestial navigation, nor did they have the equipment necessary for the long flight over neutral Spain to north Africa. The paratroopers could see trouble ahead.

After the decision was made in Washington to devote the major American effort to the war against the Germans, General Marshall felt it necessary to explain the decision to General MacArthur and the leaders of the Allied forces in the Pacific. Among others, he sent Lieutenant Colonel Reeder to the Pacific to do the job. That fall Reeder was promoted to colonel and sent to England to take command of the Twelfth Infantry Regiment of the new Fourth

Division. He checked in with Gen. Raymond Barton; then he was sent down to see General Roosevelt, the assistant division commander, who told him something about his new command. It was going to be tough: the Twelfth Infantry had a bad reputation in the division.

That was ominous. More ominous, after Colonel Reeder had arrived at the regimental headquarters at Higher Barracks, near Exeter, was a warning from a young platoon leader, 2d Lt. John Everett, who told the colonel that his platoon was not sufficiently trained to go into battle. So more training was in order.

7

READY FOR
THE WAR

Soon enough the First Division was "socked in" at Tidworth Barracks. Pfc. Moglia's company was assigned to a brick building with double-deck wooden bunks, straw-stuffed mattresses, and straw-stuffed pillows. The squad room had a wood-burning stove. Unlike the arrangement in American barracks, the toilets, basins, and showers were located in a building across the way in the center of the cobblestoned quadrangle. A British NAAFI (Navy-Army-Air Force Institute) canteen was nearby, and there the men could buy beer and snack food. The beer bottles were returnable for cash, so the soldiers kept an eye out.

Life was very definitely different. The time, for one thing: Britain was on double daylight savings time, which meant that during the summer the hours of darkness were few. Also, there were customs to be learned.

In his innocence, Pfc. Moglia one day took the bus to Salisbury, the site of one of England's most hallowed cathedrals. He saw an inn in Salisbury called "The White Hart" and decided to have lunch there. What he did not know was that by custom The White Hart was an English officers' club. No British "other rank" would have thought of trying to penetrate the doorway. But Pfc. Moglia charged in, and found himself the guest of several British officers who fed him lunch and even arranged transportation back to Tidworth Barracks at the end of the afternoon.

The next time Pfc. Moglia went to Salisbury, however, he knew better, for after a few weeks the cheery welcome to the Yanks began to wear off a bit.

The men of the First Division were a rough and ready lot, and this was encouraged by their officers. The men of the Sixteenth Infantry arrived without complete proper uniform; they did not have Class A uniform as required by the regulations, and this meant they should not be allowed off base. But when a couple of men were picked up for being out of uniform in town and brought back under guard by local MPs, General Roosevelt interceded. From then on, he told the MPs, they would not interfere with the men of the First Division unless they were out of order, not out of uniform. In fact, the less they had to do with the men of the division, the better—let the First Division MPs handle the First Division. Since the local MPs had plenty to do as it was, they turned the blind eye the general advised.

So the men of the First Division enjoyed unprecedented freedom off the post.

For the GIs, going to town meant looking for girls. One afternoon Pfc. Moglia and Pfc. Al Klimek went to Salisbury on pass. They had "seen" the cathedral. They had been in England long enough that the buildings and the cobbled streets no longer impressed them. They were lonesome and homesick. They saw a redheaded young woman standing alone on the street, and Moglia went up to her.

"Pardon me, miss. Can you please tell me the time?"

She looked first at the large clock on a pole next to them, and then at Pfc. Moglia's wristwatch. She pointed to the clock and then to the watch.

"Didn't your mother teach you to tell time?"

"Oh, I didn't see the clock. I didn't know if my watch was correct."

The young woman did not reply.

"Do you know if there is a theater nearby?"

"Yes, but it's closed."

"Why?"

She looked exasperated. "Because of the war."

"I thought you people liked movies and still went to them."

"Movies?"

"Movies. You know, moving pictures. Films."

"Oh. The flicks. Why didn't you say so?"

"I'm sorry. I didn't know. I hope you don't think I was rude. By the way, my name is John."

"My name is Ruth."

"Are you waiting for your boyfriend?"

"No. He's on duty. I'm waiting for a girlfriend."

"Are you going anyplace in particular?"

"None of your business."

"I just wondered. I'm hungry and I'm looking for a place to eat. Perhaps you can direct me."

She pointed to a tearoom across the street. "That's where I'm meeting my girlfriend, Lucy."

"Is she alone?"

"Yes, I think so."

Moglia then turned and called his friend Klimek, who was lurking a few doors away.

"Hey, Al. We got company for lunch."

Ruth's eyes opened wide.

"Are all you Yanks like this?"

"No, miss, a lot of them are a bit pushy."

But Lucy turned out to be very pleased to meet the Yanks, and the four had a pleasant lunch. From that day on they saw the girls frequently: a meal, "the flicks," and then a walk or the pub, with a lot of chatter.

It was not long, not long at all, then, before Tommy Atkins and his friends (the British soldiers) began to take a considerably different view of the Americans, whose odd ways appealed to the local girls, as did the Americans' supplies of various Post Exchange items that otherwise were hard, if not impossible, to get in England. The American troops had gotten a big pay raise, too, in 1942, and seemed to have money to burn. That irritated the British men as much as it delighted many nubile young Englishwomen, including some who ought to have known better.

So was coined the British expression that accurately described the situation of the American troops in Britain: "Overpaid, oversexed, and over 'ere."

When Lieutenant Miller learned that the Twentieth Engineers were not going overseas, it was a real shock. All the more so because Camp Kilmer was a staging area and had no facilities for troops who were not going anywhere. So the Twentieth Engineers were ordered south to Camp Pickett, Virginia, for more equipment. They were going *tomorrow*. He spent the night pushing around sleepy men to make them load up what was left of Company D's gear. They pulled out at 10 a.m. on Monday on a slow train, naturally, that stopped at every siding, it seemed. Philadelphia, Baltimore, and Washington crept by, until finally they arrived at Camp Pickett. Here they would wait for trucks and bulldozers and jeeps, and here they would train all over again.

But first they would build their camp. When they arrived at midnight at Camp Pickett, they were directed to their housing area. The housing consisted of tents put up in the middle of a cornfield. No latrines, no streets, just tents. Lieutenant Miller worked again until 3 a.m. getting the place habitable for his company. All the next week was spent building latrines, kitchens, roads, and drainage systems. At least this was the sort of thing engineers were supposed to do.

By the end of the week Lieutenant Miller was becoming acclimated again. Then Colonel Caffey threw another of his bombs: the captain in command of D Company had offended him, so he broke up the company and sent the officers flying like tent pegs to half a dozen other companies.

"I still think we had one of the best companies in the regiment," Lieutenant Miller wrote home, "but the colonel is the boss. So I have to leave all my boys just when I had got to know them and like them."

Colonel Caffey loved to give "good news" to his officers. He called them together and announced that they would soon be going further south. Cotton uniforms were to be drawn. They were going to become assault engineers, and all the officers would be issued tommy guns. They would be the same as infantry, except that they would blast pillboxes with TNT instead of artillery and bazookas.

"Anyhow," Lieutenant Miller wrote home, "we're probably going to make beach landings somewhere. God knows where. Sounds rough as hell. The colonel says we won't many of us come back. Oh, well...."

Everywhere in America in 1942 the pace of training became frenetic. Lieutenant Shebeck, who had enjoyed such an unorthodox wedding night on the train to New Orleans, had scarcely gotten his feet on the ground at Camp Wolters, Texas, when he was assigned (in February 1942) to the cadre that would help General Bradley put together the Eighty-second Infantry Division. The staff really liked General Bradley.

Shebeck said: "He had a rather quiet, fatherly manner and, unlike a lot of West Pointers, he seemed to look more favorably on Reserve officers, probably because of his own ROTC duty at South Dakota State College shortly after World War I."

By May 1942 the division was in good enough shape to stage its first review. The guest of honor was Sergeant Alvin York, the World War I hero who had been a member of the old Eighty-second Division. The showing was so good that Bradley was transferred out in June to take on the troublesome Twenty-eighth Division, and Gen. Matthew Ridgway, his chief of staff, was made commander of the Eighty-second. The Eighty-second's new chief of staff was Col. Maxwell D. Taylor.

Lieutenant Shebeck, now division special services officer, was promoted to captain. The USO was not yet organized to tour army camps, so Captain Shebeck organized his own USO. He found an old vaudeville promoter who had a half-dozen acts and signed a contract for these players to come to various units on a rotating basis. Just about anybody who could pluck a guitar or shake a leg was eligible as an entertainer, it seemed. The promoter's musicians were mostly over 70 and his dancing girls about 14. The camps had pianos, usually donated by some citizen, and not all the keys always worked. But it was recreation, and the soldiers came and enjoyed it.

In the reorganization of the U.S. Army early in the 1940s the General Staff in Washington decided it was high time the United States had a real force of airborne troops, not just a token battalion or so. The idea was actually as much American as it was anybody else's; in 1918 Billy Mitchell had asked General Pershing for permission to train a parachute division. Pershing okayed the idea, but the war ended before it could be carried out; after the war the army reverted to ultraconservatism. The idea of parachute troops languished along with that other Mitchell concept: that airplanes could sink battleships.

The Russians and the Germans picked up the paratroop idea. The Germans showed its effectiveness in May 1940 when seventy-eight airborne soldiers landed on top of Belgium's "impenetrable" Fort Eben Emäel in ten gliders and in an hour opened it up like a sardine can. Glider troops also captured the vital Meuse River bridges and made the blitzkrieg possible. A year later German paratroops and glider troops captured the British-held island of Crete in the Mediterranean. The cost was high—Hitler lost about a quarter of his men in Crete—so in his omniscience Hitler abandoned the airborne concept. But in the west the British and the Americans picked it up.

One of airborne's most stubborn advocates was Gen. Lewis H. Brereton, who had been Billy Mitchell's operations officer in 1918. In the reorganization of the army the airborne concept was accepted, and a "test platoon" of airborne infantry was organized at Lawson Field near Fort Benning. By April

1941 Benning had a parachute school run by Lt. Col. William C. Lee. By the spring of 1942 more than twenty parachute battalions were training. The Second Battalion of the 504th Parachute Infantry Regiment under Major Raff had been sent to England to train under a British general, F. A. M. Browning. The British were quite advanced in their thinking; parachute troops were shock troops, to be landed behind the enemy, thus forming a part of a pincers movement.

But back in Washington, parachute troops were regarded as very special troops, suitable only for opening up forts and investing islands under certain conditions. General Brereton and Colonel Lee persisted in arguing otherwise. Ultimately, General Marshall was convinced enough to order the development of two airborne divisions. Bradley had done such a good job with organizing the Eighty-second Division that it was cracked in two: half remained as the Eighty-second Airborne Division and half became the 101st Airborne Division, under now Brigadier General Lee.

Captain Shebeck stayed with the Eighty-second Airborne. In the reorganization the division was supposed to have one parachute regiment and two glider regiments. The 325th and 326th Infantry regiments were retained and now called glider regiments—whatever those were. There was little immediate change. The 504th Parachute Regiment (except for the Second Battalion), training at Fort Benning, was assigned to the Eighty-second Airborne Division. The 327th Infantry went to the 101st Airborne Division to become its nucleus.

So by the end of August the U.S. Army had two airborne divisions and not much of an idea of what they could do or what could be done with them. It was a case of letting the commanders feel their way. By October the two regiments were moved to Fort Bragg, North Carolina, and the airborne center was established. It did not seem to make a lot of difference to Captain Shebeck. Special Services was still the same, organizing athletics and shows. It became much easier, because Fort Bragg was an enormous installation and the USO had several centers there. But things changed. Colonel Taylor was a physical fitness advocate, and he told the captain to organize a hiking program for the division staff—"They need some toughening up," he said. So Shebeck laid out an 11-mile hike, and Taylor took him on it with the assistant division finance officer. The colonel outdistanced his two younger companions and after 7 miles he was out of sight.

Shebeck was not particularly high on the parachute jumping business, but the pressure was on. By October more than half the staff were jumpers. So Shebeck took a course of instruction and made one jump. But that was not

enough; jumpers were in demand. Soon Shebeck was transferred to command a
company of the training battalion of the 326th Glider Regiment, and there he
was "converted" to a glider soldier. Afterward he became regimental special
services officer of the 325th and assistant regimental supply officer.

The Eighty-second Airborne continued to change. The 326th Glider Regiment was transferred out, replaced by the 505th Parachute Regiment. The
emphasis on *airborne* grew ever stronger, and by autumn the idea that these
troops were just ordinary infantry who would be delivered to fight by air was
beginning to be modified.

Pfc. Moglia was promoted to corporal. He continued to train at Tidworth
Barracks with the others of the Sixteenth Infantry. He also continued to visit
Salisbury and chase girls. One day his "usual" date did not appear, but in
her place was a British Army Pay Corps corporal named Lilian Deane. A
real romance was born.

The romance flourished, but the U.S. Army took a hand, and in October
the Sixteenth Infantry was moved back aboard the *Duchess of Bedford* and
sent up to Scotland for the amphibious training of the regiment.

Moglia and his friends lived aboard the ship during this training. They
made several practice landings on the Scottish coast under the supervision
of the British Commandos. They marched inland, fortified by the usual three
sandwiches—cheese, jelly, and "Donkey Dick."

On one landing they were really put through their paces: they landed at
2 a.m. with full field pack and heavy winter coat, and covered 60 miles in
the pouring rain before coming back to the ship. Occasionally they had passes
to go into Glasgow. But only occasionally. The division was preparing to go
somewhere, that much was clear.

Lieutenant Downing also sensed the mood of preparation down at Tidworth
Barracks. He had a pass for the weekends to go into London, where he, too
chased girls. Back at the barracks after one such spree, he found that the
training was getting tougher for the Eighteenth Infantry. Mail was censored,
and Downing was one of the censors. He pored over as many as 200 letters
a week, and soon learned to look only for place names and dates and other
purely military information, which had to be blacked out.

General Allen decided that every officer and man had to show his fitness
for combat, and that meant *every* man, including the cooks, supply sergeants,

and clerks, whose exercise was usually confined to stirring pots or sitting on their butts. So one day all these specialists were assembled in full field gear, and Lieutenant Downing was selected by Captain Williams to lead the Company F contingent on a long walk in the country. He assembled the men that morning and led them out on their 25-mile hike, while the rest of the company stood by and jeered as they stepped out in a ragged line.

Major Chase, the battalion executive officer, supervised the march that day. They were to follow the usual drill: one hour of march, fifteen minutes of rest, one hour of march, ten minutes of rest. But the major had a problem: he was not used to planning military maneuvers through the English countryside. At the end of the first hour they found themselves in a town. Since part of the purpose of the halt was to let the men relieve themselves, the major marched on, and on, and it was an hour and a half before they got back into the countryside and he felt they could stop. The trouble was that the platoon the major led was now in the countryside, but Lieutenant Downing's platoon was on the edge of a village, where it took the men a long time to find a secluded culvert. Downing's platoon was still strung out when the order came to march again, and the cry went out, "Run to catch up."

They marched until noon. Trucks came out with their lunch. After half an hour for lunch they marched again. By late afternoon they had marched around in a circle and were headed back to Tidworth Barracks. They came into the compound, and the major marched them right on through. He did not want to interrupt the exercise that was taking place on the drill field. So they marched out and around the hills and back again before dismissal. Everybody made it. The cooks and bakers and supply clerks had passed the test.

When the whole company marched, from time to time General Roosevelt joined them. He was driven in a jeep by his aide, and everyone knew the jeep because it had a brigadier general's star on a red background fastened to the bumper. As the jeep came up to the column, he would stand up in the front seat, wave his riding crop, and shout at some old sergeant he knew from years past. If the unit was stopped, everybody snapped to attention, but the general put them at ease. One day he stopped at the barracks square of Downing's F Company as the company was being dismissed from drill. The general looked around, saw Sergeant Merrill, and grinned.

"Goddamnit Merrill, but you're ugly. You're getting uglier every day."

Merrill beamed at being singled out. He snapped to attention.

"The general isn't a handsome man himself," he said.

Roosevelt laughed and slapped his leg with his riding crop, and the aide drove him off, just as if he were making a stage exit. It was a fine performance and accomplished just what the general wanted. For days the men of Company F remembered, and Sergeant Merrill's status with the men went up just a little bit.

Lieutenant Colonel Campbell was as busy as an autumn squirrel, but he was also having the time of his life. Belfast, London, Tidworth Barracks, Bristol— he was moving around, finding housing for the American troops who were pouring into the British Isles. But on Thanksgiving Day he was in London. He attended services at Westminster Abbey in the morning, and at 3:15, by invitation, he and many other American staff officers went to Buckingham Palace to meet the royal family and drink large quantities of the royal Scotch.

In October the Eighteenth Infantry was moved up to Rosneath, Scotland, for amphibious training. Their instructors were the British who had staged the Dieppe raid. Day after day one great bit of wisdom was dinned into the officers: Get off the beach! Get off the beach! Getoffthebeach!!

Downing's company was broken down into thirty-five-man boat groups, each led by an officer. Downing had two rifle squads, a light–machine gun squad, Sergeant Merrill, and a handful of runners. Their first "landing" was made from an LCT loaded with 350 men. They went aboard in late afternoon. Downing and two other company officers found a place to huddle on the ramp at the bow. They nearly froze until a British officer who was part of the training crew took them into the ship's galley to thaw out.

As Downing went back to the bow of the LCT, he saw Captain Williams, the Company F commander, just coming out of the nice warm LCT wardroom, which was supposedly forbidden to the soldiers of the training mission. Rank Has Its Privileges....

Dawn had not yet broken when they landed. The ramp stuck as the crew tried to lower it, and there was much smashing and swearing, but they landed and headed up the stony beach.

Get off the beach!

Get off the beach!

Get off the beach!

Downing had learned his lesson well. He hurried up the beach and found a break in the brush, turned off, and came out on a road. He had been instructed what to do in that case, too:

Get off the road!

Downing ordered the men off the road. They crawled off the side of the road in little groups and waited in the ditches. They were waiting for Captain Williams, the company commander, to come up and tell them what to do next. They waited. Eventually Captain Williams showed up and they followed him up a hill. They did not know where they were going, or anything else about the maneuver. Finally Williams stopped and said the maneuver was over. Downing took his platoon into a field for a smoke. They waited for daylight to break. A runner came by and ordered them to march up the road. They came to a village where the people were just getting up, and the villagers stared at them silently as they came through. The LCTs were drawn into a line on the beach at the village shore. The troops got in and the LCTs churned around and headed back to Rosneath. Lieutenant Downing settled down, very dissatisfied. He hoped that when it came to the real thing it would be a lot different. He hadn't known where he was going or what he was doing. The war had to be a lot better organized than this.

Back in America the brass was trying to organize the war just as quickly as possible. Their problem was how to bring millions of young Americans into the service, train them as thoroughly as possible, and get them into the war overseas. The war effort was moving just about as fast as it could.

That fall millions of young Americans were preparing for the draft. Others, the youngsters, were enlisting so that they could choose the branch of the service they wanted. Bill Haemmel and his buddy Gilbert J. Van Elk enlisted in New York City and soon found themselves at Fort Knox, Kentucky. They had opted for the armored force, and they were now to undergo basic training. Haemmel lied a little, saying he had driven a tractor, to be sure he got an assignment as a tank driver—but that wouldn't be for a while yet. Now there were shots, and calisthenics, and close order drill, and instruction in weapons, and—KP. Private Haemmel was the "G-man," which meant that he collected all the garbage, saw that all the cans were emptied by the pickup trucks, and then washed out the cans. He ended his first week in the army with fifteen hours of KP. But soon the two young recruits were learning to drive tanks, between spells of guard duty and more study of weapons. In January they finished their basic training and were split up. Private Van Elk was soon to go overseas to north Africa. Private Haemmel was to stay on for a while at Fort Knox, the armor center.

8

THE TROOPS GO
TO WAR

Shortly after Pearl Harbor, ex-marine Barnett Hoffner had the itch to get back into the service, but his wife was still adamant. He had done his part, she said. Let someone else carry the load. So Barnett Hoffner had continued his job with the Veterans Administration in Washington. But then in the fall of 1942, walking by Walter Reed Hospital one day, Hoffner encountered an old buddy from the Marine Corps, just back, wounded, from Guadalcanal. He got the itch again, and this time he learned that the army was looking for second lieutenants. He applied and went before a screening board. He did not pass: the army wanted college graduates, not professional soldiers. So Barnett Hoffner continued in civilian life, but not for long. That fall he was drafted. When he appeared at the assembly point, he went to the Marine Corps desk with his credentials, honorable discharge, and medals. The marines wanted him, but the army had priority, so Marine Hoffner became Private Hoffner, AUS.

He was sent to Fort Dix for a week of indoctrination; old soldier Hoffner was given orders and put in charge of a slough of draftees, and off they went to Camp McCain, Mississippi, a collection of tar-paper barracks on a sandy plain. There these young men learned they were going to be a combat engineer battalion.

The commander of Hoffner's Company B was Lieutenant Witherough, who also had been a marine. He took one look at Hoffner's previous service record, and the private had a promotion to sergeant. His first job was to take charge of the weapons squad: .30-caliber water-cooled machine guns, .50-caliber machine guns, bazookas, mines, and demolition charges. Training started with four hours of close order drill every day. Every day they dug ditches, a process that separated the weak from the weary. On the basis of performance some men (over 26 years old) were transferred out. Day after day and ditch after ditch, they trained.

At first they trained with British Enfield rifles. Then they got the Garand M-1s. The difference between Marine Corps and army training showed: Sergeant Hoffner never could remember the number of his Garand.

Soon the Eighteenth Infantry moved from Rosneath to Corkerhill Camp, which was the golf course of the Pollick family estate. The troops lived in British tents. The washrooms were open sheds with long metal troughs for basins, with cold-water faucets placed at intervals along the troughs. The latrine was a sheet-iron shed divided into doorless stalls with heavy iron buckets under board seats. The mess was a large hospital tent furnished with long wooden tables. Mud was everywhere. Lieutenant Downing took one look and felt the camp was so miserable that the Eighteenth was surely going to be there a long, long time.

There was one great consolation. They were just a tram ride from the fleshpots of Glasgow and the Beresford Hotel. Downing's favorite place, it always had plenty of Scotch whiskey.

The officers and men of the Eighteenth Infantry settled into a routine: Train all day. Shave. Eat supper. Get into Class A uniform. Walk to the tram stop. Take the tram into Glasgow. Go to a dance hall or another den to find girls. Eat, drink, make merry. Return to camp as late as possible.

There was more training: amphibious landings from the *Llangibby Castle* and the *Reina del Pacifico*. There was a war game against the British Ninth Commando, "fought" in mud and rain. By this time, when Lieutenant Downing saw a K ration, he had a wish: that all the American nutrition experts who had devised the K ration could have all the cans of chopped ham and eggs crammed where it would do the most good.

And his war hadn't even started yet!

Even the war game made him miserable:

On October 19 the soldiers were aboard their transports again, preparing to be landed yet another time. However, there was a difference this time, although Lieutenant Downing did not know it: the war game was being watched by Lt. Gen. Dwight D. Eisenhower, the man chosen by General

Marshall, with the approval of Prime Minister Churchill, to head the invasion of French north Africa.

This time Lieutenant Downing was aboard the *Reina del Pacifico*, which—along with four other transports—would land the troops against the Number 9 Commando near the small towns of Dunoon and Innellan. Only one map was available to the company, so Downing made overlays for himself and his platoon sergeant.

The ships moved out late in the afternoon. That night, long before dawn, Lieutenant Downing was awakened in his berth by the squawking of the loudspeaker: "All officers assemble in the troop compartments."

He went down to his men's quarters and sat at a mess table, and there they waited for the magic call. They were Serial 135.

On deck they could hear the sounds of running feet and the thumping against the sides of the ship as the assault boats came up.

"Serial 135, repeat, 135 muster at sally port S-1, repeat, S-1."

The platoon joined the clattering, boarded the landing craft, and sat down astride low benches beneath the gunwales. Lieutenant Downing was in the bow, facing aft. An automatic rifleman occupied the little steel nest for automatic weapons next to the bow.

Ahead were Red beach, White beach, and Green beach. The Second Battalion was going in to Green beach. The landing craft moved through the choppy water and then landed with a bump. The ramp came down and Lieutenant Downing stepped out into ankle-deep water. He ran to the beach with his boat group behind him. They ran straight up and off the beach. A company runner took them along a dirt trail into a field. Downing saw Captain Williams there. Williams looked annoyed; maybe they had been too long in arriving. The captain got up and took his company headquarters group out of the field and up the trail inland.

The other platoons began to move. Lieutenant Downing's weapons platoon followed the second platoon. The third platoon followed his.

He moved out in the dark and the rain, stumbling, not knowing where he was going:

"The column would halt and the man behind me would bump into me. I'd stand still while the rain pelted on my helmet and trickled down my neck. The column would move on again at breakneck speed and I'd run off after it. My sole purpose in life at the moment was not to lose sight of the man in front of me or lose contact with the man behind."

They turned off the trail, crossed another field, and started up the side of a hill. They stopped. The captain came back, leading the column in the opposite direction. The ridiculousness of it struck Lieutenant Downing; the company was like a snake, turning back on itself. The company was disoriented, lost. The men of the weapons platoon began to bitch quietly.

"What the hell!... Even the captain doesn't know where he's going."

They waited; when the last of the column from up front passed them going back, they turned and followed. They were moving along an almost nonexistent track, and then they turned sharply up another hill that was overgrown with brush and had no track at all. The column came to a dead halt.

After a few minutes Lieutenant Downing worked his way up to the head of the column. There on the hilltop was Captain Williams, with his headquarters group around him. The atmosphere was unhappy and strained. They sat around under a tree smoking. Then up came one of the officers who had gone to find the battalion command post. He reported that the battalion commander wanted to see Captain Williams. The whole company headquarters group moved off, and Lieutenant Downing returned to his weapons platoon.

The rain was still drizzling down—"mizzle," the British called it—when the company began to move again. Lieutenant Downing's platoon passed a lone stone house, which had already been "captured" by another company. After they had moved on a short distance, a few shots rang out. Some British soldiers in the house, now "prisoners of war," were having fun shooting off their supply of blank cartridges. Lieutenant Downing's platoon plodded slowly up the hill. The ground was covered with thick grass. Beneath was mud. It was the first time Downing had seen a swamp on high ground.

When they reached the grass line up above the beach they stopped. They were in communication with battalion headquarters by radio. Orders came to halt and take up an attack formation. The company deployed along a low stone wall. Downing got his mortars and machine guns into position and then moved up to company headquarters.

He found Sergeant Merrill eating a K ration. Captain Williams was asleep, huddled up against the stone wall. A group of officers were crowded together. Downing joined them, and they sat, waiting, smoking, and griping. After a while a report came over the radio that the maneuver was over. A runner woke the captain. Downing returned to his men and formed them up in a column of twos. They walked down the hill, through the backyard of a house, into the town, and then to the dock area. The LCTs were waiting there to take them back to the ship. That was the end of the exercise. Lieutenant Downing and his men did not know where they had been or what they had done.

They all took off their wet clothes and climbed into their bunks, although it was midafternoon. They were tired and cold, and there was nothing else they had to do. That evening after chow there was a continuous party in the wardroom bar, and the Americans were introduced by their British hosts to

a ballad called "The Ball of Connemor," which consisted of scores of bawdy
verses, all of which were known to at least one of the British officers. The
Scotch whiskey flowed copiously until very late in the evening. All those
officers in the assault craft wardroom were very happy, indeed.

But in a special railroad car, riding back along the track from Inverary
to Edinburgh, and then toward London, General Eisenhower was very unhappy. He had seen the U.S. First Division in action in maneuvers. At that
moment the First Division was America's best in the European theater and
was going to be a key to the north African invasion attempt. This division
was *it*, and he was not pleased. In three weeks those troops would be dis-
embarking in earnest on what might be enemy shores. As far as Ike was
concerned, they were anything but ready. During the landings General
Roosevelt had come up all smiles and enthusiasm to tell Ike what a great job
his boys were doing. But what Eisenhower saw was failure of the leadership
at the battalion and company level. It was as if he had been watching the
Second Battalion of the Eighteenth Infantry that day, with his eye especially
on Company F.

The trouble was it was too late to do much, if anything, about it.

The training went on. The U.S. First Ranger Battalion arrived at Corkerhill
Camp. The officers and men of the Eighteenth were not favorably impressed:
"They were a cocky bunch of men and swaggered around like old combat
soldiers, talking knowingly of the Dieppe raid. Our men were impressed for
a while, until we found out that only a small fraction of the battalion had
been at Dieppe and not all of those had returned."

The rangers were extremely uniform-conscious. To avoid muddying their
meticulously shined boots when they headed for Glasgow, they drew extra
socks from the supply tent. Each night the rangers would put a pair of socks
on over their boots, walk through the mud to the tram stop, and then take off
the socks. Coming home, they didn't give a damn. When the rangers left,
the area around the tram stop was littered with army socks.

That was not the only mess the rangers left for others to clean up when
they swept out of the camp. They discarded clothes, rations, equipment,
ammunition belts, even weapons. It was the ranger creed never to take along
anything that was not necessary. The outfit believed that somebody else was
going to clean up after them, and somebody did: the British detailed a special unit to clean. What they thought of the Americans was not recorded.

*

For the men of the Eighteenth Infantry it became obvious that something was going to happen soon, because new equipment began to arrive: antigas ointment, antigas shoe impregnant, gas capes, sulfa tablets to take if wounded, water purification pills, M-1 rifles for the officers because there was a shortage of ammunition for the carbines, and three cans of American beer per man. The beer, a sort of sacrificial offering, was even more convincing than the announcement Colonel Greer made to the Eighteenth when he came back from a hurry-up visit to London:

"We're a goin' fightin'."

Almost everyone sensed that the Eighteenth was indeed about to go into battle. Also, Captain Williams, who had shown a growing distaste for maneuvers in the field, had been transferred out of the battalion to a training battalion at Tidworth Barracks. Lieutenant Spinney took command of F Company, and Lieutenant Downing now became executive officer again.

And then came the day that the officers were told to pack their footlockers, which would be stored in a warehouse outside Glasgow. A Captain Penick showed up to take over the company. Lieutenant Spinney reverted to executive officer. Lieutenant Downing reverted for the second time to command of the weapons platoon. But the one to feel sorry for was Captain Penick, assigned on the eve of combat to take over a company entirely strange to him, and to take it into battle. He was not even from the First Division, but had been transferred from the Twenty-ninth Division that had taken over the Tidworth Barracks when the First Division was detailed for combat.

Lieutenant Downing and his men believed that all this came about because Captain Williams wanted out on the eve of combat. But the fact was that when Ike had returned to London he had spoken his mind, and the word got down to General Allen and the colonels that something had to be done about the division at the company level. Period. And so came the changes.

The next day the men assembled in the usual drizzle and splashed their way out of Corkerhill Camp. They had the first inkling of their destination when they reached the high road and were told to take off their overshoes and leave them standing in the road. A detail of service of supply troops came up and took the overshoes away. The men of the Eighteenth marched to the railroad station, boarded the train, and were on their way to war. What part of the war, and where, they did not know—except, theoretically, it was not going to be a sea of mud.

*

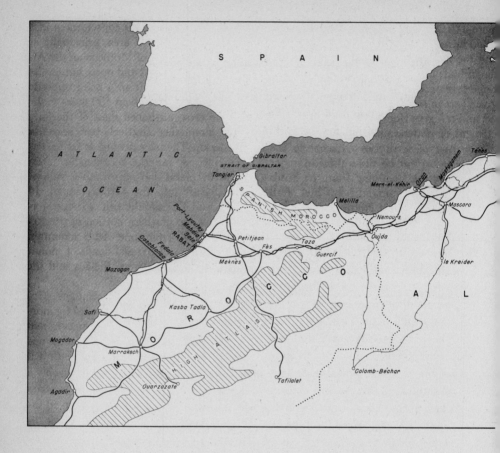

On the day that General Eisenhower traveled north to observe his army in action, the plan for Operation Torch, the invasion of French north Africa, was as complete as it could be. There had been many hitches, including the enormous difficulty of putting together enough ships to take the Americans and their equipment to Africa. However, not everything was bleak. As Eisenhower had noted, the troops of the First Division showed enormous enthusiasm and liveliness, but the preparedness of the officers and noncommissioned officers for battle was even now almost as dubious as Lord Ismay had indicated that summer. Well, summer was only just gone; it was the pace of the war in Europe that made time seem to move so swiftly.

Ready or not, the troops would go into battle.

*   *   *

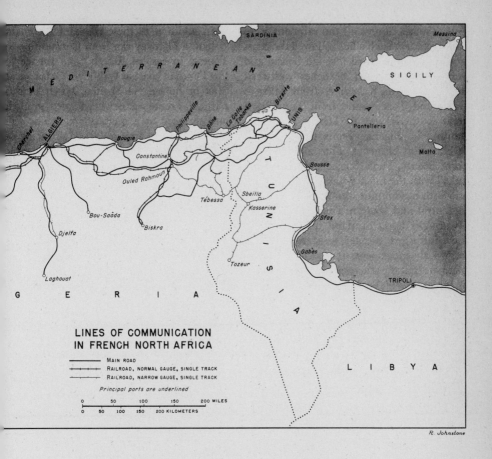

LINES OF COMMUNICATION
IN FRENCH NORTH AFRICA

———— Main road
+-+-+-+ Railroad, normal gauge, single track
———— Railroad, narrow gauge, single track

Principal ports are underlined

0   50   100   150   200 MILES
0 50 100 150 200 KILOMETERS

R. Johnstone

In north Africa the major question was political: How would the French there react to this move? Vichy France was subservient to the new German empire, but north Africa was across the Mediterranean, and Hitler's long arm did not control everything there just yet. The French attitude was a question for the politicians and the generals. As far as the GIs were concerned, they were going on an invasion, a fact they discovered as their ships and planes set forth. The invasion would involve 107,000 men of two armies in three forces under General Eisenhower. The American First Infantry Division would come from England. So would the Thirty-ninth Regimental Combat Team of the Ninth Division, which had been sent over to Northern Ireland first, and then hustled up to Scotland. The rest of the Americans and most of the supplies would come from the United States in an 850-ship convoy.

The Western Task Force was under the command of Major General Patton, who had come a long way in the preceding two years. His force included the regimental combat teams of the Forty-seventh and Sixtieth regiments of the Ninth Division, as well as the Second Armored Division. The idea of a regimental combat team was a new one to the U.S. Army. What it meant, in effect, was that the regiment became the key command factor. The Forty-seventh and Sixtieth RCTs would be the infantry for General Patton, just as the Ninth Division's Thirty-ninth RCT would make up about half the infantry for Gen. Charles W. Ryder's Eastern Task Force. A major reason for this sort of management was the state of training of the American army: some regiments were—or almost were—combat ready; some were a long way from it. In preparing for action, units had to be tightened and some quick replacements made.

The American system of troop transport had become considerably more sophisticated in the days since the First Division shipped out of New York harbor on the *Queen Mary*. And, true to his promises, President Roosevelt was sending the new troops that Prime Minister Churchill wanted for Northern Ireland.

The Thirty-ninth RCT left Fort Bragg on September 17, bound for Fort Dix, New Jersey. Seven days later the team moved to Staten Island and boarded five U.S. naval transports. On September 26 they sailed for Belfast, by way of Halifax, escorted partway by the battleship USS *Arkansas* and the rest of the way by British and Canadian destroyers and corvettes.

Each of the three battalions of the Thirty-ninth was sent to a different camp: Sunnyland Camp at Carrickfergus, Downpatrick Base Camp, and Camp Laughermoor at Temple Patrick.

More training and more hard marches were in store at these camps. The regimental service company was taken on to Scotland. It was all very confusing, but this sort of confusion seemed an unavoidable consequence of the hurried attempt of the Americans to get into the war in time to stop the Germans before they took all of north Africa. In the summer of 1942 that appeared to be a very distinct possibility. On September 1 the Germans were 20 miles from Alexandria, and were stopped there by the British at the battle of Alam el Halfa. But whether the Germans would attack again, and break through, was still the big question.

In the tension that accompanied this parlous state of affairs a plan was no sooner made than it was discarded. As these confusing movements were thrusting American troops hither and yon, the British were suffering one defeat after another by the Afrika Korps.

*

The Thirty-ninth RCT would be part of the infantry of the Eastern Task Force, under Major General Ryder. Another part would be the 168th Regimental Combat Team of the Thirty-fourth Infantry Division, together with the First and Sixth battalions of commandos, which were British and American troops (the First Battalion was the outfit that had given the men of the Eighteenth Infantry such a pain in Scotland), and the Eleventh and Thirty-sixth regimental groups of the British Seventy-eighth Infantry Division.

On October 17 the three battalions of the Thirty-ninth were moved to Scotland, and after all that wasted effort, the entire regimental combat team was reassembled at Inverary. Then came some rushed amphibious operations practice, even less successful than that of the First Division because there was not enough time. The men of the Thirty-ninth had one little taste of the political side of war: every soldier was issued an armband that was actually a small American flag. The order was that the flag was to be worn into combat on D day. The reason, which nobody told the GIs, was that the High Command was trying to persuade the French people of north Africa that the entire invasion they were about to undergo was an American show. Virtually everything was to have a U.S. flag on it, "every goddamn truck"— every battalion would fly the flag.

The Central Task Force, under Maj. Gen. Lloyd Fredendall, included the First Infantry Division, Combat Command B of the First Armored Division, the First Ranger Battalion, and various special troops.

The problem for the logistics experts was ensuring that the American troops from America and the American and British troops from Britain would all arrive off north Africa at the same time—and would arrive safely. Given the growth of Admiral Dönitz's U-boat force, this was not easy, and at least part of the reason for the success of this attenuated operation was two different British plans of deception. Throughout the war deception was one of the most effective British weapons, and its success in confusing the Germans as to where in north Africa the blow was going to strike saved the lives of hundreds if not thousands of GIs. One rumor had it that the effort would be made at Dakar, which seemed likely enough as this would have been much safer than heading into the Mediterranean. The other indicated that the convoy from Britain was headed to Malta to shore up the defenses. So the Germans had most of their defenses in the wrong place at the wrong time as the convoys came in toward Gibraltar, the fortress lent by Prime Minister Churchill to General Eisenhower for mounting the invasion of French north Africa.

Down from the British Isles in one large convoy went the five ships carrying the Thirty-ninth Regimental Combat Team.

From the decks the men of the Thirty-ninth could see ships around them from horizon to horizon: transports, with the assault landing craft hung on their sides; cargo ships, belching smoke, their decks laden with camouflaged weapons and vehicles; destroyers and corvettes and even smaller warships, convoying them through the dangerous waters. The convoy kept changing course, zigzagging, and the men below sensed each change. They began to speculate. Some said they were going to Norway: "We still got our ODs." Why else would they have the woolen uniforms?

Some said Dakar; that was the rumor the British liked best and had been encouraging for weeks. Some said Egypt, which was not only logical, but close. Some said French north Africa, which was exactly right.

In that same convoy were the ships bearing the First Division. Lieutenant Downing's Second Battalion of the Eighteenth Infantry was again aboard the *Tegelberg*, from which the troops had "assaulted" the British on the Scottish coast.

But what a difference. During the training they had been playing by British rules, which meant a nice comfortable bar for the officers and nice special arrangements for the senior sergeants in the chief petty officers' mess. But this time the rules were different. Lieutenant Downing had snugged down his men in their bow compartment, with the long mess tables and wooden benches, the hammocks rolled and stacked against the bulkheads, and after he had his dinner in the wardroom, he headed for the good old bar he knew so well.

"Whiskey," he said to the Dutch bartender.

"Sorry, sir. No alcoholic stimulants."

"What do you mean?"

"General Eisenhower's orders."

It was true. Unlike his British counterpart, the American fighting man, on sea or shore, was never trusted around alcoholic beverages, and Ike wasn't going to start trusting now. He had issued special orders to the transports that no liquor was to be served to Americans. The officers of the Eighteenth Infantry drank orange squash and cursed the brass.

A special battalion court-martial had been appointed for Monday by regiment before the troops left Scotland, and by God, it was held, although the Atlantic that day was on the side of the accused and made life rough for the court-martialers. Lieutenant Downing, the trial judge advocate, got seasick. After the accused was satisfactorily found guilty and sent to the brig, which was a chain locker, Lieutenant Downing went below, to Company F's quarters in the bow of the ship.

What a mess! The bow of a ship in an Atlantic gale was not the place to be, the men of F Company discovered. As Downing stood talking to Sergeant Merrill, the deck heaved beneath them as the ship surged forward, then the deck sank beneath them as the ship fell back. To support himself, Downing grabbed the big trash can in the middle of the deck. Four men were hanging onto it, retching. Two others sat on ammunition boxes, puking into pails. All around the hold men were lying on the deck, their steel helmets ready for emergency. A few were mopping up the mess made by men who could not contain themselves.

There were a few men, cordially detested by the others, who were not affected by the sea. One, Private Day, Downing's former machine gun sergeant who had been afflicted with an attack of AWOL, came up to Downing to tell him that he had never had it so good.

"There's all kinds of chow," he said. "And these guys aren't eating a lot."

Private Day had unquestionably learned British understatement. Lieutenant Downing hung around the hold for a while, but the stink suddenly got to him and he rushed out and up onto the deck for fresh air.

Eat or not, one thing the men were going to put down their gullets was Atabrine tablets, which would suppress the symptoms of malaria. The junior company officers served four-hour duty details in the hold with the men. Under the supervision of an officer, Sergeant Merrill personally dispensed an Atabrine tablet to each man each day and watched him swallow it.

Aboard the *Tegelberg* the officers were assembled on November 1 and told their destination:

They were six days out and well into the Atlantic. They were going to French north Africa. The First Division was to take Oran, Algeria. A bundle of maps of the Eighteenth Infantry's sector was passed out to the officers, along with a copy of the operation order and an intelligence summary.

Aboard each transport the drill was the same: the officers were given their instructions and maps, and they passed the word down to the troops. The men of the Thirty-ninth learned that their objective was Algiers.

*

The Western Assault Force was to attack western Morocco, seize Casablanca, cripple the French air force, and capture at least one airfield by the end of D day. The objectives were to be Fédala, Port Lyautey (now Kenitra), and Safi.

The Atlantic convoy of the Western Task Force began sailing on October 23, 1942—100 ships, 35,000 men, and supplies for thirty days—and was assembled at sea on October 24. Its story was almost the same as that of the convoy from Britain, except that the men of the Forty-seventh Infantry did not have to wait so long to learn where they were going. On the second day out they were told that their objective was to be the town of Safi, 130 miles south of Casablanca in French Morocco. With them would be most of the Second Armored Division. Strange names: Rabat, Marrakech, Mogador, Fédala—all these had to be learned. And strange geography, too. To help, General Harmon, commander of the Second Armored Division, had maps put up on the bulkheads of the wardrooms so that the junior officers could practice orientation.

Aboard the eight transports carrying the Sixtieth Regimental Combat Team the word was passed that the invasion point for the regiment would be Port Lyautey. And whoever heard of that place? General Patton's planners simplified matters by referring to most details under the code name "Operation Goalpost." It was the smallest force in Patton's command: Brig. Gen. Lucian D. Truscott, commander of the Ninth Division, was in charge. He had Col. Frederic J. de Rohan's Sixtieth RCT and Lt. Col. Harry Semmes's First Battalion Combat Team of the Sixty-sixth Armored Regiment—that meant a single battalion of the Second Armored Division and a handful of special troops. The first thing the men learned aboard ship was that when the battalion commander talked about the importance of capturing the Kasba, he was not talking about a movie with Hedy Lamarr and Charles Boyer, but about a very stout fort that would probably be heavily defended. The Kasba was the key to Port Lyautey, said regiment. The men would capture Port Lyautey and its airport; then they would turn south and take the airfield at Salé, 20 miles away.

Easy, said the planners. Easy. Intelligence indicated the French would be defending the Port Lyautey area with a single regiment (3000 men), about a dozen antitank guns, and a handful of engineers. Their reinforcements would have to come from Meknes and/or Rabat. They could be substantial—45 tanks and about 1200 mechanized cavalrymen—but it would take them from one to three days to arrive. By that time the situation should be well in hand.

The 39th and the 168th regimental combat teams were to land on two sides of Algiers. They were not to start shooting unless the French shot first. Many people thought the French would not shoot at all. In that case, after the landings the other divisions available would be funneled through the area quickly, taking all of Tunisia. It all seemed quite simple if you believed that the French weren't going to fight.

Aboard the SS *Tegelberg*, Lieutenant Downing studied the intelligence report. His Eighteenth Regiment was to land at Arzew, march 20 miles to the outskirts of Oran, and then take up residence on a high, forested mountain called Djebel Khar ("Lion Mountain"), which commanded the eastern section of the city. He had an aerial photo of Arzew and the countryside around it and a detailed map of the city, as well as a smaller-scale map of the countryside in the Arzew area. The only trouble, from Lieutenant Downing's point of view, was that he could not tell much about the nature of the terrain because the British system of making contour maps was different from the American.

The intelligence summary talked about the French: "They are rated as second- or third-class fighters, except the French Foreign Legion, which is rated as first-class."

Nobody knew how French intelligence rated the Americans. As Lord Ismay had? As second- or third-class fighters?

After the troops in the two convoys were told where the operations would be held, the regiments began handing out special weapons. The Americans got American weapons—the Americans who came from America, that is. The Americans who came from Britain got many British weapons. American rifles had to have American ammunition, because their calibers differed from those of the Brits. Same for machine guns and mortars. Grenades were another matter. There was a shortage of American grenades, so Lieutenant Downing's weapons platoon got British grenades—fragmentation, concussion, and thermite. To blow up and lacerate, to stun, or to burn. They were quite different from the American sort, Downing soon discovered. Somebody played a joke on him by pulling the pin on one and handing it to him. When his blood pressure returned to some semblance of normal, he was informed that the grenade had to be fused before it could explode; if it wasn't, the pin didn't make any difference.

Now he knew. Once you knew, there really wasn't any trick to the British grenade. It was just like everything else. It all looked easy enough.

9

LANDINGS

On November 5, 1942, General Eisenhower and his staff flew into Gibraltar in five B-17 Flying Fortresses, and almost immediately the conferences began. Politics, politics, all unknown to the GIs in the transports at sea not far from the "pillars of Hercules."

On the night of November 6 the convoys began slipping through, past Gibraltar. All around the blacked-out ships was the dense darkness of the tropical night; the only sound that could be heard was the slapping of waves along the sides of the ships. As the men's eyes became accustomed to the darkness, they could make out on the Spanish side the great haystack shape of "the rock." On the African side they saw the bright lights of the Spanish city of Ceuta, for Spain, being theoretically neutral—although practically pro-Axis—paid no official attention to this war.

But the army paid official attention to everything. Despite the fact that the convoys were carrying the GIs to Africa to fight, the usual levels of military discipline continued. On November 6 the combination of boredom of the voyage and tension over the next few hours created some problems.

Aboard the *Tegelberg* Lieutenant Downing had drawn this day as O.D. He put on the official armband and held a guard mount at 1 p.m. on the promenade deck. He looked over the weapons, grabbing one or two (the trick was to get them before the man let go; the GI's trick was to let go just before the officer grabbed). He looked over his guard to see that uniforms were clean, buttons buttoned, shoes shined, and faces shaved. All was well. Then he posted his guards and went back to his cabin for a nap.

All remained quiet until 9 p.m. Then a runner brought a call from the ship's chief steward. Trouble.

Lieutenant Downing tied his necktie and put on his web belt, with the pistol and cartridge case, and his steel helmet. He found the chief steward (Dutch) and two of his bakers (also Dutch) chattering excitedly. Two soldiers had threatened the bakers. The soldiers had been hanging around the bakeshop and when the bakers told them to get out, saying there would be no handouts, the soldiers had left muttering.

Lieutenant Downing calmed the civilian bakers and they went back to work. The steward offered Downing a cup of tea.

While he was drinking the tea, one baker came rushing back.

"Those men, they're out there now."

Downing put on his helmet again and walked to the bakeshop. Two soldiers, one of them wearing a navy watch cap (out of uniform), stood against the bulkhead.

"What are you doing here?"

"We ain't botherin' nobody."

"The bakers told you to stay out of this passageway."

No answer.

The lieutenant called up the nearest sentry and ordered him to walk behind the men. He then led the way to the brig, in the chain locker a deck below F Company's quarters. He locked the pair in the brig. Then he went back to his cabin for another nap.

About ten minutes later, Lieutenant Downing was awakened by the corporal of the guard. Some soldiers had broken into the beer storage vault. Off he went again with pistol belt and helmet.

Down to the beer hold, way below decks, down to a catwalk, down a long steel stairway, and into the liquor stowage, a large room, completely encircled by the doors of locked lockers. One locker had been invaded; the door hung loose, a beer case had been dragged out, and several empty bottles lay on the deck. Four men of the Third Battalion were standing against the lockers, guarded by the corporal of the guard and the sergeant of the guard, who held pistols on them.

The miscreants had discovered the location of the beer storage, and the location of the guard post at the top of the stairway. They had created an alarm a long way back up the passage, and when the guard hurried back to investigate, they had sneaked down the stairway and into the beer storage.

When the guard came back, he heard voices down there. He started down, and was threatened. He stopped, went back to the top of the stairs, and guarded them, preventing the thieves from coming up, until the corporal of the guard came by on his tour. Then the corporal found the sergeant and together they went down.

Lieutenant Downing pulled out his own pistol, pulled back the slide, shoved a shell into the chamber, jammed the weapon into the back of one man, and told him to march.

"Follow the sergeant," he ordered.

The file followed the sergeant up the stairs. When they reached the open deck, two of the prisoners took off in the darkness. But they still had the other two. Two more for the brig. Downing reported to Major Powers, the battalion commander, and was chewed out for losing two prisoners. (The next day one of them was identified because the first sergeant of his company held a head count on the men's movement in and out of the company area.)

So on the day before the invasion of north Africa the company officers of the Second and Third battalions, Eighteenth Infantry Regiment, First Division, were busying the clerks with the paperwork for courts-martial.

As H hour approached, the brass was getting very nervous. Lieutenant Downing was still O.D., but even so he had to inspect his weapons platoon to see that the men were ready. As he was doing this, he heard the rattle of machine gun fire from on deck. Then a guard brought down a member of Downing's weapons platoon, under arrest. Major Powers had done the arresting.

What was the crime?

The soldier had been standing at the rail, blowing up condoms into balloons, tying them off, and throwing them overboard. The noise Downing had heard was the firing of the ship's machine guns to sink the condoms so that they would not leave a trail for the submarines the ship's captain knew would follow the convoy.

"Why did you do such a damn fool thing as that?"

"I dunno. I was just watching them bouncing on the waves."

Down to the brig again went Lieutenant Downing, with his new prisoner.

"I think he's a spy," said Major Powers, and he proposed that the soldier be sent back to England and tried there for treason. The soldier could not have chosen a more dangerous moment to call up the U-boats and the Stuka dive-bombers that infested the Mediterranean, bombers that were based within 100 miles of the convoy.

Downing argued (successfully) that the soldier was one of his best men, and just a plain fool; in so doing, he saved the man.

Then the corporal of the guard reported a sentry asleep at his post. Downing went to the post, his sergeant of the guard behind him. There, by God, was the sentry, leaning back against a companionway ladder. His arms were folded over the muzzle of his rifle. His head was on his arms. The lieutenant stood in front of him. The man did not move. The lieutenant called the man's name. No movement. The lieutenant grabbed his arm and shook him. The soldier woke up.

"Pull his belt and take him to the brig."

Yes, fuses were very short that day before the invasion.

The brig was just about full that afternoon, when regiment called an officers' meeting. Lieutenant Downing would remain as O.D. until 9 p.m. Then all guard would be called off, and all men would report to their company compartments.

Oh, yes, the Protestant chaplain would hold interdenominational services on the promenade deck at 6 p.m.

Down went the company commanders and the platoon leaders to the troops. Every man had to shed everything on his person that might identify the regiment. Pockets were turned out, wallets opened, and old garrison passes, checks, railroad ticket stubs, and driver's licenses were handed over to be thrown into the GI cans.

Just before 6:00 Lieutenant Downing made his last inspection; then he went to the brig and released all his prisoners to their companies. Major Powers had cooled down, and the balloon flier was told that his fate would depend on how he comported himself in combat.

Chow time. Lieutenant Downing ate in the wardroom; then he went to his cabin to check his maps, routes of march, and intelligence summary. He had sewn his little American flag onto the arm of his field jacket. Someone reminded him that somebody was going to have to carry the 3- by 5-foot American flag (issued aboard ship). Who was going to be the lucky target?

"Volunteers?"

No volunteers.

The mess sergeant got the accolade.

Thank God he wasn't in their boat group.

Six o'clock came, and the Protestant chaplain's interdenominational services. The promenade deck was so jammed with men that Lieutenant Downing gave up trying to make his way to the rail for a breath of air, and for a look at what was around them.

*

It was a long night for Company F in the bow hold, and for the company officers in their bunks on the deck above.

The convoy was in position more or less on time, around midnight. The First Rangers were to go in first. Lieutenant Downing's F Company was way down on the list of serials. The landings would begin around 1 a.m. Weapons platoon was not scheduled to go ashore until 7:00.

When the ship stopped, Downing awoke and went down to the wardroom. The Malay stewards were moving around, pouring lots of coffee. Some men were eating cold cuts and bread. There didn't seem to be a lot of enthusiasm for the food. Lieutenant Downing only half-noticed that the coffee was still that dreadful British mixture, "arf-an-arf" coffee and milk.

Below, the men of Company F were downing beef stew and tea.

No, not even General Eisenhower knew what was going on along the north African beaches that morning. The sort of news he was getting was all very confusing. Were the French going to fight or not? The first real news Ike had (apart from all the politicking with General Giraud and the others) had come on Saturday morning. It was not the sort of news that does a commanding general's heart good at the opening of a battle.

The USS *Thomas Stone*, carrying the Second Battalion of the Thirty-ninth Regimental Combat Team, was torpedoed just at dawn as the convoy was going to General Quarters. A torpedo hit the ship under the fantail.

To be sure, the torpedo had to have come from an Axis submarine, so it did not answer any of Ike's questions about the French. It did raise the level of tension at Eisenhower's headquarters.

When the news reached Gibraltar that morning, it conjured visions of Admiral Dönitz's U-boats in great packs, attacking the invasion convoys. Fortunately for the invasion the visions were not true, nor was the *Thomas Stone* sunk. But she was damaged. And to the men of the Second Battalion that meant something—they were out of the first stage of the battle. The Third Battalion would lead the assault wave against Algiers.

Was that lucky?

Well, for anyone who liked the idea of sitting in a crippled ship, waiting for a tow 160 miles from shore, surrounded by enemy bases and perhaps by enemy submarines, it was a great moment.

The Second Battalion was out of it, but the convoy moved on, toward Algiers.

Lt. Col. Walter M. Oakes, the commander of the Second Battalion, was not enamored of his position on the sitting duck *Thomas Stone*. He decided to load his men into the landing craft and sail to shore to fight. So he did, and 700 men with all their equipment got into the landing craft and set sail for north Africa. But even though the weather was clement, the matchbox fleet failed, and it was not many hours before even the commander agreed that they would never make it. So the battalion was loaded aboard the British corvette that had been escorting them, and all the LCVPs were sunk. Onward they went, toward the field of battle.

It was 1:30 in the morning when the ships were in position, and the Third Battalion of the Thirty-ninth was ready to go against Algiers. The Third Battalion, aboard the SS *Leedstown,* had its troubles. The *Leedstown* suffered an electrical failure before the landing craft were lowered. The boats would not go down. The electricians were two hours in making repairs.

So it was the men of the First Battalion of the Thirty-ninth—not the Third—who climbed down from their ship into the landing craft and hurried toward the shore in the dark hours of early morning.

All day Saturday, November 7, the ships carrying the men of the Western Task Force were moving steadily toward French Morocco in the convoy led by the USS *Augusta*. That meant two-thirds of the Ninth Division, and most of the Second Armored. If the conditions borne by the men coming down in the convoys from Britain seemed rough, they were much worse in the convoy that came all the way across the Atlantic. Evidence of the American transport shortage was easy to see: four-tier bunks, crowding so severe that men preferred to sleep on deck if the weather permitted. In the daytime a place to sit on deck was a prize. Most of the GIs had to wait in line. At first the waiting was two and a half hours; toward the end of the crossing it had come down. There was still at least an hour's wait for meals, and then most of the men ate standing.

The junior officers had it better. By the luxury travel standards of the past their situation was not good, but compared to that of the enlisted men it was heaven. The junior officers were jammed together, a dozen to a small stateroom, and they too had long waits for food. But what a difference! Armies hark back to the nondemocratic past: officers are gentlemen. Enlisted men are, as the British put it so nicely, "other ranks." And by 1941 the United States had found no way to transfer the egalitarianism of American civilian life to the military.

On the third day out the word had been passed that Safi, French Morocco, was to be the Forty-seventh and Sixtieth regimental combat teams' destination. Also heading there was most of General Patton's armor, which was coming in the sea train *Lakehurst*. With the news came the maps and the poop sheets, the intelligence reports and the orders. Two rifle companies of the Forty-seventh, K and L, were transferred to the destroyers *Bernadou* and *Cole*, which had been disguised to look like French destroyers. Theirs would be the touchy mission of rushing in to capture Safi harbor before the enemy could blow up the installations or bring in reinforcements.

Lt. William G. Duckworth and five enlisted men were riding in a submarine. Their task was to get ashore in a rubber boat and place an identifying infrared light on the end of the long mole that jutted out into the Mediterranean, to guide the two destroyer transports into the harbor.

Saturday evening. Something was up, and if the troops had not been told, the chow would have said it: steak, chicken, and turkey for that last evening meal, much better fodder than that served aboard the British transports. The last instructions were given, the company officers went to join their men, to check that the Ninth Division's octofoil insignia was on the left arm, and the American flag armband below it.

What was the announcement for? President Roosevelt, who thought he knew his Frenchmen, suggested that if the French discovered that they were facing the Americans, they would not fight. The President had a highly idealized view of French attitudes, perhaps stemming from his days at Groton and study of the American Revolution. Well, it was better than that; his recollections went back to World War I when he had served as assistant secretary of the navy. During and after World War I Franco-American amity had hit an all-time high.

That was a long time ago, as General Eisenhower's political officers were discovering in their attempts to persuade the French to allow their north Africa to be invaded. Aboard the transports, the American flag insignia seemed a foolish idea of the brass, giving the enemy a lovely target. But orders were orders.

The plan called for arrival off Morocco around midnight, with some four hours for the navy to unload and to pass the command to the ground forces. But everything was late. The Port Lyautey force was supposed to arrive offshore at 11 p.m. At 11 p.m. the ships were still four hours away. The Safi force was on time.

As the troopships neared their destinations, a broadcast to the French from President Roosevelt went on the air.

The Americans, he said, were coming to restore French liberty, equality, and fraternity, religious freedom, and the old democracy of the Third Republic. They were not coming to occupy French territory; they would leave as soon as the German and Italian enemies were driven out.

"*Mes amis*, we have come among you to repulse the cruel invaders.... Have faith in our words....I am appealing to your sense of realism, self-interest, and ideals," said the President. "Help us where you are able. *Vive la France*."

What a stupid move! Not the President's broadcast, but the timing of its release. It was an enormous fuckup.

Not many GIs knew about that broadcast, but Gen. Lucian Truscott, commander of the Ninth Division and a GI general, did, and he swore. The broadcast was supposed to accompany the landing of the troops, but the ships were delayed, and actually it came an hour before, thus destroying all the element of surprise that the planners had tried so hard to create.

"If the French aren't waiting beside their guns we'll be lucky," was the remark General Truscott made for publication.

The general might have been a prophet.

The invasion was ready to begin, now that the French had been properly warned.

*   *   *

Algiers, Algeria: The First Battalion of the Thirty-ninth Infantry moved into the landing craft just after 1:30 a.m. and headed toward Aïn-Taya, 15 miles east of Algiers. At least they were right on schedule. Good.

The Second Battalion was wallowing at sea in the corvette. No good.

The Third Battalion was hung up aboard the transport *Leedstown*, waiting for the electrical system to be fixed so that the assault craft could be lowered. No good.

The 168th Regimental Combat Team landed in good order west of Algiers and took Fort Sidi Ferruch without firing a shot. The 168th then moved quickly against very light opposition to the eastern limits of Algiers. Marvelous.

Oran, Algeria: The First Division ships were on time. The landings began. Good.

Safi, Morocco: The transports were 8 miles offshore at midnight. The landings began at 1 a.m. Good.

At 4:28, guided by the infrared light (invisible on shore) the American destroyers nosed into Safi harbor. From the cliffs above, two 75-millimeter guns fired a challenge. The *Bernadou* answered with its 3-inch gun, firing the same pattern. It was not the recognition signal, but it confused the enemy for a little while. The ships came in under the guns. But then the *Bernadou* ran aground.

The men of Company K were below deck.

"Anybody hurt?" asked Capt. Gordon Sympson, the company commander.

"No."

"Well, let's get the hell out of here."

One, repeat *one*, net was flung over the side and the men clambered down the ropes and onto the beach. Offshore, the American destroyer *Mervine* began firing at the French guns on the cliff, and kept them occupied. The stranded *Bernadou* knocked out a 25-millimeter shore gun.

That was one way to deliver the men ashore. The *Bernadou* was stuck, tight. She sat there.

The *Cole* made it into harbor, and then rammed the merchandise pier, virtually shaking the GIs off. That was another way to land the men. Capt. Thomas Wilson's Company I hustled ashore.

Port Lyautey, Morocco: The landings were supposed to begin at 4 a.m. Confusion. A fleet of five French destroyers cut across the path of the convoy. One lone American sympathizer flashed a message, picked up by the U.S. destroyer *Allen:*

Be warned. Alert on shore at 5 a.m.

The presidential message had backfired.

The men in charge in Morocco saw their enlightened self-interest: stick with the Germans; they're winning, aren't they?

The landings at Port Lyautey did not start until 5:30. The French were ready to fight at 5:00. Dreadful.

Mehdia Beach: The ships carrying the Sixtieth Infantry were late. More confusion. The landings began at 5:30. The enemy was fully alert. Horrible.

Oran: The Oran portion of the convoy had arrived nearly on time, and the First Division assault began. The men of Company F, Second Battalion, Eighteenth Infantry, were huddled in their bow compartment of the SS *Tegelberg*, waiting.

The loudspeaker in the wardroom began to squawk:

"The first assault craft have reached the beach. No opposition."

Conversation became a little louder. A lieutenant speared a piece of cold meat and made a sandwich.

"The rangers have taken Fort du Nord. No casualties."

Broad smiles. More men began making sandwiches. They drifted out on deck in twos and threes, and the East Indian stewards began clearing up the tables, carting off trays, crumpling up the tablecloths.

Soon the order came for officers to report to their companies, and they went down. A few delayed to make more sandwiches.

Lieutenant Downing went back down to the bow compartment and sat on the deck next to the door. He leaned against the bulkhead and spread his gear around him, just like everybody else. The lights went off, and they sat in the dim glow of the blue emergency lamps. They waited.

The greasy beef stew and the tension did not mix well for all the men. Some began running for the latrine. The others sat. They could not smoke below deck. There was nothing to say. Their equipment was all around them: cartridge belt full of M-1 ammunition, two extra bandoliers, M-1 rifle, two canteens of water, compass, first aid pack, trench knife with brass knuckles, suspenders holding up the cartridge belt, musette bag with change of socks, shorts, water pills, gas mask, and steel helmet. Anybody who had anything else except the partial roll of toilet paper in the helmet was a damned fool.

Sergeant Merrill sent a runner up to the main deck to report when their serial number was coming up. They could hear clanking and the clatter of feet, and almost automatic orders, delivered in an upper-class British voice, dispassionate, controlled:

"Serial 123, muster at sally port No-1...."

They began to drift off to sleep. Men moved around a little to shake their legs.

Six o'clock came. Seven o'clock. Eight o'clock...

Eight o'clock? They were supposed to be ashore at 7:00.

Several of the company officers got up and went out on deck to look over the shore through their field glasses. Low shoreline, rising to small hills, a few straggly trees and orchards, a few scrub bushes. Mostly sunbaked brown earth, shining in the sunshine. There was Arzew, the little town at the foot of the hills: red tile roofs, pastel stucco, a church tower; the smokestack of the sulfur refinery, just as it was on the map.

They cupped their ears. Once in a while they heard a rifle shot. Then troops could be seen moving up a hill; they were Americans. Then a shrill scream, a flat explosion, a sort of crrruuuump, and a spurt of water, 30 yards off the shore side of the bow. They all ducked. Another scream, another burst, another geyser, this time off the seaward side. Somebody was shooting at them.

Shooting at them!

But not only shooting at them: that somebody had them zeroed in.

They waited for the third shell. It did not come.

Why?

Cautiously, Lieutenant Downing went below. So did all the others.

When they got back below, the men wanted to know what was going on up there. The officers didn't know.

What was going on up there?

Nobody could answer the question. Not even Eisenhower.

What was going on was the war. The F Company serials began to come up: 133, 134. Then came the serial of the weapons platoon, 135. "Muster at sally port S-2."

"Let's go," said Lieutenant Downing.

The war began.

10

FIGHTING THE FRENCH

The men of the First Division's Sixteenth Infantry had come in ships just like those that had carried the Eighteenth Infantry, and the conditions were the same: the officers crowded into staterooms like boys in a YMCA dormitory, the men crammed into hold compartments as tightly as sardines in a can, sleeping in hammocks at night, rolling and stowing the hammocks by day so that they could use their sleeping room as lounge and mess hall.

The Sixteenth was scheduled to hit Arzew beach on D day; as on the SS *Tegelberg*, religious services were held on every ship the night before, and on every ship the services were jammed.

On the night of D − 1, Corporal Moglia was on the deck of his transport, looking out over the peaceful sea at the Big Dipper, when he was approached by Smitty, a friend from Virginia.

"I just wanted to say goodbye, John."

"What do you mean, goodbye? I think it's going to be a long war."

"Not for me. Tomorrow I die." Smitty held out two cigars to Moglia. "Promise me that when things quiet down you'll smoke one for me."

Not ten minutes later, Bill, a friend from New Jersey, also approached Moglia, and insisted on shaking his hand. "The last time, buddy," New Jersey said. "Tomorrow I will have had it."

And within the hour, Mike, a third friend, came to Moglia with the same tale, that he, too, was destined to die on the shore of north Africa.

*

In those dark hours before the dawn, the men of the Sixteenth clambered into their boats and headed for the shore to assault their beach and then Oran. Corporal Moglia swore that he was carrying equipment that weighed more than he did. In addition to the infantryman's usual load of weapon and extra ammunition, gas mask, pack, and the like, Moglia was carrying a mine, grenades, and smoke pots. His company commander had decided (quite rightly) that this was the only sure way to get a lot of equipment ashore in a hurry, where it would be at the disposal of the company should the men need it.

After the troops hit the beach, Corporal Moglia was assigned to scout as the company moved up toward La Macta. He moved out ahead of the company to find the enemy. It was elusive. He came to a pretty little farm with white stone buildings capped by red tile roofs. Everything was still—no chickens, no other animals, no people. It was as still as death, and indeed, death is what it was. The French farmer had killed his wife and his three children and then committed suicide as the Americans approached, rather than have his family fall into the hands of "these barbarians."

Early that first day Moglia spotted a plane with circular markings of blue, white, and red. It swooped down low. Moglia stood up and waved as the pilot came down, and the pilot waved back. Ah, thought Corporal Moglia, what a comfort to have the British overhead. It was only later that Corporal Moglia learned how lucky he had been that the plane did not strafe or drop any bombs, as the French planes had been doing all morning. The French tricolor insignia was a circle of blue, white, and red, so very much like the British red, white, and blue.

The Sixteenth moved on, and fought. At the end of that first day, Company E assembled to bivouac and the first sergeant counted noses. Missing were Smitty, Bill, and Mike. "What happened to them?" asked Corporal Moglia. "KIA," said the sergeant tersely. *Killed in Action*. Corporal Moglia pulled out Smitty's cigar, still damp from the surf and the sweat of the day, and smoked it down.

Eons ago, in that summer of 1942, the American paratroop battalion in England had trained very hard under British paratroop chief General Browning. General Eisenhower had decided to use the American paratroops in north Africa to see what they could do. A lot of ironing-out had to be done: Lieutenant Colonel Raff was in charge of the paratroop battalion, but the command was in the hands of Col. W. Bentley of troop carrier. So it was sorted out in London that three squadrons of transport planes would carry the 520 men of the battalion to jump in the Oran area, and the moment they jumped, command would pass to Colonel Raff. That was the sort of thing Ike's headquarters did a lot of that summer.

But by October the role of the paratroops was as confused as anything in the north African invasion could be. Would the French cooperate? If so, then the paratroops would be landed by the transports—no airdrops involved.

At four o'clock on Saturday afternoon (November 7) thirty-nine air transport command C-47 cargo planes took off from British bases, bound for La Senia and Tafaraoui airports near Oran to land or air-drop at dawn. General Browning and other paratroop enthusiasts had promised Ike that he would really see something when the paratroops got into action. What better test was there than to assign them to capture an airfield? Airfields would be needed desperately in those first few hours of the invasion if the French decided to resist. The British could supply plenty of fighter planes, but the problem was range: British fighters had been developed for the defense of the British Isles, and their range was very short.

Airborne operations were something brand new to the Americans. Troop carrier command was virtually untrained for the job; some of the navigators had been assigned to the planes just hours before takeoff. Most of the pilots had no experience in night formation flying.

The bad news: The flight took twelve hours, and by the time the formation should have been over Gibraltar, it was hopelessly mixed up, lost and confused. No more than six planes were together. Fog rose over the Spanish coast, which did not help matters. A warship stationed 25 miles off Algeria was sending homing signals—on the wrong frequency.

The good news: From Gibraltar came the word to Colonel Raff in his aircraft: satisfactory arrangements had been made with the French. It would be a peaceful landing; there was no need to drop.

As dawn came up only half a dozen transports were on course, but some others managed to correct in the daylight. Colonel Raff's plane headed in toward Tafaraoui field and was immediately assailed by flak bursts from antiaircraft guns. That did not square with what Gibraltar had said, but someone was certainly trying to kill them. The C-47 came in low and Raff saw an armored column on the road and fighting on the ground. So he decided that his men would parachute, but not into the teeth of that armored column. They would land on the Sebkra, a dry lake bed about 25 miles west of the airfield. Before the day ended, a little over half the men of the battalion arrived on the scene. They were dressed for winter in northern Europe: long woolen underwear to begin with. On the ground in the desert they began to feel the heat, and the long woolen underwear was left for the local inhabitants.

When they were down and the colonel counted noses, there were some 300 paratroopers, but they were 35 miles from the airfield they were supposed to occupy. And there was that armored column to contend with. With great effort Colonel Raff got three C-47s operational on the second day, and flew to Tafaraoui to make another airdrop on the field. But the French air force was on the alert, and the three defenseless transports were jumped and shot up by four French fighter planes, which were in turn jumped and shot down by six British Spitfires. The C-47s managed to make crash landings, but three paratroopers were killed and fifteen wounded. And when they got out of the planes, they were surrounded by Americans. The airfield had already been occupied by an armored column from the First Armored Division. The paratroopers were assigned to the defense of the airfield, but the brass was not highly impressed with the performance.

*   *   *

Just before the troops of the Thirty-ninth Regimental Combat Team began moving to attack Algiers on D day, two British destroyers moved into the Algiers harbor. They were loaded with the troops of the First and Sixth commando battalions—American and British troops. The idea was to surprise the French and seize the port before the defenders could pull themselves together. But the French were not fooled, and they were far better organized than the Allies expected. The destroyers had been picked up by sound devices as they came in; the port searchlights were trained on them; and the shore batteries began to fire. One destroyer took several hits; and then it turned around and escaped the port. The other moved in and landed its troops, but they were immediately pinned down on the beach. The mission failed. By 9 a.m. the second destroyer had turned and was running the gauntlet back out to sea.

The Thirty-ninth's First Battalion got ashore at Aïn-Taya against very little opposition, and it moved toward its objective, Maison Blanche airport. It took a little over five hours to cover that 12 miles. At the airport the battalion hit its first real opposition, French infantry with tanks. But the French enthusiasm for the defense seemed limited, and by 8:30 a.m. the airport was in the hands of the Americans.

After a delay of three hours the *Leedstown*'s electrical system was repaired and the assault boats lowered. The Third Battalion then landed near Fort Jean Bart, and swept westward along the coast to Fort de l'Eau. Here was another fight, again not a very hard one, and the opposition vanished. Soon British fighter planes were landing at Maison Blanche airfield.

On the west side of Algiers the 168th Regimental Combat Team had almost the same experience as the Thirty-ninth RCT, except that its capture of Fort Sidi Ferruch was made without firing a shot. And only a handful of troops potshotted at the Americans as they moved eastward toward Algiers. Already, the French in Algiers, led by Adm. Jean Darlan, were negotiating with the American brass for an armistice, which was really a surrender. At the end of the first day, then, Algiers was in American hands for all practical purposes.

The only outfit missing from the Eastern Task Force was the Second Battalion of the Thirty-ninth, refugees from the damaged USS *Thomas Stone*. Their corvette pulled into harbor on the morning of November 9. The only major loss (the *Thomas Stone* was salvaged with all its cargo) was the SS *Leedstown*, which was attacked by the German bombers and set afire. The *Leedstown* had been carrying the Thirty-ninth Regiment's kitchen. Fortunately that was saved before the ship sank with a loss of twelve lives, five of them GIs.

On the other side of north Africa the Western Task Force moved against Casablanca and the rest of French Morocco. General Truscott's eight transports were late, and by the time they were off the beach the presidential message to the French that was supposed to make the First Division's way easier had alerted the defenders, who had decided to fight.

November 7, 4:30 a.m.: The first three waves of infantrymen were climbing down the assault nets and into the LCVPs. The tanks were to land inside the breakwater at Port Lyautey just before 8 a.m. But the tardiness of the attack had changed everything: the tides were wrong, the surf was terrible. Three landing craft bringing in armor were swamped immediately; a light tank, a half-track, and a scout car were lost. The end of the light tank was spectacular, if tragic: it had been "amphibiously sealed" with a compound redolent of fish oil. The tank was released from the landing craft and began moving in through the breakers; then it suddenly turned, circled, and went out into deep water. Then the tank sank with all its crew. "Gassed by that goddamn fish oil," was the dogface comment.

It would be a while before the dogfaces would get any help from their armor.

The LCVPs sped in toward the shore, their wakes kicking up strings of foam behind them. The landing craft were 700 yards offshore when a French searchlight picked up one boat. A red flare went up at the mouth of the Sebou River, and the French shore batteries began firing, mostly on the transports and the warships offshore. With the loss of surprise, the warships began shelling the coast.

It was 5:40 when the Second Battalion of the Sixtieth RCT hit Mehdia beach, south of the point where the Oued River flows out to sea, creating a lagoon that protected the Kasba. If the GIs were expecting machine guns and pillboxes, they were pleasantly disappointed; but a few minutes later in the growing light, French planes came in and strafed, and American soldiers began to fall.

The First Battalion was lucky in a way; the landing took place a mile and a half below its assigned beach. No casualties, but the troops had a way to go to get to their objectives.

Over on the far side of the Oued, Lt. Col. John J. Toffey Jr.'s Third Battalion, aboard the transport *Susan B. Anthony*, got the brunt of the enemy air attack. Two landing craft were swamped by near-misses of French bombs. They had overshot their beach, and they landed at 6:30 in full light of day. French planes strafed. American antiaircraft guns shot down two French planes. In that landing was Sgt. Wilfred M. Thornton's Company M. He was section leader of heavy machine guns.

It was a difficult landing in several ways. The water was rough, and a number of men were sick—or maybe it wasn't the water as much as the tension. But they made the shore, and then for the first time in their lives they came under artillery attack. Real guns were firing at them, and trying to kill them! With that realization they were on the way to becoming combat soldiers.

The First Battalion was facing elements of the French Foreign Legion, including tanks and cavalry. All day long the First Battalion would be fighting on the low ground west of the Oued River's lagoon and the edge of the Mamora Cork Forest.

The Second Battalion seemed to have it better, as it moved forward to-

ward the Kasba fort. But the French managed to knock out the ship-to-shore
communications between the infantry and its supporting warships, so the
GIs had no more naval gun support. The tanks were not yet ashore, nor was
there any artillery except the 37-millimeter antitank guns, which were no
match for the French 75s. The French also put Renault tanks into action in
this area.

The Second Battalion had three objectives: the Kasba, the lighthouse on
the point, and the coastal batteries that were banging away at the ships.

To get to the Kasba, the Second Battalion had to cross the lagoon or go
down around it. Part of Company F crossed in rubber boats. E Company was
assigned the lighthouse; 2d Lt. Charles Dushane, Cpl. Frank L. Czar, Pfc.
Theodore R. Bratkowitz, and one other private made the attack. They crossed
over barbed-wire entanglements, under fire, and charged inside the lighthouse. They captured twelve prisoners, and the rest of the French retreated
from that position.

One objective taken.

Company E and Company F now joined forces. They discovered that a
system of trenches connected the lighthouse and the Kasba. The Americans
began working their way forward and soon had taken about fifty prisoners.
They captured a French antitank gun, but the enemy had removed the firing
pin.

The fire from the French was steady and fairly heavy. Almost as troublesome was the fire from the American warships offshore, now shelling the
Kasba, but also shelling all around it, including the American troops attacking the fortress. Since they had lost communication with the ships, there
was no way the Second Battalion could stop the shelling. The "friendly fire"
was as dangerous as the enemy's.

Around noon the Second Battalion had reached the "cactus village," between the lighthouse and the Kasba. The French launched a counterattack,
supported by armor. The Americans began to fall back; they had no armor at
hand, no antitank weapons, not even grenades. The French pushed forward
toward the lighthouse. Lieutenant Dushane and Corporal Czar of Company E
figured out a way to use the captured antitank gun: Czar aimed the gun at
the advancing French tanks, and Dushane set off the projectile with fire from
his tommy gun. They destroyed one tank, but Lieutenant Dushane was killed.

The destruction of that one tank stopped the French advance long enough
for the Second Battalion to organize an attack. Another tank was knocked
out. The French then retreated into the shelter of the Kasba fortress, from
which they poured out heavy fire.

Pfc. Clarence L. Mohler and Pfc. John R. Fisher worked their way up to the base of the fortress, dodging fire. They climbed the wall, and from the top began firing into the parade ground inside, while other men of the battalion stormed the main gate, grabbed some prisoners, and retreated. As the shadows began to lengthen, the Second Battalion moved back into the protection of the forest and dug in for the night. More waves of infantry were coming onto the beach, but so were more French defenders moving toward the Kasba. By the end of the day half a dozen American tanks had reached the beach, but Lt. Col. Harry Semmes's First Battalion Combat Team of the Sixty-sixth Armored Regiment was not ready to go into action. It would not be ready until the next day. Semmes's unit moved into position south of the lagoon.

The Third Battalion reached its first objective, called Hill 58, by 10 a.m. The hill was an admirable artillery observation post, and from it the spotters directed the fire of the American warships offshore. Unfortunately, they did not know what the Second Battalion was facing. The spotters assumed the Americans had captured the fortress, as planned. The day ended with the issue far from decided. The French had lost half their aircraft in the area, but they held the Kasba and the coastal batteries. The Americans were still confined to the beach.

The Forty-seventh Regimental Combat Team's objective of Safi was regarded as absolutely vital to the whole operation. By capturing Safi and holding it, the regiment could prevent the French garrison at Marrakech from reinforcing Casablanca. Furthermore, Safi was a good port, and the Allies needed a good port quickly. That's why most of the Second Armored Division's tanks were assigned to this operation.

After the failure of the *Bernadou-Cole* operation to capture that port in a surprise attack, the 450-man Safi garrison prepared a warm reception for the Americans. But the USS *Cole* had gotten inside, and Company L of the Forty-seventh settled down in the dock area to prevent the French from destroying the port. One platoon moved forward to capture the Shell Oil Company tanks.

Offshore, the USS *New York* and USS *Philadelphia* engaged in a battle with the four 130-millimeter coastal guns. By 4:45 the coastal guns were out of operation. At 5 a.m. the Forty-seventh's reconnaissance platoon hit the beach, and so did the First Platoon of Company B of the Seventieth Tank Battalion. They came in on both sides of the grounded destroyer *Bernadou*. The infantrymen seized the telephone-telegraph exchange; then they knocked out a 25-millimeter antitank gun across the street from the post office. A platoon from Company B went up the hill and occupied a battery of big field guns that had been deserted by the French.

But on the high ground northeast of the harbor the foreign legion troops were much tougher, and the advance was hung up for an hour. Rangers, who had crossed the beach, scaled a 300-foot cliff. The First Battalion went up the hill.

The Second Battalion did not get ashore, 8 miles south of Safi, until 9:30. Then the Third Battalion and the Eighty-fourth Field Artillery Battalion came ashore near the center of the town.

The Second Battalion was under heavy attack and needed help. It got help from the Third Battalion, which used rifle grenades to knock out three Renault tanks. Company M brought up 81-millimeter mortars, which began firing steadily on the French barracks across the harbor from the post office.

At noon General Harmon began bringing the armor ashore; first the light tanks and then the medium tanks from the seatrain *Lakehurst*. Light tanks went down the road toward Marrakech to be sure the French did not bring up reinforcements from that garrison. The other armor prepared for the assault on Casablanca.

By four o'clock in the afternoon of that first day most of the opposition at Safi had been overcome. The Forty-seventh was holding a 10,000-yard beachhead. The last of the shore guns had been abandoned by the foreign legion. On the docks regiment established its command post in the Phosphate Building. Col. Edwin H. Randle was appointed military governor of the district. The Forty-seventh would hold Safi while the Second Armored Division drove on to Casablanca. So Safi had been taken. But Port Lyautey had not.

November 9: At 4:30 a.m. a French column with fourteen tanks was spotted on the move from Marrakech. Navy planes from the carrier *Santee* took off and attacked the leading elements. But the French armor eventually was knocked out by Colonel Semmes's tanks. Early that morning the tankers fought two tank battles and one battle against French infantry, stopping the enemy at a cost of four American tanks. The French made a new move, bringing up thirty-two tanks. Ten more American tanks from Company C of the Seventieth Tank Battalion came up and helped defeat the French again, this time driving them inland and causing them to abandon twenty-four of their tanks.

In the Kasba area attack and counterattack alternated all day long. The French brought up reinforcements against the First and Second battalions of the Sixtieth Infantry. In late afternoon of the second day the French still held the Kasba and the airport, where several artillery pieces were located.

The Sixtieth Field Artillery's Battery C was brought up to fight there. In its drive toward the airport, the Third Battalion of the Sixtieth RCT made the first American river crossing of the European war by rubber boat. But the second day ended with the French still in control of the Kasba and airport.

November 10: Night attack. The First Battalion started off in the rain, but it ran into heavy opposition and the three companies got separated in the woods. As day dawned the French launched a cavalry attack. But the troops did not fight; the French said they had word of an armistice (which did not exist). There was a lot of confusion in the Kasba area that day. Major McCarley, commander of the First Battalion, was captured with his battalion staff during the morning. Near dusk he escaped and moved back toward the U.S. lines. He ran and hid and ran some more, all night, arriving in the morning. His First Battalion companies moved into Port Lyautey that day and captured the town. American troops began moving toward the airport, taking many prisoners. By midnight it was nearly all over: the First Moroccan Regiment fought hard until the colonel suddenly gave up and announced surrender. The airport was then in the hands of the First Battalion, Sixtieth Infantry.

Only the Kasba remained, a powerful bastion in French hands. On the morning of November 10 the armor was well ashore, and two self-propelled 105-millimeter howitzers were brought up to help the men of the Second Battalion as they attacked the Kasba. Supported by navy planes and the artillery, the troops blew open the gates of the fortress and attacked inside. The French fought, but then, suddenly, the fortress was captured. The cost was high—215 casualties to the Second Battalion in that one morning.

The Third Battalion took heavy artillery fire on the night of November 9. That night its Company M came under both artillery and machine gun fire. At 2:30 on the morning of November 10 the battalion attacked the bridge at the entrance to Port Lyautey. This was very rough, and men fell, killed or wounded. The battalion was shaken up and scattered. It was raining. The men of Sergeant Thornton's Company M had no entrenching tools, so they had to dig foxholes with their helmets and knives.

Morning and daylight of November 11 found them huddling in the wet foxholes. Counts found that many of the battalion's weapons were missing.

But the objectives had been taken.

On November 11 the Third Battalion went on guard duty on the north side of the city, just over the river.

*   *   *

In the middle of French north Africa, the U.S. First Division, with Combat
Command B of the First Armored Division and the First Ranger Battalion,
had been attacking in the Oran area since before dawn.

Now it was almost the turn of Company F of the Eighteenth Infantry and
Lieutenant Downing's weapons platoon. It was about nine o'clock when Serial 135 was called, and Downing and his men backed out of the sally port
and down the iron ladder of the SS *Tegelberg* into the LCA assigned to them.
Automatically Downing moved forward to the bow and stood with his back to
the ramp. Just like Scotland. Pfc. Zaitz, the BAR man, came up into the
automatic weapons nest next to the lieutenant's place. The men came down,
one by one. Sergeant Merrill was the last man into the boat. The loading
officer waved, Downing waved back; then he gave the signal to the coxswain
to move the boat out. He peered over the ramp, waiting for that first shot.
None came.

Seventy-five yards offshore the coxswain cut the engine.

"Can't go in any further. Might run aground. You'll have to wade in."

The ramp went down. Lieutenant Downing stepped off into the water. It
was cold, and it reached his waist. He held up his rifle and plodded ashore.
The others splashed along after him. They reached the beach and a company runner came out to guide them. He took them across a railroad track.
Dogfaces were lying in the shelter of the embankment.

"Look out for snipers," said the runner. With that comforting word, he
left them.

They moved ashore, Downing's feet squishing in his wet boots. They hit
a field, the company assembly area at the foot of a hill. The town was off to
the right, about 400 yards. Downing told the light—machine gun squad to set
up in an irrigation ditch, pointing toward the town. Any attack would come
from there. He deployed his riflemen facing the town, and told them to take
it easy. He sat down under a tree next to Sergeant Merrill and took from his
pocket the ham sandwich he had made so long ago in the *Tegelberg* wardroom.

As he ate, he watched. Soldiers were coming in. One rifleman was prod-
ding a French native soldier wearing a tunic, khaki turban, and baggy trousers and boots. They moved on through toward the beach.

Slowly, the boats brought in the whole weapons platoon. A runner came
from Captain Penick. Downing went forward and got orders for the men to

stack packs in a company pile and then prepare to move out. The packs
would be brought up later by service troops. He dropped off his musette
bag, and then led the platoon along a dusty road up the hill—single file on
each side of the road.

Somebody up front stepped up the pace. The men of the weapons platoon began to yell. They were loaded down with mortars and machine guns,
panniers of mortar ammunition and boxes of machine gun ammunition belts,
plus their personal weapons and equipment. The pace was too fast—it would
have been too fast for a training march, and was certainly too fast for men
who had been cooped up aboard ship for days.

On top of the hill Downing saw that the platoon was strung out. The ground
leveled off to dry plowed fields, punctuated only by a tree here and there. In
the distance was a line of telephone poles that meant a major highway. Company headquarters was nowhere to be seen.

Downing tried to keep up. His platoon began to string out. The men passed
around machine gun ammunition, cartridge belts, packs, mortar ammunition,
gas masks, gas capes, and other items of equipment. Strained by the pace, the
men of the Third Battalion up ahead were dumping their equipment.

"The molten sun was still glaring down. My pants and shoes had dried
but my feet were getting sore from the wet socks. Sweat streamed down my
face from the hot and heavy helmet. It trickled down my armpits and the
small of my back. The gas mask was heavy and awkward under my left arm.
I wanted to throw it away, but abandoning equipment was a court-martial
offense. The heavy cartridge belt and the two bandoliers I had slung on my
chest pulled on my shoulders. The rifle got heavier with every step."

They passed through a small town—white houses, tan houses, and red
tile roofs faced the dusty road on both sides. The barefoot Arabs wore long
brown burnooses and dirty white turbans or red fezzes. There was silence as
the troops passed the adults, but when they passed the children, small Arab
boys ran alongside yelling. At first the dogfaces could not understand—then
they did understand—the kids were screaming for candy.

So this was war?

They passed through the town. Lieutenant Downing decided to stop to
try to form up his platoon. He picked a spot on the side of the road where
there were no other soldiers, and motioned the handful of men with him to
fall out. They sat in the ditch and smoked. Every time a weapons platoon
man came along, Lieutenant Downing called him over to join them.

After an hour he had about three-quarters of his platoon, all the mortars,
but only one machine gun. He started the troops out again, a file on each

side of the road. Now, from up front, came the sound of sporadic rifle fire, emphasized by the crump of a mortar or an artillery round.

A civilian truck came toward them from up front. It stopped. Captain Green, the regimental communications officer, called out to Downing to hurry forward. Every man was needed.

An amphibious jeep came down the road, two officers in the rear seat and two enlisted men on the rear platform, rifles ready, looking for snipers. It was Gen. Clift Andrus, chief of division artillery.

"Get your men forward. The French are getting ready to attack on this road."

Lieutenant Downing saluted and started forward again. A few yards down the road he met Lieutenant Spinney, the F Company executive officer. He was trying to collect the company. Captain Penick had gone forward and disappeared. An attack was coming.

Downing started forward again, leaving his men with Spinney, but taking Private Massa, a runner.

He passed more abandoned equipment—always a bad sign. A single shoe. First aid kits, opened. Empty cartridge cases, helmets, packs, gas masks, green gas capes. Somebody had been having a hard time here. A few men were sitting in the ditch, smoking, saying nothing. They looked all in.

He came upon a dead American soldier. He was lying on his back, a hole through his head, with hands raised toward his head. There was an expression of tension engraved on the dirty face. A staff sergeant. A dead dogface.

Lieutenant Downing thought he was going to be sick. So the maneuvers were over. This was war. There would be no recall bugles in the evening. It was going to go on for a long time, and the only way out was to be carried out on a stretcher, or to lie in a ditch like this sergeant.

He moved on to a break in the hedge. A soldier on the other side shouted, "Don't cross there. Sniper."

A soldier was crawling along the ditch on the other side of the road. When he was opposite the opening, he poked his head and rifle over the edge of the ditch and fired a full clip.

What to do? You had to make your own decisions.

Downing stood up. He gathered his muscles and sprang across the opening. Nothing happened. Massa came after him. Nothing. He moved up the ditch. Now the firing up ahead was more evident. But no signs of a command post. He sat down. He was getting too far away from the company, and he wasn't learning anything. It was growing late. An old-fashioned French ambulance came up the road from where he had been; the driver saw the sergeant lying dead, and he stopped. A man and a girl got out and put the body onto a stretcher, put it inside the ambulance, turned, and drove back down the road. Major Sternberg, the regimental intelligence officer, came by. He waved at Downing.

Downing went forward. He found Captain Penick sitting in a ditch, looking at a map. The captain looked up.

"Where's the company?"

"Back down the road."

"We've got to get it up here right away. We're going to make an attack at four o'clock."

Downing sent Private Massa back to bring up the company. Captain Penick turned back to his map. Downing lit a cigarette. He saw Sergeant Richter, the mess sergeant. He wasn't carrying that big American flag. Downing wondered what he had done with it.

Rifle bullets spattered overhead. Downing crouched down into the ditch.

Lieutenant Spinney and Sergeant Merrill came up the ditch followed by the rifle platoon leaders. They gathered around Captain Penick. He pointed at his map. Here was their road. Over here was the town of St. Cloud. The First Battalion had run into trouble there this morning. It lost three company commanders and was completely disorganized. That accounted for the abandoned equipment on the road, but not for the single shoe.

"Okay, here's what we're gonna do. . . ."

They were going to move out across the field to the left of the road, bear right, and head toward the town. Very simple. If you didn't get killed.

As the riflemen of F Company came up, the platoon leaders moved them out across the road. The weapons platoon came up. Lieutenant Downing moved the platoon up behind the rifle platoons, in a line of squad columns. Their field was a vineyard, geometric rows of low bushes, about a foot and a half high. Not even any grapes. It was the wrong time of year.

The sun was setting and dusk was coming fast. Too soon it would be dark. What was the recognition signal? They had been given all that on ship. What was it?

Oh, yes. The challenge: "Hi yo, Silver."

The response: "Awayyyyyy."

They crossed the vineyard. Nothing happened. They moved on, into a plowed field this time. Halfway across, Downing heard a zip. Then zip-zip. Rifle bullets. The man in front of him hit the dirt. So did Downing. A bullet smacked into the ground 2 yards to his right. He dug his nose into the dirt, and felt as if his back were a mile high.

A rifleman got up and ran toward a low, white stone wall up front. There were trees on the other side. Another did the same. Downing got up and ran. He could hear the bullets zip-zip-zip. Crrump. A mortar shell out in the field. Twaing...the mortar fragments sang over their heads. He made the wall and dropped behind a tree. A black horse wearing a French army saddle, bridle dragging, walked up, stopped, and grazed on the grass 5 yards away. The horse saw Downing, lifted his head, and whinnied.

On the left was the railroad embankment. Downing saw riflemen heading that way. He looked back. He couldn't see his platoon, but he waved back at the men anyhow and dashed forward to the embankment. He lay in the shadow of the rail line and panted. Two riflemen sat in the culvert that cut through the embankment.

"That town is full of troops. You better watch out. Snipers'll get you. Our company is all shot up. Lost the captain."

"What outfit?"

"First Battalion, Company A."

Lieutenant Downing jumped up, leaped over the embankment, and fell flat on his face. He got up, saw others, and moved toward the town. It was growing dark. The firing would die down, and then a machine gun would pick up ratatatatatatatatat. Rifles would start, popopopopopopop...pop. A grenade would blow, broomh. A mortar shell would hit. Carump. Then it would all stop again. He heard the clock in a steeple chime six times. Six o'clock.

He bumped up against the man in front of him, Sergeant Vaughan of his company. The weapons platoon was right behind, Vaughan said. The column had stopped. Riflemen came up, looking the troops over, trying to find their platoons. They passed on. Downing and Vaughan sat. The lieutenant realized he was hungry and thirsty. He reached into his hip pocket and found two D-ration chocolate bars. He took one out, broke off two squares, and ate them; he drank a little water and thought about the officers' club at Fort Benning. Pinks and greens, dress uniforms in the officers' club... And pretty girls.

Suddenly it was pitch dark. No moon.

Lt. Labombarde from the battalion came down the line.

"We're going to move out. No smoking, no talking. Watch out for infiltrators. Pass it on."

The column began to move. The embankment ended and the railroad line passed through a small cut. It started to rain. The troops passed three covered bodies. What nationality? The blankets bore no flags. They came to the First Battalion again. The column stopped. Along came a French officer, long overcoat flapping around his legs, odd-shaped steel helmet on his head. Behind him were two Zouaves in turbans. Behind them was a dogface with his rifle at their backs. They passed down the line to the rear.

The soldiers saw two men crossing the field ahead, from the town.

"Hi yo, Silver!" one soldier called out.

No response.

Downing aimed his rifle at the belly of the leading figure, slipped off the safety, and tracked.

"Hi yo, Silver!"

The two figures stopped.

"Awayyy . . ."

Downing lowered his rifle and slipped on the safety.

Some dogface had just barely saved his own life.

The company moved on to a lone house surrounded by trees. They would spend the night there, said the captain. One officer would be on watch at all times.

Lieutenant Spinney took first watch. Downing lay down with his helmet under his head, clutching his rifle. The town clock chimed every quarter-hour. A dog barked. The clock chimed. Another dog barked. A rifle popped. A dog barked. And then Spinney was shaking him, and it was his turn to stay awake. He got up and went out to inspect the outposts. The clock chimed. It was cold and the rain continued. The clock chimed. Then it was time to wake up Lieutenant Hughes. His turn. Downing lay down on his belly, buttoned up his field jacket, and tilted the helmet over his head. The clock chimed, but only once. Then a rooster crowed.

Downing was just waking up, feeling the stubble on his face, eating a piece of chocolate with dirty hands, when Captain Penick came up.

"Get your platoon together. We're moving out right away."

So they attacked. And they learned to tell that when the rifle bullets were zipping they were on your flank, and when they were cracking they were overhead.

They attacked through St. Cloud.

They came to a factory, Downing leading his mortar squad, setting up, firing, and moving on. He heard bullets cracking and hit the dirt. A bullet cut off a plant a few inches above his head. Another shot was just as close.

They fought their way through most of the town and got all mixed up with Company G. On the afternoon of the second day they still had not taken the whole town. They were very tired. First Sergeant Merrill had been shot in the head—the bullet went clear through, in behind his ear and out the other

side, without hitting any vital parts. Unbelievable! Merrill walked to the ambulance that was to take him to the hospital. Captain Penick was missing.
They moved on. They passed a farm and saw soldiers sitting in the kitchen
drinking wine. They crossed a valley, and battalion told them that a large
force of French from Sidi-bel-Abbès was moving down to attack them at daylight of the third day. Downing asked somebody what day it was. Somebody
said it was November 9. The men were almost exhausted. Sometimes they
balked. Downing had to talk them up:

"I went over to one of the squad leaders and squatted down beside him.
I talked to him, knowing that all the others around would be listening. I
pointed out the line of trees in the distance. I told him that we were going to
halt there and dig in, in preparation for the attack in the morning. I told
everyone to rest where he was until he felt able to move and then head for
the trees, call my name, and I'd answer him and tell him where to set up. . . .

"I arose and started out toward the trees. I heard the men behind me
getting up. 'If we made it this far,' one said, 'I guess we can make it to the
trees.'

"I felt better."

At the end of the third day Downing realized he had lost his gas mask,
his gas cape, and, somehow, the field glasses out of his field-glass case. He
couldn't remember losing any of them.

They attacked and attacked again. Finally they came within sight of the
spires that marked Oran. They passed through a dozen vineyards, and stopped
where they could see the high green slope of the mountain ridge of Djebel
Khar.

A runner came up shuffling in the dirt.

"All platoon leaders report to the CP."

Downing got up wearily, slung his rifle, and followed. Without interest
he saw that Captain Penick was back. He and eight men had been cut off at
St. Cloud, but they'd gotten away, found a rear command post, had a good
night's sleep and a hot meal, and then had come up. They were feeling great.
Great! The company had been fighting in the rain and dirt and dust all the
way, and the last meal had been a handful of cans of C ration issued by the
battalion supply officer the day before, one meal to each three men. Cold
stew and biscuits.

Now the First Division was going to attack Oran.

More C rations—if the men were lucky. Certainly no sleep.

But it never happened. For the brass made a deal with the French, and the word came down that an armistice had been signed.

It was November 10. Algiers had fallen to the Thirty-ninth Regimental Combat Team. The flanks of Casablanca had been taken by the Forty-seventh and Sixtieth regimental combat teams and the Second Armored Division, and General Patton had been prepared to launch a drive against that city when the armistice came. Much of French north Africa was in Allied hands. The American war against the Germans could now begin.

11

AGAINST THE GERMANS

November 11, 1942: It seemed fitting that this was Armistice Day in north Africa, reminiscent of a day twenty-four years earlier when the Germans had surrendered to the western Allies. But on this Armistice Day the Germans were moving fast to take possession of Tunisia, before the French could surrender that part of north Africa to the Allies. So all this armistice meant to the American dogfaces at war was that they were not going to have to fight the French any more, at least not in Morocco and Algeria.

In the next few hours the American High Command completed the negotiations with Admiral Jean Darlan, whom *they* designated the "senior French official in North Africa," while the Germans rushed to strengthen their position in Tunisia. As far as the GIs were concerned, this was all beyond them.

After the unsatisfactory airdrop aimed at Tafaraoui, Lieutenant Colonel Raff of the Second Battalion of the 503d Parachute Infantry had gone to Maison Blanche airfield to await orders. Most of the orders were administrative. At about this time he learned that the composition of the 503d Parachute Infantry had been changed, and his unit was now the Second Battalion of the 509th Parachute Infantry. The rest of the 503d was on its way to the Pacific.

Just about the time of the armistice, the Second Corps called Raff to warn him that he was about to go into action again. Intelligence had learned that the French had important stores of gasoline at an airport near Tebessa on the Tunisian frontier. Raff and his men had best get ready to capture the field and deny the gasoline to the Germans, who were assembling all the supplies they could in Tunisia.

On November 11 Sergeant Thornton's Third Battalion of the U.S. Sixtieth Infantry Regiment was on guard at Port Lyautey. The battalion would pull guard duty for most of the next week.

On November 12 only 150 paratroopers could be found at Maison Blanche. Some, like Sgt. Charles Doyle, had walked to Tarafaoui. Some had come in on those crash-landing transports. The others were scattered all over the lot, the result largely of the bad navigation of the troop carriers. Raff was still assembling equipment, which had ended up in a dozen different localities. By November 13 about 150 more of Raff's troopers had shown up. With the help of Brigadier Flavell of the British paratroop division they put together enough equipment to make an airdrop.

By that time intelligence had come up with some more facts; the drop was to be made against the airfield at Youks les Bains. At eight o'clock on the morning of November 15, thirty-three C-47s took off from Maison Blanche. The brass had learned something: this time the transports had an escort of six fighters to fend off the French air force.

The Youks les Bains mission was a lot different from the record long-distance flight made by the troop carrier planes from England to Tarafaoui.

Two and a half hours out the aircraft reached their objective. There on the field below was another armored column. This time, however, it was French. The enemy would do some shooting. The sergeants opened the rear doors of the C-47s, and the men hooked up and jumped as the planes came over the field.

As they came down, they expected to be shot at. But no! The French were ducking into trenches.

Afraid?

Yes. The French were afraid of being hit on the head by the American equipment. Much of it was coming down in wicker baskets lent by the British, but it still had a terrific bounce.

There was no fighting because the commander of the Third Zouaves, who were occupying that field, was an adherent of Admiral Darlan and accepted the need to cooperate with the Americans. So a truce was negotiated right there on the field between Lieutenant Colonel Raff and the French. Raff could report back to Algiers that Youks les Bains was now in friendly hands— Americans allied with the French Zouaves. The 509th had suffered fifteen casualties, all of whom were injured in the actual jump, not in battle.

The most important result of the Youks les Bains jump and successful mission was an improvement in Eisenhower's opinion of the airborne, even though the results had not been victory in battle. A few days later General Eisenhower gave Lieutenant Colonel Raff a field promotion to full colonel, which was a mixed blessing, for Raff was still commander of a battalion, and the promotion was resented within the airborne establishment.

While the Second Battalion of the 509th Parachute Infantry was in action in those early days of the North African campaign, the vast majority of American units were sitting on their heels.

The Sixteenth Infantry moved into quarters with the French Zouaves in Oran. The fleshpots. Pretty lucky.

The men of the Eighteenth Infantry also marched into Oran to be greeted by thousands of cheering civilians, and kids running along the sides of the formation shouting "Hi yo, Silver." Lieutenant Downing wondered how they had ever picked that up... so quickly!

An old lady came up with a basket of oranges and passed them out. Another woman handed around opened bottles of wine. Two pretty dark-haired girls came up to Lieutenant Downing with a basket of vegetables, and these Spanish-speaking Berbers tested his high school Spanish with much laughter and many provocative looks. Sergeant Merrill, who had talked his way out of the hospital, showed up with his head bandaged and his uniform jacket covered with his own dried blood just as the men of Company F found their quarters in a large, roofed marketplace with iron gates around it. The worst thing that had happened to Merrill apparently was that the shot that went through his head had broken his false teeth.

A woman and her black-eyed daughter came to the marketplace and asked to come in. They were carrying a huge pot of coffee and some cakes. They came in, squatted down, and poured out the coffee for the men, and the girl produced a bottle of pinkish liquid. Lieutenant Downing had to sample it to see if it was okay for the men to drink. He sampled it three times and found that it improved his outlook immeasurably.

Ah, the fleshpots. The men could hardly wait to enjoy the pleasures of

Oran. Tomorrow. Tomorrow they would shave and bathe and clean up and go on the town. This night they would sleep. And they did.

The next morning, First Sergeant Merrill was his old self, it seemed, yelling for a reveille report. The men of Company F were preparing to clean up and go out when a platoon leader's meeting was called. They were told that they were going to march to southern Algeria to go on outpost duty.

Oh, those friendly, olive-skinned, black-eyed girls and all that wine! The men went back to their platoon and passed the bad news. They policed their platoon areas of the marketplace; the company troops fell in, dressed and covered, and counted off. Captain Penick shouted the commands, and they marched out of Oran in a column of twos. They moved out toward Les Trembles.

F Company marched just outside town and then was ordered to stop. The Second Battalion was waiting for orders from regiment. The company command post was in an alley between two buildings, a point, they soon discovered, where the local Arab workmen came to relieve themselves. The flies knew it, and they buzzed around all afternoon. The stench was terrible. It was 4 p.m. before the battalion moved out, to march on until dark. The company jeeps came up with some blanket rolls (enlisted men) and bedding rolls (officers). Lieutenant Downing looked for his. It wasn't there, but the rolls of some of the casualties (nine killed, eleven wounded) were. He broke open one of those and wrapped up in blankets. He had no sooner fallen asleep than a runner came up to tell him he was wanted at the battalion command post. He and Lieutenant Hobratschk of H Company had been picked to take out patrols. Downing was to take two jeeps and reconnoiter the road to Les Trembles, their objective.

They moved out, through one town where an old lady told them there were no troops. They drove on.

"There was no traffic on the road and no sign of human activity anywhere. Suddenly out of the darkness we came upon a wrecked truck lying on the side of the road. I dismounted with the intelligence man and we looked it over carefully. It had been a French army truck, loaded with mortar ammunition and probably had been strafed by a plane. It was burned to a skeleton. Probing around the wreckage I turned up a few charred letters in French, a snapshot of two French soldiers, and the torn collar of a blouse. The collar tab was that of the Ninth Chausseurs d'Afrique, a French armored regiment. I cut off the tab with my trench knife to bring back for intelligence purposes. There was nothing left of the driver and his assistant except some red scraps, a few pieces of their blouses, and one shoe with the foot still in it. . . .

"Continuing on a short distance farther, we found an American half-track mounting a 75-millimeter gun off to the right of the road. It had been hit through the rear with an artillery shell and was completely burned out. The explosion had certainly given them a quick death."

They rode on, more cautiously. They came to a French tank, its muzzle pointing down the road. Downing got down and looked it over. The gun was loaded but the breech block was open. There did not seem to be anything wrong with it. Afraid of booby traps, he did not handle anything. They went on.

More disabled tanks, so many that Downing quit noting their locations on the map. Finally they came to a manned tank. The troops were two soldiers of the Second Regiment of Chausseurs d'Afrique. They were friendly and exchanged souvenirs with the Americans. Downing gave the sergeant a bar of chocolate. The sergeant gave him his regimental insignia.

They came to Les Trembles. More French troops, but no trouble. They turned back. On the return trip they ran out of gas. Downing left the jeeps and crews, took two men, and started the hike back to the battalion for help. But on the way he felt exhausted and stopped the others; they lay down and fell fast asleep. Downing awoke with a start to the sound of roosters crowing. It was broad daylight. They found a railroad station, traded cigarettes for a gallon of gasoline, found the jeeps, got back to the battalion bivouac, and found that the battalion had moved out. Major Chase had decided that since Lieutenant Downing and Lieutenant Hobratschk had not come back, they were dead. Downing met Sergeant Merrill. He was going back to hospital on orders from the major, who was afraid his wound would get infected.

They shook hands.

"Goodbye," said Merrill. "I'm afraid my field-soldiering days are over."

Downing left his patrol at the bivouac area with the service troops, and headed up the line. He caught a ride with a passing jeep and rejoined the column. The lieutenant told Major Powers about the abandoned tanks and all the rest, and the major radioed the information to regiment.

Finally they arrived at Les Trembles. The next day they set up company housekeeping on a level field of a farm behind the town. That afternoon trucks came up bringing the bedding and baggage from the ship. The battalion's jeeps had picked up the gear left on the beach so long ago. All of it had been looted by American troops. Downing's musette bag had been robbed of cigarettes, rations, shaving articles, and even his clean underwear. It was almost certainly some American service of supply troops, rear-echelon heroes, who had been the thieves.

A few of the men of Company F had a word for that: "Goddamn."

*

In the Ninth Division the Forty-seventh Regimental Combat Team stayed on in Safi. The MPs arrived and the "chicken shit" began.

Rules of conduct:

Soldiers will not enter, smoke, sit, loiter or stop in front of mosques; make noise or stare while Moslems are praying; drink liquor in front of Moslems; make fun of the natives; show disrespect to Moroccans; or wear the uniform improperly.

The Thirty-ninth marched to Algiers and set up its command post there. The men would have several months of the fleshpots, interspersed with missions to protect lines of communication.

On November 17 Sergeant Thornton's company marched 7 miles south of the city of Port Lyautey to the Mamora Cork Forest. Thornton was not sure he could make it: his feet had gotten wet in the landings and had not been dry since. It was a relief to go into a sort of garrison life in the forest. That's how it was for the next ten days. On November 28 the troops marched into Port Lyautey for a victory parade, and then back to camp. Training began: the firing of weapons and a 10-mile compass march on the last night of the month.

The Sixtieth had set up in the Mamora Cork Forest, along with the battle command of the Second Armored Division, to guard the troublesome Spanish Moroccan frontier. The Spanish were not friendly, and no one was quite sure the Americans would not be fighting them soon. They kept threatening to move in and extend the borders of Spanish Morocco past the place at which the Americans were encamped. General Patton gave a little show of American tank firepower to the Spanish commander, who had no tanks. Thereupon the border quieted down, and Spanish mischief was reduced to allowing Axis agents free passage through the Spanish territory.

General Harmon established a marketplace where soldiers and civilians could meet. "Souk el Harmon" it was called. At night the soldiers cooked their goodies over stoves made from No. 10 cans filled with sand and soaked with GI gasoline. They were using about 500 gallons a week in this fashion, and General Patton's inspector general complained. But Patton was wiser; he said to hell with it. It was a great morale builder, and the great "chicken shit machine" turned its head the other way. The GIs continued to burn up gasoline valued FOB north Africa at $8 a gallon.

Capt. Tom Wishard discovered that he had a great talent: the ability to distill wine and make Kickapoo Joy Juice (from the comic strip "L'il Abner"). It had the kick of a Berber donkey, but it could be tamed with canned grapefruit juice. All went well until the "revenooers" found the still.

With the establishment of higher and higher headquarters the "chicken shit" proliferated. Sgt. Frederick Morse went on leave to Algiers. He came back to camp and was stopped at the main gate by the MPs.

"Ya gotta take a pro," said the MP.

"Christ. I haven't done anything. The undipped wick."

"T.S. buddy. Orders from First Corps." (First Armored Corps, a brand new headquarters, undoubtedly manned by officers who had arrived *after* the invasion, as any GI would swear.)

"But I tell you, I'm clean as a whistle. No action."

"Ya want the red stamp?"

"I don't give a damn."

"No red stamp, you're AWOL."

"Shit."

But he submitted. There was no other way. Without the red stamp he would be declared AWOL.

All sorts of units now began to arrive from America to play their part in the expanding war. The infantry regiment elements of the Ninth Division had all come to fight in the invasion, but the Ninth Division headquarters had remained in America. Now it would come to establish itself in Casablanca. All this was part of a major buildup that would bring many thousands of troops to Africa in a hurry.

Such, for example, were the Twentieth Engineers, who had been brought back up from Camp Pickett to Camp Kilmer and shipped out to Africa on November 1. The First Battalion was aboard the SS *Cristobal*, a banana boat converted to a troop carrier.

Lieutenant Miller and two other junior officers were very lucky; they were assigned a small stateroom that opened out onto the upper deck of the ship. They ate on linen tablecloths—the food was excellent—and in a way it was like a free cruise across the Atlantic. But for the enlisted men of the battalion, of course, it was dreadful. They lived where the bananas had once lain. They were fed twice a day, and spent much of the time during the daylight hours waiting in line, for chow:

"Many a man sweated out several hours in the chow line just to lose his grip on his stomach when his nose caught the first blast from that mess hall."

The *Cristobal* was part of the first big convoy for the buildup at Casablanca. It was in mid-Atlantic when the news came of the landings.

Colonel Caffey had his tommy guns ready. He was sure that the Twentieth Engineers were probably going immediately into combat. Or maybe they were going to land and wait a few days before going into combat. Whatever it was he was discussing at whatever moment, he was damned sure of it. So the men practiced rolling full field packs every morning. Then they rolled combat packs in the afternoon. And then they rolled full field packs again every night.

The *Cristobal* arrived at Casablanca dock on the afternoon of November 19. Out came the men of the First Battalion of the Twentieth Engineers, in full uniform, full field pack, with gas masks, arms, and enormous barracks bags. They dumped the barracks bags, and under the eyes of the colonel the battalion formed up, the band played, and triumphantly the troops marched through the streets of an unwary and astonished Casablanca. The war could go on. The Twentieth Engineers had arrived.

12

DUBIOUS
BATTLE

Colonel Caffey was very much disappointed to learn that the Twentieth Engineers were not going to be hurled into combat immediately to save the day for the invasion. No, they marched to a bivouac area in Casablanca and a day or so later moved to another, the Hippodrome, where they were to stay for a while. For they had a job.

The ships that had tied up at the Phosphate Dock of Casablanca had dumped out their cargoes and then turned around and gone away to make room for more ships. The docks were jammed with a great mélange of material, most of it highly explosive or inflammable: gasoline, bombs, ammunition, rations, and clothing. One saboteur could send the whole Casablanca waterfront up in a roaring fire. So the Twentieth Engineers got the job of cleaning up, loading supplies into the miniature French railroad boxcars, and leveling the area so that trucks could run right up to the ships. They learned in short order how to be port engineers. A new convoy came in, loaded with materials. The port engineers cleared it up in a hurry. Capt. Jonathan E. Sonnefield was the commander of the First Battalion. Soon he and Lieutenant Miller and the other officers and men were experts, and one of the things they were expert in was finding the delicacies deep in the holds of the ships and short-circuiting a certain amount for the men of the Twentieth Engineers. *Vive la rear echelon!*

*

In Algiers, where General Eisenhower had established his headquarters on November 24, the generals were pinning medals on each other. Why not? This was their game, and the medals were their reward for all those years between wars in the civilian wilderness. They had their hardships: the St. Georges Hotel, headquarters for Ike Eisenhower, didn't even have central heating!

Neither did Corporal Moglia's quarters in the Casa Neuf in Oran, where the Sixteenth Infantry was living companionably with the French Zouaves.

Corporal Moglia's platoon was responsible for patrolling and manning roadblocks on the outskirts of Oran. Life settled down to a twenty-four hours on, twenty-four hours off proposition. One night, while on duty, Corporal Moglia heard vehicles approaching his roadblock. He ordered the lead vehicle to halt, and all concerned to dismount.

The riders dismounted and they turned out to be French foreign legionnaires, all armed to the teeth: hand grenades, pistols, rifles, swords, bayonets—all dangling from them like ornaments on a Christmas tree. Some of them spoke English. They were overjoyed at finding the Americans. They came, said the spokesman, from Sidi-bel-Abbès. They had had a little problem there: their colonel wanted to fight the Americans but the troops did not. So the troops disposed of the colonel, and here they were. They insisted on presenting Corporal Moglia, the senior officer present, with the late colonel's uniform and sidearms.

"Where do we go to join the American army?" they asked.

Corporal Moglia explained that recruiting wasn't done at the roadblock; but he told the legionnaires that when they got to Oran, all would be fixed up. So the legionnaires gave the Americans all their guns, swords, bayonets, grenades, and rifles, and a flask of cognac, and after a series of warm embraces and hearty handshakes, they got in their trucks and zoomed off for Oran.

The Sixteenth Infantry also did some patrolling. The Germans were spending most of their effort strengthening their positions and their reserves in Tunisia for the coming battles. But they were moving around, too. They used both glider troops and paratroops, it was said. One day there was a report from the Second Corps that the Germans had air-dropped near Tebessa. Elements of the Sixteenth Infantry were sent out to find them, engage them, and destroy them. Company E of the Second Battalion was involved.

The battalion moved up toward the area where the Germans were reported to be. That night, said the battalion commander, there would be no gunfire. It was to be a surprise attack, and the troops would go in with bayonets and trench knives.

"Don't, repeat, don't fire your weapons," said the battalion CO. "Any firing will be construed as enemy action, and you're likely to get a bayonet in the belly."

Pleasant thought. But not horrifying, because the men of the Sixteenth had been trained thoroughly in bayonet work and the use of the trench knife with its brass knuckle-duster.

As they moved along in the darkness, all Corporal Moglia could hear was the squeaking of the sand under his own boots. Suddenly, directly in his path loomed a crouched figure with arms spread out, inviting him to hand-to-hand combat. All his bayonet training was flashing through his head: long thrust—short thrust—parry left—parry right—jab—jab—recover—on guard—

What to do?

"I crouched and charged with a long thrust, and then—an awful pain in the pit of my belly, and I had lost my rifle. The dirty bastard had disarmed me! He had kicked me over on my back.

"I whipped out my trench knife and drew my legs back with bent knees. 'Okay, you dirty S.O.B. You haven't finished me off yet. How would you like two size nine-and-a-half army boots in your crotch?'

"The bastard didn't move. Why not? I sprang to my feet and began to circle my adversary, like a boxer. Still he refused to react. As I closed in to kill or be killed I discovered why: my enemy was a tree!"

Moglia swept up his rifle and hurried after the rest of the platoon. Nobody had seen. And, until now, nobody ever heard the tale!

That night one German parachute unit was discovered—not by Corporal Moglia—and captured.

Captain Penick, the men of Company F of the Eighteenth Infantry soon discovered, was a teetotaler. Worse, he seemed to be an evangelistic prohibitionist. No booze for the company. No wine. Think of that! In the heart of north Africa, tripping over grapevines at every step, practically every civilian holding out bottles of wine as the men passed, and the captain says, "No booze, no wine!"

When a medic walked past him with a bottle of wine in his hand, the captain stopped him.

"Soldier, what have you got there?"

The medic paused. What the hell did the captain think it was, a urine specimen?

"A bottle of wine, sir."

"Get your entrenching tool."

The soldier went off and got his entrenching tool.

"Now dig a hole."

The medic dug his hole.

"Now empty that bottle into it."

The medic emptied the bottle, looking mournfully into the hole. But he looked no sadder than did Lieutenant Downing and everyone else who watched the disgusting performance.

Of course, the prohibition campaign did not work. Obviously, Captain Penick was no student of the Napoleonic wars or any others; he hadn't learned what soldiers were like. The dogfaces had their ways.

But what Penick's campaign did do was make it impossible for Lieutenant Downing and the other company officers to take a drink openly. The GIs didn't offer them anything, either, because the officers were the enemy; they were of the law-enforcement class.

Less than a week after the invasion, then, the men of Company F were settled down in Les Trembles—not happy, but alive and bitching.

"C rations again," they complained when the trucks came by and dropped off a few cases of cans.

"I heard that those guys on the beach are getting a new-type ration—canned steaks, cheese, pudding, chocolate."

"Where'd you hear that?"

"I dunno. A guy in D Company...."

"Goddamn, those rear-echelon guys...."

A couple of days after they settled down, Sergeant Merrill appeared, looking much, much better. He had gotten a new uniform, or at least a different one, without any dried blood all over the shoulder, and he had had a bath. The men of the company were getting baths, too, helmet baths. But with their baggage having come up, they had clean clothes and they felt a million times better. They also began to get some sleep. If only the army would get them something decent to eat...

The C rations kept coming.

Merrill was having trouble eating because of his busted choppers, but he was afraid to tell it even to the chaplain because he knew Major Powers was already thinking about shipping him back to the rear, permanently. One day

Merrill and Lieutenant Downing went into town to get Sergeant Merrill something decent that he could eat. He particularly wanted some soft bread, because he couldn't gum the C-ration biscuit. They stopped at a café and got their canteens filled up with wine at 5 francs a canteen. They paid with "yellow seal" dollars—just like regular U.S. dollars except that the seal of the United States was yellow instead of blue. Seventy-five francs to the dollar. What Captain Penick couldn't see wouldn't hurt him.

There were patrols. Lieutenant Downing drew more than his share of them because he spoke Spanish, as did some Berbers. Lieutenant Labombarde drew more than his share because he spoke French. The patrols were uneventful, but they usually lasted all night.

It was so dull that rumors started:

The Eighteenth was going back to the states to train other units in amphibious landings.

The division was going to be broken up and made into cadres for new divisions.

Selected personnel would be sent back to New York to set up a recruiting station in Central Park. That was the most imaginative of all.

The rumors spread through all the other regiments. Finally General Allen put out a memo announcing that the operation just past was but the first of a long series of combat operations for the division: "Nothing must delay or stop the First Division."

That settled that.

Finally the troops began to get some new rations. British. The "composite ration pack" arrived in long wooden boxes, each a complete ration for fourteen men for one day. So they began to dine on beef and kidney stew, steak and kidney pudding, meat and vegetables (more popularly known as "M and V"), sardines, bangers (sausages made of cereal, which the GIs said was sawdust), bacon, oxtail stew, powdered tea, treacle (molasses pudding), plum duff, rice pudding, and seven British cigarettes per man per day. Except for the tea and cigarettes, it all went down very nicely.

They began to encounter more "chicken shit." They set up a defense perimeter, more for something to do than as anything useful. They practiced digging foxholes. Lieutenant Downing's weapons platoon had lost a baseplate for one mortar, and he took a jeep patrol back over their route to try to find it. They found that every bit of equipment dumped by the Americans had been salvaged by the Arabs. No baseplate. No nothing.

Why not use this chance to get a little wine when the captain isn't looking?

They stopped the jeep at a likely looking farmhouse and asked about buying some wine. As if by magic an elderly lieutenant colonel with MP insignia appeared in the farmyard. He had a pistol at his waist, and a soldier with a bayoneted rifle held at high port covered him.

"What are you doing here?"

Lieutenant Downing turned the bar on his collar so the colonel would see it.

"Looking for lost equipment."

"You won't find it here. You'd better get back to your unit."

"Yessir."

They went, musing on the unfairness of a war that let the rear areas fill up with soldiers unfit for combat, who hoarded all the good stuff for themselves and made damned sure the unwashed line soldiers didn't interfere with the goodies. *Screw la rear echelon!*

The battalion CO, Major Powers, and his executive officer, Major Chase, were transferred out of the Eighteenth Infantry, back to Oran on special duty. Major Sternberg and Captain Peckham would take over the battalion, coming down from regimental headquarters. That was the way the professionals took care of their own. Sternberg and Peckham were being given a chance to earn promotion. But as for the battalion's civilian soldier officers—no changes, no promotions.

The war had a garrison feel about it. There were leaves in Sidi-bel-Abbès. Then the regiment moved, without notice of course, to the village of St. Denis du Sig. Training. Replacements. The replacements were mostly former coastal artillerymen, and they came in with Springfield 1903 rifles. They were given M-1s, and the men of the battalion set about teaching the new soldiers the art of war.

The town of Mascara was assigned as the recreational center for the Second Battalion. Lieutenant Downing was assigned as battalion provost marshal to work the Saturday night shift in the town. The principal form of entertainment was the brothel. Higher authority had decreed that only European brothels were acceptable for Americans. So, with the Arab establishments off limits, the single European brothel was it. The house was in a courtyard, with the girls' rooms off a balcony on the second floor. The girls hung over the balcony, blondes and brunettes, and looked over the MPs without much interest, not even opening their kimonos. They knew the cops when they saw them. Downing made arrangements to set up the prophylactic station in a small room near the entrance. A detail of medics would operate it and see that everyone who indulged took his pro.

That night the house did a land-office business. Even the madame had to help out a bit. The price was 35 cents American. It was done with soldierly precision: as soon as one soldier came down from the balcony, he was grabbed by a medic and taken into the pro station, and another GI went up. The departing soldier was "processed" by the medics, his leave ticket stamped, and he went on his way.

The men of the Second Battalion also got to know some of the French legionnaires they had fought against in the beginning. The interested ones began to learn a little about north Africa and the Arabs. Real American rations began to arrive in the form of frozen beef, flour, coffee, and white bread. A laundry was set up for the troops. Blouses (jackets) were made compulsory for all visits to town. Captain Peckham, the new battalion executive officer, borrowed the regiment's "dance band" and the battalion held a dance at the city hall; the local girls who came were heavily chaperoned. The Red Cross showed up and began to arrange entertainments. A real garrison life was developing.

Just then the war heated up.

On December 6 British Lt. Gen. Sir Kenneth Arthur Noel Anderson, who was leading the maneuvering on the Tunisian front, announced that he had just been attacked by the Germans. That was a bit of British understatement. His infantry brigade group had been decimated. American medium tank units of the First Armored Division, which had been operating with the British, had been heavily damaged. The German dive-bombers had also done serious damage to American artillery units operating with the British. General Anderson had been in Algiers, conferring with Eisenhower. While he was away, his army had suffered a major defeat.

The men of Company F, Second Battalion, Eighteenth Infantry, were sitting down to their evening meal when a runner came from battalion to announce that they were alerted to move out for Tunisia in three hours. Only rolls and light packs would go.

A noncom from each platoon was sent out to round up the men who were in town. Extra men were assigned to KP to help the kitchen force load up.

But of course it was hurry up and wait. In the rush neither the company officers nor Sergeant Merrill could keep track of canteens and wine. The men loaded up and waited. There was a lot of surreptitious drinking, and then the boozing became very unsurreptitious, and soon empty bottles were littering the company area. The 2½-ton trucks showed up and the men got aboard. It began to rain, and some of the trucks were not covered. More bottles began clanking onto the cobblestones. The trucks moved out to the rendezvous point. They stopped and sat. Hours went by. The GIs were noisy, singing and throwing out bottles. But the bottles ran out, and the GIs pooped out and sat, miserable, in the rain, with memorable hangovers from that red north African wine that left so notable an imprint on the digestive systems of the overimbibers. At last, early in the morning, the column moved out, heading for Tunisia.

They bivouacked outside Algiers at a village called l'Arba. Orders had to come down from on high to send them to Tunisia. They waited. Lieutenant Downing left F Company to go up to regimental headquarters. He was, said Colonel Greer, going to be a regimental liaison officer. A whole new life was waiting. His first task was to go to Algiers to pick up $20,000 for emergency regimental purposes. He did. He spent the next few days buying fruit from merchants, buying barber's supplies for the regimental barbers, and waiting. He had become a purchasing agent, it seemed.

December 15: New orders. The regiment moved out. Next stop Ghardimaou, the last stop before Tunisia. Here the troops were bombed by German planes, and here they were told that they would become a part of General Anderson's British First Army. The Eighteenth Infantry was attached to the British Seventy-eighth Division, along with the U.S. Thirty-second Field Artillery Battalion. They also learned that elements of the U.S. Second Armored Division would be coming up to join them. The first attack by the regiment would be on December 24.

What a Christmas present!

13

MEANWHILE...

Three landing teams of the Second Armored Division had gone into north Africa on November 8. "Hell on Wheels," as the division was called, was dashing for Casablanca when the armistice was signed. But only part of "Hell on Wheels." The balance of the division was at Fort Dix, waiting for the word to go and for the ships to take the men to their buddies in north Africa. On December 11, 1942, the ships were there and the division loaded up and headed for Casablanca. The soldiers arrived on Christmas Eve, and after undergoing one German air raid there, they moved on to join the other units at the Mamora Cork Forest. The Second Armored would play only one part in the Tunisian campaign: some 2000 officers and men of the division would be transferred to replace casualties of the First Armored Division before the Tunisian campaign ended. Many of their vehicles would be commandeered also.

In the last few months of 1942 a lot had happened to Sergeant Elburn's Twenty-ninth Infantry Division. The "old men" of the National Guard were advanced as the raw recruits came in. The Twenty-ninth, having moved to England, took over the Tidworth Barracks when the First Division moved out to begin amphibious training for north Africa. There was a certain amount of difficulty because of the timing. For a while Elburn's 115th Infantry Reg-

iment was quartered at Cowley Barracks, near Oxford. Then, when the last
of the First Division had moved out of Tidworth, the Twenty-ninth was put
together again.

If Staff Sergeant Elburn and his friends of the 115th thought they had
trained before, now they went on a seven-day-a-week training program, with
one forty-eight-hour pass per month. Lord Ismay's predictions had to be
proved wrong, and there wasn't very much time. Soon the 25-mile hike was
SOP; then it was two 25-mile hikes or one 40-mile hike per week. Anybody
who couldn't make it was transferred out. Nobody, but nobody, escaped the
drill. By General Gerow's orders checkers were stationed along the route of
march to intercept the shortcutters, and a roll call was taken at the end of
the trek. It was the same with the 116th, the Virginia regiment, which had
been at Tidworth since the beginning of the stay in England. Pvt. Robert J.
Emert, of Company D of the 116th, was now going to undergo rigorous training as a mortarman. That meant every day.

Christmas 1942: While General Roosevelt was off in north Africa, Mrs.
Roosevelt, now of the American Red Cross, was ensconced at Tidworth
House, the Duke of Wellington's manse, as a sort of supermama to the troops.
There were receptions and dances where the local girls and the local service-
women mingled with the Americans, reinforcing the Tommies' feeling that
everything was going to hell at home with the Americans around.

Early in December Staff Sergeant Elburn, Private Emert, and their friends
were exposed to the demands of the media: they faked a Christmas celebration for the press, British and American. Their pictures and voices were
sent home for airing at Christmastide.

Just before Christmas a new unit was formed out of the Twenty-ninth
Division. The Twenty-ninth Provisional Ranger Battalion was organized to
train to replace the First Rangers, who had gone off to Africa. The British
had their commandos for conducting raids on the enemy coast, like the one
at Dieppe. Now the Americans had to learn how to raid.

Many changes were coming to the Twenty-ninth Division, and many new
people. Sergeant Ogden was among them. His career had prospered since
he left the narrow-minded confines of Fort Monroe, and he was a natural
candidate when the Twenty-ninth Ranger Battalion was established.

The Twenty-ninth Rangers began training. Soon they would go with the
British up to Scotland, to learn the act.

*

Back home in Louisiana, First Sergeant Chattaway's Twenty-eighth Division was shaping up, after General Bradley's shuffling of officers and noncoms to break up the village cliques. When the fall Louisiana maneuvers ended, the troops knew they were going somewhere soon. For one thing, the inspections were more frequent, and tougher.

One day Sergeant Chattaway was accompanying the battalion executive officer on his daily inspection of the company area. They got to the mess hall, and there found the mess sergeant *himself* busily stirring an enormous cauldron of vegetable soup. All the time they were looking around the kitchen, the mess sergeant was fooling with his soup, and the battalion exec was impressed by the tender loving care. He picked up a clean ladle, walked over to the cauldron, and sampled the soup.

"That's good soup, Sergeant," said the exec.

"Thank you, sir," said the mess sergeant, stirring vigorously.

Inspection over, Sergeant Chattaway came back to the mess hall.

"How come the big act with the soup?"

"Keerist, Charlie, one of them goddamn pea-brained KPs dropped a dish cloth in just before you guys got here. What do you think the captain would have said if he had seen that? I had to keep it down."

Orders came that month for the Twenty-eighth Division to move to Camp Gordon Johnson (Carrabelle) near Apalachicola, Florida, on the Gulf of Mexico coast, the site of the Army Amphibious Training Command.

Talk about the end of the earth! Carrabelle was it. Within a couple of weeks the dogfaces had it taped in a poem of eleven stanzas that related their woes, a few of which are below:

> *The Devil in Hell, we're told, was chained,*
> *And a thousand years he there remained.*
> *He neither complained, nor did he groan,*
> *But determined to start a Hell of his own....*
>
> *He scattered some chiggers along the road,*
> *Lizards in the grass, an occasional toad,*
> *The Gulf has sharks, barracuda, stingrays,*
> *And, in the sand, he mixed millions of fleas.*
>
> *To the tail of the jellyfish, he added a sting,*
> *Then the dragonfly, he put on the wing.*
> *He added some typhoid to all of the drink,*
> *With a pinch of sulphur, to make it stink.*

The rattlesnake bites you, the horsefly stings,
  The mosquito delights you with buzzing wings.
Sandburs cause you to jig and to dance,
  And those who sit down get ants in the pants....

The heat in the summer is one hundred and ten,
  Too hot for the Devil, too hot for the men.
Come see for yourself and you can tell,
  It's a helluva place, this Camp Carrabelle.

Every day they trained. Dog Island was the usual "enemy" beach on which they landed time and again. They dug, and dug, and dug. They marched 4 miles in forty-five minutes. They marched 16 miles in eight hours. They went back to their huts with sand floors, scorpions, tarantulas, and coral snakes, and they sacked out, exhausted.

Sergeant Chattaway's wife found a place to live in Tallahassee, and as a senior NCO, Chattaway managed to make the 55-mile trip most weekends. But on Sunday afternoons it was back to the tarantulas...

Toward the end of 1942 it was still possible for youngsters to enlist in the army, navy, or Marine Corps. Elwood Zeitz, a 17-year-old farm boy, decided he wanted to join the horse cavalry, and he did. He enlisted in the Fourth Cavalry Squadron of the Seventy-seventh Regiment, made famous by George Armstrong Custer, and soon found himself in Fort Meade, South Dakota. For the next twenty-two weeks, Private Zeitz learned how to be a soldier. Then there was a fourteen-day Christmas leave, and Private Zeitz went home to Houghton, Michigan.

In London, just before Christmas, Prime Minister Churchill suddenly realized that all the promises and plans for 1943 had been overoptimistic. Britain and America had confidently promised Stalin a real second front [an invasion of Fortress Europe] and now it was apparent that they could not bring it off. They were 35 divisions short of the men needed, and they did not have the shipping or the landing craft to perform.

The problem, as seen in Algiers and Washington, was to get moving and get out of Africa as quickly as possible. Rommel had been defeated once, and the Germans could be defeated again. But when? The Allies had reached

Djedeida, just 12 miles from Tunis, but there the Germans had counter-attacked, and forced the Allies back to Medjez. The plan for the capture of Tunis before year's end had bogged down in the rain that now assaulted the land, putting an effective end to the fighting for weeks.

In the United States the military buildup continued as fast as Washington could push it. All those cadres, sucked from divisions like the Eighty-second and Twenty-eighth, were now expanding to become divisions themselves. The plans of young Americans were cast to the winds. Tom Inglis, an orphan boy in New England, had spent his childhood proving himself. He had played so well at baseball that he was offered a contract in the Boston Braves farm program. But the draft did not come from the Braves, it came from the U.S. Army, and on the day before Thanksgiving 1942, Inglis found himself on his way to the Thirtieth Infantry Division at Camp Blanding, Florida. On December 7 he started basic training.

Times had changed with the speedup. The soldiers of the Thirtieth Infantry lived in tents ("I never saw a barracks again until the end of the war"). They ate from their mess kits from the beginning. After basic, "it was all war games and maneuvers." There was to be one year of this playing at war.

The Army Air Forces, Coast Guard, marines, and navy were all speeding up their efforts, too, for the war against the Axis. Seabees Chief Machinist's Mate Lorne D. Porter was sitting in the replacement battalion headquarters at Camp Bradford, near Norfolk, when the call came for chiefs to set up a new battalion, the Thirty-fourth Naval Construction Battalion. Their recruits were just breaking boot camp. So in came the boots, 300 whites and 900 blacks—the first black men to get a real chance in the navy, the first to be assigned to anything but menial waiters' jobs.

Chief Porter trained a platoon. At first there was a little queasiness about the unusual racial mix, but "it turned out to be one of the best battalions in the naval service." In mid-November the men went to camp near Gulfport, Mississippi. Three weeks later they were in Port Hueneme, California. They did not yet know it, but they were on their way to the Solomon Islands, where Adm. William F. Halsey had a desperate need for air and naval bases. Chief Porter had been in service for three months. That's how fast the American buildup had become. Moving fast and breaking old taboos; that was the way of war.

*

At Fort Bragg, during that Christmas season of 1942, Captain Shebeck was training his battalion of the 326th Glider Regiment. It was one set of rookies after another, Shebeck pushing them out to take their places in the ranks of the nonparachute units of the Eighty-second Airborne Division. That assignment ended; he was transferred back to the staff of the regiment. This was part of the changing nature of the airborne; the Eighty-second would now have two parachute regiments and one glider regiment. The tempo of training increased so fast that it seemed certain the time for the Eighty-second to go overseas was approaching.

Up in Northern Ireland the staff of the Fifth Corps was planning for the invasion of the continent. At first they were located at Lurgan, but in the fall they moved to Belfast. The chief planning officer was Lieutenant Colonel Campbell, who at the end of December was appointed G-3, operations officer, of the Fifth Corps. His main job, just at this point, was reconnoitering virtually every road between Wales and Southampton, to plan for the logistics of bringing thousands of vehicles and hundreds of thousands of troops to the point where they would be loaded on transports for the crossing of the English Channel.

Considerable time had now passed since President Roosevelt's 1940 orders mobilizing the National Guard, and in that time the American army was becoming more professional every day. An example of this professionalism was a 21-year-old captain, Archie W. Stewart, Jr. He had gone the whole route of the citizen soldier so far. He had lied about his age in 1936 to join the Texas National Guard. The reason was that he needed the shoes, socks, and warm wool shirt the National Guard issued. He could take these home on the pretense of washing and polishing and keep them until the next Tuesday drill night. Meanwhile, he could wear them; he had no other warm clothes, and northeast Texas was anything but hot in the winter.

Private Stewart was paid his dollar a drill night. He was promoted to corporal, which raised his pay 20 cents a night. Not much of a raise? It was the price of a hamburger and a Coke. When the Texas National Guard was mobilized, he had finally achieved the ripe, proper age of 18; he was 6 feet 2 inches tall and weighed 145 pounds; and he was a sergeant with four years'

service. Fort Benning Officer Candidate School made him a second lieutenant, and then he was assigned to the 103d Division at Camp Claiborne,
Louisiana, where he was promoted to first lieutenant. Then he went to Camp
Shelby, Mississippi, and was promoted to captain. At 21, with six years of
military service, Captain Stewart was one of the most experienced of American
citizen soldiers.

Lt. Henry G. Spencer, another citizen soldier, was at Camp McCoy, Wisconsin, with the First Battalion of the Twenty-third Infantry that Christmas
of 1942. His outfit had been chosen for a noble experiment: they were to
show how long it would take a foot soldier division to convert to a ski-trooper
unit—one that would use skis, snowshoes, sleds, weasels, and other cold-
weather equipment. The Japanese, remember, had landed at Kiska and Attu
islands in the Aleutian chain, and the army was preparing for a Japanese
invasion of the rest of Alaska.

At Bowman Field, outside Louisville, Pvt. Charles Bortzfield was sweating
out his basic training. He was another sort of soldier, a "limited service"
man. He had graduated from Brooklyn's East New York Vocational High
School that spring, and had tried to enlist in the Army Air Forces. But he
was turned down for defective vision. Then Charlie Bortzfield played his trump
card: he told the army (truthfully) that he knew a lot about aircraft mechanics from high school. That information changed the picture. The army gave
him a special test and declared him fit for "limited service only." And off he
went to boot camp.

Nobody knew quite what that meant. But then, in that Christmastime of
1942, there were a lot of things nobody knew.

14

TUNISIA

Things were very tough for the Eighteenth Infantry that Christmas season of 1942. The men had moved up to join the British drive to Tunis, but the drive had bogged down. The tanks of the First Armored Division had reached the outskirts of Tunis, but the British infantrymen who were supposed to come up in support had not arrived, and the tanks had gotten into trouble.

At the moment, of course, Lieutenant Downing did not know anything about that. He was on the road with a convoy. It still felt strange to be a staff officer with regiment, and not a company officer with a platoon to worry about. He really wanted to get back to his company. The idea of a company command appealed to him most of all.

But no, he was riding in the back seat of a jeep, his overcoat buttoned up tight around his neck, with instructions to keep his eye out for enemy aircraft. That was what being a staff officer was all about.

December 15: Late in the afternoon the convoy stopped. It was raining hard. The men of the regimental band set up the colonel's tent.

"Here is how it works," said Lieutenant Newkirk, the executive officer of headquarters company.

"First there is the colonel's tent. Then the exec's, and then...."

"Just as soon as all the senior officers are fixed up, the men will help you set up your tent, lieutenant."

Lieutenant Downing stood in the rain for five minutes, growing distinctly more uncomfortable every minute. He went to the baggage truck, pulled out his bedroll, found a level spot on the plowed field next to "headquarters," undid the bedroll, pulled out his pup tent, and put it up with the aid of a rock to pound the pegs in. He draped his raincoat over the entrance and crawled inside. He felt his face and the stubble of beard. He poured half a canteen of cold water into the cup and shaved by flashlight. The razor pulled like the devil. But he forgot that in five minutes. He was asleep.

December 16: A hot breakfast of pancakes and coffee! Then back on the road again. The rain stopped, but the cold wind started. Late in the afternoon the column stopped again. The colonel requisitioned a farmhouse on the outskirts of a village. Lieutenant Downing was lucky enough to be able to share a room with Lieutenant Moore, another junior liaison officer on the staff. That night, as they lay in their bedrolls, they heard the sound of planes overhead. The noise grew louder, then *wham, wham, wham*. German planes had bombed somewhere very close by. Downing could hear mumbled noises in the next room and the grinding of field phones.

December 17: Downing awakened and went out into the cold morning. The convoy began again and drove through the village. On the far outskirts were three large bomb craters in the area where the Third Battalion had bivouacked. Nobody had been hurt.

Late in the afternoon the long column wound its way down a hill onto the broad plain of Ghardimaou. This was almost the end. From here the troops would move into combat. As Downing was setting up his pup tent, Lieutenant Newkirk came around and told him to get some branches. Camouflage. The colonel didn't want any more German bombs.

That night the sentries had orders to enforce a strict blackout. Inside his pup tent, Lieutenant Downing lit a furtive cigarette.

"Put that goddamn light out," somebody shouted.

Then there was a shot.

It didn't come his way. Somebody else. Nobody was hit, but there was lots more shouting and some shooting that night. The whole regiment was on edge.

December 18: The colonel sent senior staff officers up to meet the British at Beja. The Eighteenth Infantry and the Thirty-second Field Artillery Battalion got the details.

The staff officers returned to report on the very scary air raids of the German Stuka dive-bombers on the British at Beja. They also reported that there was a handful of American troops already with the British—what was left of Combat Command B of the First Armored Division.

What a story they had to tell. The men of the First Armored had nearly reached Tunis, gotten into the suburbs, in fact, and then had to fall back because the Limeys hadn't sent up their infantry. Coming back they had been stopped by a bombed-out bridge over a stream. The Stukas and Messerschmitts had caught the column there and knocked out most of the tanks and half-tracks. Many men were killed, and the desperately wounded had to be left behind. The survivors had limped back, without equipment, and were now bivouacked at Souk el Arba, an armored command without any armor. Replacements and tanks were coming from the Second Armored Division in the Mamora Cork Forest, but they would be a while in getting there. Meanwhile the British-American attack force had no armor.

Even without the armor there was to be an attack.

December 20: The colonel held a staff conference to issue his regimental attack order. Lieutenants Downing and Moore were allowed to sit in since they were going to go up to the British as liaison and had to know what was going on. The regiment would drive toward Mateur, and eventually into Tunis. To start with, the First Battalion would take a piece of high ground called Longstop Hill to protect the flank of the attack. The Second and Third battalions would push up the valley toward Tebourba and Mateur. The First Battalion attack would be made on December 24.

December 22: Regimental headquarters pulled out of Ghardimaou at dusk. The column traveled blacked out in the faint moonlight, watching and listening for German planes. The troops passed through several blacked-out villages and over a submerged bridge that had been built by the British engineers. Since it could not be seen from the air, it was not bombed. There was no question about who had air superiority. The Germans did.

They began seeing burned-out vehicles beside the road, the legs of dead mules and horses sticking up from their bloated bodies. Then they came to the ruins of a town: Medjez el Bab.

The column stopped at a farmyard. British sappers (engineers) were billeted in the house, but the colonel got the barn. Lieutenants Moore and Downing got a two-wheel, two-seat buggy with a leather top that was in the barnyard. They wrapped up in blankets, put their overcoats on top, lay down on the seats snug and warm, and went promptly to sleep.

December 23: Dawn. A runner awakened Lieutenant Downing. He was to report to the regimental operations officer, Captain Colacicco, for instructions. What a marvel. All the British, officers and enlisted men, were shaving. They shaved every day!

Captain Colacicco was looking at his map. Lieutenant Downing was to take a jeep and report to the British Seventy-eighth Division headquarters at Beja, as liaison. "Look, here's the route." Captain Colacicco traced it out on the map.

Pop-pop-pop. British Bofors guns opened up. Overhead the loud sound of an airplane was very close. *Ratatatat*. Downing rushed out to look. A machine gun. *Zooom*. The plane passed overhead and out of sight. Lots of shooting. No hits.

He went back inside the building.

"Now you take this turn...."

After the briefing, it was bangers, crackers, and tea at the British mess.

While Lieutenant Downing was showing Private Foote, his jeep driver, the route on the map, up came Lieutenant Moore.

"Wanta hear the latest scoop?"

"Sure."

"Well, there was this artillery liaison officer, see, and he was riding in a jeep up that road you're gonna take one day last week. Suddenly, *ratata-tatat*. A Messerschmitt had glided up behind the jeep with its motor off. One each driver, one each liaison officer, deader'n mackerels. Cheers!"

"Ha, ha, ha," said Lieutenant Downing.

If you like driving through junkyards, you would have loved the journey to Beja. Private Foote steered the jeep past dozens, scores, of burned-out tanks, trucks, half-tracks, and other vehicles that were nothing but blackened junk. Except for the scenery it was like a Sunday drive in the country. Not a shot, not a zooming plane. Nothing.

At the British headquarters Lieutenant Downing met Captain Francis, the Seventy-eighth Division chief liaison officer. He also met Lieutenant Tosh of the Argyll and Southern Highlanders; Captain Carter, of the Monmouthshire Regiment; and Lieutenant Chevalier, a French cavalry officer.

Afternoon tea was at 4:30 at the officers' mess—for subalterns, that is, a handful of lieutenants. The other officers—more senior officers, that is—messed at the general's house. The tea and other meals would be prepared by the batmen, personal servants. Just like the old U.S Army. Not like the new army of the United States. Lieutenant Downing had no batman. He wouldn't know what to do with one.

"That's all right," someone said airily. "The others will take care of you. You and Chevalier."

Tea, biscuits, jam, and tinned sardines. The other officers' batmen didn't

seem overjoyed at having a new American officer and a new French officer
to feed.

Dinner at the British officers' mess was preceded by drinks. One of the
officers had invented a cocktail called "the Phantom": half a glass of gin in
half a glass of local wine. It didn't take many to make one see double. At
dinner the British talked mostly about the goose they would have for Christmas
dinner, and Lieutenant Downing put up his 200-franc assessment. Not a word
was said about tomorrow's attack.

December 24: The assault on Longstop Hill began. Downing drove out to
the regiment. The intelligence probe attack of the night before had run into
heavy opposition. That indicated the First Battalion of the Eighteenth Infantry was going to have trouble. From the farmyard of the regimental headquarters Downing could see shell bursts and the haze and smoke over the
attack area. The rain was not helping. Casualties were heavy and hard to
move. Late in the afternoon the attack plan was called off. Now the problem
was for the First Battalion to hold. Regiment moved its headquarters to a
new location near Teborsouk. Downing returned to the British.

Christmas day: Back at Eighteenth Regiment headquarters Downing followed the progress of the First Battalion attack. The battalion had run into
trouble, in spades. The men were still out there on the hill in foxholes. The
Germans had half the hill. Two companies of tanks from the armored division had come down to help in the attack. The Allies were convinced that
the Sherman M-4 tank was going to be superior to anything the Germans
had. "Invincible."

No. Vincible. The Americans had a new learning experience—about
German antitank weapons. Of those two companies of tanks, only one tank
came back from the attack. The hillside was full of burned-out, blasted M-4
tanks.

Christmas dinner: Lieutenant Downing was in the wrong place, at First
Battalion CP. No Phantom cocktails. No roast goose. A plate of meat and
vegetable stew, eaten in the rain with rainwater sauce. Back to the British,
late in the day.

December 26: It was cold. Downing was wearing long johns, wool shirt,
wool pants, sweater, field jacket, and mackinaw, but still he was shivering.
He drove back to regiment. The First Battalion was still on Longstop Hill.
Colonel Greer told Downing to ask the British First Guards Brigade to relieve the First Battalion. Downing drove to the British brigade headquarters
and found British Brigadier Copeland-Griffiths. He relayed the request. The
brigadier showed Downing the situation map, and said he would relieve the
battalion if possible, but there probably wasn't any need because the situ-

ation had "stabilized." That meant the Allied attack had failed and was not going to be repeated, as General Anderson had already informed General Eisenhower.

What everybody in the Third Battalion of the Sixtieth Infantry hoped was going to be a nice, quiet, relaxed Christmas with turkey and all the trimmings turned out to be a mess. On December 24 Company M was alerted and reminded that there was a war on. Why, the men did not know, but they were ordered to set up their machine guns for antiaircraft action and keep those guns manned around the clock during the holiday. It ruined Christmas, and nothing happened.

The only one to get a present was Sergeant Short, Thornton's platoon sergeant, who was promoted by field commission to second lieutenant on Christmas day. Thornton then became platoon sergeant.

While the U.S. High Command was pulling up its socks in Algiers and moving troops up to the Tunisian border in anticipation of the drier day when British General Anderson was supposed to launch a new offensive against Tunis, Allied activity against the Germans on that front was limited to harassment. Conspicuous among the harassers were the French Zouaves and the 509th Paratroopers.

On the day after Christmas Colonel Raff got orders for a new mission. His paratroopers were to drop behind the German lines in Tunisia and blow up a railroad bridge 6 miles north of El Djem. That would stem the German advance to the Tunisian-Algerian frontier.

Colonel Raff was not to lead this minor mission; it was a task for a company officer. The leader would be Lt. Daniel DeLeo. He would have with him demolitions expert S. Sgt. James W. Collins and five other demolition men, plus twenty-one paratroop riflemen and two French soldiers who spoke Arabic.

Before midnight on December 26 the team boarded three C-47 transports at Thelepte, at the foot of the mountains, and headed for El Djem. The men had been briefed by Colonel Raff, who had especially warned them against the Arabs.

"Don't have anything to do with the Arabs," he said. "They're for the enemy. If you see them, kill every Arab bastard you see. Don't take any prisoners."

It was a bright, moonlit night. They flew 60 miles behind the lines and jumped at 300 feet. Just as they had hooked up and were ready to go, they saw a highway down below and on it a convoy of Germans moving toward the front. The Germans began firing at the planes. But then the green light went on, and it was time to jump.

They got down. It took a while to assemble. Then they found they had only half the explosives they needed—500 pounds of TNT in 25-pound packages. The other 500 pounds had been lost somehow in the drop. The demolition men had trouble carrying the load. They "requisitioned" a donkey from an Arab, but the donkey collapsed under the weight. They had to carry the TNT themselves. The demolition men wanted to kill the Arab, but DeLeo made them let him go.

Bad navigation by the air transport crews caused the paratroopers to drop in the wrong place. When they assembled and found the rail line, they were completely disoriented. They thought they were a mile north of their objective. Actually they were a mile south of it, and every foot that they moved southward took them further away. Finally Lieutenant DeLeo told the demolition men, who were worn out from carrying the TNT, to hole up in an olive grove while he and some of the riflemen went scouting to see where they were.

The rest of the riflemen stayed behind with the demolition men. Guards were supposed to be posted, but were not. The next thing the stay-behind Americans knew, it was broad daylight and they were surrounded by Arabs. "There must have been 400 of them."

There was already speculation that some of the men sent out on patrol had been captured.

Starting up the track in the direction they thought would lead to the bridge, they came across several Germans on a section car. The Germans began firing. Some of the paratroopers fired back. The Germans then ran their car off along the track and disappeared.

The paratroopers found a rail center—crossings, tracks, and a control building—but as they approached the building, they saw Germans coming up all around them in trucks. The Americans blew the rail switches, the power lines, and the tracks, using up all the TNT, and then headed back the way they had come. But the Germans had them encircled.

The Americans finally came to an irrigation ditch. Germans were everywhere. Lieutenant DeLeo and Sergeant Collins consulted. Collins said he was going to break his detachment into small groups to try to get through. He did so. So did DeLeo.

Sergeant Collins had his men pair off. He and Private Caruso took off

together. They got into a ravine, and ducked into a hole in the side of a
bank, with the bank hanging over. The Germans walked right past them.

Dusk was falling.

Then a German spotted them and fired a shot. It grazed Collins's face.
Suddenly there were a dozen Germans around him, and his choice was either surrender or die.

Collins was thrown into solitary confinement. The Germans then moved
out, either forgetting Collins or abandoning him. For three days he sat, without bread or water. Then a German tank-destroyer group came by, heard
Collins yelling, and rescued him. But he was a POW, and soon he was taken
off to Sicily. Collins eventually ended up a POW in Germany.

As the German and Italian patrols continued to move around, Lieutenant
DeLeo grew ever more nervous. It was his responsibility to get the men back
to Allied lines if he could. That meant a march of 70 miles.

The Germans were methodical. They also had the resources to surround
the area in which they knew the Americans were located. Steadily the circle
grew more concentrated, until by three o'clock in the afternoon, the paratroopers saw so many troops in so many directions that they knew the enemy
was closing in. It would have been suicidal to try to make a stand with thirty
men. Lieutenant DeLeo told them to try to slip through the circle of the enemy.

He and three riflemen and the two French soldiers stuck together. They
encountered an Italian driving a truck and captured him. DeLeo sat up front
with a gun on the Italian while the others hid in the back of the truck. They
passed a patrol of Germans who were taking time out and smoking on the
side of the road. The Germans ignored them. They went on until the truck
ran into the mud. Then they abandoned it and continued on foot. Through
the French soldiers they made some contacts with Arabs and Frenchmen,
and got some food and directions. They moved up into the mountains, making as much progress westward as possible, but wandering around in circles
particularly at night. Finally they got back to their lines.

Pvt. Michael Underhill and two demolition men were assigned to break out
together. Underhill had his M-1 rifle (its sight had been damaged in the drop),
sixty rounds of ammunition, and four hand grenades. The demolition men,
having jettisoned their explosives, now were armed only with .45-caliber Colt
automatic pistols. They began walking west, through the desert, toward the
Algerian border. Suddenly, Private Underhill dropped to the ground and motioned to the others. They went down, too. Ahead, on top of a hill, they saw

a machine gun. They were behind a sandy rise. Underhill began working his way to the top of the rise. Ahead he saw an Italian patrol, about a platoon of men. One man saw him and shouted, and the machine gun began firing. Underhill motioned the two demolition men to go back, and he covered them with rifle fire. The Italians did not seem overly eager to attack. Underhill held them off for two hours and then worked his way back to the others. The Italians did not follow.

They continued to go west. The demolition men argued that they would never make it. They wanted to surrender, but Underhill was adamant. They could make it if they tried, he said. Eventually the argument reached an impasse. They came to another Italian position, and the two demolition men said they were going to surrender. Underhill told them to go ahead, and they parted company.

Late that afternoon a truck came up within 500 yards of Private Underhill. Men jumped out and began moving toward him. He waited. He then lobbed a grenade and two men fell. The others picked up their comrades, took them back to the truck, and drove off.

Private Underhill continued to move west, holing up at dawn and moving by night. He lived on the K rations he had brought and on eggs bought from local Arabs, who also warned him of the positions of Axis troops. He was very lucky to meet the right people. No one betrayed him, and he finally reached the Allied lines at Foudouk.

Sgt. Manuel Serrano was on that mission. He was a dark-skinned, dark-haired, six-footer from Puerto Rico via Brooklyn. As the men tried to get through the cordon of German troops in small groups, Serrano was unlucky and he was captured. After four days he was taken to an Italian prison camp in Sicily. He spent nine months in Italian prisoner of war camps, and then escaped and joined the Italian partisans.

The mission was a bust. The initial problem was improper delivery. But once they were down, the Americans were disoriented; that was what really killed the mission. Had intelligence materials and their French guides been able to give a better picture of the terrain, they might well have succeeded. As it was, the stories of Lieutenant DeLeo and Private Underhill are prime tales of bravery and survival, but that was not the point. Colonel Raff saw that in any major operation involving paratroops the matter of getting the men to the

right place was all important; he also saw how easy it was to fail. So he and
his men began to work on a technique that they called "Pathfinder." This
involved close study of intelligence materials, very careful selection of a drop
zone, and the dispatch of highly trained men to that drop zone to mark it out
with flares and offer whatever communication they could to aircraft bringing
the paratroopers (and gliders) to the destination behind enemy lines.

Back in Washington just then, the War Department offered General Eisenhower an unusual unit of troops: the 100th Infantry Battalion—made up entirely of nisei, Japanese-American offspring of Japanese immigrants. These
nisei soldiers were all U.S. citizens, and all volunteers.

The Allied drive on Tunis was literally bogged down in the mud. General
Eisenhower, who made a trip on December 26 to visit General Anderson's
British headquarters at Souk el Khemis, had himself seen four men trying to
push a motorcycle through the muck without success. So, after talking to
local people and finding out that the rains would persist until February, the
offensive was postponed for six weeks. But of course the GIs did not know
anything about that. The First Armored Division was going to move to Tebessa, to be ready at first chance to start raiding. It was also to become the
striking force of Second Corps. Just as all these plans were being made,
Eisenhower was called back to Algiers that day with the news that Admiral
Darlan, the head of the French "cooperators" (collaborators was a term reserved for the enemy), had been murdered. General Henri Giraud became
the new chief of the French forces in Allied-controlled north Africa, a change
that was made without a whicker as far as the GIs were concerned. They
didn't know at the moment that one of Giraud's first acts was to put the bite
on Ike to cut the dollar-franc exchange rate in half, from 75 francs to 38
francs. One other change would affect many of the GIs. General Mark Clark
was put to work assembling a unit that would be known as the U.S. Fifth
Army. General Fredendall would command Second Corps.

On the night that Admiral Darlan was assassinated, the men of Corporal
Moglia's Company E of the Sixteenth Infantry were still living in pup tents
near Tafaraoui. Moglia learned about the assassination because that night
the guard was doubled: the sentries walked in pairs. Had Moglia known of

the decision made at Souk el Khemis that day to postpone the invasion of Tunisia, he would have approved heartily.

"Isn't it ever going to stop raining?" was the question of the day in the Company E area. The men had no change of uniform and they were constantly soaked to the skin. It rained when they marched. It rained when they slept. It rained when they ate, so none but speed eaters ever had a hot or dry meal.

In the excitement over the Darlan assassination, rumors flew. The Germans had dropped a parachute unit near Tafaraoui, came the word from regiment. The Second Battalion was to send out patrols to find the Germans.

Corporal Moglia was detailed to one patrol. He was acting as scout. After plodding along the wet sand in the rain for an hour, he suddenly heard some strange sounds, about 50 yards ahead. People chuckling, or giggling, more likely. He moved up slowly. Now it sounded like a crowd of old men laughing.

"Germans. They were laughing because they had dropped into our area undetected and would now move in to sabotage."

The patrol began to encircle the laughers. The men were ready with their M-1s to open fire and eliminate the Germans.

"When we moved in close enough for the kill, we found a very strangely camouflaged enemy parachute unit. How did they manage to make themselves look like laughing hyenas?"

The patrol returned to base, and the lieutenant had to write the report. Corporal Moglia oozed into his soggy tent and stretched out in his damp blanket bag. He slept.

Sometime late in the night he awakened. Something was nibbling at his boots. Something that smelled wet and hairy. He opened one eye. A large "dog" was at the foot of his bedroll, apparently interested in eating his feet. Moglia kicked the animal in the nose and grabbed his rifle. He started yelling and a dozen soldiers appeared and began pursuit of the hyena. They chased him into an outhouse.

But how had the hyena gotten into camp? He had to have followed them back from their patrol. The men of Moglia's platoon knew; just like those French legionnaires, the hyena had decided to join the American army.

15

KASSERINE PASS

Christmas, still.

The transports *American, Ancon, Argentina, Brazil,* and *Chiriqui,* and the seatrain *Texas* arrived at Casablanca, carrying the rest of the Second Armored Division. They were met with bands and much ceremony. Even the Germans showed up with an air raid.

The troops went to the Cork Forest for training.

On December 26 the First Battalion of the Eighteenth Infantry was withdrawn from action against the Germans at Longstop Hill and moved to Teborsouk. There it was discovered that, despite the British brigadier's insouciance, the battalion had suffered more than 40 percent casualties and had to be reorganized by transfer of men from other battalions. They were lucky to get out when they did; that same day the Germans attacked the troops of the British First Guards Division, who had gone up onto Longstop Hill, and drove them off. That was the last gasp of General Anderson's Christmas offensive.

January 1943: Big doings. General Fredendall was planning an armored thrust to Gabès, and then a drive north to take Sfax on the tenth day. This move would clear the way for General Anderson to take Tunis. At Eisenhower's headquarters they were talking about clearing Tunisia of Axis forces in six weeks.

At Casablanca the Twentieth Engineers had finished their job on the docks. Every day they set a new record in unloading ships until mid-January, when the regular port battalions arrived and they were relieved. Immediately Lieutenant Miller and his men had a new job; they were to build barbed-wire entanglements around the lovely Hotel d'Anfa, high on a hill overlooking Casablanca. Soon enough they found out why. On January 17 the real big-wigs arrived for a conference at Casablanca: U.S. Admiral King, British Admiral Dudley Pound, a whole raft of generals, President Roosevelt's adviser, Harry Hopkins, and of course President Roosevelt, Prime Minister Winston Churchill, and General Charles de Gaulle, leader of the Free French. Their discussions were miles above the heads of the dogfaces, most of whom, in one place or another, were still stuck in the mud. Company A of the Sixty-seventh Armored Regiment was brought up from the Cork Forest to serve as an honor guard. The Forty-first Armored Infantry was assigned to guard the prime minister's and President's villas. What a job they did! One night when Prime Minister Churchill was returning to his villa he was stopped by a guard.

"Halt. Advance and identify yourself."

"I am Prime Minister Winston Churchill."

The guard recognized neither voice nor figure, and called the sergeant of the guard.

"Hey, Sergeant. There's some guy out here who claims he's Churchill, the prime minister."

The sergeant came, the prime minister was mollified, and identified, and all was well.

The Eighteenth Regimental Combat Team was transferred to the command of the British Sixth Armoured Division. Lieutenant Downing continued as liaison officer with the British. He got a Christmas package from home and copies of his college newspaper, *The Michigan Daily*. The war didn't get as much coverage as Michigan football!

Then Downing came down with an attack of dysentery. With no bathing facilities, it was rough:

"That night was a sleepless one for me. With only the slightest warning, I would have to scramble out of my sleeping bag, pull on my shoes, pick up my entrenching shovel, and run naked a safe distance from my tent, shiver-

ingly pay homage to the local virus, cover it up with dirt, and return to my
bed for another short nap."

The regimental surgeon gave him pills, but it was a week before he felt
enough confidence to wander far from a slit trench.

The war in Tunisia that January settled down to a series of raids. The
British planned the "Bubble and Squeak" raid, which was carried out near
Medjez el Bab. Mostly what it proved was that the mud was too deep for
tanks; they lost a number, which stuck in the mud. The crews escaped back
to the infantry lines, the Germans destroyed some of the tanks, and the Royal
Engineers went out that night and destroyed the rest of them.

Lieutenant Downing was a witness to the battle of Bou Arada, a tank
battle between British and German units. It went on for several days and
ended with the Germans taking the territory but the British destroying the
German armored striking power.

The Germans bombed the surrounding area nearly every day, both during and after the battle.

"I waited around until I had collected all the details of the battle and
then started out with my driver, Foote, to make my report to regiment. As
we left Bou Arada driving slowly, I kept looking right and left to see the
results of the bombing. I noted two French civilian women lying in a ditch
beside the road, their faces turned up toward the sky. I looked again to see
if they were dead. They saw me looking and pointed excitedly upward. I
took one look, slapped Foote's arm to stop the jeep, grabbed my helmet, and
jumped over the side. Foote followed after me. We ran off the road and into
a small cactus patch, dropped down, and hugged the ground. The dive-
bombers were back again. We lay there and sweated. They screamed down
and the bombs slammed with almost automatic regularity, making the ground
tremble under our bodies. Fortunately for us, the bombs landed inside the
town and not in our area."

There was a good deal of milling around in those weeks. Bubble and
Squeak ended, and the Eighteenth Infantry was transferred back to the
Seventy-eighth Division. The First Armored Division combat team was get-
ting new weapons by stripping the Second Armored Division. Lieutenant
Downing could sense that something was cooking.

The Germans began shelling Medjez el Bab every day between 2 and 4
p.m.; regimental headquarters and the battalions on the hills were the targets. But the German shelling was not as big a problem as the lice. The men
had been too long without bathing facilities and change of clothing. A shower
unit was set up in back of the battalion positions, and men were withdrawn

a few at a time for baths. Some of them were shaved from head to toe, daubed with ointment, and given clean clothes. The clothes had to be British, for there weren't any American ones. So the Eighteenth began to look like a gypsy outfit, with half-American and half-British battle uniform.

At that time Lieutenant Downing saw his first American planes over Africa, a flight of P-38s. Progress. January came to an end. The whole First Division was now converging on Tunisia; units of the Sixteenth Infantry and the Twenty-sixth Infantry were joining the Eighteenth. Things were beginning to move. On the last day of January Lieutenant Downing, who hadn't had a bath or a change of clothes since mid-December, got a new blanket-lined combat jacket, purloined for him by the headquarters company supply sergeant. Such garments were meant for the armored troops, but a few had made their way into the sergeant's hands. The sergeant felt sorry for Downing; the lieutenant's field jacket was greasy, his mackinaw had come apart under the arms, and the right side was impregnated with mud and grease thrown up by the jeep wheels. Now, the lieutenant felt that he cut a splendid figure.

At regiment that day Lieutenant Downing was ordered to deliver a big blond German lieutenant and about twenty German prisoners to the British POW cage at Beja. He was also given a packet of records tied up with rope.

They set out. The American jeep driver and the German lieutenant were in the front seat, and Lieutenant Downing was in the rear, with a .45-caliber pistol in his hand, shell in chamber. The German enlisted prisoners were in two deuce-and-a-halfs, with American guards on the tailgates. They started out late in the afternoon toward Beja.

Darkness came. Downing turned around from time to time to see the outlines of the trucks behind him. He had just turned back when he saw another jeep hurtling straight at his own. He opened his mouth to yell, there was a crash, his helmet pressed down hard on his head, and he blacked out.

He came to, kneeling on all fours on the road. Downing still had the pistol in his hand, but he threw it away. He still had the bundle of records under his arm, but he was bleeding and there was something wrong with his face. Blood kept running down his chin. The men got him into a truck, and they went on. After delivering his prisoners to the POW cage and handing over the records, he was taken to a British aid station. His nose had been nearly severed from his face, so he was moved to a hospital, where a British surgeon sewed him up. He had a nose again. He also had a banged-up leg and a broken kneecap, which was put into a cast.

While Lieutenant Downing was recuperating in the British hospital, he noticed a red-headed American soldier who came around the ward every day selling eggs to the British officers at 5 francs apiece.

Vive la rear echelon!

And then he was taken back to a British general hospital in Algiers. As he became ambulatory, he was allowed out on the town on pass. On the street he passed a woman dressed in khaki with the stripes of an American staff sergeant on her arm. What was this creature? He learned that he had just seen his first WAC. For the next few weeks what he knew about the war he learned from the news broadcasts. It was a lot more than he had learned before. The battle for Tunisia was beginning to unfold.

A great deal of what would happen depended on geography. In the north lies the great Tunis Plain, surrounded by mountains (*djebels*), which form a barrier that definitely favored the defenders because the few passes are very narrow. These mountains are joined by a range of hills that ring Bizerte north of Tunis.

The port of Tunis is on the plain. To the south are Zaghouan, Pont du Fahs, and Enfidaville. South of Pont du Fahs is a high range of mountains, the pivot of which is Maknassy, and from Maknassy the mountains extend another 50 miles southwest. Four main passes extend to the west: Foudouk, Faid, Maknassy, and El Guettar. Then, beyond this eastern ring of passes was a secondary group, to the west: Dernia, Sbiba, Thala, and Kasserine. The area was easily supplied from the sea. German General Jürgen von Arnim had a powerful defensive position, which he knew how to exploit.

Except for the First Armored Division, a few elements of the Second Armored Division, the Second Battalion of the Ninth Parachute Infantry, and the Eighteenth Infantry, the Americans had not yet really been involved in the war against the Germans in north Africa. General Eisenhower was itching to go, but his supply wallahs kept telling him that they could not throw the Second Armored into the battle and supply the troops. Besides, the combat team of the First Armored Division was in such terrible shape, "equipmentwise," that the Second had to be cannibalized to feed the First. But there was already on hand infantry to burn.

The Ninth Division's Thirty-ninth Regimental Combat Team had not been allowed to rot in the stews of Algiers for very long. It had been spread out through Algeria. In December Company C had the bad luck of being as-

signed to the First Armored's Combat Command B, which had been decimated in that first abortive drive on Tunis. In January the Second Battalion
moved into the Atlas Mountains. Under the British First Army, it was to
guard lines of communication between the Allied elements in Tunisia and
Eisenhower's headquarters in Algiers. The Thirty-ninth antitank company
moved up by truck to Biskra. The Third Battalion went to Souk Ahras. The
First Battalion went to Bougie (now Bejaïa).

The Sixtieth Infantry was detailed for guard duty in Algeria. Sergeant
Thornton had gotten the rank to go with his new job in Company M as platoon sergeant. Now, on January 31, 1943, Staff Sergeant Thornton was alerted
to get ready to move out. The platoon packed up and marched to Port Lyautey.
At the railroad station the soldiers boarded a train, thirty men to a boxcar
(40 *hommes ou* 8 *chevaux*). They were moved by train to Oran, to relieve the
135th Infantry on guard.

The Forty-second Infantry was committed for the Tunisian battle.

The Thirty-fourth Infantry Division moved up to prepare to fight.

On January 21, 1943, the Third Battalion of the First Armored Division arrived at Sbeitla, Tunisia, and moved into an olive grove to bivouac. This
completed the force of Combat Command A under Brig. Gen. Raymond E.
McQuillin. The units were the First and Third battalions of the Sixth Armored Infantry Regiment.

The first move was made by the Germans. They attacked Faid Pass, 130
miles to the southeast, where a French garrison was in place. The French
called for help, and General McQuillin sent his reconnaissance company
toward the pass.

That afternoon the Luftwaffe attacked the column on the road. Pvt. Peter Torgerson was killed and Pvt. Donald Mertens was wounded. A little
later the column was attacked by American A-20 attack bombers and P-39
fighters. Fortunately the American aim was not as good as the German. No
casualties.

The air attacks, particularly by the Americans, caused a lot of confusion
in the column, and General McQuillin put off the attack on the Germans
until the following day.

Company H then assembled at Lessouda, 7 miles from Faid village. That
night Capt. James Stepro, commander of Company H, went around to buck

up the men. "Remember to keep your heads down," he said. "Just keep those heads down." At 6 a.m. the company began to move. Four German planes attacked, coming in low out of Faid Pass. Sgt. William Treter of the Third Platoon shot one down with the .50-caliber machine gun on his tank.

The troops moved on, not knowing that the Germans—those canny Germans of the Afrika Korps, so long engaged in this sort of warfare—were laying a trap for them.

The Germans had moved eighteen tanks into defilade positions on the banks beside the pass. They also had dug in antitank guns, machine guns, and mortars. Not only had they made the best use of the terrain, but the geography was in their favor, as well. The Americans were attacking from west to east, and the bright morning sun was in their eyes.

The three platoons of Sherman M-4 tanks began to move. The Germans began firing, and Stuka dive-bombers joined the action. When the American tanks were in range, the Germans increased their fire. Soon ten of the U.S. tanks were disabled. Eight stopped and began to burn. Lt. Gilder S. Horne's tank was stopped, but continued to fire. Then flames shot out of the turret, and the gun quit firing.

By 11 a.m. the American tanks that were not burning were in retreat, stopping to pick up the survivors of the shot-up tanks. Even the retreat was ragged. Lt. Laurence Robertson's tank backed into a wadi that turned out to be wet, and it bogged down in the mud. The German gunners found the stuck tank and soon set it afire.

When the survivors finally stopped, they counted noses. Three men had been killed in action; three men were missing, from Horne's tank; and four other men were wounded, including Horne's driver. T/4 Elmer Farmer and bow gunner Pfc. Edward L. Stieren were the only men in Horne's tank to escape. They had been trapped at first because the turret had been swung around and the radio bulge in the back kept them from opening their hatches. The tank burned. It looked like it was about to explode. Then another German shell hit the tank, shearing off the hatch. It wounded Farmer, but both men were then able to escape the burning vehicle.

On the night of January 31 Company H received new tanks. The next day it attacked again, with the infantry. Once again the attack was a failure. The new toll: six men dead, four wounded, and eleven tanks gone. The men in the American armored divisions had boasted that their Sherman M-4 tanks were the best in the world. Now they knew better, and they knew that the German 88-millimeter gun was more than a match for the American 75-millimeter.

They had about two weeks to think it over. The company was sitting in a cactus patch east of Sidi-bou Zid, dug in so that only the turrets stuck up above ground. It had fifteen tanks now.

The Arabs, who moved back and forth between German and Allied lines, retailing everything from eggs to intelligence, told the Americans of a powerful new German tank. "Sure," said the GIs, "sure."

Valentine's day, February 14, 1943: The Germans launched a new attack at dawn. The tank battalion was spread out, too little and too scattered; the Germans moved straight up toward Faid Pass, and then split into three forces. At 7:30 a.m. they engaged the ten tanks of Company I and Company H. The Luftwaffe came in, too. Sgt. Robert G. Von Staden, a tank commander, counted eighty—yes, eighty—German tanks moving southwest around Djebel Lessouda. Most were Mark IV, but several were the new Mark VI Tiger tanks with their 88-millimeter guns. The 88s began firing before the Germans came within range of the American 75s. There was just no way the American tanks could match up, and they were pushed into retreat again. More tanks were lost, three from the Third Platoon alone.

The retreat would have been a rout had the Germans known the extent of their victory and followed, but they stopped and the Americans continued to retreat to the west. The results: 44 tanks and 4 half-tracks had been lost; 6 men from the battalion had been killed; 22 were wounded; and 136 were missing! Captain Stepro, the commander of Company H, was one of those killed, and most of his crew had been captured. That night the men of Company H laughed at the gallows humor: an 88 shell had blown off Stepro's head—*Stepro*, the man who kept telling everyone to keep his head down.

The battalion had taken a tremendous beating: G Company lost all but two tanks; H Company lost all but five (of fifteen); I Company lost all but three. In Company H's Second Platoon, only Von Staden's and Lieutenant Hillenmyer's tanks survived.

The Third Battalion of the First Armored Regiment was out of action. Next day, the men of the Third watched the continuation of the battle: they saw the Second Battalion of their regiment annihilated.

The American tanks moved south along the road toward Sidi-bou Zid, and the Germans slaughtered them. The attack began at 1 p.m. Four hours later the whole battalion was wiped out: 313 men were missing in action; of 50 tanks only 4 survived; and the commanding officer, Lt. Col. James D. Alger, was a prisoner of war.

The Germans could have walked right through the remnants of the Third Battalion, as every dogface there knew, but for some reason they did not.

February 16: All was quiet. The Americans began to withdraw, and the Germans followed. The American withdrawal became a panic, units breaking up as individual vehicles rushed to the rear. The Germans staged a night attack, lighted by flares, and more Americans panicked and deserted the field. But Company H, fighting a rearguard action, held. That night some M-3 tanks were brought up. What good they would do against 88s was extremely questionable, but the addition was comforting. The Americans moved back to new positions north of Sbeitla.

On the night of the seventeenth the British sent up troops to try to stop the American disaster. But the Americans moved on back until their forward positions were 12 miles south of Tebessa.

Not only the Americans but also the French had taken a terrific beating from the Germans, who mopped them up, destroying eighteen battalions. General Fredendall's first move, an attack on Maknassy, did not succeed. Another attack on Faid failed. General Anderson then withdrew the Allied forces "to compress the lines." That meant evacuating Gafsa. Once again the Americans were learning that the German panzer equipment was superior to the Sherman tank. About 120 tanks had been lost in this series of actions, plus guns, howitzers, and half-tracks; about 2000 Americans had been captured by the Germans. The First Armored Division's Combat Command B was virtually knocked out. General Fredendall had tried to get reinforcements from General Anderson, but General Anderson had not sent them until the Americans were in a rout. This cooperative venture did not seem to be working out very well.

The Americans had been entrusted to hold Kasserine Pass and they had failed. General Fredendall had not instilled in his men any confidence, and the morale of the troops was dreadful. The Americans were learning almost too fast; they discovered in a hurry that their M-3 Sherman was *totally* ineffective against German armor. The M-4 with its 75-millimeter gun was better, but the tankers were so dispirited that many did not believe in even the limited capabilities of their vehicles. The 75-millimeter half-track was no match for a German 88-millimeter gun, nor was the 37-millimeter antitank gun effective against German armor.

The airfields at Thelepte, where the paratroops' abortive mission against the bridge at El Djem had begun, had now fallen into German hands.

Fredendall did not know it yet, but he was through, and on his way to a training command where, as Ike's staff said so sweetly, "his fine qualities, particularly for training, would not be lost to the army." *Those as can, does; those as can't, teaches.* At that moment the emergency was such that there was no time to sort out the matter, and immediate relief of Fredendall might have made matters worse. So General Eisenhower called on General Harmon, commander of the Second Armored Division, to go up front "to advise." Harmon went up front and took command temporarily.

February 17, 1943: The Ninth Division artillery was preparing to hold maneuvers in the desert south of Tlemcen. At 10:30 in the morning the phones were ringing. The artillery was needed up front, in the Tebessa area. The Germans had broken through and were threatening the enormous supply dumps that had been established there for the coming Allied offensive in Tunisia.

It was snowing. The snow changed to rain. At 4 p.m. the artillery caravan pulled out: the Thirty-fourth Field Artillery, the Sixtieth Field Artillery, the Sixtieth Cannon Company, as well as the Headquarters Battery of Divarty. They would pick up the Eighty-fourth Field Artillery and the Forty-seventh Cannon Company. Ahead of them: a march of 777 miles. On they went, through Sidi-bel-Abbès, Orléansville, Affreville, l'Arba, Sétif, and on to Aïn-Beïda. After they had reached the mountains, casualties began. The road was narrow and slippery with hairpin turns. Some vehicles slipped off or stuck in the mud of the road shoulders. They were abandoned and the columns went on.

On February 20 the Germans made their first move through Kasserine Pass toward Thala. Field Marshal Rommel came up personally to lead this probe.

February 21: The Ninth Infantry Division artillery reached Aïn-Beïda, where the Americans were stopped by the British. No one knew what was happening up front. Perhaps Rommel had captured Tebessa already.

At noon the Ninth Division artillery was ordered on, through Tebessa, to Thala. There the Americans had to stop the Germans. The road was clogged by ambulances, vehicles, and retreating troops who told them it was no use. They'd better move back while the going was good.

But the Ninth Division artillery had its orders: hold Thala at all costs.

Up front were the remnants of three platoons of British infantry and three platoons of HM Leicestershire Yeomanry with twenty-four British tanks. Coming up were three battalions of German infantry supported by forty tanks. The British and Americans were 3 miles south of Thala. The enemy was 2500 yards away, which meant almost flat trajectory firing.

February 22: At 7 a.m. the Germans opened a tank attack up the Thala defile supported by artillery fire and Stuka dive-bombers. Battery C of the Eighty-fourth Field Artillery was moved forward. Its 105s were lowered and used as antitank guns. The Germans had never before encountered 105-millimeter antitank guns. Two guns were hit, but the battery continued to fire. So did the others. And they stopped the German armor cold.

The battle lasted all day long.

Combat Command B, that unlucky First Armored Division unit, counterattacked against the retreating Germans. But the Americans could not go very far. There was nothing behind them to support them. B-17s bombed the Germans as they went, not very effectively. But the Twenty-first Panzer Division drive on Tebessa had been stopped at Gafsa, which had earlier belonged to the Americans.

The problem of the Germans was really consolidation, for the British were pressing Rommel very hard in Libya and the Germans were retreating into Tunisia.

The major result of the loss of the battle of Kasserine Pass was the official relief of General Fredendall. General Patton, who was preparing for the invasion of Sicily, took over the Second Corps temporarily. And the changes reverberated all the way back to Camp Carrabelle, Florida, where Sergeant Chattaway's Twenty-eighth Division was training. Overnight the division lost its commander, General Bradley, who was ordered to Algiers as a sort of utility infielder. Before he got there, the situation in Tunisia grew so much worse that he was immediately assigned as General Patton's assistant in command of the Second Corps.

The war, as far as the Americans were concerned, was not going very well. But what could they expect? They were brand new at the war business, while the Germans and British had been at it for more than three years. At least what they were learning in north Africa the hard way could be transmitted to the troops back home, such as the Third Armored Division, in training at Indiantown Gap. The shock of the defeat at Kasserine Pass resounded through that division. General Rommel had impressed the Americans mightily with his use of armor. Half a dozen more U.S. armored divisions were to be developed.

*

There was not much left of the First Armored Regiment. What was left was reorganized temporarily into the Twenty-third Provisional Medium Tank Battalion. When the action ended, the Third Battalion was reconstituted and Maj. Lydon Cole became the new commander. The whole battalion had to be rebuilt. From the Second Armored Division, the First Armored got 2000 GIs; Company H had its share. Also, from Camp Campbell, Kentucky, 4000 "armored" dogfaces were about to be sent to Tunisia.

February: The Thirtieth Infantry Division arrived in England and moved to the Beaconsfield area. Tents on one side of the road. Twenty-five-mile hikes. On both his heels Private Inglis had blisters as big as half-dollars. The regimental surgeon warned the regimental commander that the men couldn't take much more. The pressure diminished a little. At night, the German bombers came over, and many an hour was spent in a slit trench, a slit trench usually three-quarters full of water and one-quarter full of soldiers.

February: Chief Petty Officer Porter's Thirty-fourth Naval Construction Battalion was aboard the cargo vessels *Alco Pennant* and *Island Mail*, on the broad Pacific Ocean, bound for Florida Island in the Solomon chain. North Africa and the European theater of operations were the furthest things from the Seabees' minds. They arrived, set up camp, and immediately began construction of a PBY seaplane base for Admiral Halsey. Out of that base the Americans would fly "Black Cat" night search planes against the Japanese who held the northern and central Solomons.

Back in England at the Fifth Corps Lieutenant Colonel Campbell continued to travel around, pulling together the odds and ends of corps planning. He did a good deal of sightseeing in Edinburgh, Glasgow, Salisbury, and London. He had a fine curiosity, which included art museums, streetcars, and Lloyd's Insurance Company, and the time to gratify it on a week's leave in January. Shortly after he returned to corps duties, he had the bad news that he was being replaced as G-3 by Colonel Schmidt, a regular army officer. That was the sort of thing a reserve officer had to live with. He was gratified to be promoted to "bird colonel" and then given the post of provost marshal of the Fifth Corps. That gave him more time to indulge in social life, and a specific as opposed to a general responsibility. Or so he believed. But then new problems kept cropping up: a conference on bomb disposal, another on traffic signs, appointment to the G-2 planning board. He was involved in a myriad of details regarding the melding of British and American military ways in this complex joint enterprise of the invasion of Fortress Europe.

The Twenty-ninth Division was still in training in England. The Twenty-ninth Provisional Ranger Battalion was learning the ropes with the British Number 4 Commando. Sergeant Ogden participated in three raids on the Norwegian coast. The first raid was a washout when the Americans ran into superior German forces while trying to destroy a bridge. They were chased back to the PT boats, which took them home. The second raid was a three-day reconnaissance of a harbor. The third raid was to destroy a German command post, but when the men of the Twenty-ninth Rangers arrived, they found no Germans. The command post had been moved. So back they went to Tidworth Barracks to train.

The brass then decided the rangers were a nuisance, and the unit was broken up. Sergeant Ogden was sent back to the 229th Field Artillery Battalion at Torquay, not far from Plymouth. The battalion trained. Sergeant Ogden was assigned to an artillery spotting section and was issued a 30-power spotting telescope. One day Ogden took a half-dozen men on a scouting mission. They came to a cliff overlooking a river, about 50 yards straight down below. There they saw some twenty girls skinny-dipping in the river. They were British WAVEs. Sergeant Ogden and his detachment spent two lovely hours on their cliff, watching. Their only disappointment was that when they got back to camp, they couldn't brag. They would have been court-martialed. *Vive les WAVEs!*

Private Emert's Company D of the 116th Infantry and Staff Sergeant Elburn's 115th Infantry were also training, the latter regiment having been separated into small units for that training.

March 1: The Sixtieth Infantry was committed to action in the Tebessa area. Staff Sergeant Thornton's Company M moved up and took up defensive positions. Part of the company was attached to Company K for defense, and part to Company L, including a section of heavy machine guns. The men were dug in, the guns surrounded by barbed-wire entanglements, and ready for the Germans to drive on Tebessa. But the Germans did not come. On March 9 Company M moved forward to a position near Thelepte. Still nothing.

*

In Alguis Colonel Caffey of the Twentieth Engineer Regiment was training
his troops for battle. Bayonet drill. A mile around the racetrack every morning, running in step. General Patton, who lived across the street from the
Twentieth's headquarters, came over to watch. The guard would not let him
through the barbed wire around the area, and made him go two blocks to the
entrance.

Colonel Caffey was certainly getting the men ready. Company officers
developed their lungs by counting cadence. The local Arabs were startled to
see the men of the Twentieth conducting assault exercises on the beach with
small-arms fire, demolitions, flamethrowers, pooled company half-tracks,
heavy weapons, and weapons squads to make a powerful striking force. They
were becoming an extraordinarily well-trained body of infantry.

The colonel loved effect. Lieutenant Miller was made the regimental demolition expert with the responsibility of devising new ways to use huge quantities of explosives on the beach to make the training exercises ever more
spectacular.

What do combat engineers do?

Colonel Caffey hadn't a clue. A few of the officers learned something
about German mines, but they were in the minority and their information
was very hazy. Nobody had bothered to find out what those British sappers
did for a living.

Colonel Caffey was always himself. Every time a GI came in late from a
pass or got too drunk, a court-martial was convened. The regiment had to
put up its own stockade. The miscreants spent their days marching at attention through the sand dunes down to the beach, filling sandbags, and
carrying them on their shoulders to add to the strength and glory of the sand
dunes.

But the excitement at Kasserine Pass changed everything; the Germans
were using land mines. What was needed was a well-trained engineer outfit
up front. The call went out for the Twentieth Engineers to head into combat.
On Sunday, March 14, the men of the Twentieth Engineers tore down their
Hippodrome city, leveled it to the ground, and got rid of the wire. All night
they loaded their vehicles. The colonel insisted on taking his stockade with
him, so a truck was equipped with a wire cage. At dawn on March 15 the
Twentieth Engineers tore out of Casablanca to move 1100 miles across the
top of French north Africa, across the Atlas Mountains, to Meknes, Fez, and
finally into Tebessa. They arrived dirty, bone-tired, and hungry. There, Colo-

nel Caffey assembled the officers and NCOs for one of his blood and thunder speeches.

Next day the officers and men learned what they were supposed to do. They were issued mine detectors and told that mine clearance would be one of their main jobs. There was a lot of searching for engineering field manuals that night. Fortunately for Lieutenant Miller, he had picked up a certain amount of information from the British in Casablanca regarding mines and booby traps.

The colonel now adopted the mine with the same enthusiasm he had recently devoted to the bayonet. Each battalion was ordered to lay a belt of mines around its bivouac area. Woe to the drunks and the innocent jackasses! Then, security ensured, the Twentieth Engineers started work on the roads. The Bekkaria-Thelepte-Sbeitla road was first; it had become the major supply road for the Second Corps. Lieutenant Miller's B Company built roads and culverts, filled holes, and dug ditches. C Company went down to Sbeitla to get road material from the debris of the battle. Digging in the debris, they ran into a field of old German S mines. One man was killed and eight men were wounded.

So, in the spring of 1943, the men of the Twentieth Engineers knew, even if their colonel didn't, what combat engineers did and what was likely to happen to them. They were no longer "rear echelon."

*   *   *

Into the battle for Tunisia now came General Bradley like a breath of fresh air from America. He had arrived in Algiers just after the debacle at Kasserine Pass had ended with the withdrawal of the German forces to face the British threat from the southeast on the Mareth line. At the moment of Bradley's arrival, Ike had not yet finally decided to really relieve Fredendall. His instructions to Bradley at the end of February were to go to the front and come back with a report. Like just about everybody else in the army, Eisenhower trusted and respected Omar Bradley's brains and sensibility. He had emphasized the fact that he was not looking for a "goat." There were plenty to share the blame, from the intelligence officers who had predicted a German attack in the wrong place, to the commanders in Kasserine Pass who had put their troops on the road and shoulders and not on the commanding mountains, to the brass in Algiers. Eisenhower wanted Kasserine to be a learning experience, not a breast-beating.

There were plenty of difficulties with Eisenhower's political management of the north African campaign. Among them were the continuing media and public reverberations after Darlan's death. But the GIs knew little and cared less about that. What Eisenhower knew, and what General Marshall knew, was that Ike would stand or fall in his command on the outcome of the North African campaign. That did involve the GIs very personally.

So in February, as the fighting continued, General Bradley went into the line as Ike's personal representative, a job that demanded all his considerable tact. He discovered that the major American problem was inexperience all the way down the line. But in the process of learning the dogfaces had lost confidence in their officers. And the senior officers, virtually all of them, Bradley found, had lost confidence in General Fredendall. When Eisenhower appeared at Tebessa on March 5, Bradley was forced to admit this to him. It had to be the kiss of death for poor Fredendall. War is a merciless master, and while error sometimes could be forgiven and forgotten, it could not if it had occasioned a loss of confidence. What was needed, Eisenhower saw, was an injection of spirit. Thus came the call to General Patton to stop his planning for Sicily and take over the Second Corps. If anybody could lift up the Second Corps, it was "Old Blood and Guts," one of the most spectacular soldiers of the U.S. Army.

What lay ahead was heralded by the manner in which Patton took command of the Second Corps.

On the morning of March 7, sirens wailing, a parade of armored cars and half-tracks moved into the square opposite Second Corps headquarters at Djebel Kouif, about equidistant between Tebessa and Thala. In the back of the leading car stood General Patton, upright as Caesar, jaw jutting out against the leather strap of the steel helmet on his head, necktie on his neck, and pistol at his hip. He was every inch the commander.

Immediately, the corps was shocked (this was Patton's ploy) by orders that everyone was to wear helmet, leggings, and necktie. A system of fines was set up to enforce the rules.

The dogfaces bitched, but they conformed. Everybody conformed, even the nurses in the hospitals and the mechanics swearing under the 2½-ton trucks. But something else very good came with Patton, and that was Bradley, already known wherever he had trod as "the soldiers' general." Patton demanded, and got, the services of General Bradley as his deputy.

The Germans had withdrawn from Kasserine Pass after the spectacular defense by the U.S. Ninth Division artillery and the British Sixth Armoured

Division. The Afrika Korps had pulled back because Gen. Bernard Montgomery had made a feint along the Mareth line on the other side of Tunisia.
Rommel had then drawn his panzer divisions from the high-water mark of
Thala back to the Mareth line. The pressure was off the Second Corps, and
there was time to plan an attack. The Americans and the British now were
able to play the Axis forces like a yo-yo; if the Germans attacked at the
Mareth line, the Allies would attack in the Kasserine area, and vice versa.

Thus was born the diversionary offensive by General Patton at El Guettar
and Maknassy. His plans were already made by the time he arrived at the
Second Corps:

The First and Ninth Infantry divisions were to move down the road from
Gafsa through the mountains in the El Guettar region. This was the key to
the offensive, because the Gafsa-Gabès road was the main route of supply
for the Axis Mareth line.

The First Armored Division would sweep down through Kasserine Pass
to Maknassy. The Thirty-fourth Infantry Division was to move down to Sbeitla
and cut back toward Foudouk, in a diversionary and holding action.

Having shocked everyone with his uniform regulations, and gotten their
attention, General Patton then called a conference of division commanders.
He briefed them on the night of March 15.

"Gentlemen, tomorrow we attack. If we are not victorious, let no one
come back alive."

With that Patton left the room.

The offensive began on the night of March 16. The First Division marched
into Gafsa to discover that the Italians who had been holding the place since
the battle of Kasserine Pass had disappeared. They had withdrawn down the
Gabès road to the hills beyond El Guettar. There, however, they had been
joined by German reinforcements, and a defensive line had been established.

On March 17 the Sixtieth Infantry Regiment moved to new positions near
Gafsa. The regiment was now completely motorized but also bogged down in
red muck a foot deep in the bivouac area. The vehicles stuck in the mud
and had to be pulled out.

On March 19 Company M was ordered to prepare for a dawn attack the
next day. The movement was to be across country by foot to the assembly
area. The objective was Maknassy Pass.

Early on the morning of March 20 the heavy weapons platoons of Company M were attached to the various rifle companies for action. The attack

kicked off at 7:30 in the morning on the pass running east and leading to Maknassy. The enemy positions were weak, and the company did not suffer any losses that day.

The regiment was on the move, but mostly by night, since it was attacked frequently and fiercely by German aircraft during the day. By the night of March 22 the Third Battalion had nearly reached the mouth of Maknassy Pass, and still Company M had had no casualties.

But here at Maknassy Pass it was a different story. On the twenty-third the fighting was very heavy. Company M went into position in support of the battalion, which was designated to capture and hold the high ground at the pass. Resistance was heavy. Casualties began to come in. Staff Sergeant Overdahl was wounded. So were Pfc. Englese, Pfc. Horton, and privates Rosero, Clary, and Clay. Pfc. Seibert and Pfc. Battaglia were killed.

The next day Company M sent out a recon patrol to find out where the enemy's heavy machine guns and mortars were located. The patrol found out, at the expense of three more casualties: Pfc. Denham, Pfc. Rucker, and Private Janolis.

Here is an excerpt from Staff Sergeant Thornton's diary:

March 25: Fighting again was heavy, our positions again heavily shelled by the enemy. Battle casualties Pfc. Aquafredda and Private Bolles. We were relieved that night by the Sixth Infantry.

March 26: Corporal Clifford missing in action. Morale quite low. Corporal Apuntius and Private Cardorick breaking down from nervous strain due to shell shock. Evacuated to hospital. Company reorganized in bivouac area 3 miles to rear of Maknassy.

March 27: Corporal Wisniewaki, Private Walflau may be evacuated to hospital due to nervous strain. Morale again coming up to normal after a good rest and mail call. Company was alerted to move into position to prevent breakthrough of the enemy.

Gafsa is where Lieutenant Downing found the command post of the Eighteenth Infantry. Downing had spent several weeks in the British general hospital in Algiers; he was discharged in March and then had to make his way back to his outfit. This, alone, was quite an accomplishment. All he knew as he stepped out of the hospital with his mimeographed orders was that there was fighting down around Kasserine Pass. He figured the Eighteenth was in it. So that's where he would go. He was traveling with Lieutenant

Mondscheim of the 168th Infantry of the Thirty-fourth Division, who had been inconsiderately shot in the buttocks at Kasserine Pass.

They got a ride to the airport, where they boarded a C-47 carrying cargo to Tlergma airport near Constantine. That city, they found, was the headquarters of the embryo Fifth Army, so they went there. At least there was a situation map in the G-1 section, and they located their divisions, both near Tebessa. A British convoy left every day for Tebessa, just like a bus service, and they each caught a ride in the passenger seat of a truck, next to the driver. They drove all day. When night came, Downing's driver turned on his lights, and so did all the other drivers in the convoy. Lieutenant Downing expressed surprise.

"We get more dustups from driving in the dark than from Messerschmitts," said the driver. But higher authority obviously did not agree. They passed through a village, and were stopped by an MP who ordered every driver to switch off his lights. Thereafter they drove in the dark. They drove on after midnight, stopped for a few hours' sleep (Lieutenant Downing had the cab but no blankets), and at dawn gathered around a fire, drank coffee, and ate cold C-ration stew. Downing looked around and realized they had reached the ration dump. He and Mondscheim conferred. They could see a cluster of mud and brick buildings off to the east. Tebessa.

The convoy commander lent them his jeep and driver to take them to town with their barracks bags. In town they found the MP headquarters; the lieutenant in charge, who was shaving as they came in, lent them his own jeep, which took them to a replacement battalion outside town. There they filled out forms and went to the officers' quarters, a pyramidal tent with a dirt floor. They went to the supply tent and each drew three blankets, mess gear, and M-1 rifle, ammunition, belt, and a first aid pouch and packet. At the pyramidal tent they learned from four other officers, all replacements, that it was a long wait to be assigned to an outfit. All the others had been there for several weeks. So they settled down. They cleaned their rifles, shaved, and slept on their new blankets. They had lunch: mashed dehydrated potatoes, Spam, beans, biscuits, canned peaches, and coffee. Very good. They could stand some more of that. Finally they reported to replacement battalion headquarters.

"Good," said the major, "we'll get you back tomorrow."

Some long stay! Downing and Mondscheim had bought some wine in Constantine. They pulled it out and with their four new friends finished it off.

Next morning, Downing and Mondscheim parted company. Downing got into the back of a deuce-and-a-half with ten other casuals from First Division. It was a sunny, cool day. The top of the truck had been rolled back, so they could watch the scenery. All of them were subdued, all deep in their own thoughts. Downing was wondering: What would happen now that he was going back into combat?

They reached Mines bou Kadra, rear-echelon headquarters of the First Division. Downing found the personnel section of the Eighteenth Infantry and reported in. Captain Worthley, the adjutant, recognized him and said he was glad to see him back. The captain was going up front in a few days, just as soon as things quieted down. Just now there was no movement because the regiment was engaged in fighting at Gafsa and El Guettar.

There was plenty of change, now that Patton had taken over, the captain said. First, Downing had to get a necktie. Patton's orders. Second, he had to wear his helmet at all times. More Patton's orders. And leggings. Ditto. No kidding, either. "Patton's gestapo," the Second Corps MPs, were real bastards about the regulations. Also, Downing saw that officers wore the insignia of their rank painted on their helmets, so he went to the infirmary, got a piece of tape, and made a first lieutenant's bar out of it.

Downing then went to headquarters and found the pile of baggage of missing men. He discovered his suitcase. His bedroll and his precious air mattress were gone. (He found them later.) He got himself issued a new bedroll, but the air mattress was only to be lamented at the time.

One of the clerks remembered the lieutenant's name. He dug around in the rear of the office and found Downing's musette bag. Downing opened it. Inside were his cigarettes, shaving articles, writing paper, and the hand grenade he had been issued aboard the *Tegelberg*. He showed that to the clerk.

"Migawd," said the clerk, "we've been tossing that bag around for months."

Imagine that! They'd been carrying his baggage all this way and never even looked at it. What if it had fallen into the hands of the real rear-echelon enemy?

Waiting, Lieutenant Downing began to learn some of the new ropes of combat. He learned about the S mine, the "Bouncing Betsy" of the Germans. An artillery captain who had been wounded in the arm by one told him how they worked: when struck, they jumped into the air about 3 feet and then exploded, sending hundreds of pellets in all directions.

Several days passed. Lieutenant Downing settled down. He got a Frenchwoman nearby to do his laundry. He found Private Fanning and Sergeant

Paddington from F Company, and they traded gossip. He told them of the glories of Algiers, where the pretty girls cost a thousand francs a night and so were out of reach of company grade personnel. They told him of the casualties in F Company.

About four days later Captain Worthley announced that the fighting had subsided and the regiment was coming out of action. The troops would leave the next morning for El Guettar.

"But you'll have to have a physical before I can take you."

"Where?"

"Casual detachment."

Downing went to the casual detachment and got the papers. He found the medical officer. The lieutenant's left knee was still swollen twice as large as the right one, and had water in it. He limped.

"What happened to you?" asked the doc.

Downing told him. The medical officer did not seem very interested.

"How do you feel?"

"Fine."

"Okay, here's your clearance."

Downing went to the French lady's house and picked up his washing. It was damp and wrinkled, but it was clean. He packed his hand baggage and put his suitcase back into the pile at personnel.

He was going back to the war.

Downing and Worthley drove rapidly along the road to El Guettar. It was cold in the morning but the sun soon heated up the day. They came down out of the hills into the plain that would lead to the Sahara Desert. By noon it was hot enough to take off the combat jacket—but not the necktie. And they ate C rations, of course.

As they drove on, the plain was cut with deep wadis, gulleys that ran like rivers in the wet season but were now dry and lifeless. They passed some Arabs with donkeys, but more with camels. They passed a field where a herd of camels was grazing.

Then the two officers began to see evidence of the war. Burned-out trucks: American, British, German. Pieces of airplanes. Solitary graves, with either the Roman cross of the Americans and British or the Maltese cross of the Germans. Piles of empty shell cases. Demolished bridges, shell holes, bomb craters. Dead horses—bloated, and busted out of their skins. Abandoned field wire. Small mounds of Teller mines.

They came to a village of sun-dried mud houses; it was Gafsa. Head-quarters was in a palm grove oasis just outside town. Downing checked in and was assigned to a junior officers' tent.

He went to F Company. Lieutenant Spinney was now commanding officer. Still a first lieutenant.

"Getting an increase in rank in the First Division is about as easy as getting admitted to King Arthur's Round Table."

Sergeant Merrill came in from having taken a shower in Gafsa.

"What happened to your nose, Lieutenant?"

"What do you mean?"

"It's all red. Accident or *vin rouge?*"

In Algiers Lieutenant Downing had bought a World War I French campaign ribbon for the sergeant. He delivered it. Sergeant Merrill reached into a pocket and pulled out a piece of velvet from a waterproof bag. Here were his ribbons: Army of Occupation of Germany (World War I), Purple Heart, Silver Star, American Defense Ribbon, ETO ribbon. He added the World War I French ribbon to the collection and put the packet back.

Sergeant Merrill. Fifty years old, ruptured, no upper teeth, and a hole in his head. Two wars, plenty of combat, and more to come. One each line company first sergeant.

Downing was "home" again.

After the Germans had retreated back through Kasserine Pass, the sector quieted down for a while. The Ninth Division had been drawn back into reserve position. General Eisenhower had decided that one of his aides, Lt. Craig Campbell, could use some seasoning with a line outfit, and so had sent him for a few weeks to the Ninth Division. Since the division was just then sitting around the Kasserine Pass area, having relieved troops of the First Division, it seemed more like a lark than anything else. Campbell went to Company E, Second Battalion, Forty-seventh Infantry. Then, without notice, the Forty-seventh was called into action on March 25.

The final drive to push the Axis forces out of Tunisia was on. Patton had put together an armored task force to drive toward the sea, an outfit commanded by Col. Clarence C. Benson. The armor was stuck for a while, but then began to move. The enemy retaliated with many air attacks. Patton complained about the lack of air support. Air Marshal Sir Arthur Coningham radioed an insulting reply, denigrating the Americans. Patton screamed like a wounded eagle to Eisenhower and the insult was withdrawn, but the memory lived on. The British had just acquired what ultimately might be regarded as one of their most effective enemies of the war. Thereafter, Patton's feeling about the British (often expressed) was that the world would be better off if their armies were all pushed into the sea.

The Patton case was the extreme. But on a command level the relations between the British and the Americans were extremely touchy. And at this point of the war the Americans were demanding a role of equality the British did not seem very eager to give them. In this final drive against the Germans the British wanted to squeeze out the U.S. Second Corps and bring the British First Army and the British Eighth Army together at Tunis.

The Forty-seventh Infantry moved up to El Guettar, relieving the Eighteenth Infantry, just as Lieutenant Downing was going back to his regiment.

The men of the Forty-seventh moved into positions 6 miles southeast of the town, and battalion commanders ordered reconnaissance of the hills on the night of March 27. The attack was set for 3:30 the next morning; First and Second battalions were to go, with the Third Battalion in reserve.

It was Sunday morning. The Second Battalion moved out first. Almost immediately Company E was caught in crossfire by German machine guns and pinned down. Company G tried to move in on the flank, but the German positions were too strong. Soon Companies F, G, and H were also pinned down. The problem was a total misestimation of enemy strength, which was more than three times as great as expected. Lt. Col. Louis Gershenow, the Second Battalion commander, was captured. So was the S-2, Lieutenant Duckworth, the man who had led the "pathfinders" in by rubber boat to Safi harbor to plant that infrared light. So was the Company E commander, Captain Ben K. Humphrey, who had been wounded in the leg.

For E Company the fight was a real disaster. The company lost 5 officers and 174 enlisted men. Company G lost one officer and thirty men. Company F's commander, Capt. Francis M. Smith, as well as his exec and five enlisted men, had been killed or captured. H Company's Capt. Horace M. Spaulding had been captured. So had Lt. Craig Campbell, General Eisenhower's aide.

By the time the fight ended and the remnants of the battalion moved back, regiment was aware of the real strength of its enemy. The First Battalion attacked, under German machine gun, mortar, and artillery fire. Company A was hit hard but managed to reach Hill 369, the objective. The Third Platoon got separated and was attacked by a large force of Germans. The platoon counterattacked with bayonets, killing four Germans and forcing the others to retreat off the hill.

Casualties continued all day. Lt. Col. John B. Evans, commander of the Third Battalion, was wounded and had to be evacuated. The commander of I Company, Capt. Richard I. Witner, was killed while leading his men. There was little further advance during the day.

On the second morning regiment ordered the establishment of a provisional battalion made up of men from G, L, F, and M companies. They moved against a hill at the front of the position, took it, were forced off by heavy artillery fire, got artillery support, took the hill again, and captured ninety-seven Italians.

After the battle was over, General Patton, who had great confidence in the American equipment, escorted British Gen. Sir Harold R. L. G. Alexander to the bivouac where Company H of the First Armored Regiment was slowly pulling itself together. Patton wanted to show off, and he began with the U.S. half-track. He brought General Alexander to a half-track that was being repaired by several GIs under the direction of Maintenance Sergeant Bob Bishop. Bishop was down on the ground, trying to put a new track on the right side. He heard General Patton telling the British general what a great vehicle the half-track was: its mobility was superb, its firepower was great, its armor would stop just about anything.

"Isn't that right, Sergeant?" asked General Patton.

"No, sir," said Sergeant Bishop, getting up. He walked around to the other side of the half-track, the generals following him, and he pointed up.

"You see this hole? One bullet from a strafer. One bullet, pierced the armor here, rattled around inside, and killed Private Torgerson. The men call it the 'Purple Heart Box,' sir."

General Patton turned pale and quickly escorted General Alexander somewhere else.

The First Armored Division spent much of the remainder of the Tunisian campaign in reserve. Company H was supposed to go into action at Maknassy Pass on March 23, but the action was called off by higher authority. Quite rightly the reentry of the First Armored Division into combat was delayed. The unit was pretty well shot, as even old Blood and Guts Patton finally had to understand.

Being in reserve did not mean you were not in a war. On March 25 Company H was on the plain northeast of Maknassy when a German air attack began. The men had moved their tanks into the wadis, and believed they were safe there. Stukas came down. Three men who had not been on guard suddenly dived under one tank to take cover. One of them was killed, and another was badly wounded in the hands. There was still a lot to be learned about when and where to take cover.

That was emphasized again on March 28, when Pvt. Raymond Kahl joined up from the "reppledepple." He was assigned to a tank in the Second Platoon, and set about learning his business. There was another shelling by the enemy. The turret of Kahl's tank was open, and he was in it. A fragment of shrapnel came in and caught him in the head. It was "taps" for Private Kahl. His fellow dogfaces of the platoon were so shaken by all that had happened to them that they would not move to reclaim his body until after dark.

In the Sixtieth Infantry sector Company M did not move out on March 28, but reconnaissance patrols went out on the left flank. That night at 7:30 the whole battalion moved up and relieved the First Battalion of the Sixth Infantry. The rest of the night was spent digging gun emplacements and getting ready for a fight.

At dawn on March 29 the battle was resumed. The Germans began shelling. One machine gun section captured eight German prisoners and turned them over to battalion. Two of the company's machine guns were knocked out by enemy artillery fire. The casualties began to climb: Corporal Schlacter, Pfc. Uiverito, and Pfc. Thornton were killed in action at the entrance to Maknassy Pass. No ground was gained that day.

The next day was a sort of respite, with heavy German shelling that did little damage because the Americans were dug in well. But morale was going down fast, until some GIs captured several German machine guns and turned them on the enemy. This raised morale for some reason—a sort of "we'll show you bastards something" attitude.

That afternoon the soldiers strung wire in front of their positions. A lull was in process. It lasted all day April 1, with the enemy shelling limited to mortars and action limited to patrols.

On April 5 the Twentieth Engineers were named Second Corps reserve and moved to Gafsa. Just in case the enemy should counterattack against the drive that had taken the Second Corps to El Guettar and Maknassy, the Twentieth would go into action.

Colonel Caffey was ecstatic. The regiment pulled into an olive grove in Gafsa in the middle of the night. The men camouflaged vehicles, dug fox-holes, and set up the "Caffey defense," with machine guns and 37-millimeter antitank guns bristling from every corner of their bivouac. When dawn came, they found themselves in the center of an American troop area. Every gun was pointed straight at some dogface's pup tent or some command post. Changes were made very quickly.

Colonel Caffey went to find General Patton and persuade him to put the Twentieth Engineers in the forefront of the next attack. The regiment sat at Gafsa in the sun of the south Tunisian desert and soaked up rest and sun-shine. Some men went swimming in the old Roman baths.

Colonel Caffey was unsuccessful, at least partly because Rommel was now in full retreat, and the Second Corps had linked up with the British Eighth Army. On April 8 the Twentieth Engineers moved back to Kasserine and began building roads again.

On April 15 General Bradley took over the Second Corps. He was now about to make one of the most masterful moves of the war: the assault on Bizerte, to give the people of America a taste of victory for a change. Lieu-tenant Miller's Twentieth Engineers were a part of this enormous troop move-ment, accomplished so slickly by General Bradley. On April 17 the troops started. They moved all night through the mountains, through Lacroix and LaCalle to Roum-es-Souk. There they spent a whole day repairing vehicles and listening to another of Colonel Caffey's blood-curdling speeches. On April 18 they moved to Djebel Abid. Their job was to make a real road out of this waterlogged trail to supply the imminent attack.

Four American divisions—the First, Ninth, Thirty-fourth, and First Armored—were assembled to drive on Bizerte. General Bradley made some remarkable innovations. Just like the British lorry driver who de-livered Lieutenant Downing to Tebessa, Bradley turned on the truck lights. There would be fewer losses to air attack than to accident, he said.

Second Corps moved on.

On April 24 B Company of the Twentieth Engineers was attached to the Corps Franc d'Afrique. B Company went ahead to clear the mines the Germans sowed so skillfully in their retreat. The French came next, and afterward the rest of the First Battalion, working to widen the road.

B Company had a hard job. The Germans had left Teller mines and S mines in the road and in all the paths that led away from it.

Still, all along the front the attack progressed.

16

ALLIED ATTACKS

Part of the Sixteenth Infantry, and particularly Company E of the Second Battalion, was in action near Robba-souk-Robba. One of the machine guns of Company E broke down—a damaged firing pin. The platoon sergeant told Corporal Moglia to go get another firing pin at battalion. That meant a half-mile run. Moglia got the pin and started back. On his way he was overtaken by a ¾-ton vehicle carrying General Roosevelt, a British general, and a French general.

"Hey, Moglia," General Roosevelt shouted, for he knew the corporal from days past.

"Who's winning this damn battle?"

"We are, sir."

"Who's we?"

"The First Division, sir. Nobody can beat the First Division, sir."

Roosevelt looked at the French general and the British general. "See? What did I tell you. These are the best damned soldiers that ever went into battle. They're unbeatable. Go get 'em corporal."

"Yessir. We will."

Whenever the action died down, the Arabs showed up—the ubiquitous Arabs. Dealing with them was always a problem, particularly for the Americans, who were not used to it. But they learned. Sometimes they learned the hard way.

One day Corporal Moglia bought a batch of pancakes that looked delectable, lightly browned, still warm, and covered with sugar. "Yum, yum," said the dogfaces of his platoon as they wolfed them down. "Yum, yum."

But half an hour later they were all puking and gasping, and after everything came up, they even had the dry heaves. The Arabs were found by the regimental MPs and interrogated with the help of the French liaison officer.

"Trying to poison our troops!"

"No, *effendi*. We are friends."

"Then why did these men get sick?"

"I do not know, *effendi*. We cooked the cakes in GI oil."

"Where did you get the oil?"

"Out of a tank, *effendi*. See, over here." He pointed to a knocked out Sherman tank on the side of the road.

Before the troops moved into Tunisia, they were issued mattress covers, two to a man. The covers were supposed to be used for mattresses—by stuffing straw into them—and for dirty clothes. There was another use, too, which the soldiers saw soon enough in battle. The graves registration people stuffed the bodies of dead GIs into mattress covers, sealed them up, and packed them into trucks for delivery to the "skull orchards" (temporary cemeteries).

But the real value of the mattress cover was in trading with the Arabs; the covers were bartered for eggs and dates and whatever the Arabs had that was fresh. The Arabs were wild for mattress covers; to them they were "garments," ready-made new outfits suitable for spring, fall, summer, or winter. All they had to do was cut an opening at the end for a head, cut two arm holes, and cut off the bottom, and *presto*, an Arab had a new suit.

In the battle zone the Arabs were detested by the brass, and particularly by the graves registration people. The locals would slip onto a battlefield and strip the bodies of everything, including dog tags. Thus the quartermaster graves registration troops sometimes didn't know if they were picking up Americans, Brits, Germans, or Italians. Down from on high came orders to shoot any Arabs on the battlefield on sight. But the dogfaces figured that once a guy was dead he was dead, and they would rather trade. Until the French gave them the word, that is.

A lot of those "Arabs" were really German or Italian agents, putting on a mattress cover to come and spy behind the Allied lines. How did the Americans know? They didn't speak German or Italian or French or Arabic. So the French policed the battle areas very closely. If they got hold of someone who didn't seem right, they gave him the business. If they didn't shoot him on the spot, they took him off for interrogation, which was worse. Run a wire to his penis and the other end to a battery-operated field telephone. Crank the handle and the victim had a hell of a shock. And afterward he was shot anyhow. Or she.

The Second Battalion was assigned to capture a rise called Connicle Hill. The Americans assaulted it and captured it, and immediately the Germans staged a counterattack and took it back. This happened several times.

At night the British, who were responsible for supply, brought hot meals up to the line. On the second night Corporal Moglia was sitting on the ground, eating. He noticed that the man next to him was wearing high black boots and a peaked cap. He couldn't recall what outfit that was, but it was obviously pretty special.

"Hey, buddy, I like those boots and that hat. What outfit are you from?"

"Austrian Alpine Troops."

"Austrian Alpine?" Are they on our side? Hell no! Here was a bloody Kraut.

"That's right," said the bloody Kraut in English again. He had made his way through the lines to surrender.

"Why didn't you say something—like *Kamerad?*"

"If I had, I would have gotten cold rations and been taken to the rear. This way I got a hot meal. Cold cans of stew?...I'm sick and tired of it."

Moglia knew what he meant. He, too, was sick of cold C rations. You see what it could do—make a man so disgusted he would surrender.

The Austrian alpiner got seconds, and then he was turned in to the MPs.

The fight for Connicle Hill went on against the Austrian alpiner's pals and their charges, the Italians. Very discouraging, both to the Germans and to the Allies. Up and down, up and down.

One afternoon, when noses were counted after E Company had been driven back down the hill, it was discovered that seven men were missing. They must have been captured by the Germans. The captain knew what to do. He reported to battalion, and battalion called for the Ghoum (*Ghoumier*) unit that was attached to the regiment. The Ghoums were French north African mounted troops, a mixed breed with dark, leathery skin, sharp black eyes, and beards. They didn't seem to be sunburned so much as sun-cured. From Moglia's experience with them they were very friendly, and smiling, and very courteous. But they had another side. They were paid a bonus by the French for killing "*les Boches et les Italiens.*" At some point a French officer had refused to believe a Ghoum report of the number of enemy soldiers dispatched, so the Ghoums had taken to bringing their victims' heads back with them. The sensitive British, concerned lest this practice be deleterious to POWs on the other side, suggested that the practice of head-hunting be curtailed.

Fine, said the Ghoums, from that point on they would bring back ears. And they did. The warriors returned on their beautiful horses from raids behind the enemy lines with strings of ears, either fresh or dried, depending on how long they had been out.

So the Ghoums came riding up to Company E's bivouac area that evening on their beautiful horses, escorted by an English-speaking French officer. They grinned and lay around smoking and drinking coffee and cadging cigarettes. Not a care in the world. The French officer called them to move out. They grinned at him and reached for more coffee. The French officer reached into his musette bag, pulled out a concussion grenade, and tossed it into the middle of the group. There was a huge bang and a spray of sand all over the place. The Ghoums got up slowly, got on their horses, and moved out.

The next day they returned with the seven former POWs of Company E and necklaces of ears. One of the guys told Moglia that the Ghoums had appeared out of nowhere the night before and in minutes had taken over the German camp on the other side of Connicle Hill. All the Germans were searched. The ones who had any American items—wristwatches, rings, cigarettes, rations—were the first to be dispatched and have their ears cut off, or vice versa. Then the rest were dealt with. A couple of Germans were left alive, minus ears, to spread the word about the Ghoums and their treatment of prisoners. That was the Ghoum way: always leave a couple of them alive to spread the word.

One night the men of E Company were all settled down snugly in their foxholes, keeping as warm as they could in the cold north African night, when Corporal Moglia heard voices. British voices.

"Shut up you guys. There are Jerries around here."

"Aha! So this is where the Yanks are! Put your gear down men, and build a fire."

Corporal Moglia was out of his foxhole in a flash.

"A fire? You guys are going to build a fire?"

"Of course, chum. We need boiling water for tea, don't we?"

Moglia was stunned. A fire on the front lines.

"You know there are Jerries in those hills up front?"

"How right you are, Yank. The deadly Boche. That's what we're here for. Tomorrow there will be no enemy in those hills."

"With all this noise and a fire, they'll probably start shooting at us any minute."

"Is that right, Yank? Shoot back at them then. You do have rifles?"

Moglia subsided into his foxhole, mumbling to himself: "You cocky bastards. You'll get your butts shot off when you attack those positions."

Strangely enough, although all the Americans expected hell to break loose, the Germans must have been more used to the British ways, for not a shot was fired; the fire blazed up brightly, and the British soldiers sat around and drank their tea and chatted. Moglia finally came out of his foxhole again; they gave him a cup of tea and told him they were of the Black Watch. He was impressed; the Black Watch was one of the most famous of the Scots units.

Eventually the Scots subsided and the fire burned out, and there was absolute quiet on the field.

Before dawn Moglia awoke, cold and cramped. He heard noises that meant troops moving out. There was no artillery barrage, not even any mortaring. There was no machine gun fire, only the sound of hobnailed boots on the gritty earth.

Then Corporal Moglia heard a voice call out:

"Fix bayonets!"

He heard the clinking sound of bayonets being attached to rifles. Then:

"Steady men. Forward!"

And—unbelievably—the squeal of bagpipes began, and off went the Black Watch in its charge up the hill. Moglia thought of all the old Errol Flynn movies he had seen. And in an hour the Black Watch had taken not only Connicle Hill, which had eluded the men of the Sixteenth for days, but the two hills on either side as well.

The First Armored Division's Company H was supporting the First Infantry Division in its drive down through the mountains. On the left was the First

Armored Division, then the First Infantry Division, and then the Thirty-fourth
Infantry Division. Hill 609 and Hill 523 stood on the sides of the line that
divided the attack zone of the First from that of the Thirty-fourth. On the
night of April 29 the First Battalion of the Sixteenth Infantry occupied Hill
523. But the next morning the Germans counterattacked and cut off that
battalion. Company H of the First Armored Regiment was given the job of
rescuing the beleaguered troops.

The Eighteenth had attacked further along the Gafsa-Gabès road, and the
fighting had been very stiff. After failing to move through the Kasserine Pass,
the Germans had holed up in the treeless mountains that jutted up 2000 feet
from the desert floor. From this position about a regiment of infantry and
about a hundred pieces of artillery protected the German main supply road
to the south, and to the rear of the Mareth line, where the Germans and
Italians were locked in battle with the British Eighth Army.

The Sixteenth Infantry was down there also, in different positions in the
El Guettar area. Corporal Moglia's Company E was down on the flat. He was
asleep in his foxhole, at dawn, when he was suddenly awakened by someone
shaking his shoulder. He looked up to see piercing black eyes staring at him
from a dark, bearded face. What a shock. But the man was smiling.

"Kaffay, kaffay," he was saying.

Moglia, soldierwise to the ways of Arab beggars, said he would look into
his pack to see if he had any instant coffee.

"No." The Ghoum pointed toward a group of men sitting around a fire.
"Come."

He led Corporal Moglia to the group, and the corporal smelled the scent
of coffee, fresh bread, and meat cooking. The Ghoums had made the bread
in a sand and rock oven. The meat was cooking over a fire, around which a
circular trench had been dug. Moglia sat down and put his feet into the trench,
as the others had done. It was nice and warm. Someone handed him a piece
of meat on a stick and said he could cook it more if he liked. He tasted it.
It tasted great. What was it? Goat.

They gave him coffee, and more goat, and fresh bread, and he filled his
belly. Before he left, he remembered: a few days earlier he had given two of
these men some of his rations and a couple of grenades. He went back to the
company area, glad that the Ghoums were on his side.

*

In the Sixtieth Infantry sector some of the men began to come back to Thornton's platoon from the hospital, having recovered from nervous shock. That helped morale. Corporal Clifford returned from being missing in action. That helped too. Staff Sergeant Thornton was feeling the tension now. But he hung on.

On April 4 Sergeant Kelly returned from the hospital, completely recovered from the shock he had received early in the battle.

All went well until the night of April 7, when the Germans laid down a heavy and accurate barrage on the battalion and company command posts, causing many casualties. The command posts were moved that night. The next day the Americans discovered that after the heavy shelling, or during it, the Germans had withdrawn. That day British Eighth Army troops moved up on both flanks of the Americans, and morale soared. This segment of the battle was over. On April 12 the regiment moved back to the Bou Chefka area and rest camp. That meant showers, new clothes, and reorganization of the companies. The shower, taken from under a GI can rigged up on the back of a truck, was the first Sergeant Thornton had taken since February 20. His uniform was so filthy that he dumped it into a bonfire with those of most of the other dogfaces.

They got clean uniforms, and then it was back into action, this time up north in the Djafied area. The regiment was going to move through the mountains to Bizerte. The movement was rapid and the pace grueling. The men were living on half a C ration a day, and filling their canteens from mountain streams they hoped were uncontaminated. The battalion advanced steadily for the next few days with no opposition. On April 26 it captured high ground overlooking the Oued Sedjarraanen. Here the Germans began shelling again and caused casualties, including the death of Private Schroder. On the twenty-eighth the American company was badly shelled and lost its first sergeant and a number of other men. The next day the battalion moved up a mountain, climbing all night, hit the top, and came under fire from snipers, again with heavy casualties. Two really rough days. Then the Germans retreated once again, and the Americans followed. It seemed to be a pattern which lasted until May 9, when the fighting ended. The Americans came down out of the mountains, dirty, tired, unshaven, with three weeks' growth of beard. Sergeant Thornton had lost twenty pounds, and his buddies said he looked like an old man.... Well, so did they.

On the night of April 29 the First Battalion of the Sixteenth Infantry attacked Hill 523. On the left of the First Division was the First Armored Division, back in action again on this drive north. On the right was the Thirty-fourth Division. This particular hill was holding up the whole advance. The GIs took it, but the Germans counterattacked and surrounded the First Battalion on its hill. The First Division called out to the First Armored Division for help. Company H was ordered to rescue the endangered battalion.

Captain Hillenmyer, the commanding officer of the company, reported in to General Roosevelt, who told him of the urgency. Company H had to get to the First before dark or there was not much hope for the encircled battalion.

Hillenmyer moved out. By 4 p.m. his seventeen tanks were in position to attack. They were supported by Company I, whose tanks tried to move along the slopes of Hill 609 but were stopped by the Germans.

The Germans also stopped Company H. It ran into concealed 47-milli-meter antitank guns. The first shot penetrated the command tank turret and killed the gunner, Pfc. Carl Brimmer. Another shell hit the front of the tank, wounding the driver, T/4 Freddie L. Blair. The rest of the crew bailed out, huddled behind the tank, and watched three more tanks get knocked out by the expert German fire. The survivors retreated on foot, under German fire. Hillenmyer finally got another tank and moved forward, but by this time it was dark and too late to advance any further.

Lieutenant Cashman's tank was hit and burned. Cashman was killed. The bow gunner, Pvt. Frank Alexander, got out of the burning tank and ran— but he ran toward the Germans and was killed by machine gun fire.

Sergeant Bowser's tank was burned. The entire crew died in the flames. Sergeant Fowler's tank was hit, but it did not burn.

So the Second Platoon was in tough shape. The surviving tanks joined the First Platoon and moved up the valley. They destroyed the two 47-milli-meter antitank guns that had done all the damage, as well as an enemy ma-chine gun position. German sniper fire was heavy, and the American infantry on the hill was still pinned down. The advance prevented another German attack on the embattled battalion, but the tanks could not get through to it. So few of the men of the First Battalion got away. On May 1 the Germans evacuated Hill 523, but they took their prisoners with them.

There were a few more engagements for the tankers of Company H, but the Tunisian campaign was winding down. Field Marshal Rommel was pre-paring to move his troops out of Africa, in what was almost a rout. The Germans moved toward Bizerte in this sector, and the Americans were in hot pursuit. Some German units gave up. Company H's last action was a charge on May 9 near the village of El Alia. The principal casualty was a horse, but behind him was a unit of German tanks that were retreating. That morning General Harmon negotiated the surrender of all German troops north of Tunis. The German tank company behind the olive grove was still fighting. When informed of the surrender, these Germans burned their tanks and withdrew.

So the battle of Company H ended, and on May 12 the company joined up with the rest of the First Armored Regiment near Ferryville. The First Armored Division now went into rest camp. It would give the men some time to think about all they had learned about the tactics they had brought with them, their equipment, and the enemy. The division had been blooded, bloodied, and nearly destroyed. But what was left was a fighting unit, and one that had become battlewise the hard way.

*　　　*　　　*

Among the officers of the Twentieth Engineers, Lieutenant Miller was not given to heroics. But it was the sort of war in which heroics were forced upon Lieutenant Miller. Now, after three months of war, he could speak casually of horrors.

"For the last three weeks, Jerry has been putting up a pretty good show," he wrote home, "and old B Company has been right in there pitching. I know now what my reactions are under fire, because I was machine-gunned three times and shelled with everything from 88s to mortars. It's just sort of exciting."

Miller and the first sergeant had a standing joke: Who was trying to get whom shot?

They were having a race to see who would get the first Purple Heart. Lieutenant Miller almost won when one day he stepped on a German mine. But for some reason it did not go off. At that point, at Sedjenane, the company was detached from the regiment and attached to the Corps Franc. The French were making their drive south of the coast toward Bizerte, and the company was to provide them with engineer support.

Part of the company was assigned to repairing the road behind the advance so that supplies could be brought up. The rest of the Twentieth worked with and in front of the infantry, removing mines so that the troops could advance.

That was, as Lieutenant Miller called it, "the hot spot." The engineers were nearly always under enemy observation, sometimes as much as a mile and a half beyond the French outposts.

Lieutenant Miller and the first sergeant would walk down the road ahead of the mine-removal party, until they drew fire. That's when Miller trod on his mine. He was not hurt. Frightening in the aftermath, but all in a day's work for the combat engineers.

One day they had "the whole French army" lined up behind B Company while it filled an enormous crater in the road and bypassed two bridges the retreating enemy had blown up.

Lieutenant Miller reconnoitered and built a road over the mountains, a road which the armored troops would use to enter Bizerte. But his engineers were the first men—the "first fool troops," he said—to enter that blasted city.

Things to remember, Miller wrote home: A luncheon in ruined Bizerte with the commandant of one of the battalions of the Corps Franc. Fish soup, a 3-inch boiled fish, spinach, cheese, blackberry jam, and, wonder of wonders, fresh strawberries. Also plenty of wine.

Other things to remember: Long strings of prisoners, a hundred or more in a bunch, trickling back from the front with two Ghoums in striped robes guarding the whole column.

And when it was all over, guess who got the credit? The company commander, Lt. Edwin M. Lutz, got the French Croix de Guerre. Such are the fortunes of war.

Lieutenant Miller was cited by the French battalion commander for a medal, but it never came through.

His reaction: "Oh well, you can't eat a medal. Had fresh hamburger today."

On May 12 Sergeant Thornton's battalion of the Sixtieth Infantry reached Bizerte and immediately was dispatched to guard the airport. On May 14 Sergeant Thornton and some of the other GIs went down to the sea for their first swim in the Mediterranean. This was the way a war ought to be fought, lying on the beach in the daytime, and in the breezes under the olives and the date palms at night.

But a month later the men of the regiment were on their way to Oran, on foot. It was a long hike.

Captain Shebeck's 325th Glider Regiment and the rest of the Eighty-second Airborne Division were on their way to north Africa in a convoy of twenty-nine ships. As the Grace liner *Santa Rosa* pulled out of New York harbor, Shebeck and several other officers were standing at the rail, watching the Statue of Liberty slide by. One lieutenant spoke up:

"I'll sure be glad when I see her again."

Naturally, he was one of the ones who would not make it.

Captain Shebeck had a dull voyage. Most of his time was spent deep in the hold packing Red Cross bags for the troops. That was his duty as special services officer of the regiment. Every man would get a bag with toilet articles, and a paperback book. Shebeck's night duty was enforcing the blackout, and he roamed the decks tapping on ports and doors from which he could see light.

They landed at Casablanca, but were soon on their way to Oujda, on the Moroccan-Algerian border. Training. At least they had a Red Cross girl to go with the bags.

Private Bortzfield spent the spring of 1943 in the Aircraft Mechanics School in Gulfport, Mississippi, learning to repair aircraft engines. He was still a "limited service" soldier.

The 110th Infantry moved up from Camp Carrabelle to Camp Pickett, Virginia. It was a relief to get away from the tarantulas and coral snakes. On the train First Sergeant Chattaway and two section sergeants shared a drawing room. RHIP. Beer and pretzels all the way north. That was one way to fight the war. Let the sergeants enjoy life while they might. Their day would come.

In April 1943 things began to happen to Sgt. Barnett Hoffner's embryo combat engineers. They had been training all along, working off the excess men, those who could not hack the grueling, dangerous job. They started building bridges in the sand hills—long bridges, short bridges, wide bridges, narrow bridges. The idea was to get them up f-a-s-t. They learned. In April 1943 their real equipment began to arrive, bulldozers and big trucks.

By June the outfit was in fighting trim; most of the weak ones had been weeded out. The engineers went into the woods to bivouac. They began working with explosives. TNT was Sergeant Hoffner's favorite. It was stable; you could cut it up and throw it around, but it would not go off by accident, as dynamite so often did. They began learning about mines—German mines, Italian mines—how to move them with a bayonet. They learned about booby traps, and one of their training casualties was one of their best sergeants. He had been fooling with a booby trap and had the pressure device upside down. It went off and he lost all his fingers.

There in Mississippi Sergeant Hoffner had his first real experience with bitter American racism. The camp was near the town of Duck Hill, and already there had been many racial incidents, including the beating and torture of some black citizens who had seemed "uppity" to their white neighbors. Hoffner's first experience came one day when he and others of the engineer unit who had passes to go into town were boarding a bus. A couple of black GIs from the adjoining quartermaster outfit tried to get on the bus along with the whites. A deputy sheriff who was standing by grabbed one of the blacks, knocked him down, and kicked him.

"Listen nigger," he said, "you-all gonna wait till all the white people get on the bus. Then, if there's any room, you can ride."

This sort of racism was new to some of the black quartermaster troops from the north. One morning at 11:00 Hoffner's company was going about its routine when suddenly came the cry, "Everybody fall in."

Into the company area rolled a number of trucks. The men were told the news: the night before, black troops from the camp had gotten into the supply room, taken all the weapons, gone into Duck Hill, and shot up the town. Men from the Eighty-sixth Division had already been sent out to bring the black soldiers back.

"I never saw a change come over these people so suddenly. Men of my own squad began shouting, 'Come on, get your nigger huntin' tools.' The cry went all through the ranks. I guess they were egged on by the southern troops. They were mostly from Alabama and Mississippi. They had a different way of life."

The trucks took the engineers into Duck Hill. Hoffner was amazed. Every doorway seemed to have bullet holes in it. The blacks were rounded up and put into the stockade. It was Hoffner's first taste of violent race relations. Who was fighting whom in this war?

Ultimately this incident and others like it brought about a distaste for Mississippi in Hoffner's unit. As the soldiers marched, and they marched a lot, they sang to count cadence:

> Left, ...left...you had a good home when you left...
> Left, right, left...

For variation, Hoffner's men began singing:

"Mississippi isn't great, it's the asshole of the forty-eight...."

But they didn't sing it long. The civilians complained to the brass and down came an order: "Cease and desist."

Then came the 50-mile hike, with light pack, each company with guidons. The temperature was about 95 that day. The march began. One hour... two hours... Men began dropping out.

Hoffner used an old marine trick: he put some pebbles into his canteen, and he kept pebbles in his mouth.

The lines were thinning out. A truck followed and picked up the dropouts. Then another truck and an ambulance. At 25 miles the men turned. Heading back now...30 miles...40 miles...By the time they got to the camp gate, Hoffner was carrying the guidon. He had seven men left in his own unit. Out of 450 men in the battalion, 40 had finished the hike.

The next day three-quarters of the company was on sick call.

There was a furlough, and then new orders sent the men to Florida, to the North Atlantic Amphibious Training Center, for underwater demolition training. They were designated "amphibious engineers."

On May 7 the Americans had forced their way into Bizerte. The only sour note for the men of the Twentieth Engineers was learning that their colonel and his executive officer had dashed into town in a jeep, looked around for a few moments, scuttled back to camp, and then written each other up for a silver star.

"Yuk," said Lieutenant Miller. "They would have made it the DSC if they'd thought they could have gotten away with it."

The war in Tunisia was over, but not the danger for the men of the Twentieth Engineer Regiment. The First Battalion moved into the Sedjenane Valley, in the shadow of Green and Bald hills, to remove all those mines in several enormous fields.

Why? Virtually everyone objected. Why? The fields had no military value; they were worked only by the Arabs. Removing the mines was enormously difficult and very dangerous, thousands of mines in thick brush and scrub that would be trod in future only by Arabs and their beasts. Almost every day there were casualties. But for the men of the Twentieth there was also joy. Colonel Caffey, wearing his brand-new Silver Star ribbon, left them to take command of the First Engineer Special Brigade.

Caffey was replaced by Colonel Arnold, a young West Point graduate who seemed to care more about what happened to the men than about how many tommy guns they had. He was immediately very popular, as he had been in England, where he was engaged to a pretty English girl named Kay Summersby. He wanted to learn from the old hands the problems of combat engineering. He went out with the men into the Arab shacks, learned how to remove the booby traps, and got himself loaded down with fleas. He learned about Teller mines and S mines. But learning is not always enough. On June 6, while working on a hillside overlooking the Sedjenane, a Teller mine got the colonel. His name did not even appear among the names of men killed in combat! In all, seven officers and nineteen men died because somebody thought it would be a good idea to clear the Sedjenane, and nobody stopped it.

A new commanding officer came in, a Colonel Daley, who was another disaster. "The Sad Sack," the regiment called him. The men would have him for a long, long time. Many of them thought he was promotion-happy, like Colonel Caffey. From regimental headquarters day after day a flood of orders came down.

It was now African summer and the sun beat down unmercifully. The colonel wanted spit and polish, so there was drill and more drill. The days were filled with infantry problems, minefield laying with the new template design, work with the Treadway bridge, range-firing of weapons, and lots of marching.

The battle was scarcely over, and garrison life had descended once again.

17

INTERLUDE IN AFRICA

The North African campaign had ended in success. In some cases good news was born from bad. An entire battalion of the Sixteenth Infantry had been captured by the Germans and put aboard a ship bound for Italy and POW camps. But the vessel had been attacked by American planes, deserted by the Italian crew, abandoned, and grounded; then the freed battalion had marched back to rejoin the Sixteenth. Several companies of the Eighteenth Infantry, captured by the Germans in those first desperate days of Kasserine, had now been released and were also to rejoin their regiment.

Lieutenant Downing learned that the whole First Division was to prepare to return to Algeria. But first Downing was determined to make a trip into Tunis. Ah, the fleshpots at last.

Downing and his jeep driver headed into the city, careful of possible mines. But there were no mines, no Germans, just British troops on the road. French civilians lined the streets and cheered at every vehicle that came through, as if it were a perpetual parade. The police kept the people from overrunning the streets. Lieutenant Downing and his driver saw a troop of Ghoumier cavalry on its way into town. They tried to get out to La Goulette air base to find some souvenirs, but couldn't find the road. The two Americans had to content themselves with a copy of a one-page English-language newspaper, edited by a British captain, J. M. MacLennan. They saw hundreds of German troops marching to the prison cages, some in the Afrika Korps khaki,

some in Wehrmacht field gray, some in Luftwaffe blue. At the end of the
column, Downing saw a handsome black-haired woman trying to gain one
last embrace from one of the German prisoners.

She wouldn't be lonely long. The desert rats of the Eighth Army, just
like the men of the First Division, had been many weeks without women.
But Tunis was not that welcoming to an American. It was a British show. So
Lieutenant Downing headed back to First Division headquarters. That night,
over some liberated wine, he and other junior officers discussed the possible
future of the division. Perhaps they would all be going home now to teach all
those other GIs how to do it.

Fat chance.

Late that evening one of the senior officers came in and said everyone
was to report to his unit the next morning. Downing knew what that meant.
They were going someplace, and it wasn't home and it wasn't to the city
stews.

The inexperienced American troops of November 1942 were now old
soldiers. The Thirty-fourth Division, which had earlier been racked up for
failure to perform—almost all its errors were those of inexperience—had performed brilliantly in the final days of the campaign. Under General Patton's
driving force, the First Armored Division had distinguished itself in the attack south from El Guettar. Under General Bradley's leadership, the whole
American force had distinguished itself on the drive to Bizerte.

The Germans, confronted by Americans en masse for the first time, simply could not understand them. Interrogation of American prisoners produced
the damnedest answers, which were duly recorded by German army intelligence:

"Why are you fighting?"

"To get rich...."

On $50 a month?

"To have an exciting time...."

In the mud of Algeria? Or on the bone-bare hills of Tunisia, battered by
sun and dust in the daytime and by cold winds at night? Subsisting for weeks
at a time on canned C rations or British compo, usually cold?

"To see something new...."

Yeah, the hold of a new ship. The back end of the guy in front of you on
the trail. If you're lucky, the canvas top of a 2½-ton truck from the inside.
If you're not lucky, the inside of a canvas mattress cover. Only you don't see
that. Very interesting.

"Because everybody else is...."

The hell they are. What about those guys in the shipyards? My gal
MaryLou wrote me last week that Joe, you remember Joe Smith, is now making eight bucks an hour at Swan Island. A goddamn welder! As a matter of
fact she wrote me a lot about Joe Smith. Maybe too much...

"Why am I fighting? For mom and apple pie.... "

"Hell, no. Blueberry. I told you, with ice cream.... "

The Americans, Hitler was told by his generals who had digested all these
intelligence reports of POW interrogations, were a nation of weak, rowdy
slobs "who cannot stand up under any emergency." They had no idea of
what they were fighting for, no political orientation at all.

"America," said Adolf Hitler, "will never become the Rome of the future."

So the Nazis, interviewing these soldiers who had come up from the farms
and factories and the shipyards and the colleges, had determined that the
Germans were still the master race. They dismissed this new enemy as they
did the British—"a nation of shopkeepers"—not understanding that one char-
acteristic the British and American Anglo-Saxon cousins shared was an in-
choate patriotism, deep-seated but seldom expressed. At home families might
fly the flag on the Fourth of July, but they didn't make any speeches about
it. The speeches were for the politicians. "Heil Hitler" was a great catch-
word, and many of the Germans really believed it. But "V for Victory" had
a lot more meaning.

Among all the war correspondents who were writing about the Americans
during World War II, one stood out as the soldiers' historian. His name was
Ernie Pyle. A small, skinny, chain-smoking reporter for the Scripps-Howard
newspaper group, he could not have weighed more than 135 pounds, soaking wet. Soaking wet he often was, because Ernie Pyle's war was up front
with the GIs, not back in Algiers at the Hotel de Paris with the generals,
correspondents, and thousand-franc-a-night girls.

Before the war Ernie Pyle had been writing a column about ordinary
Americans, you know, Kansas farm boys and sand hogs working to build the
New York subway. That sort of thing, the sort of thing that Charles Kuralt
would do on television for another American generation. When Ernie Pyle
confronted the war, he did so in the same fashion, a fact that caused a good
deal of unfavorable talk among the "more serious" war correspondents.

"I'll tell you something, Ernie," United Press Association correspondent

Reynolds Packard said one day. "You're on the wrong track. Nobody cares about these GI stories you write from the line. You've got to learn how to analyze the communiqués that come out of Eisenhower's headquarters. That's the secret of being a war correspondent. Figuring out from all that what is really going on."

"You're right, Pack, absolutely right," said Ernie Pyle miserably. "I'm a lousy correspondent. I know it. I'm trying. Believe me. I'm trying. But I just can't seem to get that stuff straight."

"I know," said Packard heroically. "It takes a lot of experience."

And so Ernie Pyle miserably went back to writing about soldiers, traveling forward to visit them in their foxholes in the line, being pushed around by the High Command, the Germans, the MPs, and the British.

One day during the Tunisian campaign Ernie Pyle had called on Ike in Algiers and had gotten a line on Maj. Gen. Terry de la Mesa Allen, the commanding general of the First Infantry Division—the Big Red One. He had then gone up front and spent some time with the First Division, and had written a number of stories that made Allen, and the men of the division, look 10 feet tall.

As it turned out, these glowing stories, while true, were not a great favor to General Allen and General Roosevelt, his second in command. The Big Red One was a problem to the higher headquarters. General Allen was an enthusiastic leader and commanded the real affection of his troops. But General Patton did not like him, because Allen insisted on doing things his own way. General Bradley concurred with Patton:

> Among the division commanders in Tunisia, none excelled the unpredictable Terry Allen in the leadership of troops. . . . He had made himself the champion of the 1st Division GI and they in turn championed him. But in looking out for his own division, Allen tended to belittle the roles of the others and demand for his Big Red One prerogatives we could not fairly accord it.

One thing General Allen and General Roosevelt demanded for their troops was that now that the fighting in north Africa was over, they be left alone by the rear-echelon MPs. They would, said General Roosevelt, take care of their own disciplinary problems. Such infractions as not wearing the necktie and not donning the tin hat were regarded by the men of Big Red One as so much "chicken shit." And their division brass supported them against the big brass. In the few weeks after the collapse of the Germans in Africa, the GIs of Big Red One were often in trouble. They were considered by the inspector generals and by the provost marshals to be a menace to the orderly management of troops overseas. The Americans were still so new in the war that some officers were unaware of the politics of command. Generals Allen and Roosevelt were of that stripe.

At the end of the Tunisian campaign Eisenhower and his generals were taking stock of their field commanders. They found General Allen a very large handful to control. They found Gen. Charles Wolcott Ryder too tame. "His weakness," said General Bradley, "was... the contentment with which he tolerated mediocrity." General Harmon, who had made a great fighting outfit out of the First Armored Division, was regarded as "constantly and brilliantly aggressive.... He was to become our most outstanding tank commander." But Bradley shorted Harmon for not making the best possible use of his infantry. Of all the commanders, closest to the heart of the brass was Gen. Manton Eddy, commander of the Ninth Division: "Though not timid, neither was he bold." Cooperative was the word. Receptive to the advice of upper echelons.

That was a war that the dogfaces knew nothing about. Their generals would have to protect themselves in the rear.

The Tunisian campaign was all buttoned up by May 13, and the big problem was getting rid of the hundreds of thousands of Axis prisoners of war who had to be housed, fed, medicated, and found some place for long-term confinement. The problem of all those mines, too, had to be met. Before the Twentieth Engineers were pulled out of the mine-defusing business, they collected about 200,000 mines in north Africa. To them the death of Colonel Arnold was really tragic. "[He] let us see what it would be like having a real soldier for a CO," said Lieutenant Miller. The only good thing to be said for that tragedy was that it caused the brass to stop and think long enough to pull the Twentieth out of that most unrewarding business of making the Sedjenane safe for Arab goats.

In a little less than two months the Allies were to take the next step, the invasion of Sicily.

The preparations were all going along as rapidly as possible.

*   *   *

Since February Battery A of the 334th Coast Artillery Antiaircraft had been stationed in Algiers, fighting off the frequent raids of the German Luftwaffe. There had been some hairy moments, as the night that the Stukas hit the convent just behind the battery's gun emplacements, killing fifteen nuns and several dozen children. S. Sgt. Charles H. Johnson listened to Axis Sally very late:

"Our gallant airmen have successfully bombed Algiers tonight and when last seen the city and harbor were in flames. Shipping was destroyed and facilities crippled. You cannot win. Heil Hitler."

Perhaps Sergeant Johnson did not, as Hitler's generals said, understand all the politics of this war. But the sergeant knew an atrocity when he saw one.

With the fighting in north Africa ended, the men of the 334th had a little time to think about tactics. One thing they had learned was that the horrifying whistle made by the Stuka dive-bomber when it lowered its flaps was really the key to its destruction. When the flaps were lowered, the bomber decelerated rapidly. That was just the point at which to track and shoot. That was a note for the future, but what the future meant was not at all certain to Sergeant Johnson and his buddies.

They were busy now checking equipment and replacing worn-out parts; ammunition stocks also had to be replenished. But there was time for some moving about. One day 1st Sgt. Fred Rupp came roaring up on a new toy, a captured German motorcycle with a sidecar, and invited Sergeant Johnson to take a trip with him to see Bizerte. So Sergeant Johnson stopped off at his quarters, grabbed two K rations and a bottle, and jumped into the sidecar.

Sergeant Rupp was apparently in training to be a racing driver. The motorcycle skidded along those narrow roads so recently checked over by Lieutenant Miller's engineers. The two men did not hit any mines. About halfway to Bizerte, they stopped to pick up a hitchhiking French sailor. But scarcely had he gotten on, and experienced Sergeant Rupp's daredevil driving, than he wanted off. So they stopped, and the Frenchman debarked, smiling.

"*Vive la France,*" said Sergeant Johnson.

"*Vive les Americains,*" said the erstwhile hitchhiker.

And with much goodwill, they waved to each other. Then the cyclists went on.

The Bizerte they found was a shell of a city: harbor jammed with sunken ships, buildings of pink and white stucco scarred and burned, red roofs blasted to rubble. They discovered the remains of an outdoor café, and set up two chairs and a table in front. They pulled out their K rations and ate them and drank their bottle of wine.

Corporal Moglia settled down with the Sixteenth Infantry at Oran again, to await developments. He collected three medals of the Order of the Purple Heart for his three wounds received in action.

The first had come in the Ousseltia River valley at the end of January. In a very confused battle Colonel D'Alary Fechet, commander of the Sixteenth

Infantry, was supposed to be in charge of defenses to hold the line, includ-ing armored elements of Combat Command B of the First Armored Division. But the French thought *they* were in charge, and Combat Command B thought it was in charge, so everything was a mess. The Second Battalion of the Sixteenth got out ahead of its support elements, and the battalion commander was told to bring the men back. All this happened on the night of January 27. A runner came hurrying up to the command post with a fouled-up mes-sage which, when translated, indicated that six battalions of German tanks were coming up the road. Since the Second Battalion's mortars were just about out of ammunition, the news was hardly comforting. The men began a very hasty withdrawal. In the commotion Corporal Moglia saw somebody stand up and throw something at him. Before he could duck back into his foxhole, the something exploded and peppered his face and upper lip. It was a con-cussion grenade. The six "tanks" turned out to be six Italian soldiers on patrol. So the battalion held, although some troops withdrew.

"How far did they withdraw?" Moglia asked a buddy later.

"I dunno. Except when we got back to guys wearing neckties we figured we were pretty far back."

That, of course, was PP—pre-Patton.

Corporal Moglia's second Purple Heart was earned—or suffered, depending on one's point of view—in the Tebessa area a couple of days later. The Second Battalion of the Sixteenth Infantry was defending Rebaas Oulad Yahia, along with the British Thirty-sixth Brigade. The men of Company E were dug in on an open sandy area and were getting the hell shelled out of them. All day long the 88s kept coming in. The soldiers couldn't get out of their foxholes.

Corporal Moglia prayed. He prayed again, and again, making personal promises to God, if only He would get Moglia out of this mess.

Then his prayers were answered. The shelling stopped. He got out of his hole to stretch.

Did God really answer, or was it just a coincidence?

Then, *blam*. An enormous explosion!

When Moglia regained consciousness, he could not figure out where he was.

Was he in a cave? Where was everybody? Where was the sky? Why was he smelling that awful stink of spent gunpowder?

He had an enormous headache. His belly hurt. When he wiggled his feet, dirt came down on his face. Finally he figured it out—he was lying upended in his foxhole. He had been blown up and set down again head first. He yelled, and somebody came up and helped him get out of the hole.

For the next couple of days Corporal Moglia kept throwing up. He had a headache all the time, and his nose bled. He went back to the aid station for some treatment.

The doctor—the GIs referred to this one as "Salesman Sam" and swore he had been a shoe salesman who had swapped his shoehorn for a scalpel when the war started—gave him a handful of APC pills and told him to take them and eat lightly. You know, lay off those steaks and fried chicken and roast turkey and gravy and pizza and lasagna. Salesman Sam didn't discuss the nutritional properties of C rations and K rations.

Oh, well. Another Purple Heart.

Both had been earned in that dreadful period referred to by British World War II historian Charles Whiting as "the slaughter" of the Americans in the first battle of Kasserine Pass, when the Americans suffered hundreds of battle casualties and more than 2000 men were lost as POWs, some 1400 of them from the First Armored Division.

The third Purple Heart came when the Americans had recovered and learned from their experiences. They were making their assault under General Patton in the El Guettar area. This time Corporal Moglia got in the way of a mortar round, and after he got up from the ground he discovered both his hands were bleeding. The shell also spoiled his shoeshine and put nasty marks in his leggings. Salesman Sam gave him another handful of APC pills and said the little finger on his left hand and middle finger on his right hand were probably broken. Too bad. APC healed all.

Three Purple Hearts, but Moglia was still around. Now, for a little while, the Sixteenth had it easy. Only a few simulated landings, to get ready for the next one. As easy as Ma's apple pie with cheese, or blueberry with ice cream. The GIs took their choice. They didn't get either.

At El Alia the men of the Twentieth Engineers spent the month of June practicing close order drill beneath the merciless Tunisian sun. There was a parade for presentation of medals. On June 23 they boarded LCIs in the Lac de Bizerte and sat on board for three days, eating K rations and wondering what came next. On June 26 they landed on Yellow beach. This was "Exercise Copybook." Then they had to march 16 miles back to El Alia in the sun. They had full field packs, gas masks, arms, ammunition, and an assault load of light and heavy machine guns, bazookas, ammunition for bazookas, mine detectors, and radios. They got back, but as a military operation, the "retreat" was a disaster. Fully half the regiment fell out along the way. It was part of the joy of having a spit-and-polish colonel.

Back in England, if any dogfaces of the Twenty-ninth Division had any illusions about the nature of the war, they must have been dispelled on May 23. Passes had been issued for leave in Bournemouth, and a lot of men had gone into town. But the Germans came that night, and dropped their bombs on the seaside town. Six men of the 175th were killed: T/4 James C. Ashford, T/5 Raymond J. Berwin, Pfc. Tony Rollick, Pfc. Stanley L. Bodziony, Pfc. Harold Parker, and Pfc. Samuel Arone. A number of men had been lost in various amphibious operations and training accidents, but these were the first actual war casualties of the Twenty-ninth.

Across the Atlantic, American troops were training, steadily and hard. At Camp McCoy, Wisconsin, the engineers of the Second Infantry Division built a replica of a section of the Siegfried line, Germany's great defense scheme. That, the troops were told, was going to be one of their objectives when the time came. Just now they were going to put on a show.

For weeks the nine battalions of the Second Infantry Division practiced attacking mock-ups of the Siegfried line. Then came the big day; the Twenty-third Infantry was going to perform. Flocks of civilian workers who had manufactured the guns and made the ammunition and other supplies were shipped in to see what their work was producing; theoretically at least, they would go back and produce a lot more. A stand was erected. The Second Engineers provided plastic explosives, bangalore torpedoes, and TNT. The three battalions of light artillery supplied the 105s, and one battalion of medium artillery the 155s; the 75-millimeter guns were provided by the tank-destroyer battalion, and lots of smoke shells were fired by the mortars. The infantry provided the assault. Major Spencer, the executive officer of the regiment, did the commentary. It was a proud moment, this prelude to attack on the German line. But then what? Everybody in the Second Division wondered exactly that. The First Division was off making heroes in north Africa. Was the Second Infantry Division going to spend the war in the United States, playing games?

*

The 325th Glider Regiment of the Eighty-second Airborne Division spent some time bivouacked at Oujda, very close to the Moroccan-Algerian frontier. About the middle of June 1943 the trucks arrived, and the regiment was on the move again. This time the destination was Kairouan in Tunisia, where the men would live in an olive grove punctuated with cacti.

The parachute regiments were not with them. They had other work.

In the spring of 1943 the most knowledgeable officer of the American airborne units had to be Colonel Raff. He was the senior U.S. officer to have dropped in combat, and he had spent every possible moment since the invasion of north Africa learning from the British and from the enemy the most effective means of using airborne equipment and men.

But General Eisenhower's field promotion of Colonel Raff had its repercussions. Some, including many of the GIs of the 509th, came to believe that General Matthew Ridgway was jealous of Raff.

Perhaps Colonel Raff annoyed the staff of the Eighty-second Airborne with some of his ideas: the Pathfinder concept was one, developed by the 509th in north Africa, and rejected out of hand by the Eighty-second Airborne that spring.

Perhaps it was because of the nature of the mission. There would be only enough aircraft available to the airborne troops to accommodate a reinforced regiment, which meant that the commander of the airborne regiment would have to be working very closely with units attached to his command. Raff and the 509th, while gaining all that experience, had lost touch with the American airborne commands.

In any event, when it came time to pick an airborne unit for the coming invasion of Sicily, the 509th was not chosen. Instead, General Ridgway selected Col. James M. Gavin's 505th Parachute Infantry. Colonel Gavin happened to be General Ridgway's brother-in-law, a fact that particularly rankled many of the men of the 509th. But was an invitation to get killed really the kind of nepotism to which one could object?

Gavin would also have the Third Battalion of the 504th Parachute Infantry, the 456th Parachute Artillery Battalion, and Company B of the 307th Airborne Engineers.

The task of the airborne troops would be to shock the enemy. The American airborne would then join General Allen's First Infantry Division. The British airborne, shocking the enemy on the other side, would join up with General Montgomery's infantry. While the glider troops went off to Kairouan, the parachute troops began intensive training again.

18

ON TO SICILY

"The invasion can't come any too soon for me," Lt. Joseph Miller wrote home from the Twentieth Engineers' bivouac in Tunisia at the end of June 1943. As far as he could see, the only reason for submitting seasoned troops like the Twentieth Engineers to constant marches was to bore them so badly and make them so tired and angry that they would welcome combat as a rest and relief. Training began at 5:15 a.m. and lasted until 11 a.m. in the burning sun, and began again at 5 p.m. and lasted until 9:30 at night. Even the brass recognized that midday was unbearable. The rest of the north African summer days was not a lot better. One day, in the middle of an exercise, Miller got so hot that he went into the ocean with all his clothes on, and afterward hiked another 9 miles. The salt in his trousers chafed his bottom so badly that he could hardly sit down.

By July 1, 1943, the men of the Twentieth Engineers were tired enough and angry enough for the invasion to commence.

Everyone knew pretty well that the invasion was going to be against some part of Italy, but that's about all most dogfaces knew. They had no knowledge of unit strength or where it was going. Only regimental commanders had any concept of what their division was doing; only battalion commanders knew what the regiment was up to; only company commanders knew where their battalion was headed. Capt. Norris Perkins, commander of Company H of the Sixty-sixth Armored Regiment, was the only man in the company who knew the details of his company's mission.

The men of the 509th Airborne Infantry were moved to Algiers, expecting that they would be involved in the next airborne invasion. They, the only seasoned American airborne troops, were the obvious choice, were they not?

No. The army did not operate on that sort of logic.

S. Sgt. Charlie Doyle and virtually all the members of the Second Battalion of the 509th were bitterly disappointed. They thought they had earned their way. (They hadn't forgotten this slight more than forty years later.)

As noted, the accolade had gone to Col. James M. Gavin's 505th Parachute Infantry, reinforced, and the troops had been training since June. There were reviews of the troops to impress politicians; there was a review to impress General Eisenhower. There was a moral briefing by General Patton, commander of the U.S. Seventh Army, who would lead the troops in the coming battle.

"Now I want you to remember," he told the troops assembled, "that no sonuvabitch ever won a war by dying for his country. He won it by making the other poor dumb sonuvabitch die for his country." What Patton was saying in his own way was that the generals commanded but when it got down to the nitty-gritty of the battlefield, with all its surprises, it was the soldiers who were going to win or lose the battle.

What the generals had decided upon was the invasion of Sicily.

The British Eighth Army would attack the Sicilian port of Siracusa (Syracuse). The American Seventh Army would attack on the left of the British. Both armies would drive along the coasts toward Messina, and when they captured Messina, they would control Sicily. British paratroops would precede their army in attack in the Siracusa area, and the American paratroops would precede the American landing forces. Opposition? Once again the American intelligence was faulty. There were virtually no Germans on the island, said intelligence. Patton's talk to the paratroops concentrated on a pornographic study of the assault, with the rapee to be the Italians. The fact was that there were two German panzer divisions on Sicily, with the most modern and powerful German armored equipment.

The American invasion force began sailing from north Africa on the Fourth of July. The first to move out was Gen. Troy Middleton's Forty-fifth Infantry

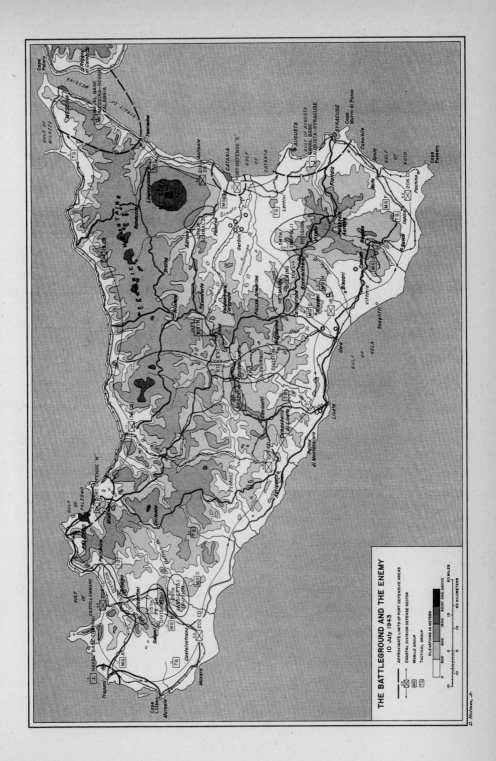

THE BATTLEGROUND AND THE ENEMY
10 July 1943

APPROXIMATE LIMITS OF PORT DEFENSIVE AREAS
COASTAL DIVISION DEFENSE SECTOR
MOBILE GROUP
TACTICAL GROUP

ELEVATIONS IN METERS

D. Holmes, Jr.

Division, from Oran. A National Guard outfit, the Forty-fifth had just arrived in north Africa from the United States in time for the show. Next came the First Infantry Division, from Algeria and Tunisia. Then the Third Infantry Division sailed from Bizerte and the Second Armored Division from Oran. The invasion craft were LCTs, LSTs, and LCIs.

The LCI, Lieutenant Downing soon discovered, was a boat with a flat bottom; it responded to every movement of the sea. For the first few days of the six-day journey the weather was fine. Well, it started out fine, but gradually worsened. The deterioration was very evident inside the LCIs. Lieutenant Downing's would rise with the wave, shiver, plunge, and then shake. By the third day it was almost impossible to remain on the rain-soaked, spray-washed deck, so nearly everyone stayed below.

There, Downing was engaged in one of the inevitable card games; his was an eight-man blackjack contest. He had $80 and he didn't care what happened to it; all he hoped was that it would keep him in the blackjack game until the boat landed. The men played constantly, stopping only for meals and a few hours of sleep, sitting on cots with an empty cot for a table. From time to time he would get up, go to the door at the head of the companionway, and look out at the storm that was building. The rolling seas made him feel seasick, so he went back and concentrated on the blackjack. Anything to keep his mind off what was coming.

On July 7 somebody came around with a bundle of maps. Downing riffled through his, found one map that gave a good view of the beach and the first few miles inland, stuck it inside his shirt, and put the rest in his musette bag.

When at sea, with his tanks in the LCTs, Captain Perkins encountered a problem. Radio silence was the rule in the invasion fleet. Company H was shipping aboard five LCTs. How was Perkins to get word to the rest of his company? In a very old-fashioned way: Lt. Cameron J. Warren stripped down and swam from one LCT to the next, passing on the captain's instructions. It was a feat worth a medal.

Aboard Lieutenant Downing's LCI on the night of D − 1 the tension was too great even for gambling. The men broke up the game. Surprised, Downing found he was a big winner, with a fistful of American dollars and Italian occupation lire. He stuffed the money into a condom and stuck it inside his shirt pocket.

He lay down on his cot, fully dressed, pulled up the blanket, and drifted off to sleep. Early on D day he was awakened by the popping of guns. He figured the fleet was being strafed by enemy aircraft, so he jumped up and ran toward the companionway, where he was bowled over by the simultaneous impact of several other soldiers doing the same. Captain Currier of battalion finally made it through, and came back to report that they were off the coast of Sicily. Land was in sight. The noise was the sound of the fleet's antiaircraft guns, popping away at the enemy.

Downing lay down again.

As the LCTs carrying Captain Perkins's tank company approached the Sicilian shore, the brand-new ensign who was captain of Perkins's ship confessed that he was lost. Perkins then made a drawing from his maps of the way the shore should look from the sea, and together they found their proper landing place, about 5 miles west.

The storm that harried the invasion fleet also blew on the C-47 transports carrying the paratroops of the 505th Parachute Infantry. The 35-mile-per-hour winds carried the aircraft far to the east of their assigned drop area. Some "sticks" from the Third Battalion and from Headquarters Company dropped in front of the British and then had trouble making their identities known. The Second Battalion landed near San Croce Camerina. Other troops landed all over the place, many of them around Vittoria. The plan had called for the paratroops to seize the high ground of Piano Lupo, a flat plateau 172 meters high, dominating the surrounding countryside. The Italians had built strong defenses there, particularly near a major road junction. The paratroops were to capture that junction and block enemy reinforcement of the Gela area from the north and east. But after the paratroops landed, so confused was the effort that only about 200 men were up on the high ground. The spread of the drop was about 60 miles. The paratroops were supposed to be in front of the First Division. One-eighth of them were; the other seven-eighths were around the landing places of the Forty-fifth Division, the British, and the Canadians.

But the paratroops of that one-eighth were in the right place. Lt. Col.

Art Gorham landed very near Piano Lupo. Capt. Edwin M. Sayre of Company A was the first to get into action there. After he landed, he found fifteen men—and an Italian pillbox. At 3 a.m. they began attacking that emplacement, but the Italians fired back so effectively that the Americans backed off, pending reinforcement. At about 5:30 another fifty men showed up, so Captain Sayre renewed his attack with rifles, machine guns, and bazookas. By 6:15 they had taken the pillbox.

Lieutenant Colonel Gorham came up with another thirty men. That made a force of about a hundred. It was a lucky break, for at about 7 a.m. a column of troops and armored vehicles came up the road. When Gorham and his men saw that column, they knew that intelligence had been wrong. The column was headed by two motorcycles and a Volkswagen command car. They were definitely German. They were also (the Americans did not yet know it) manned by soldiers of the famous Hermann Göring Luftwaffe Parachute Armored Division, on their way from the division headquarters near Caltagirone to find out what was going on down here.

Lieutenant Colonel Gorham told his paratroops to hold their fire until the lead vehicles had passed into the American perimeter. They did. When they fired, the three vehicles were knocked out.

The German armored column then stopped, not quite 2 miles from the American First Division's positions on the hillside. The German commander, seeing that he was faced with infantry, sent his own infantry, about 200 men, out across the plain to the hills where the Americans were dug in. Since the Americans were armed only with eight infantry weapons and a few bazookas, Lieutenant Colonel Gorham again told the men to hold fire, which they did, until the Germans had come to a point not a hundred yards away. Then the Americans opened up with everything they had. The German infantrymen were pinned down on the open ground, and most of them were killed there.

"... won it by making the other poor dumb sonuvabitch die for his country"

The German armored vehicles then began to move up. On the sides of the road the American bazookamen waited for the tanks, and when they came up close they opened fire. Two tanks were knocked out of action. Two more were damaged. The German commander turned the column around and retreated. But Lieutenant Colonel Gorham was not under the illusion that he had just won the war. The Germans would be back in strength.

Using prisoners to carry the American wounded, Lieutenant Colonel Gorham moved his slender force up to the Piano Lupo. Off to the northeast was a fork in the coast road: one branch led to Gela; the other to Niscemi and, behind that town, to the Hermann Göring Division. The road fork was controlled by a surrounding group of Italian pillboxes. Gorham sent Captain Sayre with about twenty men to take the emplacements.

Sayre positioned his men in a wide range around the whole circle of pillboxes and made a lot of noise. Fired on automatic, the M-1 could make a fearful racket, and the Italians on Sicily were not used to Americans yet. Sayre then yelled at the Italians that they were surrounded by a huge, powerful force, and the Italians agreed. They surrendered. The Americans then took over the pillboxes, and the rest of the force moved up to that key position.

Sure enough, the Germans came back with more tanks, but the paratroopers fought them off. Before 11 a.m. troops of the U.S. Sixteenth Infantry showed up on the Piano Lupo, and Captain Sayre went back to find a radio. Proudly, he sent word to General Ridgway that the 505th had taken its objectives and had linked up with the First Division, as ordered. The statement was true enough, but it had all been done by about 200 GIs and one battalion commander. The activity of the rest of the regiment that morning was strictly supernumerary. Well, that is not quite true. The real value of the rest of the American airdrop was the confusion it caused among the enemy commanders, who saw so many small units of paratroopers arriving in so many places. That certainly had a military value, too.

The American seaborne troops began landing at about 3:30 a.m. The landings were strung out over 70 miles of Sicilian beach in the Gulf of Gela. On the east was CENT force, the Forty-fifth Division, landing at Scoglitti. In the center was DIME force, which consisted of the First Infantry Division and the Second Armored Division, without Brig. Gen. Maurice Rose's Combat Command A. DIME would land at Gela. On the west was JOSS force, the Third Infantry Division, including Combat Command A of the Second Armored Division.

The plan for the Sixteenth Regimental Combat Team was to land on the beach not far from Biviere Pond, to cut the coastal highway, and then to move up to Piano Lupo to join the paratroopers. From there the Sixteenth would drive on Niscemi.

Company E's boats got away from the ships all right. Corporal Moglia's entire squad was loaded into one assault boat, but about halfway in to shore the boat's motor quit. The troops were drifting in wind, tide, and current. It took the coxswain twenty minutes to get the boat going again, and by that time he did not know where they were. None of the landmarks were familiar.

"Who cares?" asked Corporal Moglia. He pulled out his compass, shot an azimuth straight ahead, and told the cox to go on in.

When the boat got inshore, and the troops moved out, the coxswain picked up their bangalore torpedoes—used to blow barbed-wire entanglements—and threw them in Moglia's direction.

"Here are your poles," said the coxswain. "This is no place for a sailor."

And away he went in a cloud of smoke.

Where were they?

Squad leader Moglia hadn't the foggiest idea. They found some men, but they weren't Sixteenth Infantry. Moglia remembered some of the maps, and began working toward the right, figuring they had drifted west. After a while they got to the place on the beach where they should have landed, found the rest of the platoon there, and then began to move forward. At about this time the Italians began firing from their pillboxes above the beach. Moglia's platoon got hit while in a watermelon patch.

"The counterattack surrounded us like a horseshoe. The sea was at our backs. I saw six men running toward a large depression in the ground. They sought a haven from the machine gun and rifle fire that was getting to us. I shouted at them not to go into that depression. It was probably a spot already zeroed in by enemy artillery."

The men paid no attention. Then came the scream of a large shell, an explosion that deepened the depression significantly, and the Sixteenth Infantry was short six riflemen.

Aboard their LCIs the dogfaces of the Twentieth Engineers sat out an air raid in Bizerte harbor; they were gratified to watch the Allied fighters make mincemeat of the German bombers. Then their ships began to move. When they were safely out at sea, the men learned that their destination was Sicily and that they were part of General Patton's new Seventh Army.

They reached Sicily in the dark hours of D day and waited their turn. It was noon before their LCIs moved in to Yellow beach, 2½ miles east of Licata.

Colonel Daley was riding in the LCI also occupied by the GIs of Lieutenant Miller's Company B. The Coast Guard crew drove the LCI up onto the beach and dropped the ramps. The colonel stood at the top of one of the ramps and motioned gallantly to his men.

"Forward," he shouted, and he stepped off the ramp, into 8 feet of water. The stone-nerved colonel sank like a stone. The men following opened their life preserver valves, moved out, and rescued their bedraggled leader. Sad Sack!

They landed. Company A was sent off to the Third Infantry Division, but the rest of the engineers moved inland and took up defensive positions on the hill surrounding the beachhead. They were right in the middle of a tomato patch.

By noon the First and Second battalions of the Sixteenth Infantry came up to the high ground, where they joined up with Lieutenant Colonel Gorham's little force. Other units came along, the rangers and the engineers and the Twenty-sixth RCT. Soon they had Gela in hand.

The Second Battalion was then south of Niscemi in the Biscari area. German Lt. Gen. Paul Conrath was just then preparing an unpleasant surprise for the battalion. At 2 p.m. he sent the Hermann Göring Division in to counterattack. The enemy fire was very heavy on the beach until the cruiser *Boise* and the destroyer *Jeffers* were called up for support; they took out the guns behind the beach. The German fire continued, and some of the Americans began heading back down toward the sand, away from the enemy. Tanks were coming, they said, Tiger tanks, the best the Germans had. And enemy riflemen with bayonets. The Americans did not have any tanks on the beach yet. Panic threatened.

One squad leader stopped in his retreat to cut a watermelon from a vine. Then he picked it up and moved back toward the beach. Corporal Moglia was having a hard time keeping his own squad from retreating. Then he saw a familiar face: General Roosevelt.

"What's going on, Corporal?"

"Some of the guys are pulling back, sir. It's pretty hot here. They're on both sides. They've got tanks."

"Why go back to the sea? We just got here. D'you know who those bastards are? The Hermann Göring Division. We beat their asses in north Africa and we're going to do it again. We'll hold this ground until our tanks land. OK, Corporal? Your men aren't backing up are they?"

"No sir, we're here to fight."

"OK, Corporal. Just help me organize the rest of the people here on that bit of high ground."

So Moglia found himself running toward the high ground. Bees buzzed around him and whips cracked. But they weren't bees and whips. He kept feeling himself, wondering why he wasn't hit, but he made it and found cover, and began firing.

General Roosevelt went along the line, encouraging the men and pushing them forward. Lt. Col. Joseph Crawford, commander of the Second Battalion, did the same.

The Germans rolled slowly past Casa del Priolo. They now threatened to outflank the Americans. More calls for fire from the ships offshore. The ships responded, and the tanks sputtered to a halt at the edge of the town. The infantry responded nobly, sharply reducing the ranks of the panzer grenadiers who accompanied the tanks. After an hour General Conrath ordered the Germans to retreat. Of course, Corporal Moglia did not know that; he saw them go, that was all. He didn't know that the little failure had just cost a German tank battalion commander his job.

Later in the day another commander led the tank column in an attack that broke through the U.S. lines in the 180th Infantry sector. That netted the Germans several hundred American prisoners, including the commander of the First Battalion, and set up a danger for all the First Division's beaches. But the Germans ran into the Third Battalion of the 180th Infantry, fresh from the reserve pool, and that battalion held. The Germans panicked and ran, and did not stop until they reached Biscari. And so the day came to an end, with the American beachhead more or less secure if the troops could get tank support where they needed it. That remained to be seen. General Roosevelt had recommended that the Second Armored Division be landed on Red Beach 2, and it was already coming. Eventually all the Germans retreated back up the slopes. Moglia found his corporal friend sitting behind a rock, eating his watermelon.

"Have a piece?"

"Thanks."

They munched in silence for a few moments.

"The Krauts are lousy shots," said Moglia. "They didn't hit me even though I was out in the open most of the time."

"That's because you're too damned skinny. Look at your pants."

Moglia looked. Eight bullet holes, four coming in, four going out. There were also holes in his underwear.

"Your pack's leaking," said the corporal.

Moglia looked. His C rations were all shot up, and stew was integrating itself with his blanket.

The Eighteenth Infantry was being held in reserve aboard its LCTs, but that afternoon of D day some of the reserves were committed because of the failure of the Eighty-second Airborne to get enough men up on the high ground. And that night the men of Downing's LCI were told to get ready to go ashore. A meal was served; then the men put on their equipment, fastened their life belts, and sat, waiting. They waited for hours, sitting and smoking. Then the landing craft turned in toward the shore. Here is the way Lieutenant Downing experienced it:

"There was a sharp jar as the LCT hit solid ground, the clanking rattle of the ramps being lowered, shouts from naval personnel of the LCT and faint answers from the beach. Someone shouted, 'Let's go.' I got in line and climbed the companionway blindly following the officer in front of me. We came out on deck. There was a faint moon overhead and the waves churned and slapped against the sides of the ship. I followed the officer ahead of me to the right-hand ramp and down the slope. I saw him walk down into the water and move away. I hesitated where the waves lapped the ramp while I pressed the valve arms on my life preserver and felt it fill instantly with air, squeezing my chest. I grabbed hold of the rope railing and walked down into the water. When the water reached my waist, the ramp ended and I plunged into the heaving sea.

"The shore was about 75 yards away. I held my carbine up with my right hand and with my left hand pulled myself along the rope stretched from the LCT to the shore. I came up to a couple of men who had stopped and were not moving inland. They seemed to be in some difficulty. I let go of the rope and tried to paddle around them. The waves washed me away from the line, but I paddled desperately with my feet and one hand to get in toward the shore. My life belt and the buoyant musette bag held me up. The waves began washing me toward the rear of some assault craft beached on the shore. Their motors were throbbing and I felt myself being pulled toward the bubbling exhausts and swirling propellers. I paddled furiously to get out of their way."

Finally Downing got ashore, water pouring from his trousers and squishing in his shoes. A beachmaster warned him not to go straight inland—mines. He went to the right, found two stripes of white tape, and followed this exit off the beach. He was stopped; when he identified himself, he was told to

wait for an officer from the Second Armored Division and to go with him to
division headquarters. He waited. The night air was cold and he was wet; he
began to shiver. He found a soaking blanket and wrapped it around his shoulders. He watched the parade. Several light tanks came ashore. They stopped
near him, the drivers gunning the engines. The loud backfires, the noisy
engines, and the clanking treads sounded as if they would awaken every
German as far back as Berlin. He walked up behind one of the tanks and
stood in the exhaust. It warmed him and dried his trousers, even if the stink
was dreadful. The tanks moved out, but no Second Division liaison officer
showed up. Downing then set out to find the Eighteenth Infantry command
post. Antiaircraft guns began opening up and red tracer bullets streaked
through the sky. He hit the sand as a German fighter zoomed overhead with
all guns blazing.

Eventually Downing found two officers from the Eighteenth, and they directed him to the CP, inland. Following the usual trail of discarded gas masks,
blankets, life belts, and machine gun ammunition boxes, he found the command post just off the coast road behind a cliff. Everyone was sitting, eating
K rations. He got a map overlay of the regiment's positions, and directions,
and was about to start back toward the beach. Just then columns of black
smoke began shooting up from the beach. The Germans were shelling.

"I don't envy you going back there," said Captain Middleworth.

Silently, Downing agreed, but he turned and began trudging toward the
beach. When he got down there, he learned that it had been an air raid, not
shelling, and that it was over. He found that his LCT had been bombed and
his jeep destroyed. His driver, Private Foote, was missing in action.

Lieutenant Downing went back to the coast road and started across country to find the Second Division. At a culvert he saw a strange-looking soldier, in greenish olive drab with baggy pockets. His helmet was laced with
camouflage rags, and he carried an odd-looking submachine gun with a metal
stock. Downing slipped the safety off his carbine as he passed. Then he saw
the double-A shoulder patch of the Eighty-second Airborne Division on the
man's shoulder. He stopped to talk. The soldier had jumped the night before, but had lost his outfit. Downing couldn't help. He went on.

He caught a ride in a jeep going back to the beach. There, all was confusion. Engineers were laying a netting of wire for the heavy vehicles. The
area was full of shattered landing craft sprawled on the wet sand; cases of
rations bobbed on the waves. Strewn across the beach were mixed piles of
barbed wire and telephone wire, heaps of artillery ammunition in black clo-
verleafs, and cases of rifle ammunition. Discarded life belts were everywhere.

Soldiers were moving around the beach doing a hundred different jobs; DUKWs came in from the sea and took off down the roads with heavy loads. Behind a barbed-wire fence sat a handful of Germans in Luftwaffe blue and Italians in black.

Broad daylight had come while Downing was searching. He found the Second Division command post and gave the operations officer the overlay that showed the location of the Eighteenth Infantry. There was great coming and going. Two Sherman tanks clattered up the road, breaking all the telephone lines strung across in front of the command post. They clanked to a stop, raising an enormous cloud of dust. A lieutenant wearing a football helmet with earphones and the armored patch on his left breast climbed out of a turret and went into the CP. A few minutes later he came out with a general. The general had his arm around the lieutenant's shoulder. They parted, and the lieutenant climbed back up into his tank, waving at the general.

"Go get 'em," said the general. "Good luck." And he turned and went back inside the white mud brick house that was the Second Armored Division command post.

The second day was well under way.

19

SICILY—II

Captain Perkins took Tank Company H of the Sixty-sixth Armored Regiment ashore in the Licata area and toward the town. He crossed the Salso River. One platoon went up the east bank. It was rough going, and Captain Perkins feared that the German armor would be on him in strength. Two of his tanks *were* knocked out of action, but not by the Germans. Mother Nature was the enemy, and mud was her weapon. The tanks were not lost forever, but for the time being they were out of it. The other tanks and the infantry moved into the town and captured the airfield against very little resistance. But then, from the hills behind Licata, enemy fire began. Perkins turned his attention to the dug-in defenders, sending one platoon around to flank and directing a frontal assault himself.

The radio transmitter in the tank of the commander of the flanking platoon was out. On the crossing from north Africa someone had left the hatch ajar; salt water had gotten in, crippling the radio. So Sgt. Herbert Gwinn was relaying instructions to the platoon from his tank. The platoon commander listened in to the radioed orders and transmitted them to the platoon by voice and hand signals to Gwinn. Suddenly Sergeant Gwinn heard a voice in English:

"Hazel Six, this is John Six. What is your position and situation?"

Sergeant Gwinn had been instructed in communications security. Be suspicious, the instructors had said: the voice on the other end of the radio could be an English-speaking Kraut trying to lead you into a trap.

Gwinn was suspicious.

"Listen you lousy son of a bitch, if you are a goddamn Nazi, just keep on listening. Maybe you'll learn something."

With that, Sergeant Gwinn signed off and went into battle. In the fight the company knocked out six 75-millimeter guns and several Italian pillboxes. Afterward Lt. Col. Amzi R. Quillian, commander of the Third Battalion, came up to congratulate the company, and he asked for Sergeant Gwinn.

"Sergeant," he said, "this is John Six."

Everywhere the Allied forces had done well on that first day, although the American armor did not really get going. The British captured Syracuse, and the Americans fought off the counterattacks in the Gela area. Second-stage troops were now moving in. The 334th Coast Artillery antiaircraft guns were brought ashore. Staff Sergeant Johnson's company was assigned to Gela airfield. As the company came up along the coast road, the troops saw wrecked tanks and trucks and broken bodies all along the way. As they approached the town, a single German fighter plane came down to strafe the convoy, and then the plane was gone, with the .50-caliber tracers from the truck turrets tailing after it.

Gela. The trucks roared through the town square, and beyond, to the airfield. Gun sites were assigned. Trucks moved up with the Bofors guns, and they were dug in and sandbagged. The .50-caliber guns were moved around. All guns were sited before the crews got down to self-protection. The trucks were moved into cover if possible; if not, camouflage nets were set up over them. Engineers came in to fill the bomb craters and mark out the minefields. During a lull Sergeant Johnson took Cpl. William Reed and the platoon jeep down for a look at the beach below Gela. Trucks were pouring ashore from the ships. Artillery was coming along, too. And out beyond the threatening gray of the war flotilla the sea was bright, bright blue.

Johnson hurried back to the airfield before he was missed. Just in time. The first sergeant was looking for him, to assign the platoon command post. They dug in on a hill facing north. The field was a natural plain, with low hills in the south, crags in the north, and flat on east and west.

The company was soon dug in, and Johnson was sent out in the weapons carrier to look for water. The men drove into Gela, and found that a water crew had already set up station at the pump in the town square. The water was filtered and chlorinated and run into the 5-gallon jerry cans. Then it was back to the airfield to await the landing of the fighter planes.

Lieutenant Miller's company of the Twentieth Engineers had been guarding the beachhead for the preceding twenty-four hours. Guarding all those tomato and melon patches. C ration laced with fresh tomato and followed by watermelon was a great improvement. How many tomatoes could you eat? It was hard to count, in and out of the slit trenches, with the German bombers and fighters coming in to hit and run. Then came orders. The engineers were to march to Licata and take over guard of the city. Engineers? Maybe Colonel Caffey had been right about his tommy guns.

Off to the northwest General Rose's Combat Command A was ordered to attack toward the towns of Naro and Canicatti to secure the hills. The reconnaissance company moved out at 3:30 a.m. The road was very bad, narrow and rutted, and the terrain was jagged, no less. The Germans showed up: snipers, machine guns, and fighter-bombers. Luckily they were not good shots in the dark.

Just outside Naro the advance column was met by two civilians, the mayor and his small son. Good news! No Germans in the town. The mayor and his son rode back in style, on the hood of a half-track. The Second Armored Division had captured its first town.

The other companies came up, and a platoon of infantry was left to guard the roads and wait for the Allied military government team that would now take over. Fast work. The rest of the combat command roared through Naro to meet the enemy.

Unfortunately for Naro, communications between the American Army Air Force and the ground force were terrible. The armored men said this was because the air force had refused to set up an air-ground liaison. And so, late that morning, Naro was very effectively bombed, and mostly destroyed— by eighteen American B-26 bombers. The mayor found it very difficult to understand.

On that morning of July 11 the Germans and Italians attacked the American invaders again.

One Axis force headed down the Niscemi–Piano Lupo road. Three armored task forces of the Hermann Göring Division converged on the area. They first made contact in the Abbio Priolo area, where Corporal Moglia's Second Battalion of the Sixteenth Infantry, as well as some paratroopers, had just arrived and hastily dug in. The Americans had the support of eight howitzers of the Seventh Field Artillery Battalion, but no armor. They also had bazookas, machine guns, mortars, and the other weapons of the infantryman's arsenal. With these they withstood the attack of the German armor, which came up to fire from point-blank range.

The pressure was somewhat reduced when Colonel Gavin organized more of his paratroopers and moved toward the Biazzo area on the Biscari road. On the highland the Germans were driving toward the Gela beaches, and for a while it looked as though they might get down there. But the Sixteenth Infantry and the paratroopers held. The German lead tanks reached the highway west of Santa Spina, within view of the sea, hardly more than a mile away. They fired into supply dumps and fired at landing craft. But finally four of the ten tanks of Combat Command B managed to get off the soft sand of the beach and engage the Germans.

On Piano Lupo the First and Second battalions of the Sixteenth Infantry held the road junction against repeated enemy attacks. Corporal Moglia skittered from foxhole to foxhole. Six German tanks managed to break through the line that afternoon. One was disabled—wonder of wonders—by a miraculous shot from a 37-millimeter antitank gun. A round from a 60-millimeter mortar dropped squarely into the open hatch of a second German tank, killing its crew. An infantryman with a bazooka knocked the tread off another German tank, and its crew bailed out and retreated. The paratroops got still another tank with a bazooka, and the last two German tanks then pulled back.

Down in the beach area the Eighteenth Infantry and the Forty-first Armored Infantry prepared to fight the Germans coming toward tree-lined Highway 115. The engineers on the beach stopped moving supplies and vehicles and established a firing line along the sand dunes. Four tanks from Combat Command B joined in. The Thirty-second Field Artillery Battalion came rushing in on DUKWs, going directly to firing positions along the edge of the dunes. Also, the indefatigable General Roosevelt had sent the Sixteenth Infantry Cannon Company by ferry across the Acate River to the dune line.

So the fight became more than a little brisk, and in the end the German armor retreated from the beach area too, leaving sixteen tanks destroyed or burning on the plain on the shoreward side of Highway 115.

*

Late in the afternoon Lieutenant Downing came trudging along an intersecting road from Second Armored Division headquarters, bearing information for regiment and again seeking the Eighteenth's command post. He was still traveling by shank's mare; it was not easy finding an unused jeep to replace the one bombed out on the beach.

The road was an inch deep in fine dust. Every vehicle that passed sent up a cloud of choking powder, and the hot sun drenched him in sweat. More like mud it seemed, when the sweat and dust mingled.

Downing reached Highway 115 and turned toward the command post. But when he got there, the Eighteenth Infantry headquarters was gone; looking across the road, he saw why. The German tanks blazed and smoked in the afternoon sun, some of them just yards from the old CP.

The lieutenant was worried, but he had to find regiment. Cautiously, he walked west along the road, where he met a two-man wire team. They told him where the new command post was located, and he set off again, this time across country. He heard antiaircraft fire from the beach and saw smoke puffs in the sky and tracers smoking in every direction. He jumped into a ditch and stared up. A German fighter plane zipped overhead from the direction of the beach, tracers following. The plane began to smoke. Something else was in the sky, drifting down. He thought it was a parachute, but it turned out to be a barrage balloon. The plane continued on, but then it fell off and crashed behind a clump of trees. A cloud of dust and black smoke rose up. The firing stopped, and the lieutenant crawled out of his ditch and got back on his way. Finally he found the command post in a small olive orchard. The Eighteenth obviously had taken over an abandoned German CP: tents, beds, uniforms, letters, books, and mess gear lay scattered all around—all German.

Downing reported to Lieutenant Colonel Williamson, the regimental executive officer, and he was invited to have some chow. Someone had harvested some of the tomatoes from the fields. As Downing ate, Lieutenant Newkirk came in, driving a Sicilian cart and mule; he had been out scavenging for fresh food.

One of the officers from the Eighteenth had some business with the Second Armored Division, so he gave Downing a ride back to that command post in his jeep. It was getting dark when they arrived. Downing could see firing from the ships offshore against the Germans in the hills and from the Germans toward the beach. The Second Armored command post was located in a farmhouse, and Downing figured the Germans had that house zeroed in. So he went into the field nearby and picked a spot next to a cactus hedge, buttoned up his field jacket, and lay down. Two soldiers were digging a slit trench. The lieutenant was too tired to make one for himself.

Then a German plane came over and dropped a bomb 200 yards away. Downing jumped up, borrowed a shovel from the soldiers, and began digging. Lucky! It was soft sand. When his slit trench was finished, he lay down in it and went to sleep. He did not see or hear a thing until morning.

So Lieutenant Downing missed the big excitement of the night. But Sergeant Johnson didn't.

Back in Tunisia the air force and army brass were planning a second airdrop. It would involve 2000 paratroopers—the 504th Parachute Regimental Combat Team. So 144 transport planes were loaded up with paratroopers and supplies.

On Sicily General Patton's Seventh Army command and the British had been apprised in the plan of attack that enemy paratroops might be expected any night for the first six days. But when the first night (D day) passed without a drop, the men in battle began to forget. Also, on D + 1 the various commands had intelligence that the Germans were going to send in glider and parachute troops that night from Italy to reinforce the defenders. General Patton had sent out a general order to watch for American parachutists on the night of D + 1, but word did not reach all units.

So when the new contingent of paratroops began to come in, there was a quick reaction. The first wave made it without interference; but as the second wave came along, so did a German air attack on the fleet offshore in the Gela area. The cruiser *Boise* was nearly hit by two bombs. Many ships were damaged by fragments. And then, just as the excitement was quieting down, in came the 504th Paratroopers. The leading flight jumped into the Gela-Farello drop zone. The second flight was in sight of Biviere Pond, the last checkpoint, when the Allied antiaircraft guns began to fire again.

Offshore, the fleet heard and saw the planes coming over, and it began firing on them. Some planes fell. Down on Gela airfield the men of the 334th manned their guns again. Here come the German paratroopers! The Bofors guns began to spit, and more planes fell before the gunners learned that they were shooting down American planes and quit firing. Some planes returned to Africa without dropping, and without being hit. But when the casualties were counted, the 504th had lost 229 men in that disastrous airdrop, and those who hit the ground found themselves virtually alone. The 504th was rendered completely confused and useless as a unit of reinforcement. For days, paratroopers kept turning up as the Allied troops moved forward. Back in Africa a board of investigation was formed to find out what had happened and why, but it ended up with the generals muttering at one another. General Ridgway took the philosophical view that "the losses are part of the inevitable price of war in human life." But down at Gela airfield the gunners of the 334th were stricken.

Among Sergeant Johnson's GIs many got physically sick when they learned what had happened.

"More than one threw his helmet to the ground in anger. Tears ran down their faces—tears of horror and frustration. Some said they would never be able to fire their weapons again. This was too much!"

Their only consolation was that they were only doing the duty assigned them by the brass, and for several days Sergeant Johnson's platoon was virtually paralyzed by the tragedy.

The platoon never did discover the extent of the damage. The marksmanship of the antiaircraft gunners was pretty good: of the 70 C-47s that came over, 23 were shot down and 37 damaged; of the 504th Parachute Infantry, 81 men were killed by "friendly fire," 132 were wounded, and 16 were written off as "missing." It was the first tragedy of error for the Americans in the European theater.

20

THE MORNING
OF THE FLIES

On the morning of the third day in Sicily Lieutenant Downing awoke at dawn, ate a cold can of chopped eggs and ham, and went over to the Second Division. The command post was still there. The Germans must have forgotten about the farmhouse. There, Downing met a tall, gray-haired colonel of Chemical Warfare Service, dressed in polished riding boots, pink breeches, and a green shirt and wearing a .45 Colt automatic revolver in a shoulder holster. Very military.

Downing hung around the CP for a while, waiting for news. There didn't seem to be much. From one of the liaison half-tracks came the sound of a radio. Axis Sally was talking about the Allied invaders—how they had been driven off the beaches of Sicily by the brave German and Italian defenders.

On the morning of D + 2 the Americans went on the offensive.

"Sock the hell out of those damned heinies," said General Allen, "before they can get set to hit us again."

One First Division force moved out north of Gela against elements of the Italian Livorno Division. Another took the Ponte Olivo airfield. The third element, Corporal Moglia's Sixteenth Infantry, along with the airborne troops it had met on the first day, began to advance up the Piano Lupo–Niscemi road. There the troops ran into Tiger tanks with their 88-millimeter guns.

Moglia's Second Battalion crossed the road and reached the ridgeline just southeast of Casa del Priolo. On the other side the Germans were digging in; the GIs could hear them. About 5:30 a.m. heavy German fire began to come into the Second Battalion's positions. The Germans threatened to cut the road and surround them. Lt. Col. Joseph Crawford, Second Battalion commander, was hit in the neck and shoulder by machine gun fire as he was going up front to see what was happening; he had to be evacuated. The exec, Captain Denno, got him back to the CP, and then went forward to take over the battalion.

The Germans were moving their tanks around, probing. Around noon six Tiger tanks came up with armored cars, half-tracks, and two platoons of Panzergrenadiers. The fighting was very rugged and Second Battalion took a lot of casualties. Artillery (75- and 105-millimeter) was brought to the line, but was soon knocked out by German shelling.

Several American tanks came up too, but so did several German anti-tank guns, and they began picking off the M-4 Shermans one by one. The armor commander said he was going to pull his tanks back until the infantry took care of those antitank guns.

Captain Denno told the tank commander that if he didn't start moving forward, the infantry would take over the tanks and run them. He asked Corporal Moglia if he knew how to operate a tank.

No, said Moglia. He had never run a tank—yet. But he would try.

The war with the Germans was suspended while the infantry and the tankers fought their own battle. But eventually cooler heads prevailed, and the infantrymen, using their bazookas—and the infinitely more effective captured German Panzerfausts, when they could find them—knocked out the antitank guns. Now the tankers moved ahead. Captain Denno counted noses. The battalion was down to about 200 riflemen, including a handful of paratroopers, all that survived of the original force that had hit and held Piano Lupo. Colonel Gorham, up front with a bazooka, was killed by a direct hit from an 88 shell.

Regiment was urging the Second Battalion to move up, for it had not taken the objective assigned and General Patton was putting on the pressure. As they moved slowly forward, Moglia and his buddies spotted a paratroop captain coming from the direction of the German lines. General Roosevelt came up. The captain identified himself as being from the 504th Parachute Infantry.

"What the hell are you doing out here?" the general asked the paratrooper.

Whereupon the captain told the story of the fiasco of the night before, when his plane had been hit by "friendly fire."

"Can I join up with you?" he asked.

"Well," replied the general, "I am glad to hear that they were able to hit something. Sure, come on along."

It was nearly dark, and the Second Battalion still had not taken its objective, Niscemi. But Moglia and the others were very tired, and their ranks were thin. Captain Denno persuaded regiment to let them stop for the night.

They stopped just short of an open field. On the other side, in a wooded area, the GIs could see a concentration of enemy tanks. Regiment thought the tanks were preparing for an attack, and it was getting ready to put the heavy mortars and artillery onto the German armor. To help the men aim, Moglia went forward to shoot azimuths at both ends of the woods. The first shells would be smoke to mark the flanks. Moglia watched as they were fired.

"The first smoke round, fired at the right flank of the woods, landed in an open tank turret, and soon a beautiful display of fireworks erupted. One less enemy tank!"

Darkness came, and with it a constant harassing fire from the Germans. Regiment continued to believe the Hermann Göring Division was preparing for an attack. But when morning came regiment was shown to be wrong. The Germans had pulled back toward Caltagirone, and the Americans moved into Niscemi without trouble.

There the First and Second battalions of the Sixteenth Infantry had to be reorganized. Both had lost their battalion commanders. In those last two days 56 men from Moglia's Second Battalion had been killed, 133 had been wounded, and 57 were missing. For that the unit got a citation.

D + 3: The armored units were organized now. Canicatti was the objective for Combat Command A. On the night of D + 2 the Italians had pulled out of entrenched positions along the narrow pass that led into the town. In the morning the Americans fired a ten-minute artillery barrage, after which somebody saw a white flag from the town. General Rose and his chief of staff started into the town to accept the surrender, but on the road they were fired on by enemy artillery and dived into the ditch. The American artillery opened up again and this time fired for thirty minutes.

The assault was made by Captain Perkins's Company of the Sixty-sixth Armored Regiment and Company G of the 141st Armored Infantry. The infantrymen rode the tanks; they had been told to jump off when the tanks stopped and then to give ground assistance. The column moved up the narrow road in the mountains. When it was about a half-mile from town, the enemy artillery began zeroing in on the road. The column stopped, and the infantrymen dropped off into the ditches beside the road. Then Captain Perkins had new orders. He was to move on, in spite of everything. The tankers looked around. They could not find the infantrymen, and their orders said to go on. So they went on, under Perkins's command, to attack with all guns firing at every window, door, and roof that might hide snipers or Panzerfausts and at every intersection that might hide an antitank gun.

The tanks sped through the town. At the north edge they began to draw fire from heavy-caliber weapons about a mile and a half away. The fire grew closer and more accurate, so Perkins put his tank behind a stone wall. An antitank gun shell hit the muzzle of his 75-millimeter gun just as Perkins was reaching into the breech to clear away some spilled powder. The impact broke Captain Perkins's arm in two places. The tank burst into flames and the crew bailed out. Sgt. Tim McMahon's leg was broken. In the next few minutes the crew of Perkins's tank splinted the captain's arm and the sergeant's leg, recovered a secret radio code from the scorched tank, and moved on by foot. By D + 4 the infantry had cleared the ground north of Canicatti.

The mystery of the white flag that was not a surrender flag was solved: the "white flag" was actually a Red Cross flag flying over a hospital, and some eager beaver had passed the wrong word.

Soon the beachhead was secure. New troops moved up to carry the assault: the 179th, 180th, 157th, 7th, and 15th Infantry regiments, and heretofore unblooded armored units of the Second Armored Division, now up off the beaches and onto the solid ground where they could move to best advantage. There was considerable trouble with hot pilots from the air force who kept mistaking American armored units for German ones and shooting them up. The Americans tried using yellow smoke to identify themselves, but that did not work very well. They switched to colored pennants on the vehicles. That worked better.

D + 4: The beachhead was secure, but, as Sergeant Johnson's antiaircraft battery learned quickly enough, that did not mean the danger had ended. Sergeant Johnson was assigned to supply detail, which meant taking a 2½-ton truck down to the beach to pick up rations and ammunition. He took a driver and a driver's assistant; the sergeant rode in the open bed in back of the cab. They picked up the supplies; then the driver had to turn his vehicle

around. The white strips denoting the safe area were still there, but Private
Sad Sack forgot, and before Sergeant Johnson could yell, they were in the
minefield. The right front wheel hit a Teller mine. The next thing the sergeant knew, he was thrown "arse over teakettle," landing with a thump on
the sand. He got up, his head pounding and his ears ringing, and staggered
to the truck. There were the driver and his assistant, blood running out of
their noses, sitting paralyzed.

"You guys all right?"

No answer.

"You guys..." he began shaking them. He pulled them out of the cab,
and they seemed to be okay except for the nosebleeds. Then he looked at
the truck. The right front wheel had disappeared. The fender and hood, too.
A great chunk of the floorboard was blown away. The assistant driver had
missed losing both of his feet by about 2 inches.

"Boy," marveled a sailor, "were you guys lucky!"

Amen.

They got a ride back to the airfield, and another truck came down to pick
up the load. The medics checked them all over and said they were okay.

D + 4: The captain told the first sergeant that there was a "helluva stink" at
the airfield. A real stink, which was dreadful when the wind blew across
from the west. He thought it might be a dead cow. He wanted somebody to
go out and find out what it was. The first sergeant told Sergeant Johnson to
take Sgt. Victor Vellekoop and Corporal Lair and a jeep to go find the cause.
After breakfast ("shit on a shingle" and coffee) they set out in full combat
gear, the jeep carrying a .50-caliber machine gun. Sergeant Johnson was
driving. Sergeant Vellekoop sat up front, and Corporal Lair kept company
with the .50 in the back. As the morning sun began to heat up the rocky
land, they left the airfield and turned up the valley road that led to the west.
About a mile and a half beyond the airfield the stink grew worse. They drove
on, and the smell diminished. They drove back and stopped the jeep on the
shoulder of the road, across from a narrow ravine that led off to the west.
The ravine seemed to be the source. They took their gas masks, and walked
carefully, watching for mines.

The ravine dropped down into a sort of pocket, and as they came to the
lip, they saw that they had discovered the source of the stink. It wasn't a
cow. The whole pocket was littered with helmets, rifles, packs, shoes, and
parts of bodies.

The air was absolutely silent, except for the buzzing of the flies. The whole area... half a helmet with hunks of bone and hair sticking to it... a shoe with a shattered leg and foot... clawlike hands... legs, arms, torso pieces... scarcely a whole body in the lot. What had happened? A bomb? Perhaps. A shell from a 155? Or ten shells? Or a whole stick of bombs? The dead soldiers were all Italian—the scraps of uniform and helmets told the story. How many men? An archaeologist might have been able to figure it out from the bits and scraps, but not a patrol of dogfaces. Maybe there were a couple of squads in the ravine? Maybe a platoon?

Corporal Lair stopped and retched before they got out of the ravine. Very quiet, very subdued, they drove back to the airfield to report. A few hours later they saw bulldozers heading up the west road. When the bulldozers came back, Sergeant Johnson stopped one of them.

"Yeah, we pushed dirt and rocks into the whole ravine until it was full up." He turned and started the dozer up again. "It's a lousy war, Sarge," he said, and drove away.

*   *   *

The days went by, and the Allies moved ahead. The Germans and the Italians fought, the Germans more stubbornly than most of the Italians, but they fought and retreated and fought again. Italians, Germans, Americans, British, and Canadians fought and died. So did civilians and cows, chickens and goats. The Eighteenth Infantry moved into Barrafranca. Lieutenant Downing had caught a ride in a weapons carrier. What a thrill it was to be cheered by the people, and to see the kids running alongside the vehicles while the GIs threw C-ration candy to them. The troops bivouacked outside the town in an olive grove. That night a flight of planes came over and bombed. The dogfaces were betting they were American planes. They were right. The planes bombed the hell out of Barrafranca, knocking down buildings and killing civilians. The debris blocked the road, which was the advancing infantry's main route of supply.

The campaign developed along a pattern. The infantrymen advanced along the paved highway until they ran into the enemy, dug in on the steep hills alongside. The American infantry then also deployed along the road, and prepared to attack at night or at dawn. The artillery came up and plastered the hills with barrages, usually during the night. The riflemen attacked and found the enemy gone or going. The next day the story was repeated. The command post of the Eighteenth Infantry moved almost daily. So did division. Downing's problem was that although he was jeepless, he still had to try to keep contact between division and regiment. So, usually, by the time he got to one place, the news he brought was outdated by events, and when he went back to the other place: ditto.

General Patton, who despised the British intensely and felt that the whole role of his Seventh Army had been subordinated to British pride, now engaged in a race for Palermo against Montgomery's Eighth Army. He assembled the Second Armored Division forces near Campobello, with troops of the Eighty-second Airborne and Third Infantry divisions, as well as the ranger battalions. The idea very plainly was to make headlines in America and prove to the British that the Americans could carry their share of this war, which the British did not seem to believe. (The British claimed surprise at this American attitude. Perhaps they *were* completely oblivious to the American sensitivity.)

On July 20 the provisional corps formed by Patton got its orders to move, and on July 23 American troops entered Palermo. The big question was, Who got there first? The Second Armored Division with General Patton at its head? Or the British Seventh Infantry?

Most of the GIs didn't know or care anything about such matters of high policy. It was theirs to plod ahead, still wearing their OD wool uniforms in the heat of the Sicilian summer, uniforms that were now gray at the neckline and armpits with sweat and dust.

The campaign was winding down, and the dogfaces of the line could relax. But, as usual, the winding down of the battle meant the return of rear-echelon discipline. The first big news to the men of the First Division was the unhappy word that Gen. Terry Allen was being removed from command, and his assistant, Gen. Teddy Roosevelt, Jr., also. The official word was that Terry Allen was suffering from "war weariness" and had to go home and rest. The truth was that Allen and Patton and Bradley did not see eye to eye. The men of the First Division had proved to be fine fighting men, but in days of inaction they were also hard to control, and General Bradley found that hard to stomach. So the brass was getting rid of difficulties. Also, Bradley wanted his own boys in charge. The new commander of the First Division was to be Maj. Gen. Clarence R. Huebner, and his instructions were to get the division under control. That meant discipline. Discipline meant close order drill and a return to fundamentals, sort of a basic training rerun. The program was not a great social success within the division.

Lieutenant Downing discovered what was happening just after the Eighteenth Infantry went into bivouac.

"It was the general opinion that this change was a bad omen. General

Allen had commanded the division through Africa and Sicily and the old rumors were being revived that we might be sent back to the states after the campaign. However, if a new general took command, we could be sure that we would continue on somewhere in combat. A new general wouldn't be appointed to lead troops back to the states."

How right they were.

Lieutenant Downing had the unenviable job of bringing the first orders from the new general to Colonel Smith, commander of the Eighteenth Infantry: the men of the regiment were to utilize the rest period to zero in their weapons and take "conditioning hikes."

When Downing showed up at regiment with these instructions, the regimental staff officers did little more than grunt. They were well disciplined. But at the company level the reaction was violent and blasphemous. Just out of combat, having been hiking and firing their weapons in battle steadily for thirty days, they were being told by this greenhorn general to get ready for combat. There was only one way to describe it: "chicken shit."

If the general had come to inspect just then, he would have been most displeased. His fighting men looked like ruffians—wool uniforms stiff with grease, sweat, dirt, and blood. The quartermasters arrived in the nick of time with brand-new cotton fatigue uniforms, and these became the new proper uniform.

The regiment was ordered abruptly (was there any other sort of order?) to move up to Randazzo. Why, not one of the GIs ever figured out. They took a few casualties from mines along the road, but since the Third Division and the Second Armored had entered Messina, the campaign was over. Randazzo, they found, had been so thoroughly smashed by artillery and bombing that bulldozers had to clear a road through the town.

Lieutenant Downing was sitting on top of the world. He had a cushy job as a liaison officer, and not a lot to do. Major Colacicco, the battalion operations officer, sent him up to division headquarters at Triata to pick up a convoy of a hundred vehicles that would transport the Eighteenth to a new rest area. Downing went by jeep to the headquarters, which was set in a cluster of handsome buildings on some nobleman's estate. He was looking forward to some good food and rest, but had no sooner gotten the dust of the road washed off his face than a major of artillery braced him. The major, it seemed, was convoy commander. He gave Downing his orders and showed him the field where the vehicles were to assemble. The next day they moved.

They got to Randazzo an hour early, which made the major happy. But when Downing appeared at the regimental area with his trucks, and they were not gassed up, the regimental supply officer was furious. Downing showed him the orders, which stipulated that the Seventh Army was to gas the trucks. The supply officer went rushing up to see Colonel Smith. Downing waited:

"I shrugged my shoulders. I would probably get my ears batted down after he told his story to the colonel. It was a not uncommon trait of staff officers to run to the colonel with stories which showed the enormous amount of work they had to do to make up for the inefficiency of other officers. You can't beat city hall."

Soon Major Colacicco came up; Downing gave him the copy of the orders, which Colacicco took away with him. Downing hoped that the major would get to the colonel before the orders for a firing squad came down.

The net result was not that serious, but Downing did lose his liaison job. Lieutenant Colonel Williamson, who had been regimental executive officer for as long as anybody could remember, was being given his chance: command of the Second Battalion. In the fall from regimental grace, Downing was assigned to H Company of that battalion.

Downing loaded his equipment onto a jeep and drove to H Company. There he found Captain Murphy, who had been CO of Company H until he was wounded, and then Lieutenant Rosie had taken over. Now, Captain Murphy had come back, and Rosie had become executive officer. But since Downing outranked Rosie, it seemed that Rosie would now slip back to command of platoon. Big deal!

It was not to be. Downing's fall from grace settled the matter. Despite his higher rank, Downing was assigned as a platoon leader.

"I reported to Colonel Williamson and received a lecture on the necessity of my working hard to rehabilitate myself in the eyes of the [regimental] colonel."

At least Captain Murphy gave Downing his choice of platoons. He chose the 81-millimeter mortar platoon.

Then Downing's personal disgrace was forgotten as the upper echelons focused their dissatisfaction on the behavior of the GIs throughout the First Division. General Huebner prepared to apply the spit and polish.

21

REVVING UP

There were still Germans to be fought in Sicily. So Allied reinforcements continued to arrive. On July 31 the Sixtieth Infantry's first ships had pulled into Palermo. The next day a two-hour air raid raised havoc in the harbor.

It began at about 4 a.m. And one man it scared very much was Pvt. Jesse Butler of Company H, Sixtieth Infantry.

Private Butler was 18 years old and brand new to combat; he had been drafted in February, just six months earlier. He had gone through basic training at Camp Croft, South Carolina, and had barely assimilated that when he was shipped overseas to the Oran replacement depot. From there he was sent off to the Sixtieth Infantry at Sidi-bel-Abbès. The Sixtieth had marched from Sidi-bel-Abbès back to Oran, with Private Butler in full field pack and carrying an 81-millimeter mortar baseplate. That was tough going, but in Palermo harbor Private Butler faced his first bit of shooting war. "A terrifying experience."

When the German planes came over, the guns of the ships opened up, and the noise was so deafening that the new men in the transports believed their ships had been hit. They all tried to run out onto the deck, but the marine guards would not let them go.

Two of their ships had gone in to dock, and both were hit. One was an ammunition vessel and the other carried vehicles. The ammunition ship began to blow up, and it continued exploding until about 11 a.m. Private But-

238

ler's transport pulled into the docks around noon. But it was three o'clock in the afternoon before Sergeant Thornton's company got ashore. The men hiked 13 miles to their bivouac, and then waited while their equipment came up. On August 4 they moved into the line. They were going up to give a hand to the First Division, which had been bogged down in the Troina area for a week. The German opposition was extremely heavy.

Private Butler's Company H started for the hills. As the truck convoy carried the troops, they could hear the sounds of battle ahead, another frightening experience for the green Private Butler. They stopped and got out. The supply sergeant was passing out C rations and ammunition. Private Butler was more interested in ammunition. He loaded himself down with bandoliers of M-1 ammo, half a dozen grenades, and a marine trench knife for hand to hand combat; then he went on.

The Sixtieth was going over the mountains, the GIs learned on August 5, and the next day they were issued mules and taught the elements of mule skinning. (Private Butler, the farm boy from Georgia, would be a natural as a mule skinner, the sergeant was sure. In fact, Butler didn't know much at all about driving a mule. But he packed the pack saddle on his mule—all the ammunition and water cans and rations on top—and tied it on by running the cinch around the mule's belly. The mule "cooperated" by sticking his belly out as the cinch was tied. Then they started out. The mule now tightened up his belly muscles, and the whole pack slid around so the load was hanging beneath the animal's belly. The whole job would have to be done again.

Mule skinner Butler learned fast enough.

They finally made it up to the bivouac area on top of a mountain at about midnight. The platoon sergeant came up and told Butler to keep things quiet and his head down. They had met the Germans; they were on the next hill.

With the Americans were some of the Ghoums. All night long Private Butler could hear the Germans firing. The next morning the GIs began marching down the hill in sunshine; halfway down they came to a spring. The dogfaces began filling canteens. Butler gave his canteen to a buddy to fill, and went on ahead with his mule. He had gone only about 15 yards when all hell broke loose by the spring.

Seven German soldiers burst out of the underbrush and opened up with burp guns on the Americans. The racket was enormous. Private Butler let go of his mule and dropped behind a rock, getting ready to fire his M-1. But the Germans, having killed a few Americans with those first bursts, quickly disappeared back into the underbrush.

The Germans began to shell the Americans then. Private Butler dug a hole and jumped in. He remained there all day. Not far from where he lay was the position of an American artillery observer. He caught a shell squarely, and it turned him into "sausage meat."

That same shell also killed Butler's squad leader; he got one piece of shrapnel right between the eyes.

It was unnerving. Private Butler could not eat for two days. He stayed in his foxhole, watching the wounded come by—the walking wounded, and the stretcher cases.

On August 6 Sergeant Thornton also left Capinizzi and marched—7 miles that day—up one mountain and down another, over narrow trails. Progress stopped until the enemy artillery on Mt. Palato could be knocked out. The First and Second battalions, in the lead, were taking casualties, but so far the Third Battalion suffered none.

The next day the Second Battalion, with Private Butler's mortar, went through the First Battalion.

Cesaro, Carmalota, Del Re: the enemy was now in retreat from the superior American force. Still no losses in Sergeant Thornton's Company M. Mt. Cacolo, Floresta, Basico, Cefalù.

Lieutenant Miller's Twentieth Engineers were practicing their trade. On August 1 the First Battalion moved along Highway 113 to open up the rail line east of Palermo in order to help supply the Third and Forty-fifth divisions. The Germans had blown all the railroad bridges in their retreat. Company A built a bridge south of Termini Imerese. B Company built a bridge east of Cefalù, and C Company built a bridge at Tusa.

On August 18 Field Marshal Rommel pulled the last German troops out of Sicily, and that was the end of the campaign. Most American troops went into bivouac. General Patton came up to make one of his heroic addresses to the NCOs of the Sixtieth.

A few days earlier General Patton had given General Allen hell because the First Division had taken a week to capture Troina. Although American intelligence had been completely inaccurate about the enemy's strength, in Patton's book there was no excuse for failure. That was the real cause of General Allen's downfall.

The rough edges of the American military were hard to smooth down.

The British had the definite feeling (although most of them were careful not to enunciate it) that the Americans had a lot to learn. Well, some of the Americans who had been in the battles so far thought so, too. One was Corporal Moglia. Kasserine Pass was now ancient history, but once in a while some of those involved in the actions stopped to think about that disaster. Moglia told his buddies that the real problem was that Americans hated taking suggestions from the British and the French. "Inexperience and pride" was his assessment of Kasserine. The French and the British employed their antitank weapons in order—the smallest furthest forward—and kept them quiet unless they could do the job. No 37-millimeter guns against Tiger tanks! The heavy artillery, which belonged in the rear, should handle such chores. In contrast, the Americans fired everything, including the M-1 rifle, at anything that moved. Against the armor of a Tiger tank, a .50-caliber machine gun was a toy.

Well, the Americans were learning, and beginning to understand some of the deficiencies of their weaponry.

Once things quieted down some more of the learning process could begin.

The Sixteenth Infantry went out of action with the capture of Messina. A division dentist came up to set up shop in an olive grove, with his portable chair and foot-operated drill. The drills got hot and the filling process hurt like the devil, but the line of patients was constant all day long. Corporal Moglia—no, *Sergeant* Moglia now—joined the line one day. As the men in the line heard the cries of anguish of their friends, some dropped out. Moglia was soon in the chair. The dentist, he discovered, was the son of Phil Datz, who ran a produce farm on Long Island from which Moglia's grandfather bought the vegetables for his stand. And here they were, the sons of a couple of immigrants, meeting in this far-off country. Small world. The chance meeting was a boon to Sergeant Moglia. Dr. son-of-Phil-Datz even let the drill cool down between grinds.

Being named Moglia was also nice, and a little *parlare Italiano* didn't hurt. The sergeant met a man who had driven a streetcar in Chicago for twenty years, saved his money, come home to Sicily, and bought a farm. Then, said the farmer, all was well until Mussolini expropriated half his farm and half his possessions as "state property."

"Hurry up and kill the Fascist bastards," said Moglia's farmer friend.

Ignazio Silone, Mussolini's propagandist, was still saying that the silly Americans didn't know what they were fighting for. Well, Sergeant Moglia knew. It was to kill the Fascist bastards for his friends.

Ah, what he learned. The mulberry fruit was ripe, and he glutted himself on the dark berries. His hands turned purple. A farmer saw, laughed, and brought up some sulfur, which he lighted. "Now, rub your hands over the fumes," he said, and Sergeant Moglia did. Presto. No more stain.

There were more serious lessons to be learned by many, including no less a figure than General Patton, the toughest (self-proclaimed) commander in the army. One day, as the campaign was ending, the general was visiting the Fifteenth Evacuation Hospital near Nicosia; he encountered a soldier from Company L of the Sixteenth Infantry. The private had been admitted and diagnosed: "psychoneurosis anxiety state—moderate severe." The general, dressed to the nines as usual, in twill riding breeches and riding boots, packing two .45s, and carrying gloves, approached the private and asked what was the matter with him.

"I guess I just can't take it," said the soldier.

Whereupon the general slapped the private across the face with his gloves, seized him bodily, and threw him out of the tent.

Not content with this violence, General Patton then returned to his headquarters and issued a memo for his lesser generals:

> It has come to my attention that a very small number of soldiers are going to the hospital on the pretext that they are nervously incapable of combat. Such men are cowards and bring discredit on the Army and disgrace to their comrades who they heartlessly leave to endure the danger of a battle which they themselves use the hospital as a means of escaping.
>
> You will take measures to see that such cases are not sent to the hospital but are dealt with in their units.
>
> Those who are not willing to fight will be tried by Court-Martial for cowardice in the face of the enemy.

Shades of Kasserine and Maknassy! Sergeant Thornton and the men of Company M, Third Battalion, Sixtieth Infantry, could have told General Patton a thing or two about shell shock. But, of course, there was no way that Sergeant Thornton and the other men of the line could get through to the general, and he did not seem to know very much about the subject.

That first incident was hushed up by the West Point protective society, as one of "Georgie's" vagaries. This was the general who said his prayers every night, and then acted violently—in one way or another—toward his subordinates every day. He had many lovable qualities, but equanimity was not one of them.

That incident was a violation of the Articles of War, but since no one said anything, it was soon nearly forgotten. Then, one week later, General Patton surpassed himself. This time his performance was staged at the Ninety-third Evacuation Hospital. Patton walked into the receiving tent to build a little morale, as well as the Patton legend. He intended to go up the line of cots, asking each man where he had been hurt and commending him. The fourth man was a soldier from Battery C of the Seventeenth Field Artillery, who had been diagnosed as suffering from a severe case of shell shock. He was huddled on his cot, shivering.

"What's your trouble, soldier?"

"It's my nerves...." the soldier began to sob.

"What did you say?"

"It's my nerves. I can hear the shells come over, but I can't hear them burst."

The general turned to a medical officer who was accompanying his tour.

"What's this man talking about? What's wrong with him, if anything?"

The doctor tried to reply, but Patton had renewed the past week's fury. He turned back to the soldier.

"Your nerves, hell. You are just a goddamned coward, you yellow son of a bitch."

Just then Col. D. E. Currier, commander of the hospital, entered, and this is what he heard and saw:

The general, every inch the fighting figure in his neatly pressed whipcord riding breeches, boots, and combat jacket, was screaming at the soldier:

"You're a disgrace to the army and you're going right back to the front to fight, although that's too good for you. You ought to be lined up against a wall and shot. In fact I ought to shoot you myself right now, goddamn you."

The general pulled one of his pistols from its holster and waved it in the soldier's face. Then the general hit the soldier in the face with the back of his free hand, and continued to scream.

The other officers stood, paralyzed. Then the general spotted Colonel Currier: "I want you to get that man out of here, right away. I won't have these other brave boys seeing such a bastard babied."

He put the pistol back into his holster and started to leave, but then he turned back and saw the soldier, openly crying.

The sight aroused Patton to new fury. He rushed back to the soldier and hit him so hard in the face that the blow knocked off the helmet liner the man was wearing. Propelled by the blow, the liner rolled all the way outside the tent. That was enough for Colonel Currier, who interposed himself between the soldier and the general.

The general then strode away.

"I meant what I said about getting that coward out of here. I won't have those cowardly bastards hanging around our hospitals. We'll probably have to shoot them sometime anyway or we'll raise a breed of morons."

And the brave general left, still fuming.

By the time Patton arrived at the Second Corps headquarters of General Bradley, he had cooled off so much that he barely mentioned the incident, and Bradley and his staff paid little attention.

But Colonel Currier had not cooled off. On August 12 a very angry Colonel Currier submitted to the Second Corps surgeon general an official report of the incident. The surgeon told Gen. William B. Kean, Bradley's chief of staff, about it. Kean got hold of the report and took it to General Bradley. When Bradley read it, he knew that this was big trouble.

His old friend had really surpassed himself this time. Among the violations of the Articles of War were threatening an enlisted man with violence, two counts of physical abuse, and at least two counts of verbal abuse. A company officer would be court-martialed for these violations.

Bradley picked up the explosive report and had it locked in the safe. The West Point protective society in action again? Well, yes and no. Bradley was still under Patton's command. The official thing to do would have been to send the report up to Patton's headquarters at Seventh Army. What would have happened to it at Patton's stronghold is an interesting question. If Patton's staff had the guts to suppress the report, Colonel Currier still might get the inspector general into the picture. Bradley, the great calmer of troubled waters, tried his hand.

There was no hope. Too many people had seen the slapping, and the word was all over the island in a matter of hours. War correspondents knew of it. Loyally (these were the days before Vietnam), they did not even try just then to press the story through censorship. But Eisenhower had the word soon enough, through the surgeon's office. For General Patton had shocked and infuriated the doctors with his brazen invasion of their turf. Soon the word did get back to the United States. It made the papers and aroused storms of passion at home, including congressional demands for Patton's head. That created enormous difficulties for General Eisenhower, whose position seemed to be far more political than moral. By making such a fuss, Patton might have "destroyed his usefulness," said Ike, who seemed more concerned about what Patton had done to himself than what his violence represented to the average dogface.

Fortunately, Patton had outraged the sensibilities of millions of Americans at home. On Sicily, as Sergeant Moglia noted, 50,000 soldiers would cheer-fully have shot General Patton on sight if he had not been out of season. There was still an element of the old U.S. Army in the American forces that the people of the new Army of the United States would never understand:

Troops are pawns.

But the enormous difference between the American army and that of Adolf Hitler was that the American generals were ultimately responsible, through the politicians, to the public. And here was the prime example. The scandal was too great to be hushed. Eventually General Patton was forced to "apol-ogize" and recant. He did so with great grace. He came up to the Sixteenth Infantry (the first soldier abused had been a Sixteenth Infantry rifleman) and made a long speech glorifying the regiment and naming the names of heroes. He never really did apologize for slapping the man. There is no indication that General Patton learned that there really is such an ailment as shell shock. The general, unlike Sergeant Thornton, Sergeant Johnson, and Corporal Moglia, had not recently had his head nearly blown off by a shell, or lain listening to the shells coming in day and night for a week. He had not seen his buddies taken off the field with "shell shock" and then returned to the line a few days later, recovered and ready to fight again. Old Blood and Guts—*our blood his guts*—still had things to learn.

The real tragedy for General Patton was that he had created trouble for Eisenhower, and that was the end of any hopes he might have had for higher command. General Eisenhower vowed after the slapping incident was over that he would never use General Patton in a capacity higher than that of commander of a field army.

The First Division now came in for more trouble. General Huebner, the word trickled down, believed that the men of the First Division were lacking in fundamental military skills. (This was an opinion passed to Huebner by Patton and Bradley, but it was buttressed by Huebner's own experience as a liaison officer with the British. He spent much of his time in Britain arguing the American cause, but he was impressed with the British feeling that the Americans were simply not up to snuff.)

How to remedy the awful deficiency?

Why, the men of the First Division would go back to fundamentals, start-ing with basic recruit close order drill. They would then progress, learning everything they had not learned before, until they were "ready for combat."

The program, eight hours a day of training, included calisthenics, close

order drill, field problems, weapons instruction and practice, and conditioning marches.

Lieutenant Downing's 81-millimeter mortar platoon of Company H of the
Second Battalion of the Eighteenth Infantry got it all. His platoon NCO was
the redheaded Sergeant Henesey, a failed OCS candidate. Not exactly failed,
actually, but a reject because he had gotten into a fight with another OCS
candidate a few days before graduation.

Downing and Henesey racked their brains to make the training interesting enough to keep the angry dogfaces from going AWOL. It wasn't pleasant
for men who had just undergone nearly a year of combat in two campaigns to
be told they did not know how to fight. The way to stimulate the troops seemed
to be competition among squads. Downing got hold of an enormous quantity
of 81-millimeter ammunition, written off as expended on the battlefield, and
thus ineligible for future official battle use. He could fire every round in
practice if he wished. And he wished. As they trained and practiced firing,
the men discovered that there were *indeed* areas in which their rapidly expanded training of the past had been less than perfect. They really were
learning how to shoot.

So it was garrison life for a while. Movies every night at the open-air
amphitheater. Bob Hope and Frances Langford came to entertain one night,
and the lady came on stage in a pair of white slacks and a white brassiere,
the first brassiere a lot of men had seen in a long time.

There were hoots and howls and wolf calls.

There was also plenty of vino. Each battalion had its own wine shop,
where vino went for 10 lire (a dime) a canteen cupful. The NCOs of the top
three grades soon had a club, and so did the officers. The officers' club was
a captured Italian wall tent furnished with two picnic tables, a homemade
crap table with GI blanket upholstery, and a long bar constructed largely
from old C-ration boxes. All the beverages were strictly European: red wine,
white wine, a half-dozen vermouths, banana gin, Italian brandy, orange gin,
liberated kuemmel, anisette, liberated cognac, and many other beverages of
various colors in bottles of various sizes and shapes. The poker game never
stopped and the crap game seldom. But at least sitting around the officers'
club drinking and gambling was better than lying around the tent area, brood-
ing on the sins of the brass. Lieutenant Downing discovered nurses at a U.S.
hospital a few miles down the road. But get a date? Not a chance. Patton's
orders were for all officers and men of his army to wear ODs, helmet liners,
and leggings at all times—not a very romantic costume. The flyboys wore
khakis or pinks, leather flight jackets emblazoned with their squadron patches,
and caps with the grommets removed, so their headgear looked like pirate

caps. They also had Scotch whiskey flown up from Cairo. Even if a nurse had a face like a catfish, she had only to crook her finger. And at whom would she crook it? Too bad for the dogface boys.

The surrender of Italy caused scarcely a ripple in the Eighteenth Infantry's training. Downing's battalion was assigned to guard an airfield for a few days to be sure the Italians did not pull any tricks. Then the Eighteenth moved to Mazzarino.

The Twentieth Engineers really had almost no respite. For once the Germans were off the island, the brass saw that an enormous rehabilitation of the transportation facilities had to be effected if Sicily were to be of use in the coming Italian campaign. Fords, bridges, and roads had to be rebuilt, and sometimes created from scratch. All along the coast from Termini Imerese to Capo d'Orlando the Twentieth Engineers were building. They had 300 Italian POWs to work for them, and apparently unlimited supplies of cement.

But their lives were not all concrete and hard rock. There were liberal pass privileges and trips to Palermo and San Agata. Ah, San Agata! This was the liberty town of the Twentieth Engineers and nobody but the Twentieth Engineers. There were several houses occupied by ladies of the evening who were more than willing to entertain the troops. The Lemon Lady and the Tusa Blonde earned fortunes that summer and fall. The soldiers lived the good life, drinking Sicilian vino, which they compared very favorably to "that varnish remover we drank in Africa." There were eggs and chickens and swimming in the blue Mediterranean and fishing from rubber boats with Teller mines, a sport best indulged in only by engineers. One platoon from Company A went up to Corsica to give the French a hand in conquering that island. The First Battalion rebuilt the runway at Palermo airport.

A startling announcement!

For the infantry, a rotation policy had been devised by the brass. Each company could send one enlisted man home, and one officer from the regiment would also get to go home. Corporal Drury was the man from H Company. He had gone through the two campaigns and had won the Distinguished Service Cross at El Guettar. When Drury was told the news, he didn't believe it for a week. Lieutenant Smith of the Third Battalion was the officer selected. The other young officers gave him a party on the last night, and Lieutenant Smith was kept very busy with the toasts. Later, the colonel walked in.

"Well, Smith, it won't be long until you're on your way back home."

"Yes, sir. And, Colonel, I want to say that this is one of the saddest
moments of my life, leaving the old Eighteenth."

You could hear the jeers all the way to the Eighteenth regimental command post.

At Basico the Sixtieth Infantry was training in field problems, but it was
easygoing after the fighting. First Sergeant Kelly was the man chosen from
the company to be rotated home, and Staff Sergeant Thornton took over the
first sergeant's duties. September was spent reorganizing the regiment. The
Third Battalion received four new officers and gave up all its weapons, which
were being taken for the fight in Italy. On September 26 at a Ninth Division
review, General Patton presented DSCs, silver stars, and soldiers' medals.
Then it was back to training exercises.

When Sicily was secured, Sgt. Charlie Doyle's Second Battalion of the 509th
Parachute Infantry Regiment moved to the island. The men were still P.O.'d
at the brass for the choice of the Eighty-second Airborne units to make the
Sicily airdrops. What happened next did not make them a lot happier. They
were bivouacked on an open plain and were restricted to that area. One con-
cession was made: the brass set up a house of ill repute for the GIs, since
they had been in the north African desert for several months. They wound
up able to find only one prostitute, and she was five months pregnant. (No
doubt by a Kraut, said everybody.) Six hundred eighty men and one whore!
The lines were unbelievable.

Sergeant Doyle, operating on the principle that Rank Hath Its Privileges,
told one of the guys to wake him up in the wee hours, when he figured all
the others would be deep in sleep. He got to the house at 2:30 a.m., and the
line was as long as it had been at 2 in the afternoon. So Sergeant Doyle
remained celibate, but very, very "hot to trot."

About the time that the 509th hit Sicily, General Huebner showed up at the
Eighteenth's bivouac and decided that the officers of the Eighteenth were
rusty in the performance of the *Manual of Arms*. The result was a blast from
regiment that sent all officers onto the drill field, each equipped with M-1
rifle and cartridge belt. The colonel was platoon sergeant. The field grade
officers were squad leaders. The company grade officers played private. They

ran through the manual, with the field grade officers walking around making corrections in stance and handling. There were many, many errors. The enlisted men hovered around the edges, getting peeks, and alternating between amusement at the discomfiture of the officers and apprehension as to what was going to happen to them when all this trickled down.

The word came that the division was going back to England. Hurray! But it was followed by other words: each company commander was to select a quota of men from his company to be transferred to the Third Infantry Division, which was going into combat in Italy.

Captain Murphy called for volunteers from Company H.

No one volunteered.

The obvious tack was to get rid of the "eight balls," but there weren't enough to fill the quota. So the captain and his officers selected the men, and kept their choice a secret to avoid a rash of AWOL fever. At the last minute the unlucky ones were told, checked off, and shipped out. Then, on October 25, 1943, Lieutenant Downing and his men boarded the *Reina del Pacifico*, an old friend, and were on their way to England.

Sergeant Moglia's Sixteenth Infantry came along, too. Sergeant Thornton's Sixtieth Infantry came in November. So did Lieutenant Miller's Twentieth Engineers, leaving behind on the Palermo docks Fuzzy, Peter, and George S. Patton, with all the other dogs collected by the regiment in Sicily. Sergeant Johnson's coast artillery antiaircraft battalion and Sergeant Doyle's parachute battalion had another destination. Long before the others shoved off from Sicily's rocky shores for England, the Italian campaign had begun, to push the Germans back up the boot of Italy.

Among those to be involved in this new campaign were Pvt. Bill Haemmel, the young New Yorker who wanted to be a tank driver. The adventures of Private Haemmel and of Private Van Elk, his buddy, indicate how complex the American military effort had become by 1943.

Private Van Elk had shipped out from Fort Knox in January 1943 to Camp Campbell, where he had volunteered for overseas duty as a tank driver. In about two weeks he found himself at Camp Kilmer, and on February 5 he was at sea. On February 20 he was in Oran, assigned to the 601st Tank-Destroyer Battalion, soon in action in the Tunisian campaign. Before he was 19 years old and less than a year after he entered the service, he was a combat veteran.

Private Haemmel had stayed on a while at Fort Knox. He was qualified

for OCS, except for his extreme youth; although he made several passes at
the school, nothing ever happened because of that deficiency, which could
be remedied only with time. In June 1943 Haemmel was shipped overseas
with a cadre of replacements for the armored corps. They landed at Casablanca on June 25. From that point on, Private Haemmel seemed to bounce
from one reppledepple to another. He marched to Camp Mareschal Lyautey,
the Second reppledepple, where he was told to keep away from the Arabs.
In July he was shipped by boxcar to the First reppledepple at Canastel, 7
miles east of Oran. Here he encountered the great heated debate between
the armored men and duly constituted authority. The NCOs at the reppledepple insisted that all troops wear their overseas caps on the right side of
the head. The armored boys wore theirs on the left.

So the battle was joined. The NCOs ordered caps on the right; the GIs
put their caps on the right. The NCOs turned their backs; the GIs put their
caps on the left.

The struggle went on...and on...and on.

At the reppledepples Private Haemmel trained. He practiced scouting
and patrolling; he did calisthenics, close order drill, and road marches.

On July 18 he was shipped, along with many others, aboard the troop-
ship USS *James Jackson*. They were going to Sicily, the GIs believed. Haemmel had visions of moving into action in the Sicilian campaign. But they did
not go to Sicily. The transports hesitated at Bizerte, and Private Haemmel
and others shipped over the side in small boats and went to another reppledepple, the Seventh this time, just outside Mateur. There Private Haemmel
was classified (light tank gunner and squad leader) and shipped out thirty-
five hours later. He had to change from khakis to wool ODs because wool
OD was the requirement of the brass. Wool OD in the north African summer! Somebody had to be nuts.

The new camp was that of the 2642d Armored Replacement Battalion. It
sounded like an improvement. Haemmel was assigned to the light tank company and shown where to pitch his pup tent. He trained again, and for the
first time he really became familiar with tanks in the field.

After the Sicilian campaign ended on August 17, the confusion seemed
to set in again. People began to ship out. Haemmel volunteered and got
shipped on August 26—back to the Seventh reppledepple. But this time his
stay was only three hours; then he and the others in his group were put on
a train. They were going to the First reppledepple. In Haemmel's group were
Privates Frank Borowski, Carl Greenwald, Andre Gutnecht, and Charles
Madsen and Corporal Stangle.

En route they had their revenge on the Arabs who bedeviled the GIs at every turn. Haemmel, Greenwald, and Gutnecht purloined a fatigue coverall uniform and set up a "trading business."

Each time their slow train stopped, the coaches were surrounded by Arabs ready to sell or to buy. They would offer to buy any item of GI equipment. Since Haemmel spoke the best French-Arab pidgin of the group, he became the spokesman.

The train stopped. Privates Gutnecht and Greenwald positioned themselves on the floor, below the window of the compartment. An Arab came up. Haemmel offered to sell him the suit of fatigues. They haggled over the price. They agreed.

"Now," said Haemmel, "we must wait until the train starts to close the deal. The captain mustn't see that we are selling fatigues."

Just at the moment that the train was starting, Haemmel leaned out the window of the coach, with the bundled-up fatigue suit in hand. The Arab took hold of the suit with one hand and held up the money with the other. He did not trust the dogface; the dogface did not trust the Arab. So both were holding the money and the suit. But the train was gathering speed and the Arab was starting to run to keep up. So he let go of the money and Haemmel let go of the suit.

But...

What the Arab did not notice was that the suit was attached to a long rope, which was manipulated by Gutnecht and Greenwald, lying doggo beneath the window. They yanked on the rope, and the suit came flying out of the Arab's hands and in the window, as the Arab stood on the edge of the platform, shrieking and shaking his fists.

They sold the fatigue suit three times and netted $17 that afternoon. Everybody said it was the only time in the history of the First Armored Regiment that in an Arab-GI transaction, the Arab was left with the short end of the stick.

At their new reppledepple, Haemmel and his buddies were paid $10 each and issued new shoes and khakis to replace the ODs. It seemed that the brass had caught up with the war, finally. And on September 2, at long last, trucks came and picked them up and took them to the headquarters of the First Armored Division. The buddies parted. Haemmel was sent to Company H, a medium tank company, First Armored Regiment. At last, out of the reppledepple, Private Haemmel had found a home.

22

SALERNO

Who ever heard of Salerno? Southeast of the Isle of Capri, northwest of the ancient city of Agropoli, it lay on the shin of the Italian boot. And in a long sprawling line the Allies were to land on Salerno's beaches, with the Americans on the right flank opposite the ancient ruins of Paestum.

American rangers were with the British up north. Taking part in the American landings were two reinforced regiments of the Thirty-sixth Division, the 141st and 142d infantries. The riflemen and combat engineers went first in LCVPs; in the second wave were more riflemen, mine-detector crews, and more engineers. The third wave was heavy weapons, battalion headquarters, medics, and a navy beach party. Later came the bulldozers, antiaircraft guns, self-propelled guns, and towed field artillery, all in DUKWs.

D day was September 8. H hour was 3:30 in the morning. The GIs were waiting, each one in wool OD uniform, with canteen, two bandoliers of ammunition, M-1 rifle, helmet, and light backpack which contained mess kit, toilet articles, two chocolate D rations, and one K ration. Everything else was consigned to the supply sergeant.

It was supposed to be easy. From up north where the British had landed first came the noises of battle. But down here the LCVPs headed inshore in calm sea, under cloudless sky. The long beach looked inviting.

Inviting, that is, until the ramps of the landing craft went down and the troops stepped into the shallow water, guns held high, to wade ashore. From

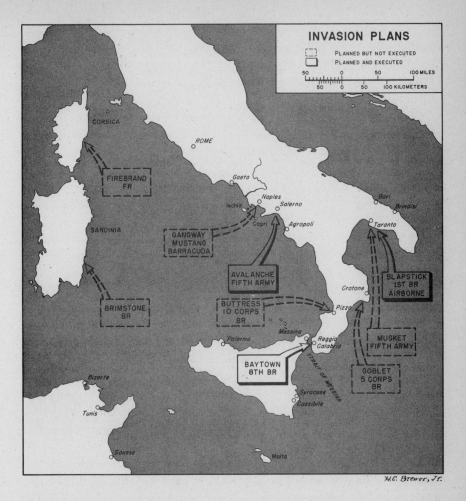

H.C. Brewer, Jr.

the Etruscan ruins of Paestum, up went flares above the beaches. From the remains of Paestum's city wall jutted the snouts of German machine guns. And beside the ruined columns of the temples squatted the German mortars.

The Americans rushed ashore, and the machine guns began burping fire. This was no north African landing, with spotty resistance and a shell here and there. It was not like Sicily, where the worst initial problem was the Luftwaffe. Here the Germans were in solid defensive positions, ordered to hold every meter of Italian ground for Hitler. These were the men of the Sixteenth Panzer Division, the best-equipped and best-trained German soldiers in southern Italy.

In the 141st Infantry's sector the First Battalion's first wave came ashore a quarter of a mile south of its Blue beach, almost unnoticed. The second wave got ashore, but the third wave caught such a blast of fire that it was pinned down on the beach. The fire continued, and the following waves were all pinned down as well.

The Third Battalion, on Yellow beach, had no respite at all. The first wave was machine-gunned and mortared as it landed, and so were the succeeding waves. The troops of the first wave struggled ashore and headed inland. A quarter of a mile from the beach they met the German infantry, and the forward movement stopped. The GIs dug in.

In the area of the 142d Infantry, the Germans were ready as the dogfaces came in on Red and Green beaches. Immediately they, too, were pinned down.

But the U.S. Navy was ready. A rocket boat came in 200 feet from the shore and fired several salvos of rockets over the heads of the GIs. The enemy fire stopped, and the American line surged forward. The German firing began again, but not nearly so heavily now.

But the concentration of fire back at the landing area increased as German artillery opened up, and heavy machine guns traversed the area from Agropoli northward. The fire was so strong that some landing craft crews turned back and had to be caught and redirected by the control boats offshore.

The beach was soon confused. Above, the flares lit the beach in grim shadows, and tracer bullets lit the sky. Offshore the darkness was broken by the surging light of burning landing craft. Men got ashore with their weapons, but without the ammunition to fire them. That was the story of one 81-millimeter mortar crew. Now the bravery began.

S. Sgt. Quillian McMichen was hit twice in the chest and shoulder by machine gun bullets before his landing craft hit the shore. Then the ramp stuck. He kicked it down and led his GIs across the sand to firing positions. He was hit again and died.

Sgt. Manuel Gonzales spotted a German machine gun in the dunes beyond the beach. He crept up under the fire and threw grenades into the position until the Germans were dead.

In the confusion men lost touch with their own units. Pvt. P. C. Jones gathered several men from other boats and led them inland, from one enemy position to another, destroying the guns.

Two companies of German infantry covered the beaches where the Americans landed. They were too few, and their defenses had been hastily erected—too little barbed wire and no minefields on the edge of the surf. The Paestum area was the hottest by far, for there the Germans had cleared land to create fields of fire.

Sgt. James M. Logan, pinned down on the bank of an irrigation canal, saw a squad of Germans coming through a gap in the wall. He killed them and then rushed forward across the open ground to a machine gun position, killed the crew, and turned the machine gun to fire against the Germans.

When daylight came, the Germans brought their armor into action, but piecemeal, one tank plus a platoon of infantry. They were met by the American infantry. Cpl. Royce Davis crept up to one tank with his bazooka, fired a round that punched a hole through the armor, and threw a grenade inside. End of tank.

Sgt. John McGill crawled up to a tank whose turret was open, jumped on it, and threw a grenade into the hatch. Another dead panzer.

But to fight tanks one should have tanks and tank destroyers and artillery—not just bazookas and grenades. The heavy weapons were delayed again by the confusion offshore. The division artillery came ashore in dribs and drabs, mostly during the afternoon. The first tanks got ashore at 8:30 a.m., but most arrived in the afternoon. The first artillery pieces to be useful were the 40-millimeter guns of the coast artillery.

Sergeant Johnson's men went ashore in the early waves. They soon were dug in and had their 40-millimeter Bofors guns in action, knocking out two tanks. The Germans brought up an 88, and one of the Bofors guns engaged it in a duel at 1300 yards. The Bofors laid down seventy-five rounds of automatic fire, and literally smothered the German gun.

By the end of the first day the entire Thirty-sixth Division was ashore and the beachhead was established. The Americans had suffered 500 casualties; the brass found that quite acceptable for an invasion.

Together the Americans and British had destroyed about two-thirds of the 100 German tanks available to the Sixteenth Panzer Division.

The question remained, however: Could the Allies sustain this invasion as the Germans brought down heavy reinforcements?

The port of Salerno was opened on September 11. Two days later the German shelling had become so severe that the port had to be abandoned. The commander of the Sixteenth Panzer Division had discovered the principal weakness of the Allied assault—a 10-mile gap between the left flank of the U.S. Thirty-sixth Division and the British units. He attacked at that gap, and the Thirty-sixth Division suffered heavy casualties. The ability to hold the positions against the German armor was so questionable that by September 12 Gen. Mark Clark was investigating the possibility of withdrawing the whole American invasion force; he had begun talking to the navy about it. The Germans attacked by air and by land, day and night. The shelling and the bombing were the worst of it. Sergeant Johnson and his men never left their guns.

"Hey, Sarge," shouted one of Johnson's privates, "a guy can get killed around here."

And indeed he could. As of the night of September 13 the U.S. Fifth Army was on the verge of defeat in its efforts to hold the Italian beachhead. The German thrust between the American and British forces threatened to outflank them. The American infantry had been hard hit in the fighting of the preceding few days: the First Battalion of the 142d Infantry was reduced to sixty men. The Second Battalion of the 143d Infantry had ceased to exist. The losses of the other infantry battalions were all serious.

The Germans were driving down to the juncture of the Sele and Calore rivers, 5 miles from the shoreline, and very close to Fifth Army headquarters. Between the headquarters and the enemy were troops of the 158th and 189th Field Artillery battalions, a handful of infantry, and a few American tanks. On the night of September 13 these units and the Twenty-seventh Armored Field Artillery Battalion, which came up at the height of the fight, staved off an attack by a company of German tanks and a battalion of German infantry. That same night the Third Division was called from Sicily, and that was when Lieutenant Downing of the Eighteenth Infantry was called on to send men to fill up the ranks of the Third.

But the Third Division could not be brought across in time to help. All the stops were pulled out on bombing, and the British were urged to press forward to save the American beachhead. The Eighty-second Airborne was now called upon to act. The division had been moved to Sicily at the end of the invasion, with the thought of using it in the Italian campaign. General Eisenhower, who had not been favorably impressed by the paratroopers' performance in north Africa or in Sicily, did not think much of the idea. A plan was made, however, to use the Eighty-second for an attack on Rome in connection with a drive by the Italian army, now allied to the Americans. But the Italians soon enough learned that the Germans were bringing new strength in to fight the battle of Italy, and they gave up the Rome operation as too risky. So here was the Eighty-second Airborne, all primed to go and itching to be used. The catch, realized by all who had been connected with Sicily, was to get the men dropped in the right place and to be sure they did not get shot down by "friendly fire" again. Learning from Sicily, General Ridgway dusted off Colonel Raff's rejected Pathfinder plan and ordered it into effect. It now became an Eighty-second Airborne invention.

On the afternoon of September 13 a pilot flew from Salerno with special orders from General Clark to General Ridgway, calling for an immediate airdrop to save the beachhead. He wanted two airdrops: one behind the American lines to reinforce the battered infantry and another behind the German lines to cause the enemy to turn away from the beach. Col. Reuben H. Tucker would lead the 504th Parachute Infantry to Paestum. Orders were given to Sergeant Johnson's antiaircraft unit that no guns were to be fired after 9 p.m. on September 13, until further notice. The drop was successful; only a few "sticks" failed to make the drop zone. The addition of those 1500 troops saved the day.

The next day General Ridgway ordered two other drops. The 505th parachute infantry would go in behind the American lines to further strengthen the Fifth Army position. The 509th would go to the north to relieve the pressure on the British Tenth Corps. That afternoon Colonel Raff got the word. The 509th was to drop behind the German lines at Avellino, disrupt German communications, control two important roadblocks, and thus prevent the enemy from reinforcing the beachhead areas.

Colonel Raff tried hard to stall the mission for twenty-four hours so that some reasonable planning could be made. But the Germans were not going to wait. It had to be that very day.

The men of the 509th were not fond of General Ridgway. "The nonjumper," they called him. Now, not knowing the desperation that had prompted these unscheduled airdrops, they were immediately critical of Ridgway's management of the operation. Not enough maps, "nothing to work with," as Sergeant Doyle put it, and no time to plan the job.

The officers had to work with 1:50,000 scale maps, which showed only Avellino—nothing a company officer could use for any guidance at all. The word came at three o'clock that afternoon. The battalion was bivouacked at Licata, Sicily, and had to board the planes at Comiso at 5 p.m., so Raff and Lt. Col. Doyle Yardley had no time even to call a meeting of company commanders.

Fortunately, the paratroopers of the 509th were used to very tough conditions. After they had gone into bivouac in north Africa, they had trained to become even tougher. One little illegal exercise pitted the officers of the command against the various enlisted units. The officers dug in on a hillside just off the main road into camp, armed with Very pistols. The enlisted men attacked them, armed with concussion grenades. Nearly every enlisted man would have given a lot to sock it to his company commander for all the "wrongs" done him in the service.

Private Doyle was particularly eager to "get" his commander, Capt. Caspar Curtis, a gentleman from down east Maine, with all that implies. Now Doyle was creeping up on Captain Curtis's foxhole, just ready to attack. He had the pin pulled from his concussion grenade and was about to lob it in. That would make up for a lot of things that had happened in the past. Then one of the officers fired a Very pistol at someone else. The red flare caromed off a rock, and socko—hit the car of the Fifth Army inspector general who was just leaving camp. The inspector general stopped the car, got out, and began delivering unshirted hell to all concerned. The exercise came to an abrupt end. What a time Private Doyle had getting the pin back into that concussion grenade!

But a few days later the inspector general was out of the way, and they were back at it again. This time it was Company D against Company E. Captain Curtis and Private Doyle were on the same hillside. Doyle was Curtis's runner, and much as he would have liked to get as far away from the captain as possible, he could not. He knew what was going to happen. The "enemy" would do its best to pile it on the captain, and that meant Doyle, also, was liable to get hurt.

And so it happened. A concussion grenade came lobbing into the position. Every man froze and just looked at the grenade. Every man but Captain Curtis. He picked up the concussion grenade and lobbed it back toward the "enemy." It exploded in midair.

Private Doyle was converted, a fan of the captain's.

So, as fighting men, the GIs of the 509th were ready enough. But what were the plans?

The men didn't know it, but Lieutenant Colonel Yardley could see that they were about to become sacrificial lambs. The orders mentioned the possibility of retreat. Private Doyle was shocked. It was the first time in his army life that he had heard that word.

If they could not accomplish the mission, they were to retreat to join the British.

In two hours the word filtered through the 509th. "Suicide mission," the dogfaces called it, and their company officers agreed. They were expendable, and they were about to be expended.

But what the hell!

They might be scared blue (as Doyle was), but they were ready. Most of them didn't expect to come back on their two feet. The best they could hope for was to be on the stretcher head first, not feet first. But morale was so high that they welcomed the chance, and they knew the beachhead was in mortal danger.

Just about everybody in Sicily knew that. Sergeant Moglia's Sixteenth Infantry was alerted to prepare for movement to the Salerno beachhead. The men were about to get into the trucks when the orders were canceled. Nobody, of course, said why.

One minute the men of the 509th were basking on the Mediterranean beach. The next they were back in their pup tents, rescuing the parachutes they had been using as pillows and preparing for work.

Private Doyle discovered an enormous centipede in his backup chute. Goodbye protection. That parachute had to be full of the centipede's brothers and sisters, all of them having chewed away at the fabric for God knew how many days.

Oh, well...

Private Doyle boarded plane No. 2. His orders were to make the jump; form up on his company commander, Captain Curtis; and then head for Avellino. Once the company took over the town, the troops were to head for the beach, to a crossroads a mile down the road, and there set up a roadblock against the Germans. Another company was to go to the right of the town and set up a similar roadblock. They were to hold these roadblocks until relieved by Fifth Army troops who would push up to meet them. Curtis's company probably would be in the line three days, the maximum amount of time a paratrooper could manage effectively with the resources dropped in with him.

Lt. Fred Perry led the Pathfinders, the scout platoon. They took off half an hour before the others. Perry's men landed just after midnight and set up their equipment; forty-five minutes later the others began to arrive. Colonel Yardley and the headquarters group were the first. Then planes came in about every ten minutes to drop. It was less than an hour before the Germans realized what was happening, and then the action began. Six hundred men against the whole goddamn German army!

Not all the paratroopers hit the drop zone. Most were scattered, some as far as 25 miles away, and much of the equipment was lost.

So the mission was fouled up. The paratroopers moved into the hills in small groups. About all they could do was harry small units of Germans, keep out of the way of large units, hope, and wait.

Captain Curtis and Company D jumped near San Lucia. When the captain hit the ground, the only man he could find was one sergeant. He and the sergeant went west to find the railroad where the company was to rally. They reached the railway line, cut the wires alongside, and headed north, picking up some other men as they went. Entering Avellino, they found it apparently deserted; then they walked west about a mile, where they found some barbed-wire obstructions which they placed in the road. As they were leaving the roadblock, a truck approached from the direction they had just come. The vehicle stopped, turned around, and then drove off. The Americans followed the truck back into town, and saw ten Germans loading it with wine and other loot from a hotel. The paratroopers captured the Germans, disarmed them, and made them unload. They were trying to figure out what to do with the prisoners when more Germans showed up: a motorcycle and an armored car. Curtis's men loaded the captured Germans into the back of the truck with a couple of paratroopers guarding them, and prepared for action. A firefight began, and Private Dean of Company D was wounded in the stomach.

Captain Curtis then set out with Private Piper in the captured German truck, with the prisoners in back. They were heading for the beach. Some of the other paratroopers were to follow in a captured German "jeep" to keep the prisoners from escaping, but they could not get the German vehicle started, so the Germans began to escape out the back of the moving truck. Seven got out. Private Piper dropped off and shot three of them. The truck driver then blundered into a blind alley, and the other three tried to escape. Piper got one more. One escaped, and Captain Curtis shot the third.

By this time more German vehicles were coming into Avellino. The Americans moved out. Captain Curtis and Private Piper made contact with Corporal Coliman and Private Beatty. Beatty had been wounded and also had injured a leg in the drop. The four hid out on a hill overlooking the town and watched. The Germans moved in. There was nothing to be done about D Company's mission; retreat was the only recourse. Hiding out in the daytime, they began to head south. Lieutenant McLean joined up, and then about fifteen more men, and all continued going south. On September 17 they joined another group of paratroopers, and finally they made their way back to the lines.

Elsewhere, Lt. Joseph J. Winsfeld of Company E dropped into a valley south of the proper zone. Eleven of the seventeen men in plane No. 11 assembled, but they could not find the bundles that held their BARs and other weapons. They circled and returned to the field to look again, but had no luck. They found only bundles of mortar ammunition. The next morning the Germans sent out six truckloads of men to comb the nearby forest, where they cornered eight men from F Company and captured or killed six of them.

Other paratroopers decided to go west to Mount Belvedere that night. Soon there were twenty-four of them, of whom five had no rifles. They cut communications wires as they went, and then turned southwest toward the lines. These two dozen were fed by Italians who helped them make contact with other paratroopers. At the east end of the Bagnoli valley the Americans found two British tankers that had escaped from the Germans. This pickup unit had to leave behind one man who had an infected foot, but finally the remainder reached the lines of the Forty-fifth Division.

That was how it went. The mission brought forth many acts of daring and heroism, but it had accomplished nothing. Ultimately about 400 of the 600 men made it back to the lines. For this action, the 509th was put in for a unit citation, but General Ridgway, who did not seem to like the 509th any more than its men liked him, turned down the proposal. The highest award for the mission was the Distinguished Service Cross to Lt. William C. Kellogg, who was not a member of the 509th but of the Eighty-second Airborne Engineers, attached to its unit. To this day many veterans of the 509th say there were plenty of other men who deserved the honor more. They lay all the slight of their unit at the feet of General Ridgway.

But there should have been plenty of glory to go around. Colonel Tucker's 504th Parachute Infantry fought hard in the Salerno area. On the night of September 16 the 504th attacked the Germans at Altavilla, and after some very hard fighting the following day the Germans withdrew; the American beachhead was again secure. The fight was over, except the intramurals. Maj. Gen. Ernest J. Dawley, commander of the Sixth Corps under General Clark, was removed for nonperformance. Some members of the American brass charged that Gen. Bernard Montgomery's British Eighth Army, advancing north from its landing at Calabria, had moved like a snail instead of a lion at a time when the British troops could have saved the very desperate situation at Salerno. Some of the British claimed that Monty *had* saved the situation, although Gen. Sir Harold Alexander acknowledged that General Clark had saved himself.

That was a feeling shared by the men of the 509th, whose affection for General Clark was as great as their dislike of General Ridgway. Many of the dogfaces, too, shared the widespread feeling that the British were too cautious and too slow to move. Fortunately for Allied amity, the opinion of the dogfaces in all this didn't amount to a hill of beans.

*   *   *

The near disaster at Salerno had scarcely been averted when there appeared on the scene that unique unit that Washington had promised General Eisenhower when he was back in Algiers. At that time of need, Ike had welcomed the prospect of the arrival of the 100th Infantry Battalion, which consisted almost entirely of nisei, Japanese-American citizens of the United States.

These young Americans and their families had suffered a great deal at the hands of the U.S. government and American citizens of white extraction. This particular group, however, had not been hurt as much as had other nisei.

The 100th Battalion was born in Oakland, California, on June 12, 1942, the direct descendant of the Hawaiian Provisional Battalion. Its members were young men of the Hawaii National Guard. The government did not know how to deal with them and made its errors, but General Marshal rectified some of them, and in that month of June GIs of the 100th were training at Camp McCoy, Wisconsin.

They trained hard and well, probably harder than any of their contemporaries, for these GIs had something special to prove to America: their unswerving loyalty despite many vicissitudes created by American racial intolerance and misunderstanding.

They had a rough time of it. President Roosevelt had personally approved the creation of a Japanese-American combat team:

> The principle on which this country was founded and by which it has always been governed is that Americanism is a matter of the mind and the heart. Americanism is not, and never was, a matter of race or ancestry.

Nice words. But easy for the nisei dogfaces to forget:

"Even during basic training we weren't trusted. I know because the sergeant in charge of basic training told me (after the war) that once a month he had to mail-drop to Hattiesburg, Mississippi, a loyalty report on each man in training," recalls one veteran of the 100th.

Nor did the situation improve much after basic:

"At Fort Riley our job was to clean out the stables. As we started to clean out the area, we received orders to drop everything and assemble on the first floor of the barracks. I looked out the window and there was a .30-caliber machine gun pointing at the building we were in. Shortly thereafter, President Roosevelt's car drove by. Here we were U.S. soldiers, in uniform, citizens, but they still didn't trust us."

And it continued:

"I was in uniform and went to visit friends in a relocation center. We checked in at the barbed-wire gate—when—wham—this guy pulls out his bayonet and mounts it on his gun, and says, 'Okay, Corporal, march.' With the bayonet right behind my back I was walking into the relocation camp. I took five steps, then turned around and said, 'Corporal, take that bayonet off and put 'um back in your scabbage.'

"He said, 'No, I have to follow you with this bayonet right in back of you.'

"So I said, 'You know I'm in American uniform.'

"He said, 'Yes, I know that, but those are my orders.'

"So I took a swing at him. Then Miyamoto and the other guy held me back."

The 100th Battalion reached Oran in September, where the nisei found out that finally they had been accepted, it seemed.

"Once we got overseas, that feeling of being watched by the army didn't exist. It really didn't exist. In the staging area we were briefed by S-2 (intelligence) and told about different weapons and armaments of the enemy.... There were no feelings of being guarded, watched, or under surveillance."

But...it seemed that nobody really wanted the Japanese-Americans—"the Buddhaheads," as they called themselves. No matter what he had said earlier, General Eisenhower didn't want them now. General Clark, who was having difficulties getting troops, accepted them with the idea that they would be turned into railroad guards. The concept that a unit of off-color Americans could be an effective fighting force was not yet recognized by the brass. Unconscious racism ran deep in the American character. The honor of the men of the 100th was championed by their white commander, Col. Farrant L. Turner. He insisted that these were fighting men. So Clark was persuaded, and Maj. Gen. Charles Ryder of the Thirty-fourth Division was pleased to have them, for Ike had just swiped his Second Battalion of the 133d Infantry as a ceremonial color guard. (Well, even in a war somebody had to wait on the brass.)

On September 19 the 100th left for Italy, full of good advice from General Ryder ("Always pin your extra socks under your arms because that is the only place they won't get wet") and facing the leftover distrust of the American military establishment for anything strange and new. General Marshall, who had gone to bat for the young Japanese-Americans, still harbored his own doubts. As he committed them to General Clark's Fifth Army he demanded an immediate report on the battalion's first military engagement.

That was a little hard to do. The men of the 100th had scarcely landed when they began to move; Montemarano was the first objective. They arrived

on September 27, a part of General Clark's drive toward the Volturno River
and the Rapido River beyond. On September 28 Sgt. Conrad Tsukayama of
Company D was hit by a fragment from a land mine. He was a lucky guy.
One each Purple Heart, for a minor wound of the face!

Then it was on to Chiusano and real trouble. The 100th Battalion was out in
front of the 133d Infantry, and the point was with the Third Platoon of Company
B. As was frequent in those early days, many of the company officers were haoles
(whites), another indication of the tenuous position of the Asian in the American
army. Lt. Paul Froming was leading. At 9:15 in the morning the GIs were moving into a clearing near a bend in the road. The Germans were waiting, and as
the Americans came up the Germans began to hit them with rifle, machine gun,
mortar, and artillery fire. Sgt. Shigeo Takata moved out in front. He advanced,
sighted a machine gun, and continued to advance, standing, firing his tommy
gun. He was hit in the head by a machine gun bullet, but he pointed out the
emplacement to his platoon. Then he died. Private Tanaka of the Second Platoon was also killed that day.

At the end of the first two days of action, the nisei had proved themselves. They had moved forward 7 miles against strong German opposition,
had suffered casualties of two men killed and seven wounded, and had learned
what General Ryder meant when he said they were going to be wet. They
had become front-line soldiers.

And they went on:

> *September 30:* Company A fired upon by enemy. Eight casualties in-
> cluding one killed—Corporal Ishii, Company D.
>
> *October 2:* Moved out approximately 3:30 p.m. to LaSera, through San
> Giorgio toward Benevento. Through Benevento to secure hill southwest of
> city to cover advance of Third Battalion (133d Infantry) the following day.
> Battalion subjected to accurate artillery fire all night.
>
> *October 4:* Passwords become effective from date indicated and continue
> for twenty-four hours. October 4 challenge: Washington; answer: Senators.
>
> *4:50 p.m.:* To all commanding officers, 100th Battalion: Patrols tonight
> same as last night except that Company A will furnish two motor patrols
> between our battalion command post and Third Battalion command post in
> Benevento. Patrols to consist of two jeeps with four men each, including
> driver. Patrols to cover each other during route.

They kept in touch by walkie-talkie. The Germans were great at inter-
cepting communications, but the nisei GIs had them stumped from the beginning with Japanese pidgin, as one GI noted:

"One time my tommy gun bolt stopped working right. I needed a replacement in a hurry. The walkie guy relays the message in a hurry: '*Hama hama tomygun boltsu, hayaku, eh?*' And we needed ammo: 'and *ammo motte kite kudasai.*'"

What was Hans supposed to make of that?

5:30 p.m.: Booby trap found at map coordinates 680720. Trap consisted of wire attached to grapevine and the other end of wire attached to an S mine which was planted in the ground.

At the end of the 100th's first week in action, the brass made its decision: General Clark reported to General Marshall that the Japanese-Americans "performed magnificently on the field of battle. I've never had such fine soldiers. Send me all you've got." Clark also reported to General Eisenhower that the 100th Battalion had seized its objectives and that the men were quick to react to enemy opposition. General Ryder ordered them to paint the Thirty-fourth Division insignia on their helmet liners. They were in like Flynn, and that would never change. The Thirty-fourth Infantry, including the new battalion, then went into reserve for a rest.

The Americans moved forward, one division leapfrogging the other, toward the Volturno River. The 100th Battalion had crossed the Volturno in style, with the GIs all yelling "Banzai" as they surged through the shallows. The German infantrymen on the other side were so shocked that they did not shoot. What was Tojo doing, sending his troops to fight with the Americans?

They learned soon enough.

The Germans contested every foot of ground. The Seventh Infantry crossed the Volturno. The Forty-fifth, the Thirty-fourth, and the Third divisions moved on, up against the German winter line south of Monte Cassino. And here the fighting slowed in November. It was apparent to the Allied High Command that there would be no hurry-up march to Rome. Hitler had elected to fight for Italy. It was going to be a long, hard battle of attrition.

23

ANZIO

Tunisia, September 11, 1943: The invasion of Italy had begun. Major General Harmon assembled the men of the First Armored Division for a talk about the future.

From its camp, south of Oran, the whole division was trucked west to a place where the hills form a natural amphitheater. Those hills were soon brown with troops, men sitting and waiting for the words of inspiration from their leader.

"Gravel Voice Ernie" was his nickname, and he was known for blunt talk. That day he spoke through a public address system. He had some misconceptions to end, he said. Some men believed that since the First Armored Division had been "blooded," it was now time for it to go home and train others. Nothing of the sort was going to happen, said the general. The role of veteran troops was to fight. The only reason they weren't fighting just at that moment was because of the shortage of shipping. That would be remedied. In thirty days they would be fighting in Italy.

The promise was met with some catcalls. They angered the general. He began to compare the First Armored Division to the First Infantry Division, which had fought through Africa and then through Sicily and had ended up fighting the MPs. That was the major reason for the command change and the other changes in that division. So General Harmon revealed to the troops of the First Armored Division what the brass had never revealed to the men of the First Infantry Division: that the top leaders had become shy of their own soldiers and that that was the reason for the reassignment of Generals Allen and Roosevelt. They had been too close and too sympathetic to their men. It was also the reason for General Huebner's "retraining" program, to tone down, and bend, the spirit of the First Division.

Let not the men of the First Armored Division get any such ideas as those the First Infantry Division had held, the general warned. There was no chance of going home. There was no chance of going back to England. Their only future was to go to Italy and fight.

By the time the general got to this point in his aggressive speech, he had lost the sympathy of whatever element of the audience he had once had. He promised more combat and the men jeered him. Their officers did nothing to stop them—a pretty good barometer of their feelings, too. General Harmon was annoyed and became more aggressive, and the men jeered harder. By the end of the speech the general was furious and growling, promising ever more dire results, and the men were openly derisive and unfriendly. The general ended his speech, turned on his heel, and got into his jeep with its two-starred flag; surrounded protectively by aides, he drove away in a cloud of dust, the curses of the dogfaces ringing after him.

As Private Haemmel had already learned, the relationships between Americans and Arabs in north Africa deteriorated steadily. After the fighting ended, the situation became very bad. One day Private Dowda disappeared when on pass to the town of St. Denis du Sig. He showed up three days later, his head bandaged, and reported that he had been assaulted by a gang of Arabs.

One of the problems was the poverty of the Arabs and the relative wealth of the soldiers. Another was religion; Islam does not look kindly on nonbelievers. Another was sex. Many a garrison tale was told of a GI found dead in the road, his penis cut off and stuffed into his mouth and the mouth sewn shut. That was the punishment for violation of an Arab woman, but there were still tales of GIs getting into the harems here and there. There were also tales of dogfaces shooting down Arabs when they encountered them on the roads at night.

So the MPs had a tough job, keeping the soldiers away from Arab women, and then away from Arab areas altogether. In the cities and towns the Arab areas were generally off limits to U.S. troops. One day shortly after General Harmon's inspirational address to the division, Private Haemmel and Pvt. Phillip Esparza went on pass to Sidi-bel-Abbès. The company truck dropped them off and made arrangements to pick them up at 11 p.m. They went into a bar and had some cognac. They went to another bar and had some beer. They went to yet another bar and had some wine. They went to still another and drank champagne. Then they stopped at a bathhouse and had tub baths— the only one Haemmel got in four months in north Africa. Cleaned up, they walked along the main street, toward the other end, where they were stopped by two MPs. The policemen took their names and told them they were off limits.

The next day the CO, Captain Hillenmyer, called them in. The MPs had reported them for being off limits, and official charges had been preferred. They argued that they did not know the main street of the town was off limits. No one had told them.

That did not help Private Esparza. He was given a summary court-martial and fined $25. But that day Private Haemmel was pulling regimental guard duty, so his trial was delayed. When it came up Haemmel argued that no one had told them that the main street was off limits, and that Bône, the last city they had visited, had been on limits except for the alleys. They had not strayed off the main street of Sidi-bel-Abbès. The prosecutor explained that the two ends of Sidi-bel-Abbès were all right but that the middle was not. How did you get to the middle of Sidi-bel-Abbès? When was the middle declared off limits? asked the court. Just *after* the two men were arrested. Oh, said the court. Case dismissed.

Private Haemmel was assigned to Sergeant McNew's M-4 tank, Duck Buggy. There he joined T/5 Leon D. Croom, who had gone all the way through the Tunisian fight, from Kasserine Pass to Bizerte. They waited for General Harmon's predictions to come true. It was hot at first, but the season changed and fall came with its rains. Unlike the rains of winter, these rains cooled off the ground but did not turn it into one great mudhole. The days passed pleasantly, light duty and lots of time for reading.

October 5: Big change. Division ordered the switch back to wool OD uniforms. A sure sign that something was up. General Harmon appeared again; this time he announced that the division was going to move into action. The men would ship to Salerno or Naples, depending on the condition of those harbors. They began packing up. By October 18 some elements were moving out.

Private Haemmel and his platoon moved aboard *LST 351* and spent the next six days crossing from Oran to Naples with three other LSTs, escorted by a minesweeper and four destroyer escorts. The vessels stopped at Bizerte, passing an outbound convoy at the mouth of the harbor. All of a sudden the destroyer escorts of the other convoy swung into action; they began circling and firing depth charges. The DEs of Haemmel's convoy joined in the fight. In about fifteen minutes a big oil slick came up. As far as Haemmel knew, the DEs had sunk a submarine, a U-boat that must have been trailing the convoy from Oran. (Postwar records show no U-boats sunk at that position that day.)

November 3: The convoy entered the Bay of Naples, and the company debarked at Bagnoli, west of the city. The troops moved on to Caivano. Up above, circling lazily, was a plane, and one of the old hands identified it: "Observation Joe," they called it, from the Luftwaffe.

November 4: The company moved to a bivouac in an orchard near Casa-puzzana. Haemmel's pup tent was pitched near an old stone wall, on the north bank of a creek. For the next three weeks the company waited as the First Armored Division assembled on the Campanian Plain. The Germans bombed Naples four times during that period. Haemmel and his buddies watched from afar as the air battles proceeded, but not in total amusement; some shrapnel from the antiaircraft guns fell on their area in the first raid. The next morning they dug slit trenches.

There was leave in Naples. Haemmel went to the opera and to visit the ruins of Pompeii. He looked at the famous Naples slums with a shudder. And using the army pocket language guide, he even began studying Italian.

The elements of the Fifteenth Army Group began to build up. The Second Corps arrived and went into the line in October. The First Armored Division assembled. The French Expeditionary Force came in and then the Second Moroccan Division in tall French helmets and American uniforms; the Third Algerian Division; the Fourth Moroccan Division; the French First Motorized Division. The British Tenth Corps and the U.S. Sixth Corps were already in the line.

After the successful crossing of the Volturno River in October, the Americans had bogged down. The reasons were weather and determined German opposition. The Fifth Army was supposed to move up from Volturno to the north, while the British Eighth Army attacked northward on the other side of the Italian boot. Very quickly a gap developed in the center. General Clark looked around for troops to fill it, but there weren't very many units to choose from. So he asked General Ridgway for a parachute regiment from the Eighty-second Airborne Division. This was all out of kilter: the parachute troops were trained and equipped to go in from the sky, to seize key positions and hold them in the expectation that regular infantry and armor would come up to relieve them in three or four days. They had not been trained in the line-battering tactics of the "leg" infantry. It was a measure of the Fifth Army's troop shortage that the paratroopers were to be so employed. But so employed they were. The men of Col. Reuben Tucker's 504th Parachute Infantry were now in the mountains of Italy, supplied by mule, in terrain so difficult that communication was often carried on by carrier pigeon.

Early in November General Clark began raising hell with General Lucas, commander of the Sixth Corps, because Lucas's divisions weren't moving fast enough. The Thirty-fourth and Forty-fifth divisions had to be gotten across the Upper Volturno to help the Third Division take the Mignano Gap and move toward Cassino. There were not very many German troops up there, said General Clark. What was holding Lucas back?

Lucas knew that General Clark did not know what he was talking about. Lucas was aware of the strong German positions on the high ground that commanded the river. But he was ordered to cross, so cross he would. The 504th Parachute Infantry would cut the Venafro-Isernia road, and the Forty-fifth Division would push up Highway 85 to Venafro, turn right, and seize Monte Sammucro, aided by the rangers.

So on November 2 the crossing began. The Fourth Ranger Battalion and the 180th Infantry reached Cannavinelle Hill, very near Venafro. On November 4 elements of the 179th and 180th infantries did reach the outskirts of Venafro. But there they were stopped by heavy German opposition. The Thirty-fourth Division crossed en masse, right into a series of minefields and booby traps laid by the Germans. The High Command could follow the progress of the troops by the explosions as GIs were blown to hell. "Not many Germans there," General Clark had said. By the evening of November 4 the Thirty-fourth Division's casualties were so heavy that General Ryder stopped the advance until he could bring up reinforcements. But by the night of November 4 General Lucas was happy. The 504th had gone over the mountains and was now protecting the Sixth Corps' right flank. "All is well tonight," wrote General Lucas in his diary.

But not for long. Although the Germans had been surprised, they recovered, dug in, and slowed the American advance to a crawl. Venafro, in the center of the Fifth Army line, was a key point. The Forty-fifth Division assaulted it, but failed to take it.

Help was needed, and this time General Clark called on the Second Battalion of the 509th Parachute Infantry, that independent outfit that had been left stranded by the promotion of Colonel Raff—a part of, but not part of, the Eighty-second Airborne Division.

Three GIs "ready to fight the forces of evil," Fort Devins, Massachusetts, 1942. (*Dubois Photo.*)

Captain Shebeck of the Eighty-second Airborne Division. He served in many capacities during the war, in the invasion of Normandy and thereafter.

Sgt. John Moglia in England in 1944. Sergeant Moglia went all the way through, from the peacetime army of 1941 until the end in Germany, participating in all the major actions of the First Division from north Africa to the occupation of Germany.

Lt. John Downing. He went almost all the way, from north Africa to Germany, with the Eighteenth Infantry.

First Sergeant Harold Chattaway of Company C, 110th Infantry, in Wales in 1944.

Sgt. Barnett Hoffner
and Sgt. Van Dorian
in England in 1943.

Some GIs got married. Sgt. John J. Moglia and his British bride, Sgt. Lilian
Moglia, in Salisbury, January 1944.

German training aircraft.

German soldiers in Paris before the invasion.

Qu'est-ce que vous préférez ?

Mourir
avec les Américains?
Ou . .

Leaflet dropped by Germans for French troops in
Algeria: (*side one*) "Which would you prefer?
To die with the Americans? Or . . .

A glider in Normandy after it ran into some *Rommelspargel*
("Rommel's asparagus")—the defensive poles erected in fields
to stop glider landings.

(side two) to live with the Germans and return home?"

Free French troops man an antitank squad vehicle.

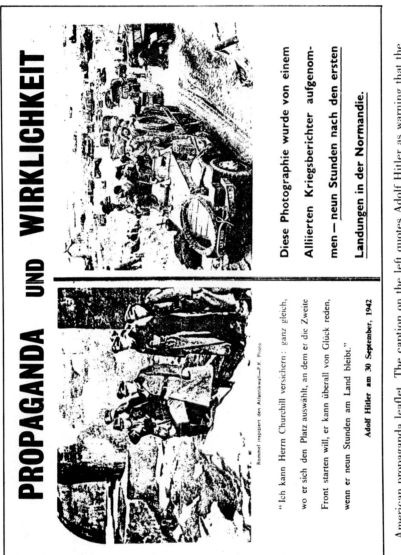

PROPAGANDA UND WIRKLICHKEIT

Rommel inspiziert den Atlantikwall—P.K. Photo

"Ich kann Herrn Churchill versichern: ganz gleich, wo er sich den Platz auswählt, an dem er die Zweite Front starten will, er kann überall von Glück reden, wenn er neun Stunden am Land bleibt."

Adolf Hitler am 30 September, 1942

Diese Photographie wurde von einem Alliierten Kriegsberichter aufgenom- men — neun Stunden nach den ersten Landungen in der Normandie.

American propaganda leaflet. The caption on the left quotes Adolf Hitler as warning that the Allies would be lucky if they were still alive nine hours after landing in France. The caption for the photo on the right says it was taken nine hours after the Allied landings.

Members of the Eighty-second Airborne Division prepare to send a 75-mm shell, via pack howitzer, to enemy objectives across the Salm River.

Cpl. Raymond Clow of Maryland at Waimes, Belgium, in his foxhole during the Battle of the Bulge.

Chow time during the Battle of the Bulge. Sergeant Moglia had a canteen cup shot out of his hand just a few minutes after this photo was taken.

Recovery of the bodies of American troops murdered by the Nazi SS during the Malmédy massacre at Christmastime, 1944. (*Army photo courtesy of Alvin B. Welsch.*)

The engineers tried to teach the infantry about mines.

Eighteenth Corps Headquarters moves into German homes in Diersford, Germany.

What was left of Gresnich, Germany, after the battle.

DIE ZEIT
DES ZOGERNS
IST VORBEI!

JEDE MINUTE IST KOSTBAR!

Durch rücksichtslosen Einsatz hat Deine Führung
bewiesen, wie gering ie Dein Leben einschätzt.

Was hat das sinnlose Opfer Deiner Kameraden
genützt? Sie alle wären heute noch am Leben,
hätten sie sich zu uns in Sicherheit gebracht.

WÄHLE

TOD

ODER EIN

NEUES LEBEN

Das neue Leben:

1) Sofortige Entfernung
   aus der Kampfzone.

2) Gleiche Kost und
   ärztliche Pflege
   wie der U.S. Soldat.

3) Sold wird
   weiter gezahlt.

4) Freiwillige Arbeit
   wird extra bezahlt.

5) Ausbildung in
   Handwerk und Beruf
   auf Fachschulen.

6) Baldige, gesunde
   Heimkehr nach dem Kriege.

MW 112

American leaflet offering the German soldier either death or new life, if he would
surrender. On the back is a pass to get the soldier through the American lines.

Officers of Company C, the 110th Infantry, in Germany. Lieutenant Chattaway is on the right.

Japanese American soldiers of the 442nd Regimental Combat Team at war's end.

Some boys of the Sixteenth Infantry with a trophy in Gresnich, Germany.

A captured German rocket in Nancy, France.

First Sergeant John J. Moglia with a disabled German tank in Bamberg, Germany.

Lt. John J. Moglia at Brig. Gen. Theodore Roosevelt's grave in Normandy, June 6, 1954.

The men of the 509th were still rankled at what they considered to be their misuse at Avellino. They had been given 250 men to replace those lost there. Now, they were told, they were going to be used as shock troops to help the tired fighters of the Sixth Corps at Venafro. Shock troops now, and not paratroopers, they would go in on foot.

When that was learned, the griping began in earnest:

"We had no idea what a straight-leg unit would do to make an attack against a fixed position," said Sergeant Doyle.

The 509th was brought up from Naples to attack. The troops went up the mountain, in the face of enemy artillery—which they had never met before—and having to contend with "friendly" artillery fire, which did not know where they were. It was 11 a.m., November 11, 1943.

They stayed up on that mountain for a month. Attack, counterattack. Attack, counterattack. Sergeant Doyle was evacuated with trench foot and then sent back to north Africa for treatment. The doctors wanted to amputate several toes. Doyle refused, even though threatened with a court-martial. They didn't know much about trench foot there. Just about then, the pressure relaxed. The Germans were pulling back to the Gustav line.

So the 509th came out, again full of resentments, not understanding what was happening up above.

The Fifth Army's drive was supposed to get moving again, and the natural route was up the broad Liri Valley, guarded by a number of mountains and the Garigliano and Rapido rivers. The First Armored Division was then assigned to participate in the attempt.

On the night of November 24 Private Haemmel's company arrived at the Volturno and crossed at Capua. Elements of the division moved into the line, but Haemmel's Company H was in reserve.

The Allied force finally reached the Rapido on January 15. The German defenses were stout; the Allies were shorthanded. Movement was very slow, and a high price was paid for every yard gained.

But that did not seem to affect the lives of the men of Company H. They sat in their field at Villa Volturno, about 25 miles north of Naples. There was no reveille for weeks and very little training. They wandered about the countryside almost at will. Haemmel and a buddy moved into a straw hut built to house donkeys. They began building wooden beds and assembling metal stoves. A service club was put up, and a tent that was found became a dayroom. It was a very nice war, particularly on December 20, when Haemmel's high school pal Gil Van Elk showed up. Van Elk's outfit, the

601st Tank-Destroyer Battalion, had been in combat for seventy days. Gil had achieved the high rank of Pfc. before being busted for disciplinary reasons.

By this time General Eisenhower had moved from the Mediterranean to London to take command of the forces that would stage the big second-front assault against Fortress Europe. At Company H it seemed obvious that the Italian campaign was now a backwater and that nothing much was going to happen very quickly.

On January 14 the comedian Joe E. Brown arrived from Los Angeles on a USO tour. He was very funny, just what the men liked—as much as they liked pretty girls. The serious actors who made the early tours fell on their faces, for there was nothing a Humphrey Bogart could suggest about toughness that matched the reality of combat.

By November 1, 1943, it was apparent to the Allied High Command that the move north from Naples was getting nowhere fast. So a new plan was devised. Gen. Mark Clark would lead the U.S. Fifth Army in an attack to take the Liri valley, 30 miles north of Cassino. To assist, the Third Infantry Division would be landed from the sea at Anzio, 30 miles south of Rome. The two forces would link up, and presto, southern Italy would be secured for the Allies.

But in November the campaign in Italy went even worse than the most pessimistic of the Allied generals expected. Terrain, weather, and experience all worked for the Germans. Their defenses were superb and their fighting spirit was undiminished by their recent succession of defeats.

The German Gustav line, which extended north and south through Cassino, stopped the Allies.

The U.S. 133d Infantry Regiment had pushed through Ciorlano with the nisei 100th Battalion in the lead, crossed the Volturno, and kept on moving. The battalion was tough enough, God knew: one day Capt. Taro Suzuki of Company B told S. Sgt. Robert Ozaki that Lt. Young Oak Kim had just been captured. Among storied men, Lieutenant Kim was a particularly fabulous character. A Korean, he had not seemed to fit in with the nisei. Anyone could understand why: Japan had colonized Korea in 1910 and had oppressed the Koreans ever since. But these were neither Koreans nor Japanese; they were young Americans. Although back in the states during training some of the leading nisei had suggested that Lieutenant Kim might want out of the outfit, he had refused and had gone along like that ever since. Now, not only was Lieutenant Kim accepted, he was one of the most popular men in the unit. So when the dogfaces of Company B learned that Lieutenant Kim was in trouble, they fixed bayonets. The men swarmed to a hedgerow, over a stone wall, over a road, and routed the enemy. There they found Lieutenant Kim hurling hand grenades at a German machine gun.

Other days too, the going was very rough. The GIs had to take one hill after another, and their mortars were the key to their advance. Lt. Neill Ray, Cpl. Katsushi Tanouye, and Cpl. Bert Higashi of Company D were forward observers, plotting the firing patterns for the mortars. On November 6, out in front of the infantry, where they were most effective, all three were killed by German artillery firing "tree bursts" of antipersonnel ammunition. It was very tough. On November 11, Armistice Day (a big laugh to the troops), the Thirty-fourth Division was pulled out of the line and the Forty-fifth went in. Of the 100th Battalion, 78 men had been killed and 239 were wounded. The Forty-fifth Division was to have the same sort of experience.

Back in the line in December, the 100th Battalion was fighting in the Colli-Atina area, trying to outflank the German defenses at Cassino. When the Americans moved, the 100th was out ahead of the other battalions, in the center.

The 100th took enormous casualties. So it went, the battle to pierce the Gustav line. The Germans held; the Americans took huge losses. The Americans bombed the abbey at Monte Cassino, but the destruction of that historic edifice did not solve their problem. In February the exhausted Thirty-fourth Division was removed from the line.

Meanwhile, the end-around move, scheduled to bring troops up by amphibious assault to Anzio, 30 miles from Rome, was not doing very well either.

Capt. Felix L. Sparks, commander of E Company, 157th Infantry Regiment, Forty-fifth Division, had been wounded in the early fighting above Salerno and had gone into the hospital. He came out in December and rejoined his division in the mountains above Venafro. On January 10, 1944, the division was relieved and sent back down to Naples. There Captain Sparks learned that his unit would be part of a Sixth Corps landing at Anzio.

*   *   *

The Germans, said G-2, were expecting Allied landings north of the Tiber River. Therefore, the actual plan—to land at Anzio—should catch them by surprise; it should all be easy.

Capt. Glenn Rathbun of Company M of the Seventh Infantry could only hope that G-2 was right. It was 3:30 in the morning, and he had just left the cocoon comfort of the LCI wardroom and stepped out onto the damp, cold deck. He felt the LCI turn to the east from its northerly course. They were going in. He stood at the rail, but there wasn't much to see. Lt. Frederick Phillips of the 81-millimeter mortar platoon came up.

"All ready, sir," he said.

The sound of gunfire from the beach ended the conversation.

"Sounds like the first wave has hit the beach. I'll go back with my boys. See you ashore, sir."

Captain Rathbun stood at the rail. The sounds of combat became louder; then the LCI ground in along the beach, and the ramps went down. He could hear the sound of a heavy machine gun firing toward the LCI. He sped down the ramp and onto the beach, and across, running as hard as he could.

For once, G-2 seemed to have been right. The opposition was only one company of German engineer troops. By midmorning the Americans had moved inland 10 miles. Then, suddenly, they were stopped by orders from the brass. Maj. Gen. John P. Lucas, commander of the Sixth Corps, was concerned lest his units be surrounded and cut off. So the momentum was lost. What the men of the Seventh Infantry had to say about that, even forty-five years later, remains unprintable.

When Captain Sparks returned to his company in December 1943, he saw that half the soldiers who'd been with him at Salerno were no longer there. It was a sobering observation.

The 157th Infantry was held in reserve at the landings. All seemed to go so very well on January 22, 1944, and the troops moved inland. But on the second day it was apparent that all was not going so well. Captain Sparks was informed that he was to take his company ashore and relieve a company on the left flank of the beachhead, bordering the sea. When he made the relief, he discovered that the Thirty-sixth Engineer Regiment had been pressed into service as infantry; that's how badly things were going. It seemed to many of the dogfaces, from information they'd learned from the grapevine, that Generals Clark and Lucas had really fouled up in choosing Anzio in the first place. So, perhaps, had others in the command echelons above. They had hoped to force the Germans to take troops out of the Gustav line to meet the new threat. But Hitler himself intervened, and new troops came into the fray with Hitler's orders to push the Allies into the sea. By the time

Captain Sparks landed, the Germans had 70,000 troops moving to encircle the beachhead.

On the night of January 17 Company H of the First Armored Regiment moved out with very little notice. Gone were the wooden beds and metal stoves and dreams of a garrison war. In a night march the company moved up 26 miles.

For the next few days the troops covered their vehicles with waterproofing material and the officers began reading up on amphibious tactics. A sea voyage and landing were in the works. The maintenance section welded hoods onto the tanks and plugged up portholes and all other crevices. On January 21 they moved back to Naples, to the Aversa staging area, and waited for a vessel to pick them up. They were going in to join the troops on the beaches at Anzio.

On January 24 Pfc. Haemmel's company, with several half-tracks and trucks, loaded aboard the British *LST 164*. Also aboard were the .50-caliber machine guns of Sergeant Johnson's 434th Antiaircraft Battalion.

On January 26 *LST 164* was off the Anzio beachhead. It was a rough morning at sea and the vessel pitched and tossed. Occasionally the bow would rise, a wave would catch its flat keel amidships, and the vessel would shudder as though it were about to break in two. By noon, however, the skies cleared, and the LST moved in to anchor just offshore. Pfc. Haemmel could see the towns of Anzio and Nettuno and the rolling hills beyond. Occasionally the men saw the smoke and dust from an exploding artillery round, but not much else.

Up ahead a ship burned. Several vessels had run into a German minefield. In the afternoon the German air raids began, and the antiaircraft crews manned their guns.

That night the air raids continued by the light of German flares.

On January 27 *LST 164* moved in toward land to discharge passengers and cargo. An ME-109 came in to strafe and bomb. The pilot dropped his bombs 200 feet off the beam of the LST. He came so close to the ship that Pfc. Haemmel could see his blond head through the canopy. Then the ship nosed up to the pier, and in a few minutes the men were ashore, moving through Anzio to a pine forest northeast of the town. They put down their bedrolls and got to work removing the waterproofing and unplugging the outlets. The crew members of Haemmel's tank, the Duck Buggy, prepared their own C-ration supper, heating the cans over a Coleman stove. Then it was lights out.

The guns of the 343d AA Battalion had been mounted on the ships in the harbor as additional firepower against the German air attacks. Sergeant Johnson was told to expect anything to happen, and then it began. The German bombers and fighters came screaming in. So did the shells from a huge German railway gun called "Anzio Annie." From God knew where, Annie lobbed rounds that broke up into fragments the size of a helmet.

Sergeant Johnson was on deck when a German shell exploded beside his LST. He staggered in the concussion, and then started across to one of the 40-millimeter Bofors guns. He stopped. In his path lay a chunk of meat. Just beyond he saw a corporal on a truck, glasses raised to scan the sky, sliding down the fender. The corporal fell and turned over, and Johnson saw the hole in his back. The piece of meat was the man's heart, blown completely through his body. The sergeant saw three more men wounded in a matter of minutes; when he came up from helping get a man to the sick bay, he saw the chaplain kneeling by the remains of one of the 20-millimeter guntubs. The tub had taken a direct hit. All that remained inside was raw hamburger and blood.

Sergeant Johnson's company went ashore that night and set up in an olive grove east of the town of Anzio. The men got the guns into place and dug in. They hoped to stay for a while, so they dug down 7 feet and built dugouts with sandbags and timber.

And they listened to Axis Sally:

"The mighty German Wehrmacht will drive you back into the sea. Adolf Hitler will send secret weapons against you soon and you will die. Give up this fight and go home to your loved ones before it is too late. Pleasant dreams, Allied soldiers."

For two days Company H of the First Armored Regiment sat in the protection of the forest as the Germans continued their air raids. On January 29 at dusk the company moved out in a column. Up front was Company I, which made contact with the enemy infantry and Mark IV tanks.

Before dawn on January 30 Company H headed into battle. Sergeant McNew placed his tank close on the tail of the one in front of him. The column rolled westward, out of the forest, and north up the Albano Highway; it turned off into a field and dispersed. As dawn came, so did the whining sound of shells and the roar of explosions. The Germans were putting shells into the road 100 yards ahead. Pfc. Haemmel, on turret guard, ducked his head back into the turret.

The German shelling ceased as quickly as it had begun. The tanks stayed still for nearly an hour; then they pulled back into the road, formed up again, and moved up slowly. A column of infantry came by, skirting the tanks, the soldiers carrying mortars, machine guns, and bazookas. Many labored under heavy loads of ammunition. This was the Third Battalion of the Sixth Armored Infantry, moving up to the crest of the hill ahead. Beyond were the Germans.

Duck Buggy began to lurch forward. At 7:15 the tanks reached the crest of the hill, moved off the road, and formed a skirmish line; the First Platoon was on the right, the Second Platoon in the middle, and the Third Platoon on the left. The Third Platoon began to go forward, covered by fire from the First and Second.

The tanks moved up into the foothills of the Alban Mountains, a grassy land, punctuated here and there by stone houses. Three hundred yards ahead lay a cluster of three such buildings. Duck Buggy began firing into them. There was no return fire and no activity. Then the platoon moved on ahead, stopped, and waited. From the turret Sergeant McNew swept the countryside with his field glasses, looking for movement. He was very careful; only the top of his steel helmet and the field glasses showed above the rim of the hatch.

Croom, the gunner, sat at his gun and chain-smoked. Driver Mosman prayed. Assistant Gunner Haemmel moved his periscope around the horizon; he went up and borrowed McNew's field glasses for a better look.

Croom's hands were trembling.

"Don't you get used to all this?" Haemmel asked Croom.

"Hell no. You can't get used to being scared. It just gets worse all the time."

Pfc. Haemmel had been instructed by Sergeant McNew to throw the used 75-millimeter shell casings out of the tank, and he had done so. Now he had to pee. The usual drill was to save at least one canister for that purpose, but Pfc. Haemmel was too green to know it. So now, Sergeant McNew had to climb out of the turret and Haemmel followed him. Haemmel had just relieved himself when there came the distinctive whine of a bullet. They scrambled up the side of the tank; Haemmel leaped into the hatch head first, and McNew followed. Gunner Croom started shooting and sent twelve rounds into the houses where the sniper was.

The day went on. If a man was hungry, he nibbled on K rations. Biscuit and water was usually enough.

At 10 a.m. the attack began again. The line of tanks started forward, one tank advancing, its section mate covering the advance by fire. Thus they leapfrogged forward.

Captain Hillenmyer was jolting forward in his command tank when the hatch cover suddenly slammed down on his hand, breaking two bones. The pain incapacitated the captain, so Lieutenant Abrams of the First Platoon assumed command of the company.

At noon the tanks stopped again. They had gained a mile and still had caught barely a glimpse of the enemy. Once Pfc. Haemmel had seen a German machine gun crew through his periscope. But only once and only for a moment.

The advance began again. Duck Buggy rolled to the top of a knoll and started down, only to mire in drainage from an irrigation ditch. The rear of the tank was up, the nose down, about as vulnerable a position as possible. The crew sat, and reported that the Duck Buggy was stuck. An hour later Sergeant Mees's tank came to the rescue, fixed two cables to the Duck Buggy, and pulled it out. Haemmel and his buddies moved ahead again, firing at houses as they went. Still they saw nothing moving.

The afternoon wore on. Loader Haemmel reported that they had only four rounds of high-explosive shells for the 75-millimeter cannon. McNew ordered the gunner to switch to the .30-caliber machine gun. It jammed. The tanks moved up to one last hill and sat there, firing, as the supporting infantry arrived and dug in. Then the tanks withdrew about a mile and stopped. That was the end of the day's battle. That night trucks came up from the service company, and the crews fueled up the tanks with gasoline from 5-gallon jerry cans and replenished their ammunition supplies. It was 9 p.m. before they dropped into their bedrolls, exhausted.

January 31: The attack was to begin again, so the men of Duck Buggy removed the camouflage net from their tank. Then they put it back up; the attack was delayed. They managed to get a hot meal, Pfc. Mosman of the tank crew cooking, while the others swabbed out the 75-millimeter gun barrel and cleared the machine guns. Coffee, cocoa, C-ration meat and beans, hash, and C-ration biscuits. It was a treat.

They sat then, and waited. It was noon before the attack actually resumed. Their platoon started forward, but it made a wrong turn and ended up with a battalion of the British Grenadier Guards. A guards captain wanted them to put some shells into a cluster of farmhouses. Sergeant McNew was agreeable, and the tank lumbered up and fired. Immediately the Germans began firing back, with big stuff—88s and maybe larger. The tank stopped firing, and moved out.

*

The battle lasted three days. When it ended, Pfc. Haemmel knew this much:

Combat Command A had been engaged from January 29 to January 31. Companies I and H had been engaged all day on the thirtieth, advancing 2½ miles. On that same afternoon Company G had moved forward, but ten tanks had bogged down in the mud. On the third day Companies I and H advanced again, while Company G retrieved its stuck tanks. Company I lost two tanks and Company H lost one to enemy action. Then came the word that the Germans were planning a big counterattack, and the battalion had been put in reserve to wait.

Combat Command A's tank battles had been only a part of the Sixth Corps attack. The rangers had led it, toward Cisterna. It had not been a success: the First and Third Ranger battalions had lost 750 men. But at this point, of course, Pfc. Haemmel and the rest of his crew had no idea that the Anzio operations threatened to become a disaster. All they knew was that as of February 1, they were in reserve, sitting in a field also occupied by a noisy battery of 155-millimeter artillery. Then they discovered that the transmission of Duck Buggy had gone bad, and a week was spent replacing it. By the time they got back to the company area from the maintenance section, they discovered the company dug in, the tanks buried 5 feet in the ground, and their buddies living in dugouts. It looked like a long war.

February 9: The crew members of Duck Buggy had just finished their noon meal when an order came to be prepared to head out to attack. The British First Division had been pushed out of Aprilia, and Cerrocento. In the latter the Fascists had built a model town with several multistory brick buildings. It had been nicknamed "the factory," and Company H was to help recapture it.

The tanks moved up, and their crews soon learned that the Germans had put antitank weapons in the upper stories of the brick buildings. The going was very poor. The Americans moved up to an overpass and stopped there. During the whole afternoon Duck Buggy fired only five rounds. Late in the afternoon the company retreated. The Germans had not been ousted.

February 10: The attack was resumed. The company waited. At noon it began to rain. Haemmel's crew was placed on a thirty-minute alert that wasn't relaxed all afternoon. But nothing happened. The Germans consolidated their hold on Cerrocento.

February 11: Company H was waiting. The 191st Tank Battalion led an attack against "the factory." The battalion reached it, but could not hold.

That night the GIs heard Axis Sally warning them that their beachhead was about to be pushed into the sea. They had better surrender before they got killed, she said. A lot of people were beginning to believe her. There was a lot of talk within the company about the prospects of becoming pris-oners of war. The officers would have it made, it was decided, since the German army was rank happy. One of the senior sergeants of the company talked about virtually nothing else. He was really scared, and he was not even one of the eighty-five men of the tank crews who really would be in danger. Not unless the defeat was total, that is.

February 16: The expected German attack began. The objective came from Hitler himself: "eliminate the abscess south of Rome at all costs."

The German attack was directed down the Albano Highway that leads from Rome to Nettuno and Anzio on the beach. The Forty-fifth Division was occupying the broad front of the beachhead. The 157th Infantry was deployed along the highway, with Captain Sparks's Second Battalion in the forward position just south of Cerrocento and Aprilia. Company E was astride the highway. F and G companies were behind, and a machine gun platoon from Company G reinforced E Company. Sparks also had an antitank gun and two tank destroyers from the 645th Tank-Destroyer Battalion.

The tankers of Company H knew about the attack hours before it came; on the night of the fifteenth the German air raids were almost continuous. Allied and German guns fired constantly.

By this time the men of Company H were emotionally exhausted. The waiting, the not knowing, had gotten to them. The company was put on alert at 8:30 a.m., and the rear echelons were ready to depart. The kitchen truck was packed up. All the noncombatants of the company were prepared to pull out on a moment's notice to escape the Germans. But, even if they did, would there be any evacuation from the beachhead? Axis Sally said no.

The Germans struck early in the morning. At 6:15 the commander in chief of the German Fourteenth Army moved to a command post 2½ kilometers southwest of Genzano. The German Sixty-fifth Infantry, Fourth Parachute, and Hermann Göring Panzer divisions attacked.

The brunt of the first attack was felt by Companies E and G of the 157th Infantry Regiment. During the first five hours half of Captain Sparks's men were killed or wounded. Around 11 o'clock a German half-track approached, carrying a white flag. As it came near a German captain stood up. The half-track stopped, and the captain got out. Captain Sparks stood up and went out to meet him. The German officer spoke, in English:

"Captain. You have many wounded and we have many wounded. Would you agree to a thirty-minute truce so that we can both evacuate our wounded?"

"Yes," said Captain Sparks.

All firing stopped, and both sides evacuated their wounded. Captain Sparks used the only vehicle he had left, a weapons carrier.

He never reported the incident to higher authority. After the half-hour, the firing began again.

Just before noon about 600 Allied bombers came up to attack Carrocento. Back at their bivouac, the tankers began to cheer. Up front Captain Sparks's infantrymen didn't have time to cheer. They were too busy shooting and ducking.

The Germans came on in force against Captain Sparks's company and G Company, on its right. The attack then enveloped the rest of the Second Battalion of the 157th Infantry and most of the units of the 179th Infantry.

February 18: By morning the Germans had penetrated the highway overpass that was occupied by Company I of the 157th. This was 2½ miles behind Captain Sparks's company. But Company I held, despite repeated attacks, and the German drive stalled.

February 19: The Second Battalion of the 157th Infantry was completely surrounded by the Germans. The battalion was told that efforts would be made to relieve it.

February 20: The relief efforts failed. Regiment and division resorted to extreme tactics. They warned the American troops to seek shelter in the caves and gulleys, and they laid down artillery fire on the American positions.

February 21: The relief failed again.

February 22: Happy Washington's Birthday! The situation was like the revolutionary war battle of Harlem Heights. The enemy still surrounded the pitiful remnants of the Second Battalion. Here is the pertinent section from the journal of the German Fourteenth Army:

The strongpoint Buon Riposo was encircled [Sparks's company]. Our attacks have confused the enemy and also brought about emergency situations in some of his units. The enemy command has repeatedly called upon isolated and dangerously placed units to hold their positions by promising reinforcements.

February 22, still: The Second Battalion of the Queen's Royal Regiment was ordered to relieve the Second Battalion of the 157th. The British moved up and reached the Americans. The men of the surrounded Second Battalion then tried to fight their way back through the German lines, with the

British, leaving their wounded behind under the care of the battalion surgeon, Dr. Peter C. Graffagnino. The British battalion suffered more than 50 percent casualties. The Germans took 402 prisoners.

That night 225 men of the 157th escaped through the German lines, the only survivors of a battalion of nearly 1000 men. Of the reinforced Company E of Captain Sparks, only two men made it back.

But they had held long enough, and the German drive to the sea had failed. The Germans took over Buon Riposo, but they went on the defensive.

Anzio was anything but a success. The Allies had a toehold, and not much more. Once again some head had to roll, and this time it was the head of General Lucas. Many of the GIs thought some others ought to have fallen, including Gen. Mark Clark, who was not the favorite of all of them, particularly after the bloodletting at the Rapido River crossing.

The German drive was blunted, but the German high command still believed the Allies could be driven into the sea at Anzio. They began to bring up reinforcements. So did the Americans. Captain Sparks got a new Company E, fresh from the United States. But even as he trained the new soldiers, he had memories of the past to sort out. One day he had a letter from a lady in Dayton, Ohio. She was the mother of Sgt. Robert L. Fremder, missing in action at Anzio. She was hoping desperately that her son might be a prisoner of war.

> The last time I dreamed of Bob was the night before we got the telegram....
> In that dream I was over there with him...in a queer looking stone house
> and shooting through the windows and any place to get at the Germans.
> Then a bomb burst just where he was. I saw him go up in pieces and also
> his gun....

Please, she asked, could the captain tell her something about what happened to her son? Or perhaps could some of the other GIs tell her?

Poor Mrs. Fremder! How could Captain Sparks tell her that there were no others to tell the tale and that, search his memory as he might, he had absolutely no recollection of what had happened to Sergeant Fremder?

24

PREPARING FOR
INVASION

England. Sergeant Moglia's Sixteenth Infantry came in from Sicily aboard the *Duchess of Bedford* and the *Malaga*, the same ships that had taken them from the United States to Liverpool, oh, so long ago. The men got off the ship and marched.

They had been warned before leaving ship that they were not to mention their experiences in Africa or Sicily. By order of General Huebner, they were to conceal the fact that they were the First Infantry Division and that they had been in combat in Africa and Sicily. Unit patches were ripped off uniforms, combat decorations and theater ribbons were forbidden, and the big red "1" on their helmets was painted over with brown paint. They were to say that they had come fresh from the United States.

And so they did. But that little white lie caused a lot of trouble for the brass in a way that had not quite been anticipated. For the dogfaces of the Sixteenth were a tough bunch of soldiers. Now, when they left the ships at Liverpool, they were marched through the streets, and they passed bands of U.S. soldiers who had arrived from America two or three months earlier and now considered themselves "old hands."

"Hey, what took you guys so long in getting over here?" shouted one old hand.

"Waiting for the war to end and then cash in on the glory?"

"Careful now, girls, don't stub your toes."

"Were you afraid to leave your mommas?"

The men of Company F gritted their teeth and marched on, except for one. He broke ranks, found one of the tormentors, and plastered his nose all over his face; then he ducked back into line.

At camp the Sixteenth was met by more "old hands," who undertook to teach them the English monetary system: this to GIs who had been dealing for months in Algerian francs, Moroccan francs, Italian lire, American occupation lire, gold seal dollars, blue seal dollars, British occupation shillings, and regular British pounds.

They were given lectures on English culture and instructed about proper behavior in pubs, tea shops, and other public places. The idiots, for so these "teachers" seemed to the men of the Sixteenth, who instructed them did not even bother to ask if they had been in England before.

Hurrah for the rear echelons!

The Sixteenth was moved to Bridport, near the Dorset coast of southwestern England. About the third day Sergeant Moglia stopped by the bus depot at Bridport and asked about the schedule of buses bound for Salisbury. Loyally, he played the charade. He wanted to see an old buddy who was stationed there, he said.

It was a lie. Sergeant Moglia wanted to see a young lady, then a member of his majesty's forces, Sgt. Lilian Deane. When he had left England on his way to north Africa, Moglia had ideas about that young woman, and they had matured in the months since, egged on a bit, perhaps, by the good-natured kidding of Moglia's buddies. ("Hey, you're not still thinking about that English girl, are you? She must have met a hundred guys by now.")

Yes, Moglia was still thinking, and ever more seriously, about Sergeant Deane.

So he spun his yarn for stationmaster Peter Picco about how he wanted to see Salisbury Cathedral, etc., etc. And when they got to talking, stationmaster Picco asked Sergeant Moglia home to dinner. Moglia went to dinner, and before the evening was over, he found himself virtually adopted by the Piccos.

What that meant! Aside from the warmth of friendship, he had hot, home-cooked meals and a hot, private bath. And Mrs. Picco even insisted on doing his laundry.

After a time the brass relented on the order that the men of the First Division were to pretend they were greenhorns. The ruse really hadn't fooled anybody, as the Piccos admitted—at least not anybody but some other Americans. The men of the Sixteenth were too quiet and too well disciplined. No bragging about what they were going to do to the Germans when they met them. They had met the enemy, and they knew. Stationmaster Picco could tell that, like the young Englishmen he knew, these Americans had been in battle. Sergeant Moglia had known too much about English currency. He had known too much about Salisbury Plain and Salisbury Cathedral. He had too much sand in his uniforms, and they were too bleached out and worn to be fresh from the states. Ah, security!

The whole First Division was under very tight security. Sergeant Moglia could not even telephone Lilian in Salisbury. Stationmaster Picco did it for him. So Lilian was invited down to visit the Piccos. She came, and Sergeant Moglia proposed, and they prepared to get married.

Lieutenant Downing's Eighteenth Infantry had a lot of bugs when *it* left Sicily. For weeks, officers and men had been fighting to keep themselves on the active list, knowing that if they went into the hospital, they probably would be reassigned to a reppledepple. Then, God knew what! Safely aboard the *Reina*, they began turning themselves in at sick bay. The infirmary soon overflowed with dogfaces exhibiting jaundice, malaria, dysentery, and trench mouth.

On the voyage back to England Lieutenant Downing learned with pleasure that he had been transferred to F Company as executive officer. F Company. His old outfit.

But what a change since the company had hit the beach in north Africa. There were more than 200 men then; now only about 30 were still on the roster. The company commander, Captain Moore, was from the Third Division. All the other officers were second lieutenants who had joined up for the Sicilian campaign.

While they were aboard ship, some literary type in the Eighteenth put himself to composing a poem, with apologies to Rudyard Kipling:

A SOLDIER THAT'S FIT FOR A SOLDIER

Now all you young soldiers who are sailing the sea,
Just drop what you're doing and listen to me.
And I'll tell of a soldier, the kind you should be.
A soldier that's fit for a soldier.

You've behaved for the most part at places we've been.
In a way that did proud by the outfit we're in.

You've established a standard, don't let it wear thin.
And lose your good name as a soldier.

Now this place that we're going, there's plenty to drink
Just remember your stomach ain't coated with zinc.
Don't take on too much and wind up in the clink
And lose half your pay as a soldier.

If you're smart you won't mix with the ladies too bold,
The native sex-sales girls are deadly, I'm told.
And any damn fool knows it's worse than a cold.
So it's best to go straight—like a soldier.

But if you take chances and some of you may
Be sure you check in by the green lantern's ray*
If you don't you will rue it for many a day.
And you won't be much use as a soldier.

And you're sure to find some, where ever you look
Who are out to get husbands, by hook or by crook
And they'll tie you up fast, by the ring and the book,
If you don't watch your step, like a soldier.

There were many more verses, which would become applicable later on.
Just now, these were enough for England.

The Eighteenth Infantry was bound for Dorchester. The troops arrived on
the anniversary of their landing in Africa, shepherded part of the way by a
lieutenant in blouse and "pinks" who wore an armband that proclaimed him
to be RTOP (rail transportation officer). He told them all about English money
and about life in a war zone. It wasn't bad, he said, except when the German
bombers came over. Lieutenant Downing remembered his assigned role,
looked impressed, and agreed that it must be hard to be under fire like that.
How long had the lieutenant been overseas?

Three months.

They moved to the town of Broadmayne, where they were billeted next to
the Third Armored Division. Nissen huts and a few frame buildings. As exec
of the company, Lieutenant Downing picked out the quarters for the officers.
One end of one Nissen hut had four cubicles: one for the captain, one for
Downing, and two for the four other lieutenants, two to a room.

---

*GI prophylactic stations were marked by a green light.

They got new uniforms. They got replacements for the men lost because of illness and the men transferred to the Third Division for combat in Italy. Downing got his bedroll, which had been shipped up from Sicily. It had been raining the day he left, and the bedroll was covered with green mold. Downing also got the footlocker he had left in Scotland in 1942, with all his clean clothes! Then the unit went back to training, especially after the quota of replacements showed up. Captain Moore got himself a job in the Transportation Corps, and Lieutenant Downing took over the company. But not for long—he was transferred to Headquarters Company of the Second Battalion as executive officer.

By the thousands, the hundreds of thousands, American troops were massing in the British Isles, tucked in wherever troops could be housed. Maj. Henry G. Spencer's Twenty-third Regiment of the Second Division had arrived at Tynan Abbey, a small village in Northern Ireland. The men lived in steel Nissen huts, went on forced marches on the macadam roads, and moved to a firing range 5 miles south of Belfast for practice. And they waited.

What they were waiting for were landing craft from America, vessels that were absolutely essential to the invasion of Fortress Europe. That invasion was now scheduled for the spring of 1944. The big problem, even bigger than the state of training of the American troops, was the shortage of landing craft and of the artificial harbors needed for that cross-Channel landing. The harbors had not yet been built. Many of the landing craft were still in American waters.

Lieutenant Colonel Snetzer's Second Engineer Battalion was stationed at Camp Drumbanagher, another estate converted with Nissen huts, 20 miles from Armbaugh. Right next door was Ninth Division headquarters. The engineers trained. The officers were sometimes invited to visit local gentry. Snetzer spent one evening with Maj. Maxwell Close, owner of Drumbanagher Estate. The whole evening was devoted to talk of fox hunting, hounds, and horses. The major was a master of hounds. "It was just like dropping back into the last century."

The battalion had traveled light, but by November 16, 1943, it had received 95 percent of its trucks and supplies.

On January 1 Snetzer and twenty-one other officers and men went down to Ilfracombe in southwest England for assault training. To prepare the troops—most of them very green—the Allies had set up an extensive amphibious assault school on the Devon coast. A whole area of the beach had

been cleared of civilians; there were buildings and roads and bridges to be
dynamited by the engineers, and there were places where minefields could
be laid. The school, conducted at the Woolacombe Hotel, covered loading
and unloading transports and landing craft. The students were taken aboard
LSTs, LCVPs, and other assault craft and shown how they worked. On the
way back north, later in the month, they managed a few days in London:
Hyde Park, Piccadilly, Trafalgar Square, Parliament, Big Ben, Westminster
Abbey, Buckingham and St. James's palaces, and St. Paul's Cathedral. They
rode the underground everywhere. They ate at the Grosvenor House (a hotel),
had tea at the Piccadilly Hotel, and saw a play at the Lyric Theatre. Then
they were on their way back to Belfast, and more training.

Almost everyone concerned with D day had to go through instruction at the
Assault Training Center. The First Division, which had made two amphibious landings, was no exception. The men went down in the winter, a long
cold drive to Braunton, to arrive at a sandy waste. There they lived in tents
furnished with canvas cots and heated by Sibley stoves. Lieutenant Downing's
Second Battalion of the Eighteenth Infantry was to train in assaulting pillboxes and using demolition charges and flamethrowers.

Most of the veteran dogfaces thought it was mostly B.S., this constant
assault on dummy emplacements by men who had been through the real thing
several times. One day, when Downing was out visiting the troops in the
field, he came upon one of the rifle platoons sitting behind a high dune on
the beach. The instructor lieutenant had the riflemen clustered around a small
fire, which they kept going by shooting flamethrower charges into the ground.
Two men were posted atop the dunes as outposts, to warn of visits by high-
ranking officers; the rest of the troops just huddled around the fire, smoking
and waiting for lunch to be brought up. No wonder: their Assault Training
Center instructor was a brand-new second lieutenant who had never been in
combat. When the dogfaces started telling him about their Sicilian and African
experiences, the lieutenant really had to shut up.

When the training time was over, the GIs moved back to Broadmayne.
Everyone was relatively happy; the brass had it down on paper that the Eighteenth Infantry had undergone its "training" and the dogfaces had gotten
through with relatively little discomfort, except that of half freezing to death.

There had been some serious and useful training on the Devon coast—a
practice river crossing in rubber boats at night, for example. Lieutenant Downing was on that mission. He got chilled, came down with recurrent malaria,

and went into the hospital again. In there he found many friends, all with malaria, jaundice, and aggravated wounds.

In a different hospital Sergeant Moglia was being treated for complications, most of them from that near escape when he had been blown "arse over teakettle" in his foxhole by an artillery round. But they were tough, these GIs, and they returned to duty.

The longer the troops waited for the invasion, the more complicated life became in England. There were just too many Americans in that small country. Frictions developed:

A YANK IN THE E.T.O.*

Where the heavy dew whips through the breeze,
And you wade in mud up to your knees.
Where the sun don't shine and the rain blows free,
And the fog's so thick you cn hardly see.

Where we live on Brussels sprouts and spam
(And those powdered eggs aren't worth a damn)
In town you eat their fish and spuds,
And wash them down with a mug of suds.

You hold your nose while you gulp it down
It bites your stomach, then you frown
For it burns your tongue, makes your throat feel queer,
It's rightly called bitter, it sure ain't beer.

Where prices are high and queues are long
And those G.I. Yanks are always wrong,
Where you get watered Scotch for four bits a snort,
And those limey cabbies never stand short.

And the pitch black nights when you stay out late
It's so bloody dark you can't navigate
There's no transportation, so you have to hike,
And you get knocked on your can by a goddam bike.

---

*A poem that mysteriously appeared on the dayroom bulletin board of Headquarters Company, Second Battalion, Eighteenth Infantry, one day in May.

Where most of the girls are blonde and bold
  And think a Yank's pockets are lined with gold.
And there's Piccadilly Commandos with painted allure
  Steer clear of them or you are burnt for sure.

This isle's not worth saving, I don't think
  Cut those balloons loose—let the damn thing sink.
I'm not complaining but I'll bet you know
  Life's rougher than hell in the E.T.O.

The reason life seemed so tough was that Americans were everywhere. The Fifth Ranger Battalion moved in with the Eighteenth Infantry. Black troops moved into the town of Weymouth. Engineers were quartered between Broadmayne and Weymouth and had better access to Downing's favorite pub, so they proceeded to drink up Lieutenant Downing's share of double Scotches. The pubs, theaters, and dance halls were jammed every night. One night Downing spent four hours in Weymouth and could not even get a glass of beer, to say nothing of a girl.

The British were getting edgy; he could tell. Outwardly they retained their quiet courtesy, but there were signs that they were becoming testy about being crowded out of their pubs, their buses, and their cinemas and having their girls monopolized by Americans. The countryside was overrunning with them.

Something had to give. The invasion could not come a moment too soon.

General Eisenhower came down to visit the Eighteenth Infantry and talked to the higher-ranking officers. General Bradley came down and talked to the officers *and the men*. Lieutenant Downing's battalion formed up for inspection. Bradley then had all the officers assemble around a jeep, and he stood in the middle and talked some more. No bullshit. He explained what was going to happen. The Americans would invade with four divisions—theirs was one of them—but behind them would be forty more.

"I wouldn't miss this show for anything in the world," said the general. "Some of you will be killed, but a person who lives through this invasion will be proud for the rest of his life for having been part of it."

They all came to attention and saluted. General Bradley drove off and left them to think it over.

*

Sergeant Hoffner's engineers sailed from America aboard the old luxury liner SS *Aquitania*. They seemed to head due north, so the dogfaces got the idea that they were somehow heading for the Pacific.

Two weeks later they landed at Greenock, Scotland. Then they went by rail through the checkerboard squares of the English countryside, dotted with sheep. They landed at Paignton, near Torquay on the Devon coast. Here they were officially designated as the Sixth Engineer Special Brigade. Sergeant Hoffner's unit was the 203d Combat Engineer Battalion.

This area had been established by Lt. Col. Paul Thompson, commander of the brigade, as a training ground. The center was named "Slapton Sands." The whole area had been cleared of civilians so that the engineers could play with their fiendish devices and the infantry could practice assaulting the beaches. The houses were rigged for door-to-door combat. As the men went from house to house, targets sprang up at them. Every major unit that was going to participate in the Normandy landings would go through Colonel Thompson's training program.

On February 23 the Second Engineer Battalion had its first casualties. The training exercise employed live mines. Staff Sergeant Robertson and Pfc. Elkins of Company C were working with antitank mines. One of those mines was activated. They lifted it, and it blew up in their faces, mortally wounding both men.

One of the awaited assault vessels still in American waters at the end of 1943 was *LCI (L) 557*.

In autumn 1943, as the American divisions from north Africa and Sicily were moving back to England to prepare for the invasion of France, CPO Lorne D. Porter of the Seabees was sweating in a tent on Guadalcanal Island. Then he was told to report to the orderly tent. That's how he learned he had just been given an ensign's commission, which came with orders to report to the General Motors Technical Center in Flint, Michigan, for training as an engineering officer in the amphibious diesel program.

Going home to see family and friends! What a break! What a war!

But it was for just a brief visit; less than a month later Porter was on duty at that Michigan school.

*

Who was to lead the invasion of Fortress Europe? Privately, the British felt strongly that their man should, but Winston Churchill knew that the Americans, who were going to be asked to supply most of the resources, would never agree to a British commander. Churchill wanted General Marshall, but President Roosevelt wanted him more in Washington. So, finally, in the late summer of 1943 General Eisenhower got the accolade. The appointment brought a good deal of sniping and backbiting, which was not to stop. Wisely, the leaders chose a Briton as deputy for air, a Briton as deputy for sea, and a Briton as deputy for land operations. This led to a British hope that Ike would be no more than a figurehead, put in to appease American public opinion, and that the British would run the war. That attitude was going to be a problem all the way.

General Bradley was appointed by Eisenhower as commander of the U.S. First Army. Poor Patton! His Seventh Army, in Sicily, was steadily cannibalized to support or create other units, and it looked as though his role in the war had ended, because of the slapping incidents and his inability to get along with the British. He certainly was not again going to be Bradley's boss. But Eisenhower and Marshall had respect for Patton's abilities as a fighting general, no matter his methods of discipline. And Patton was by far the leading American expert on armor. So he, too, was to be brought to London. His first employment would be to command a mythical army, headed theoretically for the Pas de Calais, around Le Havre, the closest continental area across the English Channel. An elaborate hoax had been established by the British, who were past masters at deception, and this was to be carried right up through the first weeks of the actual invasion on the Normandy coast, near Cherbourg on the Cotentin Peninsula. Patton was promised that later on he would get into the fight with a new Third Army, which would feature armored operations.

Col. Arthur Campbell's war was hell. At Fifth Corps it was one conference after another, one more committee detail after each previous one. There were compensations, such as seeing Queen Mary when she came up for a ball game and being introduced (along with scores of others) at tea. Ditto the Duchess of Kent.

In September 1943 the advance headquarters of the Fifth Corps had moved to Taunton, but Colonel Campbell's various committee duties kept him in Bristol.

He met Omar Bradley just after the general came to England. Then he went to Taunton and was made provost marshal of the Fifth Corps.

*

Fifth Corps and Seventh Corps were now designated as the two field headquarters that would command the American sectors of the Normandy invasion. For months subordinate units such as the Twenty-ninth Division had
been in England training for that day. Now a whole series of mock invasion
exercises was planned. Operation Duck was one of the first, held in Colonel
Thompson's bailiwick on the English coast shortly before Christmas, 1943.

The pace was increasing. Colonel Campbell went down to Operation Duck.
He was now "Bigoted"—that meant he was one of the relatively few officers
who knew the major secrets of the coming invasion of Europe: the time (May)
and the place (Normandy). The "Bigots" were scrutinized and superscru-
tinized by higher authority to be sure the secrets were kept. For the real
problem of the coming invasion was not the crossing of the Channel—
American and British air and sea power had already made that a certainty—
but the ability to hold the beachheads and supply them, and then get well
inshore before the Germans could bring up the major forces they had available to repel the invaders. The Americans had learned in the Pacific that
many more invaders were needed than defenders. And at Salerno two companies of Panzer troops had fought well enough to delay the GIs so much
that the Germans were able to launch a counterstrike on the American left
flank and very nearly push the invaders back into the sea.

So secrecy was all important. One air force general was sent home for
talking too much at a dinner party at Claridge's Hotel in London. One sergeant at SHAEF was put under deep suspicion because he had a German
name and absentmindedly misdirected some papers to his sister in Chicago.
An enormous flap was created when some "Bigoty" papers blew out a window of the War Office in London one day and were scattered from hell to
breakfast around Whitehall. Everybody in brassland, British and American,
was enormously security conscious. And well they should be, for the secret
they carried was so delicate that some did not believe it could be preserved.

From America's point of view perhaps the greatest security risk of all
was General Eisenhower. For Ike had done better by Kay Summersby, his
English driver, than simply solace her for the loss of her lover, Colonel
Arnold. The general had taken her to his bed, and she shared his innermost
secrets, in the manner of the mistresses to the great from time immemorial.
One of the still-kept secrets of the war is Kay Summersby's relationship to
British military intelligence. If she wasn't an agent, then the British had

certainly missed a bet. All during the war they had spied on their American
Allies in New York and Washington.*

To believe that the British would have missed this chance to keep tabs
on the biggest fish in Europe was to be naive. As the British knew better
than most Americans, British and American interests coincided only up to a
point. But, of course, in military and political circles the general's most im-
politic liaison was totally ignored. General Bradley never referred to it, even
in the memoirs he wrote long after the war. Captain Harry C. Butcher,
Eisenhower's naval aide, refers to Kay Summersby only as "Ike's driver"
and later as "his personal secretary" in a long, intimate memoir. That particular military secret of Ike's clandestine love life was very well kept—but
only from the American and British public. *Autre temps, autres moeurs*. In
the manner of the day, the large number of war correspondents who were in
on it said not a word. One can't blame them; they would most certainly have
been banished from SHAEF and probably sent home if they had revealed
the guilty secret. Besides, who cared? If Sergeant Doyle and Lieutenant Downing and all the others were "hot to trot," why shouldn't their supreme commander be? All any of them would have asked for was the chance to change
places with Ike for one night.

The exercises went on. Operation Fox was staged at Slapton Sands on March
11, and Colonel Campbell went down there. So did Sergeants Ogden and
Elburn of the Twenty-ninth Division. The men disembarked from landing
craft and LSTs. The engineers hit the beach and practiced getting rid of
obstacles and minefields and moving traffic inland. The place, on the Devon
coast, was chosen for its topographical similarity to the actual invasion site
across the water.

The exercises were pretty ragged. After all, most of these young men had
not yet fired a shot in anger. There was plenty to be learned, and nothing
could substitute for a twenty-four-hour baptism of fire. Captain Rathbun and
his men on the Italian front could certainly attest to that. Because of the
foul-up at Anzio, in March 1944 the Germans were about to launch a new
offensive. In and out of the line, the Seventh Infantry had been fighting for
six weeks.

*

*The book *A Man Called Intrepid* gives some of the details of this activity.

Sergeant Chattaway's 110th Infantry Regiment had come across the Atlantic
with the rest of the Twenty-eighth Infantry Division in October on the good
old SS *Cristobal*. It was the usual trip, moderately painful for the officers,
miserable for the dogfaces; half the men were in the hold, the other half
were wherever they could find space, alternating every twelve hours. They
landed, went to Pembroke, in Wales, and trained. Chattaway's Company K
was stationed at Pembroke Dock and then at Fishguard. The infantrymen,
too, went down to the Assault Training Center in Devon for some practice
for the big assault to come. Then they spent three weeks on maneuvers on
the Gower Peninsula. The men figured they were going in as part of the D
day invasion, but they were wrong. On April 12 the Twenty-eighth Division
was removed from the roster of the Fifth Corps and assigned to Patton's Third
Army. The Third would not invade; it would wait until the invasion was established, and then move through the First Army to make the dash across
France.

All that winter of 1943–1944 Ens. Lorne Porter was training for invasions.
Six weeks at Flint, and then he went back to the Solomons, but this time it
was Solomons, Maryland. His task was to organize an LCI crew and to train
the crewmen for amphibious operations.

In January he was sent to New York to fit out *LCI (L) 557*. On a Monday
morning he and Lieutenant Edman, the commanding officer, reported to a
small shipyard at Barber, New Jersey, and watched the ship workers lay the
keel of Porter's ship. On the following Monday they returned to the shipyard, this time to commission the vessel. They moved to Pier 42, North River,
for outfitting and stores. In the last week of February 1944 they sailed for
Solomons, Maryland, at the upper end of the Chesapeake Bay. Despite bad
weather and the lack of a full crew (only two officers to conn the ship), they
got there and reported to the group commander, who would have twelve LCIs
under his control. Soon a flotilla (thirty-six ships) was assembled, and they
trained.

Early in April 1944 the good ship *LCI (L) 557* and the eleven other craft
of Group 33 set sail for England, leaving Norfolk in a raging storm. They
picked up an Atlantic convoy bound for the Mediterranean, and were put on
the outer fringes to shield the big ships from torpedo attack. Inboard from
them were the wooden-hulled minesweepers, also destined for England.

It was a rough crossing. Three days out of Gibraltar, they were detached
from the big convoy, which turned south toward the Rock. Then they ran

into a terrible storm; the little LCIs were lashed by enormous waves, but ultimately they made land at Horta, in the Azores, and at the end of April arrived at Land's End.

The new date for the invasion was June 5. Although Ensign Porter and the men of *LCI (L) 557* did not know that, they had just a month to complete their manning and their training.

General Patton was now touring England, making "inspirational" addresses to the troops. On April 2 he was in Belfast, addressing the Second Division.

"Usual blasphemous talk attributed to him," said Colonel Snetzer.

The general did not impress the troops as much as he impressed the other generals with the notion that he impressed the troops. Most of the GIs regarded Patton as the biggest "B.S. artist and asshole" in the army—no reflection intended on his command abilities, of course. The Second Division and its engineers would be part of Patton's Third Army.

In private the GIs took a very practical view of the exhortations of their generals. The Ninth Division, fresh from the Mediterranean, was now stationed at Crawley Court, a few miles from Winchester, where the men lived in Quonset huts. S. Sgt. Frank W. Kalich of Company C of the Ninth Medical Battalion lived in one hut whose back wall was plastered over, making a fine "canvas." General Eddy gave a pep talk to the troops one day, promising them that in view of their Mediterranean service they would all soon get to go home. Next day on the wall of Sergeant Kalich's Quonset hut there appeared a painting of the general, unmistakably their general, driving a jeep over rocky terrain, pulling a trailer. The trailer was full to overflowing with dog tags, the personal identification discs that were worn in pairs by every GI, giving his name, rank, serial number, and blood type. When a soldier was killed in action, the graves registration people collected one dog tag and left the other on the body. So the pretty picture of General Eddy showed him hauling dog tags "home." It sounds insubordinate, and it was, but merely a typical bit of GI gallows humor, not meant to imply any hatred for the general. (Maybe!) The painting remained, a symbol of the healthy GI cynicism about the promises of the brass, until the battalion CO came in one day on inspection, took one look, and ordered it erased.

*   *   *

April: The movement was faster now. April 5 brought orders that no more furloughs or overnight passes would be issued. That order was effective all

over the United Kingdom. Everything was tightening up. On April 16 the
Second Engineers were shipped to Cardiff, Wales. On May 1 they received
the Second Division operations order for the invasion. Lieutenant Colonel
Snetzer commented:

"Roads are full of American convoys moving to various new areas. This
country is really overrun with Americans and American equipment everywhere."

The British sappers taught the engineers how to blow a hole in a seawall.
Every night now the officers had an hour of French lessons from a local priest.

On May 15 the Second Engineer Battalion had its orders to move into
the marshaling area. The next day the battalion moved out, all its trucks
loaded with equipment, ammunition, weapons, and explosives. All the men
carried their personal weapons and full combat equipment. They were bound
for Bournemouth.

On April 28 Sergeant Hoffner's engineers prepared for their final training
exercise, Operation Tiger, and amphibious landing test of the U.S. Fourth
Division. This was the new outfit to which General Roosevelt had been assigned as assistant division commander, after the shake-up of the First Division.

Two battalions of engineers were loaded aboard three LSTs for the exercise. They were to come ashore with the infantry and take out the obstacles set up by Colonel Thompson's men.

The exercise began on schedule. The Fourth Division came ashore in
smoke and confusion, with rockets firing; it was almost like the real thing.

Actually, it was more real than any of the men yet knew. Two elements
of German E-boats had crossed the Channel and gotten in among the LST
convoy that was bringing engineers, tanks, and other vehicles to participate
in the landing. One of the principal units involved was the First Engineer
Special Brigade, commanded by Col. Eugene Caffey. Yes, he was that same
Colonel Caffey who had brought the Twentieth Engineers to north Africa
equipped with tommy guns, the colonel who had planned to play a leading
part in all subsequent invasions, rather like Teddy Roosevelt (Sr.) and his
Rough Riders.

Since north Africa the colonel had been in Italy, and now with his 3500-
man brigade he was to have an important role in the Normandy invasion.
Here was his big test. The colonel rode in on a landing ship, but many of his
junior officers and noncoms were on the LSTs.

For this last big exercise the brass appeared in force. Ike came down. So did Monty. Air Marshal Tedder came. So did Admirals Ramsay and Kirk, Gen. J. Lawton Collins, and U.S. Army Air Force Gen. Lewis H. Brereton. They assembled very early in the morning on LCIs just offshore; from there they would watch the war game. What they saw was most disconcerting. The air force, which was supposed to bomb and rocket the beaches, did not show up. Some tanks had been specially waterproofed—a brand-new technique that was supposed to let them swim into shore and take off immediately for the battle. One of the tanks sank as the brass watched. The crew climbed out ignominiously to be rescued. Landing craft came up to rocket the shore, but the rockets all hit short of the beach. Sergeant Hoffner's 203d Engineer Combat Battalion then went in and began to clear the obstacles. This was all as it should be. The battalion had had a lot of practice under Colonel Thompson and did an efficient job. Then the second and subsequent waves were supposed to be managed by Colonel Caffey's First Engineers, whose job it was to direct traffic; they were to keep the supplies and troops from piling up on the beaches and to see to it that the men and matériel moved inland.

This part of the exercise was a mess. It was such a disaster that when General Bradley saw it, he told General Collins, commander of the Seventh Corps, to get a new engineer officer to replace the beach commander for the actual invasion. The guilty party seemed to be Colonel Caffey. What Bradley did not realize at the time was that part of Colonel Caffey's First Engineers had been wiped out in the sinking of two of the LSTs of the convoy. One unit, the 3206th Quartermaster Company, was almost completely destroyed. So Colonel Caffey had an excuse of sorts—perhaps not one that would justify the confusion on the beach, but enough of an excuse to cause Bradley's staff to conveniently mislay the order for the change.

Before the day was out Eisenhower and the other top commanders knew about the E-boat attack that had disrupted the invasion exercise, causing about 800 American casualties, most of them drowned. It was all hushed up, but for two weeks the brass lived in the shadow of the incident: what if the Germans had captured some "Bigoted" personnel and dragged from them the two secrets of the invasion: where and when? Ultimately all bodies were accounted for, and it was determined that the Germans had not discovered the secret. As for the GIs, anyone who knew anything at all about the events on Slapton Sands and in the nearby Channel was threatened with the direst of punishments if he talked.

On the second day of the exercise Sergeant Hoffner and his men were walking along the beach; they saw some bundles at the tide line and a group of men standing around looking down. As Hoffner and his men approached, one of the others detached himself from the group and took a few steps toward them.

"Well, what are you staring at? Haven't you ever seen a dead man before?"

The questioner was wearing the two stars of a major general. (He was General Huebner of the First Division, one of the observers of the exercise.) Sure enough, there on the beach were bodies clad in U.S. Army fatigues.

Two days later Hoffner's men learned the whole tale, and the need for silence was impressed on them.

On April 30, while packing up to return to Paignton, Sergeant Hoffner was injured when a training mine exploded. His helmet was badly dented and he found he could not move his arm. He had suffered a broken wrist that earned him a week in hospital at Newton Abbot. He went back to duty with his arm in a sling.

Then it was time for the big invasion. Everything began to close down.

April 25: Lieutenant Downing was sleeping in his Nissen hut when he was awakened by an explosion. He sat up and lit a cigarette. Antiaircraft fire was tearing into the sky. He wondered if he ought to go out to a slit trench, but he did not want to appear panicky. Then explosions shattered windows in his hut and threw the doors open. Hesitating no longer, he dashed out of the hut in his underwear, shoes, and helmet and plunged into a slit trench. So did the others. They crouched, shivering in the cold, and watched the searchlights and listened to the AA guns until the firing died down.

The next morning Downing learned that German bombers had hit the camp down the road. One headquarters company man and one cook had been killed. Lieutenant Downing had to make a report and handle the personal effects of the headquarters man. It seemed a little early for casualties from this campaign, but there it was. There really was a war on in the English countryside, too.

Since the fall of 1943, as the plans progressed in London for the invasion of Fortress Europe, an unusual group of volunteer soldiers was training at the Congressional Country Club outside Washington. This was the Norwegian Special Operations Group, formed from the Ninety-ninth Infantry Battalion, a ski outfit stationed at Camp Hale, Colorado. Almost all the men were Scandinavians; indeed a knowledge of Norwegian and skiing were required to get into the special unit. A number of the soldiers were Norwegian former

seamen, stranded here and there by the war, who had made their way to the
United States.

The training camp was under the command of Col. Serge Obolensky,
once a Russian prince. It was a hush-hush Office of Strategic Services project,
designed to harry the Germans in Norway.

Privates Borge Langeland and Leif Oistad, both Norwegian seamen, were
members of this organization. Langeland had been a radio operator aboard a
Norwegian ship that had been torpedoed. Oistad had been a sailor aboard
another Norwegian vessel.

The OSS was not stingy with its training. The group was taught guerrilla
warfare and hand-to-hand combat at camps around Washington. Then the
men went to Martha's Vineyard off Cape Cod to make amphibious landings
from canoes and rubber rafts. Late in 1943 they were sent to England and
stationed at the OSS camp about 90 miles from London. The British Airborne Command trained them in parachute skills. In the spring of 1944 they
were waiting for the invasion to make themselves useful.

Sergeants Moglia and Chattaway would never have recognized the new Fort
Dix had they suddenly been whisked home from Europe in 1944. For in the
few months since they had left, that American military installation had burst
into full bloom. Fort Dix now covered 65 square miles and housed virtually
every sort of army unit: WACs, recruits, units shipping out, and even POWs.
It was a symbol of the enormous effort that America was capable of when
aroused, and of the new army that had been built. The United States was
mass producing soldiers.

Pvt. Norman R. Adolph 12227653 was one of this new breed. He was a
boy from the Bronx, with some college background. He enlisted and was
sent to the 1229th Reception Center at Fort Dix. On January 17 Private
Adolph and the rest of this new batch of recruits of Company C were issued
their uniforms and gear. They were told to stuff it all into a long green duffel
bag and to haul it to Barracks 14, where they were housed. "It weighed at
least a hundred pounds," Private Adolph wrote his mother that night.

He didn't much like Fort Dix, although there were five different camp
movie houses, and shows and dances on the post every night. His barracks
was not lovely—plain board walls and exposed rafters ("a little different from
Princeton"). He did not like the food or the service: "disagreeable guys on
KP who hand out the food with dirty fingers...silverware always greasy...
food trays not too clean."

The next day Private Adolph started "processing." Up at 5:45 for reveille formation. Back to the barracks to make the bed, sweep up, shave, and brush teeth. Breakfast at 7:00. Detail formation at 7:30. The recruits were too green for details; they had a physical examination that morning. Sausage and potatoes for lunch. Coffee dipped out of a big pot "which ten KPs had already had their fingers in. I thought I saw some dead flies floating in the pot so I skipped coffee."

In the afternoon they marched under the direction of a lordly Pfc. At 3:30 they were dismissed to go back to Barracks 14 to organize their belongings. Private Adolph's belongings now "weighed 150 pounds and occupied two barracks bags."

Supper: cold macaroni, chopped frankfurter soup, and leftover potatoes.

At 6:30 p.m. there was a formation to announce the names of those shipping out. Private Adolph was now a "veteran" of three days, and it was his turn to lord it over the new recruits.

The following day Private Adolph had an IQ test, as well as some other tests and a classification interview. He signed up for a $10,000 GI life insurance policy, and he went to the post exchange and bought a 25-cent bar of Nestlé's almond chocolate for 12 cents.

The next night he went to the movies (*Ali Baba and the Forty Thieves*). And on January 20 old soldier Private Adolph (four days) pulled KP from 6 p.m to 4 a.m. Fifteen KPs working for one night cook. Private Adolph spent the night washing potatoes. Around midnight the cook made each KP a steak sandwich! Oh joy! They didn't have to eat the greasy potatoes and sausages they were preparing.

Private Adolph was already snapping into shape; one could see that. He had learned fast to bitch about the food. He bitched about the police detail (picking up litter in the company area). Finished at 9 a.m. "Why shouldn't they let us go back to the barracks? No. Take them to the drill field and run through a couple of hours of drill."

He bitched about the drill field: too many frozen footprints.

He bitched about the shots.

He got put on a garden detail, and he bitched about that. The corporal in charge made the GIs spread fertilizer around the barracks lawns. A lieutenant came up and chewed out the corporal and then made them rake it off. Private Adolph bitched about the inefficiency of the army.

If he wasn't on a detail, he bitched about not having anything to do.

After a week it was obvious that Private Adolph was a fine, well-adjusted young man learning to be a soldier.

On February 1, 1944, Private Adolph and a large number of other young men were sent to Fort Benning. They did not know where they were going, of course; they knew only that they'd been put aboard a train, three men to a section (two in the lower berth and one in the upper).

At Fort Benning Private Adolph was assigned to a unit of the Army Specialized Training Program. This was a program begun a year earlier to produce specialists and officer material. Young men with a high IQ (123 and above) were tested for various programs.

What a difference in their surroundings! Family-style meals at tables set with silver. Waiters to fill the food platters, delicious chicken, corn, sweet potatoes.

First, thirteen weeks of basic training. A pep talk from the sergeant, who told them how lucky they were to be in the ASTP. He also gave them a little warning: if they didn't make it, they would be shipped out to combat units.

Private Adolph vowed to work hard, and he did, plowing through all the early detail of basic training, plus tests, interviews, and more classification. He passed the tests to go into an advanced engineering program consisting of integral calculus, mechanics, and the like.

Then on February 19 the battalion commander called the men together. He smiled broadly as he announced "good news."

"Men," he said, "the ASTP unit has been disbanded."

The sergeants and the corporals all smiled, too, and were almost benign in their pleasure. Afterward they indicated what they had felt all along about the "coddling" of intellectuals.

"You guys had better get on the ball now."

"You ain't goin' back to any college. You guys are soldiers."

Basic training was resumed with great vigor. One day Private Adolph had a four-hour right-way, wrong-way demonstration on scouting and patrolling. His company marched a mile into the woods to a small valley with a grandstand at one end. The trainees were seated in the grandstand. A voice materialized over the loudspeaker system.

"Can you see where I am?"

No one could see the speaker.

Then a man stood up in the brush—less than 50 feet away from the trainees—and walked toward them. He was wearing a camouflage suit and his helmet was covered with grass. Private Adolph was very impressed. The man had been completely invisible.

From that point the trainees began to learn how to see "invisible" men. After some instruction they began to pick them out. They picked out one, then another, and another, until finally they were sure they had found all the men hidden in the field.

"Is that all?" said the voice.

"That's all."

"Okay, that's all."

And then, out of the brush, jumped a "Japanese" who charged toward the grandstand, yelling "Banzai." From a tree 50 yards away another invisible man fired, and the "Jap" fell "dead."

What a lesson! Private Adolph agreed with the instructor. Never be too damned sure that you've got 'em all.

So not only had the army grown in size, but its techniques of instruction were new and impressive.

On March 27, 1944, Private Adolph was transferred to Company L, 397th Infantry Regiment, 100th Division. It was a brand-new division made up of brand-new regiments, the 397th, 398th, and 399th infantries.

The division was full of intellectuals, the harvest of the abandoned ASTP.

The men moved to Fort Bragg. More hard-slogging training. The training was much more difficult and much more effective than Sergeant Moglia's had been four years earlier. No sticks for machine guns, no trees for field pieces, and no Bull Durham sacks for grenades these days. By April 26 Private Adolph and his friends were practicing with dummy grenades on various sorts of targets, throwing from standing, kneeling, and prone positions at rows of trenches, 15, 20, 25, and 30 yards away. It was very dull because the grenades did not explode, not even as much fun as heaving snowballs or rotten apples which at least splattered when they hit. Two days later they were studying booby traps and mines; films illustrating German mines were supplied by training units.

May came and Private Adolph went on war games into the North Carolina woods. It was hard training, with field problems and live ammunition. By the end of May Private Adolph, with only five months in the service, was a "trained rifleman."

May: The Eighteenth Infantry was moved down to its final marshaling area in southwestern England. The troops were behind barbed wire, and British soldiers patrolled the perimeter. No one could get in or out without a special pass.

One morning all the officers of Lieutenant Downing's Second Battalion were assembled and marched out in a column of twos past the sentries and up to the former staff officers' quarters, to the dining room. The doors were

closed and guards were posted. Colonel Smith then gave a little speech, and
Majors Colacicco and Middleworth, using maps, briefed the junior officers
on what was going to happen.

The First Division was going to land on the coast of France, east of the
Cotentin Peninsula, at a place called Omaha Beach. The Sixteenth Infantry
would land first and clear the beaches. The Eighteenth would land behind
the Sixteenth, move through, and assemble at the town of Colleville-sur-Mer;
the Eighteenth would then march on to Mosles, where it would set up a roadblock and await an enemy counterattack.

Lieutenant Downing and the other junior officers had hoped that somebody else was going to be making the assault. But at least their job was
easier than the Sixteenth's, and that made them all feel better. Going in
behind another regiment gave Downing the feeling that he had a better chance
of coming through in one piece.

The company grade officers were issued maps that day and told to brief their
men. The maps were clear and accurate (Downing hoped); made from photographs that had been taken from a submarine, they showed enemy installations
and gave an idea of the lay of the land as it would appear from an assault boat.

Then the officers were released, and Lieutenant Downing went back to
his company. He explained the projected assault, using his new maps. Nobody showed much enthusiasm, but nobody complained, either. The men
accepted the coming of the invasion and their part in it.

All sorts of new equipment began showing up. The "assault jacket" replaced the pack, with pockets in front, on the sides, and in the rear. When
a man put it on with all those pockets full, he was really loaded down. Gas-
proof underwear, shirts, socks, leggings, and trousers were issued, too. They
were virtually airtight and made everyone sweat. There was also shoe impregnant. Downing treated his shoes; it made them gas resistant and waterproof,
but also airtight. His feet began to sweat.

The soldiers got small blocks of nitro starch, with a fuse and igniter, to
blast foxholes instead of digging them. They got waterproof plastic bags as
covers for their weapons, field glasses, and radios. And they got compasses
and small silk maps of France. Cutting files wrapped in waxed paper and
magnetized pencil clips, to be used as emergency compasses, were issued
for escaping from prison camps—a comforting thought. They also received
paratroop first aid kits, with syringes of morphine. The battalion surgeon
showed the officers and top three grades how to use them. They were issued
sulfa tablets. The troops got back their First Division insignias for their helmets, and some were to have stripes on the back of their helmets—vertical

for officers and horizontal for noncoms. They were also issued green camouflage nets for their helmets. Too many cases of cigarettes, candy, and toilet articles were delivered, so the excess had to be abandoned.

Lieutenant Downing put his money and ID papers into condoms. He
loaded his carbine clips with cartridges and put two extra clips in his assault
jacket. Downing also took a new ration: a can of pea soup that looked like a
big firecracker. There was a thermite charge fitted in the center of the can
and a fuse that came out on top. You punched holes in the top of the can,
and lit the fuse, and the thermite charge heated the soup. The lieutenant
also took two wax heating units. He gave his field glasses to one of the S-2
officers, who said he needed them. Then Downing sorted through the maps,
took the ones that he thought would be useful, and stuffed the others into his
bedroll. He took off his officer insignia and reminded himself to get rid of
the officer ID marks on his helmet as soon as he could. After two invasions
he knew whom the Germans shot at. Downing hooked his canteen, compass,
trench knife, carbine clip pouch, and first aid packet onto his web belt. He
would wear his assault jacket over his combat jacket. He was almost ready.

Lieutenant Downing and all the rest had to get short haircuts. No lice
were wanted. Downing was also advised that he and his men could write
letters home; they would be kept until after D day and then shipped out.

There was a very welcome issue of liquor: every officer received a pint of
gin and a bottle of Scotch whiskey. That night the officers threw a party.
They toasted everything, from underwater obstacles to enemy pillboxes. They
drank the whisky and started on the gin. They began roughhousing. Lieutenant Downing got very drunk. He awoke the next morning in his cot, with
his carbine barrel in his mouth; some joker had put it there. The metallic
taste was only a part of his hangover.

Time was running out fast.

Regiment ordered a final drive to sign up every man who would do so in
the National Service Life Insurance scheme, which provided $10,000 to the
family of a soldier who was killed. At that point the insurance policies were
very easy to sell. There were also changes in pay allotments. Some replacements came in at the last moment, and their paperwork had to be brought up
to date. The first sergeant got sick and had to go to the hospital. He had
been briefed on the invasion, so MPs took him to the hospital and he was
put into a private room under constant guard until the invasion began. Downing appointed Supply Sergeant DeSantis as acting first sergeant.

All this activity brought Lieutenant Downing's company up to the first of
June 1944. It was nearly time.

25

"THE SKY IS
FULL OF
BODIES"

June 5, evening: The airfields of southern England were black with planes, most of them the squat twin-engined Douglas C-47 transports that would open the greatest battle of World War II by dropping thousands of troops from the sky.

As darkness came, the thousands of men began assembling on tarmac, preparing to board the planes that would take them to face the great question mark. Men slumped on the ground around the planes, sharpening knives, blackening their faces, struggling to get dozens of pieces of equipment into place so they would survive the harsh shock of landing.

The men of the airborne were getting ready to go into action.

The plan for the Normandy invasion called for the use of three airborne divisions: the British Sixth Airborne to pave the way for the three British landings, and the U.S. 82d and 101st Airborne divisions to prepare for the landings at Omaha and Utah beaches in the American sector. The tasks of the airborne troops were to seize bridges and main road junctions, to prevent the Germans from flooding the estuarial lands behind the beaches more than they already had, and, above all, to stop any German counterattack before it could get organized and threaten the beachheads.

Air Chief Marshal Trafford Leigh-Mallory, General Eisenhower's air com-

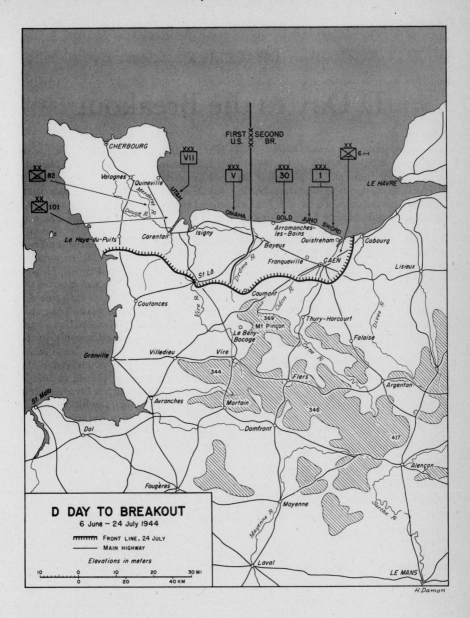

CHERBOURG

Valognes   Quineville   UTAH   FIRST U.S. / SECOND BR.   6 (-)

82   Merderet   LE HAVRE

101   Douve R.

La Haye-du-Puits   Carentan   Isigny   OMAHA   GOLD   JUNO   SWORD   Cabourg

Arromanches-les-Bains   Ouistreham   Lisieux

Bayeux   Franqueville   CAEN

St Lô   Dives R.

Coutances   Caumont   Orne R.

369   Mt Pinçon   Thury-Harcourt

Le Bény-Bocage   Falaise

Granville   Villedieu   Vire   344   Flers   Argentan

Avranches   Mortain   346

St Malo   Dol   Domfront   417

Alençon

Fougères

D DAY TO BREAKOUT
6 June – 24 July 1944

╥╥╥╥ FRONT LINE, 24 JULY
———— MAIN HIGHWAY

Elevations in meters

Mayenne   Sarthe R.

Laval   LE MANS

H. Damon

mander, opposed the airborne operation in the planning stage and, indeed, up to the eve of the invasion. He argued that there were not enough suitable drop zones in the Normandy beachhead area and that the casualties would be enormous. Ergo, the airborne operation would fail. Even after the decisions were made, Leigh-Mallory continued to believe the airborne troops were going to their doom.

The major problem, which was not often discussed in polite company, was the lack of experience of the American pilots who would carry the parachute troops and haul the gliders to their destinations.

These tyro pilots were the fliers of the Ninth Air Force Troop Carrier Command. Most of them had never flown a plane in combat, which meant they had never experienced the sensation of watching the black and white puffs of antiaircraft shells searching for them in the air or of feeling the concussion of a near miss that sends the wings fluttering wildly or turns the fuselage at a sharp angle. They had never known the horror of seeing the next plane get hit and begin to burn.

This lack of experience would be the most important factor in the management of the American airdrops. The senior American air officers were painfully aware of the deficiencies. But there was nothing to be done about it. The one way to gain experience in combat was to go into combat.

The British glider transport pilots were much more experienced. The British used bombers to tow the gliders, and virtually every bomber pilot in Britain had already experienced more than his share of flak. The British had been fighting the war far longer than the Americans. Their paratroops were extremely well trained, and so were their glider pilots and glider crews. The British equivalent of the American troop carriers had hauled gliders and paratroops, both in training and in combat.

The British paratroops, then, were assigned to the area considered by ground force commander Montgomery to be vital: the eastern end of the invasion front.

The major German reserves, particularly the panzer forces, were located east of Caen. The capital of the Normandy district, Caen was the transportation and communications hub, out of which streamed five rail lines and eleven major roads.

The British and the Germans regarded Caen as the key point in Normandy. If the German reserves were to be kept out of action during the crucial hours on the invasion beaches, they would have to be stopped at Caen. The city was on the list of D day objectives for Gen. Miles C. Dempsey's British Second Army.

The British airborne troops were to demolish five bridges over the River Dives. That action would effectively prevent the Germans from bringing armored forces up to Caen. The airborne troops were also to capture a bridge across the River Orne, which lay between Caen and the beaches that would be invaded the next morning. They were also to capture and hold a bridge across the Caen Canal, for precisely the same reason.

The British plan was as audacious as anything ever attempted. Maj. Gen. Richard Gale, the commander of the Sixth Airborne, planned to crash-land gliders *on the bridges to be saved* and, by achieving this total surprise, to overwhelm the enemy before it could either sound an alarm or destroy the bridges. The less delicate mission of destroying the Dives River bridges would be carried out by the parachute troops, and they would also clear landing zones for the main glider force of seventy-two gliders that would come in shortly before dawn.

The British plan had been fixed for months before the invasion. General Gale's men were able to build mockups of the bridges, accurate down to details, and to work out all aspects of their plan as well as could be done in training. By June 1 the British airborne troops who would participate in the operation were as familiar with the target as men could be.

The British were the first to go. The first troops took off well before midnight, in Horsa gliders pulled by Halifax bombers. Landings began shortly after midnight. Six gliders led. Three would crash on the Orne River bridge, three on the canal bridge.

One of the three canal bridge gliders came down in precisely the right place, and Maj. John Howard's company captured the bridge in short order. The second glider assigned to that bridge broke in half in the middle on landing, and many men were killed or injured. The third glider came down a short distance away, and its occupants joined the fight. When the bridge was secure, they helped to hold it.

The Orne River bridge was captured in the same way, although only one of the three gliders got close to that span.

Then came the effort of the British parachute troops, who were to destroy the five bridges across the River Dives and also a powerful battery of coastal defense guns near Merville at the mouth of the Orne River. If they remained in operation, those guns could create trouble for the troops storming the beaches.

To begin with, the airdrops were not all the parachute troops thought they should be.

Col. Terence B. H. Otway of the Ninth Parachute Battalion was dropped by a nervous pilot who took evasive action to avoid flak, and a perverse fate carried Otway into the garden of a German battalion headquarters. But Otway got out of the garden under fire and rallied his scattered men. Other officers did the same. By dawn the British Sixth Airborne Division had achieved every one of its objectives.

The story of the American airborne drops was something else.

In the first place, the specific assignments of the American airborne troops were kept "fluid" for many months, until General Eisenhower's staff decided on the western limits of the American invasion area. Then the 101st Division was assigned to drop in the Utah Beach area, to stop German reinforcements from coming up from the south. The Eighty-second Airborne was assigned to drop much further south, around St.-Sauveur-le-Vicomte in the middle of the base of the Cotentin Peninsula.

Altogether the two American airborne divisions were assigned areas much larger than the compact one given to the British.

Shortly before the invasion target date, word came from agents in France that the German Sixth Parachute Regiment had just been moved into this area to join the Ninety-first Air Landing Division. These were formidable troops, and the invasion planners did not want to send their own paratroops against such defenses when there was no real need.

So the plan for use of the American paratroops was not completed until shortly before the invasion. The drop zones were changed. The 101st Airborne was to seize the western edge of the flooded area behind the beach, between St.-Martin-de-Varreville and Pouppeville. It was also assigned to destroy two bridges. One bridge was on Route Nationale 13, the main highway leading from Carentan to Ste.-Mère-Église and then to Cherbourg. The other bridge carried the railroad west of the Carentan road.

The next tasks given the 101st were the seizure of the La Barquette locks on the Douve River and the establishment of a bridgehead across the Douve northeast of Carentan. So late in the planning were these decisions made— in May—that neither officers nor men had time to become familiar with the territory into which they would move. They would have to "play it by ear."

The 501st Parachute Infantry Regiment of the 101st Airborne Division was stationed at Lambourne, about 20 miles west of Newbury in southwest England. Toward the end of May it became apparent that the invasion was close at hand because the regiment's company officers were assembled day after day for vigorous "sand table" briefings. Maps of their drop areas were shown to them, and the officers were made as familiar with the terrain as could be done in a few days.

Then each officer took his new knowledge to a briefing of his own for his sergeants and the other paratroopers.

1st Lt. Sumpter Blackmon of Company A, First Battalion, was leader of the First Platoon of the company. His platoon's mission was to take and hold the locks at La Barquette, a mile from Carentan. These locks controlled the flow of the tide up the channel of the Douve as far as St.-Sauveur-le-Vicomte. If the Germans destroyed the locks, the water would rush in to flood both the Douve and Merderet rivers. The flooding would present a new obstacle to the troops landing on the beaches. The remainder of Company A was supposed to blow up the bridges over the river north of Carentan.

The other two parachute regiments—the 502d and the 506th—had similar orders covering the other assignments of the division in the area around the base of the Cotentin Peninsula.

The Eighty-second Airborne was to land to the west and south of the 101st. It was to clear the east bank of the Merderet River down to the beachhead and to clear the Douve north to Ste.-Mère-Église. It was also to establish a beachhead on the west bank of the Merderet. The 505th Parachute Infantry Regiment was to capture Ste.-Mère-Église. The 507th and the 508th were to accomplish the other tasks. If there was a point of focus for the Eighty-second, it was that crossroads town of Ste.-Mère-Église.

The briefings were much the same in every American unit. They concluded on June 3. The troops were taken to the airfield at Merryfield. Then came an announcement of another briefing of officers. This one turned out to be a pep talk by Maj. Gen. Maxwell Taylor, the division commander, but a pep talk with an ominous ring. He spoke about taking prisoners:

"We will have no place to keep prisoners tomorrow," the general said.

The message was clear.

That same day the pilots of the Ninth Troop Carrier Command were also briefed on the drop mission.

"Ack-ack will be light, if any," they were told. "You are to take no, repeat, no, evasive action."

On paper it was a simple mission: the pilots of the 501st's planes would fly between two of the Channel Islands off the coast of Normandy. The islands were occupied by the Germans, but the planes would not come close enough for antiaircraft fire to bother them. As they reached the French coast, they were to turn inland and ten minutes later they would be over the drop zone. Pathfinder planes would go ahead, and parachute troops would land and make signals to guide the 501st's planes into the drop zone.

Each group of planes would be led by a lead navigator; all any pilot had to do was follow the leader. It was important that the navigators hit the drop zone and that the pilots drop the troops from just high enough to permit the parachutes to open, but not so high that the troopers dangled in the air as floating targets for German gunners.

Oh, yes, almost as an afterthought came the word about the weather:

Overcast to 3000 feet, but changing rapidly. It might be a little spotty, the meteorologists said.

Late in the afternoon the officers and men of the airborne divisions picked up the last of their gear, which included about $10 worth of French francs. Each man had his own idea about necessities, which ranged from toilet paper to explosive charges.

Lieutenant Blackmon and his men assembled at the airfield at Merryfield on the afternoon of June 4 and waited. But the operation was called off that day. On June 5 they repeated the performance, along with the other 13,000 American paratroopers who would be flown off in 825 planes.

In the evening, as they waited, General Eisenhower showed up at several of the airfields to wish the troops Godspeed. After that they lazed around the aircraft, some sleeping, some worrying, some "shooting the breeze." Some adjusted their equipment, which was so abundant and binding that a few troopers had to lie down on the ground and get their buddies to zip them in. They could scarcely move unassisted; all that was to be remedied by a slash or two with a knife when they landed.

Around ten o'clock the pilots began to come out to the planes. It was nearly time to go. The officers and men of the First Platoon of the 501st's Company A joined hands and prayed that God guide them. Lieutenant Blackmon led his "stick" of eighteen men onto his aircraft. Lieutenant Puhalski took another stick onto another plane. The remainder of the men of the First Platoon were to jump with Captain Paty, the commanding officer of the company.

Just after 10:30 that night the planes took off. They moved above the airfield, circled, and waited; then they began forming up in Vs. It took an hour to get into formation. The lead plane then headed for the Channel Islands.

The V was so perfect that Lieutenant Blackmon could have pitched a grenade at the plane just outside the open cargo door of the C-47.

Right on schedule the formation turned inland. That was the moment when all the planning crumbled and their war against the Germans began.

"Light flak?"

Someone had certainly been misinformed. The sky around them erupted in fireworks.

No evasive action?

Planes were jinking and diving on all sides of Blackmon's, but the pilot of Lieutenant Blackmon's plane (Blackmon never learned his name) flew the course without a tremor. He flew directly into a fogbank, and then all the other planes disappeared; when Blackmon's plane came out, it was alone.

Lieutenant Blackmon was standing at the cargo door with the equipment bundle (machine gun and ammunition), ready to kick it out when the jump light came on. He saw the proper landmarks come up but felt no tap from the No. 2 jumper, Pvt. Thurman Day, or from Sergeant Adams, who was watching the green light. Then the ground disappeared, and he saw whitecaps. They were back over the sea.

Private Day pulled Blackmon back from the door and shouted that the pilot wanted to see him. Blackmon threaded his way up the narrow passage to the pilot's compartment.

The pilot looked worried.

"Lieutenant, we missed the drop zone and are over the Channel, headed back to England. What shall we do?"

"Take us back to land, and we'll get out," Blackmon replied.

Blackmon went back into the body of the plane, moving down the line, telling his men that the pilot had gotten lost and that they were to assemble on Blackmon when they got down. Then they would decide what to do next.

The pilot dived into a left turn, came around, and headed for the French shore again. He took the transport down just above the waves to evade the flak as he came in over the shore. As the plane reached the shoreline, he put it into a climb so steep that it threw several men off their feet. He leveled off.

Lieutenant Blackmon decided it was now or never. He pushed out the equipment bundle, hooked up his chute ring, and followed it. The plane was very low.

Jerked by the ring, Blackmon's parachute opened automatically just before he hit the ground. One or two seconds more, and he would have been dead.

The shock of the landing was hard. But Blackmon knew he was a lucky man. Hundreds of troopers and most of the equipment of both the 101st and the 82d Airborne divisions were lost in the confusion of the drop.

Some pilots became so frightened by the antiaircraft fire that they paid no attention to altitude or the drop zones. Some men were dropped high and floated down into trees, where they were prime targets for any German rifleman at hand. Some were dropped so low that their parachutes did not open at all, and that was the end of their war. Some were dropped into the swamps created by the German flooding of the low fields. Many of these troops drowned, particularly those men who were laced like mummies into their jumpsuits and hampered by too much equipment.

The important matter, however, was that the airdrops had been made and the airborne troops had set foot within Fortress Europe. The battle for Hitler's control of his empire was about to begin.

*   *   *

When Lieutenant Blackmon reached the ground, he cut himself loose from his parachute. Right beside him he found the equipment chute in a low tree that was part of one of the Normandy hedgerows—thick, nearly impenetrable lines of trees and bushes that separated the local farmers' pastures and growing fields. The red light attached to the equipment pack was showing clearly. He pulled the light down and turned it off, and he got his carbine ready for action. Then he crawled into the hedgerow and began to look around for friends. He listened. There was no sound. He waited and listened again. Finally he heard noises, and Private Day, the second man to jump, came up.

With his flashlight Lieutenant Blackmon tried to orient them. He got out his map, but he could not find any points of terrain that matched. The reason was simple enough, although it didn't seem that way at the time: they had jumped "off the map."

Blackmon and Private Day waited for what seemed like hours, but no one else showed up. Blackmon knew that the pilot had turned left to bring them back to land. He decided that he ought to be somewhere to the south of where he now found himself. So he took out his compass. He and Private Day picked up the machine gun and two boxes of ammunition out of the equipment bundle and took off across country, heading south.

After they had gone half a mile, both men were nearly exhausted. The machine gun and ammunition were too heavy. So they stashed them in a hedgerow, covered them with leaves, and moved on.

The two paratroopers came to a road. About 300 yards up the road they could see figures moving.

"You take the first man," Lieutenant Blackmon told Private Day. "I'll take the second. Then keep firing until your weapon is empty. We'll meet at that big tree back there." He pointed to a tree they had just passed.

Blackmon moved up the road about 10 yards to get out of Day's line of fire. The first man came down the road. Blackmon thought he saw an American flag on the man's arm, of the sort the paratroopers wore for recognition. The second man passed, and Blackmon was sure. He jumped out into the road.

"Don't shoot!" he shouted at Private Day.

Blackmon was right. One of the men was a major from the Eighty-second Airborne. He had collected thirty-four men, five of them from Blackmon's platoon. The major's group was just as badly lost as Blackmon and Day, and had decided to head north. Blackmon convinced them that they should go south, and they all set off along the road.

"I felt as if I had an army," Blackmon said.

After a short hike the men approached a village. They came to a house on the outskirts and saw a light; Lieutenant Blackmon decided to try out his French. The others surrounded the house, and Blackmon went to the door and knocked. A woman came to the door, and as she opened it, he could see another woman sitting at a table in the kitchen, three empty chairs, bread on the table, and two bottles of wine. Apparently they had interrupted the family at a meal.

The woman was not very friendly, and she appeared to be monstrously stupid. She did tell Blackmon where they were: Foucarville, near the fourth causeway that led to the beach road—about 3 miles from Utah Beach, 5 miles southeast of Ste.-Mère-Église, and nearly 10 miles northwest of St.-Côme-du-Mont, where Blackmon was sure he would find elements of his battalion.

These causeways stood well above the flood stage of the marshy fields, and they joined to create a transportation system in any sort of weather. They were a major factor in the planning for the Normandy landings. They must be seized so that the Germans could be prevented from moving mechanized units up to the beaches.

Now knowing approximately where he had landed, Lieutenant Blackmon asked the way to St.-Côme-du-Mont. The woman did not understand, or said she did not. He repeated the question. She became sullen. He identified himself as an American paratrooper, and her eyes widened; she shouted something and tried to run out the door. Blackmon halted her by sticking his carbine in her belly. She stopped. He could see that he would get no more information there—whether they were German collaborators or just frightened he did not know. The paratroopers met both sorts of Frenchmen that night. Blackmon told the woman to sit down at the table; when she did, he closed the door firmly and gestured to the men to get out of there. They went back to the road.

They moved around a bend in the road, and there ran into their first enemy fire. Had there been men in the farmhouse, and had they run off to warn the Germans? The way the action developed, it seemed likely the Germans knew that they were coming and that they were Americans. They turned the bend, and a burst from a German light machine gun swept the road. It sounded like someone was tearing paper. A sergeant from the Eighty-second Airborne had the point, about 10 yards in front of Blackmon. He was hit in the arm. The Americans dropped and crawled off the road to the left to get away from the enemy. They found themselves in a field of grain and soon learned that the machine gunners had moved to intercept them. The tearing-paper sound started up again. Blackmon got up and started to run. He saw a ditch ahead and got ready to jump it. Just then a German soldier stood up in the ditch and raised his hands. He said something Blackmon did not understand. At that moment that German was living on borrowed time; the men of the 101st had been told there was no place for prisoners in their operations.

But this German was lucky because Pvt. Nick Denovchik came up. He was one of the men of Blackmon's platoon who had ended up with the major from the Eighty-second Airborne. Denovchik said the German was speaking Polish, which he understood. They began to talk.

The German machine gun had been firing from the road through the grain field, but apparently the gunners decided the Americans had moved on, for the firing suddenly stopped and was not resumed. The Polish-German soldier told Denovchik that he and his buddy were manning an aircraft listening station. He shouted and his buddy stood up about 50 yards away and joined them. After some more talk the two Poles led the Americans to a pillbox buried underground in a grove of trees. Above was the listening device, four large instruments perfectly camouflaged in the trees. Inside the pillbox was a big radio set and enough ammunition to withstand a minor siege: potato masher grenades, antitank weapons bigger and more powerful than the American bazooka, burp guns, and rifle ammunition.

The two captives helped them destroy the listening device, blow up the ammunition dump, and wreck the radio—and in the process saved their lives. The Americans accepted them as allies and tacitly agreed that they could come along with them.

The captives showed them the way to the causeway, and the whole group moved onto it at Exit 4, near St.-Martin-de-Varreville. By this time dawn had broken. They were still a long way from Blackmon's assigned objective, the locks of the Douve. It was nearly time for the troops of the Fourth Division to be landing on Utah Beach. Lieutenant Blackmon could only hope that someone else had taken care of his task of capturing and holding the locks at La Barquette.

Someone had. Col. Howard R. Johnson, the regimental commander, had landed near the locks and assembled men until he had about 150. He sent a detachment in to take the lock and hold it. The Americans arrived before the Germans knew what was happening, and they dug in on the west side.

Some parachutists, like Colonel Johnson, were lucky enough to land either in or near their assigned objectives. General Taylor was supposed to land west of Ste.-Marie-du-Mont, but he dropped so deep in the maze of hedgerows that he was some time in working his way out. He moved east toward the coast, picking up troops as he went. By dawn he had assembled about eighty men, including another general, Anthony McAuliffe, his artillery commander. As dawn came up, Taylor found himself looking at the distinctive bell tower of the church of Ste.-Marie-du-Mont. His group was 2 miles from the end of the southern causeway.

The men of the Eighty-second Airborne Division were also scheduled to drop near Utah Beach, on both sides of the Merderet River, and then to capture Ste.-Mère-Église, thus cutting the main road from Carentan to Cherbourg. They were also to capture two bridges across the Merderet and hold them. These bridges would be useful later in the American drive up the Cotentin Peninsula to cut off Cherbourg.

Maj. Gen. Matthew B. Ridgway, the division commander, dropped and found himself in a cow pasture. It took some time for him to begin building up his headquarters staff so that he could function as commander of the division.

Brig. Gen. James Gavin got into action much more quickly. He dropped into an apple orchard that was populated by cows. He found himself entirely alone. Most of the planes of his formation had dropped their men and equipment into the flooded fields around the Merderet. The entire 507th Parachute Infantry Regiment was dropped into the swamps, and its casualties were so high that it was destroyed as an effective fighting force. Many men had drowned and most of the equipment—all the heavy equipment—had been lost.

Soon stragglers began to show up. Gavin assembled his men in a field in the Merderet valley, just north of Ste.-Mère-Église. A German patrol found them and began an attack. Gavin's men fought off the Germans and went on, toward the Merderet River bridge.

The only accurate drop of American airborne troops was that of the 505th Parachute Infantry Regiment, which was assigned to capture Ste.-Mère-Église. The planes found the drop zone and put the troops down in the approved manner northwest of the town. They were lucky: there was no German opposition there.

Lt. Col. Edward C. Krause's Third Battalion moved swiftly into the town and captured it from the somnolent German garrison before dawn. This move gave the Americans control of a key point on Route Nationale 13, which was also the main road from Cherbourg to Paris. When the Germans began to counterattack, Lt. Col. Benjamin H. Vandervoort's Second Battalion moved out south of Ste.-Mère-Église to stop them. As it moved up, the German 1058th Regiment, assigned the recapture of Ste.-Mère-Église, was harried by small bands of paratroopers who had been misdropped, but whose very scattered condition made it difficult for the Germans to deal with them. So did the absence of key German commanders, from Rommel, who was visiting in Germany, down to regimental commanders, who had gone to Rennes for a meeting called by Col. Gen. Friedrich Dollmann, commander of the German Seventh Army. Lt. Gen. Karl-Wilhelm von Schlieben, commander of the 709th Division, who was directly responsible for the defense of Ste.-Mère-Église, was also in Rennes, as was Maj. Gen. Wilhelm Falley, commander of the Ninety-first Division at St.-Sauveur-le-Vicomte. These two had also taken key regimental commanders and staff officers with them. And to add to the troubles of the Germans, the French Resistance began to act in response to the BBC code call from London: *"Blessent mon coeur d'une langueur monotone."* The underground moved out to begin cutting telephone and telegraph wires. German units, seeking orders, were out of communication with their headquarters for precious hours.

Shortly after one o'clock in the morning messages began coming into one German headquarters after another that Allied troops were landing near the

Orne estuary, around the Carentan-Cherbourg road, on both sides of the Merderet, and at Ste.-Mère-Église. The Germans began picking up some prisoners, unfortunate paratroopers who were dropped virtually in their laps, whose chutes hung up in trees, or who were injured in the drops. The Germans did not try to capture all of them, by far. Among the first paratroops to land in Ste.-Mère-Église was one unlucky trooper whose chute hung up on the steeple. The Germans had plenty of time to shoot him dead as he dangled.

The word reached Gen. Erich Marcks, commander of the German Eighty-fourth Corps, at 1:11. Was this the invasion? He thought so, but Field Marshal von Rundstedt, German commander in chief in the west, had warned that the Allies would make a feint at the Cotentin Peninsula to cover the main invasion attempt in the Fifteenth Army's defense zone around the Pas de Calais. The reports of the parachutists were so varied, and they came from so many places, that it was hard to get any clear picture of what was going on. General Marcks could do little but wait to see what happened.

Half an hour later came reports that several units were holding prisoners from the American 101st Airborne Division. At 2:15 German Seventh Army headquarters ordered an alert in the Eighty-fourth Corps area. Five minutes later Rear Adm. Walther Hennecke reported parachutists had landed near his Marcouf coastal gun battery. In Paris radar technicians saw so many blips on the screens of their search radar on the Channel coast that they believed they were caused by interference. But gradually the reports began to sort themselves out. At the Seventh Army headquarters, Chief of Staff Gen. Max Pemsel was sure that the invasion had come, and that it was the true invasion, not a fake. The word went to Hitler's headquarters in East Prussia. It also went to Field Marshal von Rundstedt and to Lt. Gen. Hans Speidel, Rommel's chief of staff. But none of these believed. Speidel released the Ninety-first Division from reserve and ordered it to attack, and he ordered the 709th Infantry Division to attack, too. But that was all standard procedure for a local problem. What nobody did, in the absence of Rommel, was get the available panzer forces moving for a major action. Nobody was looking toward the sea.

Lt. Col. Friedrich-August Freiherr von der Heydte, commander of the first-rate Sixth Parachute Infantry Regiment, was at his command post north of Périers when the parachute troops began to come down. He tried to get through to the Ninety-first Division and the Eighty-fourth Corps, but the French Resistance fighters had destroyed all the lines. Finally, at six o'clock in the morning, he got General Marcks on a field phone, and only then could von der Heydte get orders to counterattack through Carentan. He then rushed to that city, but he found no enemy troops there. Perplexed, he ordered his troops to assemble southwest of the town, and at St.-Côme he climbed up into the church steeple and looked out at the surrounding countryside. He saw no enemy troops anywhere, but he did see something else: a vast armada of ships in the English Channel, a fleet that extended as far as the horizon. There could be no further doubt. The invasion was on.

26

SOME CAME BY
SEA

The invasion force was milling around, waiting. Offshore, Capt. L. S. Sabin, Jr., commander of the gunfire support ships for the entire American effort, led his vessels in—ships that ranged from a 1000-ton destroyer escort to a PT boat. Captain Sabin was a professional naval officer, one of the handful in his flotilla.

Captain Sabin was a worried man that morning. He also had in his charge Convoy O-2, 304 vessels vital to the invasion. They carried amphibious tanks, troops, guns, and ammunition for the assault. His own small craft would deliver the cargoes to the beaches and then stand off and fire in support. He personally commanded the Omaha Beach group; his deputy took charge of the Utah Beach force.

Problems had bedeviled Sabin's command from the beginning. His men had been trained hastily in the United States for the invasion; they had been shipped to a base in Scotland at the end of December 1943. Their landing craft were supposed to have been there when they arrived, but not a single one was to be seen. The vessels were so slow in coming that the men despaired; the last two were delivered less than a week before the invasion.

Sabin had to get the boats, then find spare parts and put the craft in shape, and then train his crews—virtually every man a landlubber, not an ounce of combat experience among them. They had to learn all the elementary lessons: seamanship, piloting, and gunnery.

When May came, and the alert, the men were not ready. "The bare fact was that late deliveries had so curtailed the time available for training that it was impossible to bring the men to a high state of readiness." Two rocket craft joined up, although the crews had never before handled the vessels and had never fired a rocket except in school.

The assault craft were assembled at Poole; they would be part of the five-convoy force that was to conduct the invasion of Omaha Beach. Sabin divided the vessels into three sections, and took section 2 himself. The craft went out just after midnight on the morning of June 4. But back at Supreme Headquarters the planners had been watching the weather nervously all day long, and at two o'clock on the morning of June 4 General Eisenhower made the unhappy decision: the landings would have to be postponed for at least twenty-four hours.

Arrangements had been made for just such a contingency. From England came an urgent coded message to the USS *Frankford*, the flagship of Commodore Harry Sanders, commander of Destroyer Squadron 18. He was at sea, screening Captain Sabin's slow convoy. Now, he was told, he must detach two destroyers and send them after Sabin, to bring that convoy back to port.

When the message arrived aboard the *Frankford*, Commodore Sanders's squadron communications officer was wading through a sea of radio traffic. He put the message into the electronic decoding machine, decoded it, and then laid it aside and went to work on the overload of messages that had backed up. Several hours passed, and Captain Sabin's slow convoy kept moving toward the coast of France. Finally, Lieutenant Wolfe, the communications officer of the *Frankford* (as opposed to the *squadron* communications officer aboard the *Frankford*) popped his head into the code room, saw that his confrere was jammed up, and offered to help out with the message pileup. Scanning the file of messages, Wolfe noticed the urgent secret dispatch that should have sent the squadron communications officer running hours ago. Immediately Wolfe rushed up to the bridge and delivered the message to Commodore Sanders. The commodore sent off two destroyers, posthaste, and they found Captain Sabin's convoy just before it was scheduled to make a turn due south. That turn would have been a sure tip-off to the Germans, if any had been watching, that the destination of this invasion fleet was the Bay of the Seine. The vital factor of surprise had been that close to compromise. Sabin brought his ships back to Poole harbor and kept them outside overnight, waiting. The false start had been bad enough; but now one dispatch boat sprang a leak and sank, and the others were tossed about all night long by the wicked weather.

Lieutenant Wolfe, the hero of the communications foul-up, was immediately dragooned by Commodore Sanders to be his squadron communications officer, and the unfortunate incumbent was shipped off that day to the South Pacific to serve aboard an LST for the rest of the war.

On the night of June 5 Captain Sabin's flotilla once again made ready to set out for France. It was an hour and a half before General Eisenhower would make the final decision about the invasion, based on the weather. The crews did not know if the invasion was on or off, but they couldn't wait around to find out. At 2:30 on the morning of June 5 the LSTs steamed at 5 knots, in single file, through the narrow, swept channel, each of them towing a Rhino ferry (a huge barge). Behind them came the smaller vessels in columns of four.

From that point on Captain Sabin was really worried. The vanguard of the American attack was in this slow, unwieldy convoy. The convoy was 12 miles long, and wide open to attack by U-boats and E-boats. Sabin had every reason to expect an attack, particularly from the latter. His force was even more vulnerable than the Slapton Sands Operation Tiger ships had been.

Privately, Captain Sabin thought the planners must be mad to devise so unsafe a manner of delivering the spearhead of the attack. But they were committed.

The first narrow escape occurred at 4:30 on June 5. Suddenly, cutting across the bow of the convoy came a huge merchant ship, followed by another. Captain Sabin had run across one of the British convoys, heading for the three British beaches on the left of the Americans. Sabin stopped his convoy in time to avoid collisions and waited an hour, but when the British convoy ships continued to straggle on, he ordered his ships to thread their way through. All of them made it safely; but then Captain Sabin ordered his ships to take their assault positions, and he went to the front of the convoy for two hours. When he returned, he found that someone had countermanded his orders and that the second two sections of the convoy were in total confusion. He never did discover who fouled up; there was no time. Every minute counted if the convoy was to achieve surprise.

*   *   *

In that first week of June the Germans were restless and suspicious. Their experts knew that tide conditions favorable for a landing would exist on June 5 and 6, and then not again for at least two weeks. But when the weather turned foul on June 3, the German High Command relaxed. That is not to say that the Germans were unsuspecting, or unaware that invasion was imminent. For months the German defenders had been awaiting Allied action, and Field Marshal Rommel, who was in charge of the defenses in Normandy, had been almost unbelieving, but pleased, when May passed and the invasion did not come. Rommel had not been "ready." He would have said he was anything but ready. For months he had been building obstacles to prevent an invasion at high tide, for it seemed axiomatic that an invading army would come in as close to shore as possible, and on Normandy's long beaches that meant high water. Germans and French forced laborers had built all sorts of tricky devices, using rails, girders, concrete, and logs. Some of the obstacles were designed to tear the bottoms out of landing craft. Some were rigged with mines to blow up landing boats. At low tide many of these obstacles were clearly visible, as far as 250 yards out from the high-water mark. They were dangerous nonetheless, particularly the mined obstacles.

To Rommel the obstacles were a beginning, no more than that. His philosophy of defense called for an immense effort from the first moment of invasion. When Adolf Hitler had enunciated his own defense philosophy late in March to the German Atlantic wall commanders, he had said just what Rommel wanted to say: "The enemy's entire landing operation must under no circumstances be allowed to last longer than a matter of hours, or, at the most, days.... Once the landing has been defeated it will under no circumstances be repeated by the enemy." Rommel might not be so certain of the future, but he agreed with the strategy. It was, in fact, his own.

To defeat the invasion, Rommel held that he must have control of attack forces, particularly panzer divisions, and over this concept he had butted heads with Field Marshal von Rundstedt, whose plan of defense called for a running battle after the invaders had come ashore. Since von Rundstedt was in charge of the entire western defense and thus Rommel's superior, he so far had prevented the Desert Fox from getting control of the mobile panzer forces and attack infantry divisions that he wanted. But Rommel was on his way to see Hitler to try to get the decision reversed in time. Reading his own meteorologist's weather report on June 4, he had seen how "impossible" it was that the Allied forces would attack in that weather. His meteorologist, however, suffered from some deficiencies. The Allies had weather stations in Iceland and the far north of Canada to tell them about the weather that could be expected from the Arctic. At one time the Germans had had weather stations in Greenland, and they once had been able to make good use of Admiral Dönitz's far-flung submarine fleet in the North Atlantic for the same purpose. But in recent months the Germans had lost the Greenland stations, and the U-boat fleet had suffered such serious losses that the submarines were no longer of much use in weather forecasting. Using the information at hand, the German High Command could tell on June 4 that the weather was such as to prevent any major military action in air or on the sea. The German weathermen, like the Allied weathermen, had predicted a period of high winds and storm.

Even with all the milling about in the Channel on June 3 and 4, the Germans did not figure out what was going on. This was largely the fault of the Luftwaffe, which had been brought low by months of Allied air attacks on its bases and aircraft factories. Bad weather inspired inadequate German naval patrol and totally inadequate air patrol of the Channel, and that played right into the hands of the Allies.

There was another factor, too: an enormously successful deception campaign that had the Germans believing the attack would fall on the Pas de Calais area, the region of France closest to the English coast. Even a few days before D day the Allied air forces were distributing their efforts so that the Pas de Calais area actually received more raids and more bombs than did Normandy. The Allies leaked that George S. Patton, Jr., the American general best known and most respected by the Germans, was lurking in camp on the east coast of England with an enormous army, just waiting for the right day. Fake tanks, trucks, guns, and invasion vessels had been situated around the area. The fake tanks even made fake tank tracks to simulate maneuvers. Through an elaborate and practically magical deception plan, the Germans were almost completely gulled into believing the invasion would come at the Pas de Calais.

Almost is the key word. Two important Germans were not convinced. One was Adolf Hitler, who predicted in May that the Allies would invade Normandy. The other nonbeliever was Marshal Rommel. Hitler's belief was based on his famous intuition, which changed several times regarding Normandy. Finally Hitler chose to believe Field Marshal von Rundstedt rather than Rommel. Rommel's belief was based on his certainty that the Allies would have to have a port city to unload their war material after the first day. The troops could not fight more than a few hours without ammunition and food. No invasion had ever succeeded without the almost immediate possession of a port. The possible ports were, from west to east, Brest, just around the corner of the Channel, facing the Atlantic Ocean; Cherbourg, at the end of the Cotentin Peninsula; and Le Havre. After that, the possibilities moved to the Pas de Calais area: Boulogne, Calais, and Dunkerque.

Brest was too far from the English staging areas, and Le Havre was too far the other way. So Marshal Rommel, who had himself captured Cherbourg just four years earlier, opted for the Normandy invasion. But so far he had enjoyed little success in impressing his belief on von Rundstedt and the others who controlled the quality of troops that would man the defense line. Nearly every defensive unit along the Normandy coast consisted of "static" troops: overage veterans, half-shot refugees from the eastern front, and "volunteers" from occupied countries and areas. Of the troops in the Normandy front-line defense on June 1, 1944, just one division could be called first class, and Rommel had only recently been able to wangle this unit out of higher headquarters. It was the 352d Infantry Division, made up of the best of German fighting troops. It was stationed in the defenses behind and overlooking Omaha Beach. Rommel had also asked for another six panzer divisions and five motorized infantry divisions to be sent to the Paris area as a floating reserve. But von Rundstedt and Berlin had dillied and dallied, and Rommel had not gotten those troops. Since the Führer had declared himself in agreement with Rommel's defense strategy, then Rommel must go to Hitler. The field marshal left by car on the morning of June 5, planning to stop over for a night at his home in Ulm.

On that same day Rear Adm. Walther Hennecke, the commander of German naval forces in Normandy and chief of the Cherbourg defenses, had a professional premonition that something was afoot. He was well aware of the tides situation for the month, and on the night of June 4 his radar officer had reported on what appeared to be heavy activity of vessels. Perhaps the German radar had picked up the Sabin convoy during those fretful hours when it was steaming toward France. But the weather belied any such radar image, the meteorologists said. And as if to settle the matter, the port authorities canceled the sailing of a German convoy from Cherbourg to Brest because of the weather. Admiral Hennecke relaxed.

At the headquarters of the German Seventh Army at Le Mans, 200 kilometers southwest of Paris, and about the same distance from the Normandy beaches, Col. Gen. Friedrich Dollmann also inquired about the weather. He had planned a conference of his senior officers to discuss the coming invasion of Europe by the Allies. It was a part of a series of such meetings, and this one would feature an exchange on the subject of airborne landings. The officers would talk about Rommel's "asparagus," for one thing—those tall slender stakes driven into many of the Normandy fields that seemed possible sites for glider landings. The asparagus should be mined as well. And although the mines were available, most of them had not been put in place.

Dollmann's problem was when to hold the meeting, since army headquarters was so far from the defensive units along the coast. Assured that the weather on June 6 would be so foul that there was no chance of an Allied landing, the general scheduled the meeting for that day.

*　　*　　*

June 5: This was the crucial day for the Allies. If the invasion were not staged on June 6, it would have to be put off for at least two weeks, and it was doubtful if the invading troops, keyed up for more than a week already, could be brought back into mental and physical condition to try the adventure again so soon. Added to that was the enormous problem of trying to disengage an entire invasion army and then reengage it. The initial action involved about a quarter of a million men, but to put them into action had demanded the activity of ten times as many, and if the attack did not come off on schedule, then much of that effort was wasted.

Thus, given a basically negative weather report by his chief meteorologist at four o'clock on the morning of June 5, General Eisenhower was willing to grasp at straws. Group Captain J. M. Stagg, the meteorologist, knew his commander's mind and problem, and he found what might be a ray of hope. The bad weather over the French shore should let up on the night of June 5 and stay relatively clear until the morning of June 6. It should be possible to make the landings, although by the evening of June 6 the foul weather would be back. Several of Stagg's colleagues disagreed, but Eisenhower went with his chief meteorologist, and gave the order to invade. It was one of the great gambles of history, and Eisenhower knew it. That day he wrote a note absolving all others of responsibility for the failure that he half-expected would follow. He would carry that note in his breast pocket as long as the fate of the invasion remained in doubt.

27

TO THE SHORE

As Captain Sabin's convoy stood off the coast of France, he felt that everything was in doubt.

"As we went in toward the beach, there was no sign of life or resistance. Approaching closer, the concrete wall just to the east of Dog Green became plainly visible. There appeared to be openings along its length. Some structures which appeared to be pillboxes, a few houses, and the church steeple of Vierville were sighted. There was an intense quiet, so quiet that it was suspicious."

Captain Sabin was suspicious because the invasion had already been "on" for more than five hours. No matter how fouled up the German communications might be, the troops on the coastal defense line must be aware of the invasion by this time. Then why did they not react?

There was a simple reason. Field Marshal Rommel, the one man who had reasoned out the Allied plan, was away from his post, in Germany, and there was not another senior officer in the command with the imagination to strike when the warnings had come.

The first warning came when the French underground was notified of the invasion. The underground was a vital part of the Allied effort in France. Already, saboteurs had helped the bombers knock out the German lines of communication between Paris and the Channel coast. For example, Lt. Gen. von Schlieben, the commander of the 709th Division, set out on the afternoon of June 5 to drive the 120 miles from his headquarters at Valognes to Rennes for the meeting with General Dollmann twenty hours later. The roads had been so badly torn up by Allied bombers and so many bridges had been knocked out by saboteurs that he worried about getting to Rennes at all.

In retrospect, the warnings of the Allied invasion should have been picked up. In fact, they were picked up. The notification of the French underground was a complicated maneuver. Long before, the underground leaders had been informed that when the time came, the announcement would be in the form of a broadcast verse from the poem *Chanson d'Automne* by Paul Verlaine. It would come in two parts, first an alert: *Les sanglots longs des violons d'automne*. Then when the invasion was less than forty-eight hours off, the second part: *Blessent mon coeur d'une langueur monotone*. On June 1 the British Broadcasting Company had sent the first line. The efficient German counterespionage service had captured several agents who had the secret, so the Germans were informed. When, on June 4, the BBC broadcast the second half of the message, German intelligence was onto it immediately.

The army High Command in Berlin was informed. So was the Fifteenth Army, charged with defenses that included the Pas de Calais area. So was Field Marshal von Rundstedt, the overall commander of the western defenses. And so was Field Marshal Rommel. But only Rommel took the message seriously enough to insist on a personal interview with Hitler to obtain additional mobile response troops, and that was where he was going on June 5, secure in his belief that the weather was too foul for the Allies to stage their attack.

The second strong piece of evidence was given to the Germans just after midnight on June 6, when the first units of three Allied airborne divisions began to drop onto French soil. Within two hours 16,000 airborne troops had arrived, and every major element of the German defenses was warned. But once again no officer present had the intuition to realize that the invasion had begun, and none had the authority to act. Higher headquarters at first held that the airborne landings were no more than a raid of the sort so successfully repulsed at Dieppe two years earlier. And the way the airborne troops came in was even more puzzling to the German defenders.

From his vantage point, Captain Sabin could see only a part of the beach. It is 5 miles long, slightly curved, and covered with clean yellow sand. The slope is very gentle, so gentle that the tidal range is 400 yards from low to high mark. That morning, according to plan, the assault force was moving just after the tide hit the low-water mark. The Germans were not supposed to expect that, and they did not.

In fact, the Germans had been caught by surprise in the earliest hours of the morning.

At exactly H − 40 minutes, right on schedule, the guns of a whole fleet began to fire on Omaha Beach, and the noise was like thunder. It was fitting; the day was gray and the clouds hung low over sea and shore. A 25-mile-per-hour wind snapped whitecaps along the wave tops, and the smaller craft plunged and wallowed in the sea.

Captain Sabin's gun ships had been assigned to various positions along the beach. They moved in. So did several destroyers. Now it was time for the heavy bombers. Lt. Gen. Jimmy Doolittle's Eighth Air Force had been given the assignment of plastering Omaha Beach with blockbusters. The minutes went by. Where were the bombers?

H − 35 minutes: No bombers. Several squadrons of P-51 fighters roared in across the beach, strafing. But strafing did not knock out big guns and pillboxes. Where were the bombers?

H − 25 minutes: The bombers still had not shown up. They never would. In the overcast conditions the lead plane had overshot the mark and the bombs had been dropped 2 to 3 miles inland, to the consternation of the Normandy dairy farmers.

A lone gun fired from the enemy shore, and a splash rose 300 yards off the starboard bow of Captain Sabin's command ship. The shell came from the east side of Pointe du Hoc, from a spot where there was supposed to be an enormous shore battery. In fact, a ranger unit had been given the specific job of silencing that battery as soon as possible.

H − 22 minutes: The gun ships moved in closer; in two minutes they would open fire. The rocket craft moved up behind them. They were to cover the beach with rockets as the troops moved in.

Captain Sabin watched as the landing craft full of men left the line of departure and began to head toward the shore. They were supposed to be in wave formation, but they were not. Some vessels were "lost." He saw one LCT coming in from the west. The skipper had gotten mixed up and gone to Utah Beach first. He would be late. And so would others. Ens. R. A. Steinberg's landing craft was lucky to get there at all. On the way across the Channel, during the night, his vessel snapped its towline and the line wrapped around the propeller. In the darkness and the heavy weather the convoy had gone on without him. His vessel drifted for hours while men went over the side and worked to clear the propeller. When he was again under way, he was hopelessly lost, with no navigation equipment aboard. Then, in the darkness, Ensign Steinberg sighted a convoy. He hailed.

"What convoy is this?"

"British Convoy for Juno. Do you want a tow?"

Ensign Steinberg remembered his orders. If he got separated from his convoy, he was to head for the enemy coast. Now he knew where it was. West of the English. He turned.

"Hell, no. I belong in the American sector. Thanks."

And after seven hours adrift in the Channel, Ensign Steinberg's small craft was on its way to battle.

Some of Captain Sabin's ships weren't so lucky. *LCT 2049* foundered and sank in the high seas on the way across, but every man was saved.

The men of *LCT 2229* were not so fortunate. Their vessel was one of the landing craft provided to the American forces by British shipyards. It was assigned a load of two tanks, two big trailers filled with ammunition, a tank bulldozer, demolition equipment, and men. The skipper was Ens. Virgil E. Wilkerson. Second in command was Ens. John M. Wilson. Both were reserve officers, and they had just recently come to the Eleventh Amphibious Force to complete the manning—two officers to a vessel. They were attached for this operation only.

For the first few hours of the crossing everything seemed to be going fine, but on the afternoon of June 5 the weather worsened as they reached mid-Channel, and the starboard bulkhead began to break up. Ensign Wilkerson called all hands who were not on duty to help shore it up, and the army lieutenant in charge of the troops brought his men up to pile up boxes of K rations, planks, and any other material they could find. The vessel had taken on some water and developed a 5 degree starboard list, but the water was not up over the floorboards, and the bulkhead seemed to hold.

Just before dark the bulkhead began to take a beating, and part of it broke away, carrying one end of the starboard life raft with it. The skipper ordered the men to haul in the raft, but the water was so rough they had to give up and cut it loose. Now the water began to come in fast; it was soon up to the knees of the men on deck.

The night grew miserable. Most of the crew and passengers were seasick, and all were wet and half frozen. At about ten o'clock the dispatch boat eased up alongside to check on their troubles. The skipper asked En-

sign Wilkerson if he wanted to leave the ship. Wilkerson replied that he
would get the ship onto the beach, so the dispatch boat went on.

The list grew worse. Wilkerson ordered the army men and the navy demolition men who were aboard to transfer onto a nearby LCM. That left fifteen
passengers (the tank crews) and the crew of the LCT. Wilkerson was still
determined to get his cargo to the beach.

Early on the morning of D day the starboard engine quit. Saltwater had
gotten into the lubrication system. The skipper ordered several of his men
below with a portable pump to try to get the water out and ease the vessel.
One engine room crewman refused to go, and Wilkerson had to threaten him
with his pistol to get the seaman down below.

The batteries went out then, and the radioman, Coxswain Bernhart Lenz,
worked the radio while Seaman Second Class George Drzka ran the gener-
ator.

Both ensigns went into the water to try to help clear the vessel and stop
the leaking, but the list grew worse. Wilkerson asked the army sergeant in
charge of the tank crews to move the last tank over to the port side to balance the ship. But the water was too rough, and the tank kept slipping back
down the incline caused by the list. Dawn broke, and they could see the
French coast ahead of them. H hour was approaching. Then the port engine
quit. One of the big trailers and the tank were slipping steadily toward the
large hole in the starboard bulkhead. They moved over to the port side. Off
the port beam lay a destroyer, and Wilkerson ordered his signalman to signal SOS to the ship. Another crewman shot off flares.

It was five minutes to six when the skipper ordered the men to abandon
ship.

The army men put over a rubber boat; some of the navy men got into a
dinghy and went over the side, but the dinghy swamped immediately. Some
others jumped over the port side. Seaman Second Class Vester Nichols went
to the stern and brought back the last life raft and put it over the side. The
remaining men began to jump. When they were all going off, Ensign Wilkerson threw his cap onto the deck and jumped after them. Drzka and Seaman McPherson were the last to leave, and the ship capsized as they were
going down the side, so they slid all the way to the bottom. Drzka could not
swim, but he held onto McPherson, who now panicked. Somehow they were
managing to keep their heads above water, but McPherson kept shouting
that they were going to drown. Finally he broke away from Drzka, and disappeared. Drzka, the nonswimmer, made it to the raft.

Twenty-three men were hanging onto the raft, including both naval of-

ficers. The American destroyer never showed up alongside. They drifted in
the chill water for hours. Finally a British minesweeper came by. Ensign
Wilkerson, who had grown very weak from immersion, asked Seaman First
Class John Rose if the rescue vessel was coming. Rose said it was, and the
skipper smiled. Rose then tied the ensign to a line so that he could be pulled
aboard the minesweeper, and then Rose clambered up a rope. Of the whole
crew only three men could make it by themselves; when all the men were
brought up on the deck, six sailors and three soldiers had died, including
Skipper Wilkerson and Executive Officer Wilson. The invasion was over for
the other men of *LCT 2229*. They were on their way back to England, their
ship the third vessel casualty of "the far shore."

As H hour approached, two other landing craft had run into serious trouble.
LCT 2307 had struck an underwater obstacle that ripped through its thin
hull. The vessel pulled back, made it out to sea again, and was taken in tow
by *LCT 2043*. Pumps began to work to keep the craft afloat. One of the tank
carriers, *LCT 2435*, collided with the gun ship *LCG 687* and tore a hole 4
feet long above the waterline of the gun ship.

By this time H hour was on them, and boats and ships were heading
steadily in toward the beach. The bombardment lifted, and the gun ships
began to fire ahead of the landing troops. The seaborne invasion was on.

28

OMAHA BEACH

June 6, 1944: D day, H hour, 6:30 a.m.

Everything to do with Omaha Beach was important. But among all the important points, one of the keys, the intelligence officers had decided, was Pointe du Hoc. Atop that tall, sheer cliff the Germans were reported to have placed a battery of six 155-millimeter shore guns. Those were large enough to raise hob with the whole beachhead.

The Second and Fifth Ranger battalions were assigned to scale the 100-foot cliff to destroy the guns. The Second Rangers were aboard two Canadian LCTs, and they set out at 4:30 for the shore. But the two LCTs somehow collided and capsized. Men were scrambling in the water when along came two more LCTs carrying troops of the 121st Engineers, bound for Exit D-1 to the causeway above the beach. Those two craft rescued about half of the rangers. The others drowned. The engineers then proceeded to land at what they thought was their objective.

Already, then, the invasion was a little bit cockeyed. The problem was a lot more German resistance than the intelligence people had indicated. The Fifth Rangers landed and immediately drew unexpectedly heavy fire from above the beach: 88-millimeter guns, heavy mortars, machine guns, and rifles. The rangers ran and crawled up the beach to the shelter of the seawall; there they were pinned down. Ahead of them was a barbed-wire entanglement in the concertina fashion. Someone had to take a bangalore torpedo up

334

there and blow the hell out of that barbed wire so they could get through. The man chosen was Pfc. Ellis E. Reed. All he had to do, they said, was get over the seawall under fire, run up to the wire, and blow it up. Just like a training exercise.

Bullets were zinging off the seawall; 88 shells were blowing waterspouts in the sea and surf. A landing craft was hit and set afire; men struggled in the water. Behind it all, the majestic battleship *Texas* thundered with its big guns against the shore.

Reed crawled to the wall, went over it as much like a snake as he knew how, crawled forward lugging his bangalore torpedo, slipped it under the concertina, and pulled the pin.

"Fire in the hole," he shouted, as every good demolitions man did when he set off an explosion in camp.

"Fire in the hole," repeated the first man who heard.

"Fire in the hole." The word was passed down the line.

"Fire in the hole. Fire in the hole. Fire in the hole. Fire in the..."

And then the bangalore torpedo went off, the midsection of the concertina wire disappeared, and the way off the beach was clear. Just like in the exercise books, including the safety warning so nobody would get hurt.

The men of Company C of the 121st Engineers and their rescued rangers headed in for the 121st's objective, Exit D-1 to the causeway. They had a bulldozer and a ton of nitrostarch that they were going to use on the concrete wall to clear the exit. There was also the matter of a blockhouse with its 88-millimeter gun pointing up the beach from the exit.

From the outset everyone knew it was a rough assignment. The company was double-manned—two captains and two lieutenants to each platoon—and even had a jeep.

The LCTs headed in and put the men and their equipment ashore. But when they were able to recover from the shock of landing under fire, the troops learned that they were at Exit D-3; a mile and a half of the most hostile territory in the world separated them from their first objective.

Col. Paul Thompson's Sixth Special Engineer Brigade was to clear the underwater obstacles on Omaha Beach and to flatten out the beach for safe landing by the landing craft. The engineers weren't worried. While they were crossing the Channel, they heard the news that Rome had fallen. A great cheer rose up on Sgt. Barnett Hoffner's transport. The Jerries were on the run. From now on everything ought to be coming up roses.

Early on the morning of June 6 the 147th and 149th Engineers, wearing their special insignia—a rainbow, a tommy gun, and an anchor—got into the landing craft and started ashore. The Germans were ready, and the two units were decimated before they ever hit the beach.

So the brigade's reserve battalion had to be called much sooner than expected.

Hoffner and his buddies climbed down the landing nets from their small transport into the LCTs. They were wearing fatigues impregnated against gas over their wool OD uniforms. Each man carried two bandoliers of ammunition, four containers of grenades, two thermal grenades to set fires, and one smoke grenade. A navy coxswain was manning the boat, and a seaman manned the .50-caliber machine gun. The LCTs raced across the water—a whole line of them, like a racing fleet, trailing their wakes behind them. As they approached the smoke-shrouded shore, the GIs saw great geysers of water rising from shell impacts.

As his LCT came closer to the shore, Sergeant Hoffner looked over the side. He could not believe what he saw.

"The surface of the water was covered with thousands and thousands of helmets [floating upside down]. God help us. Most of them bore the insignia we carried on our helmets, the rainbow, the tommy gun, and the anchor. So we knew what had happened to the 147th and the 149th.

"It seemed that everything went wrong."

Sergeant Moglia's LCT was lying off the shore of France, 10 miles from Omaha Beach. He was assigned as a platoon sergeant for the landing. Company E of the Sixteenth Infantry would land on Easy Red beach, and it was nearly time.

Moglia and the other eleven men of his landing craft huddled in the hold of the LCT, preoccupied with their thoughts. The face of each man, seen faintly in the dim blue light of the hold, reflected those thoughts. The stink of the diesel oil and the smell of salty metal no longer bothered them. Above, the naval guns and bombing planes were working over the coast, but the soldiers scarcely heard. Each was making peace with his God in his own way.

The harsh blare of the claxon interrupted their reverie, and Sergeant Moglia led them into the DUKW that would carry them to the beach. Gears clashed and chains clanked, and the ramp in the front of the LCT opened.

The DUKW was deposited into the sea—and what a sea. The severe storm that had already caused postponement of the invasion was still kicking up out there. Sergeant Moglia had the feeling that he was being dropped into a huge black hole completely surrounded by giant walls of water and then that he was becoming airborne, appearing at the top of a water mountain, looking down into a black canyon. Then down the DUKW dropped, faster than a roller-coaster car, and then back up again. Up and down, up and down, it traveled around in circles, waiting for the other landing craft to assemble so that the troops could make their concerted assault on the beach. Sergeant Moglia's stomach moved with the boat; when the DUKW rose, his stomach went down. When the DUKW went down, his stomach rose. All this while it was pitch dark. He thought he was going to die. Then he thought he wasn't going to die but felt it might be a better idea than what he was going through. A look at the faces around him showed that he was not alone.

They moved around a French warship and the sailors on deck waved. *"Vive la France. Vive les Américains."*

Les Américains waved back feebly, and leaned over to feed the fishes more.

The British battleship HMS *Rodney*, with the biggest guns in the fleet, began firing, and her red flashes were joined by those of scores of other ships. They lightened the darkness. Then the milling landing craft began to move inshore.

Sergeant Moglia thought about Lilian, the bride he had left behind him in England. What was she doing this moment? He thought of his blessings. What a relief it was to be out of that boiling concoction called the English Channel. Or should he feel that way? This was his third invasion. Was his luck running out? Was the guardian angel who had looked after him through the accidents of training, through north Africa, and through Sicily still guarding him now? Would he survive? Or would Lilian be added to that "instant widows" list that was growing longer every day?

He thought of the lieutenant who had been taken up to Salisbury to marry his sweetheart, and brought back to the assembly area under guard. Would the lieutenant survive?

The thoughts rolled around in his head. Then the DUKW scratched bottom; the men jumped out and began to run for the beach. Moglia saw a man ahead of him go down. He stopped, grabbed the man up by the shoulder, and dragged him 30 yards before he realized he was pulling a deadweight. It was too heavy. He let go, looked down to apologize, and saw that half the man's head was missing.

Moglia looked up the beach. Fifty yards away he saw a DUKW of the sort that carried automatic weapons. As he looked there was a bright flash, and the vehicle disappeared. A mine? A German shell? A short round from the fleet at sea? The vehicle had vanished, pouf, just like that.

For this invasion Moglia was platoon sergeant of the Second Battalion's antitank platoon. But until the antitank weapons could be gotten ashore, he was just another infantry sergeant, leading a rifle platoon.

The first task was to get off the beach and through whatever minefields there were. The second was to move inland through sniper fire to Colleville-sur-Mer, on the high ground to the east. That place had to be taken and the roads held to cut German lateral communication. Sergeant Moglia headed for the grass above the beach, but he was stopped cold, right there at the water's edge, along with the other men of the Sixteenth Infantry. The Germans, who were supposed to have very little defense in this area, had reinforced it.

But as Moglia knew from experience, the Germans were very methodical in defense. You could set your watch by the intervals at which they swept the beach with their mortar and artillery fire. They would drop a round, and then one to the right of that, and one to the right of that, marching across the beach. The lieutenant was nowhere in sight, so Moglia took his men forward, toward those green hills, as the shelling moved away.

In the Twenty-ninth Division sector the First Battalion of the 116th Infantry was supposed to land to the left of a church steeple in Vierville. In those last few hours before the invasion, many of the older men had written letters, while some of the more bloodthirsty of the younger troops had sharpened their bayonets and looked to their other weapons. Pfc. Richard Dantini of Company A strapped a trench knife to his leg, a knife made for him by his father. At 3 a.m. the men had an enormous breakfast of steak and four eggs, but Dantini could not manage it. He got down a cup of coffee and some crackers, and stuffed some candy bars into his jacket. Then the troops took their seasick pills and got into the boats.

The boats circled and waited. Then they headed in to Omaha Beach. Rocket ships went ahead of them, and Dantini was comforted by the sight of the flares rushing in to hit the beaches. It was even more comforting to hear and see the naval bombardment. After all that, the Jerries had to be shaken up, and it ought to be easy.

Ought to be...

The landing craft came in near the shore. They began to take water, and the men were told to use their helmets to bail. The boat on Dantini's right was swamped. Dantini watched in horror as his friend Private Padley drowned. There was nothing he could do to help.

That shock was followed by another: the boat on his left took a direct hit from an artillery shell, and the men left alive were spilled into the water. More friends lost.

Dantini's landing craft dropped its ramp, and the soldiers got off into waist-deep water. As they waded toward shore, the German mortars and machine guns began killing them.

"Like clay pigeons," said Private Dantini. They had landed between two pillboxes and were exposed to the crossfire of machine guns.

Lieutenant Tidrick, the combat team officer, went off first, and was hit in the throat. He made the beach, and dropped dead.

Sergeant Thurman took over.

No sooner had Private Dantini moved off the boat than the men behind him were hit by a mortar shell and killed. A direct hit struck the landing craft of Captain Fellers, the company commander, and all the men aboard fell dead.

Dantini managed to hide behind one of the beach obstacles, a big, round log projecting up at an angle; the obstacle had been designed to smash in the bows of landing craft when they came in at high tide. The private was still in the water. He fired one clip from his M-1. Bullets were whizzing all around him and smacking into his log. He looked up. On the end of the log was a Teller mine, put there by the Germans. If a bullet hit that...

Dantini got the hell out of there, wading through the water and holding his rifle up to keep it dry.

On the way in to shore, Dantini was hit in the right elbow. He dropped the M-1 into the water, and he fell, fearful that his arm had been shot off. He struggled to get up.

"Help," he shouted.

There was no one to hear. Everyone around him had been killed or wounded. It was every man for himself. He could not get up, overloaded by his equipment. Then he remembered his father's trench knife, inside his legging. Dantini got it out and cut the laces of the heavy combat jacket until it fell off. Then he could get up. When he reached the beach, he lay down, exhausted, on the gravel. Then he saw the seawall ahead and decided to make a run for it. But when he got up to run, he was immediately hit in both legs by machine gun fire, and felled. He tried to get up again but could not. Then he noticed that he was bleeding badly.

Dantini realized that to stay where he was was to die, so he put his shattered arm behind him and began to crawl, using his one good hand and his hips and thighs. He could move only a short distance before stopping to rest.

Dantini's mother had sent him a Balaclava watch, which he wore proudly on his left wrist. Now the friction of the sand pulled it off. He was feeling around for it when, on the bluff above, a German soldier stood up and began firing at him. Bullets hit the sand on both sides of his body. He froze. The German did not fire again. Dantini remained frozen for ten minutes; then he continued on, to the cover of the rocks at the side of the cliff. The Balaclava watch was no longer so important. There he passed out.

The second wave, which was Company B, met the same fate. The beach engineers, the wire cutters, the demolition men, the experts who were to prepare the beaches—all were shot down before they could get to work.

Then came C and D companies in their landing craft. It was more of the same. The Germans were no dummies. The airborne troops of the Eighty-second Airborne Division and the 101st had already landed, hours ago. In fact, German officers, looking out from steeples and other high points of the towns inland, could see the enormous Allied fleet lying there off the French coast, and the telephone wires were abuzz.

C and D companies were the heavy machine guns, the mortars, the head-quarters. As they came in, the shore defenses were ready for them. When they were still a mile from shore, an 88-millimeter shell caught the landing craft in which Capt. Walter O. Schilling, commander of Company D, was riding. He was killed instantly.

The boat moved on in to shore, but it was at the wrong beach, Dog Green. The first man off was Pfc. George Kobe, who was carrying a mortar baseplate. He had rigged up the baseplate with a Mae West life vest, but the plate and vest went straight down to the bottom anyhow. Kobe had no time to stop. The air was full of flying lead, and he ran toward the hilly land inshore. Somehow both Kobe and his buddy John B. Stefko made it to a seawall at the end of the beach. There they crouched. Every time a man raised his head, the Germans fired at it.

Hoffner's LCT approached the shore, which was shrouded in smoke. Smoke covered everything, so the LCTs could not find their assigned beaches. Hidden in the pall, landing craft were burning and bodies covered the sand. Amidst the chaos Hoffner's boat finally hit the beach.

"It seemed we had entered hell itself. The whole beach was a great burning fury. All around were burning vehicles, piled-up bodies, the swimming tanks; none of them had made the shore. Flames were coming from most of them. The water was burning."

Reaching the beach was like coming into a rain cloud, but instead of raindrops falling it was machine gun bullets from one end to the other. The Germans had the beach enfiladed. The machine guns were placed to fire interlocking paths across the beach; the mortars were aimed to do the same; and the 88-millimeter guns were trained on the waters just offshore to smash the landing craft.

Every time a ramp opened, an 88 shell would come at it. A ranger boat was lost this way, the boat and all the men.

The landing craft stopped. Hoffner and his men got out. They found themselves on the shingle, something like steps of gravel that led up to the old sand prewar bathing beach. They all crouched behind the shingle, which gave some protection. Bodies were strewn to the right and left. Rifles, carbines, gas masks, blankets, anything and everything. Tanks sitting at the water's edge burning. Overturned artillery pieces. They finally had landed on Omaha Beach. Easy Green.

They lay there on the shingle. Between Sergeant Hoffner and the cliffs was a great roll of concertina strung along the beach. Someone brought up a bangalore torpedo and blew the wire. The GIs surged through, made their way up the beach under fire, and reached the shelter of the cliff. Then they went up the draw, the mine detectors in the lead, and established a path to the causeway, taped it, located the minefields and indicated them, and came back down to the beach to help the combat engineers who had gotten there first. They had landed on the wrong beach, so it was not easy to make contact.

The combat engineers had come with four bulldozers. Only one remained seemingly whole, and it started to smoke as Hoffner watched. It must have been hit. The engineers' immediate problem was getting back out to the underwater obstacles. These consisted of logs driven into the sand at 45 degree angles to rip open the bows of oncoming landing craft; tetrahedrons, steel triangles implanted for the same purpose; and element C, which were large steel doors with steel rails sticking out at 45 degree angles, also to hang up landing craft. All these obstacles were mounted with mines, and mines festooned the wires that connected them. The early party of engineers had managed to attach explosives with time fuses to many of these obstacles. The fuses were set to go off as the tide rose. But the tide was rising fast on the steep beach, and in the meantime many troops of the Twenty-ninth Division had landed and taken refuge behind those same obstacles. Hoffner and his men began swimming out to them to defuse the charges. But it was too late. The charges began to blow, and the unfortunate infantrymen who were hiding behind them were blown up with them. Parts of bodies began flying through the air.

Giving up the impossible job, Hoffner's engineers headed up the draw to the causeway. They came to a large field, which was clear of the enemy. The Germans had begun to withdraw from the beach area. Hoffner's party came to a road and started to move up it. They passed dozens, scores, of wounded infantrymen, sitting and lying alongside the road, waiting for medics to come and evacuate them to the hospital ships.

Down on the beach below, Medic Leo Scheer was with Platoon B-5 of the Seventh Navy Beach Battalion, assigned to cover the Twenty-ninth Division sector of Omaha Beach. The battalion's job was to come ashore with the first waves; the doctor and eight medics of each platoon would work with the army medics to get the wounded down to the landing craft and back to the hospital ships. The eight motor mechanics would keep traffic moving along the beach by repairing stalled vehicles. The eight seamen would help the beachmaster and his assistants direct traffic and would handle rifles to protect the platoon. A couple of signalmen would maintain communications with the ships.

Medic Scheer's platoon was riding in the after hold of *LCI 94*. In the hold up front was a unit of army combat engineers. Down below it was hard to know what was going on all night long as they crossed the Channel, stopped, circled, slowed, stopped again, and then moved. Around 6:30 a.m. the LCI speeded up and hit the beach. It sat there for a while; then the vessel pulled off again. An officer came below and told the men the water had been too deep to wade through. They were going to make another landing.

The navy men were now very nervous, mouths dry, hands fidgeting. They felt the ship start forward again, hit, bounce, move forward, hit, bounce, move forward again. Then they heard and felt an explosion up forward. They heard shouting and men running topside, and then another explosion forward. Their hatch was dogged down from the outside, so there was no way for them to get out. Then the hatch clanged open, and a crewman came to the edge shouting at them to get out, dump their packs and gear, and get over the side and swim for it. The ship was on fire.

Medic Scheer came up the ladder. Forward he saw flames leaping above the hull. The entire party of engineers had been wiped out by enemy shellfire.

He dumped his blanket and clothes pack, two large medical packs, his gas mask and belt with canteens, knife, and more bandages, and he jumped over the side. He went under; his helmet came off and sank. Then Scheer came up, inflated his life vest, and began to swim. It was hard; he was wearing a tanker's coverall, and over that another impregnated against mustard gas. The clothing weighed him down, but he struggled on.

He came upon a man who was thrashing, apparently unable to swim. Scheer tried to help him by putting him up on one of the antitank barriers. But the barrier held an antitank mine, and the flailing man seemed about to hit it. Scheer ducked and went on his own way.

Closer to the shore Scheer came upon an army engineer struggling with two large radio packs. Scheer suggested that they jettison them, but the GI would not. It was his duty to get the packs ashore and he damned well would. Scheer pulled and swam and struggled along with the engineer until they suddenly realized they could stand up, and they moved onto the beach. The engineer stopped and waved Scheer on. Shells were falling all around them, and Scheer waved back and hurried to the water's edge. He saw a helmet and picked it up, put it on, and felt better. Then he ran up the beach. Ahead he saw the breakwater. He sank down on the sand from exhaustion; then pulled himself up and began to crawl to the breakwater. Some of his buddies were already there, and they shouted him on. He made it and lay down in the protection of the barrier.

Company C of the Sixteenth Infantry started ashore. Platoon Sergeant Royal Kleinhardt's LCVP grounded 60 yards offshore. The Coast Guard coxswain tried to back off, failed, said he could go no further, and dropped the ramp. Lieutenant Scott, who was 6 feet 4 inches tall, stepped off, and immediately found himself swimming. The other twenty-eight men got off, and then Sergeant Kleinhardt, who was 5 feet 6 inches tall. It soon enough became apparent that if he did not get rid of that rifle he was going to drown. Down went one M-1 rifle into the sea. Like most of the other GIs, Sergeant Kleinhardt had cursed the gas mask carrier that higher authority had thrust upon the troops. Now he came to bless it, for its buoyancy saved his life. The equipment he was carrying was so heavy that the life vest was not enough.

He floundered ashore, breathless, and lay down on the beach oblivious to the firing. He turned. An unfamiliar dogface lay 2 feet from him.

"Help me," cried the stranger.

Kleinhardt saw that one of the GI's legs looked strange. He got up and hooked one arm under the soldier.

"Now shove with your good leg."

The GI said nothing. Kleinhardt looked at him. The man seemed to be in shock. The sergeant let go of the man and ran up the beach to a 3-foot stone seawall. He made it, and ducked down with the others who had made it.

Twenty men were crouched there. He had never seen any of them before. Scores, hundreds of others came up. He crawled along, looking for men of his company. Slowly he began to find them. The corporal of his mortar squad said he had lost his mortars. More men had lost their M-1s. Kleinhardt stopped to administer morphine to a GI who lay with a wound in the groin.

Someone shouted.

"Lieutenant Scott wants Sergeant Kleinhardt."

Kleinhardt started in that direction. He found Lieutenant Scott, who grinned at him wanly. The lieutenant was holding his bloody field jacket at the shoulder.

"It's all yours now, Sergeant. I've got a million-dollar wound."

It wasn't the first time. One of the company jokes was the lieutenant's luck. He had gotten hit early on in Africa, and thus had missed most of the heavy fighting.

"I haven't even got a rifle," said Sergeant Kleinhardt.

The lieutenant gave him his carbine. Kleinhardt went off to find more men of the company. That was the last he saw of Lieutenant Scott.

The GIs huddled behind that low stone wall. More assault craft kept coming in. The men who made it across the beach joined up under the wall. If anyone raised his head, the Germans shot; he was either killed, wounded, or scared back behind the wall. For several hours they lay there, more and more of them. A one-star general appeared at the breakwater and moved along, urging the men to put their weapons over the top and fire.

Medic Scheer saw the men of one machine gun crew arguing with the general. If they put their machine gun over the barrier and fired, they would draw fire—and they couldn't see what they were shooting at anyhow.

"Goddamn you, get that machine gun up and start firing!"

The machine gun began to fire.

Maj. Sidney V. Bingham, Jr.'s Second Battalion of the 116th Infantry was cold as ice, coming in on its assault craft, every man soaking wet and most of them seasick.

The battalion had one bit of luck. As the craft came in, the wind was blowing the smoke from grass fires started by the naval shelling, and the wisps of smoke that trailed out to sea partially hid the vessels from the enemy gunners. The battalion suffered no losses on the way to the shore.

The landing craft dumped the men opposite the seawall at the Les Nicilius exit to the beach. The men scrambled ashore and ran for the seawall. There, under cover of the wall, Major Bingham conducted a weapons cleaning formation. Most of the men had managed to preserve their weapons. But rifles, carbines, and machine guns were fouled with sand from the struggle up the beach, and they would not function. So they had to be cleaned. They were, and most of the impedimenta of headquarters was dumped: assault jackets, gas masks, and anything else that was not really needed to survive.

Somehow, one of the dozen 105-millimeter howitzers of the 116th Infantry's support artillery made it to shore. Miracle! The other eleven howitzers, all loaded into DUKWs, had been swamped. And there was Major Bingham behind the seawall, without any communications. No radio. No wire. He had runners, and that was it. It might as well have been the Battle of Waterloo in terms of communication.

*   *   *

This was the crucial period. All along the beaches of the Omaha sector it was the same. Intelligence had indicated that the Americans would have it easy, a stroll to the causeway and the towns beyond, over the old men and children the Germans had pushed into their coastal defense divisions. But something new had been added; the German 352d Infantry Division, one of the crack units of the Wehrmacht, had been brought up. And here it was, on the other side of the stone wall.

Also, much more apparent to the GIs behind the wall than to General Bradley aboard the *Augusta* was the lack of damage done by the "softening up" of the beaches. The men had been told that thousands of bombers would plaster the area and that they would not have to worry about land mines because virtually all the mines would be detonated by the saturation. Nor would they have to worry about cover, for the bombing would create plenty of craters. Now the men who were behind the wall looked around. No craters on the beach. Plenty of mines everywhere.

The command ship of Force O, the Omaha Beach landing group, was the USS *Ancon*. This was where the Fifth Corps brass was. Early that morning of

June 6 Maj. Kenneth Lord, assistant operations officer of the First Division, was enormously impressed with all the communications machinery in the map room of the *Ancon*.

But by eight o'clock it was apparent that the machinery had fouled up somehow. Colonel Talley of the Fifth Corps was on the beach, and so was General Wyman of the First Division. But there were no reports to the *Ancon*. The only way the offshore brass was learning what was happening was by messenger.

By nine o'clock the brass knew a lot of the bad news. First, as the dogfaces could see and bitch about bitterly, there were no craters on the beach. The official explanation of the moment was that the air force could bomb only behind the beach, lest the bombs hit the troops. But that was *now*. What about the night before, when the air force had completely missed the beaches? Well, if the planes had bombed the beaches, then the troops coming to shore would have drowned in the shell holes. That was what was being said aboard the *Ancon*. (A lot of men on the beach would have been glad to test the theory.)

The GIs were wondering what had happened to the rocket ships that had been advertised as prepared to blast everything in sight as they came in. But as the brass had learned in the exercises at Slapton Sands, the rocket ships had been an overrated weapon. They weren't really very accurate, and they could be used only on the flanks. Used frontally, they might have sent their rockets right into the troops.

And then there was that question about the German 352d Infantry Division, which was waiting with open gun muzzles for the Americans where the GIs were supposed to find only children and old men:

Well, the Germans had just been moved up the night before. (Not quite.) And the Germans were as surprised to see the Americans as the Americans were to see them! A freak happening, said the brass, and what could you do about that?

All this information was trickling in, and in the absence of more, the staff officers talked about the reasons for the failures. The two engineer assault battalions that were supposed to make paths to the beach had been destroyed almost completely by German guns, and only a few paths had been blown through the underwater obstacles.

The army had set great store on a secret weapon: duplex drive tanks that were supposed to be amphibious. That meant float. They had been dropped in shrouds into the water, and virtually all of them had sunk. Fortunately someone was skeptical, and an LCVP had been sent in behind each amphibious tank, so most of the crews were saved.

The one positive action that had been taken was the diversion of the 115th Regimental Combat Team of the Twenty-ninth Division to Red beach when the brass learned that the Sixteenth Infantry had made it up to the seawall. That's how Sergeant Elburn landed where he did.

At 10 a.m. General Gerow sent the Fifth Corps' first report to General Bradley aboard the *Augusta*. It must have been a difficult one to write, knowing what the staff then knew! But after all, General Gerow's neck was on the line, and there might be some sort of miracle. The report was terse and could hardly be called positive. Things were not going at all as expected. The enemy fire was heavy; the minefields were tough; most of the amphibious tanks had sunk. General Gerow did not have to say it; even from the *Augusta* General Bradley could sense that everything on the beach was a mess.

Fortunately the miracle was about to appear, in the shape of a U.S. destroyer.

Offshore the destroyer *Frankford* had been assigned to work as part of the screen of the landing force on the night arrival in the landing area, and it was not released from this duty until 8 a.m. When the word came, Comdr. James L. Semmes brought his ship up off Omaha Beach to see what he could do for the troops. It was apparent from the sea that somebody had better do something for them soon.

"In clear daylight I could see that things were going very poorly on Omaha Beach. All the soldiers on the beach were huddling low behind stone walls, and no movement up the hill and off the sand could be seen. Wave after wave of assault craft LCVPs loaded with assault troops were stalled a couple of hundred yards off the beach, waiting for clearance to run it."

The destroyer's radio operator kept trying to make contact with the army fire-control men on the shore to arrange firing missions. It took a long time, because the army's communications equipment was so badly scattered, and the observers had to get organized.

The navy operator was growing frantic when finally the army shore party message came in.

But the army fire-control men on shore reported that they could not see well enough in the smoke and haze from the shelling and the fires to call fire missions for the destroyer. If the *Frankford* was going to save the troops, it would have to do it all by itself.

"With a sick feeling in my stomach that we were facing total fiasco, I left my assigned sea area and moved in as close to shore as I could without bumping the bottom. This gave us an extra mile to improve vision for picking up targets of opportunity. My gunnery officer in the gun director found pillboxes, machine gun nests, and other targets by telescope. Also tommy gun tracer fire by GIs behind the wall was a help in finding the targets. We began to bang away."

Seeing the action of the *Frankford*, the other destroyers in the squadron also began moving in close. The USS *Harding* moved in so close that she banged her sonar dome on the bottom—the sonar dome extended down 2 feet below the keel.

Then more destroyers came in, and the pillboxes on the hill began to fall apart. The miracle was working. Germans began to come out with hands up and surrender to the American troops.

Just before noon General Huebner felt that he would have to move his First Division headquarters ashore if he was to have any reasonable information about what was happening. So Major Lord and the general and all the rest got into a PT boat and started for the beach. Offshore they encountered General Gerhardt, commander of the Twenty-ninth Division, observing from an LCM. They stopped and the generals had a little talk. General Huebner and Major Lord learned that nothing had yet been able to get off the beach in the Twenty-ninth Division sector. The Germans were using napalm-filled mortar shells, said General Gerhardt.

The First Division crowd transferred to an LCM and headed for the beach. They had to get out and walk, in water up to their necks. So that was how it felt! Except that the enemy shelling had quieted down.

They found an abandoned German pillbox near the beach and set up headquarters. General Wyman and General Hoge, the commander of engineers, came up. Hoge had been wounded in the leg, but he was still operating what was left of his shore brigade.

They learned that the fearsome guns of Pointe du Hoc had been moved inland 1200 yards, not really set up, and that the rangers had taken enormous casualties in trying to get at the site. When the American troops attacked the inland spot where the guns actually were, the Germans had blown the breechblocks and retreated.

*

S. Sgt. J. J. P. Corrigan was a member of the Fifth Corps advance headquarters group, which went across the Channel in the command ship USS
Charles Carroll. On the night of June 5 Corrigan and his buddy T/4 Francis
Cottave went to mass and took communion together. Cottave was married to
a very successful New York photographer and he was extremely proud of
her; he talked about her all the time. As they returned to the spot they had
staked out on deck for sleeping, Cottave spoke up:

"Do you think you're going to come out of this okay?"

"Sure. Why not?"

"I don't think I'm gonna make it."

"Come on. Think about that next leave in London."

"Unh-unh. Maybe. I don't think so. The worst thing, you know, is my
wife."

Corrigan kept trying to buck up Cottave, but he could see it wasn't working. Finally, as they lay down on the steel deck, he said: "Remember one
thing. Until we get up that draw at Colleville-sur-Mer, it's every guy for himself. So don't waste any time."

Corrigan was thinking about that advice himself hours later, after noon
on D day. The advance headquarters group had been scheduled to land on
the beach as soon as the troops were established, but at H + 7 they still
weren't. With the heroic actions of the destroyers the blockage was reduced,
and now Corrigan's team was going in. "Every man for himself"—he must
not forget it.

The port gangway of his team's LCI was fouled, so everybody was going
off the starboard side. The men came up from below as the craft neared
shore. Corrigan and a dozen others huddled down below the rail on the right
side of the deck. A shell struck on the starboard bow, and a fragment hit a
signal battalion GI standing in front of Corrigan. The soldier was hustled
below.

Just as the shell struck, the LCI grounded on a sandbar. The craft was
300 yards from the beach.

"This is it," said the skipper of the LCI, and the gangway clattered down.
The men inflated their life vests and stepped off, one by one. The water was
over 6 feet deep.

Sergeant Corrigan was burdened down with a carbine and a big map case,
the contents of which were to be used at the command post with an overlay.
Listening to the firing above the cliffs, and remembering "every man for

himself," he treaded water and wiggled, and finally got ashore, although he lost his carbine in the process.

Then he heard shouts behind him.

"Help! Help! Help!"

Some GI had been hit by a fragment. But there was nothing Corrigan could do.

Later he wondered. T/4 Cottave was four men behind him. Cottave was 5 feet 7 inches tall. Cottave never made the beach.

The beach was still under sporadic fire from the heights. It was a junkyard and charnel house of overturned DUKWs, piles of bulk supplies, blankets and other cast-off personal equipment, and that was to say nothing of the thousands of bodies and body parts. The GIs were still pinned down in this sector behind the seawall. Staff Sergeant Corrigan looked over the heads of the troops at the poppies in bloom in the sand dunes. Then he scurried another 200 yards up the line and again sought shelter. Brigadier General Helmick was there, the senior officer present at the time. An artilleryman, he moved back and forth along the line, standing exposed, encouraging the GIs to make a run for it up the draw.

And they moved. Staff Sergeant Corrigan moved, too, with the others of the advance team.

*   *   *

With the slackening of German fire as the destroyers smashed the pillboxes and machine gun nests, the engineers made it up to the barbed-wire entanglements and blew them with their bangalore torpedoes. Then the men behind the stone wall began to move forward up the draw. The impasse was broken. Sergeant Kleinhardt and his men saw some Germans running to their right. Having no mortars, the mortar squad leader threw rocks at them. The GIs continued to move up the draw to the top of the hill; there they waited for enough men of the company to come up to organize. They foraged among the dead for weapons and had no trouble finding rifles, BARs, and light machine guns.

Navy Medic Scheer heard the whistles blowing and the orders. It was not his job to go up that draw, so he put his back against the wall and made a step with his clasped hands, helping the GIs go over and marveling at their bravery. It came to him that he, too, might get killed here, and he worried about how his mother and father and other relatives would take it.

He looked around. There was no one left but a few of his fellow medics, the wounded, and the dead men. He met Medic Mullen from his outfit, and they began finding and treating the wounded. They had lost their kits, but they used the bandages that each man carried. They found dead bodies and stripped off the bandage kits and the canteens. There were plenty of dead and plenty of bandages. The medics needed them. Scheer and Mullen used fourteen bandages on one army engineer before they left him.

A beachmaster came up and told them that they belonged over to the right. So they crawled along the seawall, making little dashes where it was not high enough for protection, treating the wounded as they went. They came to a draw. One of the handful of tanks that had made it ashore was sitting on the narrow service road above the beach. The Germans were firing at it and their shells were overshooting, hitting the beach in front of the tank. They waited. The fire slacked off.

"Let's run past the tank," whispered Mullen. He got up.

Scheer pulled him back.

Whang! An 88 shell hit just in the place they would have been if they had run forward.

They lay there, and then Scheer realized that he could time the shots. He guessed there was just one gun firing at the tank. The next time a shell came in, they immediately rushed forward, passed the tank, and were safe. The next shell followed seconds later.

Sometime during the afternoon Sergeant Moglia learned that the lady with the tea leaves in Bridport had been almost right. She had said Pfc. Eddie Krotz would never see combat again. Perhaps Eddie did not see anything as he went in. He would not see any more combat, anyhow. He never made it off Easy Red beach. Neither did the lieutenant who had gone back under guard to marry his English sweetheart.

Further down the beach at H hour, troops of the Second Engineer Combat Battalion came in. Their job was to blast gaps in the steel and concrete obstacle course so that the armor and the artillery could be gotten ashore. But most of the men in the advance party were killed, and the battalion's objectives remained to be achieved.

*

LCI (L) 557 was carrying Capt. William Spry's Company I of the 116th Infantry of the Twenty-ninth Division. It had been a rough crossing. Theoretically the twelve LCIs of Group 33 were to stick together in two 6-ship divisions. But the weather was too rough for that, so rough that 90 percent of the troops were seasick on the crossing, and the LCIs ended up operating almost independently, instead of in divisions.

LCI (L) 557 was to drop its human cargo at Dog Red beach, but by the time Lt. (j.g.) Charles Edman, Jr., conned the ship up to that beach, there was no place to land. The beach was full of wreckage, small craft zooming in and out dangerously, and gunfire. The Germans were using their 88-millimeter guns very effectively, and on the hilltop above the beach they had their mortars zeroed in on the waterline. Edman tried several times to find an opening on Dog Red beach, but he was driven off each time.

Also destined for Omaha that morning of June 6 was Sergeant Emert's company of the 116th Infantry. It too was to land and move up to the top of the cliff overlooking the beach. By 11 a.m. the troops should have that cliff line, and then the 115th Infantry would move through them and go inland.

Sergeant Emert's E Company was to land on Easy Green beach. The assault companies were organized into six assault teams of thirty men each: riflemen, flamethrowers, demolitions, wire cutters, light machine gun, 60-millimeter mortars, and BAR men. Each thirty-man team was assigned to a specific LCI. Emert was leader of the mortar squad of his team.

In the darkness his LCI bucked and plunged toward the coast, every man soaked through to the skin. The LCI commanders made some mistakes going in, and the current, tide, wind, and human error took the troops a mile to 2 miles east of their assigned landing spot. The first consequence was that the gun ships and rocket ships did them no good at all in softening up the enemy.

As they went in, it didn't seem to matter. Emert's first wave of LCIs moved right up to the beach without any enemy fire—until they came within range. Then the Germans really began shooting those airburst shells, antipersonnel shells that were set to explode just above the surface of the water. Emert watched men die in the boats. A shell burst just above his company commander's landing craft, and the whole boat disappeared beneath the waves.

Then Emert's boat hit the beach. He was out and running, 700 yards of open beach before there was any shelter at all. Many men were down. The survivors of the wire-cutting team were inching across the beach with their tools and bangalore torpedoes. The infantrymen crouched, jumped, ran, slid on their bellies, and started up again, trying to get inland. Every few seconds a figure would stop and drop, and then would not move. Others were hit and calling for the medics.

Emert was ashore, heading for the high ground above the beach with his mortar squad. Three minutes after the first wave the second wave was supposed to come in, but it did not. The second wave was confused, and when some of the LCI commanders saw the carnage on Omaha Beach, they held off landing.

Sergeant Emert had five men still with him. He led them on a crisscross route across the beach, hoping to confuse the German gunners. It didn't work very well. One of his men fell, and then another. By the time he crossed through the barbed wire (courtesy of the wire cutters), he and one ammunition carrier were alone. His first gunner was just behind him. Then Emert heard a loud explosion; he turned just in time to see the gunner fall dead on the spot Emert had occupied moments before. Emert hit the ground. A few seconds later he crawled back to the gunner and took the mortar from the dead hands. Emert was then carrying full field equipment, the mortar, and a bag of ammunition.

He moved up. There was an enormous crash behind him and a shock to his head. He knew he had been hit. Land mine? Mortar shell? Artillery? He never knew. It knocked the breath out of him. Emert did not know if he was dying. He lay on the ground until he gained strength enough to move.

The wire team had opened a gap through the second barrier of rolled barbed wire above the beach. So Emert wriggled through with his weapons and looked for the enemy and a place to set up.

His assault team leader was just ahead of him. Emert came up, and the leader pointed out an enemy machine gun. Emert moved down behind a hillock and set up the mortar. He fired several rounds. The machine gun went silent.

He was all alone. One member of his squad arrived, but the man was so paralyzed with fear that he was useless. It was half an hour before he regained his spirit and could help.

Emert crawled up to the top of his little hill. He saw a pillbox so expertly camouflaged that he had to look several times to be sure it was really there. A machine gun pointed out of the central slot. The team BAR man came crawling up beside Emert, and the sergeant showed him the pillbox. It took a little looking at, but the BAR man then fired a long burst at that machine gun snout. The gun tilted down, and the pillbox was silent.*

Emert looked along the grass line above the beach. Quite nearby he saw a very large pillbox, which housed a heavy coastal gun that was firing out to sea at the approaching landing craft. He set up the mortar at a very sharp angle and fired one shell. It was a case of great good luck: the mortar round landed right in front of the pillbox and blew. Inside, the Germans must have thought they were zeroed in, for they hastily evacuated the position, and the gun fell silent.

Emert moved on up the hill to join the handful of men who had made it from this first wave of the 116th. On top of the hill he found a sergeant who had been shot in the abdomen, and in falling had tripped a land mine, which tore his foot up pretty badly. When Emert stopped to help, he realized that he could not see out of his left eye and that it was bleeding. A lieutenant came up and told both wounded men to go back to the beach and await the medics. Emert helped the other sergeant down to the beach; as soon as he got there, he began digging a slit trench. Just as he completed it and pushed the sergeant into it, the Germans began shelling that section of the beach. A round burst right next to the slit trench, throwing Emert on top of the sergeant and covering them both with sand. A medic saw, and came over to dig them out.

8:30 a.m.: LCI (L) 557 was two hours overdue in landing its troops. They came in to Dog Red beach only to be told by the beachmasters that they must move over to Easy Red beach where there was some room. Low tide had ended at 6:30; now the tide was rushing in, concealing the landmarks and obstacles that had been portrayed for them in the secret orders. The whole area was dotted with sunken LCVPs, LCIs, tanks, floating bodies, and the flotsam and jetsam of failed landing attempts. Above this beach Lieutenant Edman also noted another unadvertised disadvantage: hidden 88s firing over and onto the landing areas. The good news was that the enemy shelling had been so heavy that the Germans themselves had destroyed some of the obstacles they had constructed.

11:30 a.m.: LCI 557's sister ship, *LCI 554*, finally nosed in to the beach, made a neat landing, and discharged its troops. *LCI 557* headed in not far

---

*Months later, when Emert returned to the beachhead, he found a plaque on that pillbox; it was the first pillbox taken from the enemy in the Omaha Beach landings.

away, and it immediately grounded on concealed wreckage 75 yards off the beach. Seaman George Schneider volunteered to take a line to shore. He did so, floating a small anchor on a life jacket. He planted the anchor on the beach, put the life jacket down on top of it, and sat on the package. He remained there on the beach until all 210 soldiers had come off along his lifeline. Miraculously there was not one casualty among the troops or the ship's crew.

Captain Spry saw his men off. He shook hands with the ship's officers and thanked them for the ride.

"Boy, just let me get on dry land," he said, and then he was off to battle.

As they unloaded, the first sergeant of the company came up to Ensign Porter, the engineering officer of *LCI 557*, and asked to use the ship's 12-foot wherry to unload heavy gear. The boat was just being put into position when another LCI slid in alongside the 557. The newcomer was ordered away by the beachmaster; in backing off, it hit the 557 and crushed the wherry, ripped off the stern safety lines and the 55-gallon spare drum of gasoline fuel for the anchor winch engines, and whizzed back out to sea, having done what the Germans wished they could have done. Ensign Porter then rigged up two rubber rafts, and the crew helped the GIs get their guns and ammunition ashore. Mortar and machine gun fire began, but still no one was hit.

As Lieutenant Edman got ready to back the LCI off the beach, the beachmaster told him to stay and wait for casualties. He stood by for 35 minutes, but no casualties appeared and the craft was released. All this while the USS *Texas*, behind Edman's vessel, was firing its big guns, and with each shot it fired, the LCI seemed to jump out of the water.

Getting away from shore, the LCI stuck fast and had to be helped. The helping LCM got into trouble and disappeared, but by this time *LCI 557* was off the beach. That afternoon *LCI 557* returned to England for another load of troops.

Among the medics on the beach was Sgt. Ed Elburn of the 115th Infantry. That morning his company was suddenly given a new mission: to go to the aid of the 116th troops who had been landed way off to the left of Easy Green beach. The skipper of their LCI had boasted out in the Channel that he was going to land them "dry." But when they came in, the LCI did not get all the way in. It grounded. Two big men carried lifelines ashore. The others were to hang onto the lines as they walked to the beach. Sergeant Elburn stepped off the ladder of the LCI into water up to his neck. The man holding the land

end of his rope either had been hit and fallen or had abandoned the line, for
as Elburn grabbed the rope he immediately went down, dragged under by a
50-pound pack of splints.

Scrambling, half-swimming, Sergeant Elburn managed to make his way
to shore. When he reached the beach, German artillery fire was falling all
around. His LCI was hit and began to burn. He looked out to sea; landing
craft were burning all around. Amphibious tanks coming ashore got stuck in
rocks and could not climb to the beach.

The First Battalion of the 115th came in at 10:30, half an hour before
the anticipated time. Those troops were needed badly.

Pfc. Frank Globuschutz's Company B went in just after 10:30. The LCI made
a perfect landing; the ladders went down, and the men stepped ashore. But
hardly had twenty of them set foot on the beach when the Germans began
throwing an artillery barrage at the LCI. Everybody dropped and stayed down.
Globuschutz lay for a while; then he turned his head and looked back. He
saw dozens of bodies floating facedown in the water. They had been hit even
before they got to the beach; now the tide was bringing them in. As Globuschutz lay there, the man next to him was killed.

The company was completely disorganized. Nobody gave an order. Then
Globuschutz realized that he had to get off that beach or die. Little by little
he inched his way across the rocky beach until he reached the shelter of the
cliff's overhang. He took refuge in a big shell hole, already occupied by two
medics and a wounded German soldier. The German had half his head shot
away, and he was moaning in Hungarian, "Oh, my God." Globuschutz knew
because his parents were Hungarian.

After a while Globuschutz started up the draw that led to the top of the
cliff. On the way up he met GIs bringing down eight more Wehrmacht prisoners. These were Mongolians! Hitler was dredging the furthest perimeters
of the new German empire for his cannon fodder.

Globuschutz got to the top of the hill. He saw a lot of Americans up
there, mostly from the 116th Infantry. He waited, but it was two hours before the company was organized. Company B had lost a lot of men; he did
not know how many. The soldiers had to make their way across a huge field,
and they were warned that it was loaded with "shoe mines," little plastic
explosives that could blow a man's foot off. The rest of the day was spent
moving inch by inch across that field in the hot sun. Globuschutz had drained
his canteen before he reached the top of the cliff, and the rest of the day was
torture.

*

Pfc. Thomas Wickham's LCI skipper was extremely nervous. He scraped bottom, let down his gangways, and passed the word to the GIs to "get the hell off the LCI in a hurry." He wanted to get out and back to sea.

Wickham was a member of the First Battalion headquarters team, and he was carrying a large rubberized bag that contained spare parts for the battalion radios. So important was communications that another GI on another LCI had a duplicate bag. Battalion was trying to take no chances.

Wickham stepped into waist-deep water and started ashore, dragging the heavy bag. When he got out of the deep water, he looked to the right, and there he saw the man with the bag that was the twin to his. He saw the man look around and then let the bag slip from his hand into the surf. Wickham knew then that he had to get his bag ashore.

He went up the beach, past a wounded man who was on hands and knees, blood dripping from his eye, moaning, "My God, my God." Wickham did not stop. He had been told the medics would do that.

He saw many corpses; the one he remembered clearly was a man with his buttocks shot away. A GI from Wickham's platoon came up and offered to help carry the bag. Each took a strap and moved ahead. A German machine gun sprayed the area, and they hit the dirt. Finally they got to the seawall and up the draw. German mortar shells then began pounding the draw. Wickham tried to dig in. He couldn't; the rocky soil was too hard. He tried to crawl under the earth. He couldn't, but he could press his face down into it. When the shelling ended, he scurried forward to the top of the hill and flopped down behind the bank. Lieutenant James, his platoon leader, was there. It seemed safe, somehow.

Sergeant Elburn tried to dig in, but the beach was almost entirely covered by small stones. It was no use. He hooked up his gear and began moving up a draw to get off the beach. Up ahead he saw bodies lying all around and fires burning in the grass. A small antipersonnel minefield had already claimed some victims.

Sergeant Elburn made his way to the top of the cliff. More mines. Rifle and machine gun fire.

His first patient was Captain Schmitt, the commander of Company E, who had been hit by machine gun fire. The captain was in bad shape. Sergeant Elburn gave him plasma, and he and Sergeant Newman began to move the captain. Then Newman was hit. Stretcher-bearers came up to carry the wounded down to the beach. Two of them were hit. Finally all the wounded were gotten down to the beach with Sergeant Emert.

They remained on the beach all that afternoon. Emert helped the medics; he had nothing else to do. He saw one of his own men with a piece out of his chest. He and a medic gave the man a transfusion there on the beach. All afternoon wounded men came trickling back to the beach, walking or on litters.

Late in the afternoon landing craft came in to take off the wounded. Sergeant Emert got into a boat and went back to a hospital ship. That night he and Captain Schmitt and Aidman Newman were taken back to England. Emert's war had lasted just about twelve hours.*

Late on the afternoon of D day some of the naval units offshore began lobbing shells onto the beach occupied by the wounded of the 115th and 116th regiments. Many were killed and wounded by "friendly fire." As the tide came in, the men on the beach stacked up the bodies of the dead like cordwood. The evacuation continued. All was done by hand; by dark still no vehicles had appeared in that sector, and there was only a handful of tanks anywhere along the line.

The reason for that, according to Sergeant Ogden, was that the U.S. naval personnel assigned to land the tanks fouled up their job. Ogden and others of the 224th Field Artillery Battalion were landed on Green beach. The artillerymen were brought in by British landing craft, and they literally did not get their feet wet. Off to the left, the U.S. Navy was supposed to land the amphibious tanks, but the navy did not get in close enough, and the tanks went in over their snorkels and sank. Many tank crews were drowned.

Ogden and others were furious with the American navy. "All they wanted to do was back out and run for the sea. If they had stayed in any longer, the GIs on shore would have picked them off. As it was, a few tracers followed them out."

But most of those tracers were German; the GIs ashore had plenty to do to survive, and most had no quarrel to pick with anyone except the Germans. For, as they were discovering, all the poop they had been fed earlier, to the effect that they would be facing "old men and kids under 16," turned out to be false. Allied intelligence had missed the movement to the Omaha Beach

---

*Sergeant Emert lost his left eye and was fitted with a plastic eye. He went back to France, was assigned to a quartermaster graves registration unit, and served as mail clerk to that outfit until VE Day, after which he went home and was discharged. Captain Schmitt recovered from his machine gun wounds, rejoined the 115th in Germany, and was killed there by a sniper. Aidman Newman was in hospital for six months and then rejoined the unit.

area of that crack German unit, the 352d Division. The first wave had been very badly hit. Sergeant Ogden was in the second wave, and it was faring just as badly against stout German resistance. Ogden's company had been fed steak and four eggs for breakfast in those dark hours of the night. Now he ran across a hundred yards of beach under heavy fire, carrying a full field pack, a radio on his back, two rolls of telephone wire, two field telephones, and a submachine gun and twelve clips in a belt. He hit the seawall, panting and exhausted. Then he gagged. The four eggs and the steak came up, and he swore. It was the best meal he had been fed by the army in two years.

Shells were falling very close, so he ran for a foxhole not far away. Crouched down in it was another man. The other ignored him. On the lip of the foxhole, Ogden looked down at the other, shouting again. The other GI was his size (150 pounds), his age (21), with red hair, freckles, and blue eyes. It was startling, like looking at a mirror. Except...the other GI was dead. Ogden turned, terrified, and ran for another hole.

The Second Ranger Battalion had come in very early with the assigned task of taking the cliffs at Vierville. On top of those cliffs, said intelligence, were important coastal guns that could play hell with the landings. The rangers had run into heavy opposition and their ranks had been thinned. There on the beach it was decided that they had to have help, and Sergeant Ogden's platoon was given the job. The platoon joined the rangers, and after some hard going they got to the top of the cliffs. No coastal guns. The Germans had moved them almost a mile inland. Sergeant Ogden set up shop as a forward observer with his radio, and he made contact with the cruisers. He called for 10-inch naval gun support. After a few rounds those emplacements were destroyed.

General Bradley was sitting off the beach in the cruiser *Augusta*. By noon he was considering diverting to Utah Beach the next force that had been earmarked for Omaha. That would have meant abandoning the Omaha Beach landing as a failure.

*   *   *

At H hour Lieutenant Miller's Twentieth Engineers were on their way in to the shore. Their task was to clear the entrances to the big causeway so that the infantry and later the tanks could move up. Miller's Company B, riding on *LCI 83*, was scheduled to land at 8:30 a.m. But by the time the craft got near, the enemy firing had made the beach too hot, so the LCI moved off. Captain Lutz and the First Platoon loaded aboard an LCVP and headed in toward the shore. The LCI lay offshore until 9:30 and then moved in during what seemed to be a lull in the firing. But the lull was illusory. The LCI took a direct hit in the forward steel "bullpen." Three men were killed, seven seriously wounded, and ten slightly wounded. Medics took the wounded into the No. 2 compartment for treatment.

LCI 83 cruised up and down off the beach, the skipper looking for an opportunity to beach. At ten o'clock Lieutenant Miller loaded the Second Platoon aboard an LCVP and started in. The coxswain was not too eager to land, because the fire there was very heavy. Finally, Miller persuaded him to take the LCVP in, and the troops landed on Easy Red beach, in the Twenty-ninth Division sector. It was covered with dead and wounded GIs and wreckage, from one end to the other.

Lieutenant Miller was in the wrong place, of course. He worked the platoon along the beach, trying to reach Fox Green, where the mission was to clear Exit Road E-3 to the causeway.

When he got to the area, he discovered that the enemy strongpoint keeping the Americans off the causeway was still there. The infantrymen—hundreds of them—were lying jammed on the beach, just below the slight ridge that protected them from the enemy. Dead and wounded lay everywhere. Mortar and artillery rounds dropped among the troops, creating more casualties every minute. If a man stuck his head up, the machine guns got him or a sniper did.

Lieutenant Miller decided to rush the platoon up the beach and into cover. Only six men followed him. He motioned them down and went on alone to the foot of the enemy strongpoint, where he was in defilade. From there he could look down on the panorama of the beach; it was a German's-eye view. He saw many grounded vessels, and he watched as the enemy shelled one LCI just as it was unloading troops.

He moved back down to the beach to find the other members of his platoon, lying among the infantrymen. They told him that snipers had been getting dozens of men.

Private Clay had been shot through the arm, and Sergeant Evans had been wounded in the hand by a shell fragment.

By this time the platoon had been ashore for about four hours, pinned down most of that time on the beach below the strongpoint. The spot afforded the only shelter in the area, but that shelter was only from direct fire. The mortars and artillery could still get at the infantrymen. Lieutenant Miller decided to get the platoon off the beach. One at a time he called the men up and directed them to run to the foot of the strongpoint. There they were to dig in. He didn't have to say that twice.

When all the men were assembled, Lieutenant Miller took a patrol to the top of the strongpoint. The Germans, he discovered, had pulled back. He walked across the top of the hill to Exit Road E-3 and met Captain Lutz with the First Platoon.

Lieutenant Miller went down to get the rest of his platoon, but when he and the men came back up the hill, they were met by machine gun fire and pinned down. Finally they got back up and around the hill, where they met the balance of the company. By this time it was late, and they dug in for the night.

Lieutenant Downing's Eighteenth Infantry was supposed to go in at about 9:30, but when General Bradley and his staff realized how tough the going on Omaha Beach was, that regiment's landing was delayed. There was no room for more troops, with the rangers, the 16th Infantry, the 116th, and the 115th already pinned down and taking heavy casualties. As the morning wore on, there were delays and more delays as Bradley and his staff wondered what to do. Should they abandon Omaha Beach (and the men ashore) and concentrate the remainder of the troops on Utah Beach? That was the big question. Until General Bradley had the advice of General Gerow, commander of the Fifth Corps and of that Omaha landing, he would not act.

Lieutenant Downing's LCI moved slowly in toward the beach, stopped, circled, and moved again. The vessel pulled in close to the shore. Downing borrowed field glasses from another officer and scanned the shoreline. He could see the poles of the underwater obstacles sticking up through the waves. He could also see the forms of GIs in olive drab lying in an almost unbroken line on the sloping gravel shelf. They lay quiet, and he wondered if they were all dead. He saw one get up and run inshore. Then another. But most lay very still. Here and there he saw a waterproofed tank, burning or inactive. All seemed to be deserted.

From Downing's LCI the scene looked so peaceful. Above the beach was the green of the grass line. Once in a while there was a puff of smoke.

9:30 a.m.: No landing orders. Major Peckham was on the bridge of the LCI with the skipper, talking on the radio. Lieutenant Downing's gear was dumped in the middle of his bunk in the deckhouse.

He began to have a sinking feeling in the pit of his stomach. This was the big invasion. Things ought to be moving on schedule. Since they weren't, then something had to be wrong. Some of the brass had fouled up, or... even worse...

Looking through the glasses at the shore, he could not tell a thing.

10 a.m.: Lieutenant Downing still had no instructions, but he put on his equipment. The men had been wearing theirs for hours, sitting down below deck, waiting and wondering. Lieutenant Harbison, the battalion intelligence officer, joined Downing on deck. They whispered their concerns—they dared not frighten the men, and some GIs were on duty on deck. The word would spread like wildfire.

An artillery shell smacked into the sea 50 yards from the LCI. They heard the zinging sound of shell fragments overhead. The helmsman speeded up and turned.

12 noon: No word. Lieutenant Downing took off his equipment. It was too heavy to sit around in. He wandered out to the deck and then back to the deckhouse. Many landing craft were cruising, as theirs was, along the beach, offshore. Something was wrong. At least the Luftwaffe had not shown up. Thank God for small favors.

An LCI from the beach area limped by. It had taken a shell aft and was low in the water. Men were jettisoning bedrolls, ration cases, ammunition boxes, and jerry cans.

Downing's LCI crew served soup for lunch. No one wanted much. The men were waiting to land.

By 1 p.m. men began to move off the beach and up the hill. Then the boats began to move in to the beach, and traffic became orderly. From inland the Germans were still dishing it out, particularly with mortar fire, which hit among the craft on the beach. Some shells even came close to the *Frankford*, but there were no hits. The destroyer took aboard a number of wounded from the boats for emergency treatment by the ship's doctor and corpsmen in the wardroom.

By 2 p.m. the situation had changed completely. The troops were moving inland at a steady pace. An hour later the *Frankford* and the other destroyers pulled out, moving back out to sea around the invasion fleet. Capt. Harry Sanders, commander of Destroyer Squadron 18, who was riding in the *Frankford*, had to put together his screen to protect the transport area for the night. So the destroyers left the battle scene, but there was no doubt in the minds of anyone on the beach that they had saved the invasion of Omaha Beach with their swift response to the emergency.

Finally, orders came for the Eighteenth to move in to shore. General

Bradley had learned what the problem had been—the existence of that crack German division behind the beach. But despite enormous casualties the men of the First and Twenty-ninth divisions had forced their way up Easy Red, Easy Green, and Fox Red beaches, and they were advancing up the hill. So the invasion of Omaha Beach could continue.

Lieutenant Downing's LCI turned. Men lined up in the companionways, ready to dash at the order. Downing crouched behind the bulkhead and peered at the shore. On the left he saw a brush-covered hill that dropped off to a sheer bank at the beach. Not a good way to go up.

The LCI touched bottom, but the craft was still 50 yards offshore. Then the ramps on the sides rattled down. The men of E and F companies dashed out and began moving down the ramps in single file. Machine guns and rifles opened up from the beach. Downing could hear bullets whanging into the sides of the LCI. He also heard cries. Peering over the metal shield the lieutenant saw that the GIs who had gone down the ramps had stepped into deep water and were floundering out ahead of the LCI. Most of them had lost their weapons and their helmets. They were sputtering and choking and yelling, for their equipment was weighing them down in spite of their life belts. Bullets kicked up spurts in the water. Some of the men struggled over to a wrecked LCA and hung onto it, the water around them jumping with fire from the beach. Some were screaming, "Save me."

A naval corpsman dashed down to the bottom of the ramp and pulled a man out of the water, dragging him back up behind the shield. The man had been shot in the belly, and a huge patch of blood stained his middle. He was alive, but his face already had that greenish tinge which, in Downing's experience, said the poor guy wasn't going to make it.

Men started to run down the ramps to help those floundering in the water. "Stay where you are, men," shouted Major Peckham.

The LCI shuddered and began to back off. The men in the water screamed louder when they saw the LCI deserting them. The craft backed away and then sped off out of range of the shelling and small-arms fire. Some shots had penetrated the hull and knocked the valve off a fuel tank in a hold. Fumes began to fill the hold, and men rushed up on deck. A runner from the bridge told Lieutenant Downing to get the men back below, as they were spoiling the trim of the vessel. The men said they were afraid a shell would ignite the fumes. Downing said they had to go back down. They went, but they stayed next to the ladder.

Now the vessel turned and came in again. By about 3 feet it missed a Teller mine attached to a piling. The LCI hit the beach with a jolt. This time

it was right on the beach. The ramps rattled down again. Clouds of smoke
and dirt rose in front of the ship. The Germans had spotted it and were laying down a mortar barrage. Shell fragments smacked into the sides of the
ship and zinged overhead. Once more the skipper pulled the vessel offshore.

Everyone was getting edgy. Lieutenant Harbison came down and told
Downing that it was too tough; LCVPs would come alongside and take the
men in. Downing said he would take the first boat.

An LCVP came up and banged against the fantail. Men began jumping
in. Downing went over the rope railing, grabbed a stanchion, and put his
foot on the gunwale of the LCVP. The smaller craft surged downward in the
sea, and he was left dangling. What if it came back up and crushed him
against the side of the LCI? But it came up gently; he felt it, and then he
jumped inside the LCVP, tumbling over, falling into the boat.

Sergeant Keeler grabbed him.

"Thought we'd lost you that time."

Downing moved into position near the ramp in front. Sergeant Keeler
was there; so was Lieutenant Johnson of the antitank company. About thirty
men in all.

Downing looked at his watch. It was now 1:30 p.m.

The LCVP started in to shore. The beach looked blank and hazy from
the grass fires of the shelling. Seventy-five yards out, the boat jolted to a
stop. It had hit a sandbar. The coxswain gunned the engine to back off. No
dice. The boat was stuck.

Lieutenant Downing motioned to the coxswain to lower the ramp, and he
squeezed the lever on his life belt to fill it. He stepped off into cold water,
up to his chest; then his feet went out. But he managed to keep his carbine
over his head as he struggled ahead, and finally he made it to the beach.
After him Sergeant DeSantis, the acting first sergeant, cut the lieutenant out
of his life belt with a trench knife. Then they started inshore, past a burning
LCI and a bulldozer. Behind the bulldozer crouched a handful of engineer
troops, using it as shelter from small-arms fire.

Up the gravel beach they went; ahead was grassy ground, marked with
white tape by the engineers to show the cleared path. Downing followed that
path, his boat group behind him. Shells were landing on the hill to their left;
they were moving to the right. When the lieutenant reached the end of the
tagged lane, he saw a number of unfamiliar troops ahead. He did not want
to get his men mixed up with other units, and while he was watching, several of the troops ahead stepped on shoe mines and fell. So he turned around
and led his men back the way they had come.

They came to another path at right angles to the first, leading off the beach. Downing dropped to the ground and crawled up to look over the situation. Another lieutenant was lying at the top of the rise; the path was clear of mines, he said, but there was a swamp at the end of it. Downing sent scouts ahead to ford the swamp and check it out. They went through all right. So Lieutenant Downing called for his mine-detector crews to come up. Only one detector was working. The two-man crew went ahead and found no mines. Downing led the others through the swamp; it was cold and muddy, and the water soon came up to his neck. Behind, he could hear the men splashing. He emerged dripping and followed the detector up the hill. So far so good. He was moving inland. The Germans would bomb and shell the beach to hinder the landings, but inland the GIs would be likely to meet only machine gun and rifle fire.

Downing went further up the hill, the men in single file behind him. Halfway up the lieutenant saw a soldier lying on his stomach, with his face and chest bandaged.

"There's mines all over here," the GI said.

Downing continued behind the mine detector. Behind him was a sharp explosion, and dirt and pebbles showered his back as he dove for cover. He turned. Private Mayer was behind him, looking at Downing with a shocked expression.

"He shot me! He shot me in the ass and in the head."

Downing looked at the man behind Mayer. It was one of the replacements who had come in after the company reached England. His face was white and he looked stunned. Downing was about to swear at him when he looked at the man's foot. It was a bloody mess. He had stepped on a mine, and in falling he had discharged his M-1; the bullet had grazed Mayer's butt and head.

"Medic-o-Medic," Downing shouted. The others filed past and went on. Then Downing started up the hill again. A shell came in close ahead. He dropped. He got up and rushed up the hill to the top, where an overhang protected the men from shelling. His men were up there, behind the cliff.

Major Peckham came up from behind nonchalantly and walked over the top of the hill, as though he were a vacationer strolling along the French coast on a fine day. Lieutenant Genua of Downing's company was right behind him. Downing admired his insouciance. Then came more shells, and he ducked again. When he got up and went over the hilltop, there in some bushes on the other side lay Major Peckham and Lieutenant Genua, being treated by medics for shell wounds. Peckham had been very lucky. One fragment had gone through his helmet and penetrated his scalp. Another was lodged in his neck. But he was still alive.

Lieutenant Genua was wounded in the leg.

Peckham told Downing to take over. He was on his way back to England.

Downing found his radio operator and told him to get in touch with Lieutenant Colonel Williamson and find out where the battalion command post was. He went on ahead to find the CP, leaving the men in cover. He passed a dead rabbit, blown up by a shoe mine. There was one mine that would not get a GI. He passed a body covered with a blanket. A carbine in a case lay beside it. The battalion supply officer, Lieutenant Pavlak, had always carried his carbine in a case. Downing wondered, but he did not lift the blanket to look.

He came to a wide field. He went back and brought the men up. They crossed the field. He saw Lieutenant O'Grady of F Company sitting on the ground. O'Grady said he had been hit in the buttocks by shell fragments and was waiting for dark to go down to the beach.

Downing crossed the field and reached the crest of a hill; then he stopped and looked down on the beach. A few shells were landing there sporadically. No landing craft were coming in. As he watched, a shell hit a 2½-ton truck that was loaded with gasoline. The truck disappeared in a flash of flame. O'Grady could have the beach. There was going to be more danger down there than up here on the hill.

Down on the beach Private Dantini woke up. Someone was giving him a drink of water. It was a medic. The aidman bandaged Dantini's wounds and gave him a shot of morphine. He also gave him a full canteen of water and a D-ration chocolate bar, as well as a promise to try to get back later. Anyhow, he said, it wouldn't be long before Dantini was evacuated to a hospital ship.

Pvt. Felix Branham of the 115th was lucky. His boat's experience was unlike that of virtually any of the others in the early waves on Omaha Beach. Branham and his team came in aboard an LCVP, with a grizzled coxswain who bragged that he had already landed 50,000 GIs in Africa, Sicily, and Italy; they were not even going to get their feet wet, he said. And despite the shelling going on all around he very nearly made good the promise.

Private Branham was a demolition man, twice a sergeant, twice busted for insubordination. His problem was the training exercises; he argued with the umpires, and so he got busted.

Branham was carrying a 50-pound satchel charge, two bandoliers of ammunition, and ten hand grenades. By this time many of the beach obstacles had been blown up in his team's area, but the GIs still faced triple concertina wire. They got off the LCVP, went down on the pebbles, and began to inch forward. With satchel charges and bangalore torpedoes they blew the wire, and again they crept forward. The thirty-man boat crew was still intact as they reached the cliff and climbed over. At the top the buckwheat was in bloom, and the poppies dotted the field they were in. It seemed very pleasant, very peaceful.

The men moved inland, passing farmhouses. Private Branham had been told that for the first three days the infantry mission was to search and destroy. The troops were to take no prisoners, to show no quarter. Anyone they met in those first three days, they had been told, was an enemy.

On the road Branham came upon a house and saw an old woman in black coming out. He raised his rifle, but it was knocked up by someone.

"They said to shoot everything," said Private Branham.

"But not that, my son"—and Private Branham saw that the man who had knocked up his rifle was a padre from the rangers.

Late that afternoon Branham's company bivouacked at the prearranged assembly point in the hedgerow country. The company commander counted noses. Branham's boat team had come through almost intact; twenty-six of the thirty-man team made it to the assembly point. As dusk fell, they could see Germans moving along the road not far away, but they could not shoot because Americans and Germans were all intermingled that night.

Sergeant Hoffner's men came across a group of prisoners. They were not German; they were speaking Polish and Russian. Very few prisoners had been taken that day in the Twenty-ninth Division sector. As Private Branham said, the troops had been told that their mission was to destroy; if they took prisoners, the captives became their responsibility. As a result, many of the enemy were shot down as they tried to surrender; but as the growing number of prisoners on the beach late on the afternoon of D day attested, not all the men could bring themselves to shoot prisoners in cold blood, no matter what the brass wanted.

*

Hoffner's platoon came to the top of the hill, to a farmyard. The farmhouse was aflame, and in the yard was a mother duck and her six ducklings walking around, and around, and around, in a 6-foot circle. Further down the road was a château, burning. As the Americans moved along the road, they began to notice equipment—German equipment—discarded on the roadside. Belts, helmets, packs, anything that would impede a man's progress. It was the other end of what they had seen down on the beach.

They went slowly along the road, looking at maps. They heard shots and spread out in skirmish formation. It grew dark as they sought the rest of their outfit. They did not reach the rendezvous point. They stopped and dug foxholes. It was cold, and they thought of all the equipment they did not have.

There were noises of aircraft overhead. The sky was crisscrossed with tracer fire—red, blue, yellow. The German bombers seemed to have come to the beachhead.

So the night went, with occasional firing on the beach and up on the ground above.

In late afternoon Corpsman Scheer, the navy medic, finally made it to his assigned beach area. There he found that Lieutenant Fox, the beachmaster, had been wounded. The company commandant was badly burned from the fire aboard the LCI, and the unit doctor was missing in action. The corpsmen were on their own.

At that point there was no way to evacuate any wounded. No landing craft were yet landing.

Scheer was worried about his buddies Corpsman J. B. Shuman and Seaman Cletus Shoptauer, but no one had word of them.

Lieutenant Downing saw a small swamp straight below; he decided to go into it.

Downing's men seemed inclined to stick to the borders of the field they'd reached; it seemed to be mine-free and protected from enemy observation. But Downing moved them along, for he knew that battalion was inland. He passed a small firefight—snipers were trying to hold up the troop movement. Captain Spinney came up with a radio; he was in touch with battalion. Lieutenant Colonel Williamson wanted to see Downing, he said, and he gave directions for reaching the CP.

Reluctantly, for it was growing late, Downing set out alone. He moved along the edge of a hedgerow, parallel to a road. There was a hedgerow on each side and the tops of the trees met above the road, creating a shady, peaceful scene. Then, in front of him, he saw a GI who stopped suddenly at a break in the hedgerow. The soldier crouched, gathered himself, and dashed across the break. A rifle cracked and a slug slapped into a tree. Now Downing came up to the break. He knew from experience that a man could not hold a rifle at the ready for very long. He waited. Then he crouched, leaped, and ran across the gap. A shot rang out. But Downing did not hurt anywhere and he was still alive, so he had made it.

The lieutenant hurried along the road. Soon he came to a crossroads and a cluster of gray stone houses. He did not know then that he had reached the outskirts of Colleville-sur-Mer. A couple of dead German soldiers lay in the road. Not far away two French civilians were standing, apparently unconcerned with the war, holding a conversation.

"Ou sont les soldats Américains?" he asked them.

They pointed down a road.

Downing went that way. He passed a dead German soldier, lying with his head supported on a knapsack—the German kind, with the furry back flap. A bloody bandage was tied around his head, and beside him there was a pool of blood. His enormous black mustache stood starkly against his greenish face. Downing stopped to look the soldier over for a luger. None.

Downing passed another dead German, lying on his stomach, shot while trying to run; the man's limbs were all akimbo. Downing searched him, too, for a luger. No. Just an empty holster. Someone else had already taken it.

Back down on the beach life was growing a bit easier. Most of the pillboxes above had been knocked out. Corpsman Scheer and the other navy medics went along the beach finding wounded men.

GIs would see their Red Cross armbands.

"Hey doc, there's a wounded guy over here."

So they treated the men, if "treated" was the word. They had no stretchers, so the really badly wounded could not be moved. They had no blankets. They kept hoping that landing craft would bring in supplies for them, and take the wounded out. But in that sector no landing craft came at all that day.

Corpsman J. B. Shuman showed up late in the afternoon. Scheer asked him about Shoptauer. Had he seen him?

"Yep."

"Was he all right?"

"Nope. He's had it."

Shuman then told how Seaman Shoptauer had been hit and had fallen on the beach; then before anyone could help him, he was hit again and killed.

Lieutenant Downing's gut feeling about the beach proved precisely correct. At 5 p.m., while he was crossing fields on the land above, the German artillery suddenly began firing again. New guns had been brought up and more heavy mortars. The men down on the beach took a fearful beating, and whole groups were wiped out by shells.

The flotilla of destroyers now headed in toward the beach in Corpsman Scheer's sector. They started shooting, apparently at a pillbox that was still giving trouble to craft out at sea. But their aim was not good, and navy shells, too, were now pounding the beach. The "friendly" shelling, together with the Germans' evening barrage, horrified the medics. One man of the detachment, Signalman Logan, stood up in plain sight of the hill above and began signaling with flag Morse out to sea. The destroyers must have read him, for they stopped firing, turned, and went back out to sea. Then, for the first time that day, Corpsman Scheer thought about food. Someone gave him a K ration. He started to tear it open, and then he looked at his hands. They were covered with dried blood.

By 7 p.m. the beach was quiet once more. But what a dreadful scene. The wreckage of the morning had been redoubled by the wreckage wrought in the evening. Burned-out trucks, bulldozers, tanks, jeeps, half-tracks, and piles of what had been supplies littered the whole shore. One man walked along the beach, counting the bodies. In 400 paces he counted 221 dead GIs.

Very late in the evening Lieutenant Downing arrived at the battalion command post. Lieutenant Colonel Williamson and Captain Randall, the battalion operations officer, were sitting on the edge of a slit trench next to a hedgerow. Williamson merely repeated Major Peckham's instructions to take over the A and P platoon. Why all the fuss? Downing shrugged to himself. He had long since given up trying to figure out the motives of higher authority.

It was growing dark, too dark to start the trip back to the field where he had left the men. He dug a slit trench next to the hedgerow, smoked a last cigarette, and went to sleep to the rattle of an occasional burp gun and the thump of a mortar, not too close by.

Over in the St.-Laurent-sur-Mer area the Fifth Corps' advance group had found a German trench and dugout, all shored up with logs. That became the command post for the night. The men settled in. That evening snipers came up to a grove of trees about 200 yards away. The GIs routed them, killed several in the trees, and captured one, wearing a white beret. He turned out to be a she, which did not make a lot of difference. The rule was search and destroy, and a Frenchwoman with a rifle, firing at the GIs, got no more consideration than any other collaborator that day.

29

UTAH BEACH

"If things look black on the beaches, hold on! Do your best to move forward. There will be no turning back. More troops and equipment will follow you. There will be no surrender unless you are wounded and out of ammunition."

Thus spoke General Bradley in his last address to Col. Red Reeder's Twelfth Infantry Regiment before the Normandy invasion.

That was something to think about on the morning of D day, as the invasion fleet approached Utah Beach. Colonel Reeder had read to the troops aboard his LCI the inspirational messages from General Eisenhower and General Montgomery. Now, in the early morning, the Normandy coast was quite visible, and through his field glasses Colonel Reeder could see two church spires. Who was to identify them? Colonel Reeder put down the glasses and moved forward. He joined a small knot of soldiers, and they shared ten-in-one rations.

Suddenly their heads came up, for the naval barrage against "the Far Shore" had begun. The initial assault against Utah Beach was to be made by the Fourth Division's Eighth Infantry. The Twenty-second Infantry would follow, and Colonel Reeder's Twelfth Infantry was to be the reserve.

The landings on Utah were what the British called "a piece of cake." There was no opposition from the Germans on the shore. Twenty-eight of the thirty-two amphibious tanks landed safely. The other four were lost when their LCT hit a mine.

One reason for the easy landings was that the navy put the invading troops down on the wrong beaches, more than a mile from where they were supposed to land. The error caused a little confusion to the company officers, who were trying to figure out the relationship between their maps and the unfamiliar terrain. But General Roosevelt, who was in the first wave, went up a hill, spotted a church steeple, and figured it all out.

Should they try to work their way down the beach to the proper sector? Hell no, said the general. Get moving inland.

And they did. Three nice roads led from the beach across the flooded area of the marshlands. The Second Battalion of the Eighth Infantry took the Pouppeville road. The Third Battalion took the La Houssaye road. The First Battalion took the road to Audoville-la-Hubert.

An hour and a half after the Eighth Infantry had moved inland, the Twenty-second Infantry landed, also without much trouble, and headed inland across the marshes toward St.-Martin-de-Varreville and St.-Germain-de-Varreville. What a contrast to the Omaha Beach landings! Utah was less of a problem than that exercise, Operation Tiger, had been a few weeks before.

On Utah Beach the engineers and demolition parties went to work calmly and without opposition, tearing down Hitler's shore defenses. The entire beach was cleared in an hour. The engineers then blew holes in the seawall for vehicles and cleared the minefields. Their only danger came from intermittent shelling.

Colonel Reeder's Twelfth Infantry landed at H + 4. The men did not expect trouble; Colonel Van Fleet had reported to General Barton that the situation on the beach was "static," which meant no enemy troops. So it looked easy enough. Going in, Colonel Reeder went to the bow of the LCVP in which he was riding. The boat came up on the shore, and he stepped off first, into waist-deep water.

By this time the Germans were beginning to pull themselves together in the area above the beach. Artillery was firing at the landing craft, and one shell struck Reeder's LCVP, killing three men.

As Reeder moved up the beach toward the sand dunes, he realized that something was wrong. He asked Lt. William Mills what it was.

"They landed us 2 miles south of where they were supposed to." And, of course, the navy had done so, with the landing craft coxswains following the route they had used before.

Ashore, and up on the sand dunes that protected the fields from the sea,

Reeder's group encountered General Roosevelt, who confirmed the error and shared Reeder's belief that it did not matter. The thing to do was to get inland.

But by this time the very success of the Utah Beach landing had created its own problems. The vehicles were coming ashore in droves, and they were clogging up the causeways leading inland. The Eighth Infantry's Third Battalion had encountered the Germans at Ste.-Marie-du-Mont, but then moved on to the Les Forges crossroads, where it was joined by the Second Battalion. The First Battalion reached Turqueville.

Thus the Twelfth Infantry faced a traffic jam. Colonel Reeder elected to go inland through the marshes because of the jam-up on the road. The Twelfth Infantry's first objective was St.-Martin-de-Varreville. To reach it that way, they had to wade and swim across the marshes, which had been flooded by the Germans. That meant holding weapons up to keep them battleworthy.

The GIs reached the village and moved on. Then they were held up by a pair of snipers, but went around them. They got involved in a firefight with a German unit on the hedgerow beyond theirs. Reeder called for artillery support, and in a few minutes he got it. This was the neat sort of war that one read about in tactics manuals and history books. There were a few oddities for the newcomers. The German *Nebelwerfer*, the multiple-rocket artillery, had a stupefying effect on an infantryman the first time a handful of rockets came spraying over. "Screaming meemies" was the GI term for them. The 88-millimeter gun was awesome to those who had not been in Africa or Sicily. But the Utah Beach landing was nothing like Omaha Beach that day, nothing at all.

Late on the afternoon of D day Col. Edson Raff, who had now been assigned to the Eighty-second Airborne Division, landed from the sea with a task force of infantry and tanks of the Eighty-second Airborne. These were to reinforce the parachute troops who had landed from the air the night before. They headed in to the Ste.-Mère-Église area. Edson had ninety infantrymen from the 325th Glider Infantry and a company of tanks of the 746th Tank Battalion. They came up with the First Battalion of the Eighth Infantry in the Les Forges area. The men of the Eighth Infantry saw no reason to attack again so late in the day, but Colonel Raff knew that a glider landing was coming in, and he wanted to clear away the area north of Les Forges, where they would land.

Raff attacked. The Germans were stronger than expected, and they had high-velocity antitank guns, which swiftly put three of Raff's tanks out of commission. So, in the failing light, the colonel had to stop the advance.

Meanwhile, Captain Shebeck's 325th Glider Infantry was coming in. Shebeck had gotten sick in north Africa and had spent a considerable amount of time in hospitals in the months since, but now he was fit and serving as assistant S-4 of the regiment. Early on the morning of D day he had headed for the English airfield where the regiment's gliders were waiting. Then he took his place in his glider, along with a staff sergeant who was the regimental transport NCO, a GI who was Shebeck's jeep driver, the jeep itself, and a load of mortar ammunition. The flight personnel were the pilot and his copilot.

Their serial got ready; the C-47 troop transports hooked up to the gliders, and they took off, one after another. Over southern England they rendezvoused with more gliders, and then they headed toward Normandy. As they passed over the towns and villages of southern England, Shebeck looked down to see the people waving at them.

Then they were over the English Channel, and he marveled at the enormous armada of ships below. It gave him a feeling of confidence—he felt that he could almost have walked across the Channel on the ships.

And then Captain Shebeck fell asleep; he dozed most of the way across. His driver, poor soul, was airsick, and spent the air journey lying on the deck of the glider underneath the jeep.

For all those last weeks before the invasion, when Field Marshal Rommel had known the Allies were coming, he had ordered many new defenses, including the placement of *Rommelspargel* (Rommel's asparagus) in the wide, flat fields of the Normandy coast. The fields were small enough and dangerous enough as it was, surrounded by the thick hedgerows that protected the animals from weather and delineated the age-old property boundaries. The *Rommelspargel* too often were wired mines. Fortunately for the Americans, the Germans had not had enough time to do their usual thorough job of preparing all the fields, and most of the ones strewn with such antiglider defenses were in the British sector around Caen. In fact, the whole German defense in the Normandy area was strongest around Caen; it was the capital of Normandy and a port. The Germans knew that the Allies would have to have ports, so Caen's defenses received more German attention than did the beaches farther east.

Captain Shebeck's C-47 pilot found a landing area north of Les Forges, a field that was devoid of *Rommelspargel*. The glider pilot released the tow, and the glider started in. But it was a small field preceded by a steep hedgerow, and the undercarriage of the glider was knocked off on the tops of the trees. The glider lost momentum fast and made a crash landing. But at least it was a crash *landing* and not just a crash, as happened to so many other gliders that day.

Captain Shebeck felt a sharp pain in his lower back, and he thought at first that his back was broken. But it was not, and in a minute he was able to scamper out of the glider with the others.

None of the soldiers were injured, but they were immediately menaced by German fire. The enemy had remained in the area in strength, and Colonel Raff had been unable to do anything about it. Now, as the gliders came in, the Germans opened fire on them with mortars and machine guns.

Captain Shebeck and his crew hauled the jeep out of the glider, hoping it would run. It did. They got in and started for the assembly point, a road junction between Ste.-Mère-Église and Chef-du-Pont.

In all, the landings were very rough and there were many casualties. Some gliders landed under the Germans' noses, and the survivors were immediately captured. Colonel Raff began bringing pilots and others into a defense perimeter, as he prepared to fight the Germans. Captain Shebeck located the service company command post and the regimental supply. Now he had the sad job of picking up the dead from the gliders and placing them on roads and trails where they would be found. His work was with the quartermaster graves registration unit, and it began immediately, on the night of D day.

30

D DAY GOES ON

The confusion of battle was the ambience of D day. Elements of the Fifth Ranger Battalion had landed on Omaha Dog White beach at about 7:30 that morning. One platoon of B Company, commanded by Lt. Matthew Gregory, worked its way inland. In the middle of the day Gregory's unit had run across Colonel Canham, commander of the 116th Regimental Combat Team. The colonel, looking to establish his command post inland, had gotten well ahead of the regiment, most of which was pinned down behind the seawall on the beach. When he was discovered by Lieutenant Gregory's men, the colonel and a handful of staff people were pinned down by the Germans in a hedgerow in what Pfc. Carl F. Weast called "a desperate situation." As senior officer present, the colonel commandeered the services of the Fifth Ranger men, and they joined up, all twenty of them. This gave Colonel Canham about thirty men all told, and with that force he had the responsibility on the night of D day for a front about 1500 yards long. It was not an easy night.

Elsewhere on that difficult Norman beach the Twenty-sixth Infantry of the First Division had come up late in the day, behind the Sixteenth and the Eighteenth, both of which had taken such a beating at the tide line. The beach was still popping as the Twenty-sixth dug in.

Everywhere on Omaha Beach the American soldiers were fast becoming combat-hardened. It didn't take long. Pfc. Curtis W. Miller was a bazooka-man, and he landed with his bazooka stuffed with two cartons of Lucky Strike cigarettes, which could be very useful in parleying with the mademoiselles. But instead of mademoiselles he encountered several guys from the Eighty-second Airborne. When they saw him, they shouted:

"For Chrissake, get down, and stick that goddamn bazooka up your ass. You're just the guy the heinies are looking for."

As for the cigarettes, they were a total loss. Miller had moved in through the lands flooded by the Germans; he stepped into a hole, and down went the bazooka. The cigarettes were soaked.

Pfc. Miller learned fast. For the rest of the day he carried that bazooka by the sling so that it hung just off the ground, and he kept along the hedgerows. Several times during the day other GIs suggested that he abandon the bazooka. He refused. Late in the day, when they had settled down in bivouac, his new friends were glad; a German tank appeared in the field ahead. Bazookaman Miller got out his weapon and began firing. He hit the tank, and the German commander decided that "caution was the better part of valor that evening, and turned the tank around and went away."

All night long, as the GIs slept fitfully in their foxholes and slit trenches on "the Far Shore," the cables hummed and the radio waves crackled with the news of the invasion of Hitler's Fortress Europe. At Fort Bragg Private Adolph and his buddies of the citizen army were delighted. It meant the goal was in sight. Private Adolph figured he would get a discharge in 1946, but if things went better and the Japanese could be finished off not many months after the German defeat, he might be out of the army by the end of 1945.

On the beachheads of Normandy the GIs were in no position to indulge themselves in such long-range thinking. The problem of the moment was to survive another day—and see what the Germans were going to do after the Allied lodgment on the beaches.

So the night passed for the men on Omaha Beach. There were some, like Pfc. Richard Dantini of Company A, 116th Regiment, who waited to be evacuated. Dantini had been in the first wave of the First Battalion, and he was one of the first to get hit. Another was Allen Langdon of Company C, 505th Parachute Infantry Regiment. That outfit had been assigned its objective: a small bridge at La Fiere. Just after the troops reached that point, Langdon was wounded, and he became another candidate for evacuation.

So that night, as the troops lay along the hedgerows and in the foxholes they had scratched out, Richard Dantini waited to begin his journey back to England, his battle nearly ended. Paratrooper Langdon and many others waited with him.

*

On the afternoon of D day, having gotten organized in a small way, Lt. Sumpter Blackmon of the 501st Parachute Infantry took his six men (Thurman Day, Nicholas Denovchik, Jack Bleffer, George Adams, Roy Spivey, and one whose name he could not remember) toward the locks on the Douve River, where they were supposed to be. On the way they passed a deserted German unit headquarters establishment, and they liberated seven bicycles. As the shadows were growing longer, they arrived at the fountain in the middle of Ste.-Marie-du-Mont, and there they felt like tourists—until bullets began ricocheting off the fountain.

In a hurry they headed for Vierville. About 500 yards from their destination they were surprised by a Frenchman who ran out of a hedge beside the road. The Frenchman waved his hands.

"Many, many Boches everywhere," he warned.

Lieutenant Blackmon was tired. The idea of running into "many, many Boches" did not appeal to him. He motioned to the men. They turned their bicycles around and headed back to the area where the Fourth Division was bivouacking.

On the outskirts of Ste.-Marie-du-Mont they came upon a German tank and a number of infantrymen. "We came within a hundred yards of the tank, and saw it getting into position to fire, with a lot of Krauts running around. We did an about-face on our bikes, and nobody even fired at us."

They took a side road that the lieutenant said would lead them to the St.-Côme-du-Mont road. But they never got there. As they passed one big field, they saw gliders coming in and cracking up against the tall poles (*Rommelspargel*) that the Germans had erected there. As the gliders halted, Blackmon's troops rushed over to them and began pulling out men and equipment and orienting the soldiers.

Having stopped for a while, they then decided it was time to seek the Fourth Division again. So they went on down their road and found the headquarters they had been seeking. They met General Barton, who talked with Blackmon about the lieutenant's adventures of the day. Blackmon showed the general on the situation map just where he had been and what he had seen. After that Barton got in touch with Lt. Col. Harry Kinnard, who was at 101st Airborne Division headquarters, and with Colonel Euell, the commander of the Third Battalion of the 501st Parachute Infantry. The three exchanged information. That was how unit commanders and staffs were getting their information that day, in little bits and pieces from the line.

There was no room for Blackmon and his men in the division headquarters house, so they went outside and sat around. After a while they decided to sack out. Having no bedrolls or blankets, they simply lay down on the warm ground and tried to sleep. They had just dozed off when Blackmon felt the patter of rain on his face, so they got up and trudged down the road, looking for shelter. They saw a barn ahead, and they approached it carefully. Inside they found two dead German soldiers. The GIs rolled them out into the rain and then went into the barn and snuggled down in the hay. They all slept very soundly until 3 a.m., when the noises of an army awakened them. So the dogfaces got up and started back along the road they had traversed the day before. At six o'clock they entered Blouseville; there they found Lieutenant Colonel Kinnard and some of the men of the Third Battalion of the 501st Parachute Infantry.

D + 1 was spent reorganizing the First Battalion of the 501st Parachute Infantry. All the battalion headquarters company officers had been killed in action the day before, and so had the commander of B Company. The commanders of A and C companies were both missing in action, and the battalion was down to less than half-strength in enlisted men.

Lt. Col. Harry Kinnard, the regimental executive officer, now became commander of the First Battalion, to the joy of the troops. He was the most popular officer in the regiment. Other officers were moved up, and some sergeants were given commands. By midday the battalion had shaped up once more.

Rifleman Thurman Day and Lieutenant Blackmon commandeered a jeep and went back to the drop zone, where they had hidden a machine gun and ammunition. They found the hardware undisturbed and brought it all back to the battalion by late afternoon. At 6 p.m. they moved into Les Droueries on their way to La Barquette, where Colonel Johnson, the regimental commander, was holding the vital lock. (This had been the original assignment of Lieutenant Blackmon's First Platoon of A Company, but in the confusion of the drop the platoon never had a chance to carry it out.)

Now, although the colonel and a handful of men were holding the lock itself, the German Sixth Parachute Regiment occupied the high ground between Les Droueries and Johnson's troops.

The colonel needed ammunition and supplies, and Lieutenant Blackmon was given the task of getting through the German lines and bringing that material to the beleaguered force. It was also important that a message be given to the colonel, warning him away from the bridge across the Douve

River. Colonel Kinnard knew that these bridges, too, had been assigned as part of the original regimental objective, but the plans had been changed by General Bradley's headquarters. The bridges would be destroyed the following day by navy battleships, using 16-inch guns. If Colonel Johnson and his men were around, they might be blown sky-high.

So Lieutenant Blackmon set off with his supplies and with the message. He took Lieutenant Howard from Headquarters Company, six riflemen, two drivers, and two jeeps with loaded trailers. It was after 3 a.m. of D + 2 when they got started.

Less than a mile from the jump-off point the column encountered rifle and machine gun fire. Lieutenant Blackmon and Sgt. Nick Denovchik were scouting on the left when it happened. They got in touch with Colonel Ballard, the commander of the Second Battalion of the 501st, and he called up the artillery. The regimental artillery was to fire a barrage at 5 a.m., and the Second Battalion was then to attack.

It was then 4:30 a.m. Colonel Ballard told Lieutenant Blackmon it would be suicidal to try to run the road before the barrage and attack. So Blackmon moved his little convoy 200 yards up, to the point where it had received that rifle fire earlier. There the men huddled in the ditches along the sunken road, and waited.

Then came the barrage. It was scary. The first few shells of the 105-millimeter howitzers hit *behind* Blackmon and his men. That did not augur very well for the future. Then came the second round of firing, and shells began falling on the road 15 feet in front of them. Dirt geysers began to erupt all around them, but no one was hit. Then the barrage moved up 200 yards in front and on.

Blackmon and his detail jumped into the jeeps and trailers and moved out along the road. They turned left and circled the wooded hill beyond. Three-quarters of a mile beyond this point the road forked. There were no signs.

Lieutenant Blackmon and rifleman Roy Spivey climbed up on the road bank to see. They were in Adeville. The map showed only one road. While they puzzled over their map, a sharpshooter's bullet caught Spivey's helmet dead center. It went through, parted his hair, and scraped his head enough for a Purple Heart. The slug put a furrow in his scalp 3 inches long, but it did not penetrate his skull. Blackmon sent Spivey back to the jeeps, with orders to head for battalion headquarters and an aid station.

Lieutenant Blackmon ran up the right fork of the road for 50 yards. He came to a curve and rounded it. Twenty-five yards ahead he saw a German tank, maneuvering into position to control the road. He turned around and ran. Back at the jeeps he picked up an 81-millimeter mortar tube and baseplate, and the driver came along with ammunition. Blackmon steadied the tube as the driver fed in the shells, and they laid down a barrage of a dozen rounds. Accuracy was not as important as making a helluva lot of noise and convincing the Germans that a strong force was assembled around that curve.

One shell came down 15 feet away from the mortar, but on the other side of the road, fortunately. But the others went somewhere out in front—perhaps even near enough to that tank to give the crew pause.

All Blackmon wanted to do was create enough confusion to get a start down the left fork of the road that, he hoped, led toward Colonel Johnson. He was not sure if it was the right road, but all he could do was take the chance.

The firing ended. Blackmon picked up the base and the tube and loaded them into the trailer. He looked around. The other jeep and trailer were gone. Lieutenant Howard had taken them back along the road on which they had advanced, assuming that they could not get through. So Lieutenant Blackmon and the driver of his jeep were the only ones left. They got into their jeep. Blackmon got behind the mounted machine gun and told the driver to take the left fork of the road. They started out, the driver leaning over with his head stuck out wheel-high on the left side for maximum protection from fire, and Lieutenant Blackmon spraying machine gun shells in all directions and sometimes into the heavens. He used up one belt of ammunition as the jeep bounced along, turning this way and that. The second belt of ammunition was just running out when they reached the lock. And then from all sides came Germans waving white flags. They thought Lieutenant Blackmon's jeep was the first vehicle in a whole column and that the German position was surrounded.

So the fight for the lock was over, the Americans victorious.

Colonel Johnson asked Lieutenant Blackmon if he had seen Father Sampson, the chaplain. No, said the lieutenant, he and the jeep driver had been traveling about 50 miles an hour as they came. They hadn't seen anybody.

The chaplain had volunteered to remain with a group of wounded at Adeville while the colonel moved on with the able-bodied men to take the lock. All that had happened long ago, on D day. No one knew what had happened to the chaplain and the wounded since. They could be in enemy hands or surrounded.

"Lieutenant," said the jeep driver, "let's go back and get them."

It was, to Blackmon's mind, one of the bravest suggestions he had heard. Since there was no fire coming from that direction just then, Blackmon agreed to make the try. They got two other riflemen to "ride shotgun" on the jeep and an assistant machine gunner to take over if Blackmon was shot out of the vehicle, and they set out for Adeville along that long, long road. They drew fire at only one point, from a house next to the road. Blackmon sprayed the building with machine gun fire, and they moved onward.

In the village they found the house where Father Sampson had the wounded, and somehow they got all of them into the jeep and trailer. Just before they left, three Germans came up with their hands behind their heads. Blackmon told them to come along in the rear of the caravan.

They got back to First Battalion headquarters about 7 a.m. The battalion had been engaged in a firefight with the Germans, and several U.S. tanks had squashed several German soldiers, making a very unpretty mess in the road.

When Blackmon and his detail arrived, Colonel Kinnard immediately assigned the lieutenant the job of getting the bodies out of the way. The burial place allocated was at Blossville. The battalion area had been cleared of all enemy soldiers, but many dead and wounded, including civilians, were lying around. "This was not the most pleasant job in the world, but it was a great education. It showed just how bad it was for infants, 10-year-olds, mothers, and grandparents. There they were, just living in their houses, when suddenly the houses caved in and a tank came through the living room. Or the roof and the rooms below were blown apart by high-explosive shells. Or both at once. But we got used to it in a hurry. We would even hold a hunk of cheese in our teeth as we swung a body onto a truck, and then wipe our hands and go right on eating."

T/5 Tom Wickham of the Twenty-ninth Division's 115th Infantry spent that night of D day in a ditch just beyond the beach huddled around a .30-caliber machine gun with other men of Company A. After dark a German plane flew over their position and dropped a couple of bombs. Now and then machine guns began to fire, then stopped. Some shells from German 88s came into the battalion area. The men were told to prepare for a German counterattack that night, so Wickham kept his M-1 braced on the edge of his hole and stayed awake, waiting nervously.

Daylight came, without a counterattack. Wickham and his buddies moved out around the village of St. Laurent. "Snipers seemed to be everywhere. I heard the pop of rifle bullets and the sound of burp guns. Crossing through a hedgerow and a field, I hit the dirt as mortar shells dropped near. I caught myself falling asleep, shook my head, got to my feet, and ran forward."

On D + 1 men of the 115th encountered some young women. At first the girls seemed friendly, and the future looked promising. But then several of the young women opened fire on the Americans. T/5 Wickham saw his first woman killed in combat, a civilian Frenchwoman, obviously fighting for the Germans, shot down by an American.

Lieutenant Colonel Snetzer of the Second Infantry Division was at sea. He came on deck at 7 a.m. and saw great columns of ships on the horizon on either side of his transport.

"Sea covered with ships. What an armada! Faintly see the coast of France dead ahead. Sky filled with friendly aircraft. Not an enemy plane.

"About 9:00 the ship turned into the wind and dropped anchor about 5 miles offshore. Ships of every nation here, French cruisers, American battleships, British destroyers, and all kinds of small craft.

"Saw a Liberty ship hit a mine.... At about 10:00 saw another Liberty ship burning and smoking fiercely and then slowly sink under the water stern first, bow high up in the air. Saw survivors go by, jammed on every inch of space on a Canadian destroyer. Two air raid alerts but no enemy planes. Landing craft busy unloading big troop transports all around us. Battleships opposite continued intermittent firing against coastal guns."

From the sea, that's how D + 1 looked to the men getting ready to land and reinforce the first waves.

"At 8:30 that night they began loading troops over the side into small boats. One LCT took 233 officers and men off Colonel Snetzer's transport and headed in to shore."

*

Also at sea on D + 1 were two sets of strange objects being towed by service craft; one group of ships headed for the American beach, the other for the British beach. These were the elements of the "Mulberry harbors," artificial harbors that were to take the place of the "big port" that the Germans said the Allies must have to launch their invasion. For many months these had been worked over and assembled in England. They consisted of an artificial quay for the unloading of ships and of a number of "blockships," freighters that would be sunk to form breakwaters to protect the artificial harbors.

Through rough waters and mines that were sinking vessels on either side, the convoys of the Mulberry harbors came toward the French coast. They neared their destination that afternoon of D + 1, and some of the vessels anchored off Utah Beach in the outer area. The next day they would begin sinking the "blockships." At Omaha Beach that morning, Capt. A. Dayton Clark of the U.S. Navy laid out sites for the first six blockships ("Gooseberry II"). Small boats went out to mark the line with buoys. At noon the blockships began to arrive. Captain Clark went aboard the first of them. It was time to begin the scuttlings.

The merchant captain and crew who had sailed the ship across now refused to participate in the dangerous task of sinking it. But Lieutenant Commander Bassett, a New York harbor tugmaster by trade, and Lt. George Hoague sank three of the ships in the right places before dark. Just after they sank the third ship, the Germans seemed to get the idea that those vessels were important, and they began firing. There were some casualties aboard the remaining blockships and on the *Phoenix* (quay), which had just been brought across.

That night the Fifth Corps headquarters landed. General Gerhardt came ashore, too, and took over his Twenty-ninth Division. The brass began totting up the casualties: the First Division had suffered higher losses than on any previous day of battle. The losses of the Twenty-ninth were also very high.

On D + 1 the Second Division arrived and began to move in, much to the relief of the battered forces ashore in France.

*   *   *

At Field Marshal Rommel's headquarters his chief of staff, General Speidel, assessed the situation as of the morning of D + 1:

> The Allies, aided by their naval and air superiority, were able to establish a bridgehead between the Orne and the area north of Ryes fifteen miles broad and up to six miles deep. [The British.] A second bridgehead was established in the southeast corner of the Cotentin Peninsula, nine miles long and two miles deep. [This was the Americans.] ...
>
> The U.S. First Army under General Hodges had landed two airborne divisions and three to four armored divisions on the Cotentin Peninsula.

[How General Bradley wished that had been so.] The German 716th and 353rd divisions held out bravely in their trenches and battle stations under a hail of fire from sea and air and then from land, fire of a previously unknown intensity. A ring of very heavy artillery fire from the Allied navies cut off the battle area from the rest of France. The Allied air forces made some 25,000 sorties during D-Day....

Without having actually experienced the force of the land, sea, and air bombardment one cannot judge its destructive effect on morale; but Hitler would not acknowledge it, in spite of the many oral and written reports he received. He reacted at first with shabby reproaches and suspicious interference with the countermeasures. He cast about for scapegoats and thought of dismissing a number of commanders. Rommel, however, shielded them.

Yes, there was confusion aboard the command vessels at sea, and General Bradley, while expressing confidence to General Eisenhower, was not nearly as confident as he seemed. But, there also was confusion in the enemy camp. The Americans were ashore. They had a toehold. The issue was still in doubt.

Although it did not always seem so, the Allies were doing something right. Field Marshal Rommel's staff thought the British were going to make a dash for Paris. Late in the afternoon of D day Rommel secured from Hitler the release of "Sepp" Dietrich's First SS Panzer Corps, and that night that unit was ordered to the Caen area. But the Allies were attacking so heavily from the air that the German troops could not be moved in daylight, and that meant they could not attack in time. "Waves of bomber attacks on roads and crossroads made all movement impossible," said General Speidel. The defense was hamstrung by Hitler, who was convinced that another landing was coming and would not let Speidel, and later Rommel on his return, use elements of the Fifteenth Army, which could have counterattacked and might have thrown the Allies back into the sea.

*

Of course the men ashore knew nothing of the concerns or actions of the German High Command. All they knew was what they saw, and that they were somehow still alive.

On Utah Beach, where life had been relatively quiet during D day, the early hours of D + 1 found men of the Forty-second Field Artillery Battalion down on the beach, salvaging two jeeps that had gone off into deep water during the day's unloading processes. The jeep crews had been drowned.

Capt. T. A. Bradley, Jr., commander of the Service Battery, was supervising the recovery, and the motor sergeant and his crew were doing the job. It remained very quiet. The troops had secured a large beachhead on the mainland, and the leading elements of the Fourth Division were far ahead, out across the causeways in the Utah Beach area. But the GIs at Omaha Beach had run into serious trouble. And although it was not Bradley's responsibility, by daybreak on D + 1 he also knew that the British had encountered very stiff resistance from armored units at Caen and had barely gotten ashore at all.

Inshore from Utah Beach, Col. Red Reeder's Twelfth Infantry had been stopped at Beauzeville-au-Plain on the evening of D day. He had planned an attack for 5:30 in the morning, but the Germans did not wait. They counterattacked that night at 9:30, drove through the outposts, and were behind hedgerows 200 yards from Reeder's command post.

"Looking at our riflemen, kneeling and firing behind a long, rugged hedgerow, made me think of Lexington and Concord," Reeder said. He radioed the artillery for help, but the Germans were too close to his own positions.

Night flights of gliders had come in over the battle, and the Germans turned their weapons on those troops still in the air. The fight kept on until absolute darkness at 10:30 p.m., and then both sides settled down for the night. Reeder's men were 5 miles inland.

The regimental command post that night and early on the morning of D + 1 was an ancient castle with stone turrets, battlements, and a walled courtyard. Very early on the morning of D + 1 Colonel Reeder felt it was possible to leave the line to visit the command post. As he approached, he saw an old French couple at the top of the stone stairs of the castle.

He looked up, and unlimbered his rusty West Point French.

"*Vive la France*," he shouted.

And the old French couple smiled.

*

Ashore on Omaha Beach the staff of the Fifth Corps had spent a wretched D-day night, out in the open without blankets, huddled in slit trenches. For the dogfaces and the Colonel Reeders trained in the field it was hard enough, but for staff officers, used to tablecloths and soft bunks, it was very tough going.

"The worst night of my life," said Colonel Campbell, the Fifth Corps Provost Marshal. On D + 1 he was up at 6 a.m. and had no breakfast. He walked along the beach to the new POW cage, which was under his jurisdiction. He spent some time there, arranging details with the provost marshal of the First Division. He went inland to see how things were going, and he saw many bodies, German and American, mostly in the ditches on the sides of the roads. How were things going? "Tough" was the answer. He also saw two men ahead of him injured on the road—one of them had stepped on an antipersonnel mine.

Traffic on the beaches and inland was getting jammed up. Colonel Campbell had spent many hours drafting instructions for engineer and supply troops to govern movement on the beaches. Now he went out to see what was happening.

"I was walking up one of the steep roads leading from the beach to the top of the cliff (on which the American Cemetery is now located) when I saw a disabled truck blocking the road so that all traffic had stopped. The driver had driven too close to the edge of the road and part of the truck had gone over the edge. The loaded truck could not move forward or backward."

The colonel had issued orders regarding just such situations.

"I decided I should obey my own order, and I instructed the driver and his helpers to push the truck and its contents all the way over the bank. Probably the only enjoyment these men had all day was watching the truck roll over and over to the bottom of the hill, spilling all its load on the way down."

By midafternoon Colonel Campbell was very hungry. He finally got some food at a chow line, and before night he secured a bedroll; at 8 p.m. he flopped into it, exhausted.

Lieutenant Miller's Twentieth Engineers had moved inland after those bad first six hours on the beach on D day, but on D + 1 they found the going relatively easy. The job was routine. Clear the way for the infantry; find and get rid of the mines. Except for some stops to eliminate or avoid sniper fire, Miller's men were moving right along. That day the lieutenant picked up a big German flag as a souvenir. He also picked up his fourth Bronze Star medal.

*

By the beginning of D + 1 in Sergeant Ogden's area of the Twenty-ninth Division sector a major change had come over the officers and men.

"After one day of combat you are a seasoned soldier."

The biggest change came to the officers. At that time (before Eisenhower put out a new order rectifying the situation) the gap between enlisted men and officers was still very great. Ogden's battalion commander, according to talk, was rough and tough, nicknamed "Thunderbolt." But on D + 1 the dogfaces had a new name for him: "Foxhole Pete." Every time the unit moved, he demanded that a bunker be dug for him, and he retreated into it, not to emerge until the next move.

Several of the lieutenants in the battalion were "snide and mean." In combat they became "shy, quiet, and frightened." "They were afraid of the enemy, and they were also afraid of the enlisted men"—not without some reason. The officers who got on well were the friendly, easygoing officers from barracks days. "In combat these men became the tigers and leaders," according to Sergeant Ogden.

D + 1 was sniper day for Ogden's outfit:

"There was a sniper in a tree about 1000 yards to our left front. No one had a sniper rifle, and he would hide behind the tree trunk when we fired at him. I got behind a .50-caliber machine gun and put it on single shot. I then used my spotter scope to find him. I got him on the third try. It was my second kill of the day."

Ogden recalls that it was also a day for windfalls:

"Normandy was all apple orchards and hard cider that was delicious and powerful. The Calvados came out 120 proof. It worked well in a Zippo lighter. A completely sober GI was hard to find in this area. We also captured a distillery. In the warehouse was enough five-star Hennessey cognac to give four bottles to every man in the Twenty-ninth Division.

"This was after the officers slipped back truckload after load for themselves and to kiss ass with the division brass. Later many medals for bravery were given out to men who couldn't remember why they were getting them."

The men of the Twenty-ninth Division had some strange experiences in those early days. On D + 2 Sergeant Ogden's platoon captured a company of Japanese soldiers! They had been sent to the west in an exchange to teach camouflage to the Germans.

In the early hours after D day few prisoners were taken. But one Twenty-ninth Division GI had a prisoner. He told his captive to double-time. When the German did, the GI shot him in the back and then signaled a nearby tank to finish the job. The tank ran over the prisoner and spun its tracks, grinding one of Hitler's soldiers into the road.

On D + 4 Ogden and his friends had been awake for seventy-two hours. They were exhausted. Ogden was looking for a bush to hide in for a few hours, when he ran across one of his buddies who was on perimeter guard. In front of the guard was a .50-caliber machine gun on a chest-high tripod. He begged Ogden to take over for him for two hours so he could get some sleep. Ogden agreed and took over the gun. Later someone approached. He swung the gun around until it pointed at that someone. It was a major, looking for men asleep on guard. The major walked on.

Ogden squeezed the trigger of the .50-caliber gun. The racket was enormous.

In a few seconds the major was back.

"What did you do that for?"

"I was just making sure, sir, that the gun was in operating condition, sir." The major frowned and moved away.

Actually Ogden was warning anyone on guard who might be asleep that the "cops" were coming. Ogden then looked at his watch. He had been sound asleep for two hours, standing at the gun.

Lieutenant Shebeck of the 325th Glider Infantry found on D + 1 that his job in regimental supply was virtually nonexistent just then. Instead, he was working with the graves registration units.

"A temporary cemetery was established in the area of Montebourg-Valognes, a few miles north of Ste.-Mère-Église. I supervised the movement of bodies to this cemetery, both German and American. There they were separated and sent to different burial grounds."

Lieutenant Shebeck supervised the pickup of the bodies:

"Many of the bodies were virtually unrecognizable and pieces of bodies such as arms or legs were not unusual. As an example, we approached the area of a still-burning tank and found the remains of an individual—nothing but a mass of intestines and a few remnants by which you could recognize that this had been a human being. Two of my men were able to sweep this mess into a mattress cover, but a third became ill and pleaded to get off the detail. Later in the day I was able to replace him with someone else....I was standing by the truck while German POWs were unloading bodies into one of the cemeteries. The truck had stopped beside what looked like a small, charred black stump. I suddenly realized that this was not a tree stump, but the burned torso of a human being."

*   *   *

At sea D + 1 began off Omaha with shelling of the German positions. Seaman Edward B. Nagel, aboard the USS *Achernar* (command ship for the First
Army and Ninth Army Air Force), lost his helmet when the battleship *Arkansas*, next door, began firing her 16-inch guns. Then, an hour later, the
ships were attacked by German aircraft. One bomb fell off the starboard quarter of the *Achernar*, about 200 yards out, and another off the port bow, 300
yards away. "I can still feel the hot spray of the water."

More ships were coming in with more troops. S. Sgt. Henry Kraft's Fifteenth Field Artillery landed that morning as part of the Second Division.
The Germans had the beach zeroed in by that time and were delivering shells
from the 88s with alarming frequency. Kraft's platoon landed and he hurried
the men along off the beach and up the long hill that led inland. They were
moving on St.-Laurent-sur-Mer. Snipers were the problem for them once they
got up the hill: "The Germans were leaving behind many snipers. It was so
bad that after a while one got tired of ducking."

Kraft's outfit also confronted heavier weapons that day. From the attic of
a farmhouse someone was operating a machine gun, which was causing many
casualties. The soldiers advanced, throwing grenades. One went right through
the window where the machine gun was located. The shooting stopped. The
Americans entered the house. Up in the attic they found the gun on its side,
and the body of a 13-year-old French girl beside it.

The Second Division troops passed through the Fifth Corps command
post and went on. In the POW pen there was a woman in a white beret, a
French Nazi sympathizer who had been caught firing at American troops. S.
Sgt. J. J. P. Corrigan saw her while he was performing his duties in Colonel
Campbell's provost marshal command. That day two newspapermen came
through the Fifth Corps, Ernie Pyle of the Scripps-Howard Newspaper Al-
liance and Jack Thompson of the *Chicago Tribune*. The command post was
still in that captured German trench just off the beach.

Seaman Leo Scheer of the navy's Seventh Beach Battalion was rudely awakened on Omaha Beach on the morning of D + 1 when a shell landed so
close to his slit trench that the sand of the trench edge came pouring down
on his face. "As I came awake, I had the goofy feeling that a cat was licking
my face." He brushed himself off and was glad it was morning, and that he
was alive.

From the beach he could hear the sound of the artillery inland, and it
seemed to be increasing.

That morning casualties came down from the hill, and Scheer and the other medics took care of them. But they still had no way of getting the wounded off the beach; no landing craft were coming in there after the Second Division landings. The medics were still short of supplies, and they continued to wander among the dead, removing their canteens of water and the bandage that every man carried. Scheer found a pair of wire cutters and went to cut the barbed wire along the road up the hill. That way the medics could place the wounded men next to the wall for more protection. There he saw a small wire running from a post into the ground.

"I pulled the grass aside and there was a Teller mine, about 1 foot in diameter." He marked it and warned everyone about it, and went on, knowing what a close escape he had just had.

Someone said that there were three wounded men just inside a hole in the wall, a little way down the road. Medic Scheer went to the place and crawled into the hole. Two of the men were dead, but the third was alive. They had been hit by machine gun fire while crawling through the hole early on D day, and the live soldier had been lying there ever since, more than twenty-four hours. What to do? The soldier was hit in the hip and lower leg, and he could not be moved without a stretcher. But there were no stretchers. So Scheer bandaged him up and left him. "I hated to leave him there, isolated, but it was the best we could do."

Scheer took the road back toward the beach. He sat down for a rest. Along came a ranger limping down the road. He sat, too, and asked if Medic Scheer could help him.

"What's wrong?"

The ranger pointed to his foot. He had a bullet hole on both sides, just between the toes and ankle.

"Let's take off the boot."

"No. To hell with that. If we take it off, I won't be able to walk."

And then the ranger got up and limped away down the road.

Another soldier came up and asked Scheer for something for a headache.

"Why? What's wrong with you?"

The soldier took off his helmet. There was a hole in the helmet. A slug had gone in, spun around inside the helmet, and dropped out. The soldier did not have a scratch, but he had "one sore head and neck."

By midmorning there still weren't any landing craft in Medic Scheer's sector that could be used to evacuate the wounded. When a British-manned LCM showed up and landed some vehicles, Scheer went aboard and asked the naval officer commanding to stick around and take off some wounded. He got no answer, but he moved some wounded down to the beach. Then the German 88s began shelling in the area again, and the LCM captain pulled up his ramp and backed off the shore.

Scheer was so angry he ran out cursing and picked up some rocks and threw them at his gallant ally. "I hoped a German shell would get them, but it didn't."

The shelling increased as the afternoon wore on, and Scheer began "practicing name, rank, and serial number" just in case the Germans were on the way. But they were not. The First and Twenty-ninth divisions' troops inland, backed now by the Second Division, were containing the counterattack. The shelling continued. Scheer's buddy Tony Campanella was bending over, treating a wounded man, when a shell hit about 200 yards away. They were showered by debris. Then Campanella put his hand back to his bottom, and it came away covered with blood.

Campanella got a Purple Heart for that, and the worst razzing of his life. "You," said one wag, "have got to have the biggest butt on the beach."

By this time, late afternoon of D + 1, the men on the beach could relax a little. They were getting used to the war. They walked around, gauging the coming of the shells. When sounds were far off, no one worried. When the sound began to pierce, they got down.

But there was bad news that afternoon on the beach at Omaha. Still there were no evacuation facilities for the wounded. Men who had been hit early on D day were still on the beach. The wounded soldier in the hole in the wall, with his two dead companions, was still waiting in the hole in the wall. Scheer went around that evening, telling the men they would have to spend one more night on the beach. He got cursed by several men, but not by the man in the hole. "Okay," the soldier said. "If that's the way it is."

One of the men on the beach was Pfc. Richard Dantini of the 116th Infantry, who had been wounded in both legs during the landing. Two guys from the 116th came by the place where he was lying against the wall and stopped to see if he was still alive. They had half a dozen German POWs in tow. One of the Americans offered Dantini his submachine gun to "get even"— to shoot the prisoners. Dantini said no. He lay on the beach all day, and got the word that it would be D + 2 before any help would arrive.

*

After a very tough D day, the men of Company B of the First Battalion of the 115th Infantry had some good news. They were dug in on the edge of the woods at the top of the hill above the beach. Around midnight word came to pack up; they were going back down to the beach to be pulled out. The battalion had suffered so many casualties in the landings that the brass had decided it was totally disorganized and useless.

But the pullout never came. D + 1 found the men still there in their foxholes on the edge of the woods. What was left of B Company was reorganized. Private Globuschutz's platoon sergeant, who had been missing during the day, rejoined them, as did some other NCOs. So they got going again. It was not easy. Snipers were all around them, and the roads and fields were mined. There was no water, and Globuschutz had drained his canteen before noon on D day, at the top of the hill above Omaha Beach. There was no water at all for him on D + 1. He could remember crossing a river, which took the company all afternoon. After that, all he could remember was that he was weary, weary, weary, and terribly thirsty.

Sergeant Moglia's company of the 116th had also taken a serious beating in the D-day fighting, which continued until 1 a.m. on D + 1, when enemy resistance ended at Colleville.

D + 1 was more of the same, heavy hedgerow fighting. Moglia was lying in a ditch during one firefight, and about 5 feet ahead of him was a life-size crucifix on a pole. He wondered what Christ was thinking about as he looked down. All Moglia knew was that he would have liked to have been wherever that crucifix had been made, with peace and quiet around him. "All of us figured that God was on our side," he said.

There in the ditch, one of his men crawled up and offered him a cold drink of clear liquid from his canteen cup. Moglia took a drink. Suddenly he was gasping for air. His throat hurt and his stomach was turning over. That was his introduction to Calvados, the fiery apple brandy of Normandy.

That evening of D + 1 a German patrol crossed in front of the position of Moglia's unit, and a firefight developed. When things quieted down, he heard a voice crying out for help.

The cry came again. The squad leader said all the men of the squad were present and accounted for. Was it a trap, or a soldier in trouble?

Moglia organized a patrol from his platoon. Three men moved forward on his right and three on his left. He stayed in the center, talking to the mystery voice.

"Help me, please help me."

"Who are you?...Where are you?"

Slowly the patrol moved forward. It was drizzling again. Suddenly the man spoke.

"Please help me for I am *vounded*."

It was a lousy Kraut!

Moglia saw him. The German soldier was lying in the ditch beside the road, his hands stretched out as high above his head as he could do. The cover patrol reached the man just as Moglia did. They laid him on the road. The German was petrified with fear. Seven rifles were pointed at him.

"Please notify my family that I died bravely as a good German soldier should," he gasped.

Desperately, he offered Moglia his food, a piece of dry bread and cheese and an onion. He offered a small cheap camera.

He told Moglia that he was surprised to see the Americans because this was the British sector. He blurted out his unit identification, regiment, division, and corps. He was a member of a patrol, most of whom were wounded or killed. The patrol had been withdrawn, but he could not move. His left knee had been shattered by a bullet from an M-1 rifle.

He gave up his rifle and several grenades. He gave Moglia the name of his sister and his family's address.

Using the German rifle, Moglia made a splint for the German's leg and used his own first aid kit to patch the man up.

"Why are you treating my leg if you are going to kill me?" the German asked. "Are you doctor?"

Moglia said yes, he was a doctor.

The German saw that he was not going to be killed. He began to cry and shook hands with Moglia.

After a while two medics came up and took the German to the rear.

The next day Moglia's battalion S-2 reported that the German would give only name, rank, and serial number when he was taken back. "Was this the same man?" he asked.

Moglia supplied the information. What a difference it made when a man found death staring him in the face and then saw the specter turn away.

*

The Second Engineer Combat Battalion also had come in to Omaha at H hour on D day. Sixty-nine men and one officer had been assigned to come in to blast away the shore obstacles. They spent that night on the beach. On D + 1 the rest of the battalion came ashore. Its objective was Trevieres—a town turned into rubble in the fighting—but the battalion came in at Vierville.

The fighting increased again, and before the men got to the job of engineering, they were used as infantry to help stem the German counterattack. They also mined the road back from the front to the Omaha beachhead, just in case the enemy broke through. These were desperate hours, and still no one knew quite what was going to happen.

Sgt. Edward Elburn of the 115th Medics was in an area where at least there were incoming landing craft to move the wounded off the beach. On D day afternoon they had been bombed by American planes and suffered heavy casualties. That was no help. By nightfall they had found themselves still in sight of the Channel. Their worst worry that night had been German planes overhead, mostly because American ships were firing at them. The shells came down too close to the troops for comfort. There was no sleep that night of D day for Sergeant Elburn and his pals. They were cold, scared, and exhausted, still trying to evacuate their wounded, but without trucks or ambulances, and with very few jeeps.

D + 1 brought more of the same. Still no vehicles. The wounded were moved back by litter, all by hand. All day long it was move and dig, fight, move and dig.

Lieutenant Downing had smoked his last cigarette that night of D day, contemplating the noises made by a group of Germans surrounded in a patch of woods in the field bounded by the road and the hedgerows occupied by his battalion. He lay in his slit trench, listening to the sound of burp guns firing into his battalion area, as the Germans sneaked up to the edge of the hedgerows and poked their weapons over. Once in a while an American outpost guard would see movement and fire back with his M-1, but usually the Germans were concealed by the darkness. At least, Downing thought, it was good that the Germans and the Americans were right on top of one another, because there was no artillery or mortar fire.

Downing slept fitfully; after a couple of hours German planes came over to bomb the beach, and he could see the red streaks of tracer bullets in the sky above the shore.

Then it was dawn, D + 1. Lieutenant Downing sat up and took off his boots and socks. He lit a paraffin fire under a can of pea soup and wrapped his socks around the can as it heated to dry them a little. Then he drank the can of soup, put his socks and boots on, still wet, and set out down the road on reconnaissance.

Captain Spinney had brought up the company during the night. Lieutenant Fanning of the antitank platoon had brought up some half-tracks and guns. Downing borrowed a half-track from him and, with a driver, headed for the beach to pick up ammunition. They drove down the road. They passed those two dead Americans, the kneeler and the other, still in position. Nobody had been near them.

Above the beach Downing saw a tent hospital that had been erected. That was progress. Ambulances were arriving and departing. Beside one large ward tent bodies were stacked up in their white mattress covers, awaiting burial.

A little further along the road, above the beach, they came to an ammunition dump. More progress. The driver turned in to the dump, and they loaded the half-track with rifle, machine gun, and mortar ammunition. The NCO in charge let them have what they needed.

The half-track turned around and headed back to the battalion area, again passing the two dead American soldiers. They now looked different, coated with a fine white dust scattered by the vehicles that sped along the road.

Lieutenant Downing and the driver returned to the battalion area and dropped the ammunition off in a field. He notified the rifle companies of its location. Then he went on foot to the battalion command post.

While trudging along, Downing heard the sound of sustained rifle fire. A firefight. As he approached the command post, he saw the riflemen strung out, firing over the hedgerows at a patch of woods. The fire was being returned by the Germans, and bullets cracked through the trees. An antitank platoon half-track came lumbering up the road and stopped. Private Iorio, the gunner, turned the .50-caliber machine gun toward the woods where the Germans were and let go with an entire belt. The heavy slugs ripped right through small trees. His firing produced good results. Several Germans came walking out of the woods with their hands up. Iorio stopped firing.

Several riflemen jumped up to go out and meet the prisoners, but their noncoms shouted at them to stop:

"Let the prisoners come to you, and then you aren't about to get killed."

Other Germans saw that these first prisoners were not being killed, and more began to run out of the woods. A few wounded came limping out, helped by their friends. As the Germans climbed through the hedgerow, they were searched for weapons and grenades.

Downing saw one German come over the hedge with his pistol and holster still on his belt. Downing made a grab for the German, but someone else got there first and snapped up the souvenir. It was Lieutenant Koenig of E Company.

The prisoners were rounded up just as another group came down the road, led by Sergeant Stanley of F Company. The two groups were sent to the rear under a guard from the A and P platoon.

Then a new advance was ordered by battalion. The men of the battalion headed south and east. Downing was in charge of a mixed group of head-quarters men.

For a while the progress was steady. The battalion was well organized by this time, most of the lost boat groups having shown up during the night. The troops passed French farms and scattered houses. The French people stood and looked at them as they went by, their faces totally impassive, as if the Americans were beings from another world.

Then opposition developed. Lieutenant Downing heard the annoying "blurp—blurp—" of the German machine pistols. He ordered his men to hit the dirt.

The riflemen ahead began to advance. Downing knew that it was not a good idea to stay there and lose contact with the rifle companies ahead, but the headquarters men showed no eagerness to advance.

"Let's go," he shouted.

Nobody moved. The men pretended not to hear.

"To hell with you," Lieutenant Downing shouted. He started forward on reconnaissance.

Private Robinson, who in garrison had been one of the "problem guys," volunteered to go along.

They found no opposition. When they arrived at a hillcrest overlooking a stream, and beyond that the gray stone buildings of a small town, Downing sent Robinson back to bring up the company. They had reached the Aure River.

Downing and his men then deployed through the woods and across a field toward a causeway that crossed the river. As they were on the edge of the causeway, along came a group of American tanks, roaring down the road. As always the tanks drew enemy artillery fire, and Downing cursed them for causing a lot of trouble. He ran headlong across the causeway and took shelter behind a stone house at the end.

With relief he watched as the tanks roared across and through the town. No more fire. Downing's men began to cross and come up to him. Then a jeep arrived and screeched to a stop. It carried mail!

Downing got the headquarters company's bag and sorted out the letters by platoons.

More jeeps came up and stopped. Soldiers were firing at something in the town. One came up to Downing and said there was a sniper in the church steeple up the street. A jeep driver asked if he could fire his .50-caliber machine gun at the steeple.

"Sure, go ahead," said Downing. He watched as the driver began firing. The church had a row of curtained windows just under the eaves of the roof. The jeep driver fired the .50-caliber gun and shattered every window.

There was no more action from the church.

The battalion medical detachment arrived and set up an aid station at a gray stone house. An ambulance jeep went forward and soon returned fully loaded.

Lieutenant Malenski of Company G had been hit in the foot. After he was bandaged up, he sat waiting for an ambulance to take him back to the beach.

A tank lieutenant was taken off on a stretcher. All his hair had been burned off, and he was black from head to waist. But he didn't seem too badly injured; he kept up a stream of conversation and smoked a cigarette as he told his story:

He had run his tank up against a hedgerow, and the muzzle of the tank's gun had filled up with dirt. When he had fired the gun at the enemy, a flashback had burned him and set fire to the tank. He had jumped out, and the Germans shot him in the thigh.

Lieutenant Downing's men finally assembled. K rations came up by jeep. A runner came back from battalion to announce that the CP had been set up on the outskirts of town and that Downing was to bring the company forward.

So he set out with his men on both sides of the road in single file. They passed through the town, following the runner. They saw a sergeant from G Company kneeling beside the road; he had been shot in the chest. They went on to a lone house and went through the gate and behind the building. There they found an apple orchard surrounded by a hedgerow. An air raid shelter built for the occupants of the house was now the battalion command post. Downing put his men around the perimeter of the orchard, and he sat down under a tree with Captain Spinney to eat a K ration. They were on the main highway. To the east was Mosles, which was occupied by F Company. The fighting was still in progress. Bullets zipped through the trees overhead.

It was late afternoon. Strays began coming into the perimeter: engineers, ordnancemen, and signal corps men who had gotten separated from their organizations. They dug slit trenches and settled down for the night.

Two trucks drove in and parked. It was quiet for a while.

Then Lieutenant Colonel Williamson called Lieutenant Downing and told him a strong German patrol had been seen in the neighborhood of G Company. Downing was to alert the CP area for attack.

Downing checked his perimeter defenses and warned the men. He ordered the service troops who had wandered in to man their share of the perimeter. Some of them began to grouse because they had already dug their holes. But when he told them about the German patrol, they stopped complaining.

Downing set up a schedule: half the men alert for half the night, then the other half. He and Captain Spinney dug their ditch next to the hedgerow. Downing took the small gas cover out of his gas mask and crawled into it. It was airtight and would protect him from the cold. It did, all right. The airtightness caused all the moisture from his body to condense, and he got wet.

That night the navy and the air forces put on a show again. The navy guns boomed, their swishing shells passing overhead and up front. When the Allied aircraft went home, the Germans took over, bombing and strafing the beach. The Germans also began firing mortars, and two shells landed in the rear part of Downing's orchard. A soldier came limping up, holding his hand to his hip, heading for the aid station. He was moaning.

When the shelling stopped, they all settled down to get a little sleep. Then someone woke Downing to take his turn at guard duty, and he spent the rest of the night prowling around, making plenty of noise so that the trigger-happy GIs wouldn't shoot him.

Finally it was morning, and he was reaching for a K ration for breakfast.

By that time General Bradley had visited the Fifth Corps command post in its ditch behind the hedgerow on the exit from Easy Red beach, had gone on to the First Division command post up front, and had also paid a visit to General Collins on Utah Beach. Bradley had conferred with General Montgomery, who was urging a quick linkup of American and British forces along the beach. And he had spoken with General Eisenhower, who had come to the USS *Augusta* for a worried look, because he had not received any information from Bradley since the invasion began. (The problem turned out to be a delay in decoding messages at SHAEF.)

There was still danger. The Americans did not have enough supplies ashore, and communications with the beach were still spotty. But General Bradley was now hopeful. Most of the worries of the past two days were over. The Germans had not released the Fifteenth Army from the Pas de Calais area, the army that could indeed push the Allies back into the sea. Hitler was still talking about the second invasion to come, gulled by the disinformation campaign of the past few weeks.

There was a lot to be thankful for and to hope for at Allied headquarters. D + 2 had begun.

31

SECURING THE
BRIDGEHEAD

On the morning of D + 2 Lieutenant Downing opened a K ration for his breakfast. He used a wax heating unit to make a cup of coffee. Luxury. It did not look like the company would move right away, so he heated water in his canteen cup for shaving. More luxury. He had a three-day growth of beard and it itched.

There was time for some housecleaning. He checked his assault jacket pockets and found a stick of TNT and a fuse, but they had gotten wet. Over the hedgerow they went. Most of his cigarettes had gotten wet, too. They followed the TNT.

There was time to kill. Some prisoners had been brought to the farmhouse nearby and were given C rations. They were being interrogated by an American captain, and Downing and Captain Spinney wandered over to watch.

The American captain might have been a German officer. He spoke fluent German, and he had a very domineering attitude.

"He would point to a man and ask the German prisoner where other German soldiers were located. If he received no definite answer, he would try to pin the prisoner down by pointing out terrain features. If he still didn't get a satisfactory answer, he would stand the German to attention, bawl him out, and again point to the map. The German would finally point to a spot, and the captain would send him back to the others."

Downing and Captain Spinney came away smiling. It looked as if the officer scared the prisoners so much they would give him any answer at all to be let off the hook. They hoped the battalion wouldn't have to rely on the information accumulated by this captain.

Replacements arrived, were sorted out, and were sent to the rifle companies. One was a short, mustached soldier in helmet and raincoat, wearing a .45-caliber pistol on a web belt. He turned out to be a major who had been assigned to replace the casualty, Major Peckham. He was the new executive officer, a tribute to the nonsense of the army replacement system.

Downing snorted: "The promotion of any of the company commanders would have been a far better and simpler solution all around. A battalion executive officer, the potential battalion commander, with no combat experience, and who couldn't even recognize the company commanders, much less the other officers, was not exactly an asset to the organization."

D + 2, then, was a day of reorganization for the Eighteenth Infantry. Lieutenant Downing went back to the beach and found the battalion motor pool. Most of the vehicles had come ashore all right. A few drivers were missing. He would have to carry them on the "missing in action" column of the morning report until he could get definite information—if ever.

Late that afternoon the regiment moved toward Mosles. Headquarters Company was behind a rifle company. The column stopped, and the firing grew loud. Downing lay down in the ditch. Two tanks came clanking by, led by an officer in a jeep. The company moved again, this time into Mosles.

As darkness hovered over the troops, a German plane came over and strafed. If the pilot had come down the axis of the road, he would have done great damage, but instead he crossed over, made two passes, and went away.

The firing grew heavy again, and the heavy weapons company took its weapons off the jeeps and set up in the fields on the sides of the road. Lieutenant Downing led his Headquarters Company into a field on the right, and he told the men to get down into the ditch and stay there. They stayed the night.

D + 3 was almost the same, with the regiment advancing slowly inland. Downing took a wrong turn at a fork in the road and got lost. But by morning the company was back where it was supposed to be.

On D + 4 the men were collecting souvenirs. A group of prisoners came in, including one very military noncom who wore the Iron Cross, the German Combat Badge, and other decorations. Captain Linde, the artillery liaison officer, eyed the Iron Cross and stopped the prisoners. He began taking the German noncom's medals. The German began to cry. An interpreter came up. The prisoner said he would gladly give up his medals, but he did not want them stripped off him. Captain Linde paid no attention; he stripped off the medals and then told the guard to march the prisoners off.

For once there was no difficulty in getting soldiers to do what seemed to be an onerous bit of duty, guarding prisoners on their way to the cage down by the beach. That afternoon Downing learned why. He saw one of his men who had volunteered to guard prisoners. The soldier had wristwatches on each wrist and his dog tag chain was festooned with finger rings.

That same afternoon Lieutenant Downing had the first indication that he and his men were winning the war. Moving down a country lane, the column passed a woman and two young girls. Their hands were full of flowers. One of the girls stopped and stuck a flower in Downing's jacket. They passed on down the line, putting flowers on everyone and kissing some of the men. Downing did not get kissed:

"I felt cheated. I wondered if I had body odor, denture breath, or stringy hair."

The Eighteenth Infantry arrived at Planquery on D + 4. The next day the column advanced along a road and finally entered a large, thick forest. On D + 6 the infantry was still on the move. Lieutenant Downing did not feel so good about that: it was hot.

"The continual moving forward, mostly by foot, the broken sleep and the monotonous diet of cold rations were beginning to make themselves felt. The antigas shoe impregnant I had put on my shoes had made them airtight and now I had blisters on each foot. My impregnated socks also helped to keep my feet sore and tender. The chemically impregnated ODs had become black and greasy looking and smelled of chemicals and sweat. The heavy canvas assault jacket weighed me down, and I longed for a chance to discard it and return to my musette bag, which I could throw in a jeep during the hikes. The men also wanted to get back to their light packs and ditch some of the assault clothing and equipment. We hiked on, stopping for the regular hourly breaks of ten minutes and stretching them out a little. Everyone was beginning to get worn out."

At the end of the first week the Eighteenth was near Caumont, where the Twenty-sixth Infantry was attacking. Here Downing's battalion settled down on a farm near a farmhouse. Captain Spinney, who went to battalion for information, came back to announce that Downing and his men would be there a few days. But the few days became a month. The Allied advance had bogged down.

*

By D + 6 General Bradley was feeling much more secure. The troops of the 101st Airborne Division had circled Carentan and had driven in to open the main road between Omaha and Utah beaches. The artificial Mulberry harbor at Omaha Beach had become the major port of liberated Europe. General Bradley's eyes were now on Cherbourg, the big French port. But the First Division had gone into defensive positions at Caumont, 20 miles south of the coast. This was the point of deepest penetration of the Allied bridgehead; it was also a point of weakness, for it was where the British and American armies joined. The British had advanced only half as far as the U.S. First Division, leaving a long open American left flank. All this meant that Lieutenant Downing's battalion was way, way out on a limb.

In one way, Lieutenant Downing and General Bradley were in the same boat. They both got clean clothes for the first time on D + 6. There was, however, a slight difference.

General Bradley's clean clothes had come from dry quarters on the USS *Augusta* on the night before he was to meet General George C. Marshall, the U.S. Army chief of staff, who was coming to inspect the results of the invasion.

Lieutenant Downing's clean clothes came up by jeep from the beach, and he felt very lucky to get them.

On the night of D + 5 it had rained in the Caumont forest and Downing's blanket had been soaked. He had sought shelter, along with men of the company, in the attic of the farmhouse. Down below in the carriage shed the medics had set up an aid station.

On D + 6 Lieutenant Pavlak brought up ten-in-one rations. These came in cardboard cartons: meat, vegetables, dessert, coffee, cigarettes, evaporated milk, sugar, biscuits, matches, and toilet paper.

Pavlak also brought up a few officers' bedrolls that he had found on the beach. But these had been looted by the service troops. The roll of the battalion commander, Lieutenant Colonel Williamson, was missing entirely. Captain Murphy's roll had been opened, all his belongings stolen, and the roll stuffed with dirty cast-off clothing. The enlisted men were finding the same thing. The beach service troops were looting again, finding anything of value that they could sell or use. In a few hours General Huebner heard about it, and the MPs were sent down to deal with the service troops. The bedrolls were put under guard.

Now the rolls began to come up in quantity. Lieutenant Downing found his bedroll, which was saved by the guards, and got clean ODs and clean underwear. He also took out his musette bag and canvas suspenders and turned in his assault jacket for salvage. ("I had had enough of that corset.") The kitchen truck and kitchen personnel arrived, and the battalion began to get hot meals. The men got daily mail deliveries, and copies of *Stars and Stripes* newspaper.

("This was sure a different war from the Mediterranean.")

Not far from Lieutenant Downing's farmhouse was the camp of Lieutenant Miller's Twentieth Engineer Combat Regiment. Miller's outfit had come up through Colleville, through St.-Honorine-des-Pertes, Les Marais, Mosles, and Balleroy to the Caumont area. The engineers had cleared mines, hunted down snipers, improved the roads for vehicle traffic, and fought as infantry on the flank of Downing's Eighteenth Infantry. So far ten men in the regiment had been killed and 172 were wounded. Miller and his men lived in an apple orchard near Castillon, with a large road sector to work on. In their spare time they played cards and they drank cider, hard cider, harder cider, and Calvados.

Lieutenant Miller recorded their progress in his diary:

"*June 9:* Went out in jeep with Sergeant Balsamo to post signs along roads cleared yesterday. Found tank with tread blown by Teller mine and cleared field for him to pull off into. Found a German CP and picked up souvenirs. Found five Teller mines.

"*June 10:* Company moved to Tour-en-Bessin. Had to bury dead in bivouac area with bulldozer.

"*June 11:* Reconnoitered roads to Campigny with Sergeant Evans. Negative. Company moved to La Roche in evening. Two Jerries flew over the area just after we arrived. First night without air raid.

"*June 12:* Worked on widening road to Subles. Ate first fresh egg in France.

"*June 13:* In evening entire battalion took up defensive position on exposed flank of First Division. Our mission was to ward off any mechanized or infantry attack until Second Division could come up on line with First Division."

(The reason: On the evening of June 12 General Bradley learned that the Germans would attack against Carentan the next day. Bradley took every action possible. Among other things, he sent the tanks of the Second Armored Division to Carentan. This took them away from the Fifth Corps area and left General Gerow in a tizzy. He feared that the Germans might be using a ploy and that the real attack would be against his exposed salient in the Caumont area. But it was not, as it turned out.)

*

Lieutenant Colonel Snetzer's Second Engineer Battalion landed in Normandy on D + 3 after several antiaircraft barrages had shot down at least one German plane. Two LCTs had come alongside the ship at 6:30 in the morning. Then more kept coming. Snetzer left the ship at about 11 a.m. and came ashore at 12:30. It was high tide. He saw a beach littered with the wreckage of trucks, tanks, personal equipment, and landing craft. Everything seemed to be smashed up. Bodies were still lying where they had fallen three days earlier. Inland the ditches along the road were strewn with the bodies of soldiers wearing the blue and gray yin-yang patch of the Twenty-ninth Division. Fighting was still hard not a thousand yards from the beach. The Second Division was now heavily engaged.

Three days later the Second Engineers were ready to go. On June 15, D + 9, they suffered their first casualties. Captain Pettit was shot in the legs by a machine gun as he was trying to place a minefield out in front of the enemy. He was evacuated to England. Two men were also hurt, and one was killed.

The infantry, Colonel Snetzer noted, was taking very heavy casualties. The Second Division had lost four lieutenant colonels in four days, all killed.

On June 16 the Second Engineers were alerted at 6 p.m. to move up to the Thirty-eighth Infantry area and fight as infantry to relieve the Third Battalion, which had been decimated in that day's attack.

At 2 a.m. on June 17 A Company had arrived on the line. The other companies also came up. At dawn they made contact. At 3:45 the engineers attacked up Hill 192, about 12,000 yards southwest of St.-George-de-Elle, and retook the line held by the infantry the day before. A Company suffered some casualties—fourteen men killed, three officers wounded. Twenty-nine men were wounded in B and C companies.

On June 18 the Second Engineers were still fighting as infantry, holding the line. More counterattacks and more shelling.

"This infantry work is really rough, hard, dirty, and deadly," said Colonel Snetzer. "Thank God we don't have to do this every day for a living. It is a hell of an existence, lying in a slit trench trying to save your hide."

"*June 19:* Continued to hold positions. Miserable cold rain all day. Wet and muddy everywhere. No blankets. No raincoats. Just mud. C Company detached from battalion and placed directly under division to place roadblocks at 6 p.m.

"*June 20:* Received heavy mortar fire on A Company. Lieutenants Lepper and Wright killed. Freddy seriously wounded and evacuated to England. Sixteen other casualties in the company.

"*June 21:* More of the same. Rain, mud, cold, mortar fire, and more casualties.

"*June 23:* Captain Huthnance killed by mortar fire at 1:30 this morning on Hill 192. One other man killed too. And battalion headquarters relieved from attachment to Thirty-eighth Infantry yesterday and moved to the vicinity of crossroads at Haute Litte in the Forest de Cerisy. B Company still acting as infantry."

The Thirty-eighth Infantry was having its troubles. The division was on the same line. It was opposed by elements of the German Third Parachute Infantry Division.

"Really giving us hell. No advance has been made for a week. The Thirty-eighth got a new commanding officer, Colonel Zwicker. He was the fourth since the regiment went into combat. The other three were all relieved, one after the other, for failure to move the regiment."

The engineers went back to engineering duty as Cherbourg was captured.

The regiment was still stuck at Hill 192.

In the Twenty-ninth Division sector the fighting was heavy. Ahead of the troops was the hill they called Hill 88, which was full of German 88-millimeter guns and "screaming meemies," the German multirockets.

A week after D day Sergeant Ogden spotted two companies of cavalry approaching his unit. The horses were all coal black and the leather gear was black, too. The riders were Russian cossacks, wearing black boots and trousers and cream-colored cossack coats that came down to midthigh, with the traditional bullet pockets on the breast. They wore wide black belts with swastika-emblazoned silver buckles, and they carried long cavalry sabers. Each man wore a long black cape with a bright-red lining, and each had a black Persian lamb hat, the top of which was bright-red felt embellished with embroidery and the front of which bore an oversized swastika on a similar red background.

When they came up to the Americans and halted, they were disarmed and taken prisoner. The officer in charge said something to Sergeant Ogden in Russian.

A Russian-speaking GI next to the sergeant said that the officer had just called him a "son of an American whore." Ogden grabbed the officer, dragged him off his horse, and smashed his face with a rifle butt.

Sergeant Ogden described another incident that happened later:

"My buddy and I spotted a British Spitfire overturned, about a hundred yards from the road. We went over to check it out.

"In the plane was a wounded British flier hanging by his shoulder straps. When we got to him, he said, 'Nice of you chaps to drop by,' and offered us a flask of brandy. That man had guts. We got him out as easy as we could and took him to the aid station; then we went back to the line."

On another occasion Sergeant Ogden came to an abandoned farm and saw a dozen pigs, each weighing about 300 pounds. They had been starving and had broken loose to forage for food. He also found a dead German and a dead American. The pigs had already eaten the soldiers' insides. Ogden killed every one of the pigs and left them lying there.

In the hayloft of the barn he and several others of his platoon found a German army field grade officer in hiding. The German said that he would not surrender to a simple soldier; he demanded that they produce an officer to accept his surrender.

That would be fine, said Sergeant Ogden. But they would have to disarm him first. So the officer handed over his pistol, and then he pulled out a beautiful knife with an 18-inch double-edged blade and a carved ivory handle and handed it to Ogden butt first. Ogden took the knife and immediately handed it back, blade first, through the officer's body up to the hilt.

"He had a very startled look on his face."

On the morning of June 13 the Germans struck toward Carentan and drove to within 500 yards of the city before General Taylor's 101st Airborne Division troops held them off with rifle and small-arms fire. Then, at 10:30, up came Gen. Maurice Rose's combat command of tanks. With the help of those tanks the 101st Airborne counterattacked and drove off the enemy, which happened to be the Seventeenth SS Panzer Grenadier Division, one of the toughest.

But at Caumont men of the Twentieth Combat Engineer Regiment had kept watch all night waiting for the German attack expected by General Gerow.

Lieutenant Miller recorded:

"Heavy firing during night but no attack. Position was near Montrachet.

"*June 14:* Pulled out and back to original bivouack. Slept during day."

Sergeant Thornton's Ninth Infantry Division had been training in England until June 10, when the men embarked for France. They landed on June 11 and went into action at Renouf and Ste.-Colombe. By June 17 they were 6 miles from Barneville. Then they moved to Reineville. Progress was good, and the regiment took many prisoners with very few casualties.

*

On Utah Beach the Ninth Division was moving ahead. The Twelfth Infantry Regiment had its problems. Colonel Reeder had been shot in the leg on D + 6, and that was the end of his war.

The Sixtieth Infantry Regiment moved inland. Pfc. Jesse Butler, who had fought with the Third Platoon of Company H in Sicily, worked in the battalion S-4 shop while the unit was in England. When the regiment moved to France, he was left behind for a brief period to tidy up details. He arrived in France on June 13 and was sent up to the Second Battalion. Captain West, the commander of Company H, called Butler up to the front line. He went by jeep. The company command post was in a gulley, and when Butler got there, the first sergeant told him to go over to the First Platoon. The First and Second platoons were equipped with water-cooled .30-caliber machine guns, but Butler had been fighting with 81-millimeter mortars. When he told the first sergeant, his assignment was changed to the Third Platoon. The switch probably saved Butler's life. The First and Second platoons suffered more than 75 percent casualties over the next few weeks. By the end of the war their casualty rate was about 300 percent.

The Ninth Division was in support of the Ninetieth Division. The Ninetieth, under Brig. Gen. Jay W. McKelvie, its former artillery commander, had been trained in England, but only for two months. Then it had come ashore to follow the Fourth Division into the line. At that point, just before mid-June, General Bradley ordered the Fourth and Ninetieth divisions to move abreast toward Cherbourg, that important port, with the Eighty-second Airborne and the Ninth divisions to cut off the Cotentin Peninsula at the neck.

So the attack began.

But immediately the Ninetieth Division got into trouble. Later, General Bradley diagnosed the trouble as "too many inept subordinate commanders." At the time no one knew that. What was known was that the Ninetieth Division was not moving and that its men were taking an enormous beating. General McKelvie was sacked.

On June 13 the Ninth Division was rushed over to help. Pfc. Butler's Third Platoon of H Company was waiting. Occasionally an 88-millimeter shell would come into the company area, but not very often. But then the sound of fighting increased. That afternoon the division was scheduled to relieve the Ninetieth. Then came word that the Ninetieth was falling apart in the face of the Germans. The men of the Ninth Division began scurrying to set up a main line of resistance.

"I expected to see Germans any minute coming across the fields and hedgerows," said Pfc. Butler.

But that did not happen.

Late in the afternoon the Sixtieth Infantry was given orders to move. The troops began trudging down a small trail until they came to the men of the Ninetieth Division. They were dug in along the trail, on the side of a grassy field. Across the field was a heavily wooded area, full of Germans. The GIs of the Sixtieth Infantry took cover behind the men of the Ninetieth Division.

The incoming artillery fire was very heavy. Butler knew that something had been going on. He had seen the large number of dead American soldiers in that area. The bodies were stacked like cordwood along one side of the hedgerow. Now the Sixtieth waited in a ditch for the time to attack.

Then came H hour, the moment to go after the Germans. It was about sundown.

"Black Mike" Kaufman, the battalion commander, stood up in the middle of the trail and waved his hand in the "Let's go" signal. Butler and the others jumped up out of their ditch and moved across the trail, heading for the tree line.

The firing increased markedly. Said Butler:

"I was scared as hell, but I kept going because I didn't want to be called chicken by the rest of the men."

They came to a spot where they had to cross a road. On the other side they were told to hold with the 81-millimeter mortars. So the platoon stopped. But not for long. A German sniper began shooting at the men. Fortunately that sniper was not a good shot. After a few rounds the men jumped back onto the old road, where they seemed to be safe.

But a moment later along came Major Kaufman.

"What are you men doing sitting down here?" he shouted.

"The Germans are shooting at us."

"Is that so? Get the hell back up there and start to shoot back."

So the men moved out. In the meantime something had happened to their sniper; they took no more fire from him.

So the 81-millimeter mortar unit moved up in the wake of the riflemen. Once in a while the GIs stopped, set up the tubes and plates, and fired a few rounds—at what, they never knew. But mostly they moved on, until eleven o'clock that night. Then orders from Black Mike came down. It was time to dig in.

Pfc. Butler and his buddy went over into a corner where two hedgerows intersected. They were too tired to dig in, so they spread their blankets and in a few moments were asleep. But about half an hour later they were awak-

ened to take their turn at guard duty for an hour. Afterward, they went back
to the sack and slept until 7 a.m.

They awoke to hell breaking loose in their area. A German Tiger tank
pulled up into the field just across from their hedgerow. Several German
infantrymen firing machine guns and rifles accompanied the panzer.

The GIs scrambled back across the hedgerow and crouched down.

Captain West, their company commander, began shouting at them to start
shooting back. He was firing his carbine. He yelled at the bazooka team to
get going and get after that tank.

The bazookamen hopped over another hedgerow about 30 yards from the
tank and began to fire on it. They fired three times and hit the tank three
times. But the first two shells bounced off its armor. (The small American
bazooka of World War II was no match for a Tiger tank.) The third shell tore
away the ammunition trailer hauled by the tank. Then the tank commander
saw the bazooka team, turned the turret around, and fired one 88-millimeter
shell into the hedgerow where the team was. The bazooka loader was hit; his
left arm, shoulder, and head just disappeared. The gunner was very badly
wounded and out of action.

While this was happening, Captain West told Pfc. Butler's squad to set
up the 81-millimeter mortar and begin firing on the tank. The men did, but
they couldn't make contact with their section leader, who was on the other
side of the tank. They needed firing instructions. Butler was ordered to trace
down the telephone line to see if there was a break. Butler took the wire and
jumped over the hedgerow. He came to the bazooka team. The wire had
somehow gotten wrapped around the body of the dead bazookaman, and that
was where the break was. Butler repaired the wire.

Soon the riflemen of the company had killed all the German infantrymen, leaving the Tiger without support. So the tank moved out, leaving the
dead German soldiers behind.

But now the company began to take sniper fire from the rear. The men
dropped down into the ditch. Suddenly a rifleman spoke up.

"I see that bastard," he said. And he grabbed his M-1 and took aim at
a tree. He fired one shot. A body came tumbling out of the branches.

Black Mike came up and told the men to get going—to resume the attack. They moved out, crossed a country road, and ran into a German counterattack. Black Mike called back to the Sixtieth Field Artillery for fire
support. The 105-millimeter shells started coming in, but the rounds were
short, and they fell on the Americans, not the Germans.

Black Mike was on the radio. "Lift that fire," he shouted.

The fire stopped and moved on.

Major Kaufman then told the 81-millimeter mortarmen to mass together and form up in a battery at the rear of the battalion, 500 yards from the front line. It was a very smart move. The concentrated fire of the big mortars beat off six German counterattacks that afternoon.

"I never again carried so much ammo as I did that afternoon," said Butler. "Our gunners were firing so rapidly that they had to have new mortar tubes brought up because the ones we had got so hot we couldn't fire them."

Thus the German counterattack that had paralyzed the Ninetieth Division was brought to an end. That night the Germans retreated to the Douve River, several miles away. The men of the Sixtieth Infantry followed them the next morning.

June 17: Moving in column, the men of H Company reached a paved highway on their way toward the Douve. Suddenly a jeep screeched to a stop in their midst.

"Get off the road," shouted the officer, standing in the back of the jeep. "German tanks are coming up the road."

So they all ducked and ran for cover off the road. Then they waited. After an hour no German tanks had come, so they moved on. The forward elements of the regiment reached the river and crossed. Then they were hit by a German counterattack, using tanks. The company's two machine gun platoons were shot up very badly and lost a number of men.

June 18: The Sixtieth Infantry was back on the attack. A forward element surprised a battalion of Germans sleeping in an apple orchard; the Germans scattered like bugs. They left behind a hundred bicycles and motorbikes.

Black Mike came up in a jeep and gleefully got on a motorbike and rode up the line telling the men that the battalion had scared the hell out of Jerry and that there wasn't a Kraut within 10 miles. Everybody was relieved.

The battalion exec came up and told Black Mike that they were very near the sea. That meant they had almost sealed the Cotentin Peninsula. Black Mike moved the rifle companies up by jeep in a hurry. Now the German troops at Cherbourg and in the north were cut off from their *Kameraden* in the south. The move was finished at midnight. The next morning, Sunday, the whole Ninth Division was there.

At about sunup a German division started down the highway. It was caught in cross fire and the Germans were slaughtered by the score. Those who escaped retreated north toward Cherbourg.

That night the GIs celebrated. Black Mike found a cache of red wine somewhere and had it delivered to all the troop positions of the battalion.

There was very little sobriety in the line that night.

*

Lieutenant Shebeck was still busy recovering bodies, a job to which he hardened himself. One of his pals, a company commander in the 325th Glider Infantry, had just been promoted to captain. There were no captain's bars available in Normandy, so he had improvised with small strips of adhesive tape on his field jacket. One day an excited French farmer came up to Lieutenant Shebeck and told him there was a dead American officer lying in his barnyard. Shebeck went to investigate. He saw the body of an American soldier, and he noted the adhesive tape insignia of captain's rank on the shoulders. As he turned the body over, he knew exactly whom it would be. After that incident not much could surprise Lieutenant Shebeck.

*   *   *

General Bradley had cause to feel elated. On June 18 he prepared for the assault on Cherbourg, with three divisions, the Fourth, Seventy-ninth, and Ninth. Everything was going according to plan. The weather was holding, despite gloomy predictions that it must change for the worse. The forecast for June 19 was "Wind N to NW, force 3 [21 mph]. Weather fair to cloudy. Visibility good. Sea: 2–3 foot waves. Outlook Wednesday to Friday, little change from above."

At Omaha Beach the unloading of supplies was proceeding very well. The artificial harbor was being improved every day, and truckloads of supplies came smoothly off the ships. On June 18 the western roadway from sea to shore was completed, and two streams of traffic poured off the sea onto the land.

On the beach life had slowed down considerably for Seaman Leo Scheer of the Seventh Beach Battalion. He and his buddy Seaman Shuman were more or less forgotten men. Their doctor had turned up missing on the D day landings and had never shown up. The battalion was fragmented, and those who were still around remained on the beach awaiting orders that did not come. They spent the days helping with the evacuation of the wounded from the beach, giving a hand to the graves registration people, and scrounging for food and drink. At the end of the first week after D day they had built a dugout in the front yard of an abandoned house on the beach. When the Germans shelled with their 88s, it was a fine place to hide. From the flotsam and jetsam of the beach they equipped the place. They made mattresses from inflatable life vests, and they began thinking about creature comforts.

One day Scheer and Shuman climbed up the hill and pawed through the German pillboxes. They found a Nazi flag, a picture of Hitler, a German rifle, and several bottles of wine and some sausage. They ate the sausage and drank the wine and came down the hill happy and more than a little drunk. A photographer on the beach took their picture with their souvenirs.

The day after that, Scheer discovered that the fire on his landing craft finally had gone out; when the tide was out, he went aboard, feeling like Robinson Crusoe. He found his backpack, gas mask, and medical packs right where he had dropped them on the deck. He went into the forward hold and saw that the first explosion had been caused by a mine. The second, which did the craft in, was from an 88 shell that had torn a 4-foot hole in the hull.

Scheer and Shuman continued to look for their doctor. They checked graves around the area and found some of their buddies, but not the doctor. He was still very much missing.

Life was becoming boring, so one day they hitched a ride on an army jeep to go up into France and see what was going on.

They went inland some 15 or 20 miles and pulled up in a field surrounded by hedgerows. They had not even gotten out of the jeep when "all hell broke loose": machine gun, rifle, mortar, and artillery fire all around them. They jumped out and lay on the ground, trying to look very small. When the firing ended, they helped the driver unload the jeep. The driver asked if they wanted to stay up there or go back to the beach with him.

"We went back. We was not as tough as we thought we was."

Life then was very easy, so they spent most of the day scrounging for things to eat and drink. One day they were loaded onto trucks and taken up to an army portable shower. Scheer took his clothes off for the first time in two weeks and had a shower, and got new underwear.

Yes, all was serene. But on the afternoon of June 18 the Channel began to rough up. At first it reminded Scheer of D day.

That morning Captain Clark left the area in his flagship, the *SC 1329*, for a meeting aboard the USS *Augusta* with Admiral Kirk. The subject was the further improvement of the landing facilities at the artificial port.

As the *SC 1329* left the harbor for the *Augusta*'s anchorage nearly 5 miles out, the boat lifted its bow as it ran through the gap in the breakwater. The bow came down with a "smack" and a shower of spray. This was the roughest weather the crew had experienced.

As the day progressed, everyone in the beach area became conscious of the change. The black DUKW drivers of the service companies came in shivering from the outer harbor, drenched by spray and chilled by the onshore wind from the north. The port command had been bringing in new Phoenix caisson units—but in midafternoon the arrivals stopped. The weather was too rough; the wind had already passed the 20-knot mark. One man summed it all up. He was Lt. Comdr. Everett Morris, a naval reserve officer who had been both yachting reporter of the New York *Herald-Tribune* and a famous small-boat sailor.

"It's going to blow like stink if you ask me."

Nobody had asked, officially, but those who knew Morris and saw the sea could believe.

But Captain Clark had checked the weather, and the meteorologists had assured him that this change was an aberration; the steadily falling barometer was nothing more than a minor depression that would pass during the evening.

But at dawn on June 19 there was no doubt about it: they were in for a blow at Omaha Beach.

Ashore, the worsening weather made little difference to the troops. General Collins's men pressed the attack against Cherbourg, starting at 3 a.m. The Americans caught the Germans by surprise and then began to move faster. But there would be no fighter-plane support for the GIs that day, which meant that the Germans would be able to move men and supplies all along the front.

Indeed, that was precisely what happened. On the morning of June 19 the dawn broke ugly. Clouds began to blow in over the shore. The wind continued from the north, shifting a little to come from the northeast, and that meant trouble. The barometer dropped from 30.04 inches to 29.92. By full daylight the wind had risen to 30 knots, and the tops of the Phoenixes, sometimes 30 feet above the sea, were now being splashed by waves. The gun platforms were slick and dangerous, and by midmorning the antiaircraft gunners were being evacuated. The job grew harder every moment as the wind increased and the landing craft had to maneuver alongside the concrete monsters.

All work on the artificial harbor stopped. Seas 3 feet high were racing through the harbor. The roads ashore began to snake and heave. Traffic to the shore was halted.

By nightfall on June 19 the storm had grown still uglier and the outer Phoenix caissons were showing signs of imminent collapse. Landing craft began dragging their anchors. During the night the storm drove an American salvage barge and five British LCTs against the east side of the center roadway ashore. The steel hulls pounded on the concrete pontoons, and the pontoons sprang leaks and sank at one end, thus heaving up the center roadway. The wind howled all night long, and the destruction continued.

The blow continued unabated on the morning of June 20. Sometime around 10 a.m. the sun came out for a few moments, and looked down on a twisted mass that had been the roadways to the shore. The men of the Mulberry unit worked interminably to get those five LCTs away from the harbor, to stop the pounding. One by one the LCTs were moved and sunk. Having opened for a few moments, the skies clouded over again, and the storm came on with new force. The wind reached force 5 (35 mph) and went higher. It blew off the tops of the waves, not in scud anymore but in flat sheets of water, an indication to a seaman of a full gale blowing.

By afternoon the beach was strewn with wreckage from the artificial harbor and the ships at sea. All the launches were sunk or abandoned. Only one tug was still operating. The seas were now sweeping across the decks and spars of the blockships. The mooring lines of the landing craft lying inside the ships parted one after the other. Liberty ships were dragging their anchors and got up steam to ease the strain. Several other Phoenix caissons had been sent from England, and these now neared the shore. But they could not come in. One went adrift and spun out into the Channel, a danger to navigation.

At the Mulberry site the piers began falling apart. The floating breakwater tore loose. Captain Clark stayed at the scene all through the night and the next day, shouting, urging, trying to save the harbor.

By the morning of June 21 it became obvious that the harbor was damaged almost beyond repair. But was it really beyond repair? That was the question. Seventeen LCTs and a number of barges and small craft had piled into the roadway area, making a horrible mess. At one point the bridging had turned until it stood on edge. And all day the damage continued to pile up as the wind continued to blow.

On the night of June 21 the storm began to subside. The next day General Bradley went down to the beach to survey the damage:

"I was appalled by the desolation, for it vastly exceeded that of D day."

That was true. As Seaman Scheer put it, "The beach was really a pile of junk after the storm was over."

From General Bradley's point of view the disaster was more than the ending of a dream of engineering conquest. It meant a terrible hiatus in supply for the forces racing against Cherbourg. No supplies had come ashore for four days, and that meant the Americans were 140,000 tons in arrears in gasoline, ammunition, and food. The storm had cost them the delivery of 20,000 vehicles, too. Some 80,000 men who were supposed to have landed did not land. There was only a three-day stock of supply ashore, and the Americans had no apparent way of getting any more soon unless the supplies came across the other Mulberry, in British territory. But that, of course, was needed to supply the British and Canadian troops.

A radio message went from Bradley's headquarters to General Collins. The forces attacking Cherbourg were now rationed, particularly on ammunition.

From then until the end of June the supply situation moved from one crisis to another, depending on landings by barges and small vessels onto the beaches.

Until further notice the offensive planned against the Germans in the neck of the Cotentin Peninsula had to be called off. This gave the enemy plenty of time to establish strong defenses, and it would lead to trouble, as General Bradley knew, but there was nothing to be done about it. He did not have the troops and the supplies to carry out the second offensive.

Meanwhile, the Germans were building their defenses; without the harassment of Allied aircraft, the Germans moved freely along the roads of France.

On June 17 Adolf Hitler met with von Rundstedt and Rommel at Margival. Hitler began by ordering that "the fortress of Cherbourg" be held at all costs. That was predictable. At that time Hitler was constantly demanding that every position be held "at all costs."

Much more to the point, Field Marshal Rommel predicted the coming fall of Cherbourg. He assessed the Allied intentions: a breakthrough from the Caen-Bayeux area and the Cotentin Peninsula, first south, and then toward Paris, and a secondary operation to cut off Brittany. Rommel now figured that there would be no new landing north of the Seine, but Hitler disagreed. And so, as so often happened, the conference solved nothing. Hitler talked about sending reinforcements, but he did not send them. He would not free the forces north of the Seine to fight in Normandy, where the battle was raging. He still believed the Allied disinformation campaign that said the real invasion would be in the Pas de Calais area. Already he was dreaming of the "secret weapons" that would win the war for him, and he spoke of the V-1, the flying bomb, that had just gone into operation against Britain on June 16.

It was beg, borrow, and steal. Maj. Gen. Elwood Quesada, commander of the Ninth Air Force, was asked to provide an ammunition airlift. His force had been established for support of the invasion, but to him support meant fighters and bombers. Now he was asked to provide C-47 transport, and the heavy planes would tear up his new fighter fields on the French shore. But that was what was needed, and that was what Quesada supplied. Even so, the shortage continued to be so serious that the Fifth Corps, which was holding the line in the Cotentin Peninsula, was restricted to twenty-five rounds per day per gun.

On the beach at Omaha business picked up. Seaman Scheer and his buddy saw more and more ships unloaded, but by barges, which then brought the supplies ashore. It was a cumbrous process.

One day Scheer was sitting on the seawall watching this show when he saw a man in uniform walking toward him. He looked familiar. When the man approached, Scheer saw that it was his doctor. He was wearing the same uniform he had worn on D day, but he was neat and clean. Scheer asked the doctor where he had been.

After their landing craft sank, said the doctor, he had jumped into the water. He had been picked up by a small boat, but the boat was heading back out to a ship, and he was put aboard and taken back to England. He had been all this time trying to get back to the beach.

Despite the ammunition shortage the Seventh Corps began to close the ring around Cherbourg. General Collins ordered a massive air strike against the Germans to speed the movement. Ten squadrons of RAF Mustangs and Typhoons were to start the action. They would be followed by 1560 American fighter-bombers and nearly 400 medium bombers. The Fourth Division was then at Edmondville. Capt. T. A. Bradley, Jr., was commander of the Service Battery of the Forty-second Field Artillery Battalion. He made it a rule that no matter where the men stopped, no matter how easy the next day looked, they would dig foxholes and be prepared to use them.

On that day at Edmondville the British and American planes came in to hit the Germans, and a number of them hit the Fourth Division. Bradley's men all leaped for their foxholes, cursing the air force. But only two men of the battery were wounded, although in other units there were more casualties.

Two weeks after D day Pfc. Globuschutz's Company B of the First Battalion of the 115th Infantry (Twenty-ninth Division) was down from 196 men to 26 of the originals. Replacements were coming in at the rate of three or four a day, but the company was losing five or six men a day.

Company B was then told to attack the town of Ste.-Marguerite. The troops would move out at 4 a.m.

The company was dug in on the side of the Ste.-Lô–Périers road. So the GIs formed up and moved out in a small formation. Every man was exhausted and half dazed from days of fighting. After marching for an hour, they began to see the houses of Ste.-Marguerite. Then the shelling began. The shells were American; the troops had been mistaken for the enemy by their own artillery observers. Pfc. Globuschutz jumped into a gulley at the edge of the road. The shells—phosphorus—kept coming in. The barrage lasted ten minutes. The casualties were heavy, and the effect on morale was worse.

"Now we knew what it was like to be on the receiving end of our artillery. The Germans, when they used artillery, used it more sparingly. Mostly from self-propelled guns moving up and down the road in the rear. Their 88-millimeter guns were deadly accurate because they had observers up in the trees. And they had everything zeroed in long before we got there."

On that mission, just as the sun began to rise, the men of B Company were told to fix bayonets. They got off the road and advanced down a gully. Halfway down, "hell broke loose." It was worse than anything they had run into up till then. They were immediately pinned down.

They had been ambushed by a German bicycle battalion. Each man was equipped with an automatic weapon, and the Germans were dug in at the bottom of the gully, just waiting; part of the unit was on the other side of a hedgerow. Globuschutz's company commander realized he would have to pull the unit out. It was very tough, the men inching their way back out of the trap. By the time they got back to the road, it was 10:30 and midmorning sunshine was streaming down. The company reorganized and dug in along the road.

The word got back to the rear that the First Battalion needed artillery support. So at about 1:30 in the afternoon a barrage was laid down in the gully. The platoon leader told Globuschutz that 5000 rounds of 105-millimeter ammunition were fired. When the barrage ended, he announced that the company could now walk in and take over. So at 5 p.m. the troops attacked again. They now had six tank destroyers to help. It was supposed to be easy.

But the story was exactly the same as that of the morning. They could not advance under the German automatic weapons fire.

They had to give up and pull back up to the road, where once again they dug in for the night. They had lost 60 percent of their company in this fight; they were exhausted and thought of nothing but survival. They figured that they were committed to die, that there would be no rest until they did.

* * *

The Ninth Division also took a pasting from the Allied air forces that night, and some of that division thereafter remained air-strike-shy. But the effect on the Germans was still excellent.

On June 23 Pfc. Butler's Sixtieth Infantry of that Ninth Division moved ahead steadily, with only a few skirmishes fought against the retreating Germans.

Butler's column halted on the highway and waited for several hours that day. Finally word came that a section of 81-millimeter mortars was wanted up front. Butler's section was first, so off he and his buddies went in two jeeps.

When they arrived at the head of the column, Black Mike Kaufman (now a light colonel) told them that Captain West, First Sergeant Krause, and some other GIs had seen a group of German soldiers on the beach a few miles ahead. The latter were obviously taking some recreation and had no idea that their enemy was so close. Kaufman wanted to catch them unaware, so Butler's 81-millimeter mortar section moved up 2 miles ahead of the front to surprise the Germans. They pulled into a field surrounded by hedgerows, got out of the jeeps, and set up their two mortars. The plan was to frighten the Germans into surrendering.

The men who were not actually operating the mortars were posted as perimeter guards. One man strung a telephone wire to Captain West's position so that the captain could direct the firing.

The loader dropped the first shell into one of the mortars, and it went off with a "poof." It had not even landed when in came an 88-millimeter shell very close to the mortars. The men dropped. Right there in plain sight, in the next field was a German tank.

Those 88-millimeter shells began exploding all around the jeeps and the mortars.

Butler and his friends went out of action immediately. They jumped into the jeeps and roared off, some of the men just barely hanging onto the jeep trailers. They roared out of that field and back down the highway with the 88-millimeter gun following them with its shells.

Captain West and the first sergeant also headed back. A German field car came up, and they fired on it, killing the driver. They captured the German sergeant major riding with him. So the German soldiers on the beach had their recreation, and the Americans went back to the column.

The area was well fortified, and the German troops were dug in. The battalion was drawn back while it waited, somewhat nervously, for an air strike. But the air strike never materialized. In the late afternoon the battalion began to move in a different direction. Even so, the German guns opened up on the Americans. So the GIs dug in for the night and prepared to attack again in the morning. This time they had tanks with them, and the loud engines of the armor brought an enormous amount of artillery fire down on the infantry. Pfc. Butler was very pleased when the men put some distance between themselves and the tanks.

Later in the day the 81-millimeter mortar platoon met a German patrol. From some woods the Germans opened fire on the platoon with small arms and machine guns. The Americans returned the fire with their mortars. The Jerries then retreated and Butler's platoon dug in for the night, even though the area was being worked over by German 150-millimeter guns.

By June 25 the three American divisions were in the outskirts of Cherbourg. During the night Captain Bradley's men of the Fourth Division entered from the east. Then began really heavy fighting to clear the streets, because Hitler had ordered the commander of Cherbourg to hold out to the death.

The Sixtieth Infantry advanced west of Cherbourg toward the English Channel. This area was full of pillboxes, but they had been worked over by the air force so many times that there was not much left. The bombs had left huge craters in the sandy soil, and in one of these Pfc. Butler's whole squad settled down with its mortars.

After the men had dug in, the section sergeant announced by telephone that there was a German tank to the left front of the squad. The men asked for permission to open fire, and the sergeant gave them the coordinates. So they opened up.

After they had fired a few rounds, the panzer began replying with its 88-millimeter gun. The Americans did not realize it at first, but every time they fired a mortar, the dry soil boiled up in a cloud of dust, so the Germans knew exactly where they were. But the tank's gun had a flat trajectory—they were so close—and it could not put a shell into the GIs' bomb crater. The German gunner was good. He managed to place several shells around the top of the crater, but for a long time he was not lucky enough to get one inside. Finally he did put one shell into the edge of the crater, and the concussion knocked out all the Americans for a few moments.

No one was seriously injured, so the men picked themselves up and started firing at the tank again. Finally they put a round into the top turret of the tank, and the battle was over.

Butler and his fellows spent the night in that hole. The next day they marched to clear the Cap de la Hague Peninsula. The Germans were fighting hard to hold the ground.

The GIs marched under almost constant fire from the German artillery. Butler's platoon moved up ahead of the column, passing a number of dead American soldiers on the side of the road, and then the squad came to a crossroads where the infantry had put up a machine gun.

"What are you rear-echelon bastards doing up here?" asked the gunner.

"We've come to help you win the war."

With that riposte, Butler's squad turned right at the crossroads and moved about 1000 yards, into an apple orchard. From there the platoon was to give supporting fire to Company E, which was starting an attack.

An open gate led into another field. One of the American jeeps pulled through the gate, and someone fired on it. The mortarmen thought Easy Company was down there.

"Hey, stop shooting. We're Americans."

The platoon runner volunteered to run over and tell them that they were Americans. He hopped across the hedgerow. At the same time, over the hedgerow from the other side came twenty-five men in camouflage uniforms, running toward the Americans. "We're Americans," they shouted. The statement would have been more believable if they had not been firing their rifles from the hip as they came.

One of the sergeants saw it first—the German helmet with its long neckline.

"Those are Germans," he shouted. "Start shooting."

There were about fifty Americans in the field, the mortar section and support. Pfc. Butler took a shot at the leader, a German lieutenant. So, apparently, did everybody else, because he spun around and fell dead 30 yards from their position. Later he was found to be riddled by bullets.

The Americans killed five Germans, and the others jumped into a ditch alongside a hedgerow. The Americans began heaving grenades, but the distance was too great for them to be effective. Then they tried to fire an 81-millimeter mortar. But the Germans were too close for this to work. Finally somebody got two flat rocks and put them under the bipod of Butler's mortar. This let them raise the tube to a nearly vertical position. The only problem was that they had to be sure there was a slight angle so that the shell wouldn't come back down on the mortarmen.

They fired a round. A sergeant watched the round as it made its arc, and then he yelled: "Duck!"

Everybody went down behind the hedgerow. The shell landed among the Germans. It also splattered the American side of the hedgerow with shrapnel.

The mortarmen fired two more rounds.

The Germans started to yell: "*Kamerad! Kamerad! Kamerad!*"

The Americans thought they were shouting "comrade," not knowing the idiomatic German term for "I surrender."

Fortunately for those Germans Captain West came up. He yelled to the Germans to come out, telling them the Americans wouldn't hurt them.

One German came out. He walked stiffly, very scared. The Americans made him empty his pockets on the ground. Then he started to cry.

"What's wrong?" asked one American.

One of the things in his pocket was a letter from his mother, said the German.

They let him keep the letter, and they gave him a cigarette to help him calm down.

One German in the ditch tried to escape by climbing over the hedgerow. Butler's squad leader saw him and shot him through the back with an M-1 rifle.

One of the American lieutenants, a sergeant, and the captured German went to the edge of the ditch and told the Germans they had to surrender.

They did.

The medics then went up to the hedgerow to pick up the German who had been shot in the back. The bullet had mushroomed in his gut, and his intestines were hanging out the front. The medics pushed them back into the hole, sprinkled the wound with sulfa, and sent him away in an ambulance.

The Americans then questioned the Germans. Why had they come running like that into superior force?

This was a German mortar platoon, and it was just setting up to fire on the forward elements of the Sixtieth Infantry. Butler's section had gotten way out ahead of its infantry and came up on the German platoon.

The Germans saw only one jeep standing in the hedgerow gate and thought the driver and sergeant were the only Americans there. They did not see the other forty-eight Americans behind the hedgerow until it was too late.

So the day had been most adventurous for the men of the 81-millimeter mortar section of Company H, Sixtieth Infantry.

The Sixtieth Infantry moved on, pushing up the Cap de la Hague Peninsula. On June 29 it took Beaumont-Hague, and the Americans stood at the end of the peninsula. For a while the Germans on the other side had shelled with their coastal artillery and made a terrible mess of Beaumont.

While the men of Company H were on the outskirts of Beaumont, Maj. Gen. Manton Eddy, the Ninth Division commander, came up in a jeep with Ernie Pyle, the correspondent.

"Where is Colonel Kaufman?"

"Black Mike's on the other side of the town with the machine guns," said the sergeant.

General Eddy and Ernie Pyle took off through Beaumont-Hague in a hail of artillery shells. Everybody wondered if they would make it, because when the infantry went through the town, the men had had to duck into doorways several times to escape the shells that were landing all around.

In that town Pfc. Butler saw a sight he would never forget. The boot of a German soldier, standing upright in the middle of the street, with the foot and part of the leg still inside. There was no sign of a body—just the boot.

And that was about the end of it. On July 1 the fight for Cap de la Hague ended. The Sixtieth moved south to Les Pieux and set up camp for a week of rest. The Cotentin Peninsula was secure.

But the Germans were still fighting in the Cherbourg area. Pfc. James Mc-Donnell's Twelfth Infantry was moving in the suburbs of Cherbourg. From June 21 the troops had been engaged in house-to-house fighting, southeast of Tourlaville.

The Germans brought up flak batteries with their muzzles depressed for

horizontal firing. Atop the Fort du Roule, General von Schlieben's command
looked down on the advancing Americans. The fort had to be taken, so General Bradley called on the navy, and Admiral Kirk brought up three battleships to shell the fortress.

On June 26 Pfc. McDonnell and his buddies fought their way into Orglandes under heavy German shelling. Other infantrymen were climbing up
the Fort du Roule to throw satchel charges into the bastion. That evening
von Schlieben and 800 troops surrendered, but the general still would not
give the order to his men to give up, so pockets of resistance continued in
the Cherbourg area.

On July 1 Pfc. McDonnell was still engaged in house-to-house combat.

It was July 2 before the local commanders of the Germans decided that
the defense was hopeless, and they surrendered. McDonnell marched some
German prisoners through the streets; French residents of Cherbourg came
out to stand on the sidelines, spitting at the Germans and throwing rocks.
McDonnell and his buddies got a great kick out of this until they met a GI
who had been captured early in the invasion and brought to Cherbourg by
the Germans. When the Germans had marched him and his fellow captives
through the streets, the French had stood on the sidelines, spitting at the
Americans, calling them names, and throwing rocks.

A few days later Seaman Scheer and the others of the Seventh Navy Beach
Battalion were told that Cherbourg had been captured and was already beginning to operate. The Allies had the big port city they needed to carry
forward their invasion of Hitler's Europe. The battered, wrecked artificial
harbor at Omaha Beach was not going to be needed anymore. No attempt
would be made to rebuild it.

So the men on the beach had become supernumerary, and they were going to be shipped back to England.

Then came the orders.

"When I realized I was going to survive this thing," said Seaman Scheer,
"I had a feeling that was new to me. I was totally depressed. I had thoughts
about how men could do these things to other men. Why was I alive and
not buried with all those other men who died on the beach? I crawled into
some bushes in front of a house and stayed there all day. My buddy wondered what had happened to me that day. I told him I just went for a long
walk.

"The next day we left France. We were all packed and waiting for a landing craft to come in and pick us up. When it came, it was a hell of a long way down the beach. And it was a hell of a long walk carrying all my gear, plus two German rifles, and other souvenirs.

"We landed on the beach as kids, and left a lot older in some ways. Most of us were proud that we did our jobs as best we could. We had seen things few men see in their lives."

32

BREAKOUT

At the base of the Cotentin Peninsula the American drive had bogged down because of that terrible storm and the concomitant shortage of ammunition, supply, vehicles, and men.

The Eighteenth Infantry continued in defensive positions. The kitchen truck came up and kitchen personnel began to serve hot meals. The men had plenty of time, so they dug sleeping holes, covered them with logs and dirt, and set up housekeeping.

Lieutenant Downing hated manual labor, so he pitched his pup tent under a tree, next to an abandoned slit trench. As the days went by with very little happening, he became so confident that he began taking off his clothes and sleeping in his underwear on those warm June nights. One night at 11 p.m. he heard a terrible crash. He felt as if he had been lifted off the ground. Downing jumped out of his tent into the slit trench. The smell of cordite was heavy in the air. A shell had landed in the next field. Then another came in, on the road just beyond his field. He jumped out of the trench and ran toward the hedgerow at the bottom of the field. There he leaped into a foxhole. Another shell landed in the middle of the field. He could hear the fragments zinging over his head. More shells came in. He kept peering out of his foxhole. The company clerk, Corporal Ricketts, saw him shivering in his underwear and threw him a blanket.

Finally the shelling stopped. Downing went back to his tent, put on his clothes, grabbed a blanket, and slept in a slit trench for the rest of the night. The following day he moved his tent near the hedgerow. That night the Germans shelled again, and he went into the field across the road, where Lieutenant Harris had built himself an underground castle covered with ammunition boxes filled with dirt. Downing asked if he could join him. "Sure thing," said Lieutenant Harris, so Downing crawled into the hole.

At 1 a.m. they were awakened by the sound of shells coming in once more. The shells came very close. When the shelling ended, Downing crawled out of the hole and checked the company. No one was hit, although many shells had landed around the company area.

At dawn he checked his tent. One shell had landed 5 feet from it. Shell fragments had punctured its canvas and his raincoat, which he had draped across the front. If he had been sleeping there, he would have been hit.

That experience was a lesson for all the men. The ones who had only slit trenches really dug in. Downing conquered his distaste for the work, took an entrenching tool, and widened Lieutenant Harris's hole to give them both more room.

The new major, the new executive officer of the battalion, the man with the mustache who would not wear his oak leaves, was having a lot of trouble with the men. As did many officers, he refused to wear that insignia of rank, knowing that the Germans looked for officers to kill. But most of the officers in most of the units were people the enlisted men knew very well. This major, a replacement, was neither well known nor well liked. Many of the men pretended not to know that he was an officer and were very rude to him. On one occasion a driver bringing up rations refused to give the major any and told him to report to the supply sergeant. And as time went on, the major still failed to endear himself to anyone. Then one day he simply disappeared. He left the division and nobody ever saw him again. Captain Carter from the First Battalion was sent over to become battalion executive officer. He was a veteran from the Africa campaign onward, and everyone agreed that life would have been a lot simpler if regiment had given him the job in the first place.

Replacements began to come up in this slack time. This, too, was not a very happy experience for the men of the battalion. The replacements included a trained motor transport officer, and an A and P officer. The latter relieved Lieutenant Downing of the A and P duties, which he had been performing in addition to his other duties since D day. The replacements also included a first sergeant, a T-4 sergeant, and several privates. The privates were just fine. They fitted in where they were needed. Of course, one of the new privates went up front, got involved in a jeep accident, and had to be shipped out. A nice short war for him. But the kind that anyone could hope for.

The first sergeant—that was another problem.

The problem was the army's system of sending up replacements with ratings without regard for the real needs of the front-line infantry organizations.

The new first sergeant, with the chevrons and rockers on his sleeve, was fresh from the United States, without an hour of combat on his record. He took over from Sergeant DeSantis, who had been acting first sergeant since the company left England. DeSantis was a veteran of the combat in Africa and Sicily; he was ideal for the job and had already been recommended for promotion to first sergeant. But it had not come through, due to a laxity at regiment. So now up came this new man, and by army procedure he took over. DeSantis was out. He had been nursing an attack of recurrent malaria. Now he said to hell with it, let the malaria build up, and he went to the aid station with a high temperature. As he knew he would be, he was evacuated back to England. And so the company lost a fine first sergeant and took on a tyro instead.

The new first sergeant was a well-meaning man who had six years of service, but the men didn't like losing DeSantis, and the new sergeant didn't have the personality to overcome the handicap. He did not know the men or the officers or anything about the way the company ran. He was absolutely no help to the company commander, and it would be months before he could learn the ropes. The captain could have busted him for incompetence, but that would not have been fair either. The sergeant held a peacetime staff sergeant's rating, and if he were busted, he would lose that, too.

Nor was that the end of the problem. The company was functioning lamely, with this replacement first sergeant in charge of detail, when suddenly it rained first sergeants. First Sergeant Gray, who had been with the First Division in the United States, had been sent to his old outfit the minute he hit the reppledepple.

First Sergeant Di Giovanni had gone off to the hospital from the Service Company. He got back to find his job taken by Sergeant McGarrigle of Company G. So Lieutenant Downing found that he had three first sergeants. That was like having three presidents of the United States in one room. It didn't work. Orders came down transferring Gray and the original replacement first sergeant out and making Di Giovanni the sole company first sergeant. Captain Murphy did not want Di Giovanni because he had already recommended the promotion of Sergeant Henesey, the mortar platoon sergeant, to become first sergeant. That would have made four first sergeants.

Captain Spinney had to sort it all out. He resolved the problem thus: Sergeant Gray took a reduction in rank to private in order to remain with the company. The replacement first sergeant was reduced to staff sergeant, his permanent rank, and assigned to the communications platoon of another company. Sergeant Henesey did not get his promotion, but remained with the mortar platoon. Sergeant Di Giovanni took over as first sergeant, and showed immediately that he knew what he was doing.

The whole problem was caused by one of those annoying failures of the army replacement system. The many capable men who were privates and privates first class when they left the states could not be promoted until vacancies occurred in the battalion. Then, as replacements were needed, these "gold rush" noncoms who had been excess in grade in the United States, and had been shipped overseas to get rid of the rank problem, would come into the combat units, destroying organization and morale.

Most of the replacements did not seem to have the staying power of the old guys. About two days after the A and P replacement lieutenant arrived in France, he turned up with an attack of dysentery, or so it was said, and he was sent back. Downing again became A and P officer in addition to performing other duties.

But here in France, in July, things had changed remarkably. At first, Downing used to take a jeep and trailer to go to the dumps on the beach and pick up barbed wire, iron stakes, and other engineering equipment needed up front. There was no formality. The stuff had all been "surveyed"—written off—before it was landed. But now, less than a month after D day, the red tape had crawled in. Several officers found that their belongings had been ripped off by the service troops on the beach. But there was no general issue. Instead, down on the beach, someone had established an officers' supply, and the officers could go down there and get clean uniforms *and pay for them*.

As the dogfaces would say, "The chicken shit brigade had landed and t.s. was back to normal."

Also, the ennui of inaction set in.

During the hard days of fighting the line companies had been told to set booby traps and mines for protection. But then the regiment went into stagnant defensive position. The brass decided that if the regiment left the area, the location of all explosive devices must be shown to the division engineers so that they could clear away the mess. But the trouble was that most of the guys could not remember where they had stashed their explosive devices.

One of Lieutenant Downing's duties was to prepare an overlay showing the engineers where the company had set up its booby traps. Thus, said regulations, when the company moved out, the engineers could come up and clean house so rear-echelon troops would not be in danger.

Very logical, yes?

When the rifle companies got the maps, they went out to search. They found most of the mines easily enough. But the booby traps were something else. The ingenuity of the fighting men had been put to the test, and they had responded. Strangely enough, many cows and pigs set off booby traps, and the platoon that occupied the area feasted on steaks and chops. But there was another aspect. An A and P platoon man went hiking through a field one day, looking for mines, and set off a booby trap. The medics picked him up, full of holes, but luckily nothing vital had been hit.

Lieutenant Robinson, of H Company, was going up to visit an observation post, accompanied by a corporal. He opened a gate in a fence, setting off a hand grenade booby trap. The corporal was killed. Robinson was hit in the face and several teeth were knocked out. Luckily he didn't lose his eyes.

During the company's stay at Caumont, some new weapons were delivered to the regiment. From the Japanese the Americans learned about the "knee mortar," the use of grenades fired by rifle. A device was brought up to make rifle grenades out of hand grenades.

Downing also saw a new sort of sniper rifle scope that used infrared light. There was only one of those in the whole regiment, so if anyone wanted a particular sniper killed, he had to apply for the use of the specially equipped rifle.

The inventory decreed by General Bradley had a bad effect on the Eighteenth Regiment. Every night every weapons company had to report on its use of ammunition, and regiment got a report every morning, If a gun fired more than its quota, explanations had to be made to the regimental executive officer, Colonel Sternberg.

So the GIs waited, small groups moving to the rear of the line each night to watch motion pictures shown by the regimental special services officer. And while the GIs went to the movies, the Germans were building up their defenses, as General Bradley had known they would.

So there they were, in early July. The First Division was out in front in its salient, with the British on its left and the Second Infantry Division on its right.

*

Before things began to happen—things began to happen. One day Downing was told to move to the rear with a detail, and they were led by the regimental headquarters company. They reached the east-west highway and turned west. They arrived at a crossroads, where the new area for the Second Battalion was pointed out. And in a few hours they were relieved by a regiment from the Fifth Division. It was apparent that the Eighteenth Infantry was about to move out again.

From that point on, all the signs began to show: movement without apparent purpose; the sight of new patches and old. Ninth Division patches seemed to be showing up again, and Ninth Division and First Division meant assault forces. Convoys came up with the troops and supplies; then a meeting of officers was called, and the attack plans for an advance were outlined: it was to be the breakout from the beachhead. The First Division, Lieutenant Downing was told, would have a "fairly prominent" position. It was to break through west of St.-Lô, capture Marigny, and then move to Coutances, opening the route to Brittany. All they were waiting for was a clear day so that the air force could start things out with an enormous bombing campaign. So the men were to be ready to move out on short notice. It all would be set off by a code word.

At that time—nearing mid-July—the American First Army consisted of nine infantry divisions and two armored divisions, as well as the two airborne divisions that were scheduled to go back to England soon to prepare for their next landings. The American front was 40 miles long, with Lieutenant Downing's Eighteenth Infantry on the left of it. At the other end, on the Atlantic coast of Normandy, was Pfc. Butler's Sixtieth Infantry. In between were the others; the key to the assault was with Maj. Gen. Charles Corlett's Nineteenth Corps, facing St.-Lô. The American force would attack against St.-Lô and against Avranches, cut off the Brittany Peninsula, and then wheel to the left, heading for Paris. The point of attack was to be along the road from La Haye-du-Puits to Coutances. But this first Nineteenth Corps effort bogged down. By mid-July it was apparent that this was not the way to Paris.

So what the brass called Operation Cobra was born. It involved the massing of two armored divisions and eight infantry divisions around St.-Lô. After a furious carpet bombing (saturation bombing) the troops would attack and break through. The assault was set for July 25.

The units that were going to lead the attack were then moved back out of

contact with the enemy. The Second Armored Division, which had been giving the British a hand on the left, was pulled back to wait. The Second Armored had been doing pretty well. Lt. Col. William Buster's Ninety-second
Field Artillery Battalion had destroyed four German tanks in one small area
in a few hours. Now the whole Second Armored Division would be moving
on its own as a part of this new drive.

For a week Lieutenant Downing's company waited impatiently. The men
played poker (and Downing lost all his francs). The Ninth Division, which
had captured Cherbourg, sent a truckload of wine to the First Division. The
Eighteenth Infantry got its share, and Lieutenant Downing's allotment was
two bottles. The liquor ration came in: a quart of Scotch whiskey and a pint
of gin per officer.

*   *   *

July 12: Pfc. Globuschutz's Company B of the 115th Infantry had been in
the line for more than a month.

"I had not even been able to change my socks," said Globuschutz. "All
we had to live on were B rations, which somehow or other kept us going. We
were too weary to eat anyhow. Sleep was out of the question. If you got an
hour of sleep a night, you were lucky. We spent all our spare time digging
in or going on patrol.

"That night two men in our company went mad. They got out of their slit
trenches and ran screaming toward the enemy position. We never saw them
again.

"The next morning at daybreak I was told I had to go on reconnaissance
patrol to the German area. I knew this would be my last day alive. As we
advanced toward them, there was an eerie silence. All we saw were bodies
lying about, but no firing. So we kept going till we were behind the position
where they were dug in. What we saw was unbelievable. There were literally
hundreds of bodies lying in the field and along the hedgerow.

"As it turned out, we learned, they had moved out during the night. The
day before, our artillery had done a gruesome job on them. To this day the
memory of that field lies in my mind. We weren't the only ones suffering
casualties in this ordeal. There were also hundreds of bicycles lying around.
I still remember the name: Hercules bicycles."

On July 12 the Twenty-ninth Division's attack on St.-Lô was resumed. Here
is the account from the division's official history, *Let's Go:*

The attack the following day—July 12—brought the capture of Belle Fontaine and La Luzerne by the 115th, while the 116th was continuing the advance westward along the ridge paralleling the St.-Lô–Bayeux road. The 175th 2nd and 3rd Battalions continued to advance behind and on the flank of the 116th, to secure jump-off positions for the attack to the southwest.

The fighting now began to show evidence of greater enemy strength as the German paratroops resisted bitterly on the city's outer defenses.

And here is Pfc. Globuschutz's observation:

"We moved ahead and the next morning [July 12] took the town of Luzerne. Here we ran into bad fire from self-propelled 88s and mortar fire which was extremely accurate, causing a lot of casualties in the company. The adjoining town of Belle Fontaine was taken by C company of our battalion.

"The next night we moved out to relieve the 116th Infantry, which had been pinned down. It turned out the Twenty-ninth Division had gone so far ahead we were surrounded on three sides. We moved up in darkness and took over at about nine o'clock at night.

"At 11 p.m. we were subjected to a bad mortar barrage till 1 a.m. When it stopped, suddenly we were counterattacked. We were pushed back 400 yards. It was very demoralizing. The Germans were using flamethrowers and automatic fire. I remember they got nine men with flamethrowers, men dug in beside a hedgerow. But the next day we regained the ground."

The Twenty-ninth's position was very, very tough, particularly that of Maj. Sid Bingham's Second Battalion of the 116th. The regiment's objective was La Madeleine, about 1500 yards from the center of St.-Lô. On July 15 an artillery barrage was laid down, and after it was over, in the evening, the First and Second battalions moved swiftly through the battered German positions. As usual the American artillery packed a big wallop. The two battalions moved too fast, in fact, and were stopped that night by division headquarters. The battalions had outpaced their flanking units and were exposing themselves.

The First Battalion got the word when it was already halted by enemy fire 500 yards from the line of departure. But the order to halt did not get to Major Bingham's battalion until it had gone half a mile further and reached its objective near La Madeleine, on the St.-Lô–Bayeux highway. When the word came up, the battalion dug in for the night. And that night the Germans surrounded the Second Battalion of the 116th.

When Gen. Charles Gerhardt, commander of the Twenty-ninth Infantry Division, discovered what had happened, he had to decide whether to order

Major Bingham to fight his way back or to stay where he was. If Bingham
came back, he would suffer heavy casualties, and the division would have
lost this valuable salient. But to leave the battalion out there, surrounded,
could also cost many lives. Gerhardt decided that the rest of the 116th would
fight up and rescue the Second Battalion. But it was easier said than done
because the Germans were launching a counterattack all along the Twenty-
ninth's line.

Globuschutz recalls:

"We were being supplied by C-54s. At one time I counted twenty planes
coming over. Nine of these were shot down by antiaircraft fire. We were
getting pounded constantly by 88s. It all seemed so hopeless because the
further we advanced, the stiffer the resistance became. We were losing a lot
of men because of combat fatigue. I didn't know if I could go on much longer.
This seemed like the end of everything to me. There was no memory of any
time before being here, under fire. That's all there was. There was only black-
ness ahead. I knew there was no way out of this. Our objective was St.-Lô,
but that seemed like a million miles away [although it was less than 2 miles
away].

"That day I ran into a fellow from my old platoon. His name was Sackett.
We talked for a few minutes. I think he was in worse shape than I was. I
found out that we were the only two men left in our platoon from D day. All
the others were replacements.

"On the Sixteenth they made me company messenger. It would be a good
way to rest up, they said. Then they told me the two previous company mes-
sengers had been killed. What a great way to rest up.

"Platoon and company command posts were about a quarter of a mile
apart. I took messages and radios to platoon. I also escorted the walking
wounded from platoon to company.

"On July 17 I was given a message at about five o'clock to take up to
platoon. Our battalion commander told me Company B was to launch an
attack on St.-Lô at 7 p.m. When I got to platoon the artillery fire was worse
than before. I lay on top of a hedgerow and looked out at the town. Finally,
at about 6 p.m., I started back to company headquarters.

"About halfway back I was running alongside a hedgerow when I was
boxed in by mortar fire. As I was running, they followed me in a pattern.
There was no way to get out. I was terrified. I finally jumped over the hedgerow
and ran through an open gate separating a field. This was the wrong thing to
do. We had been cautioned many times not to do this because all these gates
were zeroed in by the enemy. I had gotten about 20 feet past the gate when

everything went red. I knew I had been hit by that mortar that was following me. I lay on the ground for a few minutes; then a patrol came along and dragged me into a slit trench until the medics came. This was the end of my army career as far as combat was concerned."

It was about 6:05 p.m., July 17, 1944.

Major Bingham's Second Battalion of the 116th Infantry had survived the night of July 15–16. The rest of the division was stalled and could not get to the battalion.

Here's the account of July 16 and 17 by S. Sgt. Ronald W. Cote, a squad leader in E Company:

"Sunday all we did was dig in. We got pretty hungry and thirsty because when we left we had only two rations apiece. Most of us had eaten both of them on Saturday night. By Sunday afternoon everybody's canteen was dry.

"We didn't do much talking Sunday. When we did talk we talked about food and something to drink and when they could relieve us. . . . Sunday night some of the men sneaked halfway down the hill behind us to a couple of abandoned houses and found water.

"That night no one got any sleep again. We could hear German tanks coming up. We couldn't send any more runners back that night because Jerry was plastering the valley with everything he had. Why they didn't come and get us that night I will never know.

"Monday morning someone slipped down to the abandoned houses and found some eggs and smoked ham and some frostbitten potatoes. They took some pots and candles and cooked their haul in the foxholes. A couple dozen of us—including me because I invited myself—ate the meal."

Through the early morning fog of July 17 the Third Battalion fought its way up with bayonet and grenade to make contact with Major Bingham's battalion. Then another attack was ordered, but the Germans had different ideas and put up so much artillery fire that the two battalions took many casualties and did not have the strength to move forward. The Germans, it was quite obvious, were preparing for a major counterattack.

July 19: Hill 192 still stood there before the Second Division. Colonel Warren, who had been wounded on June 17, returned from England to again

take command of the battalion. The troops were waiting for an order to resume the attack on Hill 192.

July 21: The assault on Hill 192 began with an artillery barrage at 5
a.m. Tanks and infantry began to move forward at 6:00. Two of the tanks
were blown up in front of Colonel Snetzer's eyes.

At 10:30 Colonel Snetzer was wounded by the explosion of an 88 shell
and was taken to the Second Evacuation Hospital near Le Molay. That same
day he was bedded down in a ward tent on a folding cot with *white sheets.*
The next day in came Field Marshal Montgomery with a toothy grin. The day
after that, Snetzer was in England.

*   *   *

On the evening of July 22 all the plans had been made for the attempt to
break through the German lines. The Fifth Corps had moved its headquarters up to La Bazoque, which just hours before had been vacated by the
Germans. Now the Germans retaliated by shelling the town. One of those
shells hit an apple tree near the spot where Colonel Campbell, the corps
provost marshal, was standing. Pieces of shrapnel zinged about. One bit of
shrapnel cut the gear shift knob off a jeep, and another piece buried itself
into Colonel Campbell's back as he stood next to the jeep. He was, he believed, the first officer of the Fifth Corps staff to be wounded.

Pfc. Butler's Company H of the Sixtieth Infantry (Ninth Infantry Division)
had moved down from the heart of the Cotentin Peninsula and was waiting at
the St.-Lô–Périers highway for the breakout.

One night a group of Germans came down the highway at midnight. They
were driving a captured Sherman tank. Several German infantrymen were
marching behind the vehicle. They turned right in front of Company H's
machine gun positions.

The GIs manning one machine gun had just been assigned as replacements. They did not know what to do. One of them woke up the platoon
sergeant. He woke up the section sergeant. The section sergeant took over
the gun. The platoon sergeant ran out and called out the password.

One of the Germans turned and fired his rifle at the platoon sergeant.
The section sergeant then began firing the machine gun and killed every one
of the German infantrymen. Three Germans in the tank hopped out and began to run. Another machine gun began firing and shot them down.

The next night along came a German kitchen on a two-horse wagon. The kitchen was loaded with hot German goulash and noodles. The two German cooks drove right into the American position and were captured. That was the best goulash Pfc. Butler had ever eaten.

Staff Sergeant Henry Kraft was in charge of the instrument and survey section of Headquarters Battery of the Fifteenth Field Artillery in the Second Infantry Division.

Once the troops had gotten off the beach on D + 1, they were astounded to find themselves in this bocage country, where the hedgerows had grown together over the centuries to make an impenetrable mass. The American tanks were useless in getting through them, until someone came up with the idea of mounting on the tanks a bulldozer blade with serrated teeth to rip through the hedgerows. The idea, said Sergeant Kraft, came from a sergeant, although an officer took credit for it.

Still there was the problem of observation in this flat area. The 105-millimeter howitzers needed "eyes," and at this stage of the war the liaison spotter plane was still highly experimental.

While the Fifteenth Field Artillery was still in Cerisy Forest, Sergeant Kraft discovered a church with a steeple 200 feet high. He volunteered to climb up to act as an observer, and the CO said sure.

So Sergeant Kraft climbed up the church stairs into the steeple and set up his observation telescope there. He had a commanding view of the countryside, including a church, St.-Jean-des-Baisants, which the Germans were using for the same purpose. He knew the Germans were in their steeple, and the Germans knew he was in his. Several times the Luftwaffe bombed and strafed the church, and many times it shelled the area, but Sergeant Kraft's steeple remained intact.

The Twenty-ninth Division slowed down enough to get a little rest. Sergeant Ogden gives a good picture of why:

"We were all issued a clean pair of socks. I hadn't had mine off for almost six weeks. I found that all I had was a pair of spats. I could actually strike a match on the bottom of my foot."

On July 17 Sergeant Kraft of the Fifteenth Field Artillery was directing fire from his church steeple when he saw a German staff car speeding along the road below. He called for a "fire for effect" on that car. Just as the howitzers fired, he saw some oncoming British fighter planes. They strafed the car, and at the same time the battery's shells landed. The car ran into a tree and stopped.

The enlisted men did not get liquor rations, but they knew where to find the Calvados. So in the evenings many of the GIs sat around and drank and told stories. There was a good deal of drinking done all along the line in those days, particularly of that white lightning, Calvados. Tales were told of soldiers going out to face the enemy, fighting, coming back, being awarded medals, and then sobering up and being unable to remember what they won the medals for.

And there were other tales. The Eighteenth Infantry's Lieutenant Rosie told a story of a cavalry reconnaissance platoon that was supposed to assist the infantry in the coming attack. This platoon leader came to Rosie and told him he wanted to have riflemen precede him along the road to flush out the Germans, since the recon cars had only light armor, which wouldn't stop a .30-caliber bullet. Rosie informed him that the riflemen had only skin with which to stop slugs. "No thanks," he told the cavalry officer.

And the men of the First Division waited. On July 18 Corlett's troops captured St.-Lô. Still the men waited. One thing they waited for was clearing weather, because the air force needed visibility for its carpet bombing attack.

It came on July 25. The morning dawned clear and bright. At midmorning the men of the Eighteenth Infantry heard the dull roar of many, many airplane engines, and they saw a huge armada of bombers come over high. The planes traveled slowly, with that air of assurance that big bombers have. Black flowers of antiaircraft fire blossomed around them, and they began dropping their bombs. The men of the Eighteenth Infantry could see the haze rising from the "carpet bombing area." In all, 1500 heavy bombers, 400 medium bombers, and 350 fighter-bombers were striking 5 square miles of Normandy bocage.

That was the theory. In fact, the bombers came in across the American troops, rather than parallel to them, and many of the bombers bombed outside the assigned carpet, into the Americans. The Ninth and Thirtieth divisions took a terrible beating from their own planes, and Lt. Gen. Lesley J. McNair was killed by a direct hit on his foxhole. But the attack proceeded as soon as the American bodies (several hundred of them) were recovered.

The Eighteenth Infantry moved out slowly. It was late evening before the

2½-ton trucks assigned to Lieutenant Downing's company set out. Downing rode in the cab of the lead truck as convoy commander. Late that night the troops were delivered to a half-wrecked farmhouse. This was the battalion operations shop. Downing lay down outside, rolled in his blanket, and slept.

He awakened at daylight and looked around. The house he was sleeping next to was a wreck. Shells had hit the house, scattering rubble all over the room. The floor was littered with empty ration cans, bits of equipment, plasma bottles, and old bloody bandages.

Lt. Col. William R. Buster came across the Channel with the Second Armored Division's Ninety-second Field Artillery Battalion. He was the new commander of the battalion, his former boss having gone to straighten out some morale problems in the Fourteenth Field Artillery. Buster was a lucky man. He had been involved in north Africa and Sicily, and he was still around. He had also served a stint with the British, who had a lot of experience in modern artillery practices through their time in Africa. Buster had learned quite a bit from the British, and his lessons were to stand him in good stead in the coming campaign in France. Except for the foray of General Rose to help out at Carentan, the Second Armored Division was not busily employed in this early campaign in Normandy. It was July before Lieutenant Colonel Buster's artillery battalion got into real action. Then his men were ordered to the left flank of the American forces. There they were to establish contact with the Royal Third Artillery for support of the troops of both armies.

The Ninth Division was fairly shy of Allied aircraft after the bombings near Cherbourg. On July 24, when the men of the Sixtieth were told that the air force was going to bomb near the front line, the GIs moved back 2 miles. The air force did bomb, and the air force did miss its target and kill a number of Americans. The men of Company H were not hurt, but when they tried to return to their positions, they discovered that the Germans had taken them over; the dogfaces would have to fight for the same ground all over again. Two machine gun section sergeants were killed in this action. The next day, July 25, the four-engined bombers appeared on the horizon.

Pfc. Butler watched from his hole:

"There were 100 bombers to a formation, and the formations stretched back as far as the eye could see. There were also tiny spotter planes that

shot colored flares to show the other planes where to drop. The big bombers
came in very low, and when they were overhead, they released their bomb
loads. That was one of the most terrible noises I have ever heard, with all
those bombs from 100 bombers falling at once.

"Just as soon as those bombs started to hit the ground, another wave of
100 bombers came overhead and released their bombs. This kept going until all the bombers had passed overhead and dropped their bombs.

"By the time that the bombing was about half over, the dust was so thick
that one could not see very far, and the concussion was so great that our
clothing was bulged out like balloons. Then something went wrong, and our
bombers started to drop their bombs short. Some of the bombs fell among
us. We sure did scramble for any hole."

When the GIs' attack began, the Americans found the Germans dazed
and confused. One German machine gun crew ran up in front of the American
machine guns and set up its gun, firing in the same direction as the Americans. The crew was captured.

*   *   *

The Second Battalion of the Eighteenth Infantry moved out on the morning
of July 26, traveling across country. Lieutenant Downing recalls:

"We began to see signs of aerial bombardment. Huge craters dotted the
fields, and the infrequent farmhouses were smashed. Some wrecked German
tanks and self-propelled guns were encountered at hedgerow corners and
near some farmhouses. We finally emerged onto a narrow secondary road
and moved up cautiously. We passed wrecked German two-wheeled carts
with dead horses lying stiff-legged and bloody beside them. Already the morning sun was bringing out the fetid odor of decaying flesh, and large green
flies covered the bodies, humming and buzzing as they went about their job
of scavenging."

The men passed some bloody American helmets, shoes, and broken weapons in the ditches. As they approached a crossroads, a shell burst overhead.
They all dropped and watched the black smoke disintegrate in the breeze,
their stomachs knotted. Downing hated airbursts. The foot soldier was not
safe from them no matter how deep his hole.

Another shell came over, bursting at their rear. They stood up and went
forward. At the crossroads Lieutenant Fanning showed them the rear CP and
Downing took the company over there. They found that slit trenches were
waiting for them, the gift of some earlier diggers.

The men settled down. Lieutenant Downing started forward to find the battalion forward command post. The road was bare and deserted. At the left of a road junction stood a stone farmhouse. Diagonally across from it was a small store building, and behind that was a smoldering German tank. That's where he found the battalion staff, in a shaky wooden lean-to stuck to the farmhouse. He joined the group and lit a cigarette.

The men from the rifle companies were strewn about, lying, sitting, standing around, napping, eating, talking, waiting. There was a lazy feeling in the midday sunshine. Off in the distance they could hear the reports from a German self-propelled gun that was shelling the crossroads where the rest of Headquarters Company was dug in. "We watched a couple of P-47s swooping down to shoot up the German gun. They were constantly around, looking for something German to shoot at. These two made several passes and then swooped off again."

A soldier whose helmet bore the bright-red crosses of a medic came walking up the road. He seemed dazed. He walked almost to the road junction, then went back the way he came. His outfit had gone down that side road, but he wouldn't go. His eyes stared fixedly. Over and over he would walk up dazedly and turn back again. Captain Murphy said he thought the guy was psycho:

"A soldier came up to our group and said two old French ladies were lying just down the road near a house. Their house had been shelled and both had broken legs. Could they be evacuated by our stretcher bearers?

"Lieutenant Colonel Williamson told me to hunt up the medics and send them for the old ladies. I did, then returned and flopped down again.

"I was awakened from a doze by a sharp report like a thunderclap. Smoke and dust were rising from the hedge across the road. A German shell. I scrambled around the corner and dropped to the ground. Another shell popped into the field behind the house. I heard yelling from across the road. I looked around the corner of the building. An ambulance was speeding up the road, flying white flags with red crosses. It stopped. A few men were helped in. You could see the field dressings they were wearing. The two old French ladies were loaded in, and the ambulance sped off back down the road at top speed.

"Then I began to notice a disgusting smell, and those around me looked at me queerly. I stood up and looked myself over. When I had run behind the house and dropped, I had fallen into a pile of excreta deposited by some former visitor. My field jacket was all fouled. A sergeant handed me a roll of toilet paper, and I went off to one side and cleaned up. When I had gotten it off, I came back and kicked dirt over the mess on the ground so nobody else would have that same bad luck."

A meeting of company commanders was called, and the officers of the

Second Battalion came drifting in. Captain Linde came around the corner of the house whistling, "When your heart goes bumpety-bump, it's love, love, love."

Linde had been across the road fiddling with the German tank. He tried to drive it; the engine worked fine, but a tread was off. Lousy luck.

A runner came up from regiment with some mail. Captain Spinney got a letter from First Sergeant Merrill, who had been evacuated from north Africa to a hospital in the United States. He was on the road to recovery from his wounds. Spinney passed it around to all the officers and men who had known Merrill.

Finally all the commanders were there, and Lieutenant Colonel Williamson outlined the plans for the next move. The meeting was then dismissed.

Lieutenant Downing went down the road to give the word to Headquarters Company. The men were grousing. The motor pool had not shown up with the jeeps. Neither had the rations for the next day. Downing told the men they were to stay where they were, to keep a line open to regimental headquarters.

Now he had a new task. He had to go find the motor pool and bring up the rations.

Downing took a lineman and a spool of wire, and they started back to find the motor pool, unreeling the telephone line as they went. Just as they ran out of wire, Downing saw a truck from an antiaircraft unit on his right. A soldier lay prone on the ground, and another soldier was lighting a cigarette for him. Up ahead Downing heard the continuous rattle of small-arms fire. As the lieutenant walked up alone, the prone man warned him to be careful. An ammunition truck was on fire in the next field. He had been the driver and had run over a mine; the explosion had broken his leg, but he was lucky that the truck had not exploded, too. The vehicle just started burning and now the small-arms ammunition it was carrying was popping off.

Downing went on. He saw a number of vehicles moving along the road. Then he saw a field behind a hedgerow, and there was his motor pool. Sergeant Usherwood, the motor sergeant, was heating C-ration cans over a stove. He invited Downing to eat, and he did. Then the lieutenant got a jeep and driver and started back for the command post, leaving word with the motor pool to come up at daylight.

The jeep driver was very jittery about going forward, but Downing ignored him. They pulled into the field where the telephone had been left, and there was the lineman, watching it.

The rations, which had come up after the men left, were dumped in the field. When Downing got out to count them, the jeep driver sped off, taking the lieutenant's musette bag, gas mask, and rations. Downing cursed the driver and then started looking for a place to sleep. He pulled the phone over to an abandoned slit trench, and lay down and tried to sleep.

He was cold and looked around for something abandoned with which to cover himself, but he did not find anything. Then he heard the drone of a plane overhead. It came closer. He heard a shrill whistle and started to run for his hole. The noise grew louder. He hit the ground before he reached shelter. The bomb exploded in the field behind the rations and sent a shower of white-hot pieces of steel through the darkness. Downing jumped up, ran for his hole, and fell in. When the plane droned away, he curled up in the hole and finally fell asleep.

He was awakened by the buzzing of the phone the next morning. It was the operator, telling him that the battalion was moving out and that the phone was being disconnected. Downing went back to sleep. The morning sunshine eventually woke him. He shivered and wondered if he were getting malaria again; then he got up.

Lieutenant Pecuniar, the new A and P officer, was moving his trucks forward along the road. He had a jeep, and he drove Downing back to the motor pool. There Downing looked up the driver who had deserted him the night before—and told him off. Then they ate some rations, and headed toward the front, taking a small convoy of jeeps and trailers. He found the rations that had been dumped in the field, loaded up, and then started to look for battalion headquarters. Now he drove through the area hit by the carpet-bombing attack. Fields on all sides were pockmarked with craters. Smashed and charred tanks, trucks, and more horse carts littered the road and sides of the road.

At a crossroads he inquired for the Eighteenth Infantry and was directed along the same road. He finally found the Second Battalion, delivered the rations to the first sergeant, and then went back and brought up the motor pool. Back at the rear command post Downing ran into Lieutenant Skogsberg of the First Division Recon troop, an officer he had not seen since Sicily. They had met when they were both in the reppledepple in Algiers, following Downing's hospitalization after his jeep accident.

The battalion was moving forward again, but Downing was told to stick with the phone and the motor pool and wait for orders. He had a radioman and an SCR-300 radio to keep in touch with the battalion and with the regiment.

It started to rain. He felt feverish, sure that the malaria was coming back. But he didn't go to the medics:

"It is a ticklish business to go to an aid station when your unit is attacking, unless you have blood oozing out of you someplace. Otherwise you create the impression that you are trying to avoid combat."

Downing dozed by the field phone. He heard sporadic artillery firing. The enemy was up there someplace. Most of the shells seemed to be directed at the town of Marigny.

Late that afternoon he got the word to go up front with the rations, since the battalion was stopped for the night. A jeep came back to guide him. He had the Headquarters Company and H Company jeeps load up with rations, and they started off. They moved toward Marigny and then turned down a side road. There they got into a traffic jam. Tanks were hogging the road. Off to the right came the sounds of bazookas and rifles and the blurp-blurp of German machine pistols. Downing kept stopping and asking individual tank drivers to let them by. The drivers were very obliging.

Finally he got up to the main St.-Lô–Coutances highway and turned right. There his convoy encountered troops of Sergeant Moglia's Sixteenth Infantry, marching along single file on each side of the road. Tanks of the Third Armored Division were in the middle of the road. The ration convoy threaded its way through and came to a hillcrest. Machine pistol fire zipped over Downing's head, and he jumped into the ditch beside the road. The GIs rushed off to the right, firing madly into an orchard in that direction. After a while the firing stopped, and Downing got back into his jeep and started forward. He and his convoy passed the head of the column; then they were alone. He got a prickling feeling in the back of his neck. He didn't know whether he was moving into friendly or enemy territory.

Up ahead Downing saw buildings burning, the fires glowing in the dusk. He was about to turn back when he saw Sergeant Wilcox in the ditch at the left of the road. Downing asked for directions to Headquarters Company, and the sergeant pointed to the side road on the right. All at once more bullets zipped by, so the jeeps quickly pulled out of there and moved down the road. Finally Downing met Captain Spinney, who told him the advance was still proceeding slowly. They had not yet decided where to stop for the night. And they didn't want the rations! Downing began cursing. He went back to the jeeps and told the drivers to drop their rations in a field and that he would then take them all back to the motor pool to pick up their loads of ammunition and equipment. He informed the acting supply sergeant, Corporal Noble, and then he headed to the rear, worrying about enemy fire all the way back through tanks and half-tracks. When he pulled into the motor pool, Downing gave a sigh of relief. It was now pitch dark, and the Germans were still shelling Marigny. The jeep convoy wouldn't be able to move out again soon anyway. The Third Armored Division had road priority all night.

Sweaty and exhausted, Downing went over to an antitank platoon half-track and lay down on his blanket; he slept away the remainder of July 27.

That same day the Second Armored Division was moving up right behind the infantry, as it had been since the attack began on July 25. Lieutenant Colonel Buster's Ninety-second Field Artillery was in position, even that first day, watching the carpet bombing. The troops did not know what was happening, but they saw the bombers coming closer and closer. The bomb that got General McNair was just about 500 yards in front of Buster's position in the middle of the Thirtieth Infantry Division. The field in front of them was occupied by a battalion. After the bombing was over, Buster's artillerymen proceeded up the field and found many scores of dead GIs, some of them in their foxholes.

The attack was supposed to start immediately after the planes had finished, but the bombing of the Thirtieth had so demoralized the division and broken down communications, and caused so many casualties, that units had to be reorganized before they could go ahead. It was not until nine o'clock on the morning of July 26 that the Second Armored Division was able to launch its attack, and even then the armored division did not have any infantry support on its flanks, as had been expected. So Combat Command A attacked south, with the artillery firing in support. That command was to attack toward the towns of Canisy and Tessy on the Vire River. Combat Command B was to follow Combat Command A to the river and then turn and launch an attack directly south.

The Ninety-second Field Artillery Battalion moved out at 7 a.m. on the twenty-seventh to help Combat Command A while Combat Command B rolled into position. Buster now saw the effect of the bombing. It was tremendous, far more effective against the Germans than General Bradley had ever expected. The crater effect of the bombing was so bad that Combat Command A had to go off the roads and run alongside. If the Thirtieth Division had been hit hard, the German troops opposing the division had been devastated. Colonel Buster likened the place to a green field in his own Kentucky, wet by weeks of rain, greened up beautifully, and then destroyed so that not a single blade of grass remained. The German troops of the First Parachute Division and other units had been completely demoralized by the bombing, and hundreds of them were suffering from concussion, so great was the effect. Two other disparate events were equally devastating to the German war effort.

First, on July 17 Field Marshal Rommel drove up to the Caen area himself to encourage the troops in their stand against the British. He visited General Sepp Dietrich of the First SS Panzer Corps and then left to return to La Roche Guyon, his headquarters. On the road that afternoon, between Livarot and Vimoutiers, enemy fighter planes caught the staff car and strafed it. Three fighters dived on the car, observers claimed. The driver was killed, and Rommel was hurt so badly that at first, when he was pulled out of the wreckage, it was thought that he was dead. The RAF got the credit, but U.S. Sergeant Kraft, the Fifteenth Field Artillery observer in his church steeple, said that his outfit's guns got Rommel.

The second event occurred on July 20. On that day a plot hatched among some senior German officers came to fruition: a time bomb placed in a meeting room exploded, slightly injuring Hitler. Then the German generals were subjected to a purge that paralyzed the army High Command for days.

In this atmosphere Field Marshal von Kluge replaced Rommel. Von Kluge was busily engaged in political affairs and was trying to run the western front as well.

Avranches must be held, von Kluge told his generals. All the reserves of the German Seventh Army were brought up to the Cotentin front. But the High Command still would not release the divisions from the Twenty-fifth Corps on the Breton Peninsula. There was too much confusion; Hitler was raging, and everyone was afraid of Hitler. So just at the critical moment of the American attack the German High Command was helpless.

The Second Armored Division continued to move forward on July 27, traveling along the side of the battered roads. As the division advanced, it kept encountering German soldiers who crawled out of their foxholes to surrender. They had been in those holes for two days, suffering from the shell shock of the carpet bombing. Many of them could not speak.

In the afternoon Combat Command B started forward. The commander, Colonel Roberts, called in Lieutenant Colonel Buster and told him to occupy a position on a transverse road between the routes of advance of the two combat commands. The road was just a country lane between the two columns. Still, it had not been cleared of the enemy. Buster protested, but he was overruled.

"My colonel was certainly bucking for a star," said Buster.

So the artillery officer took his jeep and a driver and, together with a warrant officer as a bodyguard, gathered up three other reconnaissance parties from the three batteries of the Ninety-second. They met at the designated country road and started out in darkness—into the "great unknown" that might conceal the enemy in great strength.

It was the first time that Buster was really scared. What was going to happen? They expected the burp guns to start firing any moment. When they got halfway in, Buster decided that was far enough. They found a position for the firing batteries and for headquarters, and he called back by radio to the battalion and told it to come up.

After the battalion got on the road, German night fighters came over and bombed the column. The Luftwaffe was thoroughly working over those roads, but the battalion came up and occupied the position. By that time it was 1:30 on the morning of July 28. And, after all that, the artillery was not called on for a single mission. Combat Command A had stopped, and there was no effort to support. When dawn came the men of the Ninety-second flushed fifty German soldiers out of the hedgerow next to their position. These Germans, like those behind, had been so thoroughly demoralized that they did not offer any resistance.

The aggressive Colonel Roberts didn't get his star. Instead, later that day he got out ahead of everybody, as was his fashion, and got himself killed.

*   *   *

On that day the Ninety-second Artillery began to take many prisoners, a great nuisance because the battalion had no way of dealing with them. Soldiers had to be detached to take the prisoners back to the rear under guard.

On the second day the Ninety-second moved down the road it was on to the route of march of Combat Command B. The troops moved behind the advance guard of the command and took position just across a bridge called Pont Brocard. The batteries were on high ground, with a valley between the artillery and the road west.

Here the action began to get hot. Combat Command B was just beginning to get into action with the enemy near Notre-Dame-de-Celigny. One battery was firing in support of Combat Command B, and one battery was firing on the road across the valley. The German antitank weapons were firing against the artillery. At the same time higher headquarters asked the Ninety-second to supply troops to help contain an infantry attack in the area the battalion had passed through the night before. So it had to get men from the Service Battery and Headquarters Battery and send them to fight a ground action. Simultaneously the Ninety-second had to contend with two air attacks.

The Germans came so close that one self-propelled howitzer was sent out
and fell into a firefight with a German self-propelled gun.

The battalion spent the night of July 28 in that place. The next night the
troops moved up to a point north of St.-Denis-LeGast. They had blocked the
German units trying to come in from the south; that same night the Germans
trapped in the American semicircle tried to break out. At 1:30 a German
column from the north started down a road adjacent to the battalion's position. The fighting grew very brisk, and machine gun bullets were whistling
through the battalion headquarters area. The batteries were firing at targets
only 200 yards in front of their positions. The battle continued until morning; in the afternoon the artillery moved back. The mission of the Second
Armored Division was accomplished, and the men now had a little respite
from the fighting.

Over on the left, abutting the British positions, was the Second Division.
Maj. Gen. Walter M. Robertson, commander of the division, had a reputation for going ahead of everybody else so that he would not have to move so
often. This created a certain confusion among the elements of his division,
as Mess Sgt. Karl A. Michel remembered:

"I was in the rear echelon, but several times we were in front of the
forward echelons due to General Robertson." The divisional headquarters
mess was famous in the line. Sergeant Michel served hotcakes and bacon
every day, and would do so for a hundred days straight.

One morning the sergeant set up his stoves in an apple orchard. On the
other side was a gully between the hedgerows. As usual, Michel was up at
4 a.m. supervising the cooking, when he heard noise in the hedgerow. He
reported to the defense platoon and the GIs investigated. In short order they
captured a dispirited German patrol.

A few days later they had moved up to a village, and a guard near a
church called out for the password when he heard a noise. Receiving no
answer, he fired a shot. His enemy fell dead. It turned out to be a 250-
pound pig.

While the action grew faster around St.-Lô, the 82d and 101st Airborne divisions were quietly withdrawn from France. As the advance began in the
south, the airborne troops were back on Utah Beach. Later that same day,
July 25, Lieutenant Shebeck's company arrived at Southampton. The men
would now rest, reorganize, and train for a new airborne operation.

*

Sergeant Chattaway's Twenty-eighth Infantry Division had approached the Normandy coast aboard troop transports on July 22. It was D + 46, and perhaps one would expect the GIs to feel a certain confidence, at least in the landing period. But not so, as Sergeant Chattaway explained:

"As our ship approached the Normandy coast, I made an effort, as first sergeant, to circulate among the 200-plus men of my company and, although none would say, I am certain that my stomach was not the only one that felt as though I had swallowed a rock, for the commitment to infantry combat was to be the 'baptism of fire' for each of us. I am certain also, that each wondered, as I did, how he would react in the face of enemy fire."

The Twenty-eighth Division's 110th Infantry went ashore on July 22 and into an assembly area. Under the original plan the 110th had been scheduled to occupy the positions of the Twenty-ninth Division. And although Operation Cobra had since supplanted that old plan, on July 23 the Twenty-eighth was committed and struck toward Percy, two days before the carpet bombing and the kickoff of Cobra.

In its first assault on Percy the 110th failed. The reason: inexperience and inadequate artillery support. First Sergeant Chattaway and three other men from A Company headquarters—the company commander and two company runners—had to fight a twilight delaying action for the successful withdrawal of their company. But the next day, having learned something, and with better artillery support, the Americans moved back and took the town. But as they moved out beyond, their column was stopped by enemy fire. When the point once more moved, the connecting files failed to relay the signal, so only half the battalion moved out. At dusk the error was discovered. Half the battalion was way out in front. The break had occurred in Sergeant Chattaway's company, so he and the two company runners had to move into what was now enemy territory, between the halves of the column, to reestablish the link. The two runners were killed.

Sergeant Thornton's Company M of the Sixtieth Infantry reached a point near Loyon on July 26, taking very heavy casualties. The fighting on the twenty-seventh was just as hard, and casualties were again heavy, but on the twenty-eighth the German resistance collapsed and the company moved up without further casualties. On July 29 it reached Carpantilly and went into reserve.

*

Lieutenant Miller went up to visit the Seventeenth Engineers on July 26 to watch their technique of mine clearing.

"I saw more dead Americans today than I have seen since D day. The Germans are planting 'mustard pots' [mines] in the ditches, and then, when they shell the roads, the doughboys jump in the ditches and blow themselves up. Our artillery are stupendous. For every shell the Germans throw, we must have been throwing over fifty, and fighter-bombers were giving close support to the tanks and infantry."

Miller saw several of the famous German Panther tanks and the first Mark VI Tiger tank he had seen in France. He also noticed that many American tanks had been knocked out by the superior German tanks and antitank weapons.

July 27: Back to the Seventeenth this p.m. My friend Captain Hagen has taken over a company to replace a company commander killed by mortar fire. The Second Armored has made a great breakthrough. The Third Armored Division and the First Division are driving for Coutances. Radio reports 12,500 prisoners and more coming in. Unable to go forward because armor had priority on all roads.

July 28: Drove through St.-Gilles and Canisy, searching for Seventeenth Engineers. I found them in latter. They were in somewhat of a storm as a result of last night when their S-4 and two men were killed and thirteen men were evacuated during an air raid. The Germans dropped AP [antipersonnel] bombs all over their bivouac.

Great evidence of heavy fighting between St. Gilles and Canisy. More German tanks knocked out than I have ever seen before. Still quite a few dead Jerries in ditches. Five American armored columns are still driving through, cutting up things in Jerry's rear.

Tonight we had the heaviest air raid since we've been in France. Starting at 10:30 there were planes over most of the night. Lots of stuff being dropped and fragments whizzing like bees. For the first time since I've been overseas, I actually got up out of my sack and hit a foxhole. Tomorrow I dig a hole and start sleeping in it.

At this point, the Americans were faced with the problem of delaying the German troops. The French Resistance was called on to help with this, and the Resistance was given some help, too. One part of that help was an American Office of Strategic Services team of forty men who were to be dropped into France to join the Maquis, report on the movements of German units, and help delay the Germans.

Eight B-24 bombers carried the OSS team over France, and the men parachuted into occupied territory. Their destination was Dijon, 208 miles southeast of Paris. They jumped from low altitude and were met by the Maquis. Sgt. Leif Oistad was one of them.

That first night they slept in a French barn. Then they set out to blow bridges and mine roads. They lost their demolitions man and then their communications expert, Captain Larsen. He was looking over a hedgerow one day and made the mistake of getting up. A German machine pistol salvo cut his body in half. Soon, ten of the Americans were dead.

It was tough and nasty all along the main battle line, too. Sergeant Ogden of the Twenty-ninth Division has a pungent memory:

"If there was a dead man on the other side of the hedgerow, you could always tell by the smell whether he was German or American. The decomposition of the uniform material gave off two distinct odors."

Strange things happened at night. One night Lt. Lucian Walkup and his driver were going down a road in a half-track when they came across a German convoy going the other way. The enemies passed, and not a shot was fired.

July 28 was a tough day for the Eighteenth Infantry. Lieutenant Downing was awakened that morning by the battalion motor transport officer, who told him that the new executive officer wanted the vehicles up front right away. Downing crawled out from under his half-track, woke the driver, and told him to wake up the other drivers. Then he started to heat a can of beans on his Coleman stove. He felt malarial, sluggish and without energy. He hoped the food would make him wake up, but after he ate the beans he got sick and vomited. He made some coffee and drank it, but soon lost that, too.

The vehicles were lined up and ready to go. The lieutenant led off in a jeep. The column went down the main highway, turned off at the bypass to Marigny, and then drove to the St.-Lô highway. Downing's jeep had a flat tire, so he transferred to the second jeep in the column.

It began to rain, and then the rain came down in sheets. Downing and the rest of the column turned off the highway to find the battalion. They drove through a large area that was like the park of an estate. They passed a few signs of war, shattered German two-wheel carts for the most part, the contents of which were strewn all over by the Americans looking for souvenirs. They saw some dead horses and a few pieces of discarded American equipment.

The jeeps passed through the village of La Chapelle. Finally they arrived at the new motor pool, and Downing set out to find the Headquarters Company of his Second Battalion. The battalion was in a defensive position around the town. The division had gotten out ahead again and was sticking out like a finger into German territory—the enemy was on three sides and the battalion had very slim control of the supply line.

"A damaged German self-propelled gun was parked in the little village square. I went over to it and looked in. The German driver was still in the front seat. His face was blackened and a square hole about 2 inches on a side was pushed through his forehead, exposing the gray brain matter. Across the road a German paratrooper was laid with his feet together and his arms by his sides. I went looking for Captain Spinney and came upon the battalion headquarters building."

There, among others, was Lieutenant Harbison, the battalion intelligence officer, occupying the building that formerly had housed a German regiment. In his office Harbison had ten cases of cognac stacked up and some brand-new German paratrooper jackets. They were knee-length camouflage coats, with an eagle and a swastika on the right breast. Downing poked around looking for German pistols but did not find any.

He went out into the courtyard in back. There he saw some German two-wheeled carts being looted by French civilians. They were loading up on black bread, cheese in tubes like toothpaste, and German cigarettes. Other Frenchmen were poking through the piles of German clothing, picking out boots, underclothing, and trousers. Odd pieces of clothing, paper, equipment, and records were strewn all over the courtyard, being trampled into a mess in the rain.

Downing went back into the building. Lieutenant Harbison had just found a cat-o'-nine-tails, a wooden-handled whip with thongs attached to the head.

"What are you going to do with that?"

"It ought to be useful on my guys in S-2 [intelligence]. Make 'em behave." He flicked the whip.

A scout entered and said two POWs had been brought in. With the whip still in his hand, Harbison led Downing out to look at them.

One was a young fuzzy-faced boy of about 16. The other was an old man with a big mustache. Harbison told the guard to put them in the corner of the courtyard. He pointed with his whip.

The old German got down on his knees and started to cry. He rattled off phrases in German, holding up his hands in supplication. The young German looked pale and scared.

Lieutenant Harbison was startled and embarrassed. Obviously the Germans thought they were going to be whipped. He called his interpreter, and when the interpreter came, Harbison instructed him to tell the Germans they were not going to be hurt. They walked away with smiles of relief.

Downing left Harbison and went to look for Headquarters Company again. He met men from that company and from H Company scurrying around with bits of loot. One man had a typewriter under his arm. As soon as the troops moved out, he would have to abandon the machine, and he knew it, but the souvenir-hunting impulse was very strong.

Downing found the company dug in on a sunken road. There he heard a story:

One of the men had jumped into a slit trench during an air raid. A bomb had killed a cow, which fell over his slit trench. Blood was running down the man's face. He dug himself out of the trench. Men gathered around him, making sympathetic noises, seeing his head, face, and jacket soaked with blood. When he told them it was cow's blood, they began jeering at him.

Now Downing went looking for the first sergeant. He came out on the main road through town and saw Father Adamowski, the Catholic chaplain, with a couple of men of his burial detail. They were trying to extricate that dead German self-propelled gun driver from his cab. Downing also saw First Sergeant Di Giovanni. He caught up with him, and they started making plans for ration distribution. Then came an ear-splitting crash. Water from a pool beside the road spurted high into the air. Di Giovanni dropped on the road. Downing dove into a slit trench alongside, landing on top of a jeep driver. They waited for the next shell, but nothing happened.

Downing got up. His right leg felt numb and wet. He turned his head and looked down. Blood was soaking through his trouser leg. He started walking fast toward the aid station. There was no feeling in his leg, but he could feel the blood trickling.

Captain Sortman, the battalion surgeon, was standing out in front of the barn he was using as an aid station.

"I've been hit."

"Sure. What else is new?"

"No. Really." Downing turned and showed his leg.

Captain Sortman took him inside, and Downing sat on a stretcher and took off his legging. He lay on his stomach. Captain Sortman looked at the wound. There was a small hole where a piece of shell had gone in, but it had not come out.

"It's not a serious wound," said the surgeon, "but we might as well evacuate you. You won't be able to hike for a while, and there's no use having you around here."

Downing did not object. He probably could have stayed with the company and favored the leg, but he wasn't feeling very heroic; he knew he had malaria, and a stretch in a hospital bed looked good to him.

Captain Spinney and Lieutenant Fanning dropped in. They had heard that Downing had been hit. Di Giovanni also came in; he hadn't been touched. The shell had hit a tree over their heads, spraying fragments all around, but none had found the sergeant.

They all stayed a while and talked. Downing thought they were a little envious. But also he thought that they had a morbid desire to look at him and reassure themselves that he really was wounded and that the wound was not serious. If a new officer joined up and got hit, it didn't have much effect on the troops. But when an officer who had been around for a long time got wounded, it was a matter of deep concern. Old officers then looked around and wondered when their time would come. They began to feel that they were crowding their luck, and they hoped that when they got it, the wound would be a light one.

The ambulance pulled up and Downing limped out and into the back. There was one other patient, another Africa veteran, down with malaria. They sat smoking as the ambulance moved on. They couldn't see anything, but they could tell when they reached the St.-Lô highway.

They drove along for a while and then heard the popping of antiaircraft fire. The driver pushed the accelerator, and they raced down the road. Over the roar of the motor Downing heard the scream of planes flying at low altitude. A deafening explosion rocked the ambulance. The driver slammed on the brakes, the assistant wrenched open the door, and they piled out. The other patient got out, and so did Downing, diving off the seat into the ditch at the side of the road. The grass was wet. He buried his face in it and waited for the raid to end. When the planes disappeared, he stood up and felt the blood running down his leg. In his jump the bandage had come off. The assistant driver helped him fix it up.

Across the road a couple of soldiers were bandaging the leg of a man who had been hit. Downing and the others got back into the ambulance and turned off at the Marigny bypass. Then they came to the receiving station of Company B of the First Medical Battalion. Downing went inside. Now he was in the hands of the medicos, out of action for a while.

*

At the front the Americans moved on. The American army in France now consisted of twenty-one divisions. And up on the Cotentin Peninsula, behind Maj. Gen. Middleton's Eighth Corps, stood Lt. Gen. George S. Patton, Jr.'s Third Army, which had moved very quietly from England. Patton had come over on July 6 with three corps. He was waiting for August 1, the day when his army would be "activated" and he would drive through the First Army toward Paris.

On July 29 Lieutenant Miller of the Twentieth Engineers went into St.-Lô. It had been a city of perhaps 40,000 people. Now it was nothing but rubble.

"This, and not Montebourg, is the most thoroughly destroyed city I have ever seen. Around the perimeter of the city there are a few houses with roofs, but in the main part there are no roofs and few walls. Bulldozers were cutting roads right through the city. Never have I seen such complete and utter destruction."

The First Division had broken through into Coutances on July 27. And then came August 1—the day that the U.S. Third Army was to come into being officially, six days after the start of the St.-Lô breakout. The war was about to change again.

33

UP FROM THE
SOUTH

June 15, 1944: On the Italian front Sergeant Haemmel's First Armored Division had been fighting almost steadily since a two-month respite at Anzio that ended on May 22. After the Americans entered Rome, the division moved up to Lake Bracciano for a short spell of rest and recreation. Then it was on into Tuscany.

That part of Italy was mountainous, with steep rises cut by deep gorges and fast streams. Highway 1 ran along the coastal plain, but in the mountainous interior there was not a single first-class road. The Germans, who knew the terrain, and who had been ordered by Hitler to hold their lines, made things even harder. They sited their guns and used demolitions so effectively that as the First Armored Division came up, the engineers found as many as two major engineering obstacles per mile.

At this point the First Armored had support from the 361st Infantry Regiment, which had arrived at Anzio early in June. They took Roccastrada on June 23. Then came Torniella, Radicondali, and Mensano. All these were hard, bloody engagements, with the Americans taking many casualties as the Germans fought tenaciously for every foot of ground.

For example, on June 30, the First Armored encountered its first enemy tanks of the Tuscan campaign near Mensano. The movement into the mountains had caught most of the German heavy armor on the coastal plain, and it was some time before the Germans could move up to contest the movements of Combat Command A.

But they did get into action in a few days. The Americans were enveloping the territory east of the village when they took fire from two German tanks, which were located about a thousand yards to the northeast. A German flak-wagon, which fired multiple 20-millimeter guns, also began shooting.

The Americans planned to deny the Germans the use of the only road in the area, so the task force established roadblocks on it 4 miles northeast of Mensano. The Germans were equally determined to hold. So a pitched battle was in the offing. The advance of Combat Command A was slowed by land mines in the road and by blown bridges. Heavy artillery fire concentrated on the road, too. When automatic fire was received, the First Battalion of the 361st Infantry was called up and attacked the high ground near Mensano. The fighting continued all day and the next day.

T/5 Nelson C. Fairchild was new to H Company. He had previously served with the 752d Tank Battalion, but at the end of May he had been assigned to Company H. He did not last long. Early on July 1 his tank took a direct artillery hit and he died.

Sgt. William M. Cochran commanded a tank of the Third Platoon, by this time reduced to only two tanks in all. The battalion was called on July 1 to support an infantry assault on a hillside. The armor moved out of the pine thicket in which it had been concealed, and immediately a German antitank gun began firing on the tanks. One projectile hit a turret door of Cochran's tank, and a fragment of the door hit Cochran in the head. He fell into the tank and onto the gunner, T/5 Yancey Cook. Cook was covered with blood and began vomiting from shock. The tank moved back into the woods, and the men got Cochran out. In a few minutes he was dead.

Late that afternoon of July 1 Captain Adams was using his field glasses. Only his head and his hands were sticking out of the turret. Suddenly the tank was hit by a 75-millimeter antitank projectile at a point about a foot from the hatch. Pieces of the turret came loose, and Adams was hit in the left hand and neck. His gunner, Cpl. James E. Bohanon, was also wounded. The tank behind Adams was hit, too, and three men were hurt.

The battle for Mensano ended on July 2. Despite their stout defense, the Germans were overwhelmed by superior force. GIs of the 361st staged a drive, and after six hours of fighting they captured the place.

Then the men of H Company took stock. The last few days of battle had been very costly. Five medium tanks, two light tanks, and one tank destroyer were damaged by mines or by enemy fire. There was plenty of work for the repair crews.

Captain Hillenmyer resumed command of the company on July 2.

*

The heaviest fighting of the Tuscan campaign was that of Task Force B at Casole d'Elsa. This little town was a natural fortress surrounded by a 15-foot wall, perched high atop a hill that offered excellent observation and several fields of fire. The road up was along ridges, commanded by the town.

Task Force B reached the town in the early hours of July 1, accompanied by the Third Battalion of the 361st Infantry. An infantry night attack was organized, supported by medium tanks of I Company. The infantry jumped off, and all seemed to be going very well. Just before dawn came word that the town had fallen. The armored vehicles moved up, but they ran into mines.

Daylight found the column stalled on the ridgeline a thousand yards south of the town. The Germans had not been driven out. They began firing with 47-millimeter antitank guns, and before the Americans could pull back, six medium and three light tanks were lost, along with two tank destroyers.

On July 2 the Americans resumed the assault. Several attempts were made to take the town by frontal attack; that was very expensive to the infantry and not successful. On July 3 Company H was shifted to Task Force B and Captain Hillenmyer brought up his few remaining tanks. More troops of the 361st Infantry also came up. That third night the advance was also supported by heavy machine guns and mortars. At 4:30 in the morning, against strong German machine gun fire, the troops of one company rushed the northeast gate of the town while another company scaled the 15-foot town wall. The Americans were inside, and by 8 a.m. the town was secured.

All the way up the Italian boot the fighting was just as hard, almost unbelievably hard for the results obtained.

The Germans had been told by their Führer to hold the Gothic line across the mountains at all costs, and they were sparing no costs to do so. But since Hitler had refused to significantly reinforce the troops in Italy, there was no doubt about the eventual outcome.

The Eighty-eighth Infantry Division joined up from the states and captured Volterra. Armored troops and the Ninety-first Infantry Division pushed north along the Era River valley, capturing Ponsacco. The First Armored Division then went into reserve at Bolgheri, and there it was reorganized, having been reduced in strength from 380 tanks to 263. Captain Hillenmyer's H Company became B Company of the First Battalion, but Captain Hillenmyer was not in command any longer.

On the way into Bolgheri the officers and men collected vino, cognac, and everything else potable that they could find, to have a party to celebrate their relief and the fact that they were still alive. They celebrated so well that next morning Captain Hillenmyer had a horrible hangover. He had a dreadful bellyache, which he attributed to the inferior quality of the cognac. He suffered with it all day long, figuring it was the wages of sin, but finally he broke down and went to the medics. Hangover? Perhaps. But what was wrong with his belly suggested acute appendicitis. So the doctors shipped Hillenmyer off to the hospital for an emergency appendectomy. Lieutenant Sturm became acting commander.

All the changes in the First Armored Division, ordained by the brass, brought the division's morale to an all-time low. The officers and men had fought gamely with inadequate weapons against the much more powerful German Panther and Tiger tanks and the German tank destroyers. They had taken many casualties, and the men who were left felt very close to one another. Why the fire teams were being broken up was not, as usual, explained to the men. Nor were they getting the new weapons that had been promised to them. They needed a medium tank with a big gun. At the end of July half a dozen tanks with 3-inch guns arrived. That was more like it! But that half-dozen was the end of the rearmament. Most of the division had to wait until just before the end of the war to get adequate weapons.

As July turned to August the First Armored Division moved into line on the bank of the Arno River. The river was 250 feet wide, but in the summer dry spell it was so shallow that the men could wade across. Screening infantry forces manned the south shore of the river, and the tanks were up in the low hills, among the trees. During August very little happened. Attention was focused elsewhere. Occasionally the tanks were called upon to fire rounds as artillery. So the tank men lived in deserted farmhouses and picked the produce in the gardens and the orchards. They lived very well that August of 1944. "The watermelons," said Sergeant Haemmel, "were particularly good."

In April 1944 the 442d Regimental Combat Team—a new Japanese-American unit—had been sent down to Camp Patrick Henry in Virginia, and soon it was shipped off to the wars. After the ships of the 100-vessel convoy were well at sea, language booklets were issued.

"*Buon giorno...*"

So the men of the 442d learned they were going to Italy. They arrived at Naples on June 2. There was a little leave. Some of the men took the opportunity for cultural exposure; they went off to Pompeii to visit the ruins and came back with exotic tales of the ancient whorehouse and with some erotic souvenirs. Then it was off to the war. By June 7 they were at Anzio, where German bombers were still raiding the supply dumps at night. That night the air raid broke up the outdoor movie, and one soldier of the 442d was hit in the helmet by a fragment of shrapnel. It was just a warning; the fragment did not penetrate.

In mid-June the 442d and the 100th Battalion got together. The place was Civitavecchia, north of Rome. The 100th Infantry Battalion had been fighting all the way up Italy with the Thirty-fourth Division. Now the 442d was assigned to that same division, and the 100th Infantry Battalion became a part of that regimental combat team, taking the place of the 442d's First Battalion, which had been left behind at Camp Shelby. But the 100th was not known as the First Battalion of the 442d. It kept its name, a special honor bestowed because of the battalion's impressive battle record. Of the 1300 Japanese-Americans who had started out from Hawaii, 900 became casualties. And many of the replacements for the battalion had come from the ranks of the 442d.

The "new" 442d, then, got into combat at Belvedere and on the road to Sassetta. It was late June. The men of the 100th taught the newcomers how to fight and die. At Suvareto the advance was held up by very heavy German resistance. Pfc. Kyoshi Muronaga picked up a 60-millimeter mortar and, by himself, took it forward to fire on a German 88-millimeter battery that was giving the troops hell. He fired so well that the Germans withdrew. But Pfc. Muronaga was killed in action that day.

The infantrymen of the 100th fought a house-to-house campaign in the streets of Belvedere, and showed their brothers how to do it. They broke up a battalion of the very tough Hermann Göring Division. And a few days later the regiment had Sassetta and Castagneto.

Early in July the 442d was fighting for the port complex of Livorno. In three weeks of combat, from July 1 to July 22, the GIs moved up across the Cecina River to the Arno.

Then there was time for a little rest and recreation. And what did that mean? As everywhere with soldiers, it meant wine, women, and song. The red wine flowed copiously in Livorno. The songs were a combination of Hawaiian, Japanese favorites, and the hottest numbers from Broadway.

The women? Sgt. Chester Tanaka remembered:

"Our house of ill repute met the specifications as prescribed by the colonel. It was run by a sergeant who relished the idea. They had a building with one madame and four girls, good looking girls. We had four bedrooms.

It was a two-story house. I was in the parlor and the sergeant was outside the door. He had a tommy gun. I had a tommy gun. And we had a cashbox and the madame stationed on the first floor. So we got three guards out there. Since the sergeant could speak Italian, he selected the girls. The girls were happy to come into the city to serve that purpose. We had no venereal disease all the time we were in Leghorn—the Pro Station was right next door."

Indeed, the 100th, while a part of the 442d, continued to sustain its remarkable reputation.

One day Gen. Mark Clark ordered the battalion to guard Livorno after it was secured. No one was to be allowed to enter without orders.

A few days later a long column of trucks started into Livorno from the south. A lone private from the 100th was standing guard on the road. He was about 5 feet tall, and he looked very insignificant—until he presented arms and stood at attention in the middle of the road to stop the convoy.

Out from a jeep at the head of the column stepped a tall colonel of engineers.

"We are here to secure the port and make it ready for the ships. Let us through," demanded the colonel.

"May I see your orders, sir?" said the private.

"I don't have any orders. Get out of the way. We must get through."

"Colonel, nobody gets through without orders."

"I can kill you right here and take my convoy through."

The small, insignificant private drew a line in the dust of the road with one foot.

"Colonel, you cross this line, you *make*."

"*Make*. What's *make?*"

"*Make* means you are dead."

"We can take you..."

"Cross the line and you *make*."

The colonel went back to his jeep. There was much hemming and hawing, much consultation with his staff. And soon the field radios and telephones began to speak. The flak got all the way up to Fifth Army Headquarters and to General Clark's office. The word came back to the engineer column.

"Return to base and get proper orders."

Later, when the engineers complained bitterly, General Clark made a special visit to Livorno. He held a press conference, and he called for the private who had held the road against all comers.

The private was brought up. The long, lean General Clark put his arm around the little private's shoulder.

"I commend this soldier to you," he said to the press as the newsreel cameras ground along. "I selected the 100th because I knew my orders would be carried out. I can depend on the 100th to successfully carry out any mission. I have absolute faith in every soldier in that battalion."

On July 15 the antitank company of the 442d was detached from the regiment and sent to camp south of Rome. There the soldiers learned that they would become part of the First Airborne Task Force. What next? They were going to take glider training and then they were going to go someplace and land from gliders. How long would they have to learn the new drill? About three weeks.

On July 25 the 442d was pulled back from the Arno line to Vada for R and R. Then came a certain amount of hoopla. General Clark presented the 100th Battalion with a presidential unit citation. The handing out of more medals began. It was a nice, lazy time.

Then on August 2 the men of the Third Battalion were ordered to attend a demonstration by the 109th Engineers. The subject was German mines, a matter with which the men of the 442d had already become quite familiar. There were Teller mines, S mines, shoe mines, TNT blocks, special detonators, and fixed grenades. The usual booby trap was a trip wire fixed to a grenade pin. A soldier hit the wire with his foot, the pin came out, and bango, the grenade went off under him. The Germans were especially adept at fixing these on the trails to latrines and in the doorways of abandoned houses.

But the Germans had more elaborate mines. One was a TNT block, a plastic charge, attached to trees along a road or trail, with a low wire strung across at the last tree. As the soldiers moved along the road, the lead soldier would trip the wire and the TNT in the trees would blow. One by one the trees would fall on the column, causing casualties and throwing the whole line into confusion.

One of the most fearsome booby traps was the "nutcracker." Three rifle rounds would be buried in the ground, attached to a pressure detonator. They would shoot straight up at the crotch of the soldier who trod on the detonator.

As in France, the Germans also strung wires at neck height across the roads. A jeep would come speeding along, the windshield usually down for better vision. The wire would pass over the hood of the jeep and catch the occupants at throat level. Several drivers and front-seat passengers had been decapitated, as in Normandy, before the engineers got wise and welded to the front bumpers tall steel bars with V notches at neck height to break the piano wire.

Sometimes, the Germans would booby-trap a dead dogface: they would fix a grenade to the body, remove the pin, and use the weight of the body to hold the trigger down. When a medic or a graves registration team rolled over the body...

All this was explained to the guys of the 442d that day, and then the demonstration ended. Most of the battalion was on the way back to the bivouac, and the engineers were reloading their truck with their deadly devices. Suddenly something triggered one of the mines. Then the rest went up. In the explosion ten men were killed: seven GIs from the 109th Engineers, two from the 232d Engineers, and one from M Company of the 442d.

After the disastrous Avellino affair Sgt. Charlie Doyle and the men of the 509th Parachute Infantry had gone into action at Menafro, Italy. The unit had received replacements for the 250 men so tragically sacrificed in the Avellino foul-up. At Menafro the paratroops were to have a new role, one already being practiced by German paratroopers, since Hitler had for some reason lost faith in his paratroops although their performance at Crete had been superb. The 509th was given the task of taking Mount Crocci, above the town of Menafro. The Forty-fifth Division had made several attacks on the mountain without much success. But in four hours, under heavy artillery fire, the paratroops did the job. That was November 1943. They held the mountain, although they had many casualties, for many weeks. Finally, they were down to five men, and Sergeant Doyle, one of those five, had trench foot. He crawled down Mount Crocci and was soon enough in the 118th Station Hospital in Naples.

The staff did not know how to treat trench foot there, so Doyle was sent to another hospital. The doctors there wanted to cut off some of his toes, since they did not know how to treat trench foot, either.

"No way," said Sergeant Doyle.

The doctors ("inexperienced types who were after all the experience they could get") threatened him with court-martial.

Still he refused to have his toes cut off.

He did not get court-martialed.

Then it was Anzio. Sergeant Doyle was in the second wave that day. He was in and out of Anzio three times because of his trench foot. And he still had that trench foot well into the summer, when the 509th was getting ready to jump into southern France. It was late July before he rejoined the battalion.

*   *   *

The 509th was on the Mediterranean coast, outside Rome. Doyle reported in to Lieutenant Colonel Yarborough. The commander looked over Doyle's battalion records. He didn't believe Doyle was ready to come back to the company, but Doyle could return if he wanted. So Doyle went back to his company. Capt. Bud Segal was the new commander. Doyle's old job as radio operator had gone to another—as had his sergeant's rank. With no particular job he was busted back down to Pfc. So now he was a parachute rifleman. But as he soon enough discovered, for the first time since it had been in combat, the 509th was going to be part of a coordinated effort, not an isolated unit asked to go in and do miracles.

Back at Fort Bragg, Private Adolph was becoming a real soldier. On May 24 he went on a 10-mile hike with full field equipment (65 pounds). Fort Bragg was dusty and hot that spring of 1944 (no rain for more than a month). It was 45 minutes hike, 15 minutes rest, 50 minutes hike, 10 minutes rest, 50 minutes hike, and then bivouack. Most of the men made it okay. Adolph was now a member of L Company, 397th Infantry Regiment, 100th Infantry Division, and not quite the raw youth he had been a few months earlier. Later that month he had a little leave and went home to New York. He knew he was slated for overseas duty because the unit already had a new post office address: APO 447.

On June 22 he was writing home from "somewhere in North Carolina." All very mysterious.

By July 20 college boy Adolph was quite the old soldier. He and his buddies were about to have a celebration: their platoon sergeant, "the dirty bastard, is leaving tomorrow for Officers' Candidate School." They were getting a new sergeant, from another platoon, a guy whom they liked. And Private Adolph was about to get a pass to go into Fayetteville. He wanted a change of scenery.

The training grew more intense. On August 15 the GIs were given a field problem: attack a pillbox with live ammunition. They used bangalore torpedoes to blow up the barbed wire around the pillbox, and they had flamethrowers to burn up the inside of the structure. They took their "objective," and the afternoon was spent cleaning up their equipment. Private Adolph's immediate worry:

"Tonight I am going to the movies to see the double feature. I hope it is not too crummy."

That night Private Adolph and his buddies went to the movies and then afterward dropped in at the enlisted men's club to hash over what they had seen.

That same night Pfc. Doyle and his buddies dropped into southern France, just outside the town of Lemais. The reporters called it the Champagne Campaign, because at first the going was very easy. The German Eleventh Armored Division had been stationed at Marseilles with its Panther tanks, but on August 13, two days before the invasion, the division was moved north to participate in the Normandy fighting. Thus the soft underbelly of France was very lightly defended.

The 141st Infantry was also involved.

The 509th and the 463d Parachute Artillery units were given the job of taking the town of Lemais. The British Second Infantry Brigade was to actually invest the town. The American paratroopers were to establish roadblocks and cut off the town from German reinforcement.

On August 12 the 509th left its Italian camp and headed for the air base at Falanizzia.

In ninety aircraft the paratroopers took off in the night. The Pathfinders got lost and did not show up for four days. The flights became separated and could not make their rendezvous over the island of Elba as planned. The second flight landed near St.-Tropez. Soon they had the artillery ready to fire, and the paratroop infantry was establishing roadblocks.

Fortunately there was very little opposition.

Paratrooper Earl Dickel landed in a tree near the drop zone about four o'clock in the morning. He had understood that the planes were off course and would make a water landing, so he had jettisoned his heavy equipment. His platoon was supposed to put outposts on the northwest ridge of the mountains overlooking Lemais. But at the moment he was more concerned about getting out of his tree.

Dickel had only his .45 automatic and some hand grenades. He called out, but no one answered. He dropped his parachute to the ground, but as he tried to climb down the reserve chute, the entrenching tool on his back caught it, and he was hanging in midair. Dickel swung back and forth, got hold of a small tree, took a knife out of his boot, and cut himself loose. He hit the ground. There was no time for relief. He had to get moving. Soon he joined up with others.

James Batton landed in a tree also. He hung there, wondering what to do. What if he were hundreds of feet in the air, over a cliff and nothingness?

He remembered a book he had read about Jimmy Doolittle's Tokyo raid. That was what had happened to one of the Doolittle fliers who landed in China after the famous B-25 raid against Japan. So Batton hung there and waited for daylight. Then he heard a voice. It was his buddy Glass, not far away.

"How the hell did you get up in this tree?" Batton asked.

"I'm standing on the ground, pal," replied Glass, "and you're only 6 feet above it."

The British Second Brigade seemed to be not very successful in taking Lemais, so the 509th came in to give a hand. Company A's First Platoon, under John Frazier, was to go in to take some houses. This was done, under small-arms fire. Led by six tanks, the platoon moved through the town and made contact with the other troops.

The town was secured in a few hours; afterward the company was pulled back and reorganized. It then started along the coast of southern France. The invasion of southern France, to divert some of Hitler's interest from the Normandy invasion, was now in progress.

Consolidation of the landing area was completed by August 18, and the troops began to move out, widening their hold in the south.

Pfc. Doyle kept falling behind on the march, though he would always arrive at the destination just in time to make the new assault with the rest of the company. Finally, one day up came Lieutenant Colonel Yarborough in a jeep. He asked Doyle what his problem was.

Doyle said nothing; his expression conveyed that he thought he was just a little slow.

"You remember what I told you back in Italy. I didn't think you were up to rejoining the company. But you wanted to, and I told you then that it might not work."

"Well..."

"Sorry Doyle, but this is the end of the line. Get in my jeep, and I'll take you to the aid station. You've done your job, as I tried to tell you back in Rome."

At the aid station the doctors took a look at Doyle's feet and sent him back to a field hospital. There, the doctors confirmed Colonel Yarborough's verdict: Doyle should not have rejoined the company. So he was sent back to Italy.

Doyle's combat days were over. Now he was detailed back to rear-echelon duty, which he hated. That's the way it was for him for the rest of the war.

Back on the French Riviera St.-Tropez was the next Allied objective. Then the invasion force pushed on. By August 25 the line had been extended west to a point south of Nimes. Soon the U.S. Seventh Army, the U.S. Sixth Army Group, and the French First Army were all involved in the campaign in the south of France, driving up along the Italian border, and then the Swiss border, heading toward Lyon and Dijon, as the troops from Normandy converged on Paris.

34

ON TOWARD
PARIS

On July 31 Lieutenant Miller was beginning to sense that the Americans were scoring an impressive victory. He knew nothing of the high policy matters, of the coming breakout of General Patton's Third Army. But he could see that something was up:

"Found Seventeenth Engineers at Notre-Dame-de-Cérilly. They report that Fourth and Fifteenth Armored divisions have taken Avranches and are headed due south. Third is cutting back east and heading south. All along the front the German lines have completely collapsed. Saw a truckload of prisoners with two Japanese in with them."

On August 2 Company B of the Twentieth Engineers was given the job of building a Bailey bridge across the Vire River to further the advance.

Lieutenant Miller went up to Campeaux and was driving south to the Vire when he met Captain Lutz, who reported that the area was being shelled. Major Argus had been wounded in the butt, he said. While the two men were talking, the Germans began laying down a heavy barrage right on the spot. Two of B Company's trucks were hit. Both burned. A house nearby began to burn. The men were pinned down for an hour, apparently from fire by German self-propelled 88s. Down the road the Germans were dropping mortar fire on the Second Platoon, and when the platoon withdrew from the proposed bridge site, it left three dead and four wounded. Sergeant Powell had a bad shoulder wound. He got the second cluster to his Purple Heart medal.

On July 31 the Second Armored Division was pushing south from Percy against scattered German resistance, especially roadblocks, which the GIs outflanked and then overran.

On August 2 the Ninth Infantry was starting its eighth straight day of attack from St.-Germain-d'Elle. The Americans drove the enemy across the Vire and were ordered to occupy the high ground on the south bank.

Once again, the engineers were in the front of it all. Col. C. J. Hirschfelder, commander of the Ninth Infantry, ordered Lt. John L. Gray, commander of Company A of the Second Engineer Battalion, to find a ford for motor vehicles and to prepare the river for a quick crossing. They discussed the possibility of bridging the river, but they decided the German artillery fire from the hill across the Vire was too tough to try that route. So Lieutenant Gray went out to reconnoiter the north bank of the river, even as the riflemen were crossing and the Germans were shooting with artillery, mortars, and automatic and small-arms fire. Gray then sent back to Lt. William Gallo for steel track to prepare a fording site. It was brought up in the three jeeps of the platoon leaders. Gray crawled up the hill through enemy fire and radioed the orders.

So in an hour the first crossing was prepared. Another crossing was made—a stronger one—for tanks, but when the tanks came up that afternoon, they took the wrong crossing and tore up the tracks. So that had to be fixed.

But by 5 p.m. Company C of the Ninth was across the river with vehicles, and by dark the engineers had built a wooden footbridge as well as two wheeled-vehicle crossings and a tank crossing.

By August 4 the Second Armored Division had reached Percy and had begun operations there. And it was there that Colonel Roberts, the division artillery commander, was killed.

The colonel was very stubborn and aggressive. Once again he was out front. He always insisted that the artillery stay right up with the armor. Many times the tanks moved through the artillery to attack. If the tanks got 5000 yards in front, then the artillery moved up.

When the colonel arrived at Percy, the column had stopped. He went to see the column commander, asking what the problem was. He was told that there was a Tiger tank in a critical position up the road. As soon as any

American vehicle appeared, the Tiger would fire. The evidence was there: a knocked-out American tank. The column commander said they had called for infantry support and were going to get the riflemen to outflank the Tiger.

Colonel Roberts did not believe this was necessary. He ordered the tankers to move on up the road with their tanks.

The tank commander refused. Colonel Roberts strode up. "I'll show you that your fears are groundless," he said.

He motioned to the forward observer, who was also mounted in a tank, to go on up and show these cowardly tankers that there was nothing to worry about.

The forward observer politely refused.

Thereupon Colonel Roberts ordered him to come along. They pulled on up the road. When they reached the point where the tanker had seen the Tiger fire on and wreck that other U.S. tank, the Tiger tank fired a single 88-millimeter projectile. It penetrated the armor of the American tank. The tank burst into flame, and Colonel Roberts and the whole crew were burned to death.

Colonel Buster gave his view:

"Sometimes bravery can be a great thing, but other times unless it is mixed with sanity and a little caution, it does not work effectively."*

Colonel Roberts was replaced by Colonel Hutton, who had commanded the Ninety-second Field Artillery Battalion until he gave it up to Lieutenant Colonel Buster. Hutton was a very effective and aggressive, but not foolhardy, commander.

The Allies were closing in on the Germans in what would become known as the "Falaise pocket." Lieutenant Miller's bridge was a definite part of it. After the German shelling, that August 2, the commander pulled the company back up the road to wait until the high ground across the river was cleared of the enemy 88s.

At about 10:30 work was started on the bridge. It was to be 110 feet long. It was finished by 5 p.m.

The next day Lieutenant Miller went down to the bank to take photographs of the bridge for the battalion's records. It was already carrying heavy vehicular traffic. On the following day B Company was asked to make the

---

*Colonel Buster followed his own advice. He survived the war and lived to become a general, although he lost a hand.

bridge twice as strong, because of the traffic that was beating it down. By late afternoon that job, too, was finished.

The engineers moved on up the line. On August 7 Lieutenant Miller visited Avranches and saw the destruction of the German vehicles that had occurred earlier all along the road. From Avranches he could see the ocean, and in the mist he made out Mont-St.-Michel.

Everywhere he saw the signs of German collapse. In Ronmay, near Coutances, he saw the remains of a German convoy which had been caught on the road by the Allied air force. The vehicles had been bumper to bumper, and every one of them was destroyed. Bulldozers had pushed the tanks, guns, half-tracks, and trucks into great piles on each side of the road.

On August 9 the lines were moving so rapidly it was hard to tell where the front existed. Lieutenants Miller and Anderson decided to find the First Engineers' command post. They set out to cut south to Mortain and soon found themselves out ahead of the front line. They ran right into a bulge the Germans had driven into the line with their panzers, in an attempt to break through. The American officers did not realize where they were until they saw P-47s diving down on the road a quarter of a mile ahead of them. Then they knew, because the P-47 was the American "tank destroyer." Along with the big artillery, the P-47 compensated for the American inferiority in tanks. When the engineer officers saw the P-47s, they hightailed it back to safety.

Eventually they found the First Engineers in Oiseau, who had been traveling with the Third Armored Division and had hairy tales to tell, such as the story of the night when twenty German tanks had tagged onto their convoy in error. When the panzers made what seemed to be a wrong turn at one intersection, a shepherding convoy jeep went after them and got shot up. The American armor then gave chase and knocked out four of the tanks, but the other sixteen got away.

Movement, movement. By the time Lieutenant Miller got back to camp that afternoon he found the headquarters was already moving again. The engineers had a new job: clean up Vire.

The job began August 9, while the city was still under fire from German guns. Lieutenant Miller drove down to see the rubble and to decide what could be done with it. The object was to put a two-way road through the town so that the vehicles could move fast.

August 10: "Sweated out a few shells Jerry was still dropping. Came back to get a water tank in a truck to wet down the dust in the roads and keep the shells away." Then Miller spent the rest of the day taking pictures of the work; he had been appointed the "unofficial photographer."

On August 11 the engineers were still clearing Vire, with six power shovels and half a dozen bulldozers.

On August 15 the command post moved outside Vire. The day was also one of tragedy for Lieutenant Miller. For weeks he had scrounged and schemed to put together a very nice trailer which he had made into a darkroom. One of the brass had obviously seen it.

"Today we were ordered by Group to turn in all 'improvised trailers.' The bastards! I had to take the chassis off my darkroom. Still have the structure itself and will try to move it by shuttling in a truck. Oh hell!"

But by August 16 he was resigned to the situation, and more interested in new developments:

"Blew up my darkroom trailer with TNT. God damn Colonel Daily!

"News today is good. Front seems to be falling to pieces. The Germans caught in the huge Vire-Mortain-Falaise trap are being pounded mercilessly."

So the Falaise trap was closing on the Germans as the Americans wheeled around to the left and the Canadians moved up from Caen to create the Falaise pocket.

The Second Armored Division's Combat Command B had swung around to the south, along with other troops. Lieutenant Colonel Buster's Ninety-second Field Artillery was at Barenton, at the bottom of the pocket. Aided by L-4 Piper liaison planes, Buster's battalion was supporting the Forty-first Infantry Regiment, which was trying to take the high ground in the vicinity of Barenton. In just a few weeks the L-4 had proved itself to be an enormous asset in conducting armored warfare. The slow-flying plane gave the armored observer plenty of time to sweep the countryside ahead of his column. Any movement of enemy armored units could be spotted immediately, as it was one day when an observer saw a panzer column heading along a side road preparing to set up an ambush for the Second Division's battle group. There was plenty of time to draw back the American column without the Germans knowing it and to zero in on the point where the side road met the main road. Colonel Buster's Ninety-second Artillery did just that, and when the German column reached the crossroads, the firing began. Within a few minutes, the Ninety-second Artillery had destroyed every vehicle in the German column.

The pitched battle had lasted for days. The artillery itself was under constant attack by German aircraft. An enemy plane came over and dropped an antipersonnel "mother" bomb, which exploded in midair, scattering miniature "baby" bombs equipped with propellers. These, too, were supposed to explode in midair, killing the personnel below. The whole battery area was scattered with these fifty sub-bombs, in the half-tracks, in the jeeps—and not one exploded!

Most of the attacks were dive-bombing attacks. There were very few casualties, but they caused a lot of excitement:

"The thing about a dive-bombing attack is that when the bomber lets his bomb go, it looks like it is going right down your throat, whether it is short or long, or whatever. Only if you watch it until it is very, very close do you realize that you are safe."

The Americans really began to move on August 17. That morning the Twentieth Engineers relocated their command post 7 miles southeast of Vire. In the afternoon they were told to get ready to move again. Just before midnight they set out to the Alençon area.

On August 18 Colonel Buster's Ninety-second Field Artillery moved. The enemy was withdrawing, and the artillery battalion's mission was to accompany the combat command in pursuit of the enemy and to try to cut the Germans off.

On August 19 Lieutenant Miller went forward to find the Ninetieth Division and the 315th Engineers. The Twentieth had been ordered up to support them in this closing of the Falaise pocket.

"The gap is now down to about 6 miles, and our artillery on the hills around the valley in which the Germans are squeezed is firing directly at them. Very effective, too."

The engineers were building bridges furiously. Miller's company built a POW cage.

Hitler had given explicit orders to the German troops to break out.

On August 20 the Second Armored Division Artillery was moving very rapidly, three, four, five times a day, in support of the tank column.

Lieutenant Colonel Buster found it necessary to be right beside the commander whose troops he was supporting, so fast was the action. And it was at Falaise that the superiority of American artillery showed itself as never before. It was, without doubt, the most effective arm of the American ground forces. The Germans, who did not have great respect for the American infantry—and, on a one-to-one basis, even less for American armor—were enormously respectful of the American artillery.

"Stick with the commander; that was the only way that I could find out what he was going to do and when he was going to do it. Otherwise, if the situation cleared up in fighting and they found nothing in front of them, they would take off. They wouldn't send you a wire and tell you. They'd just get up and leave. And if you weren't ready to get your artillery back on the road too, you'd find that you were sitting back there and that the troops you were supporting moved out of range. Then you had no protection if they got too far ahead of you, because the enemy could move in behind them, and you would have to find them. So as soon as they would start to move, then we would start to move too. In those days you had no assurance that there wasn't something to the right or to the left that might close in. It was a very tense time."

So Colonel Buster traveled with the commander of the combat command all the time. Buster relayed the situation and plans to his own executive officer, who actually ran the battalion. If he thought the tankers were getting ready to move, Buster would tell his exec to get ready. All this information was communicated by radio; Buster's jeep had two radios for the purpose.

Despite the speed of the advance, it was tough going. On this drive the division lost three armored battalion commanders and several infantry battalion commanders. Buster's old West Point roommate, Art Bailey, was killed in this push. As a staff officer with Combat Command Bailey was killed by a bombing attack on the column as it was moving at night. It was at Vernuers.

It was hard going indeed. One day the column traveled 58 miles.

At the same time, General Patton's Third Army forces were on the right flank of the First Army, and they were barreling ahead to break out and head for Paris. The Germans were trapped on the Second Armored Division's left flank.

On August 20 Lieutenant Miller was told that his Twentieth Engineer Battalion was now supporting Maj. Gen. Horace McBride's Eightieth Infantry Division. He went up to see the infantrymen and found them very green and ignorant. It was their first military action; they had left the United States in July and landed in France on August 6. This same situation applied to the Eightieth's own engineers, the 305th Engineer Battalion. So down came an order from Major General Gerow at Fifth Corps that the Twentieth Engineers were to put all available people on the job of clearing traffic through Argentan, from west to east, lest the advance be stopped. The town was reported by the Eightieth Division to be heavily mined.

The Eightieth Infantry had gone in at 11 a.m. Lieutenant Miller got up there at 1 p.m. and found that the town had been badly shelled and that there were many dead soldiers lying along the roads. Most of them were Germans. The 305th Engineers were working with detector crews on both sides of the town, but they were not marking the roads they swept, so all was confusion. The Twentieth put in a command post and put two companies with bulldozers onto the job. By 6 p.m. the task was done and two-way traffic was established. Lieutenant Miller moved up to stay with the 305th Engineers to keep them from getting the Twentieth into trouble through their inexperience.

Colonel Campbell, provost marshal of the Fifth Corps, had a new problem:

"I will never forget the surrender of the German troops at the closing of the Falaise pocket on August 19. The enemy foot troops were deployed on a fairly level plain, nearly surrounded by hills from which our artillery poured shells into them. When the enemy surrendered, they were in a state of shock, and had only one thought in mind: that was to get as far away from the battlefield as possible and as soon as possible."

For two days Lieutenant Colonel Buster's artillerymen kept running into small groups of Germans trying to fight their way out of the pocket. That meant setting up roadblocks and experiencing many delays in their progress to keep up with the combat command they were supporting at that time.

But Colonel Campbell had to deal with the prisoners. He had some 20,000 of them:

"I commandeered all available transportation in Fifth Corps and had it drive to the battlefield. There was no problem in getting the Germans into the trucks. The problem was in keeping them out. Two-and-a-half-ton trucks that normally carry twenty passengers were soon filled with fifty or sixty, and when we could not get another one on with a shoehorn, many wanted to hang onto the sides and the rear. As far as I know, it was the first time in history that prisoners of war were given taxicab service from the battlefield."

The Germans had set fire to the buildings in the villages in the battle area, and the roofs of most of the structures had collapsed. There were too many prisoners to deal with in a few hours, so as night fell the GIs put the prisoners back into the buildings, or what was left of them. It rained all night, and the prisoners had a wet night.

Meanwhile, the armies drove on, with General Patton racing along the road for Paris, more concerned about his logistics, particularly the shortage of gasoline and diesel fuel, than anything else.

The Second Armored Division was driving ahead, day after day. On August 21 the division traveled 40 miles, the artillery moving four different times. German resistance was getting stronger as the pocket was closed. The armored divisions were bypassing the towns, and that meant the infantry would have to come in and clean up.

On August 21 Lieutenant Miller of the Twentieth Engineers was living with the 305th Engineers, and he did not find the experience stimulating:

"What a comparison with our efficient, smooth-running organization. These people know almost nothing about mine clearance except to be scared of them. I find today that they are putting up signs reading 'Danger, Mines in Shoulder,' along roads we've been using for a week. They have no signs reading 'Road Surface Only Cleared,' and they figured these would do the job. As a result everyone is alarmed, and two of our companies have detector crews out working roads around the bivouacs.... Tonight the chief of staff of the Ninetieth Division ordered us to clear every road in a division assembly area of about 25 square miles. The Sad Sack (Twentieth Division engineer) was up there and graciously volunteered the services of the 1340th and the 20th. We had to furnish nine crews, the 1340th twenty crews. They didn't get started until 7:20 p.m., and it immediately began to pour. Meanwhile the division had already assembled in the critical area without harm. A very snafu job.

"*July 22:* 305th has no record of the roads they cleared last night, so we sent out two companies to clear every road not marked.... Went to Argentan this ,p.m. This was the biggest railroad yard I've seen in France. There must have been half a hundred locomotives, most of them pretty well shot up. This is a beautiful example of the job the air force did of crippling the French railroads before the invasion.

"More about the 305th Engineers:

"These people seem to think that it makes you more warlike or heroic or something to live a dirty, uncomfortable existence. In spite of heavy rains lately, most of the officers still don't put up their shelter tents. They spend most of the day drying out their clothes and bedding. Their camp is filthy, with no organized latrines or sanitary facilities. Many of their officers are loud, bragging, and ignorant. The CO is a West Point 8-ball, class of 1939, and still a major. His vice is stupidity. The exec is an unlettered boastful hillbilly who knows as much about engineering as I do about radar. The whole staff lives at the division CP. The organization struggles along as best it can. Oh, well, maybe they'll shape up—but I doubt it."

The Falaise gap was cleared now, but the prisoners kept coming back.

On August 23 the Second Armored Division artillery moved four times and traveled 22 kilometers, and on that day the Twentieth Engineers were relieved of the Eightieth Division ("Thank God") and put on alert. They were now to move fast, a hundred miles up to the Seine, northwest of Paris! That day Lieutenant Miller saw twenty-two truckloads of prisoners pass by. Out on the roads the French were appearing now, beginning to relax, laughing at the prisoners, shaking their fists and cracking their arms at the elbow (which in French means "Fuck you").

Occasionally now Lieutenant Miller ran into old acquaintances from the French Second Armored Division, which was operating there, on the road to Paris. Friends from the Corps Franc d'Afrique comprised the nucleus. But what a difference. They now had all American equipment, including their uniforms, which they wore with a French flair. They wore berets, French conical helmets, or red overseas caps with red pom-poms, as well as every other sort of gear. They drove along the roads like maniacs, and the French girls came out to cheer, and cheer, and cheer.

On August 24 Colonel Buster's battalion moved to Sesseville.

On August 25 the batteries moved up to Mandeville to support the attack southwest of Rouen on the Seine.

The Americans waited for the French, who were to have the honor of liberating Paris.

On August 25 the French drove into Paris and pulled up in front of the Hotel de Ville.

On August 25 at 4 a.m. Lieutenant Miller's Twentieth Engineers were on the move. They packed up and headed for Nogent. They arrived there at 8:30. They were to be met by a representative of the Fifth Corps who was to tell them where the regiment was to go and the route to follow. Then they were supposed to pick out bivouac sites. They waited three hours, but no Fifth Corps representative showed up. Later they learned that Captain Poussy, the Group S-2, was to meet them, but he had gone to the wrong town named Nogent. They got to Fifth Corps headquarters to learn that Colonel Daly, the corps engineer, had already picked out bivouac sites for them, south of Versailles. Of course, he had done it from a map. When the Twentieth got to the area, they found they were supposed to bivouac in a mudhole.

So Lieutenant Miller, with curses under his breath against the brass, scouted on foot and found a suitable site for his company.

On August 26 Lieutenant Miller went out to scout for Germans. Captain Poussy had reported that he ran into some Tiger tanks in the area. ("Hah!") The men of the Twentieth didn't find any Tigers or any tanks, or any Germans, but thanks to Captain Poussy they did manage to get into Paris, on the St.-Cloud–Sèvres–Versailles road. They were the first Americans to show up in that area. What a welcome they had!

"The broad avenues were lined from curb to curb with laughing, crying, waving Parisians, and the moment we stopped our vehicles, we were practically mobbed. They wanted to touch us, shake hands with us, thank us.

"Lindbergh himself never received such a reception as we had in our three jeeps and command car. The excitement was so contagious that we hardly knew what we were doing. This one morning made all the time we've spent overseas seem worthwhile.

"It's almost impossible to imagine or recall the happiness and excitement of these Parisians, who, after having waited through four years of Nazi rule, finally found themselves free once more and able to greet their 'liberators.'

"Three beautiful girls ran up to our jeep and kissed me. Wow! A man came running up and put 3 quarts of beer in the jeep. An old lady with tears streaming down her cheeks grasped my hand and said in passable Anglaise, 'We've waited for you for long years. Thank you. Thank you.'

"So much emotion has an intoxicating effect. When we got home we were almost exhausted.

"Tonight none of us pitched tents because we were expecting to move in the morning and the sky was clear. Of course it rained like the devil and everyone was drenched. It serves us right for acting like rookies.

"*August 27:* This morning I was sent to the Second French Armored Division, whom we are to support. We found them set up in Les Invalides, apparently having one hell of a good time. The job they wanted us to do was to examine the Seine River bridges for signs of demolition, and then guard them. What a swell job! However, by the time I could report back, we were relieved of the guard detail. We saw a little of Paris, the Seine and the bookstalls, the Louvre, Chamber of Deputies, Montparnasse. Went back to Fifth Corps where we found all the brass considerably more interested in visiting Paris and getting a woman than in fighting the war."

*   *   *

Fifth Corps headquarters was moving up on Paris all right. On August 25 the headquarters reached Chevilly-Mazarin, about 15 miles outside the city. Gen. Dietrich von Choltitz, the German commander of Paris, had surrendered that afternoon after some grenades were thrown into his headquarters at the Hotel Meurice. He was brought to Fifth Corps headquarters and questioned; then he was sent to First Army headquarters. Colonel Campbell, the provost marshal, took charge of von Choltitz and his staff for the night. The general's aide, who spoke perfect English, gave Colonel Campbell a souvenir:

"Colonel, here is the key to the room in the Meurice Hotel that General von Choltitz had occupied. I am sure he will not need it for a long time."*

The following day the Fifth Corps staff rushed into Paris. Colonel Campbell visited several compounds containing German prisoners. Invariably, when the Germans saw him, they assumed that he was there to arrange for their shipment to the United States.

And so Paris was liberated.

On August 28 Lieutenant Miller used an order to search for water sources as an excuse to squeeze in a visit to some of the rest of Paris. He went to the Eiffel Tower and the Place de la Concorde. He took some pictures and stopped at some camera shops, but there were no cameras available.

"The French people seem to have quieted down quite a bit from a few days ago, although every time the jeep stops they practically mob it. There's something about this Paris that gets in one's blood. In spite of the war and its privations there's a gala air about the city. Perhaps the abundance of bicycles and beautiful women has something to do with it. Anyway I can understand why people go AWOL in a place like this."

That evening Lieutenant Miller was back in Paris, to watch the 502d Engineers put up a grandstand out of Bailey bridge parts for a big parade that was to be held the next day.

A key figure in the management of this parade was Colonel Campbell of

---

*The anecdote has a sequel: Colonel Campbell kept the key for ten years. Then he planned a trip to Paris and reserved a room at the Meurice Hotel. He wrote to General Eisenhower, who was then President of the United States, and told him about the key. It was, Campbell suggested, one of the last symbols of the occupation and liberation of Paris. Perhaps the President would like to have some State Department official present the key, he wondered, because he could remember how the French loved ceremony.

President Eisenhower replied that although he liked the idea, times had changed. Now, he said, in 1954, Americans were trying to get along with the Germans, so such a ceremony would create problems. Would Colonel Campbell please restore the key and give the President's regards to his old friend, the manager of the Meurice?

And so Colonel Campbell gave back General von Choltitz's key. And the German general never did get proper credit for his greatest military act: the salvation of Paris. In those last months before the surrender, Adolf Hitler had reason to suspect that his war was lost, and his bitterness was like gall. Once, he had vowed to make Berlin the garden city of Europe, surpassing Paris. But in 1944 Berlin was being battered daily by bombs, and the great buildings were beginning to crumble. Paris, saved from German destruction by the French surrender of 1940, was a symbol of Hitler's hatred for the western Allies. The Führer telephoned von Choltitz early in August and ordered him to burn the city. Von Choltitz stalled for weeks. Ultimately von Choltitz defied his commander in chief and placed his defenses outside the city, thus saving the glory of Paris for the world.

the Fifth Corps. He did not know why the parade was being held—whether to celebrate the return to Paris of General de Gaulle or to show that the United States was behind de Gaulle, or to show the French what American weapons looked like. But there was some discernible purpose. The parade featured the Twenty-eighth Division and the Fifth Armored Division, which were scheduled to attack the very next day.

The big parade was held on the afternoon of August 29, with the reviewing stand at the Place de la Concorde. All the available members of the brass were there: General Bradley; Lt. Gen. Courtney Hodges, commander of the First Army; Major General Gerow, commander of the Fifth Corps; and, of course, General de Gaulle.

The crowd was huge. Lieutenant Miller and his friends were there, taking pictures. Four columns of tanks abreast came rumbling down the Champs-Élysées from the Arc de Triomphe and split into two lines of two before the reviewing stand at the base of the obelisk.

Colonel Campbell was very busy, moving the troops and taking care of security at the same time.

After passing the Place de la Concorde, the troops were to continue by column. The first three columns continued straight ahead, as they were supposed to do, but the fourth column turned to the right and crossed the River Seine to the left bank—and disappeared!

Colonel Campbell had set up a system of guides and guards, using men from the Twenty-eighth Division. But none of these men had ever been in Paris before, so the colonel never did figure out whether the men in the missing column had erred on their own or had been directed where their hearts would have led them. Nor did he ever discover how many of those dogfaces who had gotten "lost" that day stayed lost in the wilds of Paris.

The parade was a great success. It was only too bad that the next day, almost all of those involved had to go back to the war.

35

PUSH

On August 30, the day after the big parade in Paris, Lieutenant Miller went looking for the Twenty-eighth Division. His battalion had been assigned to support the 103d Engineers of that division, to teach them the ropes. He found them near Le Bourget Airport. That night he slept in the 103d command post, a modern apartment building with running water and real beds!

Next day he awakened to discover that his "faithful" jeep driver had gone AWOL with the jeep, Miller's M-1 rifle, and most of his personal belongings, including his camera and all the souvenirs he had bought in Paris. Miller got another jeep and driver, and found the 103d Engineers at Senlis. They wanted a Bailey bridge, so A Company of the Twentieth Engineers put it up for them. Miller spent that night in the command post, an old château, "a beautiful place but a bit smelly." It had been a German headquarters earlier.

For the next few days, as the Twenty-eighth Division moved ahead, Lieutenant Miller's men were building bridges. They bridged the Aisne at Compiègne. They had to. The infantry had sat on the near shore and let the Germans sneak back after a retreat. The Germans blew up the permanent bridge. So it was the engineers to the rescue again.

What a mess it was. A Company had been ordered to build the bridge. Then the commanding general of the Fifth Armored Division came up and ordered the Twenty-second Engineers to build it. Then more brass arrived and decided that the Twentieth should build another bridge. Miller spent half the night trying to find the bridge train, which had all the parts.

"What a horrible night. The damn convoy kept breaking in two every mile or so and pieces of it would get lost. It was cold as hell [sic] and dark as sin, and around six o'clock, six or eight 'buzz bombs' [V-1 rockets] sailed right over our heads. What a terrific racket they make! Right at daylight, while one truck was broken down in a little town and the rest of the convoy had wandered away, a French family brought us coffee. It was terrible stuff, but it was hot."

On September 2 Miller was in the Forêt de la Compiègne, where the armistice of 1918 was signed. The forest was filled with Germans. That night he was to make a 50-mile march with the 103d Engineers. The route was from Compiègne to Noyon. At the latter place he found people skinning German horses killed by American tanks, and cutting off steaks. On he went to Chauny and La Fère. Then Miller went up to check a blown bridge at La Fère. It was blown all right, and the 109th Regimental Combat Team was lined up on the road trying to get across the canal locks there. The men of the 103d were trying to build a timber bridge. Finally they succeeded.

After a long day and a hard night, Lieutenant Miller finally bedded down in an abandoned butcher shop. Next morning he slept till 10:00, got up, ate biscuits, jam, strawberries, and unripe pears he found in the backyard of the butcher shop, and discovered that the battalion had moved to Chauny.

The army was moving. On September 5 Miller found himself in rolling country, near Poix-Terron. This was newly liberated land. The battalion arrived in the little town of Touligny.

"We were completely surrounded in the village street by a cheering crowd and I was thoroughly kissed by about eighty women whose ages ranged from 1 to 80 years. Lots of them were between 16 and 20 though. All the women were on my side of the jeep and all the men were on the driver's side. He just got to shake hands. The mayor's wife brought out Calvados and we both had stiff jolts. When I told them in my broken French that there would be *beaucoup de soldats* there tonight, all the girls cheered. Someone is going to have a good time tonight!

"*September 6:* Stayed in camp all day and wrote up the monthly unit history and the afteraction report. All three companies were engaged in repairing a blown railway bridge, removing the rails and converting it for vehicular traffic. It rained like hell all day. The only bright spot was four fried eggs, which I cadged....

"*September 7:* Battalion moved to Sedan.... The Germans are supposed

to be in the woods about 3 miles across the river. We have our headquarters
in an old château. In the upper stories are a swarm of Polish slave laborers
brought to France to do farming. They were kept inside a barbed-wire en-
closure and seem very pale and undernourished. Also very glad to see us.

"*September 8:* Received orders to have headquarters cross the river by
1800. All our trucks are hauling doughboys; also we shuttled in weapons
carriers across the Meuse, and on the outskirts of Sedan.

"*September 9:* Followed the Fifth Armored on its motor march from Sedan. Well into Belgium. Red, black, and yellow flags are flying everywhere,
and there are more enthusiastic crowds in the villages. B Company is building a floating Bailey bridge across the Meuse at Sedan.

"*September 10:* Made Luxembourg border. They told me division was held
up at the capital. Went on to Luxembourg and met the Eighty-fifth Recon
Team in the western side of town. Our people were shelling over the city.
Went through town with some Eighty-fifth Recon boys and watched our artillery shell positions across the valley. Saw a half-track of Germans pull
into position and draw fire. Back into the city and saw the Grand Duke Felix,
in British uniform, being acclaimed by the citizens. Left town when the Fifth
Armored Division began to pull through.

"On the way back turned off north to go into Arlon. The town had apparently just been liberated. The people were having a tremendous celebration,
marching through the streets, carrying pictures of Der Führer for everyone
to spit on. When our jeep stopped, about fifteen girls piled onto it. Then
they began bringing out the drinks. Wine, anisette, something they called
'whiskey,' and other marvelous but potent beverages. They 'dragged' me into
a bar where an impromptu dance was going on, and of course I was the high-
light of that particular function. By this time both my driver and I were quite
plastered...so we drove on to find the command post at its new location at
Heinsch.

"*September 11:* The people of Hebray-la-Viele, a little town near our command post, took a German colonel from a truck of prisoners at night and
hanged him. He had been in command of the area and the last act of the
Nazis before leaving was to shoot fifteen of the villagers. *Sic semper tyrannis.*"

Lieutenant Downing was evacuated to England after he had been hit by that
bit of shrapnel in Normandy. But not before he spent a night at the Seventy-
seventh Evacuation Hospital.

"When I had been checked in at the receiving tent, a soldier guided me to the ward tent. A nurse assigned me to a cot. I undressed and climbed into bed. No sooner was I between the sheets than I suffered a malarial chill. When the nurse came by, I asked her for more blankets. She put some more over me and I tried to go to sleep, but a light was shining directly over my face and kept me awake. There seemed to be a lot of confusion behind me. I sat up in bed. The large hospital ward tent was crowded with cots. Behind me, our heads together, was a young German soldier lying on his cot. He kept moaning for '*Wasser.*' A blood plasma bottle was slung over his head, the tube leading to his arm. Across from him was an American soldier who tried to explain to him in German that he couldn't have water because he had been shot in the stomach and had to be operated on. The nurse came by, held the German's hand a while, and tried to soothe him to sleep. When the nurse left, the German moaned again. The soldier again explained that after the operation he could have coffee, water, fruit juice, anything he wanted, but now he couldn't drink because of the operation. The German got angry and pulled the tube out of his arm. The American soldier yelled and the nurse came running over. She sent an orderly for a doctor. When the doctor arrived, he found that the German had messed up his vein in that arm. He inserted the tube in the German's other arm and left. The German again moaned for '*Wasser.*' The nurse came down and swabbed his forehead. Orderlies brought in more wounded and the nurse left to look after them. The German tossed around and cried insistently for '*Wasser.*' The American soldier again started to explain. At this point I got fed up with the whole routine. I wanted to sleep. I yelled out:

"'*Du verdammt Schmutzige, deutsche Schwein! Wasser ist verboten.*'

"I doubled up my fist in front of his face. He shut up and I dropped off to sleep."

The next day a doctor tried to take the piece of shell out of Downing's leg, but he had to give up. It would work its way out in time. The following day, after an air raid, Downing was evacuated by C47 transport to England.

"After a short drive we arrived at a permanent hospital installation. The buildings were all Nissen huts connecting by an interlocking system of roofed pasageways.

"We reported in and gave our names to the registrar. We were told to sit outside until our names were called. This was a large concrete courtyard with grass borders. I lay down on the grass border and relaxed. Nearby were a couple of wounded German soldiers guarded by a soldier with a carbine. They wore the black uniform of the SS panzer troops. Most of the Americans ignored them except one who tried to talk to them. This character wore a khaki summer uniform and low-cut, buckled officer's dress shoes. Over his long Hollywood-style hair was a long-billed air corps ground crew cap. Those were probably the first Germans he had ever seen, and he acted as if he was playing with the animals at the zoo. . . .

"I found out that this was the 186th General Hospital, located at Hereford, England."

Downing stayed in the hospital. When the wound began to heal, he started to walk. "At first the walk to the mess hall was slow and difficult for me, but daily I picked up speed until soon I could walk as rapidly as before being wounded."

Then the doctor rated him fit to return to duty, and around the middle of August he drew new clothing and equipment.

"The news of the war that came over the radio was cheering. There had been tough fighting around Mortain, Avranches, and the Falaise Gap, but now it looked good; the Third Army had punched through the hole made by the First Army and was overrunning the Brest Peninsula."

Downing was ready to go back into the war.

Lieutenant Colonel Snetzer had been evacuated to England with the wound in his leg and was sewed up and fed and coddled until the end of August, when he was declared fit for combat once again. On August 27, D + 72, he landed again on the sands of Normandy at Utah Beach. Then he began looking for Second Infantry Division.

On August 29 he found the division near Landerneau, near Brest. It was now fighting as a part of the Eighth Corps of General Patton's Third Army. Then it was back to his battalion of the Second Combat Engineers, and the shooting war:

"*September 5:* Tuesday. Been back a week now. Still slowly closing in on Brest, hedgerow by hedgerow, just like when I left in Normandy. Deadly, sticky fight. Lots of mines and booby traps to clear. German Second Parachute Division reinforced by sailors and marines putting up a devil of a fight. Making a regular Bataan. Lieutenant Lee and two sergeants were killed yesterday by an exploding antipersonnel mine.

"*September 12:* Battle for Brest still rages viciously. We are now into the outskirts of the city, fighting house by house. Have had marvelous air support on closing in. All day long the air corps has bombed and strafed. The city is being utterly destroyed. City burns continuously, but we still haven't reached the inner wall. And the Germans fight though we have taken over 7000 pris-

oners already. General Ramcke, the German commandant, refused to surrender
today in blunt terms. The Eighth Division has been pinched out."

The area was so small that only the Twenty-ninth and Second divisions
could operate against Brest, supported by artillery.

"*September 16:* Closing into center of city of Brest now. Troops are massed
around the outskirts of the old city wall, which is a real obstacle. Direct fire
of 105-millimeter self-propelled guns and 76-millimeter guns is being used
against the wall. The Thirty-eighth Infantry captured a magnificent naval
hospital. The Germans fought from floor to floor. Machine guns were firing
out of the third-story windows.

"All front-line infantry is living in apartment houses, sleeping in beds
these days. More captured wine, cognac, perfume, toilet articles than can
be used.

"*September 18:* Brest surrendered at 1500 today. Early in the morning I
went over the wall with supporting infantry. Hundreds of prisoners were being taken. We were the first into a captured pillbox, and I picked up a Luger,
another pistol, and three pairs of binoculars. The battalion was busy opening roads into the city. I was present in President Wilson Place as the surrender took place. It was a dramatic moment as the immaculately clad German
officers, many with their Iron Crosses, stood in the center of the horribly
burned and destroyed city. A mockery of Wilson's dream that this most
vicious battle ends here in his square. It was exactly like the end of the
football season in which the home team just lost the last big game and the
captain was cheering the men up on a good show. Colonel Pietzonka, the
commanding officer of the German Seventh Parachute Infantry Regiment,
called his officers around; they gave the Nazi salute, shook hands, and he
pinned a medal on one of his surviving '*Hauptmanns*.' Battalion after battalion of Germans were led out of their deep shelters by the officers and
taken over by MPs.

"The city is utterly destroyed. All buildings left standing are completely
gutted by fire. We brought up three bulldozers and spent the night opening
up a couple of streets through town, bulldozing the fallen walls of the buildings into the basements. Witnessed the hoisting of the French *tricouleur* and
singing of the '*Marseillaise*' by the Free French left. It was strangely silent
in the city, no artillery fire passing overhead. No rifle fire."

On September 19 the engineers finished the opening of the key streets of
Brest and the entire division moved out of the area to assemble near Landerneau.

The Second Engineer Battalion moved into a big château. Higher head-quarters issued all kinds of cognac, wine, and other liquors that had been captured from the enemy. On September 21 the engineer officers organized a party at the château.

It was a blast.

"Plenty of liquor, plenty of nurses, division dance band, and all."

Vive la Guerre!

*   *   *

From where Lieutenant Downing sat in England, the news indicated that the war would be over in a matter of weeks. He was out of the hospital but still was assigned to spend a couple of weeks in a convalescent home before thinking about getting back to the war.

"We traveled first class and after a ride of a few hours arrived at our station. When the train pulled out, we looked around in dismay. We had been the only passengers getting off. The station was a tiny, one-room building. There was no town in sight, only rolling fields, hedges, and in the distance, scattered farmhouses."

One of the officers went to the stationmaster's office and put in a call to Preston Hall. That was the rest home.

Soon a civilian car came up, driven by an officer accompanied by a Red Cross girl.

"They called us over and we piled in. The driver gave us a big buildup about what a swell place the rest home was. I mentally reserved judgment. We drove through a tiny village into the grounds of an estate and pulled up before a long, low, gray-stone manor house. We went inside and were greeted by an army nurse and an elderly civilian lady. The grayhaired lady showed us to our rooms. We dropped our baggage and made a tour of exploration. The house belonged to a retired British general who had donated it originally as a rest home for flak-happy air corps pilots. Now it had degenerated into a convalescent home for shell-happy infantry officers. The grounds were beautifully laid out with flowers and shrubbery. The middle-aged British lady gave us a hearty welcome. She showed us where the croquet and archery sets were kept. She also issued us a pair of civilian slacks, a civilian shirt, a pullover civilian sweater, tennis shoes, and sweat socks. All during the day we could wear the civilian clothes, but at the evening meal we had to wear uniform.

"Every afternoon there was tea at 4 p.m., and at 6 p.m. there was a cocktail hour at which we could get one, repeat *one*, shot of gin or Scotch before the evening meal. A record was kept, and we paid for the drinks before we left for the replacement depot. We were also given the information that everything was informal, rank did not count, and you could call everyone by his first name. That made everything just ducky. Some of the officers were knocking themselves out over this setup, but it did not appeal to me. The only redeeming feature was that it was a two weeks' vacation. One drink a day was a pretty slim ration and poor compensation for the doubtful privilege of calling field officers Charlie or George. There were no women in the vicinity, and the local pub only sold beer. When I looked forward to two weeks of hitting croquet balls, shooting arrows, and drinking tea, I was bored already."

After the two weeks Downing was shipped off to the Tenth Replacement Depot at Litchfield. There, he found that he had been awarded a Bronze Star medal for his activity on D day. That same day he was transferred to a branch camp called Pheasey Farms. It had been a housing development, completed just before the war started. Before the red-brick houses could be occupied by civilians, they had been requisitioned by the British government. Since then, they had been lend-leased to the American army, and a whole succession of casuals had passed through. Downing was assigned a small room furnished with a steel army cot, mattress, sheets, pillow, and blankets. He hung his clothes on nails in the walls. The company grade officers sat at long wooden tables in the mess hall, on wooden benches, and brought their own mess kits. Field grade officers ate at small tables for four with tablecloths and waiter service. There was a pub that sold beer.

But... "A large section of the local female population thronged the place, and any enterprising officer or soldier could establish an acquaintanceship sometime between 6 p.m. and the closing hour of 10:00. Since the casual troops arrived and departed at frequent intervals, life held infinite variety for those local belles who were willing to exchange their favors for American affection, cigarettes, candy, or British pounds."

Soon Downing was assigned to a "package" of officers and men destined to return to France. They went to Tidworth Barracks, where Downing's First Infantry Division had stayed on arrival in England in 1942. It seemed a long, long time ago. From there they moved to Southampton and a ship. Two days later the ship was anchored off Omaha Beach. The LCT tied up at a floating pier, and Downing walked ashore.

"Guides started us along a path down the beach. I noticed shattered concrete pillboxes and thought of my former landing here a couple of months before. A high wooden archway had now been erected over the path. It read:

"'Along this path have walked the finest combat troops in the world.' The Hollywood touch!

"We struggled up the steep hill. Loaded as we were with equipment and just out of the hospital, a lot of men began dropping out. Officers and men mingled, and we walked along independently. I reached the top of the hill. I turned and looked back at the beach. I shook my head in wonder at how we had even gotten ashore on D day. From the hill the beach looked like a perfect death trap for troops coming ashore. There was little cover and the hill completely dominated the shore. Having seen the beach from the hill, I would have hated to have to try the landing again."

The new arrivals went into bivouac. Lieutenant Downing passed some British and American vehicles, the soldiers wearing the patch of SHAEF. He figured that SHAEF was moving the headquarters over from England. He also saw troops wearing the shoulder patch of the Ninety-fifth Division. "It looked as if the U.S. Army was finally making the supreme sacrifice of depleting the garrisons of the USO clubs to help augment the troops in the combat zone."

After several days at the airstrip bivouac the men were taken ahead by truck. The group arrived at Le Mans and then went on to Étampes. From there Downing and several other officers made a trip into Paris. They ended up in Montmartre, toured the nightclubs, and stayed at the Hotel Bourges, paying 65 francs ($1.35) for a room. They did not find any girls.

The next day they got on the Paris Metro and toured the city, winding up their visit by buying some ice cream from a pushcart at the Eiffel Tower. Finally they hitchhiked back to Étampes.

Downing came down with an attack of malaria, and that meant a month of the new treatment with Atabrine, the malaria suppressant. He got sent back to England again.

Meanwhile the war went on.

After the closing of the Falaise pocket, the Second Armored Division had moved to an assembly area on the west side of the Seine. It crossed the river in the wake of General Patton's Third Army. The Fifteenth Corps had crossed on August 19.

Then the Second Armored headed for the Belgian border. Its orders were very simple: "The division will advance, as far as gasoline will permit."

So the GIs advanced, draining the gas out of nonessential vehicles into the tanks of the self-propelled guns and essential vehicles and supplying the tanks as best they could.

On September 2 they reached Aix in Belgium. There they set up camp because they were virtually out of fuel. It was raining and cold. They remained until September 6. Gasoline began to arrive and they planned for future operations, courtesy of the "Red Ball Express," the fleet of supply trucks hastily organized to get fuel and other necessities to the front.

Sergeant Thornton's Sixtieth Infantry was moving fast through Belgium, with the rest of the Ninth Division, on the heels of the retreating Germans. But the Sixtieth suffered heavy casualties in several battles, and the need grew ever greater for experienced officers. On August 18 Sergeant Thornton was commissioned second lieutenant. By September 14 they had reached the German border.

"*September 15:* Today we started out with trucks until we contacted the enemy. We pushed through a German railroad station taking many prisoners and then advanced into Monschau, taking the city. We had to leave the trucks and tanks and climb a big hill to get on the high ground. That night we were under a lot of small-arms fire, and the first platoon suffered casualties from tank fire.

"*September 16:* Today we made an attack reaching the road, and then our tanks came up after getting around a German tank. We pushed to the town of Hofen. We got through many big pillboxes and took a lot of prisoners. We entered the town and put up roadblocks. Just after that a German tank broke through and tore up the town all night, and knocked out a lot of our guns.

"*September 17:* This forenoon we were surrounded by Germans and had a terrible fight, until our tanks got to us. I wounded three Germans at very close range. Tonight we remained on the same block with much better luck than last night.

"*September 18:* Today we advanced about 700 yards and put up some more roadblocks. Company K took many prisoners. Tonight I got a blackout room and wrote four letters by the light of a candle.

"*September 19:* This morning we were replaced by the First Battalion and we moved north by truck convoy through Monschau to an assembly area.

"*September 20:* Today we jumped off on the attack and made 2000 yards without meeting any resistance.

"*September 21–25:* During these days we moved around in the woods meeting some resistance; casualties were light.

"*September 26–28:* These three days have been rough with many pillboxes to crack and many casualties. The weather has been bad with lots of rain and mud.

"*September 29–30:* These days have been at a standstill, just holding our position."

On September 11 Lieutenant Miller drove through Bastogne and into northern Luxembourg, behind the Twenty-eighth Division. He reached Troisvierges just as the Luxembourgers were celebrating, passing out glasses of cold beer. He and a friend rode back and forth through the town until they had been given three beers each. "It was wonderful beer, almost like Budweiser, with a beautiful head."

On September 12 Lieutenant Miller drove to Clervaux, a little resort town in a deep valley. He drove on till he looked over into Germany. It looked just like anyplace else he had seen.

On September 14 Miller drove across the German border at Welchenhausen. "The only people I saw were quite old, and they just glowered at us."

In the morning the Twenty-eighth Division began an attack designed to force the Siegfried line.

That same day Miller's jeep driver asked to be relieved. He complained that the lieutenant was always going off and poking his nose into dangerous places. So Miller got a new jeep driver that day, Private Rogers.

On September 16 Lieutenant Miller went up to Weiswampach and Marnach to watch the shelling of the Siegfried line with phosphorus.

Then, on September 17, came more big news: The Allies had landed a whole airborne army in Holland, and the First Infantry Division had broken through the Siegfried line and was heading for Cologne. The Twentieth Engineers moved that night to Clervaux and took up temporary residence in the monastery there.

By mid-September the Canadian First Army had isolated the Channel ports of Le Havre, Boulogne, Calais, and Dunkerque. The Twenty-eighth Division had also come very near the Schelde Estuary in Holland. The British Second Army had reached Antwerp and had put a bridgehead across the Schelde Canal. The American First Army was on the Siegfried line from Aachen to Luxembourg, and the U.S. Third Army in the south had established bridgeheads across the Moselle River around Nancy.

That airborne army in Holland consisted of the U.S. 17th, 82nd, and 101st Airborne divisions, a Polish brigade, and three British divisions.

The 101st Airborne landed in Eindhoven in an area around the road from the Belgian border north to the Zuider Zee. The road, about a hundred miles

long, was very important: it was just about the only way to bring armor over
the canals and rivers that crossed this part of Holland.

The 506th Parachute Infantry Regiment landed on the afternoon of September 17 around 1:15. Its mission was to secure bridges over the Wilhelmina
Canal at Zon. In that town the paratroopers came under fire from a German
88. The unofficial division history reported it this way:

> The advance party, one platoon from Company D, swung out to the right
> and around the first row of buildings. Its members were protected from the
> fire of the gun by the surrounding houses and walked to within fifty yards of
> it without any difficulty. Evidently the Germans had put out no flank pro-
> tection.
>
> With his bazooka, Pvt. Thomas G. Lindsey of the 2nd Battalion Head-
> quarters bazooka section, fired one round at the 88-mm. gun. The rocket hit
> the gun near the elevating mechanism and the gun was finished. One German
> was killed by the blast and six others fled toward the bridges.

The paratroopers killed them all. And then another 88 was knocked out
near the first one. The action was over in about twenty minutes.

But the Germans were not finished.

As the Second Battalion of the 101st moved toward the center bridge,
the troops saw a few Germans run from buildings. The center was receiving
fire from a house on the far side of the canal. The battalion began to take
casualties, and soon ten men were wounded. Heavy American fire was then
concentrated on the house by rifles, machine guns, bazookas, and mortars.
The men in the house stopped shooting.

The Americans advanced onto the bridge. Parts of three rifle companies
got within 50 yards of the bank. Suddenly the bridge went up with a roar.
Debris fell all around the infantrymen. They found three Germans crouched
under the concrete of the north pillar, unharmed. They had done their job:
they had blown up the bridge.

And then Colonel Sink, commander of the regiment, learned that the
other two bridges across the canal had been blown up by the Germans several days earlier. So it was not going to be a "piece of cake" after all.

And it was not. The Germans fought stoutly for the whole area. Eindhoven
was supposed to fall swiftly. It did not.

The Germans staged a counterattack on D + 5, September 22. The point
was Vechel on the long road. The Germans used the 107th Panzer and 280th
Assault Gun brigades, plus elements of the 347th and 59th Infantry divisions.

The Americans, warned by the Dutch underground, hustled the 506th Parachute Infantry up to Uden; the Germans cut the road just after the 506th arrived at 11 a.m. Or at least Headquarters Company of the 506th and a platoon of the Second Battalion made it to Uden that day. And they held the town.

The Second Battalion of the 501st Parachute Infantry was at Erp, where it was attacked by a German column. As the fighting grew desperate, up came the men of the Second Battalion of the 506th. They had a 57-millimeter antitank gun, and they got into action against a German Mark V tank.

Said one man from the 101st:

> There was no time for Colonel Cox and his crew to get into a covered position. Swinging their 57 around in the middle of the road a hundred yards from the tank, they jumped to the ground. As they started to ram home a shell, they saw the gun on the Panther swing over toward them. The tank fired first; they felt the flash and thought they were goners, but the shell hit the house behind them and merely showered them with masonry. Squinting through the dust, Colonel Cox aimed and fired. His shot hit the tank, disabling it. His second shot, quickly gotten off, set it on fire.

So the fighting went on, very brisk fighting as the Germans got their second wind.

*　　*　　*

Headquarters Company of the 501st's Second Battalion crossed the Nijmegen bridge and holed up in an orchard to get away from the almost constant shellfire on the road. After waiting a few hours, toward dusk the company moved up to replace a British contingent.

The main line of resistance was on the reverse slope of a dike, 15 to 20 feet high, with a road on top. It was a real hot spot, and the company suffered some casualties. Cpl. Glen A. Derber was one of the soldiers in this unit.

He was ordered to take over a machine gun whose crew had suffered a direct hit from a mortar shell. Derber moved up to a spot about 600 yards from the German line. He began firing his machine gun and sent the Germans hunting for cover. But a few minutes later a mortar shell dropped very close to his position. He stopped firing the machine gun and jumped into a foxhole. It did not seem deep enough to him, so he dug it deeper. Then he slipped out and fired the machine gun again. This time he got more mortar fire, and it was too close for comfort. He jumped back into the hole. He also decided that the machine gun made him too attractive a target.

He tasted his first C rations that day. After eating British rations for several weeks, they tasted good. Then he settled back down to his war.

Corporal Derber was an old-fashioned soldier; his favorite weapon was a 1903 Springfield rifle. He borrowed a pair of field glasses and set up in business as a sniper.

I saw a Kraut about six hundred yards or so away, lying outside his hole in the warm sun, so I tried a shot. He didn't move. I guessed the bullet couldn't have gotten to him so I set my sights up to seven hundred yards and tried again. He scrambled to his feet and ducked into his foxhole, then looked around wondering who was shooting at him. The next time I fired he ducked into his hole. When he came up to look around again he had his rifle. I tried another shot, and down he went again. I checked with the field glasses after each shot and when I looked after my last shot, he was aiming at me!

I got ready to fire again and a bullet cracked above my head. It seemed pretty wide to me and I was all for this game. . . . The next shot I fired must have hit him in the head for he bounded out of his hole as if by reflex action and went tumbling head over heels down the side of the dike. Some other Kraut came over to take a look at him and I scared him off with a shot.

I had a lot of fun that afternoon, wounding two more and two probables. That not being enough excitement for one day I spied some wild ducks in a pond to the rear of our lines and started chasing them around with my .03 [1903 Springfield rifle]. I finally hit one. That done I went off to one of the nearby houses, or what was left of it, and went into the fruit celler and found a couple of jars of canned cherries.

That night Corporal Derber enjoyed a celebrated continental entrée: roast duck with cherries.

The following day Derber did some more sniping, but without results. He and the others held the line.

The days went by.

On D + 21 the Germans began to probe. They moved 400 yards down the dike on Derber's right, and they dug in directly across from the position of the 501st. The American lines were on one side of the dike, and 30 feet away were the Germans.

It was very hard for the Americans to get at the enemy on the reverse side of the dike. When the GIs threw grenades, they rolled past the Jerries, down to the bottom of the dike. So somebody had a bright idea: attach a length of parachute suspension line to each grenade, making the whole about 40 feet long. Then when the grenade was thrown, it could roll only to the end of the line.

Corporal Derber was there when somebody came along asking for a rifleman who could use a grenade launcher to try to knock out a machine gun position down the dike. So he took the job. The machine gun was located about 75 yards out. The only way to reach it was to stand up and shoot the grenades. So he did, while other soldiers covered him with their M-1s. He put three grenades into the position; then he went back for more grenades. But when he returned, the Germans had pulled out, leaving their gun in the ditch. Then along came the first sergeant of Headquarters Company to ream out Corporal Derber for leaving his machine gun position and going off to play games.

By D + 22 Derber's platoon had been cut down by attrition from eight gun crews to five. When Derber was not on duty on the line with his crew, he was off sniping, but with little success. The 1903 Springfield was not really the best sniper weapon in the world.

After a few more days the company went into division reserve, and the men marched 7 miles back to an orphans' home where they were billeted for five days' rest.

On their thirty-first day in Holland they moved up to the line again. This time they were in static situation, a sort of trench warfare that lasted for ten days. They were well dug in; so were the Germans. They ate well; so did the Germans. They got mail; so did the Germans. The Americans saw virtually no enemy infantry. They just got mortar and artillery fire to keep them on their toes. They were in the middle of a group of orchards, so there were plenty of apples. On the forty-first day they were relieved again and marched back to the orphans' home.

A few days later it was back to the front once more. This time they did not have to march, but were sent up in trucks. What a relief. The fact was that the life was so soft that Corporal Derber was putting on weight and was no longer in very good condition.

On their first night back in the line he and his pals saw what looked like meteors. The next day they saw one in daylight, a missile rising high in the sky with a long trail of smoke in its wake. It was one of the new V-2 rocket bombs. The Germans were using them on Amsterdam.

The war continued, a slow, lazy war for Corporal Derber.

On Armistice Day, November 11, which "celebrated" the end of World War I, the regiment arranged its own celebration. At 11 a.m. every American weapon in the area began to fire: artillery, 81- and 60-millimeter mortars, bazookas, machine guns, grenades, M-1s, and Corporal Derber's old Springfield. The Germans responded in kind.

On the fifty-seventh day Derber's company was relieved again, but on the sixty-fourth day it was back.

"No one seemed happy about going this time, for by now we had all become pretty much sick of the whole thing. We knew winter would be setting in and we wanted action. The positions at the dike were a mess now. The rain had leaked in. . . . Most of the foxholes on the dike were soaked, and it was impossible to keep dry. All holes on the level ground were filled to within 8 inches of the surface. The only dry places to stay were the basements of demolished houses. There was no shelter near enough to my gun position to be made use of because we had to stay on the gun, especially at night. During the day all but one of us would go to an old barn for shelter. We cooked meals there and built a fire to dry out. I used an old raincoat over my machine gun to try to keep it dry, but to no avail. It was just mud and water everywhere. The side of the dike got so greasy with mud that we could hardly crawl up to our gun position, and steps had to be cut in. One poor chap got caught in a mortar barrage while traveling on level ground to the barn. He jumped into a foxhole and was soaked to the waist."

Thanksgiving came. As a special treat the GIs were supposed to have some American ten-in-one rations. But the boys in the rear echelons got them; the front line did not. They were told there would be no food at all for Thanksgiving. But someone discovered a cow that had been "killed by enemy fire." So Derber's platoon got the liver, and from one of the wrecked houses the men got potatoes. That night they had fried liver and potatoes instead of turkey and trimmings.

And the next day they got a real present. The Canadians moved in to take over the paratroopers' positions. When the men of the company marched out, Corporal Gerber counted noses. Of the men who had dropped with him into Holland two months earlier, only half were left. He had gone through three gun crews. Of the eight gunner corporals only three remained to march back.

And so the 101st Airborne Division was pulled out of Holland, and moved to Mourmelon-le-Grand, in France. It was late November.

*

Private Adolph's L Company of the 397th Infantry of the 100th Division moved overseas. From Fort Bragg the men had traveled to Camp Kilmer, New Jersey. From there they took ship. Private Adolph wrote to his grandmother from the mid-Atlantic:

"Don't worry, I'll be back before you know it. It's just like being away at a distant camp in the U.S. only its overseas and we won't have a chance to come home as often as before."

He said virtually nothing about the voyage, and yet there was a nice neat half-a-sentence-long hole in the letter; some zealous company officer had just preserved the unit's security.

And so in late October Private Adolph and his outfit landed in southern France to join the battle against the Germans. But first they got a little time off.

They were allowed to go into a town he identified only as C. The passes lasted from 9 a.m. until 6 p.m. Private Adolph and his pals hitched a ride in a 2½-ton truck.

"There are many nice stores and fancy ones, too, where we bought a few odds and ends. We walked into a parfums shop and I got some shaving cream...and the other guy with me bought some toothpaste. They cost 15 francs apiece. We really should have had tickets because everything is rationed, but they gave it to us free. There is absolutely no soap in France, and the black market pays 50 francs a bar."

Private Adolph also noticed: "On some of the streets it seems there never was a war. The boulevards are as clean and neat as Fifth Avenue. The sidewalk cafes flourish with plenty of customers."

But within a few days the respite was over and the 100th Division was engaged in battle, moving toward the Vosges Mountains, and Germany. Adolph was writing to his family from a pup tent, sitting on a helmet, using a package from home as a desk. Occasionally the men spent a night in a farmer's house or in a barn. One evening they were lucky enough to get a home-cooked farm meal; a grateful farm family had killed several chickens and brought out the canned cherries, the potatoes, and the *eau de vie*, and had fed Adolph's squad royally. But as the GIs moved forward into the borderland between France and Germany, the populace became less friendly, more sullen.

And then the Americans were in real battle, trying to take a certain hill— Hill No. (military secret) according to Private Adolph. The Germans were dug in about a third of the way up the rise, with good position and fields of fire, and plenty of automatic weapon and mortar support. Adolph's platoon was in the assault force. The troops tried to take that hill twice on the first day, but failed. Private Adolph was now acting squad leader, a job for a staff sergeant. There was no one else to handle it. The casualties were high.

That night the artillerymen unlimbered and fired everything they could find at the Germans on the hill.

The next day the American infantrymen attacked again, and once more were sent reeling back. Only in the afternoon, after more artillery and mortar support, did they take the objective.

"The bastards shoot and kill as long as they can, and then they bring out their white flags and surrender."

A few days after this desperate assault Private Adolph became Staff Sergeant Adolph. He was 19 years old, and an old hand, who was writing home about wine, *eau de vie*, and cognac with the assurance of a man who knew whereof he spoke.

It was just before Christmas 1944.

On November 5 Colonel Campbell had been given a rude shock. He was advised by General Gerow that he was being declared excess. The problem was that Corps Headquarters had too many West Point officers, so the civilian soldiers like Colonel Campbell had to go. The general did not say that, of course. He said he was sorry. What did Colonel Campbell want to do?

Colonel Campbell wanted to go back to America and go on inactive duty. He was, after all, a retread from World War I and could have opted out of this war a long time ago.

But all the questions regarding rank and the problems of professional as opposed to citizen soldiers were soon moot, for the colonel developed a pain and went into the hospital a week after the capture of Metz. Diverticulitis was the diagnosis, and he was slapped into a general hospital. On December 10 Colonel Campbell was on his way to England, to the Tenth reppledepple, to be processed to go home to America. On December 15, as the Germans prepared their big surprise for the Allies, Colonel Campbell was alerted for return to the states. He boarded the USS *Wakefield*, and so he missed the coming big German offensive. The colonel's war was over.

It wasn't easy near the German border. On October 18 Captain Miller was awakened in the middle of the night by the sound of an explosion, and then he saw a huge fire a few miles away. The next morning he discovered that a German Ju-88 had crashed into one of the engineer unit's buildings at Camp Elsenborn. Fortunately the dogfaces in the barracks escaped without injury.

By the end of October the Twentieth Engineers had moved to the German border. Captain Miller drove up to Aachen on October 29 to look over the ruins of that city. It had been bombed very heavily and then damaged more severely by artillery. Then it was captured by the Big Red One.

There was a certain relaxed feeling in the air at that time. Lieutenant Lyons came back from leave in Paris, bringing Scotch whiskey and champagne. They all had a little party in the S-3 tent, and Miller was much amused by Sergeant Evans's cat, which they got drunk on Scotch.

Lieutenant Colonel Sonnenfeld went up to look at Aachen, too, and came back to agree with Miller's opinion.

The next day the engineers had new orders. They were to prepare to follow close behind the 112th Regimental Combat Team, building a main supply route from Germeter to Vossenack, across the river to Schmidt, and building a bridge if necessary. It was called Operation X. The plan was to get ready to hit the Cologne Plain. But to do so, the reservoirs feeding the Roer River had to be seized, lest the Germans blow up the dams while the Americans crossed the river below, destroying the attacking forces. The little town of Schmidt, standing above the dams, controlled the approaches. Miller's battalion moved into Germany, first to Schmidthof and then into the Huertgen Forest near Germeter.

But that operation was postponed due to the bad weather that was closing in over northern Europe. When new operations began on November 2, they did not go smoothly. The enemy reacted with heavy mortar fire in the valley west of Germeter. Company C did not move out of the valley. Miller went to the 112th CP, a pillbox up front, and learned that the First Battalion had been pinned down just 400 yards from the line of departure. But on the next day, November 3, the Third Battalion attacked south from Vossenack and crossed the river. In order to do their job, the engineers had to get into Vossenack.

"The latter town was receiving quite heavy enemy fire and there were snipers in the houses a little way from us. I wanted to move on into town badly, but the situation looked pretty grim. After a while I met Captain Lutz and a platoon of B Company, which had come up to clear rubble in town. We decided to try another road into Vossenack, and worked along the road back to Germeter. We then struck out across country, aiming for the church tower in Vossenack, and bypassing a column of doughboys. Just as we were approaching the edge of town, Jerry laid down a nasty mortar barrage all around us. In town we found the street leading south blocked by a tank with a track blown off, so we put a platoon to work building a bypass through the house yards. At the infantry command post in a cellar we were informed that tanks were vitally needed on the other side of the valley, that the stream was fordable. Lutz and I decided to take a look for ourselves, and by dodging artillery and mortar fire made our way across the open country into the woods in the valley. Now we found a weasel with a load of wounded and a thrown track blocking the one-way road through the woods. The river bottom was being shelled intermittently as we reached it.

"We were overjoyed to see a perfectly good stone arch bridge spanning the river. The existence of this bridge had apparently never been known by anyone until we saw it. I classified the bridge as 3D, perfectly capable of carrying tanks. We made our way back up the hill and back into town, and the climb just about killed me. I'm certainly out of condition. We reported this dope to the tank commanding officer and advised him to send his tanks down, yank out the weasel, and go on across. Captain Lutz took a platoon along with the tanks. But just as they reached the open fields, they came under heavy observed artillery fire. He pulled them back, and the tanks followed shortly afterward to secure in town for the night. Just at dusk Company A arrived in the town and another platoon of B Company."

On November 5 at dawn Captain Miller headed back for Vossenack. He had a radio and four runners. When he reached the town, he found the B Company command post in a concrete pigpen. That morning six American tanks came along the road to the bridge. Three of them made it, but each of the other three threw a track and stalled. In the afternoon the Germans counterattacked with tanks at Schmidt, and American dive-bombers came in to break up the German attack. It was a very impressive show, but the dive-bombers bombed American troops instead of German.

Late that afternoon the battalion command post ordered Captain Miller to come back. He started off. In the town he encountered Colonel Daley, the commander of the Twentieth Engineers, with Major Argus of his staff. The colonel was known for his aversion to experiencing any sort of violence. Just then he and the major were creeping down the ditch alongside the road. Captain Miller stopped when they flagged him. But artillery was coming in, occasionally, landing up near the church. A round fell and the colonel jumped into a cellar. Then he wanted to borrow Miller's jeep to go down to B Company's command post, and he climbed into the vehicle.

Along came an infantry lieutenant in another jeep.

"Don't go down there, Colonel," the lieutenant called.

And before anyone could take another breath, Colonel Daley was back in the cellar again. Miller calmed him down and the colonel got into Miller's jeep and driver Blankenship drove away.

"Blankenship was back in a very few minutes and told me that on the way to the church, a wire crew waved them down, and The Sad Sack [colonel] was out of the jeep and into the ditch before he could say a word."

The fight for Vossenack continued. On November 6 Captain Miller went up front to learn that the Twenty-eighth Infantry Division had withdrawn from the town and that it was being held for the time being by only two platoons of his own B Company. They, too, were being pulled back. Captain Lutz came up, deaf and dazed for the moment; he had been stunned by a shell which had killed Lieutenant Gray. The third platoon and Lieutenant Osola were missing. Miller went back to base camp and there was ordered to reassemble B Company and bring it back out of Vossenack; the company would go back in as infantry and retake the town. At Germeter Miller met Brig. Gen. George Davis, the assistant division commander of the Twenty-eighth, who was storming around trying to round up the 146th Engineers to send in as infantry as well.

Colonel Sonnenfeld and Captain Lutz took two platoons of B Company into town. Captain Miller stayed at the radio car and tool dump just west of Germeter and spent a cold, wet, horrid night in a foxhole.

November 7: All the companies of Miller's battalion of the Twentieth Engineers and the companies of the 1340th Engineers were committed as infantry in the fight for Vossenack. The men of B Company were brought out.

What had happened? A German counterattack had once again seized the area around the bridge, and the American attempt to take Vossenack was a failure.

"*November 9:* Went down the hill to where B Company's provisional platoon was dug in. The Germans still hold the bridge and can place fire on the vehicles if anyone goes near them. Around 1500 a message came on the radio for A Company and the 1340's B Company to move down to where C Company of the 1340th was dug in near the bridge. The officers and men looked like people who had just read their death sentences. Darkness was approaching, and the men were so exhausted they would be unable to dig suitable shelters before dark. The A Company commander radioed back for confirmation while the men loaded up the machine guns and entrenching tools, explaining that he would not be able to set up before darkness. Just as the two companies were ready to move, the order was rescinded. About 1530 I received a radio message for Lutz and myself; our party was to report back

to the command post. Lutz was down at the bottom of the hill with his people; when I contacted him by runner and radio, he refused to come back but
sent Lieutenant Horn. I led the group up the hill into Vossenack without
incident until, just as we reached the town, Jerry began lobbing them in.
The first round of small-caliber high-velocity stuff landed about 20 feet from
me, and I plopped into a doughboy's rifle pit. There were two doughboys in
it already, and I couldn't get below ground level. The next round also was
about 20 feet away and threw snow and dirt all over me. There were about
a dozen more, and then I took a group on into Vossenack and back to our
forward dump, where we found a weapons carrier. Coming back the jerk
driver ran off the road and tossed me into a couple of feet of mud, onto my
belly. When I got back to the CP after bumming a ride, I found I had been
elected to take a platoon formed from elements of B Company back out to
the bridge to hand-carry and lay antipersonnel mines. I went to bed early
and was awakened at 2300 by the joyful news that the companies were being
relieved during the night and we would not have to lay the mines. Sixteen
antipersonnel bombs fell in the company area during the night and wounded
six men.

"*November 10:* A Company and the platoon of B Company returned this
morning. During the p.m. I had to make a rush run to Group for some recon
dope. I found it was the same road net up front that I know by heart. So I
just phonied up the recon report and rode back to Group in the dark. . . .

"*November 13:* The engineers had the mission of blowing up that noto-
rious bridge below Vossenack. We had a platoon alerted to do the job if they
failed. At about 2300 their commanding officer notified the platoon leader
they had failed and told him to make roadblocks of mines near the bridge.
They had one man wounded in this attempt. Lieutenant Codey of C Company laid the mines without incident."

The attack on the Roer River dams had failed. It had cost the Twentieth
Engineers dearly: two officers killed, two missing, seven enlisted men killed,
thirty missing, fifty wounded and evacuated, and people still going to the
hospital with trench foot and frostbite.

Now the Americans were planning a big attack to retrieve a badly bun-
gled situation. Captain Miller's company was notified to build splinterproof
shelters for all the men. They would be occupied during a tremendous bombing attack, code-named "Prairie Dog," that was to precede the big attack.

"The weather is beastly, snow alternating with rain. I guess the rest of
the year is going to be just plain hell for us outdoor boys."

*

In the sector occupied by the 142d Infantry, the Americans faced very tough infantry of the German SS. They called for some help from the 132d Field Artillery, and that battalion sent up elements from Battery C. Included were five forward observers: Lt. Robert Lang and dogfaces Omar Lewis, Esquell Jaques, Lem West, and Amil Kohutek.

They assembled in a schoolroom for a briefing. The officers who did the briefing stood before a big picture of Adolf Hitler (which was in every German schoolroom) and worked on the blackboard, outlining their war picture:

Over the next hill was the town that had been given to Company K of the 142d as its next objective. The town was being bombed by American aircraft at that moment. (The men could hear the racket.)

It had been raining all day. The ground was wet and muddy. The sky, however, had cleared, and the late evening sun went down behind the mountains to the west.

Now here was the word: *Every* man was needed, so the observers from the field artillery were to join Company K and fight as infantry. Capt. Albert Kudzia was very short of men. Altogether he had fewer than ninety men— less than half his normal company strength. They would work in four platoons.

The company moved out that evening, single file, following a muddy stream that ran toward the town. The five artillerymen were in the second platoon. Soon they came to a cemetery wall and began moving up in its cover. Then came a call from the head of the line. A BAR man was needed.

Up came a BAR man named Brumley. As he passed Private Kohutek, he nodded.

"Be careful," said Kohutek.

He watched as Brumley moved forward. The man had not gone ten steps when suddenly he dropped his BAR and raised his hands. He walked forward and disappeared.

Kohutek moved back and whispered to his section what he had seen. The group pulled back a hundred feet, and then one of the artillerymen crawled forward to scout. He came back to report that the whole area was literally crawling with Germans.

Two platoons of the 142d had walked into a nice neat trap. Most of the officers were captured.

Soon a big German mortar began shelling the area along the cemetery wall. But the ground was so sloppy that the first shell buried itself and then exploded with a cruuump that sent a small geyser straight upward. The Americans moved back and regrouped.

They watched as the Germans marched their captives to the rear. Then they watched as L Company of the 142d Infantry came down the hill on their left. They heard rifle fire and saw that company also decimated by the Germans.

So the four artillerymen were now alone, and trapped behind the German line. They moved to the edge of the town and saw that most of the buildings were burning. Only two houses seemed to be intact, but the GIs could not get to them.

They crawled out behind those buildings and found an outhouse. It was a typical farm outhouse, with a two-hole seat—not very big, as any farm kid would know. But somehow, urged by the sounds of battle all around them, the four artillery observers with all their equipment crowded into that outhouse.

The door sagged, and they could not shut it. There they were, jammed into the privy, watching the burning town. Kohutek struggled with the door again and finally got it shut, but the motion had obviously caught somebody's attention, because they all heard a thud against the door. They knew what that had to be. They waited—but nothing happened.

They waited until dawn. The sector was quiet. Slowly one of them opened the door. Right next to it lay a German potato masher grenade, which somehow had failed to go off.

The four men made it back to the American lines, and there they told the story. Of course, nobody believed them. Not the part about the grenade not exploding—that was common enough, and at this stage of the war the Germans had lots of duds. No, what was unbelievable was the part about the four big Americans with all their gear jammed into a German privy. It had to be a crock, said everybody.

On November 15 Captain Miller went up to the First Division's CP to call on the First Engineers and tell them how the Twentieth had held the bag at Vossenack for the 103d Engineers of the Twenty-eighth Division. The others were not surprised, for they had heard stories about the "Bloody Bucket Boys."* The news came down that the Twenty-eighth Division was being relieved by the Eighth Division, and the Twentieth Engineers cheered.

They had indeed held the bag in that previous fighting, and when they were relieved on November 10, they had suffered 144 casualties, their high-

---

*The Twenty-eighth Infantry Division's shoulder insignia was a red keystone. German troops during World War I had noticed its resemblance to a bucket of blood, hence the nickname.

est number of any battle in the war. Now up came the Eighth Division and the Fifth Armored Division to try to do the job.

Now, the Twentieth Engineers said, they might have someone more competent to support. Bitter memories of Vossenack remained. It had been an enormous failure at high level, and the Twentieth Engineers certainly had taken the brunt of it.

On November 16 the bombers started over. All the people on the ground sought their shelters. The planes came over continuously until 1:30. Fortunately nothing was dropped on the GIs.

That afternoon, Colonel Daley and the commander of the 1340th Engineers called a critique.

"It was pretty much of a frost. The Sad Sack [Colonel Daley] did all the talking. He emphasized his own courage and the faults of the Twentieth."

Up top the blame for the infantry failure apparently was put on the engineers. The infantry didn't want the blame. Colonel Daley did nothing to protect his men from getting it.

"But that's war. You have to fight the enemy and your own brass hats too."

On November 17 the First Division took over the attack in that area. The Twentieth regained confidence.

"If anyone can do it, those First Division boys can. Our barrage is deafening and continuous."

On November 17 Captain Miller got a new officer's trench coat—water repellent, with a warm lining. Within hours he had it covered with mud from riding on the sloppy roads. It was no longer pretty, but it was still warm. He also had some combat trousers and heavy lined overalls with a zipper up the front. With these clothes he thought he was ready for the winter.

The war was not going so well there in the edge of the Huertgen Forest.

On November 20 the 121st Infantry was scheduled to attack so that the Fifth Armored Division could take the town.

"That's dreadful country, that Huertgen Forest," said Captain Miller. The attack jumped off on November 21, and it went slowly.

"When I was back at the First Division quartermasters at Waldheim I saw the graves registration people loading bodies into trucks like so much cordwood. A very pitiful sight. German artillery is responsible for much of this."

Captain Miller's Thanksgiving was much better than Private Adolph's. He had real turkey and apple pie for dessert.

But the next day it was back to the war. A combat command of the Fifth Armored Division went over the road the Twentieth Engineers had been cultivating for weeks, and tore the hell out of it in one day.

On November 23 Captain Miller went up to join the Twelfth Engineers as liaison officer for the corps. The Eighth Division was attacking Huertgen. Miller now had a pyramidal tent and a stove. Life was not so bad:

"Lieutenant Markovich and his driver moved in with me, and we had a very pleasant evening drinking gin and grapefruit juice."

On December 1 he learned that the Eighth Division was driving on Brandenberg, 2 miles east of Huertgen. If the division made it, the Seventh Corps would secure on the Roer River line.

The fighting continued. The going was very slow. On December 5 the Eighth Division took Bergstein, about a mile and a half southeast of Brandenberg.

But on December 16 Captain Miller had a feeling that something else was happening. The German activity on his front was increasing markedly.

Lieutenant Downing had the feeling that autumn that the war was passing him by. His malarial attacks had caused him to be put into a medical ward where he took Atabrine every day and was told to take long walks. One day he met a paratroop officer he had met previously in his first hospital stay in England. This officer had returned to his outfit, made the Arnhem jump, and been shot in the neck, and he was now back in the hospital. Small war.

Downing was hoping to be sent back to the states; he had served twenty-eight months in Africa, Sicily, and France, been wounded, and suffered five attacks of malaria. But a survey board came by and found him quite fit for duty. He was to go back to the Eighteenth Infantry.

By reading *Stars and Stripes* Downing knew that the First Division was in action around Aachen. On October 30 he got his orders to return to the Tenth Replacement Depot at Litchfield. It was not long before he was in LeHavre, where he saw patches of the Seventy-eighth Infantry Division. So a new outfit was coming over. By boxcar he moved up to Paris; then he went on to Étampes, where he spent Thanksgiving. Turkey in a mess kit. Downing ate it standing up at a table of boards laid across sawhorses in a dim tent with a mud floor.

Two days later his orders came. He was to be in temporary command of a platoon of men returning to the First Division. The GIs marched to the railroad station and boarded boxcars. They drew K rations for the trip and settled down. The air was cold and frosty. Downing learned from a sergeant

who had been in Company F that Lieutenant Caswell had been killed. He
and Caswell had gone on several benders in England before D day. The news
of Caswell's death gave Downing a feeling of depression that lasted all day.

The war had changed. People had changed.

At Charleroi he noticed a shabbily clad pale-faced Belgian who was trying to buy a chocolate bar from the American soldiers. He had money. He
kept waving francs at the soldiers, but they ignored him. They wanted wine.

"Finally one of the soldiers kicked at the man's face and yelled at him to
get away. He stepped back a little, looking like a whipped dog. That was too
much for my stomach. I called him back and threw him a D-ration chocolate
bar. He offered me the money, but I waved him away. I didn't know whether
I had been imposed upon or had done someone a favor, but I felt better. It
made me crawl inside to see grown people feebly and falsely laughing while
taking abuse and insults all to get items which they wanted desperately and
could get no other way. It's a disgusting situation when a human being has
to exchange a part of his human dignity for a chocolate bar."

Finally the train stopped in Belgium. Downing saw a V-2 rocket as it
sailed overhead emitting a trail of fire. It was aimed at Liège and the port of
Antwerp, and he was at Verviers. There he saw men of the new 104th
"Timberwolf" Infantry Division, which was commanded by Gen. Terry Allen,
former commander of his First Division. And then it was time to go back
toward the front line.

A three-piece soldier band consisting of a saxophone, an accordion, and
a guitar was playing popular tunes on the street outside the line of trucks
that assembled to carry the troops. A signal was given, and the truck drivers
started their engines. The band began to play "Auld Lang Syne."

The men on the trucks yelled: "Blow it out your ass. Go fuck yourself.
Don't get hurt back here, you bastards."

The band quit playing abruptly and left.

Bitterness. The bitterness of old soldiers in winter, going back to face
death another time.

The convoy sped along the road. The fields were still green, but Downing felt winter in the air. The trucks passed blasted farmhouses and a rusty
burned-out tank. They drove by the big green concrete pillboxes of the
Maginot line. In the distance the troops could hear the rumble of artillery.

They passed a sign: "You are now entering Germany."

The road ended and the convoy entered a shell-cratered, blasted stretch
with ridges of frozen mud. Shattered trolley-car tracks and poles appeared
on the right. The troops had reached the outskirts of Aachen.

"The whole city was torn apart. You couldn't see a single untouched build-

ing standing. The streets were piled with debris. Occasionally we saw a dingy-
looking civilian walking quietly along the street. We pulled at last into a
large courtyard. When we detrucked we noticed that the rumble of artillery
was more distinct. There was no joking or horseplay among the men. Everyone wore a strained, poker-faced look. This was the last stop before get-

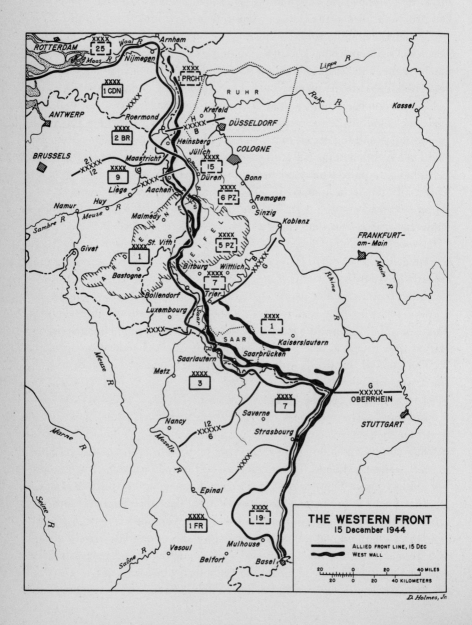

THE WESTERN FRONT
15 December 1944

⸻⸻ ALLIED FRONT LINE, 15 DEC
⸻⸻ WEST WALL

D. Holmes, Jr.

ting back to the outfit. In too short a time the gamble against the odds would begin again."

Downing's casual platoon was quartered in a half-destroyed apartment house. Outside the wind began to blow hard. The men waited there for trucks from the First Division to come and pick them up.

When Downing got to the Eighteenth Infantry and met the officers he had known so well before, they seemed years older than when he had last seen them. They told him of some of their adventures and of how the regiment had been badly shot up in the Huertgen Forest. They named the names of officers who had been killed. Captain Spinney had been transferred up to division headquarters. It all seemed very strange. "The more they talked, the more I felt like the ghost of the feast."

Lieutenant Downing was assigned to the cannon company. That meant the six 105-millimeter howitzers on 75-millimeter gun carriages. Downing would be forward observer with the Second Platoon, which supported the Second Battalion of the regiment. His predecessor had been wounded by a shell that broke both arms and both legs, someone told him.

Swell!

Downing went to Second Battalion headquarters. He met a new captain, fresh from the states, who had been given the Headquarters Company once promised to Downing.

The regiment was in a static situation, under heavy German shellfire. The American advance had obviously been stalled. A few days after Downing's arrival, the First Division was pulled out of the line and replaced by the Ninth Division in the Langerwehe area.

R and R was in the town of Plombieres in Belgium. Downing and the other forward observer of the cannon company occupied a pleasant room above a drug store. But...

"The town was blacked out. We slopped through the mud and darkness to the factory for evening mess. The kitchen had a hot meal ready. It was an exceptionally good meal, but the atmosphere of the place was depressing. The dark room, gritty with coal dust, crisscrossed with narrow railroad tracks where the coal carts were shunted around, and lit by a couple of unshaded bulbs, had a somber appearance. We ate and returned to our room. There was no place to go, nothing to do, and nothing to read. We wrote a couple of letters and then huddled next to the stove, sipping out of a bottle of gin."

For the first time since D day in June, the Eighteenth Infantry was enjoying a rest. But the weather was freezing and wet, the sky was gray, and

even though the infantry was out of action, life seemed very grim. It was
December 15, 1944.

*   *   *

Captain Shebeck's war had taken a strange new turn. After his Eighty-second
Airborne Division was sent back to England, Shebeck was transferred to the
Tenth Replacement Depot at Birmingham. He was apparently too senior in
grade to stay with a glider company, and there was not enough room at the
top. So he found himself assigned as assistant operations officer at Pheasey
Farms, where Lieutenant Downing spent quite a stretch. Shebeck's task was
to retrain wounded officers and men and to train people coming in from the
states in some of the lessons of survival learned by the troops at Normandy.

What a different life it was: the Victory Club; the Perry Barr Racetrack;
the Princess Hotel, where Allen Rook and his three-piece string ensemble
held forth each afternoon.

Alas, that idyll ended too soon and Captain Shebeck found himself assigned to the Third reppledepple at Verviers. He arrived just a few days
before December 16, 1944.

Sergeant Moglia and the men of the Sixteenth Infantry had spent a hard,
unpleasant autumn on the German border and in the Huertgen Forest. They
took Eilendorf that fall and settled in to occupation. The town was just outside Aachen; Crucifix Hill stood between the Eighteenth and that big city.

In Eilendorf the railroad station was still intact. A small park nearby
seemed almost unhurt. Across the street was a row of apartment houses, and
on the corner stood a tavern, all battered, but still more or less in one piece.
Sergeant Moglia set up his platoon headquarters in the railroad station, but
the Germans kept hurling 88-millimeter shells at it, so the group moved.
The move was hastened by the appearance of a sniper. He was a very odd
sniper. His activities were irregular, and as far as Moglia could make out,
the man had to be the worst shot in the German army. He never hit anything. But the sniping was still irritating, pop-pop-pop, like a kid with an
air rifle, but... you never knew when...

So the platoon moved into the basements of the apartment houses and
into the tavern. That was easy to do because parts of the adjoining buildings had been blasted, and it was only a matter of clearing a passage in
the rubble. In the new quarters the men were very pleased to discover,

along with safety, a number of barrels of preserved hard-boiled eggs and pickles, casual food for the good burghers who had come to the tavern in better days.

But the sniper fire continued, and it worried Sergeant Moglia just about every day. Sergeant Moglia began a check of the area. The sniper had to be within a block or two, or he could not have observed their activities. So it was look here, look there.

One afternoon Moglia heard footsteps on a large patio. It was just about 150 yards from the platoon's underground castle, just right for a sniper to feel comfortable. When Moglia checked the building and the broad flat space, he again heard footsteps. He motioned his men back and ducked into a doorway. The footsteps grew closer. Soon the stranger and Moglia were nearly face-to-face. Moglia jumped out and seized the man, and two of his riflemen got the drop on him.

It was a German soldier. Or was it? It was really an old man in his sixties, thin, his field-gray uniform bagging on his skinny frame. Yes, a German soldier, or so said his identification card. They took away his rifle and his ammunition and then hustled him back to their radio room in the basement of the tavern. A door led to a bombed-out room next door. Moglia told the poor old man that he was a POW and was going to be sent to the rear of the Allied lines. The G-2 people didn't like snipers, he said.

The old man looked very worried and very sad. Moglia then put him into the room next to the radio room, a room that had been hit by a bomb and in which one window to the outside was completely missing. After announcing loudly that the prisoner would be secure there, the Americans shut the door, leaving it open only a crack. Then they watched as the old sniper climbed out the window, and skedaddled from the area. There was no more sniper fire in their pleasant little block after that.

That was how it went in the late autumn of 1944. Life seemed to have quieted down. It was almost as if a period of static warfare, almost like the trench war of 1917, loomed ahead. That's how it seemed to many of the dogfaces on the Siegfried line in mid-December 1944.

First Sergeant Chattaway of the 110th Infantry had been with the company all the way through: Compiègne, Creil, St.-Quentin, and into Belgium. He had come very close to getting killed at Neufchâteau when the company was held up by artillery fire. He dived into a ditch and felt a shell graze the back of his combat pack. A few moments later he felt an unexploded shell, still hot, lodged in the bank behind him. It had creased his pack and then buried itself halfway into the far side of the hole.

Sergeant Chattaway had fought through the "dragon's teeth" tank barriers of the Siegfried line, and he had lived through German flamethrower attacks—something entirely new. The Germans mounted their flamethrowers on half-tracks, and they came at the enemy at night, with searchlights. That sort of attack was particularly frightening and devastating to the replacements. He had lived through "Screaming Meemie" attacks and had learned that the Germans called those multibarreled rocket discharges *Nebelwerfer*. He had received a battlefield commission as second lieutenant, the second awarded in the division, and his new gold bars had been pinned on by Maj. Gen. "Dutch" Cota, the division commander. Chattaway had taken over a rifle platoon; then he had taken a piece of shrapnel in his arm and had been sent back to England. After several weeks in the hospital he had followed Lieutenant Downing's pattern, more or less, and had been ordered back to duty with his regiment early in December. Through the maze of reppledepples he had been making his way across the continent, toward Germany. He was aboard a boxcar on December 15, on his way from LeHavre back to Belgium, to rejoin the 110th.

In the fighting of all those months Staff Sergeant Thornton of the Sixtieth Infantry also had become a lieutenant through a battlefield commission. That's how it was very often among the old-line units that had been fighting since Africa. The army was learning: a first-class noncom with plenty of experience was worth a half-dozen shavetail lieutenants straight out of OCS in the states.

Lieutenant Thornton's Sixtieth Infantry also fought the battle of the Huertgen Forest in that fall of 1944. The infantry took particularly heavy casualties near Vossenack in mid-October. Like the other American units, the Sixtieth was held back by the Germans along the west wall that Hitler had built five years earlier.

November 1944 began with the Sixtieth in reserve in the southern end of the Huertgen Forest. But again, "reserve" did not mean taking it easy. Not in Germany. The Germans infiltrated at night. On Sunday, November 5, the company moved to a new area. As Pfc. Post was driving a jeep in the company area, he ran over a mine that had been there only a few hours. It blew. He died in the field hospital.

The casualties had been so heavy and the replacements so many that Lieutenant Thornton spent a lot of time giving lectures on battle procedures,

such as the use of the machine gun. The weather was miserable. It had turned
from mud to snow. In midmonth the Sixtieth was relieved and went back to
Camp Elsenborn, and the Ninety-ninth Division came into the line. Lieutenant Thornton mailed out his Christmas cards on November 17. Some of
them he wrote a little self-consciously. Plenty of time to get there for Christmas. It had stopped snowing and was raining again. Cold rain.

On December 1 the Sixtieth Infantry moved to Muetzimid, in defensive
position on the front line. Ten enemy planes came over on December 3.
Four were shot down.

On December 5 Thornton's battalion was relieved by Sergeant Moglia's,
the second battalion of the Sixtieth Infantry. But that did not mean much to
Thornton and his boys, because the next day their battalion moved up to
Langerwehe to relieve Lieutenant Downing's battalion of the Eighteenth Infantry.

On December 10 the Sixtieth Infantry attacked at Langerwehe, supported
by 132 tanks, and took many prisoners. On December 13 the Sixtieth Infantry reached Rothouse, Germany. The next day Lieutenant Thornton's battalion reached the river facing Düren. That afternoon Lieutenant Thornton
was sent along with four other officers up to the Seventh Corps headquarters
to observe a weapons demonstration. They spent the night in Maastricht,
Holland. On the fifteenth they went back to Aachen for more demonstrations. Then they went to Liège and spent the evening at a nightclub where
they saw a fine floor show. Plenty of girls. Plenty of legs. On December 16
they left Liège at 6 a.m. and returned to the battalion.

Lieutenant Colonel Snetzer's Second Division had been in Germany since
early October, too. His Second Engineers were on the Siegfried line. The
men lived in the German forts they had captured, and on sunny days they
brought out their laundry. The British popular ditty of 1939, "I'll hang my
washing on the Siegfried Line," an old song now, had become a reality.

The engineers' portion of the line was on the edge of a great pine woods,
overlooking the farm countryside, with 88s dug in between the forts—now in
American hands. One day Snetzer visited a huge underground machine shop
built by the Germans in a railroad tunnel at Bleialf. It was 700 meters long,
all drills and lathes. The job of Snetzer's Second Engineers was mostly road
maintenance and other support of the Twenty-third Infantry. On November 2
B Company blew up forty-nine German pillboxes as the Twenty-third withdrew a bit. They were in the First Army sector. It was very quiet.

On November 9 Snetzer made a trip to Brussels with a French interpreter to pick up stovepipes. They went up through Namur, driving in a deuce-and-a-half through rain and snow. They went to the Belgian stove company and did their business; then they parked the truck in a British parking lot and found a hotel.

"City is British pass town and full of British and Canadian troops. Only a few American airborne and air corps troops there. Twenty-first Army Group Headquarters is here. They are very strict about no one being in town except on orders. Spent evening visiting several of the multitudinous joints, drinking beer, and watching lousy floor shows."

Snetzer returned to the Siegfried line on November 16, D + 163.

"It's positively beautiful up in the Siegfried line now. There is about a foot of snow over everything. A regular winter wonderland. Reminds me of Ski Training in Michigan. Down in valleys to the rear snow melts, but up in Schnee Eifel it all remains. Rest of First Army and Ninth Army launched an attack today north of us. Third Army has been progressing slowly in attack in Metz area for a week."

On December 10 the Second Division moved out in preparation for an attack in the Fifth Corps sector, about 20 miles north of Snetzer's camp. It was snowing heavily around Malmédy, where his engineers were bound. He took stock of the battalion after six months in combat: casualties, 429; authorized strength, 32 officers and 632 enlisted men; actual strength, 32 officers and 605 enlisted men. Not bad. That night the staff had a big party, saying goodbye to the farmhouse they had commandeered for two months. Champagne, piano music, and community singing. "Very pleasant. Not more than a little rowdy."

"*December 12:* The Second Division moved to Elsenborn and prepared to attack on December 13.

"Roads are getting pretty bad. Passed the poor doughboys this evening moving up to the line of departure for tomorrow's jump-off. I could cry for sorrow at them as they wearily plodded forward through the deep snow, with enormous rolls on their backs, their faces brown with cold and several days' growth of beard, their overcoats steamy with melting snow. Tonight they lie in the snow in the desolate wild forest waiting for tomorrow's battle. The poor devils are being asked to do too much. It isn't fair. They get along without the very necessities of life and die so miserably...

"*December 13:* Nineteenth Division jumped off at 8:00 a.m. and moved through snowy, foggy forest. Engineers cleared main supply route right behind them, finding Teller, Riegel, and S mines. Snow and terrain big obstacle for infantry until they bumped against a fortified position.

"*December 14:* The infantry bumped its head against that fortified position all day but did not get anywhere. Casualties are running 50 percent in the assault companies. Heavy artillery and mortar fire and many antipersonnel mines in the woods. Infantry is suffering horribly from the cold and snow as they try to live in the woods with no shelter at all and are soaking wet. The rate of combat exhaustion is up. This is the hardest battle yet as far as the infantry is concerned.

"*December 16:* The day began with a vicious shelling of our command post area by the Krauts at 5:30. All took refuge in the basements of our houses as hill we stay on was plastered with some big stuff. No casualties to us. Buzz bomb hit in division ordnance company at same time, causing heavy casualties and completely wrecking the motor section. Fighting goes slowly against tough terrain, snow, and concrete pillboxes."

November 1944: The Second Armored Division had crossed the Meuse River into Holland, had crossed the Wurm River into Germany, and had gone through the Siegfried line. Victory seemed imminent to many in the division those days. They spent a lot of time listening to Armed Forces Radio. Colonel Buster, a West Pointer, was pleased to note that on November 4 Army beat Villanova in football, 83–6.

Captain Knight made a bet with Lieutenant Colonel Buster that the war would end before Armistice Day, November 11, 1944. Well, it did not, and a few days later the Second Armored was engaged in the toughest tank battle of its history. In the end the Second Armored captured positions controlling the Roer River. Late in November the division was moved into reserve to prepare for the next step of the assault on Germany.

Life quieted down. On December 15 Lieutenant Colonel Buster's executive officer went to Paris. Troops were also going on leave back to Belgium for a little wallowing in the fleshpots. Some went on pass to Brussels.

On December 16 Lieutenant Colonel Buster began to hear a little about the possibility of a German counterattack. On December 17 there was definite indication of a German counterattack in the direction of Liège. Buster was moving among his various batteries, giving situational talks to the men. It was still very relaxed, still very much like a static war.

General Bradley was at SHAEF headquarters in Paris on December 16. Field Marshal Montgomery was at his headquarters in Belgium.

The Germans, said Monty in a situation report to Eisenhower that day, were fighting a defensive campaign on all fronts. There was no chance they could stage a counteroffensive. Under no conditions could the Germans permit the war to get into a mobile phase; they had neither the fuel nor the transport to do so. The German tanks could not compete with the Allied armor in such a fight.

Yes, the Germans were in bad shape. But that being said, the Allies must not relax. They must continue to push the Germans, to keep them off balance; they must not give the Germans time to recover their strength.

Because of all that, said Montgomery to Eisenhower, he was issuing orders for his big operation: an attack from Nijmegen southeast to clear the west bank of the Rhine. But Montgomery's real reason for this letter was to request that he be allowed to go to England to spend Christmas with his family.

Of course, said General Eisenhower. And he joked about a wager he had with Montgomery, who had bet that the war would not really end before Christmas. Eisenhower had bet that it would end by then, but they were not really in disagreement—just very, very confident.

On the evening of December 16 General Bradley arrived to spend the night with Eisenhower. Ike's mistress was banished while the two commanders discussed the problem of getting replacements up to the fighting divisions.

Maj. Gen. Maxwell D. Taylor, the commander of the 101st Airborne Division, was off in Washington inspecting airborne installations and new equipment. On December 16 and 17 the newspapers carried some speculative stories from correspondents in Europe: the talk was about a German counteroffensive.

Nonsense, said General Taylor. The German troops his division had been encountering indicated that the Wehrmacht was virtually finished. Morale was poor and "the fighting edge" was gone.

And so the Allies settled down for the coming of Christmas, the mess sergeants scrounging at the depots for goodies, the special services officers looking for booze, every dogface and officer who could manage it trying to get leave so he could spend the season in some city or big town, away from the line, among real people, and, above all, with a girl. Paris was beginning to show a little of its old prewar glamour, despite rationing, shortages, and the cold.

It really did seem to nearly everyone that the Germans were losing their grip, that it was just a matter of time.

36

COUNTEROFFENSIVE

The German scheme for a counteroffensive against the American and British armies was arguably the enemy's best plan of the war. For several reasons the Germans had a real local advantage in the Ardennes at the end of 1944.

First, they were fighting in their homeland. The very successful Allied intelligence network that had worked so well in France did not work in Germany. The Americans and British had to depend on aerial observation and POW interrogation for news of German activity.

Hitler's plan was to drive to Antwerp, splitting the American and British forces, and severing their supply line. To do this, he assembled thirty-six divisions. They included eleven panzer divisions with 600 tanks. The Allies did not believe that Hitler could amass so much might, and thus they were relaxed and unprepared in that Christmas season.

It didn't help much that the weather had been continuously cloudy and overcast and that, as a consequence, Allied air observation had been very limited since December 13. It was "German weather," and it permitted Field Marshal von Rundstedt to mass his troops without Allied knowledge.

The strange, almost disembodied war of the preceding few weeks had led the newspapermen to call this the "ghost front." The war situation had some of the aspects of the "phony war" of 1940. Training in lieu of fighting, weapons demonstrations, and a lot of leave to the cities were becoming commonplace.

It was quite apparent that most American and British soldiers thought that the war was just about over. In fact, General Eisenhower and Field Marshal Montgomery had a friendly bet of £5 as to whether the war would be over by the end of the year. And down the line the opinion was pretty clear that the dogfaces thought they would be going home very, very soon.

In a leisurely way, the Allies were planning a big push across the Rhine, scheduled for just after the first of the year. Just now, at the Christmas season, they were relaxing. General Bradley was in Paris, visiting General Eisenhower. General Ridgway, commander of the Eighteenth Airborne Corps, was in England. General Maxwell Taylor, commander of the 101st Airborne Division, was in America. Many, many high-ranking officers of all the divisions and armies were in Paris or Brussels or elsewhere on leave.

But on December 15 the Germans set out to change things. Three German armies came up along a front of 70 miles. The Sixth Panzer Army was on the north, the Fifth Panzer Army was in the center, and the Seventh Army was on the south. Opposite them were only three American divisions, the Ninety-ninth, which had just arrived from America, the 106th, which was still unblooded, and the Twenty-eighth, which had been beaten up in the Huertgen Forest battles. A screen was provided by the Fourteenth Cavalry.

The main assault was to be made by the Sixth Panzer Army's First Panzer Corps. The leading element was the First SS Panzer Division, whose spearhead battle group was led by Col. Jochen Peiper. The division set out.

On December 16 Lieutenant Thornton returned from Liège to the Sixtieth Infantry encampment at 6 a.m. He did not know it, but half an hour earlier the Germans had unleashed their counteroffensive with an enormous artillery barrage along a broad front. Their main armored attack was launched against two divisions, the tired Twenty-eighth Division and the untried 106th Division. The latter had just been brought into the line by the Americans and had no experience in combat.

That night of December 16 Captain Miller and his men noticed an enormous increase in German air activity. The Luftwaffe was really on its toes, dropping flares and bombs. Paratroops were also dropped—at Verviers, Eupen, Monschau, and other places—to further confuse the Americans. The real objective was the coast, and the cutting of the Allied line so that the northern sector could be completely destroyed or driven into the sea.

By morning Captain Miller knew the Germans were attacking on a 60-mile front from Luxembourg north. All the talk about the "big push" by the Americans was called off.

On December 17 Lieutenant Thornton's company was still on the river at Düren, patrolling the bank. The German offensive was south of the Americans.

General Bradley left SHAEF that day in a hurry and sped to his own headquarters at Spa. The weather was still terrible, no chance of getting a plane; he drove from Paris. A look at the situation map showed a big battle beginning. And from Bradley's point of view it could not have come at a worse moment. He did not have a single division in his army group reserve. The only two uncommitted divisions available to the Americans just then were the 82d and the 101st Airborne, both pulled out of the line for rest and refitting after the struggle in Holland.

About all Bradley could do that day was call General Patton, in the south at Nancy with his Third Army, and ask that the Tenth Armored Division be put on the road toward Luxembourg.

Colonel Peiper's First SS Panzer Division was forging ahead, carrying German paratroopers as infantry on the tanks. Before dawn on December 17 he reached Honsfeld, a rest area for the Ninety-ninth Division. Peiper had not fired a shot. Then he hit Büllingen. He thought by this time that he had achieved a complete breakthrough of the American line. The panzers went after B Company of the Second Engineers and broke up that resistance. Then they moved on.

Just after noon Peiper's column encountered an American truck convoy, moving south, about 3 miles south of Malmédy on the road to St.-Vith. It was part of the U.S. Seventh Armored Division, which had been ordered to St.-Vith to strengthen the line. Three hundred yards behind the crossroads of the cutoff for St.-Vith the convoy was surprised from the woods by German machine guns and mortars.

The Germans also surprised an American MP who was directing traffic at the crossroads. He ran for shelter behind a house and soon was joined by half a dozen soldiers from a truck.

All the American vehicles stopped, and the GIs jumped off and took cover in the ditches at the sides of the road.

Pvt. Warren R. Schmitt jumped off a truck and crawled to a small stream 40 feet from the road, where he covered himself with grass and mud. He lay there for two hours, listening to the sounds of shooting and the cries of wounded men. He became so numb that he couldn't move the lower half of his body. Crawling on his elbows, he eventually dragged himself into the woods. There he had to stop and rub himself to get the circulation going again. Then he found his compass and got back to the road well past the scene of the battle. He went down the road until he was stopped by an American guard and taken to an aid station.

Lt. Virgil Lary of Battery B headed for that same house. A captain from his battery also followed. A tank came up the road, and Lieutenant Lary put his hands up. A German officer stuck his head out of the turret and aimed his pistol at Lary. Lary ducked, and the shot missed. The officer then aimed at the captain. He fired and missed again. Lary jumped into the ditch.

By this time three more tanks had come down the road. They were Tiger tanks, and they were moving along the ditches spewing machine gun fire. One German tank shot up an American ambulance; other German tanks knocked out twenty-four American vehicles. Colonel Peiper then took his task force onward and left the mopping up to the parachute troops, with a few tanks.

Thus was the 285th Field Artillery observation column ambushed that day. With only small arms to protect themselves, all the Americans soon surrendered. The MP and the others who had hidden behind the farmhouse, and then in its barn, found they were surrounded, and they too surrendered.

The German infantry had taken more American prisoners. They included five military policemen, two ambulance drivers, a mess sergeant, several medics and engineers (probably from Company B of the Second Engineers in Büllingen), infantrymen, and members of an armored reconnaissance unit. Altogether there were about 150 POWs.

The Germans were in a hurry; their object was to drive through the American lines, not shepherd prisoners.

They herded the American prisoners together. A half-track came up and tried to put its gun onto the prisoners but could not depress it enough. So the Germans set up machine guns on the ground. The infantrymen searched the Americans for wallets, watches, gloves, rings, cigarettes, and weapons. All these were taken from the men. Then they were ordered to line up in a field south of the crossroads; they were to stand with their hands over their heads.

In the front row were medics and others. No effort was made to segregate the noncombatants from the "shooting soldiers." Tanks then parked at either end of the field, with their machine guns covering the American prisoners. Then a German command car drew up to the scene.

One German spoke up: "You *will* go across the Siegfried line, will you, you dirty swine!"

The officer in the car stood up, took aim at an American medical officer, and fired his pistol. The medical officer fell. The German fired again and another American dropped. Then the two tanks opened up with their machine guns.

As the men dropped, those who were not hit had the good sense to fall along with the others. Lieutenant Lary was hit in the arm. The German soldiers came along with pistols and rifles and shot some of the wounded and bashed the heads of others with rifle butts. There was even more grisly work done that day. (When the bodies were recovered later, at least one man was found with his eyes gouged out. These Germans all belonged to the SS, which included more than its share of perverts and sadists.)

The Americans were flat on their stomachs with their faces in the snow and mud. The tanks moved up, continuing their machine gun fire. Along the ground walked German soldiers to finish off the Americans who were not dead. All the Americans still alive were lying there. Some were moaning and crying.

The Germans came up.

"Is he dead?" one asked another. Then he reached down with the butt of his gun.

The closest they came to Lieutenant Lary was 10 feet. He was stretched out with his hands extended, and he could feel the blood oozing from his arm and from his foot, where he also had been hit. Wet now, and starting to shiver, he was afraid the Germans would notice him, but they did not. He kept his head down, so he did not see them, but he heard. He heard the sound of pistols firing, and of the squashing noise made when a rifle butt connected with a skull.

Others did put their heads up. They saw.

The Germans came up and kicked a man, maybe in the face. If a man moved, they shot him. One American medic got up to bandage the wound of another man. The Germans watched him do the job; then they shot the medic and his patient.

The German infantrymen hung about the area. The living prisoners lay there waiting.

About an hour after the armored column moved off, several of the survivors decided to make a break for it. One of these men was Pvt. James P. Mattera. He got up and made a break. Seeing that, fourteen others did the same. They jumped up and ran north up the road toward Malmédy. The Germans opened up with rifle fire and machine guns. At the crossroads the Americans were fired on by another German machine gun that had taken up position there. Twelve of the Americans hid in that house again. The other three rushed into the woods. One of these men was Private Mattera. The Germans at the crossroads saw them, but they could not fire behind the house. The Americans then played dead. A German in an SS uniform came over and looked them over. He had a pistol, but he did not fire. For two hours the armored column continued to pass. Fast stuff, all tanks and half-tracks. Then the road quieted down. Lieutenant Lary and another American got up and ran from the house. Two Germans sprayed after them with machine gun fire, but they continued to run toward Malmédy. Lary and the other soldier ran for 2 miles, and then a jeep came along and picked them up and brought them in.

Mattera and his two companions lay there until dark, and then skidded under a hedgerow. Later they found a man from their division headquarters, a staff sergeant, who had been shot in the arm. Then they all started to walk, but stayed 200 yards off the road. Later they met a medic who had been shot in the foot. They also met another soldier. They all got in safely. After dark T/5 Theodore J. Paluch moved on through the woods and finally got back to the engineering battalion of their outfit.

Meanwhile, the Germans closed in on the house, and set it on fire. When the Americans tried to escape the fire, through the door and windows of the blazing building, they were shot down. All of them died there in the building.

After that first break, several other Americans tried to run from the scene of the massacre. A few got away into the woods, but most were killed by the German riflemen. Night fell, and more Americans tried the break. More were killed.

Many lay in the freezing weather until after midnight, when they were sure the Germans had left the scene. Of the 150 Americans who had been captured at that crossroads, only 43 are known to have escaped, and three-quarters of those were wounded.

*　　　　*　　　　*

As the Americans who had escaped the massacre came limping in to the aid stations, they were met by two war correspondents, Hal Boyle of the Associated Press and Jack Belden of *Time* magazine. So in a matter of hours the world knew of the German action, which was labeled "atrocity."* The word of Malmédy soon permeated the whole Allied line.

From that point on Germans who were captured in this fierce struggle could expect very little mercy from the Americans, who knew the story. Largely because of the massacre, three Germans who had been captured wearing the American uniforms given out by the SS for a deception operation were sentenced to death as spies. None of the Germans in that particular trio had fired a shot, but such was the fury of the Americans over the Malmédy massacre that General Bradley, usually one of the most compassionate of men, confirmed the sentence without a whicker. Later, it was indicated that the American High Command had panicked and that it had ordered this execution (and the execution of Pvt. Eddie Slovik, the only U.S. soldier ever shot for cowardice in World War II) in order to bolster morale. Perhaps, but that could not be the reason the Americans took so few prisoners during the next few days.

It was Sunday, December 17. Lieutenant Downing got up early and went to mass at the local Catholic church. He walked slowly back to his quarters above the shop. The sun tried to come out and blinked weakly through the cold air. Maybe it would make it sometime during the six weeks the regiment would be hanging around here.

All around him Belgians were out in their Sunday best, greeting each other and stopping to chat in little groups. But when Downing reached the Eighteenth Regiment's billeting area, he saw men scurrying around. Several men came out of a house with blanket rolls over their shoulders.

A lead weight dropped into Downing's stomach. Something was up. He looked around. Over on one side men were loading up half-tracks and hitching up the guns.

Downing hurried to the orderly room. The first sergeant told him the company was on alert to move at a moment's notice. He was to pack up,

---

*At the trial of various Germans in connection with the Malmédy massacre, the Germans claimed that it was an act of war, that they killed the Americans because they had no time to take prisoners. They also claimed that the Americans had done the same. The stories of various American soldiers regarding D day indicate that this was true, and one or two anecdotes about American torture of German soldiers in interrogations indicate that if such actions were called "atrocities," these cruelties were common to both sides. To match the tale of the American with his eyes gouged out is the story by Felix Branham of the Twenty-ninth Division about the German soldier who was emasculated in a Normandy barn before the eyes of his buddy, to convince that comrade to talk about German troop dispositions.

assemble his forward observer group, and report to Second Battalion headquarters.

What was it all about?

"Damfino," said the sergeant. "The Jerries have broken through somewhere."

Six weeks rest? The troops had been here just eight days.

Downing went to his quarters and picked up his gear. A jeep roared up,
and an orderly came in to get his cot and bedding roll to the supply room.
Another jeep rolled up carrying Downing's driver, radio operator, and the
instrument corporal. Sergeant Brown, the man he really needed, was off in
Paris on a pass. They drove over to Brown's billet and picked up his gear,
particularly his artillery binoculars, and then went up to the Second Battalion area.

The Belgians, who had been chatting and laughing around the church,
were now silent, and their faces were blank. Downing could sense their concern: the Germans were coming back.

Everybody was gone, it seemed. Downing went inside to report. Major
Colacicco was in charge; the commander, Lieutenant Colonel Williamson,
was off on leave.

Downing got a little real information. The Germans had broken through
in the Ardennes sector and were pushing toward Liège and Antwerp. Paratroops had been dropped. The front was "fluid"—which meant nobody knew
what the hell was going on.

Still, the American army was so used to victory now that even to Downing the reverses did not seem too serious. The Krauts couldn't have much
left, everybody said.

He sat around the headquarters with the others, shooting the bull and
waiting for orders. Jeeps roared up, and people kept coming in to join the
crowd: battalion staff, cannon company, antitank company, field artillery,
rifle company commanders. They sat until late afternoon. Then regiment finally sent down orders.

The Eighteenth Infantry was going to advance to the threatened sector in
short moves, making sure that the Germans did not infiltrate behind the infantrymen. In other words, the Eighteenth itself would establish a line of
resistance.

Darkness settled down over Belgium. The air grew colder and fog set in again.

The vehicles began to move. Now MPs were seen at all the crossroads, checking. It seemed strange. Downing did not then know about the infiltration of the Germans: special German units had air-dropped behind the American lines in GI uniforms, speaking American English and equipped with jeeps and American weapons, and they were having some success in confusing the troops.

It was a slow caravan; the night was dark, and Downing's jeep driver was guided by the small red taillight of the jeep ahead. At one point the driver ran the jeep off the road, and they had to get a 2½-ton truck to pull the vehicle out of the ditch.

Downing got lost. He retraced his steps and found the battalion back at a tavern. The staff was huddled over a table looking at maps by flashlight.

The convoy got started again. Bumper-to-bumper traffic—slow and slow and slow. Now the men could hear explosions in the distance. It sounded as if German planes were bombing and strafing the convoy up the road.

When the convoy stopped again, Downing got out of his jeep to see what was happening, but he saw the jeep move, so he dashed back to it. He ran into the fishpole aerial, which jabbed him in the forehead; the blood ran down into his right eye and sealed it shut. The vehicles got going again and arrived at the battalion command post. There, Downing found the aidmen, who cleaned up his eye and the cut and bandaged the wound. Half an inch lower and he might have lost that eye.

Downing went to the headquarters billets that were set up in a barroom. The windows were blacked out and the room was lighted by two battery lamps. A door led to the cellar, which was occupied by the battalion commander and the staff. The first sergeant of Headquarters Company gave Downing a cot. People were heating rations over a Coleman stove in the next room. Someone was heating water, so Downing filled his canteen cup and made coffee to go with his K ration. Soon he was asleep.

At midnight he was awakened by the sound of antiaircraft fire. He heard planes coming closer. There was the scream of a diving plane, but it pulled up and away. Then it came back, and the plane dove on the town. Bombs exploded a few blocks away, shaking his building. Downing wanted to run to the cellar, but he didn't want to be the first man to run.

More bombs came down. He was scared. He stumped down the cellar stairs and backed against the stone wall. Lieutenant Colonel Williamson and Major Colacicco and some civilians were billeted down there. Everyone was sitting up, waiting. But finally it all quieted down.

*

The Second Infantry Division was in the thick of the trouble.

At 6:30 Lieutenant Colonel Snetzer was alerted. The German Fifth and Sixth Panzer armies had broken through at Manderfeld and a column of armor and infantry had rushed into Büllingen where it overran B Company of the Second Engineers. The Germans also wiped up the quartermaster dumps, and the signal dump, and then headed into Wirtzfeld. Their tanks reached within 1000 yards of the division command post. American tank destroyers fought them off. All the troops in the town, cooks and bakers and everyone else, were thrown into the line on the outskirts of Büllingen. The Second Battalion of the Twenty-third Infantry was brought up to hold, and the division command post was moved by foot to the rear. All day long the Americans fell back, giving ground. C Company of the Second Engineers placed mines as it retreated, along with the Thirtieth Infantry, to Krinkelt. A Company was thrown into the line there at 11 p.m. to prevent a German breakthrough. All night long the troops fought at Krinkelt. Battalion moved its headquarters back to Camp Elsenborn.

December 18: General Eisenhower decided to commit the reserves to the battle. That meant the 82d and 101st Airborne divisions. General Ridgway was still in England. General Taylor was still in America. The 101st's assistant division commander was in England. Yes, everybody had expected things to be soft that Christmastime. The senior officer of the 101st present that day was Brig. Gen. Anthony C. McAuliffe, the artillery commander. So, as ordered, he moved the troops to Bastogne, the headquarters of the Eighth Corps.

December 18: Lieutenant Downing got up and went outside to look at the bomb damage done by the planes that had come over during the night. The town was a mess.

Then the battalion moved out, on to another town where its CP was to be established. Sergeant Brown showed up; he had hitchhiked to make it back to the outfit. So had many others. All day they kept coming in.

The rifle companies were deployed to constitute a main line of resistance. Downing could not zero in his guns because a mixed force of rear-area units were in front of them, left over from the panic. So he waited.

That day he moved into a two-story house. The Belgian civilians were still there, but they slept in the cellar because they were afraid of buzz bombs. The Americans moved in with them; Downing, Lieutenant Fanning, and Sergeant Brown slept on the big double bed, in their clothes. The jeep driver slept in blankets on the floor.

December 19: The battalion was relieved by a cavalry recon group. The new men didn't know what they were doing, and Downing could see it by the way they dug in. They drove up in 2½-ton trucks and left their .50-caliber machine guns mounted on the trucks. If the Krauts ever came, the trucks wouldn't last fifteen minutes.

December 19: Other divisions were coming down alongside the Second Division to hold the Germans. But the enemy had penetrated 20 miles next to the Second Division. The front-line troops were taking heavy shelling but were destroying many panzers. A Company was running the evacuation road; C Company was placing mines; and the remnants of B Company were being reorganized. An air attack on Camp Elsenborn raised hell with the motor pool, killing nine men, wounding four, and knocking out the whole operation. The Ninth and Thirty-eighth divisions were moving out of Krinkelt and Wirtzfeld. That included Lieutenant Thornton's Sixtieth Infantry.

Captain Miller's Twentieth Engineers were to move, too. The situation of the Eighth Corps was critical. Miller learned that the Germans had 150 soldiers in American uniforms, riding around in American jeeps, who were to blow up headquarters and major installations. Miller headed for Eupen for orders. He was stopped by MPs and soldiers and challenged a dozen times. Traffic in Eupen was heavy as units were funneled in to meet the German attack.

December 20: Downing had a message to go up front with Company H, his old company. He found Captain Crouthamel, now commanding the company, and Lieutenant Hobratschk was the exec. Henesey, the former platoon sergeant, was now first sergeant. He had finally made it! Not too many first sergeants to go around just now.

The company jeeps were ready for action with .50-caliber machine guns mounted. It grew colder. The troops stopped that night at a road junction. They saw red and green parachutes—German parachutes. The riflemen deployed and captured some paratroopers.

December 20: Captain Miller's men moved at 8 a.m. through Eupen and Spa to La Reid. He saw that First Army headquarters had left Spa. Everywhere, the brass was evacuating.

*

The situation was thoroughly confusing. Lieutenant Thornton's Sixtieth Infantry was not having any trouble. He moved the company command post to Mariaweilerhausen. Then he learned that the Thirtieth Division had gone south to try to help the 106th.

December 20: The Second Engineers were under heavy fire. The whole First Army front was desperate. The Twelfth SS Panzer Division had tried and failed to break through the Second Division. But the First SS Panzer Division had broken through deep into Belgium.

The weather was German weather still—fog and rain. And mud. There were virtually no Allied aircraft flying, but the Luftwaffe flew. Nobody even thought about mail or Christmas or hot meals. The cooks and the mail clerks were all in the line, fighting as infantry. One week of action had brought 25 percent casualties to the Second Engineers—4 officers missing in action, and 144 enlisted men killed, wounded, or missing.

The Twentieth Engineers moved again. They were going to Robertville this time, to keep up with the corps command post.

December 21: Everything was confused. Lieutenant Thornton's Company M of the Sixtieth Infantry was relieved at Marieweiler and then moved to Stolberg. Then the Sixtieth was moved out of Stolberg to drive all night to take up a position close to the Meuse River near Huy.

The Second Armored Division was not quite sure what was up, even yet. On the eighteenth the men were ordered back, but then for a moment it seemed that the Germans had been stopped. So everyone relaxed. That was December 20. On December 21 Lieutenant Colonel Buster's Ninety-second Field Artillery Battalion was told to get ready to move the next day.

December 22: B Company of the Twentieth Engineers was laying mines alongside the roads and in the battalion area.

December 22: Lieutenant Downing was having a hard time keeping up. Battalion headquarters kept moving. No sooner would Downing get set up in some nice warm house than a new order would come down. He moved to Camp Elsenborn, but he missed a turn because some MP told him to go straight ahead. Soon he found himself out in a field where dogfaces were setting up and digging foxholes. This was not the Second Battalion command post.

"Nope," said a dogface. "This is the Second Division, Lootenant. And right over there, where you're going, is where the Jerries are."

So Downing turned around fast and got the hell out of there, stopping enroute only to chew out the MP who had given him the wrong directions.

*　　　*　　　*

Maj. Gen. James M. Gavin, who was General Ridgway's assistant commander of the airborne corps, assigned the Eighty-second Airborne to move into position to block the Germans at Werbomont. The 101st moved into Bastogne.

Lieutenant Downing moved up to the forward position of the Eighteenth Infantry on the north edge of the "bulge" where the First Division was keeping the Germans from widening the penetration.

The commander of Company G bragged to him that he had made an excellent observation post at a CP he had dug on the foremost part of the forward slope of the position. So Downing took his men and drove up to a place where the fence-line hedge ended. He went forward first. The radio operator and instrument corporal followed him. He crawled to the crest of the hill, along a line of brush, and saw the log- and dirt-covered command post down the slope about 25 yards away, across a flat snow-covered piece of ground. Holes from shell bursts ringed the position. He grabbed his carbine, gathered his legs, and sprinted across the ground to the hole entrance and tumbled in.

Two G Company soldiers were squatting on the floor, heating C rations over a can of gasoline-soaked dirt. They stared at him. He told them he was the forward observer for the cannon company. They began griping at him. It was American artillery, not 88s, that had made all those holes around the CP that morning.

As they were talking, Downing's two men also tumbled into the command post. This made it pretty crowded in there. And then they heard the scream of an incoming shell. Everyone flattened on the bottom of the hole. The shell whammed in, not 20 yards away. Then another came over.

"This is a helluva CP," said Lieutenant Downing. He could tell he and his men were not very welcome. He decided to get out of there. But who was going to go first? Naturally Downing had to lead. So he did. A shell came whining over. After it burst, he jumped out of the hole and ran across the open ground before the Germans could fire another. He slipped and stumbled in the snow, but he finally reached the brush line and ran down the hill. Partway down he dropped behind a tree and lay gasping for breath. The Germans had seen him. A shell landed in the field to his left. He ran to the jeep, dropped down, and sucked in gulps of cold air. Still the others did not show up. He decided to go back to the inn alone. He walked along the jeep track. Suddenly salvos of shells began arriving. He saw a foxhole on the right and jumped in. Shells slammed into the field. One landed 15 yards from his hole, making his ears ring with concussion. He stayed quiet. Finally the shelling stopped.

On December 19 men from the shattered Twenty-eighth Division began moving through the lines of the newly situated 101st Airborne Division east of Bastogne. Many of these men were in no condition to fight further; they were suffering from exhaustion and shock.

But not all. A battalion of field artillery, the 109th, joined up with the 907th Glider Field Artillery. Some groups from the Ninth Armored Division, which had withdrawn from the Longvilly road, came to the Bastogne area and set up to resist. Seven tanks from the Ninth Armored Division showed up and stayed. They would be a little task force operating with the Second Battalion of the 501st Parachute Infantry for the next few days.

And they came just in time. At 5:30 on the morning of December 20, the 501st Parachute Infantry had a patrol out in front, on the big hill to the east. Three thousand yards away were six German tanks, coming up from the southeast. Sgt. Floyd Johnson led his section to the hill north of the Bizory. He put two tank destroyers out, one on each side of the road. Lt. Frederic Mallon went to the higher ground southeast of town and waited for the German tanks.

The enemy came up at about 7:30, a Mark IV tank and Mark V tank and two self-propelled 75-millimeter guns. Behind them were a full battalion of German infantrymen.

The tanks and tank destroyers began shooting. One American tank destroyer was disabled by a direct hit on the turret. It limped away. But the second tank destroyer knocked out the Mark IV and then pulled back to Bizory. But the driver ran the gun up against a building and damaged it. That tank destroyer, too, was out of action. The second section of tank destroyers fought another tank and a self-propelled gun and destroyed both of them. From Bastogne, General McAuliffe's artillery blasted the German infantrymen, who then moved off to the north to escape the fire.

That day the 501st and 506th regiments linked up. By the morning of December 21 they had firm possession of the road to Bastogne from the east and north.

*

The German effort now was concentrated in the Noville area. On the left flank of the 506th Parachute Infantry was the 502d. A pair of German tanks came roaring up through a field on the Houffalize road and stopped behind the first building of Noville. What they did not see was a bazooka team. The bazookamen fired a rocket, and one tank was set on fire. The Germans also did not see an American tank commanded by S. Sgt. Michael Lesniak. He heard them coming, got down from the tank and onto the main street for a look, spotted the German tanks, got back into his tank, and moved down the street. He fired before the enemy had more than a glimpse of him, and his first round finished the second German tank. A third German tank saw what was happening and stayed north of the town, along the road, hiding in the fog of the hollows. From there it fired several shells, one of which hit the turret of Sergeant Lesniak's tank, damaging it.

The fog that morning around Noville was very thick. No one could see much outside the town. Then at 10 a.m. the fog lifted for a while and out there in the field were fifteen German tanks moving back toward their own lines. They were about 1000 yards away. The American tank destroyers began firing and disabled four of the panzers.

One German Tiger tank charged into the middle of Noville. It stopped right in front of the command post of Company B of the Twentieth Armored Infantry Battalion. The tank swung its gun slowly toward the door of the building.

Capt. Omar Billett looked at it in dismay.

"Don't look now," said some joker behind him, "but there's an 88 pointed at you."

Not for long. Sergeant Lesniak's tank was just 20 yards away, hidden from the enemy by the fog. He had a bead on the Tiger. He fired three rounds of 75-millimeter ammunition. This did not seem to damage the Tiger at all, but the panzer driver shifted into reverse. He ran over a jeep, fouling a track in the wreckage. The track began to slide off, but he continued to back up. He collided with a half-track, and the tank slid over to one side. The crewmen opened up, jumped out, and ran out of the town toward the German lines. The fog was so thick that the GI riflemen did not even get a shot at them.

As the fog lifted and lowered, it became apparent that the Germans had Noville surrounded, with tanks between the town and Bastogne. And so during the morning Maj. Robert Harwick was ordered to withdraw the Third Battalion of the 506th Parachute Infantry from the town. The move began at about 1:15 that afternoon. The Americans blew up the ammunition dump and started out. The fog had settled in again, which was to their advantage.

An armored car led the van. It sped off into Bastogne without drawing fire. One of the five escorting tanks broke down and had to be destroyed by thermite. The column continued on toward Foy. Then came a comedy of errors—if you could call it that.

The column was moving toward Foy and safety. The vehicles were abreast of a farmhouse about 500 yards from the village.

On the leading half-track the shutter dropped down and the driver could not see the road. The driver raised his arm to move the shutter. The commander, Maj. James B. Duncan, thought the driver had been wounded and was putting his hand to his face. So he slammed on the brakes. That stopped the column. The second half-track rammed into the back of the first. The third half-track pulled up right behind. Then they began to feel fire from both sides of the road as well as from the house. The three half-tracks began fighting. The riflemen dismounted and blazed away with tommy guns. In ten minutes they had dispersed a large group of Germans.

But after that the battle deteriorated rapidly. The fourth half-track had withdrawn. Duncan called on the tanks to come up and fire on the house.

But the tanks did not move. The crewmen of the first tank said they had no ammunition. The second tank said the machine gun was jammed and there were no shells for the big gun. Then two tanks did come up and shell the house until it caught fire. But they were attacked by three German tanks which came up through the fog from the east; first one American tank was knocked out, and then the driver of the second was wounded.

Capt. William G. Schultz, the tank unit commander, was in the fifth tank. He walked up to the third tank, got in, and drove along the road toward Bastogne, figuring the others would follow. But they did not. And on the way Schultz's tank was disabled by fire from a German tank. But Schultz and the crew got out and hoofed it into Bastogne safely.

Back by the burning house: fiasco!

A U.S. tank destroyer came up to look for German tanks. A Sherman tank began backing into the tank destroyer; the driver reversed course and crushed a jeep. The Sherman tank moved up and was hit by a shell from an unseen German tank. The Sherman exploded in flame. Its turret blew off into the middle of the road and blocked passage. The fifth tank was left without a crew, since Captain Schultz had gone on to one tank and the driver to another. Major Hustead of the 506th came up to try to get the column going again. But there were no tank drivers available. He asked all around. Nobody admitted to being able to drive a tank. The paratroopers concluded that the tankers were crapping out, and they walked up and down the line cursing them as yellow bastards. But the fact was that the "tankers" were right. Most of the men were replacements, and they didn't know "shit from Shinola," as the dogface phrase would have it. Some of them were cooks. Some were mechanics. Some were riflemen. None of them was a driver. These guys were tankers only because they had been assigned to a tank unit by the replacement depots. Hurray for the reppledepples! Round pegs in square holes!

So the men of the 506th had to abandon the road and the vehicles and move through the fields on both sides, toward Bastogne. The troops in the right-hand column made it all right, and so did the tank destroyers that were following them. The troops on the left ran into fire from two tanks, but they called on the tank destroyers, which came back around and destroyed one tank. The others escaped over the hill, and the infantrymen forged on.

Finally, what was left of the column made its way into Bastogne. That fifth tank, which had had no driver, finally got a driver when a bunch of paratroopers got aboard and decided it was time to learn "how to run the son of a bitch." And somehow they did!

At dusk on December 20 the column, including the trucks and ambulances with the wounded, made its way down the road and inside the perimeter of the Third Battalion of the 506th Parachute Infantry.

December 21: The Second Armored Division was warned to get ready to move.

It was raining and snowing at Robertville, and the men of the Twentieth Engineers were thoroughly miserable, but they saw no action.

Artillery fire in the sector manned by the Second Armored Division was intense on both sides. Guns belched night and day. For once the Germans seemed to be throwing as much artillery as the Americans.

On December 21 the Germans seemed to have lost interest in breaking through to Bastogne. The action at Neffe and Mont, just east of Bastogne, was confined to sparring. Patrols moved around in all directions. On the night of December 20 the Germans had moved onto the road to Neufchâteau, southwest of Bastogne. General McAuliffe had come out along the road that evening to meet with General Middleton, the corps commander. They talked about the prospects. McAuliffe was sure he could hold out for forty-eight hours, no matter what. Middleton warned that the 116th Panzer Division was on its way to attack. General McAuliffe went out of the corps headquarters and hurried along the road back to Bastogne. A few hours later the road was cut.

When General Middleton learned this, he put General McAuliffe in charge of the defense. McAuliffe had his paratroops and armored troops. And that night General Middleton gave an order to Combat Command B of the Tenth Armored Division: Bastogne must be held at all costs.

At this point, General McAuliffe received a gift of two days from the Germans, who were having troubles of their own with supply, now that they had gone out on the limb that was supposed to take them to Antwerp. The German troops were going hungry. The German artillery was growing short of ammunition.

On December 21 the Neufchâteau road to Bastogne was cut, but off to the left Mande-St.-Etienne was still no man's land. But on December 22 the Germans closed in, and Bastogne was completely surrounded.

December 21: In the morning a patrol from an armor unit went down the Neufchâteau road to see what the Germans were doing. The patrol consisted of a single tank destroyer and two squads of infantry. They met a 101st Division patrol 1½ miles southwest of Bastogne. A little further on they found an enemy force, and then they turned around.

Another armored patrol observed a force of Germans riding in American vehicles and dressed in American uniforms. But when they encountered, fought, and captured some of those Germans, they found that each enemy soldier had kept his dog tags or some part of his equipment so that he could claim he was still in German uniform.

Near Senonchamps an American armored force of fourteen tanks and 200 infantrymen came to grips with a German force that slipped off into the Bois de Fragotte. The American 420th Field Artillery Battalion and the 755th Field Artillery Battalion got into action there and began giving the woods a heavy shelling. The Americans knocked out an enemy self-propelled gun. The Germans disabled an American tank, which had to be destroyed. The American force stayed in action all evening. At night 300 American infantrymen and 19 U.S. tanks were fighting in a sector 4000 yards long, from south of Senonchamps to the Neufchâteau road.

The surrounding of Bastogne solidified the defense. It also created problems of communication, and ultimately General Middleton expected that Bastogne would be cut off. But not yet. Lt. Col. Harry Kinnard, the 101st Airborne operations officer, was talking to corps that night. Corps wanted information. Kinnard did not want to give it to the Germans, whom he knew were listening in. What was the situation? asked corps.

"You know what a doughnut looks like?" asked Kinnard. "Well, we're the hole in the doughnut."

December 22: At 3:45 a.m. the Second Armored Division moved out from its encampment, bound for the battle zone. It passed through Aachen and then through Huy. The march was miserable—cold, raining, and wet. The vehicles had to drive so close together to keep sight of the taillights in front that the drivers were under constant strain. The march went at 6 miles an hour, and it was 78 miles of march. Every turn had to be marked; every crossroads had to have its MPs to direct the traffic properly. "A memorable event," said Lieutenant Colonel Buster. Not pleasant, but memorable.

None of the jeeps had windshields; they had been discarded because the reflection of light could give away position. The command cars and weapons carriers were also without them. It was the same for the tanks. The quota of general misery was very high; the commanders had to stand with hatches open, helping to guide the drivers.

"And we were not really equipped for cold weather. Facing freezing rain."

What they needed were lined boots and multilayer garments to keep in the heat. At this stage of the war they did not have such niceties.

From a logistic standpoint it was a good march. The Second Armored Division lost only about thirty-five vehicles from the whole division, and all these were repairable. The division was in very good shape.

It had moved 14,000 men and 3000 vehicles 78 miles. Generally speaking, the column was strung out for a hundred miles.

There were plenty of rumors. The story of the Malmédy massacre had gotten out and had been amplified. Other tales of horror, of German infiltration, passed up and down the line as the men of the Second Armored Division moved.

The division moved through Eichen, through Eupen. Virtually all the towns along the way were bombed-out relics of the war.

At 5:45 on the afternoon of December 22 the troops reached Paar and bivouacked there. Lieutenant Colonel Buster's headquarters was in a château that belonged to Madame de Piemont. The Americans found her very gracious in giving them plenty of room and support. The Second Armored was now the Seventh Corps' reserve. It was ready to help fight the battle of the breakthrough.

*   *   *

December 22: At 11:30 in the morning a German major, a captain, and two enlisted men came up the road to Bastogne from Remoifosse, which was just south of the Marvie section of the defense perimeter. They were carrying a big white flag. They were met by three GIs of the 327th Glider Infantry. Pfc. Ernest D. Premetz, a medic, could speak German.

They wanted to talk, said the Germans.

The dogfaces took the Germans to a house that was the command post of the 327th weapons platoon. The German enlisted men were left there, but the two officers were blindfolded and taken up to the command post of Capt. James F. Adams of Company F. Adams called battalion. Battalion called regiment, and regiment called division. The word was that the Germans wanted to talk surrender terms. Division also happened to be Bastogne defense command, Brig. Gen. McAuliffe presiding.

Along the line the dogfaces got the idea that the Germans wanted to surrender. That sounded very good. Everyone relaxed.

That was not quite the way it was. The Germans met with Maj. Alvin Jones and gave him this message:

To the U.S.A. Commander of the encircled town of Bastogne:

The fortune of war is changing. This time the U.S.A. forces in and near Bastogne have been encircled by strong German armored units. More German armored units have crossed the River Ourthe, near Ourtheville, have taken Marche and reached St. Hubert by passing through Hompre-Sibret-Tillet. Libramont is in German hands.

There is only one possibility to save the encircled U.S.A. troops from total annihilation; that is the honorable surrender of the encircled town. In order to think it over a term of two hours will be granted beginning with the presentation of this note.

If this proposal should be rejected one German artillery corps and six heavy A.A. battalions are ready to annihilate the U.S.A. troops in and near Bastogne. The order for firing will be given immediately after this two hours' term.

All the serious civilian losses caused by this artillery fire would not correspond with the well known American humanity.

The German Commander

So, said the Germans, Bastogne must surrender or it would be destroyed.

The German officers were left with Captain Adams, and the note was taken to General McAuliffe. He knew that his position was pretty strong and he expected help. He thought the demand was funny.

"Aw nuts," said he, as he read the note. But he really didn't know quite how to phrase his reply, until Colonel Kinnard came through with the solution. At the colonel's suggestion, McAuliffe's initial reaction to the note was the answer given to the German officers:

"Will you surrender?"

"Nuts!"

Colonel Harper of McAuliffe's staff took the message to the German officers who were waiting at the command post of Company F.

"I have the American commander's reply," he said.

"Is it written or verbal?"

"It is written. I will stick it in your hand."

"Is the reply negative or affirmative? If it is the latter, I will negotiate further."

"The reply is definitely not affirmative," Colonel Harper said. "If you continue this foolish attack, your losses will be tremendous."

Colonel Harper then put the two German officers into a jeep and took them back to the main road. The German soldiers were waiting there with their white flag. Colonel Harper then removed the blindfolds from the German officers.

"If you don't understand what 'nuts' means, in plain English it is the same as 'Go to hell.' And I will tell you something else. If you continue to attack, we will kill every goddamn German that tries to break into this city."

The German major and captain saluted.

"We will kill many Americans. This is war," said the captain.

"On your way, bud," said Colonel Harper. "And good luck to you."

So the Germans walked down the road. It was 1:30 p.m.

The rest of the day was quiet, no matter what the Germans had said about the war starting again at 3 p.m. There was an attack just before four o'clock against Company F, but it involved only about fifty enemy troops, and it was beaten off. Another strike came an hour later, but this too was repelled.

But that night, December 22, the Luftwaffe was over Bastogne in force, and bombing. That was no joke.

The situation was not quite so serene at Bastogne as General McAuliffe had indicated. That night the defenders reached the low ebb of their capability. He had the men. He had the guns. But he did not have the ammunition.

The 463d Field Artillery, in support of the 327th Glider Infantry, had only 200 rounds left. All the other artillery battalions were in about the same state. General McAuliffe was just issuing an order that would restrict the artillery to ten rounds per day!

One commander telephoned headquarters: "We are about to be attacked by two regiments. We can see them out there. Please let us fire at least two rounds per gun."

The answer came back: "If you see 400 Germans in a 100-yard area, and they have their heads up, you can fire artillery at them, but not more than two rounds."

There was one good word: headquarters said that a column from the Fourth Armored Division was coming up from the southwest to support the 101st Airborne. But could it arrive in time?

The Germans were quite well aware of the American ammunition shortage. They knew the American artillery and how it operated, and they could tell that this American artillery was not firing its usual patterns. Therefore they moved troops around Bastogne in the open, with the utmost contempt for the defenders' guns.

Then came the word that the air supply for Bastogne would begin at 8 p.m. The spot designated was a hillside near the 101st Division command post.

The regiments were ordered to send ¾-ton trucks to the field.

So the trucks arrived, but the supplies did not. The drop was canceled. Bad weather. The C-47s would drop the supplies on the "first flyable day."

And when would that be?

Nobody knew.

December 22: Lieutenant Chattaway was still living aboard his "*40 hommes ou 8 chevaux*" boxcar. He had expected to be delivered swiftly to his destination, but the train was shunted from one siding to another, with no explanations. He knew absolutely nothing about the German breakthrough in the Ardennes. The worst thing about the boxcars was that there were no sanitary facilities. When the train was on a siding, it wasn't so bad. But when the train was moving... The boxcar began to smell like a pigsty.

Captain Shebeck's Third Replacement Depot was moved to Waremme, a city about 12 miles west of Liège on the road to Brussels. There was very little training. Mostly he and the others were sorting out replacements, some of them pretty green, and sending them to the line units to try to plug up the holes created by the Germans. In addition to his other duties, Captain Shebeck was put in charge of security for Waremme. He had a detail of forty MPs to do the job. There were reports of Germans having infiltrated the area; but if so, they had taken what they wanted and left, because he did not find any of them.

*

December 23: For three days artillery fire had boomed continuously in the area of the Second Engineers.

"My God, it is an awesome sight and sound to live with," said Lieutenant Colonel Snetzer, "with this constant wrath of the gods of war."

It was cold and crisp on the twenty-third, and he could see high-altitude aerial battles going on, with the planes crisscrossing and leaving vapor trails. The word came down that the German push had been stopped in the engineers' area. The First Army was back under the British, the men were told.

December 23: A patrol of Colonel Merriam's Eighty-second Reconnaissance Battalion ran into a German unit on the road south and west of the American lines, not far from the Meuse River at Dinant. The patrol had been ordered to maintain radio silence so that the enemy would not know of the arrival of the Second Armored Division in that area. Because of that order the leader of the patrol could not give any instant warning. Instead, he returned to the unit command post and reported. Fortunately the command post was just across the road from division headquarters, so the commander of the unit went across and reported to General Harmon's staff that the Germans had "damned near reached the Meuse." Harmon's staff was under the impression that the Meuse was the German objective, not realizing that Hitler had predicated his offensive on going all the way to the sea. He planned to do again in 1944 what he had done so successfully in 1940—cut the Allied forces in two. So there was a lot of talk at Second Armored Division headquarters. Also, General Collins, commander of the First Army, had indeed been placed again under the control of Field Marshal Montgomery, and Montgomery had the nice, tidy idea that the German advance could be allowed to move in and that the forces could then be sealed off and decimated. General Collins did not share that view, but Montgomery was the boss.

So the Second Armored Division waited. And waited some more. The division waited on the twenty-third, having given Montgomery the information about the German infiltration. The division waited on the twenty-fourth. It was not until December 25 that General Collins said to hell with it and told the Second Armored Division to get going and stop the Germans.

December 23: Bastogne. It was certainly a flyable day. Everyone was waiting for the C-47s. Around 9:40 the Pathfinder jumpers appeared, bringing the word that the C-47 supply train would arrive in about an hour and a half. So the drop zone was again delineated and the men were again out, waiting.

The planes began to come in. By 4 p.m. nearly 250 planes had dropped 1450 bundles into the mile-square drop zone. Ninety-five percent of the dropped material was recovered. That was more than excellent.

Of course, darkness came very early in those winter days, and the crews on the ground worked hard. By 5 p.m. they had almost all the bundles in jeeps, trucks, and other vehicles and were bringing them back to the Bastogne defense. The artillery could begin firing again, and it did.

But then the supply people began counting. They found that they had an overabundance of .50-caliber machine gun ammunition, but they needed 75-millimeter ammunition for the pack howitzers and 105-millimeter ammunition for the bigger guns.

By nightfall there were still shortages. The defenders had only 445 gallons of gasoline, and the 26,000 K rations would supply the men for only one day. So the troops were ordered to forage. From the ruins of Bastogne, from army and enemy and civilian supply, they found that they could raise flour, lard, salt, and coffee. There were potatoes and cows and chickens. Someone found an extra 450 pounds of coffee. And a lot of—yuck—Ovaltine. In a civilian warehouse a supply officer found margerine and jam. And somebody found 2000 burlap bags.

The last were invaluable. The infantrymen did not have weatherproof boots, so 1000 soldiers got burlap bags to wrap around their feet. It was just like Valley Forge!

December 24: Captain Miller observed that the air force johnnies were certainly earning their pay. All day long he saw the Allied bombers and fighters overhead. That afternoon B Company went out to build a Bailey bridge across the lake east of Robertville. All Christmas eve the men worked on the bridge. They did not finish until two o'clock on Christmas morning.

Lieutenant Thornton of M Company of the Sixtieth Infantry was made commanding officer of the company that day. The company moved into Klaterhelberg.

December 24: Lieutenant Colonel Buster and the rest of the Second Armored Division were waiting. They knew the Germans were moving, but what could they do but follow orders?

That day the division prepared to move out. Lieutenant Colonel Buster's artillery was assigned to support Combat Command A's coming attack, set for December 24.

The artillerymen were to support Peewee Collier, the general commanding Combat Command A, a very determined, very tough, bantam rooster of a commander.

December 24: The day passed and Christmas eve arrived at Lieutenant Downing's battalion command post of the Eighteenth Infantry's Second Battalion. The men sat around the table in the parlor of the inn that they had taken over. Some of the command post group had gotten packages from home. They shared. They spread out the canned meat, cheese, crackers, and candy for everybody. Someone found a bottle of cognac, and they passed that around, drinking to Christmas.

Merry Christmas everyone! (Krauts excepted, of course.)

The warm, lighted parlor produced a feeling of well-being and comfort. But still everyone "was silently imagining how it would be to be back again in the states, opening presents around a tree and drinking Tom and Jerries in the comfort, cleanliness, and security of civilian life."

If anyone doubted, he was brought back to sudden reality at about midnight by the roar of a tank engine. The driver outside was performing his nightly ritual, starting the engine and rocking the tank backward and forward a little to break the hold of the ice on the treads. The roar of the exhaust was the only clue to the driver's activity; the vapor, which might have given the tank away to the enemy, was screened by the darkness.

A pair of unshaven, dirt-encrusted riflemen, looking like the prototypes of Bill Mauldin's cartoon characters—the dogfaces Willie and Joe—came in, their faces red with cold, overcoat collars standing high, and brought with them a deserter from the First SS Panzer Division. He was interrogated there in the warm inn early that Christmas morning and then sent to the rear. The riflemen each got a drink of cognac and then reluctantly went back out to return to the cold and their holes in the ground. Lieutenant Downing lay down on the floor in his sleeping bag. His mind wandered back to other years:

Christmas 1942. He had been in the rain at Medjez el Bab in Tunisia, just getting ready for that dreadful, abortive attack on the Germans. At least he had survived.

Christmas 1943. The Nissen huts at Broadmayne, England. Safety, but not much comfort.

Christmas 1944. Butgenbach, Belgium, and who ever heard of that?

Christmas 1945. ??????????

Would he be in Europe, or would that war end and would he be in the Pacific. Or would he be back in the states?

After twenty-nine months overseas, and particularly the way the war was now going, he could not imagine its ever ending.

Finally he fell asleep.

*　　　*　　　*

Christmas eve. Bastogne.

General McAuliffe wanted to raise morale. He issued a communiqué:

Merry Christmas

What's merry about all this, you ask? We're fighting—it's cold—we aren't home. All true. But what has the proud Eagle Division accomplished with its worthy comrades of the 10th Armored Division, the 705th Tank-Destroyer Battalion and all the rest? Just this: We have stopped cold everything that has been thrown at us from the north, east, south, and west. We have identification from four German Panzer Divisions, two German Infantry Divisions, and one German Parachute Division. These units, spearheading the last desperate German lunge, were headed straight west for key points when the Eagle Division was hurriedly ordered to stem the advance. How effectively this was done will be written in history, not only in our division's glorious history but in world history. The Germans actually did surround us, their radios blared out our doom, their commander demanded our surrender.

Then McAuliffe told the story of the German officers who came up with their surrender flag and of his reply—"Nuts."

He explained the situation on that Christmas day:

Allied troops are counterattacking in force. We continue to hold Bastogne. By holding Bastogne we assure the success of the Allied armies. We know that our division commander, General Taylor, will say "Well done."

We, who are giving our country and our loved ones at home a worthy Christmas present and being privileged to take part in this gallant feat of arms, are truly making for ourselves a Merry Christmas.

Well, that was the rhetoric.

In fact, on the telephone that night to General Middleton, who was well outside the danger zone, General McAuliffe said that the best Christmas present the troops could have was a relief the next day. Because who knew what was really going to happen?

Christmas eve had its ironies. The town of Bastogne was bombed, and of course a bomb hit a hospital, burying twenty patients and killing a Belgian woman. Good will to all men, all right. Another bomb knocked down the Christmas tree of Combat Command B's headquarters. One of the sergeants picked up a mangled doll, inked a purple heart on it, and hung it on the tree.

But really, all was quiet on the Bastogne front that night. The snow fell. Men on the perimeter shook hands and said goodbye. They were not really very impressed with General McAuliffe's words.

The officers knew that the "tactical situation is strong." The trouble was that the men knew that things were dreadful.

At the 502d Parachute Infantry headquarters the officers had a lovely time, hearing mass in the tenth-century Rolle Château chapel. The Belgians turned out with sides of beef and other goodies. The officers drank and ate very well and stayed up until 1:30.

At 2:45 on Christmas morning they were suddenly awakened from their stupor. The Germans were coming. At 3:30 Capt. Wallace Swanson of Company A, out on the perimeter, announced that the Germans were on top of his troops; then the line went out. A few minutes later he and his men were in hand-to-hand combat with the enemy. It was house-to-house fighting.

So much for General McAuliffe's confident words.

The Germans were moving all around. At Champs, where the road led down to Hemroulle, and then to Bastogne, the fighting was desperate. Tanks were coming up fast. The point of juncture with the 327th Glider Infantry was threatened.

"There are seven enemy tanks and a lot of enemy infantry coming over the hill on your left," said Lt. Samuel B. Nickels, charging into the sacred château where the 502d officers were just waking up.

So out of the Rolle Château poured the men of the 502d headquarters—cooks, clerks, radiomen, chaplains, and staff officers—and they rushed to the next hill. They had to stop the German column if it was not to take Hemroulle and then threaten Bastogne.

From the château stable came the walking wounded. Maj. Douglas T. Davidson, the 502d surgeon, stood by and handed out rifles as the men hobbled up. Then he led them out to fight the tanks.

The 327th Glider Infantry was engaged by the Germans. First the tanks hit the positions of companies A and B and broke through to the battalion command posts. At 7:15 the commander of the Third Battalion announced that the tanks were on top of him.

"How close?" asked the colonel.

"Right here," said Colonel Allen. "They are firing point blank at me at 1150 yards. I've got to run."

And so Christmas day broke...

The main body of the German armor broke through the 327th's lines at Company A. They were beautifully done up, those tanks—all in white covers to camouflage them in the snow. But the men of the company stayed in their foxholes and let the tanks go by. When the tanks passed, four men of the company died and five were wounded. But sixty-eight survivors were still fighting, and now they were behind the enemy, a very nice place to be.

On the ridge, past the company, the German armor split. Half went toward the château. Half went toward Champs. And there, waiting for them, was the 705th Tank-Destroyer Battalion.

The Americans had finally found a way to make their 37-millimeter guns effective. They could be used to fire "canister," or small shot, that scattered widely from a 37-millimeter projectile; it was useful against troop concentrations. So one of these fired at the German infantry. A tank destroyer went ahead to a house where thirty Germans had taken cover. Sgt. Lawrence Valletta moved up and blew the place apart.

South of Champs the Germans forged ahead. They knocked out two American tank destroyers in short order. Confident now, the Germans came rushing ahead, not seeing the concealed American tank destroyers in the woods. The Germans charged in, firing at the American infantrymen, but the fog helped protect them. Company C of the 705th then began a hasty retreat. From a point in the woods the Americans rallied and began potting at the German soldiers riding the tanks, and with good effect. The panzers then moved along the top of the ridge, and the hidden American tank destroyers opened fire. Three German Mark IV tanks were knocked out quietly. Two more panzers were stopped by bazookamen. The German infantry now was battered and confused. The Americans counted sixty-seven German dead and thirty-five prisoners taken around the wrecked tanks. One panzer broke through Company B and into Champs. But there it was hit by bazookas or by a 57-millimeter shell, or both. Nobody quite knew what stopped that tank, but something did.

And, finally, six of the seven tanks of the German attack were accounted for.

So the first German attack of Christmas had been fielded, and the lines had held.

So had the 327th Glider Infantry next door, which had faced eighteen tanks. All eighteen of those panzers were captured or destroyed that day. By nightfall the perimeter was again solid. Any Germans who had gotten through had not gotten out again. Colonel Harper was keeping his promise to that German major, made as the German parley party had left Bastogne.

But on Christmas night the situation still did not look very good for the men of the 101st in Bastogne. The brass sat down to dinner: a can of sardines and a box of crackers. Things never look good under those conditions.

"We have been let down," said General McAuliffe. He had expected relief that day.

December 25, Christmas: The weather was still holding up in the Twentieth Engineers' sector of the front, and Allied aircraft were hitting the Germans hard. Nothing much was happening on the ground. The engineers had a lovely Christmas dinner. That took care of that. In the afternoon Captain Miller went over to the Robertville dam to check on the possibility of opening the gates to lower the water level. First Division was asking that the level be lowered so that if the Germans blew the dam upstream, this one wouldn't be wiped out, too.

Captain Miller had an argument with the guards on the dam, but he finally convinced them that he was real, and not a German spy. They let him go in. He went down to the bottom of the dam and opened a valve. A stream of water 5 feet in diameter started to shoot out. "A beautiful sight," said the engineer in him.

December 25, Christmas: Lieutenant Thornton's Company M moved to Mutenich into a defense perimeter. The lieutenant was not above a little fraternizing on Christmas, particularly with women, and he spent the evening "having a little party with a couple of German girls." They danced a little. And then...

What the hell, even if there was a war on, it was Christmas, wasn't it?

*

December 25, Christmas: It was also D + 202, and the war seemed a long way from over. In the sector held by the Second Infantry Division the day was cold and clear; the infantrymen, too, watched the contrails of the air force boys as they came over to sock the Germans. Their Christmas entertainment was watching the air force perform.

That day there was one lucky German pilot. His plane was shot down over the Second Engineers' position, and he parachuted down. Waiting for him were his enemies and a Christmas dinner of turkey, dressing, cranberries, asparagus, and even beer. Then, of course, it was off to interrogation and to a cold POW cage.

December 25, Christmas: Lieutenant Downing awakened on the nice warm floor of the inn, stowed his sleeping bag, and went out to the outposts to see what was happening, in case the efforts of the cannon company should be needed. During this round he received word from the radio operator that he was wanted back at the cannon company command post.

"Come and bring all your equipment," was the order.

Puzzling.

He picked up all the stuff and drove over the icy road to the CP, which was in a farmhouse. It had been shelled two nights earlier and looked dreadful.

What was up, the lieutenant asked.

Nobody knew, except that orders had come down asking that Downing be transferred to Company D. No details were available.

So Lieutenant Downing picked up his sleeping bag and his musette bag and took his jeep driver back into the middle of the town of Butgenbach. They found the First Battalion headquarters. There he met the battalion commander, Lieutenant Colonel Leonard, a young-looking regular army officer who had come from the Second Armored Division a few days earlier. Downing was to go to D Company, said the colonel. So the lieutenant went to D Company's orderly room in another shell-battered house.

Captain Bowers invited Downing to Christmas dinner. It was the same—turkey and all the things that went with it—except that the first sergeant had also made a pot of soup from scratch, using an old family recipe. Captain Bowers, Lieutenant Downing, the executive officer of the company, the first sergeant, and the company clerks all ate around the kitchen table in the Belgian farmhouse. After dinner Captain Bowers told Downing he would become a section leader of the company's mortar platoon.

It was a nice quiet Christmas afternoon for Downing. Nice, quiet, and lousy. He had just gotten another demotion.

Downing was furious, and he went to the battalion commander. Could he be reclassified and transferred out of the Eighteenth, he asked. Lieutenant Colonel Williamson knew what that would mean: an officer transferred out of a combat outfit during combat was in real trouble, no matter the reason. But the colonel also seemed to understand Downing's frustration.

He would never hurt an officer who had served as faithfully under him as Downing had, he said. "Carry on this assignment, and I'll see what I can do."

But Downing was seething. He borrowed a jeep and went up to Nidrum to see Colonel Smith, commander of the regiment.

"Why can't you get along with your company commanders?" the colonel asked.

"I haven't had any trouble that I know of," said Downing.

The colonel looked angry. He picked up the phone and asked the operator to get Lieutenant Wohlers on the phone. He got him. The colonel asked why Wohlers had asked for Downing's transfer out of the company.

"He uses too many rounds on a target," said Wohlers.

"That doesn't sound like much of a reason to transfer an officer out," said the colonel. Then he called Lieutenant Colonel Williamson.

Williamson said that Downing had good recommendations from Captains Murphy and Spinney, but that he did not have enough experience to take over a company. And if he came back to the Second Battalion, that's what he should have.

So the colonel hung up the telephone thoughtfully. Perhaps he was getting a glimpse of the real problem: Downing was an old hand, in it from the beginning, and these new replacement commanders resented and feared him. That's the way it was going in that winter of 1944–1945.

"Go on back to your company and do your job, and I'll see what can be done," said the colonel. Downing saluted and left.

December 25, Christmas morning: For two days the Germans who were surrounding Bastogne did not make a serious move. That meant the Americans had a little respite. But Christmas? It dawned with the knowledge that this was going to be a K-ration day at Bastogne.

December 25: The Second Armored Division was fighting in the Celles pocket. Lieutenant Colonel Buster's Ninety-second Field Artillery fired 648 rounds of 105-millimeter ammunition.

December 26: The Second Armored Division was still fighting hard in the Celles pocket. Buster's battalion fired 985 rounds.

December 27: The fighting continued, toward Rochefort; another 600 rounds were fired.

December 26: The air force was back with more airdrops over Bastogne. At three o'clock in the afternoon a combat command of the Fourth Armored Division arrived at the high ground overlooking Clochimont. This was about 4 miles southwest of Bastogne. Lt. Col. Creighton W. Abrams, commander of the Thirty-seventh Tank Battalion, and Lt. Col. George L. Jaques, of the Fifty-third Armored Infantry Battalion, decided to make a break for Bastogne. They had been fighting hard, and the tank unit had been cut down to only twenty tanks. The armored infantry battalion was at less than one-third strength.

They drove hard, and five tanks and one infantry half-track burst through toward Bastogne. When three tanks got out ahead, the Germans strewed Teller mines between the tanks and the rest of the force. Then the half-track hit one of the mines and was knocked out. Finally, three tanks of the Fourth Armored Division drove through into the lines of the 326th Airborne Engineer Battalion. The German encirclement was broken. In this drive near Assenois the Americans captured 428 prisoners.

December 26: Lieutenant Downing assembled his equipment and got into a jeep with a sergeant and a radio operator. They drove out of town and stopped behind a long reverse slope of a hill. The work of spotting for the artillery was about to begin again.

In his defensive position at Mutzenich, Lieutenant Thornton was moving his men around. He changed the position of the machine gun, as much to confuse the Germans as anything else. It would never do to have them zero in on the gun. It was very quiet in this sector of the Sixtieth Infantry.

In fact, all the Fifth Corps was very quiet, too. Captain Miller drove around on various errands and found no activity. He saw many Allied planes overhead. A very comforting sight.

*

On December 27 Lieutenant Downing came in from the cold to C Company's "rest home." The men of platoon headquarters were heating water in the kitchen, so he decided to shave. There was a mirror hanging over the sink, and he looked into it. He saw a gaunt face with long uncombed hair, matted and sprinkled with dirt from the sides of his foxhole up forward. He had a three-day growth of beard streaked with soot from the gasoline lamps they used at night. The folds of his neck were crusted with dirt, and his shirt collar had greasy piping around the edge.

After Downing washed and shaved, he found the corporal who cut hair and he got a haircut. And after that Downing got mail!

He hadn't had any mail for months. Now he had half a mail sack full. Some of it had been written before D day. There was fruitcake, and an absentee ballot that should have been cast in November. There was an invitation to attend the First Division annual banquet at the Waldorf-Astoria Hotel. Reading the mail took all afternoon.

December 28: There was no change in the Sixtieth Infantry's position. But that day the weather turned foggy again, and the Germans awoke at Robertville. They began shelling the place. Still, the barrage was not followed by an attack.

It had begun to snow on Christmas day, and it snowed heavily all week.

December 28: The Second Division was taking a lot of enemy fire. It was bombed, strafed, and shelled every day. The Second Engineers alone took half a dozen casualties daily, and the Germans were still pouring through the gap alongside the division.

It was quiet in Bastogne. General Taylor arrived on December 27 to congratulate General McAuliffe and to take over again as commander. Various other commanders congratulated McAuliffe. The fact that there was now time for congratulations meant that the German offensive was already blunted. Troops were now being assembled to come to Bastogne to start a counterattack. General Patton launched such an attack on December 30.

December 30: Lieutenant Downing was awarded a Bronze Star medal. Colonel Smith pinned it on him—and he remembered Downing's name!

"Good work, Downing," said the colonel.

Lieutenant Downing put the ribbon into his pocket alongside the Purple Heart.

New Year's eve.

The engineers laid 28,000 mines in front of the First Division's positions. That would give any advancing Germans something to think about.

Lieutenant Thornton and a couple of pals had a big party with their German girls, Paula and Wilhelmina. Lucky Lieutenant Thornton, enjoying the joys of fraternization!

During the day the Second Engineers moved their headquarters back into French-speaking Belgium to escape the continual shelling of their area. The temperature was 20 degrees Fahrenheit. The engineers and the Second Division both got many replacements.

That same day the Ninety-second Field Artillery moved back to the vicinity of Soree. Lieutenant Colonel Buster received orders to move out the next day.

Lieutenant Chattaway, trying to get back to his outfit from the reppledepple, was still being shunted about in his boxcar. On New Year's eve he and his buddies found some tank cars in the train yard. They were full of wine! Out came canteens, canteen cups, and helmets. Several of the 500-gallon tanks were shot up with M-1 fire. Many men got very, very sick that night.

January 1: Lieutenant Downing went to mass at the village church.

"After I entered, the church gradually filled with soldiers, all carrying their weapons. The rifles and helmets clattered against the wooden pews and kneeling benches, as the men took their seats. A few civilians, mostly elderly women, were scattered through the building. In the rear pews were some black-garbed nuns and small children. Captain Adamowski said the mass, served by two soldiers. The nuns and children sang. One of the hymns, sung in German, was 'Nearer My God to Thee.'"

When the mass was over, Downing went back up front, to his hole in the snow. The temperature fell to 10 degrees. It was a miserable time, day and night.

"After dark we had our evening meal. We never washed, shaved, or took off our clothes. At night I would crawl into my issue sleeping bag, fully clothed with shoes and field jacket on. I would pull my wool knit cap down over my ears, rest my head on my helmet, pull my overcoat over me, and go to sleep."

*

The Germans were still pushing on Liège and Antwerp, but they were not trying to widen their penetration. The Americans planned some attacks, but they were invariably called off. It was a stalemate on the First Division front just then.

All during that first week of January Allied reinforcements came up, but there was little fighting. It continued to snow heavily all around that area of Germany and Belgium.

Lieutenant Thornton was bored. January 6 was the anniversary of his promotion to first sergeant. The important thing was the snow, more and more of it. Some men went to Paris on leave. Otherwise it was patrol, patrol, with an occasional change in position.

It was the same in Captain Miller's area. The officers lived in a villa beside a lake. Villas by the lake are nicer in summer than in winter. One night they "had a little party and drank thirteen bottles of Heidsick Dry Monopole champagne, 1937 vintage." The next day the temperature dropped to 7 degrees. How many of them could feel it? Miller and some friends went deer hunting but did not see any deer. Just tracks.

January 12: "Jerry is pulling his armor out of the salient quite rapidly now."

But the fact was that even a month after the beginning of the December 16 offensive, the Germans were still deep inside the Allied lines. But now the enemy was trapped. In the month of battle the Germans had suffered 250,000 casualties, 36,000 of them POWs. The problem now was to escape out of the trap, and it was a miserable time for the escapers. Short of food, short of ammunition, short of clothing, they struggled back across the Siegfried line. It was the end of January before the German rush to get back was over, and stragglers were coming through for days.

*   *   *

The Americans and the British were regrouping, getting ready to go back on the offensive. On January 17 Lieutenant Colonel Snetzer assumed command of the Second Engineer Battalion. Colonel Warren had been transferred up to the Ninth Division as chief of staff, part of the rebuilding of that shattered division.

The snow continued to be very bad, falling every day and blowing into big drifts. The engineers were using tank bulldozers, truck plows, and every possible means to keep the roads open.

Lieutenant Downing's battalion of the Eighteenth Infantry was relieved by the Second Battalion and moved back to Nidrum, where it settled into a training routine.

Lieutenant Chattaway finally reached the village of Boullon. He found that his 110th Infantry had been badly hurt by fighting parts of four divisions in the last battle and was being completely reorganized. His earlier wound undoubtedly had saved his life; most of his friends were gone, and as a shavetail he might have been expected to be right up front in the action. Chattaway was assigned to Company C of the First Battalion.

As one of the old hands he was made executive officer of the company. They were billeted at Fumay, awaiting the campaign in the Vosges Mountains.

S. Sgt. Robert Adolph was also waiting. He and his buddies were holding the lower flank of the Third Army, camped on a mountain, in a fixed position—waiting. On December 30 Sergeant Adolph smoked his first cigar and was very proud of himself for not getting sick. He was, in many ways, still a child, this 20-year-old staff sergeant of the Army of the United States. He had already won the Bronze Star.

The 397th Infantry had moved up to Mouterhouse. The Germans had attacked several times after Christmas. Finally, on January 10, the 397th had to withdraw. As platoon guide, Sergeant Adolph had to stay with the command post. But at least that was better than living in a foxhole in the snow. His principal job was bringing K rations to the others. Once in a while there was also a sandwich and some coffee. But one day when he was out, the Germans zeroed in on the command post. So the brass in the rear decided to move the company out, and Adolph and friends hiked back 5 miles to a town. There they were examined for trench foot. With his red feet Sergeant Adolph was a suspect. So he was ordered to take it easy. He had been in the line for sixty-six consecutive days without a rest.

But soon enough he was back again.

In the new position Sergeant Adolph was in charge of booby traps for the platoon. He set one with a white phosphorus grenade. On the night of January 21 a German soldier, creeping up to observe the Americans' position, tripped the booby trap. Nobody saw it go off, but the next morning the Americans found the German's rifle, his gloves, his white forage cap, and his white cape all burned up by the phosphorus.

"I'll bet that bastard will have a scarred face for life and I dood it. Aren't we mean?"

*

By the end of January the Americans had eliminated the "bulge" and were facing the Siegfried line once more. Lieutenant Downing's First Army was concentrated between the Huertgen Forest and St.-Vith. Then came the Ninth Army. Patton's Third Army, of which Sergeant Adolph was a part, was around the Moselle River, the Luxembourg border, and near Saarlautern. Now forty-seven U.S. divisions were committed to the western front.

The forces of the western Allies were now concentrated on Germany itself. During the autumn the First Armored Division and other elements of General Mark Clark's Fifth Army had been fighting vigorously against the Germans in northern Italy, but this was hardly the center of the war. The enemy often counterattacked, as at Lucca late in December. Fighting along the Serchio River continued for a week. It was tough. The Ninety-second Division fell back, and the 366th Infantry came past. The First Tank Battalion stopped it. On December 28 the First Armored Division was relieved by the Ninety-first Division. The armored division, said the brass, would not be used again during the winter months. And now the talk was that the First Armored was no longer needed and that the troops would be reorganized into infantry. Sure, said Sergeant Haemmel and his friends. But not for long. Once they got out of the mountains, there would be good reason to use the armored once again.

37

THE LAST DAYS

After the failure of Hitler's great western counteroffensive, it was just a matter of time before Germany was finished. On the eastern front the Russians were driving hard that winter and were nearing Berlin, as the Allies were inside Germany on the west. The end might have come more quickly except for a political quarrel between the British and the Americans over the best method of getting through Germany and the decision to let the Russians take Berlin. But these were matters beyond the purview of the dogfaces, who did not give a damn who took Berlin as long as somebody did. What they were interested in was getting the war over with and going home. All they knew in January 1945 was that the war was still on, that they were still getting shot at, and that Germany in the winter was not a very comfortable place to be.

The fighting in January had been very expensive to the First Infantry Division. On January 22 the First Engineers asked the Twentieth Engineers to give them a hand by moving their forward line to the Weismer-Butgenbach road and maintaining all roads north of that line. The division had halted its attack, having reached its assigned objective. But the costs were high. Many wounded men were buried in the falling snow, and no help could get to them in time to save them. Some men from the Eighteenth Infantry lay in snow for four days and nights, and were found, remarkably, still alive.

"It's a nasty damn war," said Captain Miller when he heard that tale.

On January 24 the First Division was attacking again. The artillery shelled

the Germans at 2 a.m. for about fifteen minutes and then quit. The idea was
to lull the enemy. Then at 4 a.m. the dogfaces moved out to try to catch the
Germans in their foxholes.

For two days the air force had been having a field day, attacking the
German armor in its retreat from the salient. St.-Vith fell to the Seventh
Armored Division that day. Wiltz and Diekirch fell to the Third Army. Cap-
tain Miller heard a radio report that the Russians were only 125 miles from
Berlin!

"Good lads," said Captain Miller.

January 27 was the last day that the Twentieth Engineers supported the
First Division. They were replaced by the 276th Battalion of the 1153d Group.

"They are green as grass, fresh from the states, with about two weeks in
combat."

The Twentieth Engineers then went to support the Ninety-ninth Division,
which was to be involved immediately in the new attack against the Siegfried
line. They started on January 30, and immediately the troops were pinned
down in the snow. Next day came a blizzard. That night the weather changed
twice, and the snow melted and then froze.

The American attack was all along the line.

The Eighteenth Infantry was called on to give a hand to the Second Division, on its right; one regiment of the Second had been held up. The Thirtieth Division on the right of the Second had reached its own objective, but
there was a gap between the two divisions, and this meant the Germans could
delay the advance of the whole line until the gap was closed. So the First
Battalion of the Eighteenth was given the job.

That night Lieutenant Downing bedded down in the parlor of the house
where he was staying. The next morning, after eating breakfast in the room,
his group went out to the trucks. When all were loaded, the convoy started.
It was breaking daylight, and the cold was bitter in the open trucks without
tops.

The convoy traveled at high speed on highways behind the American
line. After a few hours the troops began to see splintered trees, scattered
dead leaves, and branches littering the sides of the road. Then they reached
a small shot-up village, where they got down from the trucks. The men lined
up in files on each side of the road and moved forward. They climbed the
road up a hill, and when the column halted, Downing went back to find
Company A's Captain van Wagoner. The captain showed him a map. They

were going to cut across country and attack the flank of the Germans holding up the Second Division.

The column moved out. As the men neared the crest of a hill, out front they saw piney slopes and snowy fields. The Germans were there. But there were no vehicle marks or footprints in the snow. A weasel came up, churning the snow as its crew laid telephone wire. Then a tank clattered by, driving all the men into the ditches and showering them with snow.

Downing wanted to get off that hillcrest. At last the troops moved down the hill, off the road, and across a field. Each man followed the tracks of the man ahead. About 50 yards from a pine forest the column halted again. The machine gun platoon came up, the dogfaces pulling their guns on homemade sleds.

As they stood, waiting, another platoon of men came up, wearing only field jackets and having a very arrogant air about them. They seemed to expect the men of the Eighteenth Infantry to give way.

"Get off the path," they yelled.

The Eighteenth men stood their ground.

As the platoon men passed, griping, Downing saw the Thirtieth Division patches on their shoulders.

"If they're so goddamn full of pep, why don't they clean up their own mess instead of getting us to do it?" groused the machine gun sergeant.

The word was passed back to the Eighteenth men to take off their overcoats, carry them, and stack them in the woods. They were getting ready to attack. The line moved forward, but nobody piled overcoats. They passed that Thirtieth Division platoon, sitting in the snow, eating K rations. They moved around the platoon through the snow, at least 12 inches deep. As they plodded, Downing broke into a sweat; the snow made the going very tough. The overcoat was very heavy, and the column was going very fast. The underbrush got thicker. From time to time they saw Thirtieth Division men, sitting around. Captain van Wagoner's column passed through and came up onto a logging road. The troops went to the right, and Downing found the machine gun platoon under the trees. He dumped his overcoat onto a pile, and sat down with the men and waited. The snow was covered with pine needles. Downing began to shiver from the cold and from the nervous feeling in the stomach that always preceded an attack.

A runner came stumbling up a slope, looking for the machine gun platoon leader. He told the officer that the attack had been called off. A patrol had found the German position abandoned. Everybody began to gripe and growl, in a very relieved tone of voice.

The men put on their overcoats and started back down the trail in single file. It was getting late in the afternoon. The trees were tall and the cold afternoon wind sang through them. The only other sound was the crunch-crunch-crunch of boots on snow and the rattling of equipment. Lieutenant Downing and his sergeant and corporal stopped and had a smoke. It would be a while before they would have another.

Lieutenant Colonel Leonard came up the path and nodded to them. He said he was going forward to find out what had caused the delay.

The column moved on. The troops found a fire lane cut through the trees and turned left.

"No talking," came the word. Off to the right they heard the blurp of a German machine pistol. A thin fog drifted in. The column halted, and moved, and halted again. The men turned into the wood. Suddenly they came on three German soldiers in white camouflage suits, guarded by an American private. To the left was a little lean-to with a fire burning in front. Apparently the Germans had been surprised here. The column moved on, down another fire lane, past an old-fashioned fire tower, and then turned deep into the woods.

"At ease. We'll stop here."

Sergeant Gulbeck and Lieutenant Downing went over to a fallen log, kicked off the snow, and sat down. Gulbeck opened a cold can of hash. They started to eat, but without enthusiasm. Then they looked for a place to dig in. The snow was 18 inches deep. Fallen pine trees littered the area. They selected a spot and started digging. The radio operator came up. He had gotten some cigarettes and an axe from a mortar platoon digging in a few yards away.

Night came down. They took turns digging. The pine tree roots made it tough. When they had a hole about 18 inches deep, Gulbeck and Downing went out to look for logs for a roof. They went to the old watchtower and tore off the wooden ladder. They lugged it back and Gulbeck began chopping it up with the axe.

Off to the left they could hear shelling in the trees. Downing went out to look for more logs. He found one near the tower, about 6 inches in diameter. He picked it up and started to drag it back through the snow. Suddenly his feet played out. He sat down on the log. He was cold, sleepy, hungry, and thirsty. He didn't care if a hundred shells landed on top of him. He was pooped.

Then he heard feet shuffling in the snow. Gulbeck came up, calling his name. Downing got up and picked up the log. The two of them carried it back to the hole. They put it on the roof and spread blankets over the floor of the hole. Then the three men crawled in and pulled the third blanket up as a cover. They slept fully clothed, even with their overcoats on. It was a tight fit, but the closeness kept them all warm. Or a little bit warm. It was a miserable night.

Downing was awakened just before dawn by a runner from Company A. He got up. The snow had drifted into their dugout. He scrambled up and went to the Company A command post. Captain van Wagoner was briefing the officers on the day's attack:

They had the Germans in a pocket. They were to attack, and would be supported by artillery that was on the other side of the Germans, in front of them. Downing went back to his hole and told the others. He was thirsty. He got out his canteen, but the water was frozen solid. His carbine was covered with ice and would not function until he thawed out the moving parts around the breech.

C Company came by. The men had picked up some bed sheets, and they were clothed all in white, like the Germans.

Downing and the others dumped their overcoats again and waited. Lieutenant Di Nucci of the cannon company came up. Captain van Wagoner came by and called Downing to go with him. Lieutenant Di Nucci stayed to follow a rifle platoon. Downing moved along the lane until he came to a clearing. The column had halted and spread out. Ahead was the rattle of rifle and machine gun fire and the shrill screams of shells. A shell landed in the clearing, up a slope to the right. Smoke drifted up from the dark smudge that blackened the snow.

Sergeant Gulbeck and Lieutenant Downing moved into some trees. Another shell screamed over and landed in the rear. Two more came in, these to the front.

Downing heard a yell.

"Lieutenant Di Nucci's been killed!"

Everybody looked back. A man of the cannon company was bending over a body in the brush.

"Get away from him. If he's dead, don't touch him," Captain van Wagoner yelled.

Machine pistols blurped from the trees in front. Captain van Wagoner called to Downing. He followed up the hill to the right.

On top of the wooded hill the captain sat down and looked around through his field glasses. Downing sat down by him, and so did several other men. A message came up ordering the captain back to battalion. He told Downing to take over for him as observer.

Downing took the glasses and looked around. He couldn't see anything but trees and snow. A shell screamed in and landed in the trees to the group's left. The men saw an abandoned German foxhole on the hill. They ran over to it and huddled in the bottom. A whole succession of shells slammed into the woods near them, while some went overhead. Someone had seen them up on the hilltop. After a while the shelling stopped. They lit cigarettes and waited. No one wanted to get out of the hole.

A while later Downing heard footsteps. He looked over the top of the hole. Captain van Wagoner was back. The men scrambled out and went after him. They stopped at the edge of the woods, in the clearing. A small group of men came down from the hill. They were all wounded and had bandages on arms, legs, and heads. One man had been hit in the buttocks; his pants were torn, and a bandage covered his rear end.

A few minutes later a group of German prisoners came down, carrying litters of German and American wounded. They looked very young.

The attack had not been very successful.

Captain van Wagoner told that to the troops, and then he told them they would go back to the former bivouac area. Downing found Captain Bowers of battalion at the company command post. His group had a nice strong dugout. At about 9 p.m. they moved back to another position, and Downing and Gulbeck took over the dugout.

On the next morning the activity began early. Lieutenant Downing was very thirsty, but his canteen was still frozen. He managed to get a C-ration can full of warm water from a soldier in A Company.

Company A was going to attack a village called Montenan. The troops started out, and Downing decided to move with the machine gun platoon until he got to the point where he would have missions to order from the cannon company.

Fog set in. To the right the men could hear the blurp-blurps that meant Germans. They went up one hill and then down, coming through a clearing with several huts in it. It was deserted. An officer from A Company told them that they were not far from the edge of the forest and that Montenan was on the other side of a field up front. Patrols were going out to find a covered route of approach if possible. Freezing rain set in. Ice formed on Downing's carbine, so he held the breech under his arm to warm it. He was thirsty again. Gulbeck ate snow, but snow did not seem to help Downing.

All day long they sat around on the edge of the woods. They couldn't build a fire since the attack on Montenan was to be a surprise. The time of attack was set twice, but each time the attack was almost immediately called off. The company would have to attack across open fields, came the word.

The snow was deep, and the area was crisscrossed by barbed-wire animal fences. So the GIs would wait until evening.

Downing began to set up for the attack. He told the radio operator to check out the radio. He called up the mortar platoon, which told him the mortar locations and Downing plotted them. He figured out the areas where he would fire and radioed that back. An hour later he tried to call the platoon again. But this time the radio would not work. The icy rain had frozen it. The operator said he would go back to the platoon and get another set. He was too eager, Downing suspected, but he let the man go. Sure enough, the operator didn't return.

Downing and Captain van Wagoner went up front. They lay down behind trees and looked over the ground. From the woods a long narrow belt of low evergreens extended about 100 yards down toward the town. From the end of this the men would have to move about 200 yards through an open field crossed with fences. Then came the first house, a two-story stone building. Since the attack was to be a surprise, Downing could not adjust the fire on the town until the attack started. More important, he didn't have a radio. He went back to see if the radio operator had returned. No.

The sun began to go down. He went out to join van Wagoner. The sky turned black. A tank on the left began firing toward the town. Then came the fire of .50-caliber machine guns. The tracers flew in a red dotted line to the town. Some hit stone walls and ricocheted more slowly into the air. A tank destroyer began firing with the tank. Then came a flash and an explosion from the tank. The tank destroyer had fired a round into the rear of the tank.

Then came the popping of M-1 rifles and the sound of grenades. A rifle platoon had worked its way into the town. Captain van Wagoner moved up toward the village with his command post group. The machine gun platoon had its guns set up to cover both the edge of the woods and the attack if a withdrawal order came. Downing then went down and collected the machine gun crews and took them into the town. He crossed a barbed-wire fence and ripped his pants.

"We climbed over a fence and slid into a ditch beside the road, landing in icy water which soaked our legs up to the knees. We started off to the left down the road. A wrecked German truck lay careened in the ditch to the right. We passed the truck, but the sound of incoming shells made us dash to get behind it for cover. The shells landed in the center of the town with a clatter. The machine gun platoon assembled down in the town."

Slowly the GIs moved through the village, taking one house after another.

On the left Downing saw a building that looked like the town hall. He went over there. Outside the building he found some Company A command post men and the exec of that company. A number of wounded men were down in a cellar, in a bunk room formerly occupied by Germans. A sentry was posted at the entrance. Downing picked up the password from him and went over to the men of the machine gun platoon, telling them to wait for Captain van Wagoner to get instructions as to where they should set up next. Then he went back to the command post.

The wounded men in the next room were having a bad time. One had a chunk shot out of his thigh, and he was afraid he was dying from loss of blood. He kept talking all the time to reassure himself that he was going to live. The other soldier was in a bad way. He had been hit in the shoulder by a piece of shell fragment, and it had gone down into his lung. Every time he inhaled, the air whistled through the hole. The aidman put a piece of tape over the hole so that the air could not pass through—and also to stop the noise, which was driving everybody else nuts.

Downing conferred with Captain van Wagoner again. They were having difficulty getting the vehicles going.

* * *

The aidman came into the command post and told Captain van Wagoner that he didn't think the man with the hole in his lung would make it unless he could be gotten to a doctor quickly. The ambulances could not come up because the Germans had destroyed the road bridge. The wounded man could not be taken back because he could not endure being carried on a stretcher all the way to the aid station. The captain told the medic to give the man morphine and make him comfortable.

Downing waited:

"The captain had to go back to battalion for a meeting with the battalion commander. There were some German prisoners upstairs who had been captured in the town. I volunteered to go back with him to see if I could get a radio operator. As we went through the next room, the aidman told the captain that the severely wounded man had died. We went upstairs and lined up the prisoners. We went through the lumberyard and across the creek. Battalion had moved to a house farther along the road to the rear. I stepped in a deep hole beside the road, sinking up to my waist. One of the Germans reached down, grabbed my hand, and pulled me out. I continued up the road, the prisoners following behind me, clumping in cadence in their batten boots on the hard, frozen surface. We passed the burning tank on the right. I saw it was still blazing. We walked past a few deserted stone barns and at length came to a large school building with vehicles of all types parked around it. A sentry halted us. We turned the prisoners over to him and went inside. The battalion CP was a small, bare unfurnished room. Lieutenant Colonel Leonard sat on the floor with a map laid out near a lantern. I left a message to be sent as soon as the wires were laid, asking for a radio operator to be sent to me, and then started back for the A Company sector."

Downing found his way back to the company CP. Sergeant Gulbeck was there, waiting for him. The CP was crowded, so they scouted around for a place to sleep. They went over to the lumberyard's sawmill. One of the rooms had bunks in it, and probably had been used by German soldiers. Equipment and torn mattresses littered the floor. "As we looked it over in the dim moonlight, we heard a shuffling and clanking in the next room." There was a Dutch door. Downing threw open the top half as Gulbeck covered it with his carbine. A donkey nosed up to Downing.

Finally they found a disused storeroom and mattresses, and they went to sleep.

Morning came, but no radio operator. Downing went back to D Company to find one. The men of the headquarters group were standing around log fires heating rations and drying their socks. Two men were sitting near a log hut. They had trench foot. The first sergeant was raising hell with them for not taking care of themselves.

"You damn fools may get your toes cut off."

Downing stopped to eat a can of C ration, picked up a radio operator, and started up front.

When they came to the open field that went down the hill to the town, Gulbeck and the operator sprinted down. Downing followed, but they got separated. He completed his dash near a shattered German tank, where now an American tank was on its side in the ditch, too. Shells started coming in to the field. He ran for the stone house. As he approached, a door opened and a GI beckoned him in. A shell struck the tree in front of the house. The troops flattened against the wall. Several women ran past them down the cellar stairs. The soldiers led Downing into the parlor. The crew of the abandoned tank was there cooking ten-in-one rations. The lieutenant asked Downing to sit down and gave him a cup of coffee and some cigarettes. They had been watching him come down the hill when the shells began coming in. They had nothing to do except wait for a tank retriever to come up and pull their tank out of the ditch.

When the shelling stopped, Downing started out again for A Company.

He passed a stopped jeep on the road. An artillery captain and his driver were eating K rations on the hood. Two German soldiers came by, escorted by an American private.

"I bet you can't get the both of them with two shots," said the artillery captain.

Downing looked at the artillery captain as if he were crazy. "If he was so damned bloodthirsty, all he had to do was go out with a rifle company and kill some for himself. It doesn't take any courage to shoot people who can't shoot back."

Finally Downing found Gulbeck and the radio operator and they began to call in fire missions for the first time in twenty-four hours.

After a while they saw American tanks moving up along the road, and they had to stop firing. The tank platoon leader told Downing that the Eighty-second Airborne and the Seventh Armored divisions were making an attack through the First Division and that the division would be relieved that night.

Downing waited. He sat in the kitchen of the house that was the CP. He was on a chair by the stove. Most of the men were lounging on mattresses on the floor. As he sat there, with his elbows on his knees, smoking, a loud explosion startled all of them. He hit the floor. His face felt wet and sticky. He looked around; there was no shell hole in the room. Then one of the men held up a tin can. It had burst. Someone had put a can of beans on the stove without punching holes in the top. It had exploded all over Downing's face. He had beans splattered over his jacket, face, and hair.

The other lieutenant said that if Downing put in for a Purple Heart he would back him up.

That night a convoy took them back to Nidrum. They were supposed to be in for a rest.

The rest period didn't last long, but long enough for Lieutenant Downing to get a promotion: he was assigned as executive officer of Company M. Colonel Smith had been thinking things over and had come to the conclusion that the lieutenant had been getting a raw deal. Downing reported in to Lieutenant Colonel Peckham, who had been Downing's first company commander back in 1942. Peckham was now commander of the Third Battalion.

After a few days the company moved out. Captain Carey, the former exec of Company M, was the new commanding officer. He went on with the battalion CP group. Downing led the company. The men headed south in the open jeeps, chilled to the bone, their faces buried deep in their overcoat collars against the icy wind. The terrain was barren, with houses very widely scattered. Only an occasional hedge broke the monotony of the snowy fields.

They came to a small town—Moederscheid—where Captain Carey was waiting. First Sergeant Donahue led them to the company CP, a shell-shattered house. A small storeroom became the orderly room. The German occupants lived in the basement, but soldiers and civilians used the kitchen.

One of the jeep drivers became very friendly with the young girl who lived in the basement and was invited to sleep down there. "For some reason it always took a lot of summoning to get him out of there whenever there was any jeep driving to do."

For Downing it was like old home week. Lieutenant Lee, who commanded the mortar platoon, had been a noncom in Africa days. Lieutenant Henesey was Downing's former platoon sergeant from Sicily days. Now he ran a machine gun platoon.

Captain Carey explained the situation:

The town had been held by the Ninety-ninth Infantry Division but had been overrun at the beginning of the Battle of the Bulge. The Eighteenth was to hold there, regain lost ground, and then continue through the Siegfried line.

Downing's job as executive officer was to organize the company. He did. The shattered living room of the house was fixed up to become a drying room for the platoons. Here the men could not only dry their clothes but wash, shave, and write letters as well.

On the second day Downing went to the motor pool and encountered a whole stack of German bodies, cleared out of a battered house to make way for an American command post. On the third day he was working over decorations write-ups and company fund accounts when up came a band of replacements. The first man to come in was a sergeant who had flunked out of OCS. He had extensive machine gun experience. Captain Carey assigned him to a machine gun platoon that might need a new sergeant soon. But the others were "a sorry lot": a few young-looking draftees fresh from basic training and a group culled out of various rear-echelon headquarters. There were several T/5s, former mail orderlies. They were all very much aggrieved at being assigned to the infantry.

"I shouldn't be up here, Captain," said one. "I can't see in the dark."

"Who the hell can?" asked Captain Carey. He assigned the T/5 to a machine gun platoon.

And then there were more T/5s. A great nuisance because it interfered with the promotion processes. They, too, were assigned to machine gun platoons.

Two days later Captain Carey came back from battalion with the plan for a new attack. It would begin the next day. The troops would move up to an assembly area in the evening and jump off just before dawn. But that order was changed. They would move up to Hepscheid and then attack. The objective was Housfeld.

Before dawn Downing was up and with the command post group. He lay listening to the pounding of the artillery and the whizzing of shells passing overhead. The artillery was working over Housfeld.

Just after dawn Downing was ordered to take his group forward. The men reached Hepscheid in their jeeps and drove up the hill. The road was cut up with deep ruts. Jeeps stalled as their undercarriages hung up on the high crown of the road. Finally they crossed the crest of the hill and sped down into town. The attack had progressed to the next village, Huenningen. They parked the jeeps off the road on the edge of Hepscheid. A tank destroyer was in position in front of a house. Downing and his group went into the building. The tank crew was gathered around a stove; one man was frying pieces of salami on the stove lid.

Downing left his men inside and went up to see what was going on. He found a man from battalion headquarters who told him Carey had moved up to the next town. After running into a traffic jam, Downing and his group got into Huenningen. They moved up, found the house in the center of town that Captain Carey had selected as the command post, and got a fire going in a Sibley stove. Captain Carey said that the attack would continue the next morning.

The troops were right up against the Siegfried line fortifications again. The following day the command post moved forward again to a wide spot in the road called Ramscheiderhoehe.

"The battalion attacked that night and next morning I went over to the aid station to check on casualties to enter on our Morning Report. I was amazed at the high number of M Company casualties to enter, since a weapons company usually suffered less than a rifle company.... Down in the celler I found Carey. He told me that just as the machine gun platoons were about to assemble near the road, to follow the rifle companies in the attack the night before, our own artillery had laid down a barrage on them. This barrage had battered up the machine gun platoons pretty badly. They no longer had to worry about that excess of T/5s in the company. Most of them had been killed or wounded by the barrage."

That day the battalion captured Ramscheiderhoehe, its objective. That was the good news. The bad news was that the troops were now on the forward slope of a steep hill that could be approached only across open ground bounded by pine forests in which German infantry were holed up. That meant a real problem of supply.

The next day at noon Downing had an order from regiment that one enlisted man could be sent back to the states for a forty-five-day furlough. This was an extension of a policy begun back in Sicily, a scheme that had been functioning raggedly ever since.

The following day Downing learned that the division had regained all the ground it had lost in the Battle of the Bulge; it had again passed through the Siegfried line. It was to be relieved by the Ninety-ninth Division.

The division moved, and the Eighteenth Infantry, and Company M. The troops came to Malmédy. They moved through Aachen and through a number of German villages, but they stopped and camped in the woods.

"The area was wet, wooded, houseless, remote, and gloomy. In a place like that we would probably stay for months."

Downing encountered Captain Murphy, also a previous commanding officer of his. Murphy had been wounded in the arm and sent back to England; he was just now returning to duty. "It boosted your morale to see some of the old indestructibles still around."

Downing learned from Captain Carey that the battalion was being held in reserve for a future attack across the Roer River. Meanwhile, it was to be fairly easy. Men would get passes to Paris, Brussels, and some even to England. Two officers could be absent from the company for twenty-four hours at a time.

When it was Downing's turn, he and another officer went to Liège in his jeep. They found rooms in a small hotel just inside the city limits. He and the other officer began to make the rounds of the bars. They wandered along the darkened streets, listening to the throbbing of buzz bombs and the explosions as they landed on the other side of town near the railroad yards. The two men stopped in every bar for a drink or two. When the bars began to close, they walked back to the hotel.

Inside, the proprietress closed up the doors, but she served drinks to them because they were residents. She brought out some fried eggs and slices of soggy, dark bread. The other officer made an amorous approach to her, and she responded very positively. At length Downing asked if she had a friend.

Yes.

She led Downing up to the next floor and rapped on a door. A girl of about 22 answered. A voluble conversation took place in French outside Downing's range. The girl went back into the room for a moment; then she came out and put her arm through Downing's. They went upstairs to his room and to bed.

Downing was awakened the next morning by the other officer hammering on the door and saying they had better get started if they wanted to get back to the company on time. The girl was snuggled next to him down under the covers. When she heard him moving, she turned over and watched him with large, dark eyes, her face flushed with sleep and her black curly hair all tousled. He sat on the edge of the bed and began to dress. He had that burned-out, bored feeling that the world was bearing down on him.

"These recreation trips were always the same. You dashed into town, drank in a hurry as much as you could hold, enjoyed a few hours of feminine companionship, and then it was back again to the tent or hole or cellar, the dirt and stench and monotony."

The girl, with the bed covering tight against her neck, lay there without saying a word. The other officer rapped on the door once more. Downing let him in and then sat down on the bed again to lace up his shoes. The other GI waited, leaning on the dresser, smoking.

Downing finished. He turned. The girl was still looking gravely at him with her sparkling dark eyes. He reached into his shirt pocket, pulled out a 500 franc note, and tucked it under the pillow. The girl's face broke into a smile. Two bare arms came out from underneath the covers, and she stretched them out toward Downing. He leaned back on the bed and they embraced warmly.

"Why the hell don't you marry her and get it over with?" growled Downing's pal. "Come on, we gotta go."

Downing stood up, put on his jacket and cap, waved goodbye ("She sure was a sweet little girl"), and waved goodbye again as he went out the door.

Downstairs in the café part of the hotel the husband was mopping the floor while the proprietress was behind the bar wiping glasses. The blackout curtains were down, and the cold morning sunshine streamed in through the glass. The jeep driver was sitting at a table. Downing went to the bar and ordered a double cognac. He gulped it down and asked for another. The driver didn't drink any and the other officer drank only one.

"You could tell that he hadn't been overseas long. In another year or two he would be drinking doubles also."

They went back to camp, and the next day Captain Carey left on his own "scheduled pursuit of happiness."

*   *   *

Sergeant Adolph's 397th Infantry was a part of Patton's Third Army, and the general was itching to go. On the night of February 2 Adolph took a twelve-man patrol out into the area between the American and German lines. The Americans were heavily armed: nine rifles, three BARs, two bazookas, two tommy guns, and dozens of hand grenades. They started out at 7 p.m. The object was to ascertain the lie of the German main line of resistance. About a third of the way out Sergeant Adolph found a booby trap, which he neutralized. But there were more of them, booby traps and barbed wire, which made it hard to travel, particularly since the night was so dark the men could not see 5 yards ahead. The snow had melted in the winter sunshine of the day, and everything was mud. They moved along. Then, suddenly, one of the scouts out in front waved his arm, signaling everybody down. Everyone took cover. Adolph and the assistant patrol leader crept up to the lead scout and looked over toward the enemy. Then they spotted a line of mounds that had the unmistakable look of foxhole edges. The Germans were only about 75 yards away, on at least two sides of the GIs.

It looked as though the American patrol had been sucked into a trap and that the Germans were all around them. But there was still the chance they had not been seen.

Adolph began to see shadowy figures emerging from the holes. He crawled back 50 yards to join the rest of the patrol. Then they all took off. They were in a big hurry. The scout was out in front again, going toward his own lines. He set off a white phosphorous grenade booby trap as the patrol came near the American line, but he was going so fast he was not hurt. Then someone took a shot at the patrol. A flare burst overhead, and an American machine gun began firing at the group.

Sergeant Adolph recognized the barbed wire and the configuration of the land ahead. He began to yell, "Hi Bob." That was the night's password.

The men in the machine gun nest answered back, but Adolph's patrol did not hear them. So there was a stalemate, almost inside the line.

Adolph crawled up to the wire, and he shouted. One of the GIs from the other side came up and showed the patrol the way through the wire, the same way the group had taken on the way out, but could not now find. Three of the men were slightly burned by the white phosphorous grenade, but the medics fixed them up easily. So everyone was back relatively in one piece.

Sergeant Adolph went to the command post and described the patrol to the commanding officer.

Now the Americans knew where the enemy line of resistance was.

The next day they learned that the Russians were supposed to be very close to Berlin and that Americans were 12 miles from Manila. Sergeant Adolph was very pleased.

"Some bright and sunny morning we are going to wake up to find this war is over. Just you wait and see," he sang.

The Roer River was reported to be still too high to be crossed, so the men of the Eighteenth Infantry waited.

The war changed. It was still deadly enough—one night the bivouac area was bombed by German aircraft—but it changed. The special services officer came back from Belgium with a number of fancy shoulder holsters for .45-caliber pistols. Downing bought one. Everybody got overseas service stripes. Downing got five, one for each six months of overseas service. They looked pretty impressive on the sleeve of his blouse.

PX rations of cigars, candy, and toilet articles showed up. Belgian beer in kegs also arrived. The men set up the kegs in the drying room.

February: The quiet period ended. One day Captain Carey came back from battalion to announce that the push across the Roer River was going to happen soon. Other divisions would make the first jump; the First Division would follow to broaden the front. They would cross at Düren and attack toward Cologne.

That night Lieutenants Downing and Henesey lay in their bedrolls in the command post log hut, nipping at a quart of gin. Henesey had been feeling pretty low, he said. He had always taken combat in stride, but recently he had begun to "sweat out" each attack. What bothered him was that he had been in a line company all the way from Africa and had never been wounded. He had made every landing and every attack. He figured that his luck was bound to run out pretty soon.

Downing said he had been in the division a long time and had had only that one little wound.

"Yeah," said Henesey, "but that wound cleared the books for you and gave you more time." If he could only get a light wound, Henesey said, he would feel better. But as it was he was expecting something more serious.

Downing was depressed by Henesey's depression. Here was the one guy he knew who seemed to take combat in stride, and now he was gloomy. Of course, Henesey should have been rotated back to the states months earlier, but at a quota rate of one officer per month from a regiment, the number of officers who got the brass ring was negligible. Henesey would have been better off if he had refused the battlefield commission.

*

One officer who got lucky that month was Lieutenant Thornton of the Sixtieth Infantry's Company M. It came as a great surprise. He was just gearing up for a lot more war. A new attack was under way by the Ninth Division.

The battalion's attack started from Monchair to Hofen on January 30 at four o'clock in the morning. It began to snow. The company ran into a lot of stout German defense. One man was killed. Captain Kytle returned to the company from England. The next day, January 31, the company moved up easily. The Germans had already abandoned Hofen. And day after that, February 1, Lieutenant Thornton learned that he was going home. As with everything in the army, it was all done without feeling. A man got killed, his name disappeared from the roster; a man got wounded, ditto; a man got rotated, tritto.

Thornton was told to report to regiment at 8:30 the next morning, ready to go home. That was all. No tender farewells. Before the next day was over, he was in Stolberg, Germany, where he was paid up to date by a bored finance clerk, given the awards and ribbons his papers said he had earned, and shipped out for Verviers, Belgium. From there he went to Le Havre. On February 22 the transport *Thomas Barry* left for Southampton, where it picked up more officers and men who were homeward bound. On the twenty-third the ship left Southampton for America. That day Lieutenant Thornton totted it up: he had been overseas twenty-eight months to the day.

The trip was uneventful. The German submarine menace was almost a thing of the past. On March 5 the ship reached Boston. The next day the men went ashore at Camp Myles Standish. That night Thornton was dancing at the officers' club. He called a girl back in his hometown, but she wasn't home. So...Lieutenant Thornton's shooting war was over.

The Eighteenth Infantry was on the attack, moving toward the Rhine.

Lieutenants Henesey and Downing stood talking as they waited for the rifle companies to move out. Then Henesey's platoon was ordered up, and he put on his pack and picked up his carbine. As he joined his platoon, he turned and waved to Downing.

"See you."

The platoon started down the road in a column of twos.

Downing got into his jeep, and the driver went down the road in his convoy of jeeps in the direction of Düren. The battalion was to attack the town of Jakobwuerresheim, a place that seemed smaller than its name. The troops attacked.

"Friendly artillery opened up nearby on our right, startling us. Out in the open ground the reports were loud and reverberant, no longer hushed by the woods. We moved through the streets of the town, where blasts of guns made me jump and start. The guns must have been set up in the fields back of the houses. As I passed the interval between two houses, I felt the muzzle blast as a gun went off. Off to the left bright flashes lit the sky, followed by resounding crashes. The Germans were sending over airbursts.

"As we passed a small village, a deafening crash drove my heart up into my throat. I heard the 'whang' as a shell fragment zipped across in front of me and struck a building on my right. By now everyone was tense. We hurried along as fast as the column would move, wanting to get out of the town into the open country. The Germans were probably adjusting to shell the town and the artillery near it.

"We came out of the town and moved across open ground beyond at a mile-eating pace. I felt better away from the buildings."

The Americans went into Jakobwuerresheim, found a house for a command post, and took over. The battalion was pushing forward to Iressheim, 3 miles further on. The town of Kelz, on the right, was to be attacked by the Second Battalion.

So the GIs had only a few hours of rest in their nice cozy house, and then they were called out to move on to Iressheim.

They crossed the railroad tracks, and soon they saw the fires of burning haystacks and houses. Suddenly they came to a fork in the road and halted. Downing had to guess—"any signs of indecision on a night movement always cause concern among men following an officer." He guessed that it was to the left, and went in that direction. It was better to be wrong than indecisive. But he happened to be right. The troops came under the fire of a German self-propelled gun and spent a lot of time on their bellies in the ditch. Then along came a handful of American tanks and half-tracks, carrying American riflemen. They went on through and, gladly, Downing and his men followed.

They passed blasted German equipment, a jeep off the road in the ditch, and L-shaped trenches. They passed two men huddled in a trench at the base of a haystack.

"What outfit is that?" asked the men.

"Eighteenth Infantry," Downing replied.

"Are you fellows going into town?"

"Yes."

"Can we go with you?"

"Come ahead."

They passed riflemen kneeling at the side of the road, firing. Downing asked if the town was taken.

"Yeah," said one rifleman. "We're just clearing out some snipers."

They went into the town and met First Sergeant Donahue. He led them down the street to a small square. They entered the square and turned into a yard. This was the house chosen for the new CP. They moved in and down into the basement. It looked like they were going to stay for a while. The battalion had taken the town but had to wait for the Eighteenth's other two battalions to come up on the flanks.

And so the regiment and the division moved, slowly, day by day.

The troops stayed in Iressheim for a few days. Then they moved on to Hochkirchen and Noervenich. There they learned that the Germans were changing tactics, concentrating on using mines again, as they had in the early days in Normandy. These new mines were rectangular wooden boxes about 3 feet long and 6 inches wide and high. The wooden construction was designed to thwart the American magnetic mine detectors. These mines were very effective and murderous devices.

Sergeant Donahue had been looking over a beer hall when a terrific explosion had made him jump for the cellar. Later he went outside. One soldier had picked up one of the box mines and lifted it onto his shoulder to carry it away. The mine had blown up, and the soldier had disintegrated. One shoe inside one overshoe with part of a foot—that was all that was left of that soldier. He would go down as missing in action, for even his dog tags had been blown to smithereens.

The Americans moved on across the Neffel River and came to Rath. They reached the outskirts of Wissersheim, where they were attacked by a lone German plane. This sort of *solo* air attack happened quite often those days; it had been a long time since the Messerschmitts had come in like schools of sharks to hit the men of the Eighteenth Infantry in Africa. The Luftwaffe was not much of a threat any more.

But still...

They were on a narrow street when the German plane came screaming down. Downing looked around. A dark alley opened on his left. He dashed into it, tripped over someone, and fell flat on his face, his helmet and carbine clattering on the cobblestones. He sat up and hugged the wall. The plane zoomed away. He asked the body who it was. A soldier from F Company. The Second Battalion was catching up.

They set up a new command post and were attacked several times by individual dive-bombing German planes that night. These attacks did little damage to the troops or their equipment, but they were certainly hell on sleep.

The regiment moved up to the Neffel River, about 10 miles from Cologne. There the men learned they were to be relieved by the Eighteenth Cavalry Group. So for the moment it was over, and they could relax.

That was the day that Lieutenant Downing learned that Lieutenant Henesey's hunch had been right. Henesey was dead.

Henesey and his platoon had made that first day's attack. He had set up a machine gun in the cellar of a house and at dawn had gone upstairs to check the field of fire from a first-floor window. He had pulled open the window, and a machine pistol blast had caught him straight in the face. A German had made a booby trap of his gun, trained on the window, so that it would fire if the window was opened. It was hard for Downing to believe that a man who had survived Africa, Sicily, Normandy, Aachen, the Huertgen Forest, and the Bulge would be killed so senselessly in a nameless little town in Germany.

Just across the Neffel, Downing saw the service company sign and had his driver stop. He wanted to see about a report of survey. Inside he found Warrant Officer Kelty, and a footlocker bearing the name Col. George A. Smith, Jr. The colonel had been transferred out to be assistant division commander of the 104th Division, and to get his star.

Downing looked at the footlocker. Colonel Smith, the officer who had looked down his nose at Downing but who had finally given him a break. The rank on the footlocker ought to be changed.

"I'm just getting it ready to ship back to the states," said Kelty.

"Oh? Colonel going home?"

"Yeah. You might say that. The colonel got hisself killed."

The shiny new brigadier general's star had hardly made a dent in his collar. General Smith had been observing when the 104th crossed the Roer, and he was killed by enemy artillery fire.

Downing thought it over. Two in one day. Colonel Smith had commanded the Eighteenth from Sicily on and hadn't gotten a scratch. Just like Henesey. So he got a new job that was supposed to be safer, and got killed in the first attack.

Downing went outside. He saw a large truck trailer parked across the road. He saw legs sticking out the end.

"Hey, Lieutenant, Lieutenant Henesey's body's in there. He was a buddy of yours, wasn't he? Wanna see him?"

Downing didn't answer.

"Let's get the hell moving back to Wissersheim," said Lieutenant Downing.

On February 1 Lieutenant Colonel Snetzer's Second Division attacked toward the crossroads and through Monschau Forest. The division passed Heartbreak Corner. The Second Engineers battalion command post moved into Krinkelt. The next day the infantry overran Schonseiffen and Harperscheid. On February 3 the infantry took the town of Etelscheid. The Germans were mining everything heavily. The engineers were busy with mine detectors, opening up the roads, sometimes behind, sometimes in front of the front line.

That day Lieutenant Colonel Snetzer learned the Russians were only 40 miles from Berlin.

On February 5 the Second Division fought at Hellenthal. The battle was fierce. On February 6 the bridges were still in enemy hands. Four of them were blown up, but that night the engineers restored two.

On February 1 Lt. Charles Chattaway's 110th Infantry moved into the Colmar area. Then the men moved to the Monschau area and were back on the Siegfried line, not far from the positions they had held in September. On March 5 they attacked. They stopped at the Ahre River and remained there until March 19. Then they moved to Andernach on the Rhine, going into defensive positions. They stayed there until March 28 and then crossed the Rhine at Hünningen on the twenty-ninth.

The armored units were moving on through Germany toward the Elbe, but the infantry were staying behind to clean up. Lieutenant Chattaway's 110th Infantry mopped up for a time; then the men moved back across the Rhine to operate control checkpoints and to patrol along the Dutch-German border. Their war changed again. Later, they moved into the Saar valley and were put in charge of a number of displaced persons' camps.

Sgt. Thomas G. Wickham's First Battalion of the Twenty-ninth Division was also waiting to cross the Roer. The troops were executing "dry runs" with the engineers. Any day now they expected to get going.

But early in February Sergeant Wickham got the welcome word that he was up for rotation home.

"I felt a little guilty to leave the battalion when it was about to make the big push. But I was the last man left in the radio section who had landed on D day, and I did not want my luck to run out."

Captain Miller's Twentieth Engineers had a rough time of it in early February. They were just about the hottest engineer outfit in Europe and everybody wanted them. The Ninety-ninth Division, to whom they were attached, was cracking the Siegfried line. On the first day one of their bulldozers hit a mine and blew up.

Miller went down to Büllingen and Krinkelt.

"My God, how we have knocked those towns apart."

There, where Colonel Peiper had laid waste with his panzers during the Battle of the Bulge, Captain Miller saw all sorts of wrecked American equipment: jeeps, ¾-ton trucks, 2½-ton trucks, trailers, half-tracks—all shot up during that battle. He also saw a lot of Colonel Peiper's German equipment that went in but never got out again: self-propelled guns, Volkswagen staff cars, and tanks. Miller saw three of the 88-millimeter self-propelled guns called Hornets; they all had been blasted within a 50-foot area—one, two, three.

On February 9 Miller learned that the Ninety-ninth Division would be relieved and that the Twentieth Engineers would now support the Sixty-ninth Division. Divisions came, divisions went, but the Twentieth Engineers just kept going on in the face of the enemy.

On February 24 Miller got some really good news. He learned that Technical Sergeant Martin had scrounged enough equipment to build a shower bath, so the captain went over to the command post and tried it out.

Hot water.

"It was the first bath other than a whore's bath out of a helmet that I've had since some time in October. Wonderful what a human body will stand."

March 1: The Second Division was preparing to attack Gemünd.

On March 5 the division was in that city, and the engineers were having a hard time of it. Mines again. Lieutenants McDougal and Delaney were wounded when their jeep hit an S mine at the end of a bridge. Two other A Company men were killed by mines that day.

The next day the Americans encountered a new wrinkle, the pressure mine. During the morning three tanks crossed the Bailey bridge in Gemünd safely. But the fourth tank activated the mine's memory factor and blew up on the bridge. The Germans had refined their mine techniques and had infiltrated again. Their infiltration was constant and a serious problem. That particular bridge explosion wrecked the division's timing, but by noon a treadway bridge was across the river and traffic was moving again.

On March 2 Captains Miller and Rogers were ordered to Paris to go to school for a week. Tough duty! They went through Malmédy, Liège, Namur, Charleroi, Mons, and St.-Quentin the first day. Captains Speer and Markovich were in town on their way back from Paris and the four officers drank three bottles of champagne and a lot of cognac. Captain Miller got "very plastered."

The next morning their jeep was broken down, so they traded it (after 35,000 miles) for a new one. Captain Miller had a terrible hangover. The men drove through La Fère, Chauny, Noyon, Compiègne, and Senlis and then on to Paris, where they registered for school at the Cité Universitaire.

Classes on engineering modifications lasted from 8:30 to 5:20. Then there was nightlife in the officers' club. And pretty French girls.

Captain Miller took the subway to Notre-Dame and went through the cathedral. He went shopping at Au Bon Marche. He went to Pigalle ("Pig Alley" to the Americans) to see the nightlife, and perhaps to grab a hunk of it.

And on March 9 he learned that the U.S. First Army had crossed the Rhine.

Then it was back to the war. On March 13 the Twentieth Engineer Battalion moved to Münstereifel. The engineers took over a German barracks that once had belonged to the Fifth Panzer Army.

On March 14 Captain Miller decided to take a trip to the Rhine. He was headed for the Remagen railroad bridge, but traffic was very heavy, so he went around by a pontoon bridge instead. At the bridgeheads the American heavy artillery was firing away merrily. It seemed very quiet otherwise. But then a German fighter-bomber came across—as they did those days, a lone plane appearing out of nowhere—and dropped a pair of bombs very close to his jeep. Then the antiaircraft guns opened up. The racket was enormous. Just another little reminder that the war was still on.

Miller stopped to visit a friend of Colonel Sonnenfeld's at the 552d Heavy Pontoon Battalion headquarters. He had just become commander of the battalion because the former CO was killed the night before. Yes, the war was still very real.

A few days after this excursion, Captain Miller took another trip, this one back to old haunts: the dams along the Roer. He went to Schmidt and Vossenack, where he had fought, and saw that they were completely destroyed. All of the equipment the engineers had put in there was still there, all beaten up, including an old bulldozer that some ordnance people were trying to move up the hill. It was still running after four and a half months of beating. There were still German and American bodies, or what was left of them, lying about in the bushes. Graves registration had fallen behind in its efforts.

The Twentieth Engineers moved again, this time to Königsfeld, about 5 miles from the Rhine. The weather was getting warm. Spring. Bodies would rot faster and stink more now. On March 24 Captain Miller learned that the Third Army had crossed the Rhine south of Koblenz.

*   *   *

March 1: Captain Shebeck was transferred to Dijon, France, to the 117th Military Labor Center. He served as S-2, S-3, and S-4. About thirty officers and a hundred enlisted men administered two POW camps, which held about 10,000 POWS.

The officers lived in a lovely hotel, the LaClose, which bordered on a park. There was very little to do except at one point, when a hurry-up call came from the brass ordering the officers to examine every POW for evidence of membership in the Nazi party. They found a few, usually recognizable because they had small swastikas tattooed on their arms. In addition to his other duties, Captain Shebeck was the president of a special court-martial and a member of a general court-martial. Most of the cases brought before him involved black marketeering. Life was getting pretty soft in the rear echelons.

On March 7, Lieutenant Colonel Snetzer's Second Division was really rolling on its drive through Germany. The infantrymen were riding the tanks and going along at full speed, maybe 20 to 25 miles per hour. There was very little opposition and it was scattered. At noon the Second Division reached Münstereifel. Cologne fell to the 104th Division and the Third Armored. The Ninth Army linked up with the British.

The troops were moving so fast that field telephones were useless. All communication had to be by radio. The Second Engineer Battalion's CP was at Holzheim. The division CP was at Mechernecht. Wire could hardly reach.

"We move in as conquerors. People are bewildered and scared. We pick out the best house for our CP and billets, kick people out, spend the night, and move on the next day. Continues to rain incessantly. Visibility zero. Weather cold and damp. Mud, mud, mud. But we are over the roads before they begin to break down.

"*March 8:* Fifth Corps and Division surged forward. The infantry cleared along the Ahr River and seized the bridges there intact. They had pinched out the Sixty-ninth and 106th divisions, moving southeast. They were moving to the Rhine.

"*March 9:* The motorized Twenty-third Infantry pushed east to the Rhine, which it reached that evening. There was virtually nothing for the engineers to do, the movement was quick, and seemed almost effortless."

On March 10 Colonel Snetzer crossed the Rhine over the great Remagen bridge, which had been captured intact.

"Doughfeet of the Ninth Division were streaming across on foot, unending columns of vehicles and tanks rolled steadily along. Most all of the Seventy-eighth and Ninth Infantry and Ninth Armored divisions are across now."

On March 11 Sergeant Adolph was walking along the barbed-wire line in his company's sector of the 397th Infantry front, when something exploded a few yards to his right and knocked him off his feet.

"I couldn't imagine what kind of hell had broken loose. I didn't hear any whine of a shell come screaming in. It could have been a mortar though, and I felt all over me.

"It's funny the kind of thoughts that pass through a man's mind in such a situation. Am I dead? Will I die? Am I wounded, leg, arm, head, body? What will happen to me now? Can I see? Can I talk? Can I hear? Mind pictures of wounds I'd seen before and what kind of injury I would have. Crippled for life?

"Sightless?

"All this takes place in three or four seconds while I'm still in the process of hitting the ground. While laying there, gathering my wits from the winds, I smell the putrid smoke of white phosphorus and still see the flaming pieces showering down on the ground. A burning sensation on the right side of my head brings me back to reality and what I should do to help myself. I glance over my body and see a few smoldering spots on my clothing, which I immediately pull off. Nothing underneath.

"Meanwhile, some of the boys have seen my plight and come to my aid. Some mud is applied to my head and I take off for the company command post, where an aidman gives me some temporary treatment and a jeep carries me back to the battalion aid station."

Sergeant Adolph had hit the trip wire of a booby trap laid by some replacement, without doubt, for it was laid on the American side of the wire instead of the German side, where it should have been.

So Sergeant Adolph was taken back to a clearing hospital, and then to a general hospital in Nancy. On April 4 he was awarded a Purple Heart medal (along with several hundred others in the hospital) "as a direct result of hostile enemy fire," said the orders. Sergeant Adolph thought that was pretty funny since the wound was caused by an American booby trap set by an American idiot.

After the Eighteenth Infantry reached the Rhine, Lieutenant Downing was transferred out of the Eighteenth to Chaudfontaine, a quiet Belgian town, famous for its mineral baths and casino.

Zut! Alors! It happened just like that. One minute he was Lieutenant Downing, proud member of a famous fighting outfit, executive officer of a line infantry company, hoping for his captaincy and command of a company of his own. But it was 1945, and the army had too many captains and not enough war left. So...one moment Downing was a hero. Next moment he was a rear-echelon pony. That was the army way. No explanations. No arguments. Do your duty soldier, and gripe all you wish.

After two and a half years overseas—Algeria, Tunisia, Sicily, Normandy, and all the rest of it—Lieutenant Downing was too tired even to gripe.

He was to work in the First Army Special Service Section, setting up leave trips for First Army people. What a comedown for an infantry line officer! But was it? Who cared?

Now he was most unlikely to go the way of Lieutenant Henesey.

Soon he was moved to Düren. There he shuffled papers all day and watched movies in the evening. It was very dull. One day a garbage can outside his window tipped over, and the contents dropped out with a rattle. Machine gun attack! Downing threw himself on the floor. The office was still, everyone looking at him. He got up.

"Sorry," he said. "For a moment I thought it was a machine gun."

"It sounded like a garbage can tipping over to me," said the WAC lieutenant at the next desk, a little primly.

Sure! That's what it was, all right. Rear-echelon garbage cans sounded like that.

He moved to Koblenz. He was shuffling his papers there when the word came that President Franklin Roosevelt had died. A ceremony was held at Koblenz the next Sunday. The headquarters personnel lined up in a field and several high-ranking members of the staff (light colonels and up) made inspirational speeches. The chaplains each outdid each other in their inspirational prayers.

Taps was sounded.

The people were dismissed. Downing spent the afternoon being sad. The war went on.

The Americans still on the front line moved deeper into Germany to keep the lines of communication with the First Army open and short. This time they set up at Weimar.

On April 15 the First Army reached the Mulde River, and the Sixty-ninth Infantry met the Russians at Torgau ten days later. Germany was now split up into individual centers of resistance. It was all but over.

In the second week of April 1945 the Ninth Army, with the Second Armored Division in front, sped toward the Harz Mountains, where five German divisions had holed up.

The Sixteenth Infantry was moving in a wooded area near Beverungen. Sergeant Moglia's company command post unit was eating a meal in a German house. Someone put some medical alcohol (200 proof) into Moglia's grapefruit juice. The sergeant was an earnest young man, not much of a drinker, and the spiked drink affected him more than a little.

In fact, he could not remember what happened next. But he took a patrol out into the thick woods that day, knocked out a German outpost, eliminated a whole German patrol, and blew up an ammunition dump.

That was for beginners.

Moglia's patrol moved very fast and soon came up to a clearing where what seemed to be a command post had been put up. A tent had been erected, and outside it a table was set and a German officer was being served food. The Americans ran across the clearing to the spot. Somehow they had gotten deep inside the German line. A platoon of German soldiers was in the area, but they were lounging not far way. So Moglia and his dozen men had the drop on the German officer. Moglia announced that the officer was his prisoner. A German soldier addressed the officer as "*Herr* General."

The general looked at Technical Sergeant Moglia's stripes and laughed. He returned to his meal, ignoring the Americans.

Moglia fixed his bayonet onto his M-1 and moved up so that the bayonet touched the general.

"You are outranked, General," he said. "You had better join up before I call our main body of troops to attack in full force."

So the general got up, very dignified, and the patrol began to escort him back to the American lines.

The group came to the road and there spotted an American half-track. Sergeant Moglia asked the driver for a ride to battalion headquarters so that he could deliver his bag.

"Get in," he said to the general, motioning to the back of the half-track.

"I am a general officer. I will ride in front."

Moglia turned to his men. "Dump him in the back," he said.

They did, and the general was unceremoniously delivered to Battalion S-2.

The next day Lt. Col. Walter T. Grant, the battalion commander, sent for Moglia. Higher headquarters was upset, he said, because the sergeant had treated a senior enemy military commander in a disrespectful manner.

The general had also complained to the commander of the Sixteenth Infantry that Sergeant Moglia and his men were crazy. They had attacked a superior German force with unorthodox tactics that were not in the book.

"Okay, Sergeant," said Lieutenant Colonel Grant, "you may consider yourself officially reprimanded. But off the record it was a job well done. Next time you capture a German general, you'd better be more careful. I don't want you getting hurt."

So Sergeant Moglia retreated and repented. But not much. Nobody ever told Colonel Grant about the medical alcohol.

The grapefruit juice cocktail's effects had gone, but the fuzziness about it all remained. He thought the general's name was Karst, but he really couldn't quite recall.*

A few days later Sergeant Moglia took a patrol out and came upon what had been (before the American push) a German rear-echelon hospital, near Paderborn. A German doctor came up.

"You Americans are butchers," he said. He swept his arm around and indicated the wards, which were full of amputees.

"Are you proud of what you're doing? Germany has already lost the war. Why do you keep killing us?"

---

*Samuel W. Mitcham's *Hitler's Legions: The German Army Order of Battle, World War II* lists a Lt. Gen. Friedrich Karst, who commanded the 262d Infantry Division in 1942–1943 and was Commandant of Brussels in 1944.

"Tell it to the General Staff," said Moglia. "We have just as many casualties. As long as the German army resists, we will fight them."

He told the doctor that all the Americans wanted to do was go home, and that they would as soon as the war was won.

"You won this one, but we will beat you in the next one," promised the doctor.

"If I had the time, Doctor, I would have you put in a hospital for the criminally insane. For Christ's sake. You'd better not follow us outside this hospital, because if you do you'll never get back in again alive."

The doctor's jaw dropped and his mouth opened, but no sounds came out. He stood there like a furious, frightened jackal.

Moglia wondered what the doctor was thinking then, but he decided it was better that he not find out.

Sergeant Adolph was in the hospital until April 11, when he began wending his way through the maze of replacement centers on the way back to his company inside Germany.

Sergeant Moglia's Sixteenth Infantry was moving along the bank of the Weser River, near Lauenford. The sergeant was chosen to take a patrol out to check the depth of the river to see if it was fordable. A group of engineers and signal people was to accompany the patrol. They were to assemble at the company command post.

A road ran along the forest to the objective. Condition? Unknown. Were there mines? Was it booby-trapped?

That night Moglia went to the assembly point. The company had moved. It seemed now to be an abandoned house. The night was pitch dark, no moon, no stars. He was challenged outside the house, but he gave the password and was let through. He explained his mission to a lieutenant who told him the others had already gone on. So Moglia set out to catch up.

He inched up the road, or rather the side of the road. Suddenly he was shocked by the sound of gunfire to his immediate front—and then to the rear. Small-arms and some automatic fire. He was between opposing American and German patrols.

When the firing died down, Moglia moved forward again, arguing with himself.

"What are you doing here, stupid?"

"Your duty. Forward."

So he stumbled forward, through woods and brush, until he reached the bank of the river. There were several houses there and the stream was fordable—he could see the marks of previous vehicles. He even tested it with some sticks.

Suddenly two German soldiers came out of one of the houses and entered another. Then another soldier joined them. They were not 20 yards away.

Moglia was scared. He stopped cold and waited. The night was completely silent.

He began inching his way backward. He walked all the rest of the night, going back to his lines. He reached the clearing where the deserted house stood forth. Then he heard a voice say, "Here comes one of them."

"What do you mean, one of them," shouted Moglia. "I'm one of you."

"Oh yeah? What's the password?"

Half a dozen rifles were pointed at Moglia, who lay flat in the grass.

"Buck Rogers."

"That's yesterday's password. What's today's?"

"How the hell do I know? I've been traveling all night, looking for my patrol."

"Stand up with your hands up."

Moglia complied.

A young lieutenant looked him over, patted him for hand weapons, and then motioned to the men to lower their rifles.

"I think he's all right."

Moglia told his story and asked where the patrol was.

"Oh, that patrol was canceled. Too dangerous."

"Great. Then where's battalion headquarters?"

"What battalion?"

"Second Battalion, Sixteenth Infantry."

"I dunno where the hell they are now. They moved out last night. They must be about 5 miles up the road by now."

So Sergeant Moglia moved out. After about two hours he came to a building and was told by another dogface that this was his battalion CP. He went inside. No one was there but a cat, stretched out on a bed on its back. He joined the cat.

He slept until late afternoon, when suddenly he awoke to find half a dozen people around him. One of them was Colonel Grant, the battalion commander.

"Okay, soldier," said a sergeant, "get the hell off Colonel Grant's bed."

So Moglia got up, apologizing. But there was no need. The others had been wanting to roust him out for hours, but Grant had let him sleep. And then Moglia told his tale about the ford. And battalion told it to regiment, and regiment issued new orders. And that night the men of the Sixteenth Infantry routed out those Germans at the ford and crossed over.

*   *   *

On April 3 Captain Miller's Twentieth Engineer Battalion moved its headquarters to Elmshausen, near Wolfhagen. They took over a 500-year-old castle from its baronial owners. What a beautiful place it was, complete with donjon, keep, and a moat full of enormous carp. There was only one little nagging problem: the baron was raising hell with every higher command he could reach because the officers of the Twentieth Engineers were drinking up all his rare old wine. That was part of the fortunes of war, said the officers of the Twentieth.

The engineers were building bridges furiously, putting back together what the Allied air forces had ripped asunder.

The Twentieth moved again, this time to the castle of the Baron von Münchhausen, (really) "a much more beautiful castle than the last one, full of hunting trophies."

On April 14 Captain Miller went out looking for Combat Command B of the Ninth Armored Division to see what was needed in the way of roads. He did not find the combat unit at the place it was supposed to be, but the Germans were there with a couple of self-propelled guns, potting at jeeps on the road. Captain Miller had to bail out of his jeep and do some fancy crawling.

On April 15 Captain Miller met Colonel Snetzer when the Second Engineers moved in to Merseberg. The Second Engineers had been having a tough time in support of the Twenty-third Infantry and the Ninth Armored Division. Large numbers of flak batteries had been set up to fire horizontally and were shooting point-blank at American troops and tanks. They were extremely effective. "Burned-out tanks and dead soldiers are left behind our slow, inching advance." The Twenty-third had fought all day to reach the heart of the city. Resistance was strong all the way.

The Second Engineers put a 48-foot treadway bridge across the damaged span of the 200-foot-wide Saale River bridge. The Saale Canal was still holding up the advance.

That day more flak batteries were knocked out. By this time the Twenty-third had captured 2000 antiaircraft guns of 88-, 105-, and 128-millimeter.

On April 15 the infantry captured 1781 prisoners. The clearing of the Ruhr pocket, now 200 miles behind the Twenty-third Infantry, had meant 317,000 POWs captured—but still the Germans fought on.

On April 16 Captain Miller and Colonel Snetzer went down to the canal to look at the bridge site. The Germans were making things very warm with their flak batteries. Shortly after the two men returned to the Second Engineers bivouac, the Germans put a barrage into the area where the Second Engineers and C Company of the Twentieth Engineers were staying. A number of vehicles were wiped out, and two men were wounded.

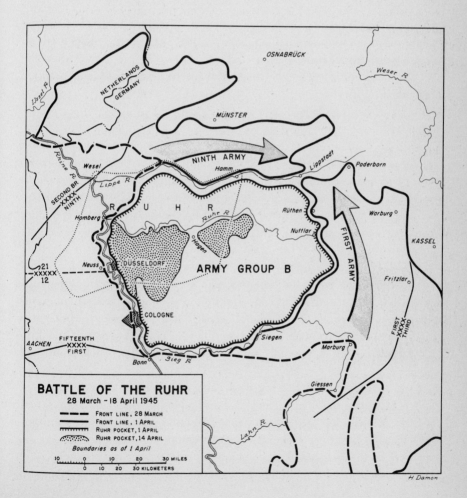

BATTLE OF THE RUHR
28 March - 18 April 1945

- ▬ ▬ ▬ FRONT LINE, 28 MARCH
- ▬▬▬ FRONT LINE, 1 APRIL
- ▥▥▥ RUHR POCKET, 1 APRIL
- ▓▓▓ RUHR POCKET, 14 APRIL

Boundaries as of 1 April

10   0   10   20   30 MILES
0   10   20   30 KILOMETERS

H. Damon

On April 19 Colonel Snetzer noted in his diary that Leipzig fell to the
Americans. He went into the city even as the combat troops were just moving through. Great crowds of civilians lined the streets, watching the Americans who came through in columns as if on parade. Further on, the parade
suddenly stopped and men headed for the shelter of the buildings. Machine
guns fired from the upper-story windows of buildings, and tanks and men
staged a battle before crossing the canal. While this was going on Colonel
Snetzer and three of his officers discovered a nice new public swimming pool
in a very pleasant building and went for a swim.

On April 20 the Second Division prepared to move out beyond Leipzig.

April 25: Pfc. Wickham had been given a thirty-day furlough from the
Twenty-ninth Division and had spent several weeks at home pigging out on
baked beans, Swedish meatballs, rhubarb, and apple pie. Now, when the
time was about up, he received word that his furlough had been extended
fifteen days.

On April 26 Captain Miller drove 40 miles east of Leipzig to visit the 269th
Engineers. Everyone there was excited about a report from a liaison pilot
that he had seen the Russians only 18 miles east of the Mulde River. Captain Miller thought the linkup could be made in a matter of hours but was
being held back. The Americans were told they could not cross the Mulde.
"Apparently this is to give all the brass on both sides a chance to congregate
for the historic meeting." The brass and the press.

April 27: Captain Miller wrote in his diary:

"Nothing much doing for the last week. All of First Army is sitting still.
Today they announced the official 'linkup' on the radio. Lots of congratu-
latory speeches by the Big Three. I went 'Burgermeistering'... and got a
scope-mounted Mauser Sportes, another Mauser Sportes, a beautiful double-
12 with rifle barrel underneath, and a Walther automatic pistol. Not a bad
haul."

April 30, D + 327: The big deal came off. Colonel Snetzer drove up
through Eilenburg to Torgau. The Russians had built a pontoon bridge across
the Elbe. It was lined with Soviet women soldiers—military police all wearing sleek silk stockings. General Hodges was up there, and he crossed the
river to meet the Russian army commander as Colonel Snetzer watched. So
did a few other people, including Ernest Hemingway, who was working as a

war correspondent, and Edward Ward of the BBC, who interpreted Russian for Colonel Snetzer's party.

The war was very nearly over, and everyone knew it.

On the evening of May 1 the men of Captain Miller's headquarters crew found a toy mechanical train in the attic of their billet. They brought it down and began playing with it. Then somebody suggested that they each put Reichsmark notes under a section of the track and then turn the engine loose; when it stopped, the guy whose track it stopped on would get all the money. It led to a hilarious evening. But before the night was out came news that was a great deal happier.

The word came that Adolf Hitler was dead!

On May 2 Captain Miller took a drive into Sudeten Czechoslovakia. He got back to the company to learn that the Germans had surrendered unconditionally in Italy.

It was the first thought that most troops in Germany had given to Italy for a long time. The war there had been more or less static throughout the year. Most of the soldiers of the First Armored Division had been dismounted and turned into mountain infantry that winter. Until April they had been in the line near Vergato on Highway 64 on the left flank of the Second Corps. But very little was happening. When two German prisoners and an agent were captured on March 28, it was a "big event."

"An even bigger event was the romance of Captain Hillenmyer, who fell in love with a dietician of the Twenty-fourth General Hospital. The romance prospered.* As Sergeant Haemmel put it:

"Hillenmyer's position as battalion executive officer and the static nature of the winter war enabled him to make many hair-raising trips over the winding slippery muddy roads, and after his return from a thirty-day furlough the couple were engaged in April."

Captain Miller also heard that day that Berlin had fallen.

"It can't be long now."

On May 5 the First Army was getting ready to attack again, this time from Liebstein. B Company of the Twentieth Engineers was building a treadway bridge for the troops. Then came the news of the unconditional surrender of

---

*They were married in May.

all German forces in Holland, Denmark, and northwest Germany. So Captain Miller and the headquarters officers of the First Engineers went to the village tavern, where they spent the night drinking Slovakian Dreams—"which are pleasant tasting Mickey Finns."

*

May 7: Pfc. Wickham arrived at Camp Shanks, New York, his last stop before shipping back out to the Twenty-ninth Division in Europe. But now he would not be going. Men with more than 85 points (1 point for each month of service, 1 point for each month overseas, 5 points for each battle star, and 5 points for each decoration) would be discharged quickly. Wickham had 107 points.

May 7: The First Division received the cease-fire order. The final surrender was to take place on May 9, the men learned.

Captain Miller was overjoyed.

"V-E day at last! Boyohboy, it's been a long time. Today is my birthday. 30 years old. The third one overseas. Two years ago today Bizerte fell and we thought the war was over, and here I am wearing five Hershey Bars [overseas stripes]. I hope I'll be a civilian next birthday."

May 8, V-E day: "This is it! This is what the Twentieth has been fighting for since we landed at Casablanca thirty months ago. I started celebrating in Scotch at noon, switched to cognac in the afternoon, went over at 2100 to help the colonel drink his bottle of Victory Champagne that he has carried since Sedan, and went back to cognac to finish up a wonderful day in a practically petrified position."

Captain Shebeck joined the thousands of people thronging the streets of Dijon. The Place d'Arcy was jammed as military men and civilians wandered from one café to another. Shebeck got to bed at 3 a.m. He was awakened by the strains of "It's a Long Way to Tipperary." He looked out the window of his hotel room. There below he saw two British Tommies staggering along the street, accompanied by a lone French civilian playing an accordion.

And so the dogfaces' war came to an end.

NOTES

It would have been impossible for me to research and write this book had it not been for the unflagging loyalty and constant effort of my wife, Olga G. Hoyt. She typed hundreds of letters and wrote many for my signature. She kept the files and the correspondence, and she was the first person to edit my manuscript.

Chapter 1

I am indebted to Edward Elburn of Chestertown, Maryland, for a long interview and for the loan of the book *29 Let's Go*. William R. Ogden sent me several letters and tapes after he ascertained that I wanted to "tell it like it was." Col. Russell Potter Reeder contributed letters and an unpublished article he had written. Barnett Hoffner lent me many pictures and documents. Charles Chattaway, now an insurance executive, wrote me several letters and accounts of his service. Harold Shebeck gave me his unpublished war memoirs. John J. Moglia wrote a whole series of letters about his service life.

Chapter 2

The men mentioned above also contributed to this chapter. So did Thomas G. Wickham, who sent me a series of vignettes of his military career. Arthur C. Campbell sent me a long letter about his career. I also used his diaries, located now in the military archives at Carlisle Barracks, Pennsylvania. The menu of the 504th Parachute Infantry Battalion was contributed by Charles Doyle.

Chapter 3

I used Gen. Maxwell Taylor's book and Gen. Omar Bradley's memoirs for this chapter. I had known General Marshall when he was commandant at Vancouver Barracks. Joseph Miller lent me his wartime diary. Friends in Hawaii contributed a great deal about the nisei soldiers. I am particularly indebted to Sohei Yamate of Merrill, Lynch, Pierce, Fenner and Smith for a number of books. William G. Haemmel lent me his unpublished history of the First Armored Division. Mrs. John P. Downing lent me her late husband's book, *At War with the British,* and a much longer unpublished manuscript about Downing's entire wartime career.

Chapter 4

The quotation from Winston Churchill comes from his six-volume history of the Second World War.

Chapter 5

The material about President Roosevelt's plans is from Omar Bradley's book. So is the material about Bradley. The rundown on the 110th Infantry Regiment was supplied by Charles Chattaway. The material about Churchill's American trip is from volume 3 of his World War II history. The story of Sergeant Merrill is from Downing's book.

Chapter 6

The story about General Roosevelt is from Moglia's letters to me. The material about Col. Thomas Sherburne is from his letters to me. The story of the Dieppe raid is from Sergeant Ogden's tapes. The tales about Colonel Caffey come from Captain Miller's diary. The stories about the Twenty-ninth Division come from Ed Elburn and *29 Let's Go.*

Chapter 7

The general material about the war is from the books in the bibliography. I used all the important accounts.

Chapter 8

The material about the north African invasion is from Downing's manuscript, Eisenhower's book, and Bradley's book.

Chapter 9

The story of the landings is from Moglia's letters, from Downing's book, and from General Buster's tapes. The history of the First Division and the history of the Ninth Division were useful here to set the scene.

Chapter 10

Lieutenant Downing's graphic descriptions of his battle were primary to this chapter.

Chapter 11

Charles Doyle sent me a whole series of tapes about the history of the 504th Parachute Infantry Battalion. He had made them in connection with his own history of that unit. I used them extensively. The histories of the First and Second Armored divisions were very useful here, as was William Haemmel's book. Colonel Caffey's further adventures came from Joseph Miller's diary.

Chapter 12

Colonel Caffey's story, as seen through the eyes of then Lieutenant Miller, continues here. Lieutenant Downing continues his adventures as reported in his book; Sergeant Moglia's letters about north Africa tell his story. The general information is largely from the Bradley book and from Harry Butcher's story.

Chapter 13

The histories of the First and Second Armored divisions were used here, and also Haemmel's unpublished book.

Chapter 14

The adventures of Private Underhill and the others of the 504th are from Charles Doyle's tapes.

Chapter 15

I used Charles Whiting's *Kasserine* for background, and also General Bradley's book. Moglia contributed the tale about Winston Churchill.

Chapter 16

The material about General Patton and his ways is from Downing and from Bradley.

Chapter 17

The material about the Germans comes from a number of sources, such as the biographies of Field Marshal Rommel. The Ernie Pyle story was told to me by George Weller, war correspondent for the Chicago *Daily News*. The Purple Hearts of Sergeant Moglia were not a matter he liked to brag about, but I coaxed the information from him.

Chapter 18

I used Gen. James Gavin's *On to Berlin* for part of the story of the Eighty-second Airborne operations in Sicily. Captain Perkins's story comes from Donald Houston's *Hell on Wheels (Presidio Press)*, the history of the Second Armored Division. Then Corporal Moglia tells his own story, as does Downing.

Chapter 19

Captain Perkins's tale is from *Hell on Wheels*. Sergeant Johnson's story is from his book.

Chapter 20

The tale that provides the title for this chapter is from Sergeant Johnson's book. The story of General Allen is from Downing's book.

Chapter 21

Jesse Butler sent me several letters and a tape about his experiences. They provide the base for this story. The story of General Patton's treatment of soldiers is from several sources, including Moglia, Harry Butcher, and the official army history. The story of the First Division's "retraining" is largely from Downing, who went through it.

Chapter 22

I used Sergeant Johnson's book here, as well as Charles Doyle's tapes and *Go for Broke*, the story of the nisei soldiers.

Chapter 23

I used William Haemmel's manuscript for the story of the First Armored Division. Capt. Felix L. Sparks provided me with a combat history of the Anzio period.

Chapter 24

The poem "A Soldier That's Fit for a Soldier" came from Downing's manuscript. Colonel Snetzer's diary was lent to me by Mrs. Snetzer. The poem "A Yank in the ETO" is also from Downing. Sergeant Hoffner's adventures come from his letters and tapes. Lorne Porter's story is from his own account. The story of the "battle of Slapton Sands" is from my own book *The Invasion Before Normandy*. Private Adolph's adventures come from an extensive series of letters he wrote home to his family from the day he joined the service, and which he kindly lent me.

Chapter 25

Sumpter Blackmon's story comes from an account he sent to me. Much of the rest of the material about the Eighty-second Airborne's landing is from James Gavin's *On to Berlin*, and that about the 101st is from *Rendezvous with Destiny*.

Chapter 26

Captain Sabin's story is from letters to me. Much of the rest comes from books about the landings and the Mulberry operation.

Chapter 27

Captain Sabin's account was very valuable. I also used Cornelius Ryan's *The Longest Day* and several other accounts of the D day operations listed in the bibliography. For the German point of view I depended on various biographies of Field Marshal Rommel and my own research materials.

Chapter 28

Almost all of my hundreds of correspondents contributed something to the stories of the landings on Omaha and Utah beaches. The Dantini story is from his letters to me.

Chapter 29

This chapter dealing with the D day landings is the most complicated in the book and depended on literally hundreds of sources. Most of them are indicated in the text, usually taken from letters or tapes or interviews with various protagonists. Sergeant Hoffner's tapes were very helpful here. Sergeant Moglia's letters gave me a great deal of information. A number of men of the Twenty-ninth Division told me about their experiences. I had assistance from army, navy, and air-force people. The major difficulty in sorting all this out came from the enormous volume of material available. That's why I tried to stay with the characters the reader had already met in north Africa and in other parts of the book.

Chapter 30

The story of Utah beach is not nearly so exciting as that of Omaha beach on that first day. And yet, Colonel Reeder's story of the movement of the 12th Infantry is very exciting, and he told it well in his own book. The continuing story of the airborne troops comes from several sources, almost always named in the text. Colonel Snetzer's diary gives a good picture of how it looked to men coming in for the second day's landings. Sergeant Ogden's story is from his letters and his tapes. All the way along, medic Scheer's tale gives the impression of a man fighting a sort of private war, confined to the beach, itself, day after day.

Chapter 31

The material about the Second Armored Division comes largely from General Buster's tapes. Sgt. Wilfred Thornton lent me his diary, which covered the war from north Africa through the Battle of the Bulge. I used it extensively.

Chapter 32

Sergeant Haemmel's unpublished manuscript was the basis for much of this material. *Go for Broke* was also used. Charles Doyle's tapes provided the story of the paratroopers.

Chapter 33

General Buster's story of the death of Colonel Roberts is from Buster's tapes. Colonel Campbell's letters to me were the source of his story of the Falaise gap.

Chapter 34

Almost all the material in this chapter comes from the letters and diaries of the principal characters. It is interesting to contemplate what might have happened to that column of men who marched blithely across the bridge to the left bank of the Seine and disappeared. Some of them might still be out there.

Chapter 35

Again, this chapter was almost entirely written from diaries and letters. The exception is the material about the 101st Airborne Division's landings in Holland, which comes from letters and also from *Rendezvous with Destiny*.

Chapter 36

The material about the German plans for the great Ardennes offensive (their drive on Antwerp) comes from research I did for my book *Hitler's War*. General Guderian's memoir was important and so was Field Marshal Keitel's. I also had a good deal of assistance from various officers and men who were connected with the investigation of the Malmedy massacre, especially Alvin R. Welsch. I used General Gavin's book *On to Berlin* for a part of the activity of the Eighty-second Airborne during the story of the German breakthrough. General Buster's tapes told the story of a part of the Second Armored Division activity. Captain Shebeck and Lieutenant Chattaway contributed stories of peripheral activities during this vital period. Lieutenant Thornton told his story in his diary. Sergeant Adolph's letters home indicated what was happening in General Patton's sector.

Chapter 37

The books of General Guderian and Field Marshal Keitel set the background of the Germans during this period, as did those of Field Marshal Montgomery, General Bradley, and General Eisenhower for the Allies. Lieutenant Downing's war moved into a long period of frustration. Sergeant Adolph was becoming very much the professional. The death of Lieutenant Henesey is indicative of the strange fortunes of war. Lieutenant Colonel Snetzer's stories are from his diaries of the period. He and Captain Miller were the only two of my protagonists who actually met during the war. Lieutenant Chattaway had now become an officer, and his war was completely changed. Captain Shebeck's fortunes waxed and waned. He got out of the heroics of the airborne and into administration which was duller but safer. None of this was his idea. The brass made the decision. Sergeant Moglia's story about capturing the German general was proved out by the facts, General Friedrich Karst was the unlucky German who ran into that American patrol.

The ending of this books seems somehow anticlimactic; after all the excitement all the way along, suddenly, it all just stopped. But that was the way it was for the GIs. One minute they were fighting and men were dying. The next minute it was all over.

BIBLIOGRAPHY

Arnold-Forster, Mark. *The World at War*. New York: Stein and Day, 1973.

Becton, F. Julian, with Joseph Morschauser, III. *The Ship that Would Not Die*. Englewood Cliffs, N.J.: Prentice Hall, 1980.

Belfield, Eversley, and H. Essume. *The Battle for Normandy*. Philadelphia: Dufour Editions, 1961.

Bennett, Ralph. *Ultra in the West*. New York: Charles Scribner's Sons, 1977.

Bradley, Omar N. *A Soldier's Story*. New York: Henry Holt and Co., 1951.

Breuer, William B. *Death of a Nazi Army, The Falaise Pocket*. New York: Stein and Day, 1985.

Brown, John Mason. *Many a Watchful Night*. New York: Whittlesey House, 1944.

Burgett, Donald R. *Currahee! A Paratrooper's Account of the Normandy Invasion*. Boston: Houghton Mifflin Co., 1967.

Butcher, Harry C. *My Three Years with Eisenhower*. New York: Simon and Schuster, 1946.

Bykofsky, Joseph, and Harold Larson. *The Transportation Corps: Operations Overseas*. Washington: Office of the Chief of Military History, Department of the Army, 1957.

Churchill, Winston. *The Second World War*, six volumes. Boston: Houghton Mifflin Co., 1948–1953.

Columbia Broadcasting System. *From D. Day through Victory in Europe, The Eye-Witness Stories as Told by War Correspondents on the Air*. New York: Columbia Broadcasting System, 1945.

Cooper, John B., Jr. *The History of the 110th Field Artillery*. Baltimore: War Records Division, Maryland Historical Society, 1953.

Crookendon, Napier. *Dropzone Normandy*. New York: Charles Scribner's Sons, 1976.

Dalgleish, Maj. John. *We Planned the Second Front*. London: Victor Gollancz, 1945.

Davis, Kenneth S. *Experience of War*. Garden City, N.Y.: Doubleday and Co., 1965.

Downing, John. *At War with the British*. Daytona Beach, Fla.: Privately printed, 1980.

Edwards, Kenneth. *Operation Neptune*. London: Collins, 1946.

Edwards, Tudor. *D-Day*. London: Wayland, 1977.

Eisenhower, Dwight D. *Crusade in Europe*. Garden City, N.Y.: Doubleday and Co., 1948.

Ellsberg, Edward. *The Far Shore*. New York: Dodd Mead and Co., 1960.

Ewing, Joseph. *29 Let's Go! A History of the 29th Infantry Division in World War II*. Washington: Infantry Journal Press, 1979.

Freidin, Seymour, and William Richardson. *The Fatal Decisions*. New York: Berkley Publishing Co., 1958.

Gorlitz, Walter (ed.). *The Memoirs of Field Marshal Keitel*. New York: Stein and Day, 1966.

Guderian, Heinz. *Panzer Leader*. New York: E. P. Dutton, 1957.

Harrison, Gordon A. *Cross Channel Attack, The U.S. Army in World War II*. Washington: Office of the Chief of Military History, Department of the Army, 1951.

Harrison, Michael. *Mulberry, The Return in Triumph*. London: W. H. Allen, 1965.

Hartcup, Guy. *Code Name Mulberry*. London: David & Charles, 1977.

Haswell, Jock. *The Intelligence and Deception of the D-Day Landings*. London: B. T. Batsford, 1979.

Haupt, Werner, and Uwe Faise. *Invasion, D-Day, June 6*. Bad Nauheim, Germany: Podzun-Verlag, 1968.

Howarth, David. *D. Day*. New York: McGraw-Hill Book Co., 1959.

Hoyt, Edwin P. *The Invasion Before Normandy*. London: Robert Hale, 1986.

Hunt, Robert, and David Mason. *The Normandy Campaign*. London: Leo Cooper, 1976.

Ingersoll, Ralph. *Top Secret*. New York: Harcourt Brace and Co., 1946.

Johnson, Charles. *A Taste of War*. New York: Exposition Press, 1969.

Jones, R. V. *The Wizard War*. New York: Coward-McCann and Geoghegan, 1978.

Keegan, John. *Six Armies in Normandy*. New York: Viking Press, 1982.

Langer, Walter C. *The Mind of Adolf Hitler*. New York: Basic Books, 1972.

Lochner, Louis P. (ed.). *The Goebbels Diaries*. New York: Award Books, 1971.

Miller, Max. *The Far Shore*. New York: Whittlesey House, 1945.

Montgomery, Field Marshal, the Viscount of Alamein. *Normandy to the Baltic*. New York: Hutchinson, 1945.

Morgan, Frederick. *Overture to Overlord*. Garden City, N.Y.: Doubleday and Co., 1950.

Overy, R. J. *The Air War, 1939–1945*. New York: Stein and Day, 1980.

Paine, Lauren. *D. Day*. London: Robert Hale, 1981.

Rapport, Leonard, and Arthur Norwood, Jr. *Rendezvous with Destiny, a History of the 101st Airborne Division*. Madelia, Minn.: Privately printed (House of Print), 1948.

Ryan, Cornelius. *The Longest Day*. New York: Simon and Schuster, 1959.

Shirer, William L. *End of a Berlin Diary*. New York: Popular Library, 1947.

——. *The Rise and Fall of the Third Reich*. New York: Simon and Schuster, 1960.

Smith, Bradley F., and Elena Agarossi. *Operation Sunrise*. New York: Basic Books, 1979.

Stagg, J. M. *Forecast for Overlord*. New York: W. W. Norton and Co., 1971.

Stanford, Alfred. *Force Mulberry*. New York: William Morrow and Co., 1951.

Swettenham, John. *D-Day*. Ottawa: Canadian War Museum, undated.

Taylor, Maxwell D. *Swords and Plowshares*. New York: W. W. Norton and Co., 1972.

Third Armored Division. *Spearhead in the West*. Frankfurt am Main-Schwanheim, Germany: Third Armored Division, 1945.

Thompson, R. W. *D-Day, Spearhead of Invasion*. New York: Ballantine Books, 1968.

Thorne, Christopher. *Allies of a Kind*. Oxford: Oxford University Press, 1978.

Trevor-Roper, Hugh (ed.). *Final Entries, 1945. The Diaries of Joseph Goebbels*. New York: G. P. Putnam's Sons, 1978.

Turner, John Frayn. *Invasion '44, The Full Story of D-Day*. London: George G. Harrap & Co. Ltd., 1959.

Warner, Philip. *The D-Day Landings*. London: William Kimber, 1980.

Weigley, Russell E. *Eisenhower's Lieutenants*. Bloomington, Ind.: Indiana University Press, 1981.

Whiting, Charles. *Death of a Division*. New York: Stein and Day, 1981.

——. *'44. In Combat from Normandy to the Ardennes*. New York: Stein and Day, 1984.

——. *Kasserine*. New York: Stein and Day, 1984.

Periodicals, Bulletins, Pamphlets

Fourth Cavalry Association. *The 4th Cavalry Spur,* various issues.

Henry, Thomas R. "The Avenging Ghosts of the 9th." *Saturday Evening Post,* July 6, 1946.

Ingersoll, Ralph. "D-Day 40 Years Later." *Modern Maturity,* June–July 1984.

Lewis, Don. "Jump into Occupied Europe." *Dixie,* Aug. 24, 1969.

Malone, Ted. "A Broadcast from the European War Theatre." July 17, 1944.

"Massacre at Malmedy." *History of the 285th Field Artillery Observation Battalion.*

Ninth Infantry Division Association. *The Octofoil,* various issues.

101st Airborne Division Association. *The Screaming Eagle,* February 1980, March–April 1982.

Second (Indian Head) Division Association, Inc. Various publications.

Snetzer, Lt. Col. Robert. *Record of Events While Overseas of Lt. Col. Snetzer, October 1943 to November 1, 1945.* Privately printed.

Time, Jan. 17, 1949.

U.S. War Department. *Omaha Beachhead.* U.S. War Department, Historical Division.

Veterans of the Battle of the Bulge. *The Bulge Bugle,* January 1985.

Newspapers

Baltimore Sunday Sun, Dec. 7, 1941.

Christian Science Monitor, June 6, 1984.

Daily Oklahoman, June 6, 1944.

London *Daily Mail,* July 11, 1944.

New York *Sun,* Apr. 5, 1955.

New York Times, June 1, 1940; June 27, 1940; June 30, 1940; Aug. 1, 1940; Aug. 8, 1940.

Stars and Stripes (Oran daily), June 6, 1944.

Sunday Ledger-Enquirer (Columbus, Ga.), June 25, 1949.

Washington *Post,* May 29, 1944.

Washington *Times,* June 6, 1984.

Miscellaneous

Adolph, Ralph. Unpublished letters, 1944–1945.

Office of Naval Records and Library, Washington, D.C. Various documents, ships' records, June 1944.

SUBJECT INDEX

603

INDEX OF NAMES